# Legal Aspects of Business

## SECOND EDITION

**P.K. PADHI**

*Professor, XLRI Jamshedpur*

and

*Former Principal, University Law College*
*Utkal University, Bhubaneswar*

**PHI Learning Private Limited**

Delhi-110092

2025

*In fond memory of **Shri Asoke K. Ghosh** (October 1942 – February 2024), Founder Chairman and Managing Director of PHI Learning, whose vision endlessly inspires.*

*The Legacy Continues....*

Published by Pushpita Ghosh, PHI Learning Private Limited, Rimjhim House, 111, Patparganj Industrial Estate, Delhi-110092 and Printed by Sanjay Printers, 12/31, Site-4, Sahibabad Industrial Area, UP -201010.

**₹995.00**

**LEGAL ASPECTS OF BUSINESS, Second Edition**
P.K. Padhi



**ISBN-978-81-19364-82-4 (Print Book)**
**ISBN-978-81-19364-73-2 (e-Book)**

The export rights of the book are vested solely with the publisher.

# Contents


*Preface* ........ *xxv*

*Preface to the First Edition* ........ *xxvii*

*Table of Cases* ........ *xxix*

**1. THE INDIAN CONTRACT ACT, 1872 ........ 1–178**

Introduction *1*
Preamble *1*
Section 1: Short title *2*
Section 2: Interpretation clause *3*
Offer *3*
Tender *6*
Standard Form Contract *8*

CHAPTER I OF THE COMMUNICATION, ACCEPTANCE AND REVOCATION OF PROPOSALS **24**

Section 3: Communication, acceptance and revocation of proposals *24*
Section 4: Communication when complete *25*
Section 5: Revocation of proposals and acceptance *29*
Section 6: Revocation how made *31*
Section 7: Acceptance must be absolute *32*
Section 8: Acceptance by performing conditions, or receiving consideration *33*
Section 9: Promises, express and implied *34*

CHAPTER II OF CONTRACTS, VOIDABLE CONTRACTS AND VOID AGREEMENTS **35**

Section 10: What agreements are contracts *35*
Section 11: Who are competent to contract *36*
Section 12: What is a sound mind for the purposes of contracting *37*
Section 13: "Consent" defined *38*
Section 14: "Free consent" defined *38*
Section 15: "Coercion" defined *39*

Section 16: "Undue influence" defined *42*
Section 17: "Fraud" defined *47*
Section 18: "Misrepresentation" defined *50*
Section 19: Voidability of agreements without free consent *54*
Section 19A: Power to set aside contract induced by undue influence *55*
Section 20: Agreement void where both parties are under mistake as to matter of fact *56*
Section 21: Effect of mistakes as to law *57*
Section 22: Contract caused by mistake of one party as to matter of fact *57*
Section 23: What considerations and objects are lawful and what not *60*
Section 24: Agreement void, if considerations and objects unlawful in part *65*
Section 25: Agreement without consideration, void, unless it is in writing and registered or is a promise to compensate for something done or is a promise to pay a debt barred by limitation law *65*
Types of Consideration *66*
Section 26: Agreement in restraint of marriage void *67*
Section 27: Agreement in restraint of trade void *67*
Section 28: Agreements in restraint of legal proceedings void *74*
Section 29: Agreements void for uncertainty *77*
Section 30: Agreements by way of wager, void *78*
**CHAPTER III OF CONTINGENT CONTRACTS 80**
Section 31: "Contingent contract" defined *80*
Section 32: Enforcement of contracts contingent on an event happening *80*
Section 33: Enforcement of contracts contingent on an event not happening *81*
Section 34: When event on which contract is contingent to be deemed impossible, if it is the future conduct of a living person *81*
Section 35: When contracts become void which are contingent on happening of specified event within fixed time *81*
Section 36: Agreement contingent on impossible event void *82*
**CHAPTER IV OF THE PERFORMANCE OF CONTRACTS 82**
Section 37: Obligation of parties to contract *82*
Section 38: Effect of refusal to accept offer of performance *83*
Section 39: Effect of refusal of party to perform promise wholly *83*
Section 40: Person by whom promise is to be performed *84*
Section 41: Effect of accepting performance from third person *84*
Section 42: Devolution of joint liabilities *84*
Section 43: Anyone of joint promisors may be compelled to perform *84*
Section 44: Effect of release of one joint promisor *85*
Section 45: Devolution of joint rights *85*
Section 46: Time for performance of promise, when no application is to be made and no time is specified *85*
Section 47: Time and place for performance of promise, where time is specified and no application to be made *86*
Section 48: Application for performance on certain day to be at proper time and place *86*

Section 49: Place for performance of promise, where no application to be made and no place fixed for performance *86*
Section 50: Performance in manner or at time prescribed or sanctioned by promise *86*
Section 51: Promisor not bound to perform, unless reciprocal promisee ready and willing to perform *87*
Section 52: Order of performance of reciprocal promises *87*
Section 53: Liability of party preventing event on which the contract is to take effect *88*
Section 54: Effect of default as to that promise which should be first performed, in contract consisting of reciprocal promises *88*
Section 55: Effect of failure to perform at fixed time, in contract in which time is essential *89*
Section 56: Agreement to do impossible act *91*
Origins: Principle of Absolutism *92*
Section 57: Reciprocal promise to do things legal, and also other things illegal *98*
Section 58: Alternative promise, one branch being illegal *99*
Section 59: Application of payment where debt to be discharged is indicated *99*
Section 60: Application of payment where debt to be discharged is not indicated *100*
Section 61: Application of payment where neither party appropriates *100*
Section 62: Effect of novation, rescission, and alteration of contract *102*
Section 63: Promisee may dispense with or remit performance of promise *104*
Section 64: Consequences of rescission of voidable contract *106*
Section 65: Obligation of person who has received advantage under void agreement, or contract that becomes void *106*
Section 66: Mode of communicating or revoking rescission of voidable contract *108*
Section 67: Effect of neglect of promisee to afford promisor reasonable facilities for performance *108*

CHAPTER V OF CERTAIN RELATIONS RESEMBLING THOSE CREATED BY CONTRACT 109

Quasi Contract *109*
Section 68: Claim for necessaries supplied to person incapable of contracting, or on his account *110*
Section 69: Reimbursement of person paying money due by another, in payment of which he is interested *112*
Section 70: Obligation of person enjoying benefit of non-gratuitous act *112*
Section 71: Responsibility of finder of goods *115*
Section 72: Liability of person to whom money is paid or thing delivered by mistake or under coercion *115*

Quantum Meruit *118*

CHAPTER VI OF THE CONSEQUENCES OF BREACH OF CONTRACT 121

Section 73: Compensation for loss or damage caused by breach of contract *121*

Section 74: Compensation for breach of contract where penalty stipulated for *128*
Section 75: Party rightfully rescinding contract, entitled to compensation *133*

**Chapter VIII Of Indemnity and Guarantee 134**

Section 124: "Contract of indemnity" defined *134*
Section 125: Rights of indemnity-holder when sued *135*
Section 126: 'Contract of guarantee', 'surety', 'principal-debtor' and 'creditor' *137*
Section 127: Consideration for guarantee *138*
Section 128: Surety's liability *138*
Section 129: Continuing guarantee *139*
Section 130: Revocation of continuing guarantee *139*
Section 131: Revocation of continuing guarantee by surety's death *141*
Section 132: Liability of two persons, primarily liable, not affected by arrangement between them that one shall be surety on other's default *141*
Section 133: Discharge of surety by variance in terms of contract *141*
Section 134: Discharge of surety by release or discharge of principal debtor *142*
Section 135: Discharge of surety when creditor compounds with, gives time to, or agrees not to sue, principal debtor *143*
Section 136: Surety not discharged when agreement made with third person to give time to, or agree not to sue, principal debtor *143*
Section 137: Creditor's forbearance to sue does not discharge surety *143*
Section 138: Release of one co-surety does not discharge others *144*
Section 139: Discharge of surety by creditor's act or omission impairing surety's eventual remedy *144*
Section 140: Rights of surety on payment or performance *145*
Section 141: Surety's right to benefit of creditor's securities *145*
Section 142: Guarantee obtained by misrepresentation, invalid *147*
Section 143: Guarantee obtained by concealment, invalid *147*
Section 144: Guarantee on contract that creditor shall not act on it until co-surety joins *147*
Section 145: Implied promise to indemnify surety *147*
Section 146: Co-surety liable to contribute equally *148*
Section 147: Liability of co-sureties bound in different sums *148*

**Chapter IX Of Bailment 149**

Section 148: "Bailment", "bailor" and "bailee" defined *150*
Section 149: Delivery to bailee how made *153*
Section 150: Bailor's duty to disclose faults in goods bailed *153*
Section 151: Care to be taken by bailee *153*
Section 152: Bailee when not liable for loss, etc., of thing bailed *154*
Section 153: Termination of bailment by bailee's act inconsistent with conditions *154*
Section 154: Liability of bailee making unauthorised use of goods bailed *154*
Section 155: Effect of mixture with bailor's consent, of his goods with bailee's *155*

Section 156: Effect of mixture, without bailor's consent, when the goods can be separated 155
Section 157: Effect of mixture, without bailor's consent, when the goods cannot be separated 155
Section 158: Repayment, by bailor, of necessary expenses 155
Section 159: Restoration of goods lent gratuitously 155
Section 160: Return of goods bailed, on expiration of time or accomplishment of purpose 156
Section 161: Bailee's responsibility when goods are not duly returned 156
Section 162: Termination of gratuitous bailment by death 156
Section 163: Bailer entitled to increase or profit from goods bailed 156
Section 164: Bailor's responsibility to bailee 156
Section 165: Bailment by several joint owners 156
Section 166: Bailee not responsible on redelivery to bailor without title 157
Section 167: Right of third person claiming goods bailed 157
Section 168: Right to finder of goods; may sue for specific reward offered 157
Section 169: When finder of thing commonly on sale may sell it 157
Section 170: Bailee's particular lien 157
Section 171: General lien of bankers, factors, wharfingers, attorneys and policy brokers 157
Section 172: "Pledge", "Pawnor", and "Pawnee" defined 160
Section 173: Pawnee's right of retainer 160
Section 174: Pawnee not to retain for debt or promise other than for which goods pledged: Presumption in case of subsequent advances 160
Section 175: Pawnee's right as to extraordinary expenses incurred 160
Section 176: Pawnee's right where pawnor makes default 160
Section 177: Defaulting pawnor's right to redeem 161
Section 178: Pledge by mercantile agent 161
Section 178A: Pledge by person in possession under voidable contract 161
Section 179: Pledge where pawnor has only a limited interest 161
Section 180: Suit by bailor or bailee against wrong-doer 161
Section 181: Apportionment of relief or compensation obtained by such suits 161

CHAPTER X AGENCY 162
Section 182: "Agent" and "principal" defined 162
Section 183: Who may employ agent 164
Section 184: Who may be an agent 164
Section 185: Consideration not necessary 164
Section 186: Agent's authority may be expressed or implied 164
Section 187: Definitions of express and implied 164
Section 188: Extent of agent's authority 165
Section 189: Agent's authority in an emergency 165
Section 190: When agent cannot delegate 165
Section 191: "Sub-agent" defined 165
Section 192: Representation of principal by sub-agent properly appointed 165
Section 193: Agent's responsibility for sub-agent appointed without authority 166

Section 194: Relation between principal and person duly appointed by agent to act in business of agency 166
Section 195: Agent's duty in naming such person 166
Section 196: Right of person as to acts done for him without his authority—effect of ratification 167
Section 197: Ratification may be expressed or implied 167
Section 198: Knowledge requisite for valid ratification 167
Section 199: Effect of ratifying unauthorised act forming part of a transaction 167
Section 200: Ratification of unauthorised act cannot injure third person 167
Section 201: Termination of agency 168
Section 202: Termination of agency, where agent has an interest in subject-matter 168
Section 203: When principal may revoke agent's authority 169
Section 204: Revocation where authority has been partly exercised 169
Section 205: Compensation for revocation by principal, or renunciation by agent 169
Section 206: Notice of revocation or renunciation 169
Section 207: Revocation and renunciation may be expressed or implied 169
Section 208: When termination of agent's authority takes effect as to agent, and as to third persons 170
Section 209: Agent's duty on termination of agency by principal's death or insanity 170
Section 210: Termination of sub-agent's authority 170
Section 211: Agent's duty in conducting principal's business 170
Section 212: Skill and diligence required from agent 171
Section 213: Agent's accounts 171
Section 214: Agent's duty to communicate with principal 172
Section 215: Right of principal when agent deals, on his own account, in business of agency without principal's consent 172
Section 216: Principal's right to benefit gained by agent dealing on his own account in business of agency 172
Section 217: Agent's right of retainer out of sums received on principal's account 172
Section 218: Agent's duty to pay sums received for principal 173
Section 219: When agent's remuneration becomes due 173
Section 220: Agent not entitled to remuneration for business misconducted 173
Section 221: Agent's lien on principal's property 173
Section 222: Agent to be indemnified against consequences of lawful acts 173
Section 223: Agent to be indemnified against consequences of acts done in good faith 174
Section 224: Non-liability of employer of agent to do a criminal act 174
Section 225: Compensation to agent for injury caused by principal's neglect 174
Section 226: Enforcement and consequences of agent's contract 175
Section 227: Principal how far bound, when agent exceeds authority 175

Section 228: Principal not bound when excess of agent's authority is not separable 175
Section 229: Consequences of notice given to agent 176
Section 230: Agent cannot personally enforce, nor be bound by, contracts on behalf of principal 176
Section 231: Right of parties to a contract made by agent not disclosed 176
Section 232: Performance of contract with agent supposed to be principal 176
Section 233: Right of person dealing with agent personally liable 177
Section 234: Consequence of inducing agent or principal to act on belief that principal or agent will be held exclusively liable 177
Section 235: Liability of pretended agent 177
Section 236: Person falsely contracting as agent, not entitled to performance 177
Section 237: Liability of principal inducing belief that agent's unauthorised acts were authorised 177
Section 238: Effect, on agreement, of misrepresentation or fraud by agent 178

**2. THE SALE OF GOODS ACT, 1930 .......... 179–235**

Introduction 179
Act in a Nutshell 179

CHAPTER I PRELIMINARY 180
Section 1: Short title, extent and commencement 180
Section 2: Definitions 180
Section 3: Application of provisions of Act 9 of 1872 181

CHAPTER II FORMATION OF THE CONTRACT OF SALE 182
Section 4: Sale and agreement to sell 182
Section 5: Contract of sale how made 186
Section 6: Existing or future goods 188
Section 7: Goods perishing before making of contract 189
Section 8: Goods perishing before sale but after agreement to sell 189
Section 9: Ascertainment of price 191
Section 10: Agreement to sell at valuation 191

CHAPTER III CONDITIONS AND WARRANTIES 192
Section 11: Stipulations as to time 192
Section 12: Condition and warranty 192
Section 13: When condition to be treated as warranty 193
Section 14: Implied undertaking as to title, etc. 193
Section 15: Sale by description 195
Section 16: Implied conditions as to quality or fitness 196
Section 17: Sale by sample 200

CHAPTER IV EFFECTS OF THE CONTRACT 200
Section 18: Goods must be ascertained 200
Section 19: Property passes when intended to pass 201
Section 20: Specific goods in a deliverable state 201

Section 21: Specific goods to be put into a deliverable state *203*
Section 22: Specific goods in a deliverable state, when the seller has to do anything thereto in order to ascertain price *203*
Section 23: Sale of unascertained goods and appropriation *203*
Section 24: Goods sent on approval or "on sale or return" *205*
Section 25: Reservation of right of disposal *205*
Section 26: Risk *prima facie* passes with property *206*

**Chapter V Transfer of Title 206**
Section 27: Sale by person not the owner *206*
Section 28: Sale by one of joint owners *210*
Section 29: Sale by person in possession under voidable contract *210*
Section 30: Seller or buyer in possession after sale *210*

**Chapter VI Performance of the Contract 211**
Section 31: Duties of seller and buyer *211*
Section 32: Payment and delivery are concurrent conditions *211*
Section 33: Delivery *212*
Section 34: Effect of part delivery *212*
Section 35: Buyer to apply for delivery *212*
Section 36: Rules as to delivery *213*
Section 37: Delivery of wrong quantity *213*
Section 38: Instalment deliveries *214*
Section 39: Delivery to carrier or wharfinger *214*
Section 40: Risk where goods are delivered at distant place *220*
Section 41: Buyer's right of examining the goods *221*
Section 42: Acceptance *222*
Section 43: Buyer not bound to return rejected goods *223*
Section 44: Liability of buyer for neglecting or refusing delivery of goods *223*

**Chapter VII Rights of Unpaid Seller against the Goods 223**
Section 45: "Unpaid seller" defined *223*
Section 46: Unpaid seller's rights *224*
Section 47: Seller's lien *224*
Section 48: Part delivery *224*
Section 49: Termination of lien *225*
Section 50: Right of stoppage in transit *225*
Section 51: Duration of transit *225*
Section 52: How stoppage in transit is effected *226*
Section 53: Effect of sub-sale or pledge by buyer *226*
Section 54: Sale not generally rescinded by lien or stoppage in transit *227*

**Chapter VIII Suits for Breach of the Contract 228**
Section 55: Suit for price *228*
Section 56: Damages for non-acceptance *229*
Section 57: Damages for non-delivery *229*
Section 58: Specific performance *229*
Section 59: Remedy for breach of warranty *229*
Section 60: Repudiation of contract before due date *230*
Section 61: Interest by way of damages and special damages *230*

**CHAPTER IX MISCELLANEOUS 231**
Section 62: Exclusion of implied terms and conditions *231*
Section 63: Reasonable time a question of fact *232*
Section 64: Auction sale *232*
Section 64A: In contracts of sale, amount of increased or decreased taxes to be added or deducted *234*
Section 65: [Repeal] Rep. by the Repealing Act, 1938 (1 of 1938), Section 2 and Schedule *235*
Section 66: Savings *235*

**3. THE CONSUMER PROTECTION ACT, 2019 .................................... 236–327**

Introduction *236*
Preamble *237*
Salient Features of the Act *238*
Objectives of the Act *238*
Constitutionality of the Act *239*
Act in a Nutshell *240*

**CHAPTER I PRELIMINARY 241**
Section 1: Short title, extent, commencement and application *241*
Section 2: Definitions *241*
Who is a Consumer? *243*
Services Marketing *255*

**CHAPTER II CONSUMER PROTECTION COUNCILS 283**
Section 3: Central consumer protection council *283*
Section 4: Procedure for meetings of central council *283*
Section 5: Objects of central council *283*
Section 6: State consumer protection councils *283*
Section 7: Objects of state council *284*
Section 8: District consumer protection council *284*
Section 9: Objects of district council *284*

**CHAPTER III CENTRAL CONSUMER PROTECTION AUTHORITY 284**
Section 10: Establishment of Central Consumer Protection Authority *284*
Section 11: Qualifications, method of recruitment, etc., of Chief Commissioner and Commissioners *285*
Section 12: Vacancy, etc., not to invalidate proceedings of Central Authority *285*
Section 13: Appointment of officers, experts, professionals and other employees of Central Authority *285*
Section 14: Procedure of Central Authority *286*
Section 15: Investigation Wing *286*
Section 16: Power of District Collector *286*
Section 17: Complaints to authorities *286*
Section 18: Powers and functions of Central Authority *287*
Section 19: Power of Central Authority to refer matter for Investigation or to other Regulator *288*
Section 20: Power of Central Authority to recall goods, etc. *288*
Section 21: Power of Central Authority to issue directions and penalties against false or misleading advertisements *288*

Section 22: Search and Seizure *289*
Section 23: Designation of any statutory authority or body to function as Central Authority *290*
Section 24: Appeal *290*
Section 25: Grants by Central Government *290*
Section 26: Accounts and Audit *290*
Section 27: Furnishing of annual reports, etc. *291*
**CHAPTER IV CONSUMER DISPUTES REDRESSAL COMMISSION 291**
Section 28: Establishment of District Consumer Disputes Redressal Commission *291*
Comments *292*
Section 29: Qualifications, etc., of President and members of District Commission *292*
Section 30: Salaries, allowances and other terms and conditions of service of President and members of District Commission *292*
Section 31: Transitional provision *292*
Section 32: Vacancy in office of member of District Commission *292*
Section 33: Officers and other employees of District Commission *292*
Section 34: Jurisdiction of District Commission *293*
Section 35: Manner in which complaint shall be made *293*
Section 36: Proceedings before District Commission *294*
Section 37: Reference to Mediation *294*
Section 38: Procedure on admission of complaint *294*
Section 39: Findings of District Commission *297*
Section 40: Review by District Commission in certain cases *298*
Section 41: Appeal against order of District Commission *298*
Section 42: Establishment of State Consumer Disputes Redressal Commission *299*
Section 43: Qualifications, etc., of President and members of State Commission *299*
Section 44: Salaries, allowances and other terms and conditions of service of President and members of State Commission *299*
Section 45: Transitional provision *299*
Section 46: Officers and employees of State Commission *299*
Section 47: Jurisdiction of State Commission *300*
Section 48: Transfer of cases *302*
Section 49: Procedure applicable to State Commission *302*
Section 50: Review by State Commission in certain cases *302*
Section 51: Appeal to National Commission *302*
Section 52: Hearing of appeal *303*
Section 53: Establishment of National Consumer Disputes Redressal Commission *303*
Section 54: Composition of National Commission *303*
Section 55: Qualifications, etc., of President and members of National Commission *303*
Section 56: Transitional provision *304*
Section 57: Other officers and employees of National Commission *304*
Section 58: Jurisdiction of National Commission *304*
Section 59: Procedure applicable to National Commission *306*
Section 60: Review by National Commission in certain cases *307*
Section 61: Power to set aside *ex parte* orders *307*

Section 62: Transfer of cases *307*
Section 63: Vacancy in office of President of National Commission *307*
Section 64: Vacancies or defects in appointment not to invalidate orders *307*
Section 65: Service of notice, etc. *307*
Section 66: Experts to assist National Commission or State Commission *308*
Section 67: Appeal against order of National Commission *308*
Section 68: Finality of orders *308*
Section 69: Limitation period *309*
Section 70: Administrative Control *309*
Section 71: Enforcement of orders of District Commission, State Commission and National Commission *310*
Section 72: Penalty for non-compliance of order *310*
Section 73: Appeal against order passed under Section 72 *310*

**CHAPTER V MEDIATION 311**

Section 74: Establishment of consumer mediation cell *311*
Section 75: Empanelment of mediators *311*
Section 76: Nomination of mediators from panel *312*
Section 77: Duty of mediator to disclose certain facts *312*
Section 78: Replacement of mediator in certain cases *312*
Section 79: Procedure for mediation *312*
Section 80: Settlement through mediation *312*
Section 81: Recording settlement and passing of order *313*

**CHAPTER VI PRODUCT LIABILITY 313**

Section 82: Application of Chapter *313*
Section 83: Product liability action *313*
Section 84: Liability of product manufacturer *313*
Section 85: Liability of product service provider *314*
Section 86: Liability of product sellers *314*
Section 87: Exceptions to product liability action *314*

**CHAPTER VII OFFENCES AND PENALTIES 318**

Section 88: Penalty for non-compliance of direction of Central Authority *318*
Section 89: Punishment for false or misleading advertisement *318*
Section 90: Punishment for manufacturing for sale or storing, selling or distributing or importing products containing adulterant *319*
Section 91: Punishment for manufacturing for sale or for storing or selling or distributing or importing spurious goods *319*
Section 92: Cognizance of offence by court *320*
Section 93: Vexatious search *320*

**CHAPTER VIII MISCELLANEOUS 320**

Section 94: Measures to prevent unfair trade practices in e-commerce, direct selling, etc. *320*
Section 95: Presidents, members, Chief Commissioner, Commissioner, and certain officers to be public servants *320*
Section 96: Compounding of offences *321*
Section 97: Manner of crediting penalty *321*
Section 98: Protection of action taken in good faith *321*

Section 99: Power to give directions by Central Government 321
Section 100: Act not in derogation of any other law 322
Section 101: Power of Central Government to make rules 322
Section 102: Power of State Government to make rules 324
Section 103: Power of National Commission to make regulations 325
Section 104: Power of Central Authority to make regulations 326
Section 105: Rules and regulations to be laid before each House of Parliament 326
Section 106: Power to remove difficulties 327
Section 107: Repeal and savings 327

**4. THE COMPANIES ACT, 2013 .................................................................... 328–447**

**Chapter I Meaning and Features 328**
Introduction 328
Definition of a Company 328
Characteristics 329
Distinction between Company and Partnership 330
Is Company a Citizen? 331
Lifting of Corporate Veil (LCV) 332
Lifting the Corporate Veil in India (LIC v. Escorts) 333

**Chapter II Kinds of Company 336**

**Chapter III Registration and Incorporation 343**
Certificate of Incorporation 344
Effect of Registration 345
Pre-incorporation Contract and its Consequences 345
Commencement of Business (Sec. 10A) 345
Who Need to File Declaration for Commencement of Business? 346
Consequences of Non-Compliance of Section 10A 346

**Chapter IV Memorandum of Association 347**
What is Memorandum of Association? 347
Contents of Memorandum 347
Doctrine of the Ultra Vires 350
Alteration of Memorandum: (Section 13) 355

**Chapter V Articles of Association 356**
Alteration of (AOA) 358
Doctrine of Constructive Notice 359
Doctrine of Indoor-management 359

**Chapter VI Prospectus 362**
Contents of Prospectus 366
Liability for Misstatements under Company Law 367
Remedies under Civil Law 368

**Chapter VII Share and Share Capital 369**
Definition and Meaning of Share 369
Equity Share Capital 371
Preference Share Capital 372
Issue of Shares at Discount 374

Issue of Shares at a Premium *374*
Employee Stock Option Plan (ESOP) *375*
Buyback of Shares *377*
Sweat Equity Shares *378*
Classification of Share Capital *379*
Allotment of Shares *381*

**CHAPTER VIII SHAREHOLDERS AND MEMBERS 382**

**CHAPTER IX DEBENTURES 385**
Characteristics of a Debenture *386*
Kinds of Debentures *386*
Difference between Shares and Debentures *387*
Types of Debentures *388*
Legal Framework of Issuing Debentures and Remedies *388*
Differences between Shareholders and Debenture-holders *389*

**CHAPTER X CORPORATE SOCIAL RESPONSIBILITY (CSR) 390**
Legal Compliance *390*
CSR Activities as per Schedule VII *390*
Activities do not Qualify under CSR Activity *391*
Amount to be Spent and where: Area of Operation of CSR *392*
Penal Action in Case of Default/Non-compliance *392*

**CHAPTER XI DIRECTORS 393**
Position of Directors *393*
Number of Directors *395*
Appointment of Directors *396*
Independent Director *397*
Woman Director *398*
Removal of Directors *398*
Duties of Directors *398*
Powers of Directors *400*
Restrictions of Powers of Board of Directors *401*
Liabilities of Directors *402*
Meetings of Directors *407*
Remuneration of Directors *408*

**CHAPTER XII MEETINGS 410**
Requisites of a Valid Meeting *410*
Kinds of Meetings *410*
Chairman *412*
Resolutions *416*
Registration of Resolutions and Agreements *420*

**CHAPTER XIII MAJORITY POWERS AND MINORITY RIGHTS 421**

**CHAPTER XIV PREVENTION OF OPPRESSION AND MISMANAGEMENT 428**
What is Oppression? *428*
Section 241: Application to Tribunal for relief in cases of oppression, etc. *430*
What is Mismanagement? *431*
Powers of Tribunal on Application under Section 241 *432*

Section 242: Powers of Tribunal: 432
Who can Seek the Remedy? 434
Class Action–Sec. 245 435
Against Whom Class Action Suit can be Filed under Companies Act, 2013? 435
What Orders that can be Sought by the Applicant [Section 245(1)] 436
Requisite Number of Members/Depositors: [Section 245(3)] 436
Conditions for Considering Admissibility of Application Filed 437
Binding Effect of the Orders of the Tribunal [Sec. 245(6)] 437
Non-compliance of Order [Section 245(7)] 437

**CHAPTER XV WINDING-UP OF A COMPANY 437**

Definition of Winding-up 438
Difference between Winding-up and Dissolution of a Company 438
Who can Apply for Winding-up? 438
Winding-up by the Tribunal 441
What is Loss of Substratum? 443
Powers of the Tribunal (Section 273 of 2013 Act) 444
Appeal from Orders of Tribunal (Section 421) 444
Appeal to Supreme Court (Section 423) 445
Consequence of Winding-up Order 445
Preferential Payments 446

**5. THE ARBITRATION AND CONCILIATION ACT, 1996 .......................... 448–520**

Preamble 448
Introduction 449
Object of the Act 450
Scheme of the Act 451
Law Based on uncitral Model Law 451
Matters not Referable to Arbitration 451
Section 1: Short title, extent, and commencement 451

**PART I ARBITRATION**

**CHAPTER I GENERAL PROVISIONS 452**

Section 2: Definitions 452
Applicability of Part I 455
Section 3: Receipt of written communications 455
Section 4: Waiver of right to object 456
Section 5: Extent of judicial intervention 456
Section 6: Administrative assistance 456

**CHAPTER II ARBITRATION AGREEMENT 456**

Section 7: Arbitration agreement 456
Section 8: Power to refer parties to arbitration where there is an arbitration agreement 459
Section 9: Interim measures, etc. by Court 460

**CHAPTER III COMPOSITION OF ARBITRAL TRIBUNAL 461**

Section 10: Number of arbitrators 461

Section 11: Appointment of arbitrators *461*
Section 11A: Power of Central Government to amend Fourth Schedule *464*
Section 12: Grounds for challenge *465*
Section 13: Challenge procedure *466*
Section 14: Failure or impossibility to act *466*
Section 15: Termination of mandate and substitution of arbitrator *467*

**CHAPTER IV JURISDICTION OF ARBITRAL TRIBUNALS 468**

Section 16: Competence of arbitral Tribunal to rule on its jurisdiction *468*
Section 17: Interim measures ordered by arbitral Tribunal *469*

**CHAPTER V CONDUCT OF ARBITRAL PROCEEDINGS 470**

Section 18: Equal treatment of parties *470*
Section 19: Determination of rules of procedure *470*
Section 20: Place of arbitration *470*
Section 21: Commencement of arbitral proceedings *471*
Section 22: Language *471*
Section 23: Statements of claim and defence *472*
Section 24: Hearings and written proceedings *472*
Section 25: Default of a party *473*
Section 26: Expert appointed by arbitral Tribunal *473*
Section 27: Court assistance in taking evidence *474*

**CHAPTER VI MAKING OF ARBITRAL AWARD AND TERMINATION OF PROCEEDINGS 474**

Section 28: Rules applicable to substance of dispute *474*
Section 29: Decision-making by panel of arbitrators *475*
Section 29A: Time limit for arbitral award *475*
Section 29B: Fast track procedure *476*
Section 30: Settlement *477*
Section 31: Form and contents of arbitral award *477*
Section 31A: Regime for costs *478*
Section 32: Termination of proceedings *479*
Section 33: Correction and interpretation of award; additional award *480*

**CHAPTER VII RECOURSE AGAINST ARBITRAL AWARD 480**

Section 34: Application for setting aside arbitral award *480*

**CHAPTER VIII FINALITY AND ENFORCEMENT OF ARBITRAL AWARDS 482**

Section 35: Finality of arbitral awards *482*
Section 36: Enforcement *482*

**CHAPTER IX APPEALS 483**

Section 37: Appealable orders *483*

**CHAPTER X MISCELLANEOUS 484**

Section 38: Deposits *484*
Section 39: Lien on arbitral award and deposits as to costs *484*
Section 40: Arbitration agreement not to be discharged by death of party thereto *485*
Section 41: Provisions in case of insolvency *485*
Section 42: Jurisdiction *486*
Section 42A: Confidentiality of information *486*

Section 42B: Protection of action taken in good faith 486
Section 43: Limitations 486

## PART IA ARBITRATION COUNCIL OF INDIA

Section 43A: Definitions in this Part, unless the context otherwise requires 487
Section 43B: Establishment and incorporation of Arbitration Council of India 487
Section 43C: Composition of Council 487
Section 43D: Duties and functions of Council 488
Section 43E: Vacancies, etc., not to invalidate proceedings of Council 489
Section 43F: Resignation of Members 489
Section 43G: Removal of Member 489
Section 43H: Appointment of experts and constitution of Committees thereof 490
Section 43I: General norms for grading of arbitral institutions 490
Section 43J: Norms for accreditation of arbitrators 490
Section 43K: Depository of awards 490
Section 43L: Power to make regulations by Council 490
Section 43M: Chief Executive Officer 490

## PART II ENFORCEMENT OF CERTAIN FOREIGN AWARDS

CHAPTER I NEW YORK CONVENTION AWARDS **491**
Section 44: Definition 491
Section 45: Power of judicial authority to refer parties to arbitration 491
Section 46: When foreign award binding 491
Section 47: Evidence 492
Section 48: Condition for enforcement of foreign awards 492
Section 49: Enforcement of foreign awards 493
Section 50: Appealable orders 493
Section 51: Saving 493
Section 52: Chapter II not to apply 493
CHAPTER II GENEVA CONVENTION AWARDS **494**
Section 53: Interpretation 494
Section 54: Power of judicial authority to refer parties to arbitration 494
Section 55: Foreign awards when binding 494
Section 56: Evidence 494
Section 57: Conditions for enforcement of foreign awards 495
Section 58: Enforcement of foreign awards 496
Section 59: Appealable orders 496
Section 60: Saving 496

## PART III CONCILIATION

Section 61: Application and scope 496
Difference between Arbitration and Conciliation 497
Section 62: Commencement of conciliation proceedings 497
Section 63: Number of conciliators 498
Section 64: Appointment of conciliators 498
Section 65: Submission of statements to conciliator 498

Section 66: Conciliator not bound by certain enactments 499
Section 67: Role of conciliator 499
Section 68: Administrative assistance 499
Section 69: Communication between conciliator and parties 499
Section 70: Disclosure of information 500
Section 71: Co-operation of parties with conciliator 500
Section 72: Suggestions by parties for settlement of dispute 500
Section 73: Settlement agreement 500
Section 74: Status and effect of settlement agreement 502
Section 75: Confidentiality 502
Section 76: Termination of conciliation proceedings 502
Section 77: Resort to arbitral or judicial proceedings 502
Section 78: Costs 502
Section 79: Deposits 503
Section 80: Role of conciliator in other proceedings 503
Section 81: Admissibility of evidence in other proceedings 503

**PART IV SUPPLEMENTARY PROVISIONS**

Section 82: Power of High Court to make rules 504
Section 83: Removal of difficulties 504
Section 84: Power to make rules 504
Section 85: Repeal and savings 504
Section 86: Repeal and saving 505
Section 87: Effect of arbitral and related court proceedings commenced prior to 23rd October, 2015 505
The First Schedule 505
Convention on the Recognition and Enforcement of Foreign 505
Arbitral Awards [Article I – XVI] 505
The Second Schedule 510
Protocol on Arbitration Clauses 510
The Third Schedule 512
Convention on the Execution of Foreign 512
Arbitral Awards [Article I – XI] 512
The Fourth Schedule 515
The Fifth Schedule 516
The Sixth Schedule 518
The Seventh Schedule 519

**6. THE NEGOTIABLE INSTRUMENTS ACT, 1881 ........................................ 521–585**

Introduction 521
Object of the Act 521
Salient features of Negotiable Instruments 522
Information Technology Act, 2000 vis-a-vis NI Act, 1881 523

**CHAPTER I PRELIMINARY 523**

Section 1: Short title 523
Section 2: Repeal of enactment 524
Section 3: Interpretation clause 524

**Chapter II Of Notes, Bills and Cheques 524**

Section 4: "Promissory note" *524*
Section 5: "Bill of exchange" *527*
Section 6: "Cheque" *529*
Section 7: "Drawer", "Drawee" *531*
Section 8: "Holder" *531*
Section 9: "Holder in due course" *531*
Section 10: "Payment in due course" *534*
Section 11: "Inland instrument" *534*
Section 12: "Foreign instrument" *534*
Section 13: "Negotiable instrument" *534*
Section 14: Negotiation *534*
Section 15: Indorsement *535*
Section 16: Indorsement "in blank" and "in full" *535*
Section 17: Ambiguous instruments *535*
Section 18: Where amount is stated differently in figures and words *535*
Section 19: Instruments payable on demand *535*
Section 20: Inchoate stamped instruments *535*
Section 21: "At sight", "On presentment", "After sight" *536*
Section 22: "Maturity" *536*
Section 23: Calculating maturity of bill or note payable so many months after date or sight *536*
Section 24: Calculating maturity of bill or note payable so many days after date or sight *536*
Section 25: When day of maturity is a holiday *536*

**Chapter III Parties to Notes, Bills and Cheques 537**

Section 26: Capacity to make, etc., the promissory notes, etc. *537*
Section 27: Agency *537*
Section 28: Liability of agent signing *537*
Section 29: Liability of legal representative signing *537*
Section 30: Liability of drawer *537*
Section 31: Liability of drawee of cheque *538*
Section 32: Liability of maker of note and acceptor of bill *538*
Section 33: Only drawee can be acceptor except in need or for honour *538*
Section 34: Acceptance by several drawees not partners *538*
Section 35: Liability of indorser *538*
Section 36: Liability of prior parties to holder in due course *539*
Section 37: Maker, drawer and acceptor principals *539*
Section 38: Prior party a principal in respect of each subsequent party *539*
Section 39: Suretyship *539*
Section 40: Discharge of indorser's liability *539*
Section 41: Acceptor bound although indorsement forged *540*
Section 42: Acceptance of bill drawn in fictitious name *540*
Section 43: Negotiable instrument made, etc., without consideration *540*
Section 44: Partial absence or failure of money-consideration *540*
Section 45: Partial failure of consideration not consisting of money *541*
Section 45A: Holder's right to duplicate of lost bill *541*

**Chapter IV Of Negotiation 541**
Section 46: Delivery *541*
Section 47: Negotiation by delivery *541*
Section 48: Negotiation by indorsement *542*
Section 49: Conversion of indorsement in blank into indorsement in full *542*
Section 50: Effect of indorsement *542*
Section 51: Who may negotiate *542*
Section 52: Indorser who excludes his own liability or makes it conditional *543*
Section 53: Holder deriving title from holder in due course *543*
Section 54: Instrument indorsed in blank *543*
Section 55: Conversion of indorsement in blank into indorsement in full *543*
Section 56: Indorsement for part of sum due *543*
Section 57: Legal representative cannot by delivery only negotiate instrument indorsed by deceased *543*
Section 58: Instrument obtained by unlawful means or for unlawful consideration *544*
Section 59: Instrument acquired after dishonour or when overdue *544*
Section 60: Instrument negotiable till payment or satisfaction *544*

**Chapter V Of Presentment 544**
Section 61: Presentment for acceptance *544*
Section 62: Presentment of promissory note for sight *545*
Section 63: Drawee's time for deliberation *545*
Section 64: Presentment for payment *545*
Section 65: Hours for presentment *546*
Section 66: Presentment for payment of instrument payable after date or sight *546*
Section 67: Presentment for payment of promissory note payable by installments *546*
Section 68: Presentment for payment of instrument payable at specified place and not elsewhere *546*
Section 69: Instrument payable at specified place *546*
Section 70: Presentment where no exclusive place specified *546*
Section 71: Presentment when maker, etc., has no known place of business or residence *546*
Section 72: Presentment of cheque to charge drawer *546*
Section 73: Presentment of cheque to charge any other person *547*
Section 74: Presentment of instrument payable on demand *547*
Section 75: Presentment by or to agent, representative of deceased, or assignee of insolvent *547*
Section 75A: Excuse for delay in presentment for acceptance or payment *547*
Section 76: When presentment unnecessary *547*
Section 77: Liability of banker for negligently dealing with bill presented for payment *548*

**Chapter VI Of Payment and Interest 548**
Section 78: To whom payment should be made *548*
Section 79: Interest when rate specified *548*
Section 80: Interest when no rate specified *548*
Section 81: Delivery of instrument on payment or indemnity in case of loss *548*

**Chapter VII Of Discharge from Liability on Notes, Bills and Cheques 549**
Section 82: Discharge from liability *549*
Section 83: Discharge by allowing drawee more than forty-eight hours to accept *549*
Section 84: When cheque not duly presented and drawer damaged thereby *549*
Section 85: Cheque payable to order *550*
Section 85A: Drafts drawn by one branch of a bank on another payable to order *551*
Section 86: Parties not consenting discharged by qualified or limited acceptance *551*
Section 87: Effect of material alteration *551*
Section 88: Acceptor or indorser bound notwithstanding previous alteration *552*
Section 89: Payment of instrument on which alteration is not apparent *552*
Section 90: Extinguishment of rights of action on bill in acceptor's hands *553*

**Chapter VIII Of Notice of Dishonour 553**
Section 91: Dishonour by non-acceptance *553*
Section 92: Dishonour by non-payment *553*
Section 93: By and to whom notice should be given *553*
Section 94: Mode in which notice may be given *554*
Section 95: Party receiving must transmit notice of dishonour *554*
Section 96: Agent for presentment *554*
Section 97: When party to whom notice given is dead *554*
Section 98: When notice of dishonour is unnecessary *554*

**Chapter IX Of Noting and Protest 555**
Section 99: Noting *555*
Section 100: Protest *555*
Section 101: Contents of protest *555*
Section 102: Notice of protest *555*
Section 103: Protest for non-payment after dishonour by non-acceptance *556*
Section 104: Protest of foreign bills *556*
Section 104A: When noting equivalent to protest *556*

**Chapter X Of Reasonable Time 556**
Section 105: Reasonable time *556*
Section 106: Reasonable time of giving notice of dishonour *556*
Section 107: Reasonable time for transmitting such notice *556*

**Chapter XI Of Acceptance and Payment for Honour and Reference in Case of Need 557**
Section 108: Acceptance for honour *557*
Section 109: How acceptance for honour must be made *557*
Section 110: Acceptance not specifying for whose honour it is made *557*
Section 111: Liability of acceptor for honour *557*
Section 112: When acceptor for honour may be charged *557*
Section 113: Payment for honour *557*
Section 114: Right of payer for honour *557*
Section 115: Drawee in case of need *558*
Section 116: Acceptance and payment without protest *558*

**Chapter XII Of Compensation 558**
Section 117: Rules as to compensation *558*

**CHAPTER XIII SPECIAL RULES OF EVIDENCE 558**

Section 118: Presumptions as to negotiable instruments *558*
Section 119: Presumption on proof of protest *562*
Section 120: Estoppel against denying original validity of instrument *562*
Section 121: Estoppel against denying capacity of payee to indorse *562*
Section 122: Estoppel against denying signature or capacity of prior party *562*

**CHAPTER XIV OF CROSSED CHEQUES 563**

Section 123: Cheque crossed generally *563*
Section 124: Cheque crossed specially *564*
Section 125: Crossing after issue *564*
Section 126: Payment of cheque crossed generally *564*
Section 127: Payment of cheque crossed specially more than once *564*
Section 128: Payment in due course of crossed cheque *564*
Section 129: Payment of crossed cheque out of due course *564*
Section 130: Cheque bearing "not negotiable" *565*
Section 131: Non-liability of banker receiving payment of cheque *565*
Section 131A: Application of Chapter to drafts *565*

**CHAPTER XV OF BILLS IN SETS 565**

Section 132: Set of bills *565*
Section 133: Holder of first acquired part entitled to all *565*

**CHAPTER XVI OF INTERNATIONAL LAW 566**

Section 134: Law governing liability of maker, acceptor or indorser of foreign instrument *566*
Section 135: Law of place of payment governs dishonour *566*
Section 136: Instrument made, etc., out of India, but in accordance with the law of India *566*
Section 137: Presumption as to foreign law *566*

**CHAPTER XVII OF PENALTIES IN CASE OF DISHONOUR OF CERTAIN CHEQUES FOR INSUFFICIENCY OF FUNDS IN THE ACCOUNTS 566**

Section 138: Dishonour of cheque for insufficiency, etc., of funds in the account *566*
Section 139: Presumption in favour of holder *573*
Section 140: Defence which may not be allowed in any prosecution under Section 138 *575*
Section 141: Offences by companies *575*
Section 142: Cognizance of offences *579*
Section 142A: Validation for transfer of pending cases: *580*
Section 143: Power of Court to try cases summarily *581*
Section 143A: Power to direct interim compensation *581*
Section 144: Mode of service of summons *583*
Section 145: Evidence on affidavit *583*
Section 146: Bank's slip prima facie evidence of certain facts *584*
Section 147: Offences to be compoundable *584*
Section 148: Power of Appellate Court to order payment pending appeal against conviction: *585*

***INDEX* .......... *587–590***

# Preface

The legal landscape is constantly evolving, and it is essential to keep academic resources up-to-date to reflect these changes. The second edition of "Legal Aspects of Business" has been thoroughly revised to incorporate significant legislative amendments and landmark judicial decisions. Key updates include:

1. **Consumer Protection Act, 1986**: This pivotal legislation has undergone substantial revisions with the Consumer Protection Act, 2019, which modernizes consumer rights and addresses contemporary consumer issues. The new edition incorporates these changes, providing a comprehensive understanding of the current legal framework.
2. **Companies Act, 2013**: To enhance corporate governance and ease of doing business, the Companies Act has been amended multiple times. The second edition discusses all these amendments in detail, ensuring that readers are well-versed in the latest legal requirements and regulatory changes.
3. **Arbitration and Conciliation Act, 1996**: With amendments in 2015, 2019, and 2021, this Act has evolved to streamline dispute resolution processes and make arbitration more efficient. The new edition covers these amendments, offering insights into the improved arbitration framework.
4. **Negotiable Instruments Act, 1881**: Amendments in 2003, 2015, and 2018 have modernized this Act to address issues related to financial instruments and enhance the credibility of cheques. The second edition includes these updates, providing a clear understanding of the current legal provisions.

Additionally, the second edition features discussions on landmark decisions by the Supreme Court of India, enriching the readers' knowledge and interest in the subject. These judicial pronouncements are crucial for understanding the practical application of laws and their interpretation by the highest court.

This updated edition is tailored to meet the needs of law and management students, ensuring that they have access to the most current legal information and can navigate the complex legal environment with confidence.

**P.K. Padhi**

# Preface to the First Edition

The legal landscape is constantly evolving, and it is essential to keep academic resources up-to-date to reflect these changes. The second edition of *Legal Aspects of Business* has been thoroughly revised to incorporate significant legislative amendments and landmark judicial decisions. Key updates include:

1. **Consumer Protection Act, 1986:** This pivotal legislation has undergone substantial revisions with the Consumer Protection Act, 2019, which modernizes consumer rights and addresses contemporary consumer issues. The new edition incorporates these changes, providing a comprehensive understanding of the current legal framework.
2. **Companies Act, 2013:** To enhance corporate governance and ease of doing business, the Companies Act has been amended multiple times. The second edition discusses all these amendments in detail, ensuring that readers are well versed in the latest compliance requirements and regulatory changes.
3. **Arbitration and Conciliation Act, 1996:** With amendments in 2015, 2019, and 2021, this Act has evolved to streamline dispute resolution processes and make arbitration more efficient. The new edition covers these amendments, offering insights into the improved arbitration framework.
4. **Negotiable Instruments Act, 1881:** Amendments in 2002, 2015, and 2018 have modernized this Act to address issues related to financial instruments and enhance the credibility of cheques. The second edition includes these updates, providing a clear understanding of the current legal provisions.

Additionally, the second edition features discussions on landmark decisions by the Supreme Court of India, enriching the readers' knowledge and insights into the subject. These judicial pronouncements are crucial for understanding the practical application of laws and their interpretation by the highest court.

This updated edition is tailored to meet the needs of law and management students, ensuring that they have access to the most current legal information and can navigate the complex legal environment with confidence.

P.K. Padhi

# Preface to the First Edition

Business law is the body of knowledge that deals with the rights, relation and conduct of persons engaged in commerce, merchandising, trade and sales. It is a broad and continually evolving field. Business law regulates various forms of legal business entities such as sole proprietors, partnerships, and registered companies with limited liabilities. Some of the business laws are statutory, i.e. legislative bodies create them while others have their origin in common law, for example, the Law of Contract. The business laws in India are mainly based on English laws.

Business laws serve several purposes. One of them is the smooth functioning of business operations. Business people need to have confidence in their dealing with other individuals, and these laws are meant to address their genuine concerns.

Though there are quite a few books on Business law available in the market, somehow they fail to treat the subject in a systematic and comprehensive fashion. I have therefore endeavoured to give an in-depth analysis of the subject for the benefit of students and professionals interested in the field of Business law.

The book discusses in detail the six Acts that pertain to Business Law, namely, the Indian Contract Act, 1872; the Arbitration and Conciliation Act,1996; the Sale of Goods Act, 1930; the Negotiable Instruments Act, 1881; the Consumer Protection Act, 1986; and the Companies Act, 1956. Topics are presented in an accessible manner so that the students can understand the concepts clearly. Many case laws are given to understand the subject in the right perspective.

What distinguishes the text is that it gives many Supreme Court and High Court judgments to reinforce the problem discussed.

The book is primarily meant as a text for undergraduate and postgraduate students of management and law, and undergraduate students of commerce. It would also prove extremely useful to those pursuing professional courses such as chartered accountancy, company secretaryship, and cost and works accountancy.

I am grateful to the editorial and production team of the publishers, PHI Learning for their careful processing of the manuscript.

Any constructive suggestions for improving the contents would be most welcome.

**P.K. Padhi**

# Table of Cases


**A**

*A. Lakshmanaswami Mudaliar* v. *Life Insurance Corporation of India,* AIR 1963 SC 1185., **351**

*A. Ramamoorthy* v. *P. Satyanarayana,* AIR 1958 ANDHRA PRADESH 550., **212**

*A. Subba Reddy* v. *Neelapa Reddi,* AIR 1966 AP 267., **552**

*A.B.C. Laminart Pvt. Ltd.* v. *A.P. Agencies, Salem,* AIR 1989 SC 1239., **75**

*A.D. Thirukoil, Palani* v. *Director General of Post Offices, Department of Posts,* AIR 2011 SC 2604., **278**

*Achutrao Haribhau Khodwa* v. *State of Maharashtra,* (1996) 2 SCC 634., **259**

*Adams* v. *Thrift,* (1915) 2 Ch. 21, **403**

*Aditya Narayan Chouresia* v. *Bank of India,* AIR 2000 Pat 222., **139**

*Agricultural Market Committee* v. *Shalimar Chemical Works Ltd.,* AIR 1997 SC 2502., **202**

*Alapati R.G.K. and Co.* v. *J. Ramanujam,* AIR 1961 ANDHRA PRADESH 408., **187**

*Alexander* v. *Railway Executive,* (1951) 2 All ER 442., **12**

*Allcard* v. *Skinner,* (1887) 36 Ch. D. 145., **45**

*Amrit Banaspati Co. Ltd.* v. *State of Punjab,* AIR 1992 SC 1075., **64**

*Amrit Lal Goverdhan Lalan* v. *State Bank of Travancore,* AIR 1968 SC 1432., **143**

*Anand Bihari Lal* v. *Dinshaw & Co.,* AIR 1942 Oudh 417., **361**

*Archana M. Kamath* v. *Canara Bank,* AIR 2003 SC 1694., **32**

*Arcos* v. *Ranaasan & Sons,* (1933) A.C. 470 102., **196**

*Armstrong* v. *Jackson,* [1917] 2 KB 822., **54**

*Arosan Enterprises Ltd.* v. *Union of India,* AIR 1999 SC 3804., **91**

*Arosan Enterprises Ltd., M/s.* v. *Union of India,* AIR 1999 SC 3804., **90**

*Arvind Mills Ltd.* v. *M/s. Associated Roadways,* AIR 2004 SC 5147., **274**

*Ashbury Railway Carriage and Iron Co. Ltd.* v. *Riche,* (1875) LR 7 HL 653., **350**

*Ashok Yeshwant Badeve* v. *Surendra Madhavrao Nighojakar,* AIR 2001 SC 1315., **529**

*Atlas Export Industries, M/s.* v. *M/s. Kotak and Company,* AIR 1999 SC 3286., **77**

*Attorney General* v. *Great Eastern Railway Co.,* (1880) 5AC 473., **351**

**B**

*B.O.I. Finance Ltd.* v. *Custodian,* AIR 1997 SC 1952, **99**

*Baldry* v. *Marshall,* (1925) 1KB 260., **192**

*Bank of Bihar Ltd.* v. *Dr. Damodar Prasad,* AIR 1969 SC 297., **138**

*Bank of Bihar* v. *Mahabir Lal,* AIR 1964 SC 377., **550**

*Bank of Chittor* v. *Narsimbulu ,* AIR 1966 AP 163., **151**

*Bank of India* v. *O.P. Swaranakar,* AIR 2003 SC 858., **2**

*Barton* v. *Armstrong,* [1976] AC 104., **39**

*BCPP Mazdoor Sangh* v. *N.T.P.C.,* AIR 2008 SC 336., **64**

*Bellachi* v. *Pakeeran,* AIR 2009 SC 3293., **44**

*Bengal Corporation* v. *Commrs. for the Port of Calcutta,* AIR 1971 CALCUTTA 357., **198**
*Bentsen* v. *Taylor,* (1893) 2 Q.B. 274., **192**
*Beswick* v. *Beswick,* (1966) 3 All ER 1., **22**
*Bevelon Investments Pty. Ltd.* v. *Kingsley Air Conditioning Pty. Ltd.,* (1971) 1 ACLR 24., **119**
*Bhagwandas Goverdhandas Kedia* v. *M/s. Girdharlal Parshottamadas and Co.,* AIR 1966 SC 543., **25**
*Bhagwati Prasad Pawan Kumar, M/s.* v. *Union of India,* AIR 2006 SC 2331., **33**
*Bharat Insurance Co. Ltd.* v. *Kanhaiya Lal,* AIR 1935 Lah 792., **425**
*Bharat Petroleum Corpn. Ltd.* v. *Great Eastern Shipping Co. Ltd.,* AIR 2008 SC 357., **34**
*Bharat Sanchar Nigam Ltd.* v. *Motorola India Pvt. Ltd.,* AIR 2009 SC 357., **456**
*Bherulal* v. *Ram Rikh,* AIR 1951 AJMER 71., **526**
*Bihar School Examination Board* v. *Suresh Prasad Sinha,* AIR 2010 SC 93., **246**
*Bihar State Mineral Dev. Corpn.* v. *Encon Builders (I) Pvt. Ltd.,* AIR 2003 SC 3688., **453**
*Bisset* v. *Wilkinson,* [1927] AC 177., **50**
*Blount* v. *War Office,* (1953) 1 All ER 1071., **153**
*Bolam* v. *Friem Hospital Management Committee,* (1957) 2 All. ER 118., **258**
*Bolton Partners* v. *Lambert* (1889) 41 Ch. D. 295., **168**
*Boomer* v. *Muir 24 P 2d 570* (Cal App. 1933)., **120**
*Brahmaputra Tea Co. Ltd.* v. *Scarth,* (1885) ILR 11 Cal 545., **71**
*Brown* v. *British Abrasive Wheels Co.,* [1919] 1 Ch. 290, **426**
*Burn and Co. Ltd.* v. *Colin Mac Donald,* (1909) ILR 26 Cal 354., **71**

**C**

*C.L. Joseph* v. *Jos,* AIR 1965 Ker 68., **427**
*Carlill* v. *Carbolic Smoke Ball Co.,* (1892) 2 QB 484., **25, 79**
*Central H.I. Trading Co.* v. *Pitty Bros.,* AIR 1962 BOMBAY 222., **235**
*Central Inland Water Transport Corpn. Ltd.* v. *Brojo Nath Ganguly,* (1986) 3 SCC 156., **18**
*Central Inland Water Transport Corporation Ltd.* v. *Brojo Nath Ganguly,* AIR 1986 SC 1571., **62**
*Chacko* v. *Mahadevan,* AIR 2007 SC 2967., **36**
*Chairman and MD, NTPC Ltd.* v. *Reshmi Constructions, Builders and Contractors,* (2004) 2 SCC 663., **19**
*Chand* v. *M/s. Jagdish Pershad Kishan Chand,* AIR 1966 SC 1427., **144**
*Chapel* v. *Cooper,* (1844) 13 M and W 252., **111**
*Chapelton* v. *Barry Urban District Council,* (1940) 1 KB 532., **11**
*Charan Singh* v. *Healing Touch Hospital and others,* AIR 2000 SC 3138., **239**
*Chettinad Mercantile Bank Ltd.* v. *P.L.A. Pichammai Achi,* AIR 1945 Mad. 445., **159**
*Chikham Amiraju* v. *Chikham Seshamma,* (1917) 41 Mad 33., **41**
*Harshendra Kumar D.* v. *Rebatilata Koley,* AIR 2011 SC 1090., **577**
*City and I.D. Corpn. of Maharashtra Ltd.* v. *Nagpur Steel and Alloys Pvt. Ltd.,* AIR 1992 BOMBAY 55., **230**
*City Union Bank Ltd.* v. *Thangarajan,* (2003)46 SCL 237 (Mad)., **160**
*Cochin Port Trust* v. *Associated Cotton Traders Ltd.,* AIR 1983 KERALA 154., **154**
*Commissioner of Income tax, Delhi* v. *M/s P.M. Rathod and Co.,* AIR 1959 SC 1394., **149**
*Commissioner of Income-tax (Central) Calcutta* v. *Standard Vacuum Oil Co.,* AIR 1966 SC 1393., **369**
*Commissioner of Income-tax, A.P.* v. *M/s. Motors and General Stores (P) Ltd.,* AIR 1968 SC 200., **181**
*Commr. of Income-tax, Madras* v. *Mysore Chromite Ltd.,* AIR 1955 SC 98., **204**
*Condor* v. *Barron Knights Ltd.,* [1966] 1 WLR 87., **95**
*Consolidated Coffee Ltd.* v. *Coffee Board, Bangalore,* AIR 1980 SC 1468., **232**
*Consolidated Engineering Enterprises, M/s.* v. *Principal Secretary, (Irrigation Department),* AIR 2009 SC (Supp), **487**
*Consumer Unity and Trust Society, Jaipur* v. *Chairman and Managing Director, Bank of Baroda, Calcutta,* (1995) 2 SCC 150., **249, 267**
*Cooper* v. *Phibbs,* (1867) LR 2 HL 149., **59**
*Costain Civil Engineering* v. *Zanen Dredging* (1996) 85 BLR 77., **120**
*Couturier* v. *Hastie, 1852,* 5 H.L.C. 673, 23 R.C. 204., 288, (1856) 5 HL Cas. 673., **58, 190**
*Craven-Ellis* v. *Canons Ltd.* [1936] 2 KB 403., **119**
*Cundy* v. *Lindsay,* (1878) 3 App. Cas. 459., **57, 207**
*Cunningham* v. *Munro,* (1922) 28 Com Cas 42., **217**
*Currie* v. *Misa,* (1875) LR 10 Exch 153., **66**

**D**

*Daimler Co. Ltd.* v. *Continental Tyre and Rubber Co. (Great Britain) Ltd.,* [1916] 2 AC 307., **334**

*Dalmia Cement (Bharat) Ltd., M/s.* v. *M/s. Galaxy Traders and Agencies Ltd.,* AIR 2001 SC 676., **522, 568**

*Damodar S. Prabhu* v. *Sayed Babalal H.,* AIR 2010 SC 1907, **567, 584**

*Darlington B C* v. *Eiltshier Northern Ltd.,* (1995) 3 All ER 895., **23**

*Davies* v. *Collins,* (1945) 1 All ER 247., **12**

*Davis Contractors* v. *Fareham UDC* [1956] AC 696., **98**

*DCM Financial Services Ltd.* v. *J. N. Sareen,* AIR 2008 SC 2255., **579**

*Delhi Development Authority, N.D.* v. *Joint Action Committee, Allottee of SFS Flats,* AIR 2008 SC 1343., **78**

*Delhi Transport Corpn. Ltd.* v. *Rose Advertising,* AIR 2003 SC 2523., **552**

*Denny, Mott & Dickinson* v. *James Fraser,* [1944] AC 265., **97**

*Derry* v. *Peek,* (1889) LR 14 APP. CAS 337., **50, 368**

*Dhanrajamal Gobindram, M/s.* v. *M/s. Shamji Kalidas and Co.,* AIR 1961 SC 1285., **78**

*Dhanyalakshmi Rice Mills* v. *Commissioner of Civil Supplies,* AIR 1976 SC 2243., **116**

*Dharampal and Co., Agra* v. *K.G. Ram Chandra Rao and Co.,* AIR 1980 ALLAHABAD., **221**

*Dharangadhara Chemical Words Ltd.* v. *State of Saurashtra,* AIR 1957 SC 264., **254**

*Digamber Pershad Kirti Prasad, M/s.* v. *State of U.P.,* AIR 1996 ALLAHABAD 1., **202**

*Dimskal Shipping Co* v. *ITWF,* [1991] 4 All ER 871., **40**

*Donoghue* v. *Stevenson,* [1932] HL 100., **20**

*Dr. Vimla* v. *Delhi Administration,* AIR 1963 SC 1572., **48**

*Dunlop Pneumatic Tyre Co. Ltd.* v. *New Garage & Motor Co. Ltd.,* (1915) AC 847., **21**

*Dunlop Pneumatic Tyre Co. Ltd.* v. *New Garage and Motor Co. Ltd.,* (1915) AC 79., **132**

*Dunlop* v. *Selfridge Ltd.,* [1915] AC 847., **66**

*Dutton* v. *Poole,* (1677) 2 Lev 210. (Court of King's Bench)., **21**

E

*E.W. Evans* v. *S. Benjamin, AIR 1951 CALCUTTA 470.,* **230**

*Economic Transport Organization* v. *Dharwad Distt. Khadi Gramudyog Sangh,* AIR 2000 SC 1635., **274**

*Edwards* v. *Halliwell,* [1950] 2 All ER 1064, **423**

*Elphick* v. *Barnes,* 5 C.P.D. 321 (1880)., **190**

*Esso Petroleum Company Ltd.,* v. *Harper's Garage (Stourport) Ltd.,* (1967) 1 All ER 699., **73**

*Esso Petroleum* v. *Mardon,* [1976] QB 801., **51**

*Eternit Everest Ltd.* v. *C.G. Abraham,* AIR 2003 KERALA 273., **197**

*Everhart* v. *Miles,* 47 Md. App. 131, 136, 422 A.2d 28., **110**

F

*Fateh Chand* v. *Balkishan Dass,* AIR 1963 SC 1405., **129**

*Fazaluddin* v. *Panchanan Das,* AIR 1957 Cal 92., **66**

*Ferguson* v. *Wilson,* (1866) 2 Ch. App. 77., **323**

*Fisher* v. *Bell,* (1960) 3 All ER 731., **6**

*Forest of Dean Coal Mining Co., Re,* [1878] 10 Ch. D. 450, **395**

*FOSS* v. *HARBOTTLE,* (1843) 67 ER 189, **421**

G

*Gajanan Moreshwar* v. *Moreshwar Madan,* AIR 1942 Bom 302., **136**

*General Manager, Telecom* v. *M. Krishnan,* AIR 2010 SC 90., **306**

*Ghaziabad Development Authority* v. *Balbir Singh,* AIR 2004 SC 2141., **269, 271**

*Ghaziabad Development Authority* v. *Balbir Singh,* AIR 2005 SC 1206., **270**

*Gherulal Parakh* v. *Mahadeodas Maiya,* AIR 1959 SC 781., **61, 79**

*Gilford Motor Company Ltd.* v. *Horne,* [1933] 1 Ch. 935., **334**

*Girdharilal, M/s.* v. *Jethmal,* AIR 1963 ANDHRA PRADESH 185., **224**

*Girija Proshad Pal* v. *National Coal Co. Ltd.,* AIR 1949 Cal 472., **215**

*Goaplast Pvt. Ltd.* v. *Shri Chico Ursula D'Souza,* AIR 2003 SC 2035., **570**

*Gomathinayagam Pillai* v. *Palaniswami Nadar,* AIR 1967 SC 868., **91**

*Gowrishankar* v. *Joshi Amba Shankar Family Trust,* AIR 1996 SC 2202., **48**

*Greenmast Shipping* v. *Jean Lion,* [1986] 2 Lloyd's Rep. 277., **120**

*Gujarat Bottling Co. Ltd., M/s.* v. *Coca Cola Company,* AIR 1995 SC 2372., **73**

*Gulabchand Rawatmal, M/s.* v. *S.C. Mfg. Co.,* AIR 1959 BOMBAY 158., **228**

H

*H.L. Bolton (Engg.) Co. Ltd.* v. *T.J. Graham,* [1957] 1 QB 169, **394**

*H.M. Corpn.* v. *M. Venkateswarlu and Co.,* AIR 1959 ANDHRA PRADESH 545., **213**

*Hakam Singh* v. *M/s. Gammon (India) Ltd.,* AIR 1971 SC 740., **75**

*Hanutmal Bhutoria* v. *Dominion of India,* AIR 1961 CALCUTTA 54., **206**

*Har Bhajan Lal* v. *Harcharan Lal,* AIR 1925 All 539., **24**

*Harbutt's Plasticine Ltd.* v. *Wayne Tank and Pump Co.,* (1970) 1 All ER 225., **13**

*Hardley* v. *Baxendale,* (1854) 9 Exch. 341., **124**

*Harman Electronics (P) Ltd., M/s.* v. *M/s. National Panasonic India Ltd.,* AIR 2009 SC 1168., **569**

*Harvey* v. *Facey.,* (1893) AC 552., **5**

*Haryana Urban Development Authority* v. *Rajnish Chander Sharda,* AIR 2000 SC 3573., **269**

*Haryana Urban Development Authority* v. *Smt. Nalini Aggarwal,* AIR 1997 SC 2582., **272**

*Haryana Urban Development Authority* v. *Jeewan Asha Garg,* AIR 2005 SC 1397; **270**

*Haryana Urban Development Authority* v. *Dheer Singh Bhatti,* AIR 2005 SC 1472; **270**

*Haryana Urban Development Authority* v. *Dropadi Devi,* AIR 2005 SC 1487., **270**

*Haseldine* v. *C.A. Daw & Son Ltd.,* (1941) 2 KB 343., **16**

*Hedley Byrne* v. *Heller,* [1964] AC 465., **51**

*Henderson* v. *Stevenson,* (1875) 32 LT 709., **9**

*Herne Bay Steamboat Co.* v. *Hutton,* [1903] 2 KB 683., **95**

*Hind Overseas Private Ltd.* v. *Raghunath Prasad Jhunjhunwalla,* AIR 1976 SC 565., **443**

*Hirji Bharmal, M/s.* v. *Bombay Cotton Ltd.,* AIR 1958 BOMBAY 411., **228**

*Hirji Mulji* v. *Cheong Yue Steamship Co. Ltd.,* [1926] AC 497., **93**

*Hiten P. Dalal* v. *Bratindranath Banerjee,* AIR 2001 SC 3897., **575**

*Howard* v. *Patent Ivory Co.,* (1888) 38 Ch. D. 156., **361**

*Howell* v. *Coupland,* (1876) 1 QBD 258., **190**

**I**

*IBI Consultancy* v. *DSC Ltd.,* AIR 2018 SC 2907., **464**

*I.C.D.S. Ltd., M/s.* v. *Smithaben H. Patel,* AIR 1999 SC 1036., **100, 101**

*I.F.C.I. Ltd.* v. *Cannanore Spg. and Wvg. Mills Ltd.,* AIR 2002 SC 1841., **94, 146**

*Indian Airlines Corporation* v. *Jothaji Maniram,* AIR 1959 Mad 285., **20**

*Indian Medical Association* v. *V.P. Shantha,* AIR 1996 SC 550., **254 – 255**

*Indo Automobiles, M/s.* v. *M/s. Jai Durga Enterprises,* AIR 2009 SC 386., **570**

*Ingram* v. *Little,* (1961) 1QB 31., **58**

**J**

*J. Spurling Ltd.* v. *Bradshaw,* (1956) 1 WLR 461., **12**

*Jacob Mathew* v. *State of Punjab,* AIR 2005 SC 3180., **262, 264**

*Jagdish Chander* v. *Ram Chandra,* 2007 (5) SCC 719., **458**

*Jagjivan Mavji Vithalani* v. *Messrs. Ranchhoddas Meghji,* AIR 1954 SC 554., **538, 546**

*Jain & Son* v. *Comeron,* AIR 1922 All 735., **153**

*Jammu and Kashmir Bank Ltd.* v. *Attar-Ul-Nisa,* AIR 1967 SC 540., **117**

*Jia Ram* v. *Sulakhan Mal,* AIR 1941 Lahore 386., **100**

*Joseph Constantine Steamship Lime Limited* v. *Imperial Smelting Corporation Ltd.,* 1942–AC 154., **93**

**K**

*K. Bhaskaran* v. *Sankaran Vaidhyan Balan and anr.,* [1999 (7) SCC 510], **570**

*K. Bhaskaran* v. *Sankaran Vaidhyan Balan,* AIR 1999 SC 3762., **560, 568, 569**

*K.K. Ahuja* v. *V.K. Vora and another,* (2009) 10 SCC 48., **577**

*K.K. Modi* v. *K.N. Modi,* AIR 1998 SC 1297., **457**

*K.L. Johar and Co.* v. *Dy. Commercial Tax Officer,* AIR 1965 SC 1082., **183**

*K.P. Chowdhry* v. *State of M.P.,* AIR 1967 SC 203., **35**

*K.P. Subbarama Sastri* v. *K.S. Raghavan,* AIR 1987 SC 1257., **133**

*Kaliaperumal Pillai* v. *Visalakshmi,* AIR 1938 Mad 32., **150**

*Kalka Prasad, M/s.* v. *Harish Chandra,* AIR 1957 ALLAHABAD 25., **227**

*Kalpavruksha Charitable Trust* v. *Toshniwal Brothers (Bombay) Pvt. Ltd.,* AIR 1999 SC 3356., **248**

*Kane Constructions* v. *Sopov,* [2005] VSC 237., **119**

*Kane* v. *Sopov* [2005] VSC 237., **120**

*Karuppayee Ammal* v. *Karuppiaah Pillai,* (1987) 1 Mad L J 138., **41**

*Kerala State Financial Enterprises Ltd.* v. *C.J. Thampi,* AIR 2000 Ker 36., **138**

*Khandas Narandas* v. *Dahiabhai,* 3 Bom 182., **538**

*Khan Gul* v. *Lakha Singh,* AIR 1928 Lah 609., **37**

*Khetarpal* v. *Madhukar Pictures,* AIR 1956 Bom 106., **136**

*KLG Systel Ltd., M/s.* v. *M/s. Fujitsu ICIM Ltd.,* AIR 2001 DELHI 357., **222**

*Konkan Railway Corpn. Ltd.* v. *M/s. Mehul Construction Co.,* AIR 2000 SC 2821., **450**
*Kotla Venkataswamy* v. *Ramamurthy,* AIR 1934 Mad 579., **359**
*Krell* v. *Henry,* [1903] 2 KB 740., **95**
*Krishna Janardhan Bhat* v. *Dattatraya G. Hegde,* AIR 2008 SC 1325., **573**
*Krishna Mohan Kul* v. *Pratima Maity,* AIR 2003 SC 4351., **45**
*Krishna* v. *Ganapathi,* AIR 1955 MADRAS 648., **162**
*Kuju Collieries Ltd.* v. *Jharkhand Mines Ltd.,* AIR 1974 SC 1892., **108**
*Kumar Exports, M/s.* v. *M/s. Sharma Carpets,* AIR 2009 SC 1518., **560, 575**

**L**

*L & A Drywall, Inc.* v. *Whitmore Const. Co., Inc., Utah,* 608 P.2d 626, 630., **109**
*L.I.C. of India* v. *Anuradha,* AIR 2004 SC 2070., **275**
*L'Estrange* v. *Graucob Ltd.,* (1934) All ER Rep 16: (1934) 2 KB 394., **9**
*Ladli Prashad Jaiswal* v. *Karnal Distillery Co. Ltd., Karnal,* AIR 1963 SC 1279., **44**
*Lakshiminarayan Ram Gopal and Son Ltd.* v. *Govt. of Hyderabad,* AIR 1954 SC 364., **163**
*Lakshmi Ratan Lal Cotton Mills* v. *J.K. Jute Mills Co.,* AIR 1957 All 311., **360, 361**
*Lala Kapurchand Godha* v. *Mir Nawab Himayatalikhan Azamjah,* AIR 1963 SC 250., **105**
*Lalman* v. *Gauri Datt,* (1913) 11 All LJ 489., **24**
*Lata Construction* v. *Dr. Rameshchandra Ramniklal Shah,* AIR 2000 SC 380., **102**
*Lata Construction* v. *Rameshchandra Ramniklal Shah,* AIR 2000 SC 380., **268**
*Laxman Balakrishnan Joshi* v. *Dr. Trimbak Bapu Godbole,* (1969) 1 SCR 206., **259**
*Laxman Balkrishna Joshi* v. *Dr. Trimbak Bapu Godbole,* AIR 1969 SC 128., **255, 262**
*Laxmi Engineering Works v. P.S.G. Industrial Institute,* AIR 1995 SC 1428., **237, 247**
*Lakshmi Ratan Cotton Mills Co., Ltd.* v. *J. K. Jute Mills Co., Ltd.,* AIR 1957 ALL 311., **360**
*Leaf* v. *International Galleries,* [1950] 2 KB 86., **53**
*Lebeaupin* v. *Crispin,* 1920–2 KB 714., **92**
*Lee* v. *Butler,* 1893 2 Q.B. 318., **183**
*Lee* v. *Lee's Air Farming Ltd.,* [1960] 3 All ER 420., **393**
*Lewis* v. *Great Western Railways,* 157 ER, p. 1427 (Ex. 1860)., **8**
*LIC of India* v. *C.E.R.C., (1995) 5 SCC 482; see also Bihar State Electricity Board* v. *Green Rubber Industries,* AIR 1990 SC 699., **19**
*LIC* v. *Escorts,* 1984 SCR (3) 643, **333**
*Life Insurance Corporation of India* v. *Raja Vasireddy Komalavalli Kamba,* AIR 1984 SC 1014., **34**
*Life Insurance Corporation of India* v. *S. Sindhu,* AIR 2006 SC 2366., **276**
*Lilly White* v. *Mannuswami,* AIR 1966 Mad 13., **15**
*Lily White* v. *R. Mannuswami,* AIR 1966 Mad 13., **19**
*Lily White* v. *R. Munuswami, AIR 1966 Mad 13; Olley* v. *Marlborough Court,* (1949) 1 All ER 127., **9**
*Lloyd's Bank* v. *Bundy,* [1974] 3 All ER 757., **46**
*Long* v. *Lloyd,* [1958] 1 WLR 753., **53**
*Loon Karan* v. *John and Co.,* AIR 1967 ALLAHABAD 308., **163**
*Loonkaran Sethia* v. *Ivan E. John,* AIR 1977 SC 336., **103**
*Lowe* v. *Fahey,* [1988] Ch. 114, **425**
*Lucknow Development Authority* v. *M.K. Gupta,* AIR 1994 SC 787., **239, 254, 271**
*Lucknow Development Authority* v. *M.K. Gupta,* (1994) 1 SCC 243., 254, AIR 1994 SC 787., **239, 271**

**M**

*M. Sham Singh* v. *State of Mysore.,* AIR 1972 SC 2440., **125**
*M. Siddalingappa* v. *T. Nataraj,* AIR 1970 Mys. 154; *R.S. Deboo* v. *M.V. Hindlekar,* AIR 1995 Bom 68., **16**
*M.S. Madhusoodhanan* v. *Kerala Kaumudi Pvt. Ltd,* AIR 2004 SC 909., **191**
*M.S.E.B.* v. *Sterlite Industries (India) Ltd.,* AIR 2000 BOMBAY 204., **231**
*M.S.E.B., Bombay* v. *Official Liquidator, H.C., Ernakulam,* AIR 1982 SC 1497., **143**
*Mahabir Kishore* v. *State of M.P.,* AIR 1990 SC 313., **117**
*Mahabir Kishore* v. *State of M.P.,* AIR 1990 SC 313., **110**
*Mahaliram* v. *Fort Gloster Manufacturing Company,* AIR 1955 Cal.132., **415**
*Malay Kumar Ganguly* v. *Sukumar Mukherjee,* AIR 2010 SC 1162., **258**
*Mallikarjun* v. *Gulbarga University,* AIR 2004 SC 716., **453**
*Manbre Saccharine Co.* v. *Corn Products Co.,* (1919) 1 KB 198., **219**
*Maritime National Fish* v. *Ocean Trawlers* [1935] AC 524., **98**

*Martin F. D'Souza* v. *Mohd. Ishfaq,* AIR 2009 SC 2049., **264**

*Maruti Suzuki India Ltd.* v. *Rajiv Kumar Loomba,* AIR 2010 SC 3141., **283**

*Marwar Tent Factory, M/s.* v. *Union of India,* AIR 1990 SC 1753., **215**

*Mc Pherson* v. *Appana,* AIR 1951 SC 184., **5**

*Meerut Development Authority* v. *Association of Management Studies,* AIR 2009 SC 2894., **7**

*Meghraj* v. *Bayabai.* AIR 1970 SC 161., **102**

*Menier* v. *Hooper's Telegraph Works,* [1874] 9 Ch. App. 350., **426**

*Mercantile Credit Co.* v. *Hamblin,* (1965) 2 QB 242; (1964) 1 WLR 423., **208**

*Metropolitan Water Board* v. *Dick Kerr,* [1918] AC 119., **96**

*Minerva Mills Ltd.* v. *Govt. of Maharastra,, (*1975) 45 Com Cas1 (Bom)., **349**

*Mithoolal Nayak* v. *Life Insurance Corporation of India,* AIR 1962 SC 814., **50, 55**

*Modern Insulators Ltd., M/s.* v. *Oriental Insurance Co. Ltd.,* AIR 2000 SC 1014., **275**

*Modi Cements Ltd.* v. *Kuchil Kumar Nandi,* (1998) 3 SCC 249., **571**

*Mohanlal Manilal* v. *Firm Dhirubhai Bavajibhai,* AIR 1962 GUJARAT 56., **222**

*Mohori Bibi* v. *Dharamodas Ghose,* (1930) 30 1A 114., **36**

*Moore & Co.* v. *Landauer & Co.,* (1921) 2KB 519., **195**

*Morgan Stanley Mutual Fund* v. *Kartick Das,* (1994) 4 SCC 225., **244**

*Morgan* v. *Fry,* [1968] 2 QB 710., **42**

*Moses* v. *Macferlan,* (1760) 2 Burr 1005., **109**

*Moti Lal* v. *Mool Chand,* AIR 1952 ALLAHABAD 242., **228**

*Mukul Dutta Gupta* v. *Indian Airlines Corporation,* AIR 1962 Cal 311., **19**

*Mulamchand* v. *State of Madhya Pradesh,* AIR 1968 SC 1218., **114**

*Murlidhar Chiranjilal, M/s.* v. *M/s. Harishchandra Dwarkadas,* AIR 1962 SC 366., **125**

*Mysore Cements Ltd.* v. *Svedala Barmac Ltd.,* AIR 2003 SC 3493., *501*

## N

*N. Rangachari* v. *Bharat Sanchar Nigam Ltd.,* AIR 2007 SC 1682., **577**

*N. Sundareswaran* v. *Krishna Refineries,* AIR 1977 MADRAS 109., **212**

*N.R. Srinivasa Iyer* v. *New India Assurance Co. Ltd. Madras,* AIR 1983 SC 899., **151**

*Narayanaswami Chetti* v. *Soundararajan and Co.,* AIR 1958 MADRAS 43., **218**

*Nash* v. *Inman,* (1908) KB 1., **111**

*Nath Bros.* v. *Best Roadways Ltd., 2000* AIR SCW 2116., **274**

*Nathu Lal* v. *Mt. Gomti Kuar,* AIR 1940 PC 160., **551**

*National Highway Authority of India* v. *Ganga Enterprises,* AIR 2003 SC 3823., **31**

*National Insurance Co. Ltd.* v. *Sujir Ganesh Nayak and Co.,* AIR 1997 SC 2049., **77**

*National Small Industries Corporation Limited* v. *Harmeet Singh Paintal and another, 2010,* AIR SCW 1508., **578**

*National Textile Workers' Union* v. *P.R. Ramakrishnan,* AIR 1983 SC 75, **439**

*National Traders* v. *Hindustan Soap Works,* AIR 1959 MADRAS 112., **200**

*National Westminster Bank* v. *Morgan,* [1985] 1 All ER 821., **45, 46**

*Needle Industries (India) Ltd.* v. *Needle Industries Newey (India) Holdings Ltd.,* AIR 1981 SC 1298, **429**

*Niblett Limited* v. *Confectioners' Materials Co. Ltd.,* (1921) 3 KB 387., **194**

*Nichol* v. *Godts,* (1854) 156 ER 410., **196**

*Nicholson and Venn* v. *Smith Marriott,* (1947) 177 L.T. 189., **195**

*Nilima Ghosh* v. *Harjeet Kaur,* AIR 2011 DELHI 104., **38**

*Niranjan Shankar Golikari* v. *Century Spinning and Manufacturing Co., Ltd.,* AIR 1967 SC 1098., **68**

*North Ocean Shipping* v. *Hyundai Construction (popularly known as The Atlantic Baron case),* [1979] QB 705., **40**

## O

*Official Receiver, Kanpur* v. *Abdul Shakoor,* AIR 1965 SC 920., **562**

*Oil and Natural Gas Corpn. Ltd.* v. *SAW Pipes Ltd.,* AIR 2003 SC 2629., **130**

*Orissa Textile Mills Ltd.* v. *M/s. Ganesh Das Ramkishun,* AIR 1961 PAT 107., **89**

## P

*P.J. Agro Tech. Ltd.* v. *Water Base Ltd.,* AIR 2010 SC 2596., **570**

*Paradine* v. *Jane,* (1647) Aleyn 26., **92**

*Parker* v. *South Eastern Rail Co.,* (1874–80) All ER Rep. 166., **10**

*Partridge* v. *Crittenden.*, 4, (1968) 2 All ER 421., **4**
*Patel Roadways Ltd.* v. *Birla Yamaha Ltd.,* AIR 2000 SC 1461., **273**
*Pavey and Matthews Pty. Ltd.* v. *Paul* (1987) 162 CLR 221., **119**
*Pender* v. *Lushington,* (1877) 6 Ch. D. 70., **427**
*Percept D'Mark (India) Pvt. Ltd.* v. *Zaheer Khan,* AIR 2006 SC 3426., **74**
*Pharmaceutical Society of Great Britain* v. *Boots Cash Chemists Ltd.,* (1952) 2 QB 795., **6**
*Phillips* v. *Brooks,* (1919) 2 KB 243., **54, 58**
*Pioneer Shipping* v. *BTP Tioxide* [1982] AC 724., **98**
*PNB Ltd.* v. *Arura Mal Durga Dass and another,* AIR 1960 Pun.632., **159**
*Ponnuswami* v. *Velliamuthu,* AIR 1957 Mad 355., **526**
*Poonam Verma* v. *Ashwin Patel,* AIR 1996 SC 2111., **261**
*Powell* v. *Braun* [1954] 1 All ER 484., **118**
*Pradeep Kumar Jain* v. *Citibank,* AIR 1999 SC 3119., **266**
*Pramatha Nath* v. *Probirendra ,* AIR 1966 CALCUTTA 405., **211**
*Punjab and Sind Bank* v. *Vinkar Sahakari Bank Ltd.,* AIR 2001 SC 3641., **573**
*Punjab National Bank Ltd.* v. *Bikram Cotton Mills Ltd.,* AIR 1970 SC 1973., **137**
*Punjab State* v. *Dina Nath,* AIR 2007 SC 2157., **453**
*Punjab Urban Planning and Development Authority* v. *Daya Singh,* AIR 2010 SC 486., **270**
*Pyrene and Co. Ltd.* v. *Scindia Steam Navigation Co. Ltd.,* (1954) 2 QB 402., **216**

## R

*R.C. Society* v. *State of Andhra,* AIR 1961 ANDHRA PRADESH 86., **226**
*R.L. Kalathia Co.* v. *State of Gujarat,* AIR 2011 SC 754., **105**
*R.S. Deboo* v. *M.V. Hindlekar,* AIR 1995 Bom 68., **19**
*R.S. Thakur* v. *H.G.E. Corporation,* AIR 1971 BOMBAY 97., **199**
*Radhey Shyam Garg* v. *Naresh Kumar Gupta,* AIR 2010 SC 3210., **584**
*Raffles* v. *Wichelhaus,* (1864) 2 H & C 906., **59**
*Raghava Menon* v. *Kuttappan Nair,* AIR 1962 KERALA 318., **198**
*Raja Dhruv Dev Chand* v. *Raja Harmohinder Singh,* AIR 1968 SC 1024., **97**
*Rajahmundry Electric Supply Corporation Ltd.* v. *A. Nageshwara Rao,* AIR 1956 SC 213., **422, 443**
*Rakesh Ranjan Shrivastava* v. *The State of Jharkhand & Anr* [2024] 3 S.C.R. 438., **582**
*Ram Chandra Singh* v. *Savitri Devi,* (2003) 8 SCC 319., **48**
*Ram Gulam* v. *Govt. of UP,* AIR 1950 All 206., **152**
*Ramniwas* v. *Commr. of Taxes,* AIR 1952 ASSAM 178., **204**
*Ramaswamy Iyer* v. *Brahmayya & Co,* [1966] 1 Comp LJ 107, **394**
*Rangappa* v. *Mohan,* AIR 2010 SC 1898., **574**
*Ravneet Singh Bagga* v. *KLM Royal Dutch Airlines,* (2000) 1 SCC 66., **249**
*Re Dinshwa Maneeckjee Petit,* AIR 1926 Bom 371., **335**
*Re Dunlop India Ltd.,* [2013] 31 taxmann.com 135 (Calcutta), **444**
*Re Lee Behrens & Co. Ltd.,* [1932] 2 Ch. 46., **395**
*Re Mackinnon Mackenzie & Co.,* (1967) 37 Comp Cas 516., **348**
*Regalian Properties* v. *London Docklands Development Corporation,* [1995] 1 WLR 212., **118**
*Regional Provident Fund Commissioner* v. *Shiv Kumar Joshi,* AIR 2000 SC 331., **246**
*Robinson* v. *Davison,* [1871] LR 6 Exch 269., **95**
*Rouse* v. *Bradford Banking Co.,* 1894-2 Ch. 32 CA at p. 75. per *A L. Smith, L J.,* **143**
*Rowland* v. *Divall,* (1923) 2 KB 500., **194**
*Royal British Bank* v. *Turquand,* (1856) 119 ER 886., **360**
*Ruben* v. *Great Fingall Consolidated Co.,* 1906 AC 439., **361**

## S

*S. Viswanathan* v. *East India Distilleries and Sugar Factories Ltd.,* AIR 1957 MADRAS 341., **369**
*S.B.P. and Co., M/s.* v. *M/s. Patel Engineering Ltd.,* AIR 2006 SC 450., **467**
*S.M.S. Pharmaceuticals Ltd.* v. *Neeta Bhalla and another,* AIR 2005 SC 3512., **576**
*S.P. Chengalvaraya Naidu* v. *Jagannath,* AIR 1994 SC 853., **48**
*Sales Tax Officer, Banaras* v. *Kanhaiya Lal Makund Lal Saraf,* AIR 1959 SC 135., **116**
*Salomon* v. *Salomon & Co.,* (1897) AC 22., **329, 332**
*Sanjay Lachhani* v. *Destination Canada (UK) Ltd.* (1997) 13 Const LJ 279., **120**
*Sanshin Chemicals Industry* v. *Oriental Carbons and Chemicals Ltd.,* AIR 2001 SC 1219., **471**
*Satyabrata Ghose* v. *Mugneeram Bangur and Co.,* AIR 1954 SC 44., **93, 96**

*Scruttons Ltd.* v. *Midland Silicones Ltd.,* (1962) 1 All ER, H L., **16**

*Shankar Finance and Investments, M/s.* v. *State of A.P.,* AIR 2009 SC 422., **580**

*Shanklin Pier* v. *Detel Products,* [1951] 2 KB 854., **23**

*Shanti Prasad Jain* v. *Kalinga Tubes Ltd.,* AIR 1965 SC 1535., **428**, **432**

*Shaw & Co.* v. *Symmons & Sons,* (1917) 1 KB 799., **156**

*Shin-Etsu Chemical Co. Ltd.* v. *M/s. Aksh Optifibre Ltd.,* AIR 2005 SC 3766., **491**

*Simmons* v. *Heath Laundry Co.,* (1990) 1 KB 543., **254**

*Sita Ram Gupta* v. *Punjab National Bank,* AIR 2008 SC 2416., **140**

*Skeate* v. *Beale* (1840) 11 Ad & El 983., **40**

*Smith* v. *Land & House Property Corp.,* (1884) 28 Ch. D.7., **51**

*Som Prakash Rekhi* v. *Union of India,* AIR 1981 SC 212., **336**

*Sorabji H. Joshi and Co.* v. *V.M. Ismail,* AIR 1960 MADRAS 520., **199**

*Spiro* v. *Lintern,* [1973] 3 All ER 319., **168**

*Spring Meadows Hospital* v. *Harjol Ahluwalia,* AIR 1998 SC 1801., **245**, **260**

*Standard Chartered Bank Ltd.* v. *Dr. B.N. Raman,* AIR 2006 SC 2810., **265**

*State Bank of Patiala* v. *Romesh Chander Kanoji,* AIR 2004 SC 2016., **31**

*State of Goa* v. *Praveen Enterprises,* AIR 2011 SC 3814., **471, 472**

*State of Gujarat* v. *Memon Mahomed Haji Hasan,* AIR 1967 SC 1885., **152**

*State of Haryana* v. *Santra,* AIR 2000 SC 1888., **261**

*State of Karnataka* v. *Vishwabarathi House Building Co-op. Society,* AIR 2003 SC 1043., **239**

*State of Kerala* v. *M.A. Mathai,* AIR 2007 SC 1537., **90**

*State of Kerala* v. *Prabhavathy Thankamma,* AIR 2009 SC (Supp) 2831., **181**

*State of Madhya Pradesh* v. *Kaluram,* AIR 1967 SC 1105., **146**

*State of Rajasthan* v. *Associated Stone Industries (Kotah) Ltd.,* AIR 1985 SC 466., **108**

*State of Rajasthan* v. *Basant Nahata,* AIR 2005 SC 3401., **62**

*State of U.P.* v. *Renu Sagar Power Company,* AIR 1988 SC 1773, **333**

*State of W.B.* v. *M/s. B.K. Mondal and Sons,* AIR 1962 SC 779., **112**

*State Trading Corporation of India Ltd.* v. *Commercial Tax Officer,* AIR 1963 SC 1811., **331**

*Stewart Gill Ltd.* v. *Horatio Myer & Co. Ltd.,* (1992) 2 All ER 257., **18**

*Subhas Chandra Das Mushib* v. *Ganga Prosad Das Mushib,* AIR 1967 SC 878., **47**

*Suman Sethi* v. *Ajay K. Churiwal,* AIR 2000 SC 828., **572**

*Sundaram Finance Ltd.* v. *State of Kerala,* AIR 1966 SC 1178., **182**

*Superintendence Company of India (P) Ltd.* v. *Krishna Murgai,* AIR 1980 SC 1717., **71**

*Sussie Atlantique Societe D' Armement S.A.* v. *N.V. Rotterdamsche Kolen Centrale,* (1966) All ER 61 HL., **13**

*Swastik Gas* v. *Indian Oil Corporation,* 2013(9) SCC 32, **464**

*Swarnam Ramchandran* v. *Aravacode Chakungal Jayapalan,* AIR 2000 Bom 410., **91**

*Synco Industries* v. *State Bank of Bikaner & Jaipur,* AIR 2002 SC 568., **266**

*Syndicate Bank* v. *Channaveerappa Beleri,* AIR 2006 SC 1874., **139**

*Syndicate Bank* v. *Vijay Kumar,* AIR 1992 SC 1066., **159**

**T**

*TCS* v. *Cyrus Investment,* 2021 SCC On Line SC 272, **434**

*Tamplin Steamship Co. Ltd.* v. *Anglo-Mexican Petroleum Products Co. Ltd.,* 1916–2 AC 297., **93**

*Tarsem Singh* v. *Sukhminder Singh,* AIR 1998 SC 1400., **57, 131**

*Tata Cellular* v. *Union of India,* AIR 1996 SC 11., **7**

*Taylor* v. *Caldwell, 3 B. & S. 826, 122 Eng. Rep. 309.,* **94**

*Tej Singh* v. *State,* AIR 1981 ALLAHABAD 103., **201**

*Thakurain Harnath Kuar* v. *Thakur Indar Bahadur Singh,* AIR 1922 PC 403., **107**

*The Commr. Hindu Religious Endowments, Madras* v. *Sri Lakshmindra Thirtha Swamiar of Sri Shirur Mutt,* AIR 1954 SC 282, **258**

*Thomas* v. *Thomas* (1842) 2 QB 851., **66**

*Thorn* v. *London Corp.* (1876) 1 App. Cas. 120, HL., **119**

*Thornton* v. *Shoe Lane Parking Ltd.,* (1971) 1 All ER 686., **11**

*Tilden Rent—A-Car* v. *Clendenning,* (1988) 1 All ER 348 CA., **11**

*Trollope & Colls Ltd.* v. *Atomic Power Constructions Ltd.* [1963] 1WLR 333., **118**

*Tsakiroglou & Co. Ltd.* v. *Noblee & Thorl GMBH* [1962] AC 93., **97, 98**

*Tulalip Shores, Inc.* v. *Mortland,* 9 Wash. App. 271, 511 P. 2d 1402, 1404., **109**

*Tulk* v. *Moxhay,* (1848) 41 ER 1143., **23**
*Tweddle* v. *Atkinson,* 30 LJ QB 218., **21**

**U**

*U. Ponnappa Moothan, M/s. Sons, Palghat* v. *Catholic Syrian Bank Ltd.,* AIR 1991 SC 441., **532**
*Ultzen* v. *Nicolls,* (1894) 1 QB 92., **150**
*Union of India* v. *Steel Stock Holders Syndicate Poona,* AIR 1976 SC 879., **2**
*Union of India* v. *Delhi High Court Bar Association,* (2002) 4 SCC 275., **240**
*Union of India* v. *M/s. Indian and Overseas Trading Co.,* AIR 1987 ALLAHABAD 196., **205**
*Union of India* v. *Satyam Computer Services Ltd.,* [2009] 89 SCL 393 (CLB), **396**
*United India Insurance Co. Ltd.* v. *Pushpalaya Printers,* AIR 2004 SC 1700., **14**
*Universe Tankships* v. *ITWF,* [1982] 2 All ER 67., **40, 42**
*Upton v. Tribilcock,* 91 US 45 (1875), and *see also Webster Co. v. Trinidad Bean & Elevator Co.,* 92 F 2d 177 (4th Cir, 1937)., **9**
*Uptron India Ltd.* v. *Shammi Bhan.,* **2**

**V**

*V. Kishan Rao* v. *Nikhil Super Specialty Hospital and another, 2010,* AIR SCW 4252., **264**
*Varkey Souriar* v. *Keraleeya Banking Co. Ltd.,* AIR 1957 KER 97., **360**
*Varley* v. *Whipp,* (1900) 1 QB., **195**
*VarkeySouriar* v. *Keraleeya Banking Co. Ltd.,* AIR 1957 KER 97., **360**
*Veera Exports* v. *T. Kalavathy,* AIR 2002 SC 38., **552**
*Vigers* v. *Pike,* (1842) 8 CI & F 562., **54**
*Virendra Singh Bahadur* v. *Nandlal Bhandari & Sons Ltd.* [1982] 52 Comp. Cas. 36 (MP), **443**
*Vimal Chandra Grover* v. *Bank of India,* AIR 2000 SC 2181., **265**
*Vinitha Ashok* v. *Lakshmi Hospital,* AIR 2001 SC 3914., **259**

**W**

*Waman Shriniwas Kini* v. *Ratilal Bhagwandas and Co.,* AIR 1959 SC 689., **105**
*Webster Co.* v. *Trinidad Bean & Elevator Co.,* 92 F 2d 177 (4th Cir, 1937), **9**
*White* v. *John Warwick & Co. Ltd.,* (1953) 1 WLR 1285., **17**
*Wimble, Sons and Co.* v. *Rosenberg,* (1913) 3 KB 743., **216, 217**

**Y**

*Y.A. Kader* v. *Muthulakshmi Ammal,* AIR 1992 Mad 208., **91**
*Yashwith Constructions (P) Ltd.* v. *Simplex Concrete Piles India Ltd.,* AIR 2006 SC 2798., **467**
*Yianni* v. *Edwin Evans & Sons,* (1982) QB 438., **18**
*York and North Midland Ry.* v. *Hudson,* (1853) 16 Beav. 485, **394**

**Z**

*Zila Parishad, Muzaffarnagar* v. *Udai Veer Singh,* AIR 1989 ALLAHABAD 64., **233**

# 1 The Indian Contract Act, 1872

## INTRODUCTION

In the business world, the person responsible for making the contract with the client, service provider or supplier or buying a product or hiring a house on lease should have full knowledge of law of contract because all business transactions are based on contracts which are regulated under the law of contract. Therefore, it is highly essential for the businessmen to manage the contract effectively whereby many unforeseen legal issues may be avoided. Both the parties making the contract may decide upon the terms and conditions beforehand within the framework of law.

In a technological era, it is seen that business houses make the contract through e-mail with their clients and sometimes they prepare their own fixed terms and conditions and upload it on the website and which are generally not flexible. While doing so, usually, they insert a disclaimer clause or limiting or excluding clause as a part of the contract. It is found that in every written agreement, the contracting parties mutually agree to pay certain amount in case of breach of contract. It is popularly known as LD Clause. The significance and binding force of LD Clause may be found in the law of contract.

The law of contract provides all relevant keys to the contracting parties which would help them in better understanding the legal and managerial issues in contract formulation, performance, and enforcement so that they can successfully avoid some of the inherent mistakes usually committed by the parties while formulating the terms and conditions for making domestic and/or international commercial contracts.

## PREAMBLE

WHEREAS it is expedient to define and amend certain parts of the law relating to contracts; It is hereby enacted as follows.

## PRELIMINARY

### Section 1: Short title

This Act may be called the Indian Contract Act, 1872.

**Extent, Commencement:** It extends to the whole of India except the State of Jammu and Kashmir; and it shall come into force on the first day of September, 1872.

**Saving:** Nothing herein contained shall affect the provisions of any Statute, Act or Regulation not hereby expressly repealed, nor any usage or custom of trade, nor any incident of any contract, not inconsistent with the provisions of this Act.

The question that arose before the Supreme Court in *Uptron India Ltd.* v. *Shammi Bhan*[1] was, whether the law of contract would be applied to industrial employment. The Court observed that the general principles of the Contract Act, 1872 applicable to an agreement between two persons having capacity to contract, are also applicable to a contract of industrial employment but the relationship so created is partly contractual and partly non-contractual as the Legislature has already prescribed positive obligations for the employer towards his workmen, as for example, terms, conditions and obligations prescribed by the Payment of Wages Act, 1936; Industrial Employment (Standing Orders) Act, 1946; Minimum Wages Act, 1948; Payment of Bonus Act, 1965; Payment of Gratuity Act, 1972, etc. The *Uptron India Ltd.* case has been further approved in *Steel Authority of India Ltd.* v. *National Union Water Front Workers*[2] (*SAIL* case), which was decided by the Constitutional Bench. The Apex Court categorically said in the *SAIL* case that the law has been correctly laid down in the *Uptron India Ltd.* case. The judgment in that case cannot be read as the provisions of the Contract Act are not applicable to relation between the labour and the management.

It is well settled that while the Contract Act merely provides certain elementary conditions under which the contract becomes binding on the parties, it does not provide any particular form or condition of a contract. It is, therefore, clear that the parties to the contract may agree to a particular form or condition or of mode in which the contract is to be executed, where the Government enters into a contract with a person or vice versa a particular form in which the contract is to be executed has been provided for by the Constitution. Section 72 of the Railways Act (1890) also provides for a particular mode or form in which the contract has to be entered into. This does not mean that the provisions of the Contract Act stand superseded either by the Constitution or by the Railways Act.[3] The Supreme Court in *Bank of India* v. *O.P. Swaranakar*[4] held that it is difficult to accept the contention raised that a contract of employment would not be governed by the Indian Contract Act. A contract of employment is also a subject matter of contract, unless governed by a statute or statutory rules. Subject to certain just exceptions, even specific performance of contract by way of a direction for reinstatement of a dismissed employee is also permissible in law.

---

[1] AIR 1998 SC 1681.

[2] AIR 2001 SC 3527.

[3] *Union of India* v. *Steel Stock Holders Syndicate, Poona*, AIR 1976 SC 879.

[4] AIR 2003 SC 858.

### Section 2: Interpretation clause

In this Act the following words and expressions are used in the following senses, unless contrary intention appears from the context:

(a) When one person signifies to another his willingness to do or to abstain from doing anything, with a view to obtaining the assent of that other to such act or abstinence, he is said to make a proposal;

(b) When a person to whom the proposal is made, signifies his assent thereto, the proposal is said to be accepted. A proposal, when a accepted, becomes a promise;

(c) The person making the proposal is called the "promisor", and the person accepting the proposal is called "promisee";

(d) When, at the desire of the promisor, the promisee or any other person has done or abstained from doing, or does or abstains from doing, or promises to do or to abstain from doing, something, such act or abstinence or promise is called a consideration for the promise;

(e) Every promise and every set of promises, forming the consideration for each other, is an agreement;

(f) Promises which form the consideration or part of the consideration for each other, are called reciprocal promises;

(g) An agreement not enforceable by law is said to be void;

(h) An agreement enforceable by law is a contract;

(i) An agreement which is enforceable by law at the option of one or more of the parties thereto, but not at the option of the other or others, is a voidable contract;

(j) A contract which ceases to be enforceable by law becomes void when it ceases to be enforceable.

## OFFER

A person who makes an offer is known as an offeror. A person to whom an offer is made is known as an offeree. An offer is made when an offeror proposes a set of terms to an offeree, with the intention that if the proposed terms are accepted, they will create a binding contract between the two parties. By accepting the terms proposed, the offeree would also agree to become legally bound by them. This acceptance would therefore form a contract. As a contract is a legally binding agreement, neither an offer nor an acceptance should be made without a willingness to accept the legal consequences.

Neither the offer nor the acceptance needs to be made in writing, or even in words. For example, when goods are sold at an auction, a contract is formed even though both the offer and the acceptance are made by conduct. Each bidder makes an offer to buy the particular lot being auctioned by making a gesture, which the auctioneer recognises as a bid. The auctioneer accepts the highest bid by banging the gavel on the table.

### Rules with Regard to Offer

1. Expression of willingness to do something or refrain from doing something by one person.

2. Made to the other person with a view to seeking his positive response to do or abstain from doing any act.
3. The person can be a natural person or an artificial person such as company, etc.
4. Offer can be a specific offer made to a particular person or persons or it can be a general offer made to a larger community.
5. Offer can be an express offer by use of words or written offer or implied by the conduct of the parties to the contract.
6. Offer needs to be communicated to the intended party to be contracted with.
7. Offer can be a plain offer or with conditions. Conditions of the offer can be in a standard form.
8. An offer needs to be distinguished from the mere invitation to offer.

***Example***: In case a company invites the public to participate in a proposed auction sale, then it amounts to invitation to offer and not the offer by the company. It is only expression of desire of the company to conduct auction sale. In case the person participates in the auction sale of the company and bids for a product, then it amounts to offer from the side of the person to the company.

### Offer and Invitations to Treat

It is important to make a distinction between an offer and an invitation to treat. An invitation to treat is not an offer. It is an invitation to negotiate or an invitation to make an offer. Advertisements can amount either to offers or to invitations to treat. If an advertisement is an offer, then a person who accepts the offer makes a contract with the person who advertised. If an advertisement is only an invitation to treat, then it cannot be accepted in such a way that a contract is thereby formed. In the following cases, the Court had an occasion to decide whether or not an advertisement was merely an invitation to treat or whether it was in fact an offer. A person advertises goods for sale in a newspaper or announces that he will sell them by tender or by auction; a shopkeeper displays goods in a shop window at a certain price; or a bus company advertises that it will carry passengers from A to Z and will reach Z and other intermediate stops at certain times. In such cases, it may be asked whether the statement made is an offer capable of acceptance or merely an invitation to make offers and do business. An invitation of this nature, if it is not intended to be binding, is known as an "invitation to treat."[5]

In *Partridge* v. *Crittenden*[6], the defendant had advertised bramble finches in a magazine at £1.25 each. A customer sent the defendant £1.25 and a bramble finch was sent to him. The defendant was charged with offering for sale a wild live bird, contrary to the Protection of Birds Act, 1964. The Court held that the defendant was not guilty because his advertisement was an invitation to treat, not an offer. As the advertisement was not an offer, the defendant had not 'offered for sale' a wild bird. (The defendant had committed a different crime, selling a wild bird. However, he had not been charged with this offence.)

At first sight, it seems as if the defendant in the *Partridge* case did make an offer. However, the Court reasoned that this could not be the case. If the advertisement had been

[5] Anson's Law of Contract, 26th edn. at p. 25.

[6] (1968) 2 All ER 421.

an offer, then the defendant would have had to supply a bird to everyone who wrote in accepting the offer. The defendant had only a limited supply of birds and so could not have intended that any number of customers would be supplied with one. Therefore, his advertisement was an invitation to treat, not an offer. Although the vast majority of advertisements will amount to no more than invitations to treat, some advertisements do amount to offers. In *Harvey* v. *Facey*[7], the defendants were the owners of the plot of land named "Bumper Hall Pen". The plaintiff being interested in purchasing the same sent a telegram to the defendants "will you sell us Bumper Hall Pen?" "Telegraph lowest cash price" (1st telegram).

The defendants replied also by a telegram "lowest price for BHP, £900 asked by you" (2nd telegram). The plaintiff immediately sent another telegram to defendants—"we agree to buy BHP for £ 900 as asked by you" (3rd telegram). The defendants subsequently refused to sell the plot of land at that price. The plaintiffs contended that the telegram from the defendants quoting lowest price was an offer and the same has been accepted by the plaintiff and thus, the contract is complete. The defendants contended that quoting the price was not an offer which could be accepted.

The Judicial Committee of Privy Council held that the exchange of the above telegrams has not resulted in a contract. It was observed that the 1st telegram had asked two questions regarding willingness to sell and the other regarding the lowest price. In reply, only the lowest price was quoted and this was not an offer but a mere supply of information as desired by the other party.

The third telegram from the plaintiffs saying, "he agrees to buy" was only an offer and not the acceptance of an offer. Since this offer of the plaintiff had not been accepted, there was no binding contract between the parties. The principle of this case has been followed by the Supreme Court of India in *Mc Pherson* v. *Appana*.[8] The facts of this case are as follows:

On receiving an offer from A for the purchase of a house belonging to B, Y who was looking after the house cabled to B that there was an offer of ₹6,000 for the house. B sent a cable in reply on the 5th August, 1944, that he would not accept less than ₹10,000. Y conveyed this information to A on the 9th and on the 14th A wrote a letter to Y stating that he thereby confirmed the oral offer of ₹10,000 that he had made to Y on the 11th. On the 26th Y cabled to B: *"Offered ₹10,000. May I sell"*? On the same day, W, another friend of B, with whom also B was in correspondence, sent an offer for ₹11,000 and B accepted it. A sued for specific performance alleging that B's cable of the 5th was a counter-offer and as he had accepted it on the 14th, there was a concluded contract for sale in his favour on that day.

The Court held that the cable sent by B on the 5th was a mere statement of the lowest price at which he would sell and contained no implied contract to sell at that price. A's letter of the 14th was under the circumstances only a fresh offer; and as B had not accepted it, there was no concluded contract in favour of A.

### Goods Displayed in Business Mall or Shop

A display of goods in a shop window or a mall does not amount to an offer to sell the goods displayed. The display is only an invitation to treat. In a self-service counter, the

---

[7] (1893) AC 552.

[8] AIR 1951 SC 184.

buyers select the goods and put them in a cart or carry them to the counter where they have to pay the money. By considering the situation and facts, it may be said that the goods displayed in the counter are nothing but an invitation to offer and when the buyer carries the products to the counter for payment, he is nothing but an offeror.

In *Pharmaceutical Society of Great Britain* v. *Boots Cash Chemists Ltd.,*[9] where the Pharmacy and Poisons Act 1933 made it a criminal offence to sell listed drugs without a pharmacist being present, the defendants displayed listed drugs on a supermarket shelf in an area of their supermarket where no pharmacist was present. However, a pharmacist was present near the till. It therefore had to be decided *where* the drugs were sold, that is to say, *where* the contract to sell the drugs was made. If the contract was made in the area of the supermarket where the drugs were displayed, then the defendants would have been guilty of the offence. If, however, the contract was made at the till, then the defendants would not have been guilty. The prosecution argued that the displayed drugs amounted to an offer and that this offer was accepted when customers put the drugs into their baskets. The Court held that the defendants were not guilty. The display of goods on supermarket shelves amounts only to an invitation to treat. A customer makes an offer to buy the goods displayed by selecting the goods and taking them to the till. The cashier can accept this offer by ringing up the price. However, the cashier has no obligation to accept the offer and can refuse to sell. So, the defendants were not guilty of the offence because any contract to sell the listed drugs was made at the till and would therefore have been made in the presence of a pharmacist.

In *Fisher* v. *Bell*[10], the defendant was charged with offering for sale an offensive weapon, contrary to the Restriction of Offensive Weapons Act 1959. He had displayed a flick knife in his shop window and a ticket behind the knife had said, 'Ejector knife—4 shillings'. The Court held that the defendant was not guilty. The display of the knife amounted only to an invitation to treat and not to an offer to sell. The defendant had not therefore 'offered for sale' the offensive weapon. Lord Parker said: "The display of an article with a price on it in a shop window is merely an invitation to treat. It is in no sense an offer for sale the acceptance of which constitutes a contract. That is clearly the general law of the country."

## TENDER

An invitation for tender is not an offer but an invitation to offer. It is something which invites and is communicated to notify acceptance. Broadly stated, it must be unconditional; must be in the proper form, the person by whom tender is made must be able to and willing to perform his obligations. The terms of the invitation to tender cannot be open to judicial scrutiny because the invitation to tender is in the realm of contract. However, a limited judicial review may be available in cases where it is established that the terms of the invitation to tender were so tailor-made to suit the convenience of any particular person with a view to eliminating all others from participating in the bidding process. The bidders participating in the tender process have no other right except the right to

[9] (1952) 2 QB 795.

[10] (1960) 3 All ER 731.

equality and fair treatment in the matter of evaluation of competitive bids offered by interested persons in response to notice inviting tenders in a transparent manner and free from hidden agenda. One cannot challenge the terms and conditions of the tender except on the above stated ground, the reason being the terms of the invitation to tender are in the realm of the contract. No bidder is entitled as a matter of right to insist the Authority inviting tenders to enter into further negotiations unless the terms and conditions of notice so provide for such negotiations.

It is so well-settled in law and needs no re-statement that disposal of the public property by the State or its instrumentalities partakes the character of a trust. The methods to be adopted for disposal of public property must be fair and transparent providing an opportunity to all the interested persons to participate in the process. The Authority has the right not to accept the highest bid and even to prefer a tender other than the highest bidder, if there exist good and sufficient reasons, such as, the highest bid not representing the market price but there cannot be any doubt that the Authority's action in accepting or refusing the bid must be free from arbitrariness or favouritism.[11]

A statement that goods are to be sold by tender is not normally an offer to sell to the person making the highest tender; it merely indicates a readiness to receive offers. Similarly, an invitation for tenders for the supply of goods or for the execution of works is, generally, not an offer, even though the preparation of the tender may involve very considerable expense. The offer comes from the person who submits the tender and there is no contract until the person asking for the tenders accepts one of them. These rules may, however, be excluded by evidence of contrary intention: e.g. where the person who invites the tenders states in the invitation that he binds himself to accept the highest offer to buy (or, as the case may be, the lowest offer to sell or to provide the specified services). In such cases, the invitation for tenders may be regarded either as itself an offer or is an invitation to submit offers coupled with an undertaking to accept the highest (or, as the case may be, the lowest) offer; and the contract is concluded as soon as the highest offer to buy (or lowest offer to sell, etc.) is communicated.

When parties negotiate with a view to making a contract, many preliminary communications may pass between them before a definite offer is made. One party may simply respond to a request for information (e.g. by stating the price at which he might be prepared to sell a house), or he may invite the other to make an offer; he is then said to make an *"invitation to treat"*. The question whether a statement is an offer or an invitation to treat depends primarily on the intention with which it is made.

The Supreme Court in *Tata Cellular* v. *Union of India*[12] has prescribed the following requisites of a valid tender:

1. It must be unconditional.
2. Must be made at a proper place.
3. Must conform to the terms of obligation.
4. Must be made at the proper time.
5. Must be made in the proper form.

[11] *Meerut Development Authority* v. *Association of Management Studies*, AIR 2009 SC 2894.

[12] AIR 1996 SC 11.

6. The person by whom the tender is made must be able and willing to perform his obligations.
7. There must be reasonable opportunity for inspection.
8. Tender must be made to the proper person.
9. It must be of full amount.

## STANDARD FORM CONTRACT

A standard form contract (sometimes referred to as an 'adhesion contract' or 'boilerplate contract' or 'compulsory contract' or 'private legislation') is a contract between two parties that does not allow for negotiation; simply it takes away the bargaining power of one of the parties and leaves him only with the option of either to take it or leave it, i.e., accept or leave the contract. It is often a contract that is entered into between unequal bargaining partners, such as when an individual is given a contract by the sales person of a multinational corporation. The consumer is not in a position to negotiate the standard terms of such contracts and the company's representative often does not have the authority to do so. In other words, one can say that 'Standard Form Contract' is a fine-print consumer form contract which is generally given to consumers at point-of-sale, with no opportunity for negotiation as to its terms, and which sets out the terms and conditions of the sale, usually to the advantage of the seller.

Contract of Adhesion means that the individual has no choice *"but to accept; he does not negotiate, but merely adheres"*. It is also known as *"compulsory contracts"* because it is nothing but an imposition to others Lord Denning in his book 'Road to Justice' described it as a *"private legisation"* because the terms and conditions are drafted by an individual.

Nearly almost all business houses nowadays are using standard form contract for their businesses, for example, rail tickets, insurance contracts, lottery tickets and mail order sales contracts. Standard form contracts facilitate business transactions. They economise time and effort and dispense with formal contract requirements that would impede business and raise the costs of products. The Life Insurance Corporation of India, for example, has to issue thousands of insurances covers every day. Similarly, the railway administration of India has to make innumerable contracts of carriage. It would be difficult for such large-scale organisations to draw up a separate contract with every individual. They, therefore, keep printed forms of contract.

### Historical Perspective

One of the earliest decisions requiring strict enforcement of a standard form contract was that of the Court of Exchequer in 1860 in *Lewis* v. *Great Western Railways.*[13] In this case, the Court of Exchequer rejected a plea of the plaintiff that a printed form in a contract was not binding on him since he could not be expected to have read so lengthy a document which was presented to him in printed form.

[13] 157 ER, p. 1427 (Ex. 1860).

Speaking for the Court, Justice Baron Bramwell said:

> "It would be absurd to say that this document, which is partly in writing and partly in print, and which was filled up, signed, and made sensible by the plaintiff, was not binding upon him. A person who signs a paper like this must know that he signs it for some purpose, and when he gives it to the Company must understand that it is to regulate the rights which it explains. I do not say that there may not be cases where a person may sign a paper, and yet be at liberty to say, "I did not mean to be bound by this', as if the party signing were blind, and he was not informed of its contents. But where the party does not pretend that he was deceived, he should never be allowed to set up such a defense."[14]

This view of the Court of Exchequer has been followed by the Courts in the United States of America.[15] The same principle was applied in the case of *L'Estrange* v. *Graucob Ltd.*,[16] but this principle of strict enforcement was rejected by the Courts of India as well as England in many subsequent cases.[17]

### Evolution of Protective Measures

The Courts have tried to provide some relief to the individuals who are considered to be at a weaker bargaining side. Since there is a possibility of their exploitation in terms of the non-negotiable terms of the standard form contracts, the Courts from time to time developed different theories and principles to provide some relief to the individual parties or to parties with less bargaining power. The trend of these principles changed from time to time and Court to Court. Most of these protective measures or principles evolved in the English law and the same are applied by the Indian Courts. They are as discussed in the following sections.

### *Doctrine of Reasonable Notice*

In the year 1875, the question related to reasonable notice came before the Court for consideration in the case of *Henderson* v. *Stevenson*[18]. The facts of the case are as follows:

> The plaintiff bought tickets for travelling in a steamer. On the face of the ticket it was printed "Dublin to Whitehaven". It looked like a usual travelling ticket. But on the back side of the ticket there were certain conditions printed and it stated that the company is not liable for any loss, injury or delay to the passenger or to his luggage. There was a shipwreck and the plaintiff lost his luggage. He filed a suit for damages.

It was argued by the defendant that there is an exemption clause printed on the back of the ticket and the company is not liable for the loss as it was a condition laid down with

[14] *Id* at p. 1430.

[15] *Upton* v. *Tribilcock*, 91 US 45 (1875), and see also *Webster Co.* v. *Trinidad Bean & Elevator Co.*, 92 F 2d 177 (4th Cir, 1937).

[16] (1934) All ER Rep 16: (1934) 2 KB 394.

[17] *Lily White* v. *R. Munuswami*, AIR 1966 Mad 13; *Olley* v. *Marlborough Court*, (1949) 1 All ER 127.

[18] (1875) 32 LT 709.

the purchase of the ticket. The plaintiff argued that he was unaware of such condition as he has not seen the back of the ticket. The Court stated that since there was no indication on the front side of the ticket about the conditions printed on the back, nor was the plaintiff told or notified about such condition, hence, the company is liable for the loss of the plaintiff's good. The House of Lords stated that it cannot be said that the plaintiff has accepted the terms which he has not seen since he knew nothing about such notice printed on the back of the ticket.

The doctrine of reasonable notice was further clarified in the case of *Parker* v. *South Eastern Rail Co.*[19] The facts of this case are as follows:

Mr. Parker left a bag in the cloakroom of a railway station. On depositing his bag and paying two pence he received a ticket, which, on its back, stated that the railway was excluded from liability for items worth £10 or more. Parker failed to read the clause as he thought the ticket was only a receipt of payment. (However, he admitted that he knew the ticket contained writing.) The question of law put to the Court was whether the clause applied to Parker. At trial the jury found for Mr. Parker as it was reasonable for him not to read the ticket.

The Court held that if Parker was aware the ticket contained writing, Mr. Parker would be presumed to know of the existence of the clause. However, it also ruled that the railway must have shown that it went to reasonable efforts to bring the condition to Mr. Parker's attention. The Court ordered a retrial for the jury to consider whether reasonable notice was given. The majority of the Court of Appeal held there should be a retrial. They said that if Mr Parker knew of the conditions, he would be bound. If he did not know, he would be bound if he was given the ticket in such a way as amounted to "reasonable notice". Mellish LJ said the following:

> "I am of opinion, therefore, that the proper direction to leave to the jury in these cases is, that if the person receiving the ticket did not see or know that there was any writing on the ticket, he is not bound by the conditions; that if he knew there was writing, and knew or believed that the writing contained conditions, then he is bound by the conditions; that if he knew there was writing on the ticket, but did not know or believe that the writing contained conditions, nevertheless he would be bound, if the delivering of the ticket to him in such a manner that he could see there was writing upon it, was, in the opinion of the jury, reasonable notice that the writing contained conditions."[20]

The principle laid down in this case can be summed up as that an individual cannot escape a contractual term by failing to read the contract, but that a party wanting to rely on an exclusion clause must take reasonable steps to bring it to the attention or notice of the customer. For this, Lord Mellish stated in the above case that there must be something written to bring the conditions in notice of the other party. Terms such as *"for conditions, see back"* printed on the tickets started appearing after the decision of this case.

The doctrine of reasonable notice evolved in these cases went through a change in the later half of the last century when a difference between documents, tickets and receipts

---

[19] (1874–80) All ER Rep. 166.

[20] http://en.wikipedia.org/wiki/*Parker_v_South_Eastern_Railway_Company.*

was made by the Court. It is seen that if a document is a receipt or some sort of proof that the person has paid the fare, it is considered different from a contractual document. These latest developments are seen in some of the cases. In the case of *Chapelton* v. *Barry Urban District Council*[21], it was held that a receipt of payment of fare for hiring chairs is different from that of travelling tickets. In this case, the plaintiff hired chairs from the council and suffered injuries due to the breaking of the chairs. The council argued that there is an exemption clause printed on the back of the receipts, but the plaintiff said that he had no idea about such conditions as he considered them as merely receipts for the payment of fare he paid to hire the chairs. The Court held that the council would be liable for damages and Lord Slesser laid down the difference that exits between a travelling ticket and receipt categorising the former as a contractual document whereas the latter a mere proof of payment and hence the conditions printed on back are not part of the contract.

In modern times, the most important case law regarding the position of the doctrine of reasonable notice is *Thornton* v. *Shoe Lane Parking Ltd.*[22] The facts of this case are as follows:

> Mr. Thornton parked his car in an automatic car parking. The automatic parking was managed by Shoe Lane Parking Ltd. Mr. Thornton slipped the money into the machine and got the parking tickets. The ticket contained the time of parking and a notice drawing the attention of the customer towards the notice at the entrance which stated that "*Cars parked at the owner's risk*" and posters inside the parking area stating the exclusion of liability of the company for any injury to the car or customer. While taking back the car, Mr. Thornton suffered some injuries and sued the parking company for damages. The parking company pleaded that the conditions clause in the posters and notice exempted its liability.

But the Court held that the parking company would be liable. It stated that the exemption condition is so wide and so destructive of rights that the Court should not hold any man bound by it unless it is drawn to his attention in the most explicit way. Lord Denning stated that in the case of issuing of ticket by an automatic machine, the point that must be considered is whether the terms of the contract or notice printed are contemporaneously given with the ticket or subsequent to it. It was further stated that the terms of the offer must be given during the formation of the contract and not subsequently or afterwards. There should be sufficient notice about the conditions during the formation of the contract. The Court further held that the customer would be bound by such conditions if they were brought to his knowledge before or at least at the time of the formation of the contract, but not after it.

The principle of sufficient reasonable notice was applied by many Courts in England, Canada and Australia to provide relief to individuals. In the case of *Tilden Rent — A- Car* v. *Clendenning*[23], the Canadian Court held the company would be liable for damages as the exemption clause was not printed properly and its contents were not visible properly. Though the driver consumed some alcohol, as in this case, the company was held liable since the plaintiff is not bound by unusual and onerous printed terms which were not drawn to his attention.

---

[21] (1940) 1 KB 532.

[22] (1971) 1 All ER 686.

[23] (1988) 1 All ER 348 CA.

### Theory of Fundamental Breach

The doctrine of fundamental breach was developed by the English Court to control the consequences of wide and sweeping exemption clauses attached as conditions to the contracts. The theory of fundamental breach is different from the doctrine of reasonable notice since, even if the notice is sufficiently served, the doctrine imposes a liability for breach of fundamental duty inspite of exemption clause attached to it in the contract.

In the case of *J. Spurling Ltd.* v. *Bradshaw*[24], Lord Denning asserted that exemption clauses are meant to have an overriding effect only to exempt a party when he is carrying out his contract, not when he is deviating from it or is guilty of the breach which goes to the root of it.

***Core of contract***: Every contract prescribes a fundamental obligation to be performed by the contracting parties, which may be called core of a contract. If the 'core' or 'fundamental' element of the contract is not satisfied, it may lead to the breach of the entire contract and liability must arise of it since, it is of fundamental nature and the breach of the fundamental element must carry some liability. Otherwise, the whole purpose of the contract would be vitiated. In 1945, in the case of *Davies* v. *Collins,*[25] Lord Greene laid down the essentials of the core of contract doctrine. The facts of the case are as follows:

> Mr. Davies, the plaintiff entrusted to a dyer and cleaner, a uniform for cleaning. The docket given to him when he handed over the uniform stated that *"whilst every care is exercised in cleaning and dyeing garments, all orders are accepted at owner's risk entirely and we are unable to hold ourselves responsible for damages, shrinkage, colour or defects developed in necessary handling. The proprietor's liability for loss is limited to an amount not exceeding ten times the cost of cleaning"*. The defendant company sent the uniform to be cleaned by a sub-contractor and it was never returned. The plaintiff sued for damages and claimed the full value of the uniform.

It was held that the defendant is liable to pay the damages sought by the plaintiff. The Court stated that the limitation and exemption clauses in the contract were sufficient to exclude any right to sub contract the performance of the substance of the contract but such limitation clause would have no application when the goods are lost or something which is done was outside the terms of the contract.

In the case of *Alexander* v. *Railway Executive*[26], Mr. Alexander deposited his luggage at the parcel office of a railway station, paying ordinary rates and received a ticket containing conditions one of which exempted the defendants from liability from mis delivery or loss of any article exceeding 5 pounds in value unless a special charge for the same was paid. The defendants allowed the plaintiff's friend to take away the luggage and in an action by the plaintiff relied on the above exemption clause.

The Court held that an essential part of the executive's duty was to take care of the deposited goods; that they had committed a fundamental breach of the contract in allowing an unauthorised person to take away the goods, and hence, the exemption clause will not have effect. It will not act as a shield to prevent the liability of the defendant.

---

[24] (1956) 1 WLR 461.

[25] (1945) 1 All ER 247.

[26] (1951) 2 All ER 442.

***Rule of construction*:** A later development in the theory of fundamental breach that took place around 1964 was that it is not an independent rule of law but a rule of construction. What is meant by rule of construction and why did such proposition evolved is much debated among the jurists. During the development of the 'theory of fundamental breach' which has overriding effect on the exemption and exclusion clauses, it was argued that this rule of fundamental breach was not an independent rule of law but a rule of construction. What is meant by this is that the provision of the exclusion clause should be construed in such a manner that it does not apply to the situation when there is a breach of any fundamental or core element of the contract. This rule of construction takes into account the intention of the agreeing parties and their business efficiency. An important case in this regard is of *Sussie Atlantique Societe D' Armement S.A.* v. *N.V. Rotterdamsche Kolen Centrale*[27], where the defendant, N.V. Rotterdamsche Kolen Centrale, entered into a contract with the plaintiff, Suisse Atlantique, for chartering its ships for carrying coals from United States of America to Europe for two years. The terms of the contract stated the rates of loading and also provided a clause which stated that in case of delay in loading, the defendants would pay demurrage, sum of $1000 per day. The defendants caused delay and therefore the plaintiff argued that the contract was repudiated because of such delay but allowed the defendant to use the ship and claimed damages as per the demurrage clause.

The Court held that there was no fundamental breach of contract and stated that the plaintiff affirmed the contract by allowing the defendants to use the ship. Hence, they cannot invoke the fundamental breach doctrine even if the defendants' action was not in lieu of the terms of contract. Moreover, the House of Lords went on to bring in the difference between an exception clause and the demurrage clause, calling the latter a mere stipulated liability for breach of contract. In this case, the Court tried to define the fundamental breach as a breach going to the root and stated two important characteristics of such breach:

(i) a performance totally different from that which is contemplated by the terms of the contract, and

(ii) a breach of contract of more serious nature than one which would entitle the other party merely to damages and which would entitle him to refuse performance or further performance of contract.

In another case, *Harbutt's Plasticine Ltd.* v. *Wayne Tank and Pump Co.*[28], the Court clarified the doubts that were created in the earlier judgment. The question before the Court was that if fundamental breach means departure from the contract, how great a departure will constitute fundamental breach. The answer of this question was that it depends on the facts and circumstances of the case. In the present case, the facts pointed towards fundamental breach. The facts are as follows:

The plaintiff company, Wayne Tanks and Pump Co., entered into an agreement with the defendant company, Harbutt's Ltd. to design and install equipment for storing and dispensing stearine, a chemical, in a molten State in their factory. The terms of the contract had a limitation clause which

---

[27] (1966) All ER 61 HL.

[28] (1970) 1 All ER 225.

restricted the liability of the defendant company, for any accident to 2330 pounds. The defendants installed pipes which were not suitable and were form of a plastic pipe. The pipes busted in the testing leading to a fire which destroyed the entire factory. The plaintiff sued for the entire loss and the defendant pleaded the limitation of their liability.

The Court of Appeal held that the defendants were guilty of fundamental breach to the contract and hence, they cannot invoke the limitation clause. The Court pointed out that it must also take into account the result of the breach and in this case the result of the breach is total destruction of the subject matter of the contract, i.e., the factory. Hence, the limitation clause also came to an end with the breach of the contract which is a fundamental breach in this case and the defendants cannot escape the full liability that arises for such breach.

***Contra proferentem*:** *'Contra'* is a Latin word which literally means "against" (contra) and the word *'proferentem'* is also a Latin word derived from *'proferens'*, meaning the 'one bringing forth'. Contra proferentem is a rule of contractual interpretation which provides that a term which is found to be ambiguous should be construed against the party which imposed its inclusion in the contract. That is, the preferred interpretation will be the one most favourable to the party upon whom its inclusion was imposed. The rule only applies if, and to the extent that, the clause was included at the unilateral insistence of one party without having been subject to negotiation by the counter party.

The reasoning behind this rule is to encourage the drafter of a contract to be as clear and explicit as possible and to take into account as many foreseeable situations as he can. Moreover, the development of this rule reflects the Court's inherent dislike of standard form, i.e., take-it-or-leave-it contracts also known as contracts of adhesion. The Court perceives such contracts to be the product of bargaining between parties in unfair or uneven positions. To mitigate this perceived unfairness, legal systems apply the doctrine of *'contra proferentem'* giving the benefit of any doubt in favour of the party upon whom the contract was foisted.

An example of this principle was found in the case of *United India Insurance Co. Ltd.* v. *Pushpalaya Printers*[29], where it is evident from the terms of the insurance policy that the property was insured as against destruction or damage to whole or part. The appellant company agreed to pay towards destruction or damage to the property insured to the extent of its liability on account of various happenings. In the present case, both parties relied on Clause 5 of the insurance policy. Clause 5 is also subject to exclusions contained in the insurance policy. That damage caused to the building or machinery on account of driving of vehicle on the road close to the building is not excluded. Clause 5 speaks of 'impact' by any rail/road vehicle or animal. If the appellant company wanted to exclude any damage or destruction caused on account of driving of vehicle on the road close to the building, it could have expressly excluded. The insured possibly did not understand and expect that the destruction and damage to the building and machinery is confined only to the direct collision by vehicle moving on the road to the building or machinery. In the ordinary course, the question of vehicle directly dashing the building or the machinery inside the building does not arise. Further, 'impact' by road vehicle found in the company

[29] AIR 2004 SC 1700.

of other words in the same Clause 5 normally indicates that damage caused to the building on account of vibration by driving of vehicle close to the road is also included. In order to interpret this clause, it is also necessary to gather the intention of the parties from the words used in the policy. If the word 'impact' is interpreted narrowly, the question of impact by any rail would not arise as the question of a rail forcibly coming to the contact of a building or machinery would not arise. In the absence of specific exclusion and the word 'impact' having more meanings in the context, it cannot be confined to forcible contact alone when it includes the meanings 'to drive close', 'effective action of one thing upon another' and 'the effect of such action', it is reasonable and fair to hold in the context that the word 'impact' contained in Clause 5 of the insurance policy covers the case of the respondent to say that damage caused to the building and machinery on account of the bulldozer moving closely on the road was on account of its 'impact'. Accordingly, the complaint was maintainable. The Supreme Court of India further observed as follows:

> "It is also settled position in law that if there is any ambiguity or a term is capable of two possible interpretations one beneficial to the insured should be accepted consistent with the purpose for which the policy is taken, namely, to cover the risk on the happening of certain event. Although there is no ambiguity in the expression 'impact', even otherwise applying the rule of *contra proferentem*, the use of the word 'impact' in Clause 5 in the instant policy must be construed against the appellant Insurance Company. Where the words of a document are ambiguous, they shall be construed against the party who prepared the document. This rule applies to contracts of insurance and Clause 5 of the insurance policy even after reading the entire policy in the present case should be construed against the insurer."[30]

### *Unreasonable terms*

Under the English law, the Unfair Contract Terms Act, 1977 applies the test of reasonableness to ascertain whether the conditions are logical and reasonable. But in India, the doctrine of unreasonable terms does provide some relief to the customers against unreasonable and absurd terms used as conditions in contract. In the case of *Lilly White* v. *Mannuswami*[31], the doctrine of unreasonable terms was applied. The doctrine states that if a term in the contract is unreasonable or defeats the very purpose of the contract or is against public policy, then it is excluded from the contract. In the above case, an example of this can be traced. The facts are as follows:

> Lilly White, the plaintiff, gave her sari which was quite new for dry wash at the defendant's laundry. The laundry receipt given to her, contained a condition that the customer would be entitled to claim only 15% of the market price or value of the article in case of loss. The plaintiff's sari was lost and she sued the defendant for damages claiming the cost of the sari. The defendant pleaded that the liability is limited.

The Court stated that the conditions stated on the back of the receipt may govern or modify simple contract but this is subject to the obligation on the part of the defendant to perform

[30] *Id* at p. 1703 per *SHIVARAJ* v. *PATIL*, J.

[31] AIR 1966 Mad 13.

the process properly and to return the article safe. The Court stated that it considered the condition unreasonable as it is a flagrant infringement of the law related to negligence and is not in the interest of the public.

In many later cases, the Court went on to declare conditions as unreasonable on the grounds of it being against the very purpose of the contract as well as public policy. But most of the cases where the Indian Courts declared the conditional clause as unreasonable are related to garment or laundry industries.[32]

### *Exemption clauses*

The doctrine of privity of contract states that a contract is a contract between the parties to it and no third party can either enjoy the benefits or sue of liabilities. This principle applies to standard form contracts also. What is important to note is that a stranger to a contract cannot sue. But this does not mean the right to sue is detached from the aggrieved person. He can sue for negligence or any other damages.

A different proposition has evolved as far as the interpretation of this rule is concerned. The Courts have developed a doctrine through various decisions where the parties cannot avoid their liabilities to other persons on the basis of exemption clause agreed between the parties to the contract. An example of this can be *Haseldine* v. *C.A. Daw & Son Ltd.*[33]. The facts of the case are as follows:

> The defendants, a contractor agrees to maintain and repair a lift in certain premises under contract with the owner which exempts him from liability. A person, not the owner, while using the lift suffered injuries due to malfunctioning of the lift. He sued the contractor for damages. The contract or said his liability is restricted due to the exemption clause.

The Court held the contractor liable for damages for the tort of negligence. The Court stated that the contractor cannot rely on the exemption clause to exclude his liability. In cases like this, the Court said, the contractor cannot avoid his liability under any exemption clause signed between him and the owners, as the life and security of millions of people would then be in the hands of two parties to the contract. But the Court went on to state that the liability does not arise of the contract between the owner and the contractor but due to the contractor's duty to the third party which is independent of the contract. Similarly, the third party, as in the above case is not affected by the terms of the contract, cannot claim any advantages from it.[34]

### *Liability under Torts*

It is a well-settled principle that, a party may claim relief and exemption from liability under the limitation or exemption clauses in the contract, but can be sued for damages

[32] *M. Siddalingappa* v. *T. Nataraj*, AIR 1970 Mys. 154; *R.S. Deboo* v. *M.V. Hindlekar*, AIR 1995 Bom 68.

[33] (1941) 2 KB 343.

[34] In the case of *Scruttons Ltd.* v. *Midland Silicones Ltd.*, (1962) 1 All ER, H L, where the Court held the contract between the shipping company and its passenger for exemption of liability for loss of goods cannot be invoked to exclude the liability of stevedores, of whose negligence the goods are lost.

under the law of torts for personal harm inflicted upon the other party or persons. It can be rightly said that an exemption clause can be an exhaustive clause to exclude all kinds of liability under a contract, but it may not exclude liability under torts. Liabilities arising out of negligence, defamation, trespass, etc., cannot be limited or excluded by exemption clauses. There are many case laws in support of this statement.

In *White* v. *John Warwick & Co. Ltd.*,[35] where Mr. White hired a cycle from the defendant's company. The defendants agreed to maintain the cycle in working order and a clause in the agreement provided that *'nothing in this agreement shall render the owners liable for any personal injuries'*. While the plaintiff was riding the cycle, the saddle of the cycle tilted forward and the plaintiff was thrown and an injury was caused to him. The Court held the defendant company would be liable for damages arising out of negligence in maintaining the cycle. It stated that although the clause exempted the defendants from the liability in contract, it did not exempt them from liability in negligence.

## Reasonableness and the Unfair Contract Terms Act, 1977 (UK)

The Unfair Contract Terms Act 1977 is a British Act of Parliament (passed in the year 1977 and came into force on 1978) which regulates contracts by restricting the operation and legality of some contract terms. It extends to nearly all forms of contract and one of its most important functions is limiting the applicability of disclaimers of liability. The Act provides for great relief to parties under standard form contract as the exemption clauses, limitation clauses, exception clauses and exclusion clauses in the standard form contracts can also be struck down, if they do not pass the test of reasonableness, as prescribed under this Act.

1. Under Sec. 1(3) of the Act, it is stated that the Act only applies to "liability for breach of obligations or duties arising (a) from things done or to be done by a person in the course of a business (whether his own business or another's); or (b) from the occupation of premises used for business purposes of the occupier."
2. Under Secs. 11 and 13 of the Act, some guidelines are provided for deciding whether a term is reasonable or not. Also, schedule 2 of the Act provides some important aspects of reasonableness with respect to sale of goods, and contractual liability.
3. Under Sec. 2(1) of the Unfair Contract Terms Act 1977, it is stated that liability for negligence occasioning death or personal injury cannot be excluded.
4. Under Sec. 2(2), exclusion of liability for negligence (other than for death or personal injury) must satisfy the requirement of reasonableness.
5. Section 3 of the Act deals with reasonableness in contractual liability. Under Sec. 3, it is stated that reasonableness in contractual liability applies against a party that drafted a standard form contract where the other party is a consumer. Exclusion of breach of the same contract (under Sec. 3(2)(a)) or performance of which is substantially or totally different of that which is reasonably expected of him (under Sec. (3)(b)) are to be tested on the ground of reasonableness.

[35] (1953) 1 WLR 1285.

6. Section 4 of the Act deals with indemnity clauses. It states that a party dealing as a consumer cannot contract to indemnify a third party on behalf of the other party, except insofar as it satisfies the requirement of reasonableness.
7. Section 6 deals with sales of goods. Under Sec. 6(3), it is laid down that implied terms as to description, quality and sample (Sale of Goods Act 1979, Secs. 13–15) may only be reasonably excluded where neither party is dealing as a consumer.
8. Section 8 deals with misrepresentation. It substituted the Misrepresentation Act 1967. Under this section, an exclusion of liability for misrepresentation must satisfy the requirement of reasonableness.
9. Under Sec. 14 of the Act, the term used is "any government department", which makes the Act applicable even to contracts drafted by government agencies and does away with the concept of sovereign immunity as applies to government contracts.

Two important case laws also provide the new aspects that Court found out in the doctrine of reasonableness. In the case of *Stewart Gill Ltd.* v. *Horatio Myer & Co. Ltd.*[36], the Court held that reasonableness is assessed at the time of contract; and that the burden of proof is upon the party purporting to have excluded liability.

Earlier, in the case of *Yianni* v. *Edwin Evans & Sons*[37], Lord Griffith provided four points that may be considered in ascertaining the reasonableness of the terms or clause in a contract. These points are as follows:

1. Equality of bargaining powers.
2. The Court must also see how practical was it for the parties to obtain independent legal advice regarding the term and is there any uncertainity with its meaning.
3. He also laid emphasis on the fact that the Court must consider the question, how difficult is the task for which liability is being excluded?
4. What are the practical consequences of ruling that a term is unreasonable, must also be kept in mind.

Hence, it is submitted that even the English Court also, to some extent, recognises that the very foundation of standard form contract, with lack of bargaining power, is unreasonable but cannot do away with it since conflict is between economy and law. The traditional contract doctrine is needed to be balanced with the economic and market theories which are in support of standard form contract. To overcome this problem, the Court adopted, from time to time, various doctrines as protective measures to help the aggrieved party and the Legislature ultimately enacted the Unfair Contract Terms Act, 1977.

### Standard Form Contracts: The Indian Experience

Section 23 of the Indian Contract Act deals with when contracts may be declared as void. The Supreme Court of India in *Central Inland Water Transport Corpn. Ltd.* v. *Brojo Nath Ganguly*[38] held that an unfair or an unreasonable contract entered into between parties of

[36] (1992) 2 All ER 257.

[37] (1982) QB 438.

[38] (1986) 3 SCC 156.

unequal bargaining power was void as unconscionable under Sec. 23 of the Indian Contract Act. Thus, Indian Courts have shown a remarkable willingness to interfere with printed form contracts where there is evidence of unequal bargaining power. It has been held that the Courts would relieve the weaker party to a contract from unconscionable, oppressive, unfair, unjust and unconstitutional obligations in a standard form contract. The Supreme Court has also held that standard form contracts drawn up even by the Government must be fair, and that these contracts are open to judicial review on grounds of unreasonableness or unfairness.[39] The Supreme Court has upheld a plea that a printed form contract was void on grounds of coercion, where the parties had unequal bargaining power.[40] A printed form in a dry-cleaning contract, exempting the dry-cleaner from any liability in the event of loss or damage to the clothes concerned has been held to be contrary to public policy and therefore void.[41] The Bombay High Court has followed this view in *R.S. Deboo* v. *M.V. Hindlekar*.[42] In the present case, the plaintiff (customer) entrusted various clothes to the defendant who was carrying on business of cleaners, dryers and launderers, for drying, cleaning and ironing as a bailee. The defendant was giving receipts for the articles received from the customers. Once the defendant failed to return some of the clothes entrusted to him by the plaintiff for dry clearing and ironing, a suit was filed for recovery of damages for non-return of the clothes. The defendant in his defence relied heavily on the laundry receipt which contained a printed condition on its reverse purporting to restrict the launderer's liability for quantum of loss to twenty times the laundering charges or half of the value of unreturned articles, whichever was less, whatever be the cause for non-return of the article entrusted by the customer to the laundry for the purpose of laundering. The defendant was prepared to pay the amount of compensation as per the condition printed on the receipt given to the plaintiff.

The Court held that the above referred printed condition was too wide, one sided and purported to restrict the liability of owner of the laundry arbitrarily and unreasonably. It was also opposed to public policy and fundamental principles of law of contract and the same was thus void under Sec. 23 of the Contract Act, 1872. No stipulation opposed to public policy can be given effect to or enforced by a Court, even where the stipulation is found to and have been assented to, by the parties voluntarily.

The application of the "reasonable notice theory", as evolved by the common law principle can be found to some extent in India. This principle states that a clause in a printed form is not binding unless the attention of the other party is drawn thereto, and such clause is to be brought to his or her notice in order to bring the party into legal net. In *Mukul Dutta Gupta* v. *Indian Airlines Corporation*[43], the Calcutta High Court held to be binding, the conditions of carriage applicable to an air ticket, which were printed in small font, on the inside of the air ticket. The High Court was of the view that sufficient steps were taken by the airline company to bring these conditions of carriage to the notice of

39 *LIC of India* v. *C.E.R.C.*, (1995) 5 SCC 482; see also *Bihar State Electricity Board* v. *Green Rubber Industries*, AIR 1990 SC 699.

40 *Chairman and MD, NTPC Ltd.* v. *Reshmi Constructions, Builders and Contractors*, (2004) 2 SCC 663.

41 *Lily White* v. *R. Mannuswami*, AIR 1966 Mad 13.

42 AIR 1995 Bom 68.

43 AIR 1962 Cal 311.

the customers. Similarly, the Madras High Court in *Indian Airlines Corporation* v. *Jothaji Maniram*[44] held that certain conditions limiting the liability of a carrier were binding, which were printed on the consignment note. The High Court was of the view that these were the conditions that the customer could reasonably expect to be bound by in the course of such transactions.

The question as to what constitutes sufficient notice of a particular clause varies from case to case. In cases of mass issuance of a printed form, such as in the case of a ticket, the consumer may notice the clause but still feel unable to negotiate the clause. Thus, there are cases where a party is either aware of or is deemed to be aware (by constructive notice) of a clause, and yet, the contract would still not truly represent the terms of the understanding between the parties. The notice theory fails to address this problem. The Standard Form Contracts are standardised contracts that contain a large number of terms and conditions in fine print and which restrict and often exclude liability under the contract. This gives a unique opportunity to the giant company to exploit the weakness of the individual by imposing upon him terms which often look like a kind of private legislation and which may go to the extent of exempting from all liability of the company under the contract.

## Privity of Contract

"Privity of contract" or "privity in contract" means party to the contract. The doctrine of privity in the common law of contract provides that a contract cannot confer rights or impose obligations arising under it on any person or agent except the parties to it. In other words, it means that a contract is a contract between the parties only and no third party can sue upon it even if the contract is made for the benefit of a third party.

The premise is that only parties to contracts should be able to sue to enforce their rights or claim damages as such. However, the doctrine has proven problematic due to its implications upon contracts made for the benefit of third parties who are unable to enforce the obligations of the contracting parties.

Privity may be of two types: horizontal and vertical. Horizontal privity arises when the benefits from a contract are to be given to a third party. Vertical privity involves a contract between two parties, with an independent contract between one of the parties and another individual or company.

In a supply chain activity, a manufacturer sells a product to a distributor and the distributor sells the product to a retailer. The retailer then sells the product to a consumer. There is no privity of contract between the manufacturer and the consumer. If we apply the principle of privity of contract, the consumer is having no right to sue against the manufacturer or a distributor or a retailer under the law of contract. However, the remedy is available to such consumer under the tort. The best example is the case of *Donoghue* v. *Stevenson*.[45]

---

[44] AIR 1959 Mad 285.

[45] [1932] HL 100.

The facts of the case in brief are as follows:

> Donoghue ordered for a bottle of ginger beer. After consuming the beer, she found a decomposed snail in the lower part of the bottle. It was brought to her notice when the beer dropped out of the bottle into the tumbler. Donoghue later complained of stomach pain and her doctor diagnosed her as having gastroenteritis and being in a State of severe shock. On 9 April, 1929, Donoghue brought an action against David Stevenson. She claimed £ 500 as damages for injuries sustained by her through drinking ginger beer which had been manufactured by him. The House of Lords held that the manufacturer would be liable under tort.

Prior to 1861, there are decisions in English Law allowing a third party to enforce the contract, of course the third party in question was having interest on the subject matter of the contract. In 1677, in *Dutton* v. *Poole*[46], a father agreed with his son that if his son (defendant) would pay £ 1000 to his sister (plaintiff), then the father would not sell the property. On the assurance made by the son, the father did not sell the property but the son (defendant) refused to pay. The sister sued the defendant.

It is very much clear from the fact of the case that the plaintiff was not a privity to contract, however, the whole object of the agreement made between father and son (defendant) was to provide the benefit to the plaintiff. Therefore, the Court of King's Bench held that it would be inequitable to allow the son (defendant) to enjoy the whole property and it may lead to unjust enrichment at the cost of the plaintiff's sister who was also having interest to her father's property. Accordingly, the Court of King's Bench held that the plaintiff, even if not a party to the contract, may sue the defendant and he was held liable.

The strict principle of doctrine of privity to contract has been applied by the Queen's Bench in *Tweddle* v. *Atkinson*[47] in 1861 where the groom's father, John Tweddle, agreed with the bride's father, William Guy, to pay the groom, William Tweddle, £200. William Guy died, and the estate would not pay. So, William Tweddle sued. His suit was not successful as it was held no stranger to the consideration can take advantage of a contract, although made for his benefit. Further, the Court held that no legal entitlement is conferred on third parties to an agreement. Third parties to a contract do not derive any rights from that agreement nor are they subject to any burdens imposed by it.

The principle of privity to contract was affirmed by the House of Lords in *Dunlop Pneumatic Tyre Co. Ltd.* v. *New Garage & Motor Co. Ltd.*[48] Dunlop made tyres. It did not want them sold cheaply but to maintain a standard resale price. It agreed with its dealers (in this case Dew & Co.) not to sell them below its recommended retail price. It also bargained for dealers to get the same undertaking from their retailers (in this case Selfridge). If retailers did sell below the list price, they would have to pay £5 a tyre in liquidated damages to Dunlop. Dunlop thus was a third party to a contract between Selfridge and Dew. When Selfridge sold the tyres at below the agreed price, Dunlop sued to enforce the contract by injunction and claimed damages. Selfridge argued it could not enforce the burden of a contract between itself and Dew, which Selfridge had not agreed to.

---

[46] (1677) 2 Lev 210. ( Court of King's Bench)

[47] 30 LJ QB 218.

[48] (1915) AC 847.

At trial, the judge was in favour of Dunlop. In appeal, the damages and injunction were reversed, saying that Selfridge was not a principal or an agent and thus was not bound. The issue put to the House of Lords for consideration whether Dunlop would get damages from Selfridge without a contractual relationship.

Lord Viscount Haldane based his argument on three fundamental principles in law. *First,* the doctrine of privity requires that only a party to a contract can sue. *Second,* the doctrine of consideration requires a person with whom a contract not under seal is made is only able to enforce it if there is consideration from the promisee to the promisor. *Third,* the doctrine of agency requires that the principal not named in the contract can only be sued if the promisee was contracted as an agent. In application to the facts, Lord Haldane could not find any consideration between Dunlop and Selfridge, nor could he find any indication of an agency relationship between Dew and Selfridge. Consequently, the Court held that Dunlop is a stranger to the contract and law does not confer any right to the stranger to take any action in the Court of law.

In 1966, Lord Denning in *Beswick v Beswick*[49] relaxed the strict rule of privity of contract that a third party cannot sue. In March, 1962, Peter Beswick and his wife were both over 70. He was not in good health. The nephew was anxious to get hold of the business before the old man died. So, they went to a solicitor who drew up an agreement for them. The business was to be transferred to the nephew and Peter Beswick was to be employed in it as a consultant for the rest of his life. After his death, the nephew was to pay to his widow an annuity of £5 per week, which was to come out of the business. After the agreement was signed, the nephew took over the business. Peter Beswick died on 3 November, 1963, leaving his widow. The nephew paid her the first £5. But he then stopped paying her and has refused to pay her any more.

On 15 July, 1964, she brought an action against the nephew for nonpayment of annuity. She sued in the capacity of administratrix of the estate of Peter Beswick, deceased, and in her personal capacity she claimed £175 arrears and a declaration. By amendment she claimed specific performance and the appointment of a receiver. The action came for hearing before the Vice-Chancellor of the County Palatine of Lancaster, who held that she had no right to enforce the agreement. He dismissed the action. In appeal, Lord Denning observed that if the decision of the Vice-Chancellor would be accepted as the law of England that a third party would not be allowed to sue in the name of privity of contract, it would be deplorable and it would lead to unjust because the nephew could keep the business to himself, and at the same time repudiate his promise to pay the widow. Further, His Lordship observed that the general rule undoubtedly is that *"no third person can sue, or be sued, on a contract to which he is not a party"*, but at bottom that is only a rule of procedure. Where a contract is made for the benefit of a third person who has a legitimate interest to enforce it, it can be enforced by the third person in the name of the contracting party or jointly with him or, if he refuses to join, by adding him as a defendant. In that sense and it is a very real sense, the third person has a right arising by way of contract. He has an interest which will be protected by law. In the *Beswick* case, the Court held that the widow here can sue in her capacity as executrix of her husband's estate (and therefore as contracting party), and also in her personal capacity. She was entitled to an order for

[49] (1966) 3 All ER 1.

specific performance of the agreement, by ordering the defendant to pay the arrears of £175, and the instalments of £5 a week as they fall due.

In 1995, in *Darlington B C* v. *Eiltshier Northern Ltd.*,[50] the English Court further relaxed the strict rule of privity to contract. The Court observed that the case for recognising a contract for the benefit of a third party is simple and straightforward. The autonomy of the will of the parties should be respected. The law of contract should give effect to the reasonable expectations of contracting parties. The principle certainly requires that a burden should not be imposed on a third party without his consent. But there is no logical reason to deny the effectiveness to a contract for the benefit of a third party where, that is, the expressed intention of the parties making the contract. Moreover, often the parties, and particularly third parties, organise their affairs on the faith of the contract. They rely on the contract. It is therefore unjust to deny effectiveness to such a contract.[51]

### Exception to Privity of Contract

In the course of time, the judiciary and different statutes have introduced a number of exceptions to avoid unjust enrichment and to provide equitable justice.

1. ***Collateral contracts***: A contract between two parties may be accompanied by a collateral contract between one of them and a third person relating to the same subject-matter. For example, in *Shanklin Pier* v. *Detel Products*[52], the plaintiffs had employed contractors to paint a pier. They told them to buy paint made by the defendants. The defendants had told them that the painting would last for seven years. It only lasted for three months. The Court decided that the plaintiffs could sue the defendants on a collateral contract. They had provided consideration for the defendants' promise by entering into an agreement with the contractors, which entailed the purchase of the defendants' paint. However, there must be an intention to create a collateral contract before that contract can be formed.
2. ***Restrictive covenants***: Restrictive covenants may, if certain conditions are satisfied, run with the land and bind purchasers of it to observe the covenants for the benefit of adjoining owners. For example, in *Tulk* v. *Moxhay*[53], the plaintiff who owned several houses in Leicester Square sold the garden in the centre to Elms, who covenanted that he would keep the gardens and railings in their present condition and continue to allow individuals to use the gardens. The land was sold to the defendants who knew of the restriction contained in the contract between the plaintiff and Elms. The defendant announced that he was going to build on the land, and the plaintiff, who still owned several adjacent houses, sought an injunction to restrain him from doing so. It was held that the covenant would be enforced in equity against all subsequent purchasers with notice.
3. ***Trust***: Equity developed a general exception to the doctrine of privity by use of the concept of trust. A trust is an equitable obligation to hold property on behalf of another.

50 (1995) 3 All ER 895.

51 www.nadr.co.uk/articles/.../Darlington%20v%20Wiltshire%201994.p...

52 [1951] 2 KB 854.

53 (1848) 41 ER 1143.

4. ***Agency***: The concept of agency is an exception to the doctrine of privity in that an agent may contract on behalf of his principal with a third party and form a binding contract between the principal and the third party.
5. ***Consumer Protection Act, 1986***: Goods are purchased but they would be consumed by the family members. If it is found that the goods are hazardous for health, the family member may sue the seller.
6. ***Contract Labour (Regulation & Abolition) Act, 1970***: There is an implied contract between the contractor (employer) and contract labour (employee) that the contract labours are entitled to get the wages from the contractor. The 1970 Act prescribes that if the wages are not paid, they may sue the principal employer who is not a party to this implied contract.
7. ***Insurance***: The nominee may sue the insurance company in case of dispute even if he is not a party to the contract. Therefore, it may be construed as an exception to privity to contract.

# Chapter I Of the Communication, Acceptance and Revocation of Proposals

## Section 3: Communication, acceptance, and revocation of proposals

The communication of proposals, the acceptance of proposals, and the revocation of proposals and acceptances, respectively, are deemed to be made by any act or omission of the party proposing, accepting, or revoking by which he intends to communicate such proposal acceptance or revocation, or which, has the effect of communicating it.

In *Lalman* v. *Gauri Datt*[54], the defendant's nephew absconded from home. He sent his servant in search of the boy. When the servant had left, the defendant by handbills offered to pay ₹501 to anybody discovering the boy. The servant came to know of this offer only when he had already traced the missing child. He, however, brought an action to recover the reward. But the action failed. The Court held that in order to constitute a contract, there must be an acceptance of an offer and there can be no acceptance unless there is knowledge of the offer.

In *Har Bhajan Lal* v. *Harcharan Lal*,[55] a young boy had run away from his father's house. The father issued a pamphlet stating that anybody who finds or traces the boy and brings him home, will get ₹500. Har Bhajan Lal, who knew of the reward, found out the boy at a railway station Dharamshala, and took him to the police station. It was held that the handbill was a general offer and therefore he was entitled to the reward as he had found the boy.

### *Offer to the Whole World*

The above discussed two cases, namely, *Lalaman* and *Har Bhajan Lal*, may be treated as an offer to the world at large. Offer need not be made to an individual. It may be made to

[54] (1913) 11 All LJ 489.

[55] AIR 1925 All 539.

the whole world. The leading case on this topic is *Carlill* v. *Carbolic Smoke Ball Co.*[56] and the facts of the case are as follows:

> The defendants manufactured smoke balls. They claimed that the use of these smoke balls cured many illnesses and made it impossible to catch flu. A large advertising campaign stated that if anyone used a smoke ball correctly, and still caught flu, they would be paid £100 reward. One advertisement stated that the defendants had deposited £1,000 in a Regent Street bank to show that they meant what they said. The claimant, Mrs. Carlill, was persuaded by this advertisement to buy a smoke ball. Despite using the smoke ball properly, she still caught flu. When Mrs. Carlill claimed the £100 reward, the defendants refused to pay, arguing that their advertisement was not an offer.

The Court held that the advertisement was an offer of a unilateral contract. The claimant had accepted this offer by using the smoke ball in the correct way and catching flu. She was, therefore, entitled to the £100 reward.

### Section 4: Communication when complete

The communication of a proposal is complete when it comes to the knowledge of the person to whom it is made.

The communication of an acceptance is complete,—as against the proposer, when it is put in a course of transmission to him, so as to be out of the power of the acceptor; as against the acceptor, when it comes to the knowledge of the proposer.

The communication of a revocation is complete,—as against the person who makes it, when it is put into a course of transmission to the person to whom it is made, so as to be out of the power of the person who makes it; as against the person to whom it is made, when it comes to his knowledge.

### Illustrations

(a) A proposes, by letter, to sell a house to B at a certain price. The communication of the proposal is complete when B receives the letter.

(b) B accepts A's proposal by a letter sent by post.
The communication of the acceptance is complete, as against A when the letter is posted as against B, when the letter is received by A.

(c) A revokes his proposal by telegram.
The revocation is complete as against A when the telegram is dispatched. It is complete as against B when B receives it. B revokes his acceptance by telegram. B's revocation is complete as against B when the telegram is dispatched, and as against A when it reaches him.

In *Bhagwandas Goverdhandas Kedia* v. *M/s. Girdharlal Parshottamadas and Co.*[57], the question came before the Supreme Court for consideration on the issue of jurisdiction. Messrs. Girdharilal Parshottamdas and Company—hereinafter called "the plaintiffs"—commenced

[56] (1892) 2 QB 484
[57] AIR 1966 SC 543

an action in the City Civil Court at Ahmedabad against the Kedia Ginning Factory and Oil Mills of Khamgaon—hereinafter called "the defendants" for a decree for ₹31,150 on the plea that the defendants had failed to supply cotton seed cake which they had agreed to supply under an oral contract dated 22 July, 1959 negotiated between the parties by conversation on long distance telephone. The plaintiffs submitted that the cause of action for the suit arose at Ahmedabad, because the defendants had offered to sell cotton seed cake which offer was accepted by the plaintiffs at Ahmedabad, and also because the defendants were under the contract bound to supply the goods at Ahmedabad, and the defendants were to receive payment for the goods through a bank at Ahmedabad. The defendants contended that the plaintiffs had by a message communicated by telephone offered to purchase cotton seed cake, and they (the defendants) had accepted the offer of Khamgaon, that under the contract delivery of the goods contracted for was to be made at Khamgaon, price was also to be paid at Khamgaon and that no part of the cause of action for the suit had arisen within the territorial jurisdiction of the City Civil Court, Ahmedabad.

The Trial Court found that the plaintiffs had made an offer from Ahmedabad by long distance telephone to the defendants to purchase the goods and that the defendants had accepted the offer at Khamgaon, that the goods were under the contract to be delivered at Khamgaon and that payment was also to be made at Khamgaon. The contract was in the view of the Court to be performed at Khamgaon, and because of the offer made from Ahmedabad to purchase goods, the Court at Ahmedabad could not be invested with the jurisdiction to entertain the suit. But the Court held that when a contract is made by conversation on telephone, the place where acceptance of offer is intimated to the offeror, is the place where the contract is made, and, therefore, the Civil Court at Ahmedabad had the jurisdiction to try the suit. A revision application filed by the defendants against the order, directing the suit to proceed on the merits, was rejected *in limine* by the High Court of Gujarat. Against the order of the High Court of Gujarat, this appeal has been preferred with special leave before the Supreme Court.

The Court observed that making of an offer at a place which has been accepted elsewhere does not form part of the cause of action in the suit for damages for breach of contract. Ordinarily, it is the acceptance of offer and intimation of that acceptance which result in a contract. By intimating an offer, when the parties are not in the presence of each other, the offeror is deemed to be making the offer continuously till the offer reaches the offeree. The offeror thereby merely intimates his intention to enter into a contract on the terms of the offer. The offeror cannot impose upon the offeree an obligation to accept, nor proclaim that silence of the offeree shall be deemed consent. A contract being the result of an offer made by one party and acceptance of that very offer by the other, acceptance of the offer and intimation of acceptance by some external manifestation which the law regards as is necessary.

The principal contention raised by the defendants raises a problem of some complexity which must be approached in the light of the relevant principles of the common law and statutory provisions contained in the Contract Act. A contract, unlike a tort, is not unilateral. If there is no "meeting of minds", no contract may result. There should, therefore, be an offer by one party, express or implied, and acceptance of that offer by the other in the same sense in which it was made by the other. But an agreement does not result from a mere state of mind; intent to accept an offer does not give rise to a contract. There must be intention to accept and some textural manifestation of that intent by speech, writing or other act, and acceptance must be communicated to the offer or, unless he has waived such intimation or the encores of negotiations implies an agreement or the course of negotiations implies an agreement to the contrary. The Contract Act does not expressly deal with the place where a contract is made. Sections 3 and 4 of the Contract Act deal with the communication, acceptance, and revocation of proposals. Section 4 deals not with the place, but with the completion of communication of a proposal, acceptance, and revocation. In determining the place where a contract takes place, the interpretation clauses in Sec. 2 which largely incorporate the substantive, the law of contract must be taken into account.

By the second clause of Sec. 4, the communication of an acceptance is complete as against the proposer, when it is put in a course of transmission to him so as to be out of the power of the acceptor. This implies that where communication of an acceptance is made and it is put in a course of transmission to the proposer, the acceptance is complete as against the proposer; as against the acceptor, it becomes complete when it comes to the knowledge of the proposer. In the matter of the communication of revocation, it is provided that as against the person who makes the revocation, it becomes complete when it is put into a course of transmission to the person to whom it is made, so as to be out of the power of the person who makes it and as against the person to whom it is made when it comes to his knowledge. But Sec. 4 does not imply that the contract is made qua the proposer at one place and qua the acceptor at another place. The contract becomes complete as soon as the acceptance is made by the acceptor and unless otherwise agreed expressly or by necessary implication by the adoption of a special method of intimation, when the acceptance of offer is intimated to the offeror.

Acceptance and intimation of acceptance of offer are, therefore, both necessary to result in a binding contract. In the case of a contract which consists of mutual promises, the offeror must receive intimation that the offeree has accepted his offer and has signified his willingness to perform his promise. When parties are in the presence of each other, the method of communication will depend upon the nature of the offer and the circumstances in which it is made. When an offer is orally made, acceptance may be expected to be made by an oral reply, but even a nod, or other act which indubitably intimates, even if the offeree has resolved to accept the offer a contract may not result. But on this rule is engrafted an exception based on grounds of convenience which has the merit not of logic or principle in support, but of long acceptance by judicial decisions. If the parties are not in the presence of each other, and the offeror has not prescribed a mode of communication of acceptance, insistence upon communication of acceptance of the offer by the offeree would be found to be inconvenient, when the contract is made by letters sent by post.

In the case of negotiations by post, the contract is complete when acceptance of the offer is put into a course of transmission to the offeror. A similar rule has been adopted when the offer and acceptance are by telegrams. The exception to the general rule requiring intimation of acceptance may be summarised as follows. When by agreement, course of conduct, or usage of trade, acceptance by port or telegram is authorised, the bargain is struck and the contract is complete when the acceptance is put into a course of transmission by the offeree by posting a letter or dispatching a telegram.

In the case of a telephonic conversation, in a sense the parties are in the presence of each other, each party is able to hear the voice of the other. There is instantaneous communication of speech intimating offer and acceptance, rejection or counter-offer. Intervention of an electrical impulse which results in the instantaneous communication of messages from a distance does not alter the nature of the conversation so as to make it analogous to that of an offer and acceptance through post or by telegraph.

In the case of correspondence by post or telegraphic communication, a third agency intervenes and without the effective intervention of that third agency, letters or messages cannot be transmitted. In the case of a conversation by telephone, once a connection is established, there is in the normal course no further intervention of another agency. Parties holding conversation on the telephone are unable to see each other: they are also physically separated in space, but they are in the hearing of each other by the aid of a mechanical contrivance which makes the voice of one heard by the other instantaneously and communication does not depend upon an external agency.

In the administration of the law of contracts, the Court in India has generally been guided by the rules of the English common law applicable to contracts where no statutory provision to the contrary is in force. Under the English Common Law, where a contract is made by instantaneous communication, e.g., by telephone, the contract is complete only when the acceptance is received by the offeror, since generally an acceptance must be notified to the offeror to make a binding contract and the contract is made at the place where the acceptance is received.

In a large majority of European countries, the rule based on the theory of consensus ad idem, is that a contract takes place where the acceptance of the offer is communicated to the offeror, and no distinction is made between contracts made by post or telegraph and by telephone or Telex. In decisions of the State Courts in the United States, conflicting views have been expressed, but the generally accepted view is that by the technical law of contracts the contract is made in the district where the acceptance is spoken. This is based on what is called the deeply rooted principle of common law that where the parties impliedly or expressly authorise a particular channel of communication, acceptance is effective when and where it enters that channel of communication.

Obviously, the draftsmen of the Indian Contract Act did not envisage use of the telephone as a means of personal conversation between parties separated in space and could not have intended to make any rule in that behalf. The question then is whether the ordinary rule which regards a contract as completed only when acceptance is intimated should apply, or whether the exception engrafted upon the rule in respect of offers and acceptances by post and by telegrams is to be accepted. If regard be had to the essential nature of conversation by telephone, it would be reasonable to hold that the parties being in a sense in the presence of each other and negotiations are concluded by instantaneous communication of speech, communication of acceptance is a necessary part of the formation of contract, and the exception to the rule imposed on grounds of commercial expediency is inapplicable.

The Court held that where the offer was made by the plaintiff by telephone conversation from Ahmedabad and the same was accepted by the defendant by telephone conversation from Khamgaon, the contract is made at Ahmedabad where the acceptance was communicated and a part of the cause of action for suit for damages for breach of the contract arises within the jurisdiction of Ahmedabad Court.

## Section 5: Revocation of proposals and acceptance

A proposal may be revoked at any time before the communication of its acceptance is complete as against the proposer, but not afterwards. An acceptance may be revoked at any time before the communication of the acceptance is complete as against the acceptor, but not afterwards.

### Illustrations

A proposes, by a letter sent by post, to sell his house to B. B accepts the proposal by a letter sent by post.

A may revoke his proposal at any time before or at the moment when B posts his letter of acceptance, but not afterwards.

B may revoke his acceptance at any time before or at the moment when the letter communicating it reaches A, but not afterwards.

An interesting case relating to the legal aspect of Voluntary Retirement Scheme (VRS) declared by nationalised banks came before the Apex Court for consideration in *Bank of India* v. *O.P. Swaranakar.*[58] The nationalised banks, with a view to downsizing their staff, floated the VRS. The Scheme required the employee who intends to seek voluntary retirement to submit duly completed application in duplicate in the prescribed form marked *'offer to seek voluntary retirement.'* The application so received was to be considered by the competent authority on first come first serve basis. The decision-making process involved application of mind on the part of several authorities. The request of employees seeking voluntary retirement was not to take effect until and unless it was accepted in writing by the competent authority. The competent authority had the absolute discretion whether to accept or reject the request of the employee seeking voluntary retirement under the Scheme. The Bank also reserved to itself the right to alter/rescind the conditions of the Scheme. The Scheme also contained a clause that an employee who has opted for voluntary retirement cannot withdraw his application. A large number of employees submitted their applications out of whom a small number of employees withdrew their offer. Despite withdrawal, the offer was accepted. The action on the part of the banks in accepting the applications of the employees concerned despite their withdrawal was challenged.

A proposal is made when one person signifies to another his willingness to do or abstain from doing anything with a view to obtaining the assent of the other to such act or abstinence under Sec. 2(a). Herein the Banks by reason of the Scheme or otherwise have not expressed their willingness to do or abstain from doing anything with a view to obtaining assent of the employees to such act. Not only the power of the Bank to accept or reject such application is absolutely discretionary, it could also amend or rescind the Scheme. The Scheme, therefore, cannot be said to be an offer which, on the acceptance by the employee, would fructify in a concluded contract. The Scheme having regard to its provisions merely constitutes an invitation to treat and not an offer. The proposal of the employee when accepted by the Bank would constitute a promise within the meaning of Sec. 2(b) of the Act. Thereafter the promise becomes an enforceable contract. In the instant case, the banks when floating the Scheme did not signify that on the employees assenting

---

[58] AIR 2003 SC 858.

thereto a concluded contract would come into being in terms whereof they would be permitted to retire voluntarily and get the benefits thereunder. Furthermore, in terms of the said Scheme, no consideration passed so as to constitute an agreement. Once it is found that by giving their option under the Scheme, the employees did not derive an enforceable right, the same in absence of any consideration would be void in terms of Sec. 2(g) of the Contract Act as opposed to Sec. 2(h) thereof. Furthermore, even by opting for the Scheme as floated by the Banks, no consideration is passed far less amounting to reciprocal promise. In the instant case, there was even no reasonable certainty that the Scheme would be acted upon. Furthermore, terms and conditions thereof could be amended and even the Scheme itself could be rescinded. The VRS was, therefore, not a proposal or an offer but merely an invitation to treat and the applications filed by the employees constituted 'offer.'

Once the application filed by the employees is held to be an 'offer', Sec. 5 in absence of any other independent binding contract or statute or statutory rules to the contrary would come into play and the offer made by employees could be revoked any time before it was accepted. As regards the clause in the Scheme barring withdrawal of the option, by making such option or *firm offer* the offeree must get some benefit or the offeree must incur some detriment. In the instant case apart from the fact that no consideration is passed, the Banks standing in the category of offeree either expressly or impliedly had not promised to do or refrain from doing something in exchange for the offeror's promise not to revoke the offer.

The plea that as soon as an offer is made by an employee, the same would amount to resignation in *praesenti* cannot be accepted. The Scheme was in force for a fixed period. A decision by authority was required to be taken and till a decision was taken, the *jural* relationship of employer and employee continued and the employees concerned would have been entitled to payment of all salaries and allowances, etc. Thus, it cannot be said to be a case where the offer was given in *praesenti* but the same would be prospective in nature keeping in view the fact that it was to come into force at a later date and that too subject to acceptance thereof by the employer. However, those who accepted the ex-gratia payment or any other benefit under the Scheme could not have resiled therefrom. Accordingly, the Supreme Court held that the employees opting for voluntary retirement could withdraw their offer before it was accepted by the Bank despite the contractual bar to withdrawal contained in the Scheme.

The State Bank of Patiala is a subsidiary of the State Bank of India. The State Bank of Patiala Voluntary Retirement Scheme (SBPVRS) is similar to SBIVRS. Clause (5) of the SBPVRS gave 15 days' time to the employees to opt for the scheme and under Clause (8) a period of two months is given to the management to work out the Scheme. SBPVRS is an invitation to offer and not an offer. Clause (5) of the said SBPVRS *inter alia* states that the Scheme will remain open during the period 15 February, 2001 to 1 March, 2001 whereas Rule 8 thereof provides for mode of acceptance by the management. It is in the light of Clauses (5) and (8) that one has to read Clause (9)(i) which provides for general conditions and under which it is provided that application once made cannot be withdrawn. Rule that *"an offer may be withdrawn at any time before it is accepted"* applies even when the offeror has promised to keep the offer open for a specified time, for such a promise is unsupported by consideration. Therefore, Clause (5) of SBPVRS gives *locus poenitentiae* to the employee to withdraw by 1 March, 2001 after which the mode of acceptance contemplated by Clause (8) of the SBPVRS would apply and the Bank will proceed to vet the applications. Since the said Schemes are funded Schemes, the management is required to create a fund. The creation of the fund would depend upon the number of applications, the cost of the Scheme, liability which the Scheme would impose on the Bank and such other variable factors. If the employees are allowed to withdraw from the Scheme at any time after their closure, it would not be possible to work out the Scheme as all calculations of the management would fail. The Bank needs time to ascertain its liability; it is required to find out the cost of creation of a separate fund which in turn depends on the number of applications and if the employees are permitted to withdraw after the date of closure, it would be impossible for the Bank to implement the scheme. Therefore, Clause (5) gives time to the employee to withdraw by 1 March, 2001 and the Bank is given time of two months thereafter to complete the designated mode of acceptance. Reading Clauses (5), (8) and (9)(i), it is held that employees are precluded from withdrawing from the SBPVRS after the closure of the Scheme on 1 March, 2001. Each Scheme for the purposes of enforceability is required to be read as a whole.[59]

The Contract Act merely provides that a person can withdraw his offer before its acceptance. But withdrawal of an offer, before it is accepted, is a completely different aspect from forfeiture of earnest/security money which has been given for a particular purpose. A person may have a right to withdraw his offer but if he has made his offer on a condition that some earnest money will be forfeited for not entering into contract or if some act is not performed, then even though he may have a right to withdraw his offer, he has no right to claim that the earnest/security be returned to him. Forfeiture of such earnest/security, in no way, affects any statutory right under the Contract Act. Such earnest/security is given and taken to ensure that a contract comes into existence. It would be an anomalous situation that a person who, by his own conduct, precludes the coming into existence of the contract is then given advantage or benefit of his own wrong by not allowing forfeiture. It must be remembered that, particularly in Government contracts, such a term is always included in order to ensure that only the genuine party makes a bid. If such a term was not there, even a person who does not have the capacity or a person who has no intention of entering into the contract will make a bid. The whole purpose of such a clause, i.e., to see that only genuine bids are received would be lost if forfeiture was not permitted.[60]

### Section 6: Revocation how made

A proposal is revoked—

(1) by the communication of notice of revocation by the proposer to the other party;

(2) by the lapse of the time prescribed in such proposal for its acceptance, or, if no time is so prescribed, by the lapse of a reasonable time, without communication of the acceptance;

(3) by the failure of the acceptor to fulfill a condition precedent to acceptance ; or

[59] *State Bank of Patiala* v. *Romesh Chander Kanoji*, AIR 2004 SC 2016.

[60] *National Highway Authority of India* v. *Ganga Enterprises*, AIR 2003 SC 3823.

(4) by the death or insanity of the proposer, if the fact of his death or insanity comes to the knowledge of the acceptor before acceptance.

**Section 7: Acceptance must be absolute**

In order to convert a proposal into a promise, the acceptance must—

(1) be absolute and unqualified;

(2) be expressed in some usual and reasonable manner, unless the proposal prescribes the manner in which it is to be accepted. If the proposal prescribes a manner in which it is to be accepted, and the acceptance is not made in such manner, the proposer may, within a reasonable time after the acceptance is communicated to him, insist that his proposal shall be accepted in the prescribed manner, and not otherwise; but if he fails to do so, he accepts the acceptance.

The appellant before the Supreme Court, namely, the customer, has urged that the National Commission is not right in holding that it relates to pricing of services rendered by the Bank. The arguments advanced before the District Forum and the State Commission have been reiterated before the Apex Court. Much stress has been placed on the point that the charge has been unilateral, without consent and against the directives of the RBI. The Court is not impressed by the submission made on behalf of the appellant. The fact is that recently there has been a large-scale change and improvement in the working and method and manner of functioning of various institutions, including Banks. Many services, which were not available earlier, have been introduced with the aid of mechanical and technological devices. Introduction of computerisation has its own effect; one of which is introduction of MICR cheques. There is no denying of the fact, from either side, that it facilitates the clearance of the cheques and avoids unduly long time-consuming process in cheque clearance, which is issued by the customer within the city or in any other part of the country. Therefore, to say that it was only for the facility of the Bank that the MICR was introduced, would not be correct nor the argument that it could not be permissible for the Bank to make up some amount of the cost incurred in introducing the new and modern infrastructure for improving its working. Accordingly, the Court held that for such small charges necessitated due general modernisation of its functioning and services, the question of it being unilateral does not arise nor the question of consent of each customer.

The other point raised that the amount was being charged for MICR cheques against the directives of the RBI. also does not hold water. In this connection, the learned counsel appearing for the respondent has drawn attention to the letters addressed to the RBI, seeking clarification and the reply of the RBI in response thereof. A perusal of the said documents only indicates that the instructions of the RBI were that the processing charges of cheque, payable by the Banks to the RBI were not to be passed on to the customers. Beyond that there was no instructions at all saying that the Banks would not be charging any amount for issuing MICR cheques to their customers or for the better services rendered for clearance of cheques by introducing any modern and new methods to undergo the whole process. There seems to be complete misreading of the letters issued in that regard by the RBI. Therefore, the appeal was dismissed.[61]

---

[61] *Archana M. Kamath* v. *Canara Bank*, AIR 2003 SC 1694.

## Section 8: Acceptance by performing conditions, or receiving consideration

Performance of the conditions of a proposal, or the acceptance of any consideration for a reciprocal promise which may be offered with a proposal, is an acceptance of the proposal.

Section 8 of the Contract Act provides for acceptance by performing conditions of a proposal. In *Bhagwati Prasad Pawan Kumar, M/s.* v. *Union of India,*[62] the Railways made an offer to the appellant laying down the condition that if the offer was not acceptable, the cheque should be returned forthwith, failing which it would be deemed that the appellant accepted the offer in full and final satisfaction of its claim. This was further clarified by providing that the retention of the cheque and/or encashment thereof will automatically amount to satisfaction in full and final settlement of the claim. Thus, if the appellant accepted the cheques and encashed those without anything more, it would amount to an acceptance of the offer made in the letters of Railways dated 7 April, 1993. The offer prescribed the mode of acceptance, and by conduct the appellant must be held to have accepted the offer and, therefore, could not make a claim later. However, if the appellant had not encashed the cheques and protested to the Railways calling upon them to pay the balance amount and expressed its inability to accept the cheques remitted to it, the controversy would have acquired a different complexion. In that event, in view of the express nonacceptance of the offer, the appellant could not be presumed to have accepted the offer. What, however, is significant is that the protest and nonacceptance must be conveyed before the cheques are encashed. If the cheques are encashed without protest, then it must be held that the offer stood unequivocally accepted. An 'offeree' cannot be permitted to change his mind after the unequivocal acceptance of the offer.

It is well settled that an offer may be accepted by conduct. But conduct would only amount to acceptance if it is clear that the offeree did the act with the intention (actual or apparent) of accepting the offer. Considering the facts of this instant case, if the appellant, before encashing the cheques, had sent the communication dated 20 August, 1993, it could perhaps be argued that by retaining but not encashing the cheques, it did not intend to accept the offer made in the letter of the Railways dated 7 April, 1993. At the same time, if the evidence disclosed that it encashed the cheques and later sent a protest, it must be held that it had accepted the offer unconditionally by conveying its acceptance by the mode prescribed, namely by retaining and encashing the cheques, without reservation. Its subsequent change of mind and consequent protest did not matter.

In the instant case, there is neither pleading nor evidence on record as to the date on which the cheques were received and the date on which the same were sent for encashment. It is, therefore, not possible to record a categoric finding as to whether the letters of protest were written after encashing the cheques or before encashing the cheques. It was for the appellant to plead and prove that it had not accepted the offer and had called upon Railways to pay the balance amount. This it must have done before encashing the cheques. If the appellant encashed the cheques and then wrote letters of protest to the Railways, it cannot be held that it had not accepted the offer by conduct, because at the time when it sent the cheques for encashment, it had not conveyed its protest to the offerer. In the absence of any pleading or evidence to establish that the encashment of the cheques was

---

[62] AIR 2006 SC 2331.

subsequent to the protest letters by the appellant, it is not possible to hold that by encashing the cheques the appellant had not adopted the mode of acceptance prescribed in the letters of the Railways dated 7 April, 1993. In the absence of such evidence, it must be held that by encashing the cheques received from the Railways, the appellant accepted the offer by adopting the mode of acceptance prescribed in the offer of the Railways. Accordingly, the appeal is dismissed, but without any order as to costs.

A contract of insurance will be concluded only when the party to whom an offer has been made accepts it unconditionally and communicates his acceptance to the person making the offer. Though in certain human relationships silence to a proposal might convey acceptance but in the case of insurance proposal, silence does not denote consent and no binding contract arises until the person to whom an offer is made says or does something to signify his acceptance. Mere delay in giving an answer cannot be construed as an acceptance, as, *prima facie*, acceptance must be communicated to the offeror. Similarly, the mere receipt and retention of premium until after the death of the applicant or the mere preparation of the policy document is not acceptance.[63]

## Section 9: Promises, express and implied

Insofar as the proposal or acceptance of any promise is made in words, the promise is said to be express. Insofar as such proposal or acceptance is made otherwise than in words, the promise is said to be implied.

It is the general rule that an offer is not accepted by mere silence on the part of the offeree, yet it does not mean that an acceptance always has to be given in so many words. Under certain circumstances, the offeree's silence, coupled with his conduct, which takes the form of a positive act, may constitute an acceptance which is known as an agreement *sub silentio*. Therefore, the terms of a contract between the parties can be proved not only by their words but also by their conduct.[64]

### *Contract between Government and another person*

**Article 299 of the Constitution of India states as follows:**

(1) All contracts made in the exercise of the executive power of the Union or of a State shall be expressed to be made by the President, or by the Governor of the State, as the case may be, and all such contracts and all assurances of property made in the exercise of that power shall be executed on behalf of the President or the Governor by such persons and in such manner as he may direct or authorise.

(2) Neither the President nor the Governor shall be personally liable in respect of any contract or assurance made or executed for the purposes of this Constitution, or for the purposes of any enactment relating to the Government of India heretofore in force, nor shall any person making or executing any such contract or assurance on behalf of any of them be personally liable in respect thereof.

In view of Art. 299(1) of the Constitution, there can be no implied contract between the Government and any other person, the reason being that if such an implied contract

[63] *Life Insurance Corporation of India* v. *Raja Vasireddy Komalavalli Kamba*, AIR 1984 SC 1014.

[64] *Bharat Petroleum Corpn. Ltd.* v. *Great Eastern Shipping Co. Ltd.*, AIR 2008 SC 357.

between Government and any other person were allowed, that would in effect make Art. 299(1) useless, for then a person who had a contract with Government which was not executed at all in the manner provided in Art. 299(1) could get away by saying that an implied contract may be inferred by the facts and circumstances of a particular case. Further, if the contract between the Government and another person is not in compliance with Art. 299(1), it would be no contract at all and could not be enforced either by the Government or by the other person as a contract.[65]

# Chapter II Of Contracts, Voidable Contracts and Void Agreements

### Section 10: What agreements are contracts

All agreements are contracts if they are made by the free consent of parties competent to contract, for a lawful consideration and with a lawful object, and are not hereby expressly declared to be void.

Nothing herein contained shall affect any law in force in India and not hereby expressly repealed by which any contract is required to be made in writing or in the presence of witnesses, or any law relating to the registration of documents.

Section 10 may be divided into two parts. The first part of Sec. 10 provides four essential elements of a contract. If one is absent out of the four, the document prepared by the contracting parties, even if in a stamp paper, such document cannot be said to be a contract. The document would be a simple and unenforceable agreement. Four essential elements are as follows:

1. Both the contracting parties must be competent to contract.
2. Both the parties must give their free consent.
3. There must be a lawful consideration.
4. The object for which the contract is made must be a lawful one.

The second part of Sec. 10 of the Contract Act provides that if any contract is required to be written and it must be signed in the presence of witnesses and further required to be registered, all necessary legal formalities must be complied with in order to make an enforceable contract. All above stated legal formalities, like writing, witnesses and registration may not be required in all contracts under the Contract Act, but these legal formalities must be satisfied if any other law specifically prescribed for. The best example may be Sec. 25 of the Contract Act that prescribes certain legal formalities to be complied with and contract relating to transfer of immovable property under the Transfer of Property Act.[66]

[65] *K.P. Chowdhry* v. *State of M.P.*, AIR 1967 SC 203.

[66] For further discussion, see the Indian Registration Act.

### Section 11: Who are competent to contract

Every person is competent to contract who is of the age of majority according to the law to which he is subject, and who is of sound mind, and is not disqualified from contracting by any law to which he is subject.

As per Sec. 11 of the Act, the following persons are incompetent to contract—

1. A minor
2. A person of unsound mind, and
3. A person disqualified by law to which he is subject

In *Mohori Bibi* v. *Dharamodas Ghose*[67], Dharmodas Ghose, a minor, entered into a contract for borrowing a sum of ₹20,000, out of which the lender paid the minor a sum of ₹8,000. The minor executed mortgage of property in favour of the lender. Subsequently, the minor sued for setting aside the mortgage. The Privy Council had to ascertain the validity of the mortgage. Under Sec. 7 of the Transfer of Property Act, every person competent to contract is competent to mortgage. The Privy Council decided that Secs. 10 and 11 of the Indian Contract Act make the minor's contract void. The mortgagee prayed for refund of ₹8,000. The Privy Council further held that a minor's contract is not only void but void *ab initio* (from the beginning). Any money advanced to a minor cannot be recovered.

Considering the facts of the case decided by the Supreme Court in *Chacko* v. *Mahadevan*,[68] it has been recorded that Chacko was not having sound mind and he was treated from 11 August, 1983 to 14 August, 1983 in Mental Hospital, Trichur for Alcoholic Psychosis. Moreover, it is established from the facts that one cent of the land was sold for ₹18,000 on 4 September, 1982 vide Ext. A2, while 10 months thereafter three cents of land was sold for only ₹1,000. This corroborates the finding that Chacko was not of sound mind at least at the time when he executed the sale deed dated 11 July, 1983. If one cent of land costs ₹18,000, then three cents of land should ordinarily cost ₹54,000. No one in his senses would sell property worth ₹54,000 for ₹1,000. According to the well-known Latin maxim, '*res ipsa loquitur*', i.e., the matter speaks for itself, it was held that Chacko sold the land by the sale deed dated 11 July, 1983 when he was not of sound mind and some fraud was played on him at that time.

A minor in law suffers from certain specified disabilities. A minor is not competent to enter into a contract. Section 11 of the Contract Act states:

> "Who are competent to contract. Every person is competent to contract who is of the age of majority according to the law to which he is subject, and who is of sound mind and is not disqualified from contracting by any law to which he is subject."

A minor suffers disability from entering into a contract but he is thereby not incapable of receiving property. The Transfer of Property Act does not prohibit transfer of property to a minor. Section 127 of the Transfer of Property Act throws light on the question of validity of transfer of property by gift to a minor. It recognises the minor's capacity to accept the gift without intervention of a guardian, if it is possible, or through him.

---

[67] (1930) 30 1A 114.

[68] AIR 2007 SC 2967.

Section 127 of the Transfer of Property Act—Onerous gifts. Where a gift is in the form of a single transfer to the same person of several things of which one is, and the others are not burdened by an obligation, the donee can take nothing by the gift unless he accepts it fully.

Where a gift is in the form of two or more separate and independent transfers to the same person of several things, the donee is at liberty to accept one of them and refuse the others, although the former may be beneficial and the latter onerous.

Onerous gift to disqualified person—A donee not competent to contract and accepting property burdened by any obligation is not bound by his acceptance. But if, after becoming competent to contract and being aware of the obligation, he retains the property given, he becomes so bound.

The last part of Sec. 127 of the Transfer of Property Act clearly indicates that a minor donee, who can be said to be in law incompetent to contract under Sec. 11 of the Contract Act, is, however, competent to accept a non-onerous gift. Acceptance of an onerous gift, however, cannot bind the minor. If he accepts the gift during his minority of a property burdened with obligation and on attaining majority does not repudiate but retains it, he would be bound by the obligation attached to it.

### *Effect of Minor's Contract*

1. No estoppel against the minor.
2. No liability in contract or tort arising out of contract.
3. No ratification of minor's contract.
4. Application of doctrine of restitution.
5. Liability for necessaries (please refer to Sec. 68 of the Act).

The application of the doctrine of restitution is having its own limitations. It is difficult to identify the same coin or notes[69] or the products which have been already consumed by the minor.

### Section 12: What is a sound mind for the purposes of contracting

A person is said to be of sound mind for the purpose of making a contract if, at the time when he makes it, he is capable of understanding it and of forming a rational judgment as to its effect upon his interests.

A person, who is usually of unsound mind, but occasionally of sound mind, may make a contract when he is of sound mind.

A person, who is usually of sound mind, but occasionally of unsound mind, may not make a contract when he is of unsound mind.

### Illustrations

(a) A patient in a lunatic asylum, who is at intervals of sound mind, may contract during those intervals.

(b) A sane man, who is delirious from fever or who is so drunk that he cannot understand the terms of a contract or form a rational judgment as to its effect on his interests, cannot contract whilst such delirium or drunkenness lasts.

[69] *Khan Gul* v. *Lakha Singh*, AIR 1928 Lah 609.

It follows from Sec. 11 that only a person of sound mind can enter into a contract and it follows from Sec. 12 that soundness of mind of a person has to be seen at the time when he enters into a contract and it matters not if such a person is usually of unsound mind but occasionally of sound mind or is usually of sound mind but occasionally of unsound mind. What has to be seen is whether at the relevant time and that relevant time is when he made the contract he was capable of understanding it and forming a rational view as to its effects upon his interest. In a case where the appellant was declared as unfit by the doctors as she was suffering from 'Schizophrenia'. To this effect the doctor issued two medical certificates on 26 October, 1989 and 10 January, 1990. But the appellant signed in two "Agreements to sell" documents on 21 February, 1985 and 7 September, 1987. The appellant took the plea that the two "Agreement to sell" document would be declared as invalid. But it was held the documents could not be declared as invalid because she was suffering from Schizophrenia' only after the signature of the documents.[70]

## Section 13: "Consent" defined

Two or more persons are said to consent when they agree upon the same thing in the same sense.

Section 10 of the Act prescribes that free consent is one of the essential elements for an agreement to be a valid and legal contract. The word 'consent' is, however, defined under Sec. 13 of the Act as follows:

> "Consent" defined: — two or more persons are said to consent when they agree upon the same thing in the same manner.

It is essential for a contract that both parties to the contract should agree to the same thing in the same sense, which is otherwise known as *consensus ad idem.*

## Section 14: "Free consent" defined

Consent is said to be free when it is not caused by—

1. Coercion, as defined in Section 15, or
2. Undue influence, as defined in Section 16, or
3. Fraud, as defined in Section 17, or
4. Misrepresentation, as defined in Section 18, or
5. Mistake, subject to the provisions of Sections 20, 21 and 22.

Consent is said to be so caused when it would not have been given but for the existence of such coercion, undue influence, fraud, misrepresentation, or mistake.

The word 'free consent' has not been defined under the Contract Act. However, Sec. 14 provides five situations where it does not amount to free consent.

---

[70] *Nilima Ghosh* v. *Harjeet Kaur*, AIR 2011 DELHI 104.

### *Consequences of Voidable Contract and Void Contract*

Where consent is obtained by coercion, undue influence, fraud or misrepresentation, the contract may be a voidable contract which may be avoided at the option of the party whose consent was obtained by coercion, undue influence, fraud or misrepresentation. Voidable contract is defined under Sec. 2(i) as follows:

> An agreement which is enforceable by law at the option of one or more of the parties thereto, but not at the option of the other or others, is a voidable contract.

When consent is obtained by mistake, the agreement is void. Section 2(g) provides that a void agreement is not enforceable at the option of either party.

## Section 15: "Coercion" defined

"Coercion" is the committing, or threatening to commit, any act forbidden by the Indian Penal Code, or the unlawful detaining, or threatening to detain, any property, to the prejudice of any person whatever, with the intention of causing any person to enter into an agreement. (45 of 1860)

***Explanation*:** It is immaterial whether the Indian Penal Code is or is not in force in the place where the coercion is employed. (45 of 1860)

### Illustration

A, on board an English ship on the high seas, causes B to enter into an agreement by an act amounting to criminal intimidation under the Indian Penal Code. (45 of 1860.)

A afterwards sues B for breach of contract at Calcutta.

A has employed coercion, although his act is not an offence by the law of England, and although Section 506 of the Indian Penal Code was not in force at the time when or place where the act was done. (45 of 1860)

An agreement would be a valid contract if both the parties must act freely and their consents should be free. In other words, parties to the contract must give their consents freely and without any duress or coercion. If one of the parties is forced to make the contract by violence or the threat of violence, that is duress or coercion, and renders the contract voidable.

The original common law of duress confined the doctrine within very narrow limits. Only duress to the person was recognised during the nineteenth century, and this required actual or threatened violence to the victim. For example, in *Barton* v. *Armstrong*[71] where A (the former chairman of a company) threatened B (the managing director) with death if he did not agree to purchase A's shares in the company. There was some evidence that B thought the proposed agreement was a satisfactory business arrangement both from his own point of view and that of the company. B executed a deed on behalf of the company carrying out the agreement. He sought a declaration that the deed was executed under duress and was void.

---

[71] [1976] AC 104.

The nineteenth century limitation on duress meant that it could not be applied to 'duress of goods'. If a person, unlawfully detained, or threatened to detain, another's goods, this was not considered to be sufficient duress to enable a contract to be avoided.[72] In recent times, the English Courts have extended the concept of duress from its earlier limits so as to recognise that certain forms of commercial pressure could amount to economic duress. In *North Ocean Shipping* v. *Hyundai Construction (popularly known as The Atlantic Baron case)*[73], the builders of a ship demanded 10% increases on the contract price from the owners largely because the value of the US dollar fell by 10%, or threatened not to complete the ship. The owners paid the increased rate demanded from them, although they protested that there was no legal basis on which the demand could be made. The owners were commercially compelled to pay since, at the time of the threat, they were negotiating a very lucrative contract for the charter of the ship being built. Mocatta J decided that this constituted economic duress. The illegitimate pressure exerted by the building company was their threat to break the construction contract. Where a threat to break a contract had led to a further contract, that contract, even though it was made for good consideration, was voidable by reason of economic duress.

The House of Lords in *Universe Tankships* v. *ITWF*[74] where A trade union had 'blacked' the plaintiff's ship, i.e., threatened to induce the crew of a ship to break their contracts of employment and so to prevent the ship from leaving port, unless the owner paid a large sum of money, partly to the union welfare fund. In view of the catastrophic financial consequences which the ship owners would suffer if these threats were carried out, it was conceded that they constituted economic duress, vitiating the ship owners' consent to the agreement. It was held by the House of Lords that these payments could be recovered.

In *Dimskal Shipping Co* v. *ITWF*[75], whilst the plaintiff's ship was in harbour in Sweden, it was boarded by agents of the International Transport Workers' Federation, who informed them that the ship would be blacked and loading would not be continued until the company entered into certain agreements with ITWF, including back pay to the crew, new contracts of employment at higher wages and guarantees for future payments. At first, the plaintiffs would not agree and the ship was in fact blacked. Yielding to the pressure, the company agreed to sign the various agreements, which were expressly declared to be governed by English law. The plaintiffs then sought to avoid the agreement on the grounds of duress and claimed restitution of all sums paid.

The House of Lords held that it constituted economic duress and observed that under English law, a contract obtained by duress is voidable and improper economic pressure (blacking the ship) constitutes one form of duress. The owners were thus entitled to avoid the agreements as they entered into the contract because of pressure from ITWF.

The Indian Contract Act has avoided the word 'duress' and in its place used 'coercion', which has been defined in Sec. 15 of the Act.

---

[72] *Skeate* v. *Beale* (1840) 11 Ad & El 983.

[73] [1979] QB 705.

[74] [1982] 2 All ER 67.

[75] [1991] 4 All ER 871.

### *Grounds of causing coercion*

1. Committing or threatening to commit, any act forbidden by the Indian Penal Code; or
2. Unlawful detaining, or threatening to detain, any property.

In *Chikham Amiraju* v. *Chikham Seshamma*[76], by threat of suicide, a Hindu induced his wife and son to execute a release in favour of his brother in respect of certain properties which they claimed as their own. It was held by a majority that the threat of suicide amounted to coercion within Sec. 15 of the Contract Act inasmuch as the attempting to commit suicide is an offence under Sec. 309 of the Penal Code, 1860 and by committing the offence he obtained consent from his wife and son to the contract and the contract therefore was voidable.

### *Duress in English Law and Coercion in Indian Law—A Comparison*

Under the English law, duress is said to consist in actual or threatened violence or imprisonment of the contracting party or his wife, parent or child, by the other party or anyone acting with his knowledge and for his advantage. But in the Indian law, coercion, as defined in Sec. 15 of the Indian Contract Act, is much wider and includes unlawful detention of the property also. Further, coercion may be committed by any person, not necessarily a party to the contract. Again, it need not be directed against the contracting party or his parent, wife or child. It may be directed against any person, even if he is a stranger. While in English Law, duress must be such as will cause immediate violence and also unnerve a person of ordinary firmness of mind, these requisites are not necessary in Indian Law.[77]

### *Remedies for coercion*

1. The effect of coercion is to make the contract voidable (not void). Section 19 of the Act provides that when consent to an agreement is caused by coercion, the agreement is a contract voidable at the option of the party whose consent was so caused. The injured party will, therefore, be entitled to have the contract set aside unless he has expressly or impliedly affirmed it. The victim of coercion must seek rescission as soon as possible.
2. Once the party rescinds the contract, by default, Sec. 64 would be applied. Section 64 reads as follows:

> When a person at whose option a contract is voidable rescinds it, the other party thereto need not perform any promise therein contained in which he is the promisor. The party rescinding a voidable contract shall, if he have received any benefit there under from another party to such contract, restore such benefit, so far as may be, to the person from whom it was received.

[76] (1917) 41 Mad 33.

[77] See *Karuppayee Ammal* v. *Karuppiaah Pillai*, (1987) 1 Mad L J 138.

3. As coercion may be equated with the tort of intimidation, remedy for damages would lie in tort.[78]

   Lord Denning MR defined the tort of intimidation in *Morgan* v. *Fry*[79] as follows:

> "The essential ingredients are these: there must be a threat by one person to use unlawful means (such as violence or a tort or a breach of contract) so as to compel another to obey his wishes and the person so threatened must comply with the demand rather than risk the threat being carried into execution. In such circumstances the person damnified by the compliance can sue for intimidation."

4. There is, as yet, no authority on the question of whether or not an injured party who has affirmed the contract may nevertheless recover damages in tort. It is submitted that damages should be recoverable, since otherwise a party who has lost the right to avoid the contract is left without a remedy for a clearly unlawful act.

## Section 16: "Undue influence" defined

1. A contract is said to be induced by "undue influence" where the relations subsisting between the parties are such that one of the parties is in a position to dominate the will of the other and uses that position to obtain an unfair advantage over the other.
2. In particular and without prejudice to the generality of the foregoing principle, a person is deemed to be in a position to dominate the will of another,—
   (a) Where he holds a real or apparent authority over the other or where he stands in a fiduciary relation to the other; or
   (b) Where he makes a contract with a person whose mental capacity is temporarily or permanently affected by reason of age, illness, or mental or bodily distress.
3. Where a person who is in a position to dominate the will of another, enters into a contract with him, and the transaction appears, on the face of it or on the evidence adduced, to be unconscionable, the burden of proving that such contract was not induced by undue influence shall lie upon the person in a position to dominate the will of the other.

   Nothing in this sub-section shall affect the provisions of Section III of the Indian Evidence Act, 1872. (1 of 1872)

### Illustrations

(a) A having advanced money to his son, B, during his minority, upon B's coming of age obtains, by misuse of parental influence, a bond from B for a greater amount than the sum due in respect of the advance, A employs undue influence.

---

[78] See *Universe Tankships* v. *ITWF*, [1982] 2 All ER 67.

[79] [1968] 2 QB 710.

(b) A, a man enfeebled by disease or age, is induced, by B's influence over him as his medical attendant, to agree to pay B an unreasonable sum for his professional services. B employs undue influence.

(c) A, being in debt to B, the money-lender of his village, contracts a fresh loan on terms which appear to be unconscionable. It lies on B to prove that the contract was not induced by undue influence.

(d) A applies to a banker for a loan at a time when there is stringency in the money market. The banker declines to make the loan except at an unusually high rate of interest. A accepts the loan on these terms. This is a transaction in the ordinary course of business, and the contract is not induced by undue influence.

The doctrine of undue influence under the common law was evolved by the Courts in England for granting protection against transactions procured by the exercise of insidious forms of influence spiritual and temporal. The doctrine applies to acts of bounty as well as to other transactions in which one parry by exercising his position of dominance obtains an unfair advantage over another. The Indian Contract Act is founded substantially on the rules of English common law. The first sub-section of Sec. 16 of the Contract Act lays down the principle in general terms. By sub-sec. (2), a presumption arises that a person shall be deemed to be in a position to dominate the will of another if the conditions set therein are fulfilled. Sub-section (3) lays down the conditions for raising a rebuttable presumption that a transaction is procured by the exercise of undue influence. The reason for the rule in the third sub-section is that a person who has obtained an advantage over another by dominating his will may also remain a position to suppress the requisite evidence in support of the plea of undue influence. A transaction may be vitiated on account of undue influence where the relations between the parties are such that one of them is in a position to dominate the will of the other and he uses his position to obtain unfair advantage over the other. It is manifest that both the conditions have ordinarily to be established by the person seeking to avoid the transaction; he has to prove (a) that the other party to a transaction was in a position to dominate his will and (b) that the other party had obtained an unfair advantage by using that position.

There may arise cases in which even though the burden lies on such a person to prove his case of undue influence, he may establish it from admissions made by the other party or his witnesses or from other evidence, and without giving his own testimony. Clause (2) lays down a special presumption that a person is deemed to be in a position to dominate the will of another (i) where he holds a real or apparent authority—over the other, or (ii) where he stands in a fiduciary relation to the other or (iii) where he enters into a transaction with a person whose mental capacity is temporarily or permanently affected by reason of age, illness or mental or bodily distress. Where it is proved that a person is in a position to dominate the will of another (such proof being furnished either by evidence or by the presumption arising under sub-sec. (2) and the enters into a transaction with that other person which on the face of it or on the evidence adduced, appears to be unconscionable the burden of proving that the transaction was not induced by undue influence lies upon the person in a position to dominate the will of the other. But sub-sec. (3) has manifestly a limited application; the presumption will only arise if it is established by evidence that the party who had obtained the benefit of a transaction was in a position to dominate the will of the other and that transaction is shown to be unconscionable. If either of these two conditions is not fulfilled, the presumption of undue influence will not arise and burden will not shift.[80]

Equity gives relief on the ground of undue influence where consent to an agreement has been obtained by certain kinds of improper pressure which is neither a duress nor coercion because no element of violence to the person is involved. A person who has been induced to enter into a transaction by the undue influence of another (the wrongdoer) is entitled to set that transaction aside as against the wrongdoer. The effect of undue influence, like coercion, is to make the contract voidable.

So far as Sec. 16 is concerned, two conditions must be satisfied to constitute undue influence that:

1. one of the parties to an agreement is in a position to dominate the will of the other; and
2. such dominate position has been exercised by the party to obtain an unfair advantage over the other.

Section 16(2) provides a deeming clause where it specifically provides that a person would be deemed to be in a position to dominate the will of another where:

1. he holds a real or apparent authority over the other, or
2. he stands in a fiduciary relation to the other; or
3. he makes a contract with a person whose mental capacity is temporarily or permanently affected by reason of age, illness, or mental or bodily distress.

Section 16(3) speaks about the burden of proof. Section 16(2) provides the deeming clause that the Court would presume at the beginning that the person who is in a dominant position might have exercised his dominant power to obtain the consent of the other party to make the contract. Here the burden of proof is shifted on the dominant person to disprove that he has not exercised his dominant power to obtain the consent of the other party to make the contract.

Relationship between the parties so as to enable one of them to dominate the will of other is a *sine qua non* for constitution of undue influence. The law does not envisage rising of a presumption in favour of undue influence. A parry alleging the same must prove the same subject, of course to just exceptions. In a given case it is possible to hold that when an illiterate, *pardanashin* woman executes a deed of sale, the burden would be on the vendee to prove that the deed of sale was a genuine document. Where it is, however, a registered document, it carries with it a presumption that it was executed in accordance with law.[81]

In the case of undue influence, the complainant only has to show, in the first instance, that there was a relationship of trust and confidence between the complainant and the wrongdoer of such a nature that it is fair to presume that the wrongdoer abused that relationship in procuring the complainant to enter the impugned transaction. In case of presumed undue influence, there is no need to produce evidence that actual undue

[80] *Ladli Prashad Jaiswal* v. *Karnal Distillery Co. Ltd., Karnal*, AIR 1963 SC 1279.

[81] *Bellachi* v. *Pakeeran*, AIR 2009 SC 3293.

influence was exerted in relation to the particular transaction impugned. Once a confidential relationship has been proved, the burden then shifts to the wrongdoer to prove that the complainant entered into the impugned transaction freely. However, it must also be shown that the transaction was manifestly disadvantageous to the party alleged to be influenced.[82]

When fraud, misrepresentation or undue influence is alleged by a party in a suit, normally, the burden is on him to prove such fraud, undue influence or misrepresentation. But when a person is in a fiduciary relationship with another and the latter is in a position of active confidence, the burden of proving the absence of fraud, misrepresentation or undue influence is upon the person, in the dominating position. He has to prove that there was fair play in the transaction and that the apparent is the real; in other words, that the transaction is genuine and bona fide. In such a case, the burden of proving the good faith of the transaction is thrown upon the dominant party, that is to say, the party who is in a position of active confidence. A person standing in a fiduciary relation to another has a duty to protect the interest given to his care and the Court watches with jealously all transactions between such persons so that the protector may not use his influence or the confidence to his advantage. When the party complaining shows such relation, the law presumes everything against the transaction and the onus is cast upon the person holding the position of confidence or trust to show that the transaction is perfectly fair and reasonable, that no advantage has been taken of his position.[83]

Such a confidential relationship can be established in two ways:

1. Certain relationships, as a matter of law, raise the presumption that undue influence has been exercised. The relationships where undue influence is presumed have been held to be: parent and child; solicitor and client; doctor and patient; trustee and beneficiary; and religious adviser and disciple.

   In *Allcard* v. *Skinner*,[84] an unmarried woman aged 27 sought a clergyman as a confessor in 1867. The following year she became an associate of the sisterhood of which he was spiritual director and in 1871, she was admitted as a full member, taking vows of poverty, chastity and obedience. Without independent advice, she made gifts of money and stock to the mother superior on behalf of the sisterhood. She left the sisterhood in 1879 and in 1884 claimed the return of the stock. Proceedings to recover the stock were commenced in 1885.

   It was held by the Court of Appeal that although the plaintiff's gifts were voidable because of undue influence brought to bear upon the plaintiff through the training she had received, she was disentitled to recover because of her conduct and delay.

   The relationship of husband and wife does not, as a matter of law, raise a presumption of undue influence and this rule too does not apply between employer and employee.

2. If the complainant proves the existence of a relationship under which the complainant generally reposed trust and confidence in the wrongdoer, the existence of such relationship raises the presumption of undue influence.

---

[82] *National Westminster Bank* v. *Morgan,* [1985] 1 All ER 821.

[83] *Krishna Mohan Kul* v. *P[illegible]ma Maity*, AIR 2003 SC 4351.

[84] (1887) 36 Ch D 145.

In the absence of evidence disproving undue influence, the complainant will succeed in setting aside the impugned transaction merely by proof that the complainant reposed trust and confidence in the wrongdoer without having to prove that the wrongdoer exerted actual undue influence or otherwise abused such trust and confidence in relation to the particular transaction impugned.

The relation of banker and customer will not normally give rise to a presumption of undue influence, but it can do so in exceptional cases if the customer has placed himself entirely in the hands of the bank and has not been given any opportunity to seek independent advice. In *Lloyd's Bank* v. *Bundy*[85], a guarantee was given to the bank by an elderly farmer, a customer of the bank, for his son's debts. The guarantee was secured by a mortgage of Bundy's house in favour of the bank. An assistant manager of the bank, with the son, later told the father that they would only continue to support the son's company if he increased the guarantee and charge. The father did so, the assistant manager appreciating that the father relied on him implicitly to advise him about the transaction. The Court of Appeal set aside the guarantee and charge.

Lord Denning held that the relationship between the bank and the father was one of trust and confidence. The bank knew that the father relied on them implicitly to advise him about the transaction. The father trusted the bank. This gave the bank much influence on the father. Yet the bank failed in that trust. They allowed the father to charge the house to his ruin. There was also a conflict of interest between the bank and the father, yet the bank did not realize it, nor did they suggest that the father should get independent advice. If the father had gone to his solicitor or any man of business there is no doubt that they would have advised him not to enter the transaction as the house was his sole asset and the son's company was in a dangerous state.

With both of the above presumptions, (1 and 2), the transaction must be to the 'manifest disadvantage' of the party claiming undue influence. In *National Westminster Bank* v. *Morgan*[86], both husband and wife owned a home jointly. The husband was unable to meet his mortgage commitments and the building society threatened to seek possession for unpaid debts. The husband made refinancing arrangements with the bank secured by a mortgage in favour of the bank over the matrimonial home. The bank manager called at the home to get the wife to execute the charge. She did not wish the charge to cover her husband's business liabilities. The bank manager assured her, in good faith but incorrectly, that it did not. It was, in fact, unlimited in extent and could, therefore, extend to all the husband's liabilities to the bank, though it was the bank's intention to confine it to the amount needed to refinance the mortgage. The wife had not received independent legal advice before executing the mortgage. The husband and wife fell into arrears with their payments, and the bank obtained an order for possession of the home. Shortly afterwards, the husband died without owing

[85] [1974] 3 All ER 757.

[86] [1985] 1 All ER 821.

the bank any business debts. The wife argued that the bank manager exercised undue influence over her and that a special relationship existed between her and the bank which required it to ensure that she received independent legal advice before entering into a further mortgage. The Court relied on the decision of *Lloyd's Bank* case.

The Court trying a case of undue influence must consider two things to start with, namely, (1) are the relations between the donor and the donee such that the donee is in a position to dominate the will of the donor, and (2) has the donee used that position to obtain an unfair advantage over the donor? Upon the determination of these issues, a third point emerges, which is that of the onus probandi. If the transaction appears to be unconscionable, then the burden of proving that the contract was not induced by undue influence is to lie upon the person who was in a position to dominate the will of the other. Undue influence may not be presumed merely because the parties were nearly related to each other or merely because the donor was old or of weak character. Generally speaking, the relations of solicitor and client, trustee and *cestui que* trust, spiritual adviser and devotee, medical attendant and patient, parent and child are those in which such a presumption arises. The circumstance that a grandfather made a gift of a portion of his properties to his only grandson a few years before his death is not on the face of it an unconscionable transaction.[87]

## Remedies

The remedy in cases of undue influence is rescission. Damages are not available. Rescission of contract is allowed in the case of undue influence under Sec. 19A of the Act. Where rescission is ordered, the whole transaction will be set aside.

## Section 17: "Fraud" defined

"Fraud" means and includes any of the following acts committed by a party to a contract, or with his connivance, or by his agent, with intent to deceive another party thereto of his agent, or to induce him to enter into the contract:—

1. the suggestion, as a fact, of that which is not true, by one who does not believe it to be true;
2. the active concealment of a fact by one having knowledge or belief of the fact;
3. a promise made without any intention of performing it;
4. any other act fitted to deceive;
5. any such act or omission as the law specially declares to be fraudulent.

***Explanation*:** Mere silence as to facts likely to affect the willingness of a person to enter into a contract is not fraud, unless the circumstances of the case are such that, regard being had to them, it is the duty of the person keeping silence to speak, or unless his silence is, in itself, equivalent to speech.

[87] *Subhas Chandra Das Mushib* v. *Ganga Prosad Das Mushib*, AIR 1967 SC 878.

**Illustrations**

(a) A sells, by auction, to B, a horse which A knows to be unsound. A says nothing to B about the horse's unsoundness. This is not fraud in A.

(b) B is A's daughter and has just come of age. Here, the relation between the parties would make it A's duty to tell B if the horse, is unsound.

(c) B says to A—"If you do not deny it, I shall assume that the horse is sound." A says nothing. Here, A's silence is equivalent to speech.

(d) A and B, being traders, enter upon a contract. A has private information of a change in prices which would affect B's willingness to proceed with the contract. A is not bound to inform B.

By "fraud" is meant an intention to deceive; whether it is from any expectation of advantage to the party himself or from the ill will towards the other is immaterial. The expression "fraud" involves two elements, deceit and injury to the person deceived. Injury is something other than economic loss, that is, deprivation of property, whether movable or immovable or of money and it will include any harm whatever caused to any person in body, mind, reputation or such others. In short, it is a non-economic or non-pecuniary loss. A benefit or advantage to the deceiver, will almost always call loss or detriment to the deceived. Even in those rare cases where there is a benefit or advantage to the deceiver, but no corresponding loss to the deceived, the second condition is satisfied.[88] A "fraud" is an act of deliberate deception with the design of securing something by taking unfair advantage of another. It is a deception in order to gain by another's loss. It is a cheating intended to get an advantage.[89]

"Fraud", as is well known, vitiates every solemn act. Fraud and justice never dwell together. Fraud is a conduct either by letter or words, which includes the other person or authority to take a definite determinative stand as a response to the conduct of the former either by words or letter. It is also well settled that misrepresentation itself amounts to fraud. Indeed, innocent misrepresentation may also give reason to claim relief against fraud. A fraudulent misrepresentation is called deceit and consists in leading a man into damage by willfully or recklessly causing him to believe and act on falsehood. It is a fraud in law if a party makes representations, which he knows to be false, and injury ensues therefrom although the motive from which the representations proceeded may not have been bad. An act of fraud on Court is always viewed seriously.[90] 'Fraud is proved when it is shown that a false representation has been made (i) knowingly, or (ii) without belief in its truth, or (iii) recklessly, careless whether it is true or false'. "Suppression of a material document would also amount to a fraud."[91]

Under the Muslim Law, a marriage is a contract unlike the Hindu Law, where it is a sacrament. In *Amina* v. *Hassan Koya*[92], the respondent-husband pleaded a case that he was not aware of the fact that the appellant-wife was pregnant at the time of marriage

[88] *Dr. Vimla* v. *Delhi Administration*, AIR 1963 SC 1572.

[89] *S.P. Chengalvaraya Naidu* v. *Jagannath*, AIR 1994 SC 853.

[90] *Ram Chandra Singh* v. *Savitri Devi*, (2003) 8 SCC 319.

[91] *Gowrishankar* v. *Joshi Amba Shankar Family Trust*, AIR 1996 SC 2202.

[92] AIR 2004 SC 1227.

and as this fact was concealed by the appellant-wife from him, it rendered the contract of marriage as void. The Supreme Court held that it is very difficult to believe that a woman who is five months pregnant will be able to conceal the pregnancy from the husband. Such an advanced stage of pregnancy cannot be concealed as the pregnancy starts showing by that time. In any case, the pregnancy cannot be concealed from the husband. A husband will at least know for sure that the wife is pregnant especially when the pregnancy is five months old. Therefore, it cannot be accepted that the respondent-husband did not know at the time of marriage that the appellant-wife was already pregnant. If this fact was known to the respondent-husband, the marriage cannot be said to be illegal or void. Conduct of the respondent-husband at the relevant time also is material. He goes through the marriage. He does not raise any objection even after the marriage. He is present at the time of delivery of the child. Presumably he gives his own name as the name of the father of the child for the official record. Even thereafter for nearly four years, he goes along with the marriage and brings up the child while treating appellant as his wife. The divorce is said to have been given after 41/2 years. Any person who learns that his newly married wife is already pregnant for five months and who does not accept that marriage or pregnancy, will not behave in the manner in which respondent husband did. A normal reasonable person would have immediately turned out the wife from his house on coming to know of the fact of pregnancy. Nobody will continue with such a marriage for four and a half years, especially when a child is born just after four months of the marriage. In the facts of the case, it has to be held that the respondent-husband was fully aware of the pregnancy of the appellant wife at the time of the marriage and, therefore, cannot avoid liability to pay maintenance to wife on ground that the marriage was invalid or void or that he had not fathered the child.

Where, according to the terms of the life insurance policy, all moneys that had been paid in consequence of policy would belong to the insurance company if the policy was vitiated by reason of a fraudulent suppression of material facts by the insured, and the contract is bad on the ground of fraud, the party who has been guilty of fraud or a person who claims under him cannot ask for a refund of the money paid. Where the policy holder, who had been treated, a few months before he submitted a proposal for the insurance of his life with the insurance company by a physician of repute for certain serious ailments as anemia, shortness of breath and asthma, not only failed to disclose in his answers to the questions put to him by the insurance company that he suffered from those ailments but he made a false statement to the effect that he had not been treated by any doctor for any such serious ailment. It was held that by the standard laid down in Sec. 17 of the Contract Act, the policy holder was clearly guilty of a fraudulent suppression of material facts when he made his statements, which he must have known were deliberately false and hence, the policy issued to him relying on those statements was vitiated. Moreover, the principle underlying the Explanation to Sec. 19 of the Contract Act is that a false representation, whether fraudulent or innocent, is irrelevant if it has not induced the party to whom it is made to act upon it by entering into a contract. That principle did not apply in the instant case. The terms of the policy made it clear that the averments made as to the state of health of the insured in the proposal form and the personal statement were the basis of the contract between the parties and the circumstance that the policy holder had taken pains to falsify or conceal that he had been treated for a serious ailment by a physician only a few months before the policy was taken showed that the falsification or concealment had an important bearing in obtaining the other party's consent. A man who has so acted cannot afterwards turn round and say, "It could have made no difference if you had known the truth." In the circumstances, no advantage could be taken of the Explanation to Sec. 19 of the Contract Act.[93]

In a famous case in *Derry* v. *Peek*[94], the plaintiff received a prospectus regarding the incorporation of defendant's company, which highlighted that the company would have the right to use steam or mechanical power. After receiving the prospectus, the plaintiff bought shares of the company, relying on the allegations of the prospectus, and believing that the company had the absolute right to use steam or mechanical power. The board of trade refused to allow steam or mechanical power, and the company was wound up, unable to complete its work. Thereafter, the plaintiff brought suit against the defendant for fraudulent misrepresentations. The trial judge dismissed the action, after coming to the conclusion that the directors knew that the use of steam or mechanical power was contingent on the board of trade and it was not unreasonable or deceitful for them to rely on the board. On appeal, the dismissal was reversed, because the Court found that the defendants may have reasonably believed the prospectus and, because they did not have reasonable grounds for what they wrote in the prospectus, they should be held liable for the plaintiff's reliance. On appeal, the issue was whether it is deceit when a company forms a prospectus to solicit investors, which later proves to be wrong. However, the shareholders' action failed, because it was not proved that the director lacked honest belief in what they had said.

**Section 18: "Misrepresentation" defined**

"Misrepresentation" means and includes—

1. the positive assertion, in a manner not warranted by the information of the person making it, of that which is not true, though he believes it to be true;
2. any breach, of duty which, without an intent to deceive, gains an advantage to the person committing it, or anyone claiming under him, by misleading another to his prejudice or to the prejudice of anyone claiming under him;
3. causing, however innocently, a party to an agreement to make a mistake as to the substance of the thing which is the subject of the agreement.

A misrepresentation is a false statement of fact made by one party to another, thereby inducing the other party to enter the contract. The effect of such contract may be a voidable one and the innocent party is having right to rescind the contract and/or claim damages.

***Guidelines as to constitute misrepresentation***

**1.** ***False statement of fact***: An actionable misrepresentation must be a false statement of fact, not opinion or future intention or law.

(a) *Statements of opinion*: A false statement of opinion is not a misrepresentation under the law. In *Bisset* v. *Wilkinson*[95], the plaintiff purchased from the defendant

[93] *Mithoolal Nayak* v. *Life Insurance Corporation of India*, AIR 1962 SC 814.

[94] (1889) LR 14 APP CAS 337.

[95] [1927] AC 177.

two blocks of land for the purpose of sheep farming. During the negotiations, the defendant said that if the place was worked properly, it would carry 2,000 sheep. The plaintiff bought the place believing that it would carry 2,000 sheep. Both parties were aware that the defendant had not carried on sheep-farming on the land. In an action for misrepresentation, the trial judge said that in the ordinary circumstances, any statement made by an owner who has been occupying his own farm as to its carrying capacity would be regarded as a statement of fact. In these circumstances, the defendants were not justified in regarding anything said by the plaintiff as to the carrying capacity as being anything more than an expression of his opinion on the subject. The Privy Council accordingly accepted this view and therefore held that in the absence of fraud, the purchaser had no right to rescind the contract.

However, where the person giving the statement was in a position to know the true facts and it can be proved that he could not reasonably have held such a view as a result, then his opinion will be treated as a statement of fact. In *Smith* v. *Land & House Property Corp.*[96], the plaintiff put up his hotel for sale stating that it was let to a 'most desirable tenant'. The defendants agreed to buy the hotel. The tenant was bankrupt. As a result, the defendants refused to complete the contract and were sued by the plaintiff for specific performance. The Court of Appeal held that the plaintiff's statement was not mere opinion but was one of fact.

(b) *Statements as to the future*: A false statement by a person as to what he will do in the future is not a misrepresentation and will not be binding on a person unless the statement is incorporated into a contract. However, if a person knows that his promise, which has induced another to enter into a contract, will not in fact be carried out, then he will be liable. In *Esso Petroleum* v. *Mardon*[97], where Esso's experienced representative told Mardon that Esso estimated that the throughput of petrol on a certain site would reach 2,00,000 gallons in the third year of operation and so persuaded Mardon to enter into a tenancy agreement in April 1963 for three years. Mardon did all that could be expected of him as tenant but the site was not good enough to achieve a throughput of more than 60,000–70,000 gallons. Mardon lost money and was unable to pay for petrol supplied. Esso claimed possession of the site and money due. Mardon claimed damages in respect of the representation alleging that it amounted to (i) a warranty; and (ii) a negligent misrepresentation. The Court of Appeal affirmed the finding of negligence applying the principle of *Hedley Byrne* v. *Heller*[98]. On the issue of warranty, Lord Denning MR stated that it was a forecast made by a party, Esso, who had special knowledge and skill. It was the yardstick (the "e a c") by which they measured the worth of a filling station. They knew the facts. They knew the traffic in the town. They knew the throughput of comparable

96 (1884) 28 Ch D7.

97 [1976] QB 801.

98 [1964] AC 465.

stations. They had much experience and expertise at their disposal. They were in a much better position than Mr. Mardon to make a forecast. It seems to the Court that if such a person makes a forecast—intending that the other should act on it and he does act on it—it can well be interpreted as a warranty that the forecast is sound and reliable in this sense that they made it with reasonable care and skill. If the forecast turned out to be an unsound forecast, such as no person of skill or experience should have made, there is a breach of warranty.

(c) *Statements of the law*: A false statement as to the law is not actionable misrepresentation because everyone is presumed to know the law of the country. However, the distinction between fact and law is not as simple as we presume. The fact of the case may be considered to know whether it is a fact or law.

(d) *Silence*: Generally, silence is not a misrepresentation. The effect of the maxim *caveat emptor* is that the other party has no duty to disclose voluntarily. Thus, if one party is labouring under a misapprehension, there is no duty on the other party to correct it.

Three exceptions to this rule are:

(i) Half truths
(ii) Statements which become false
(iii) Contracts uberrimae fidei

Contracts *uberrimae fidei* (contracts of the utmost good faith) impose a duty of disclosure of all material facts because one party is in a strong position to know the truth. Examples would include contracts of insurance and family settlements. A material fact is something which would influence a reasonable person in making the contract. If one party fails to do this, the contract may be avoided. Where there is a fiduciary relationship between the parties to a contract, a duty of disclosure will arise, e.g., solicitor and client, bank manager and client, trustee and beneficiary, and inter-family agreements.

2. ***The misrepresentation must have induced the contract***: The false statement must have induced the other party to enter into the contract. The requirements here are that (a) the misrepresentation must be material and (b) it must have been relied on.

(a) *Materiality*: The misrepresentation must be material, in the sense that it would have induced a reasonable person to enter into the contract.

(b) *Reliance*: The contracting party must have relied on the misrepresentation. There will be no reliance if the contracting party was unaware of the misrepresentation. There will be no reliance if the contracting party does not rely on misrepresentation.

### Remedies for Misrepresentation

Once an actionable misrepresentation has been established, it is then necessary to consider the remedies available to the other contracting party.

***Rescission***: Rescission, that is, setting aside the contract, is possible in all cases of misrepresentation. The aim of rescission is to put the parties back in their original position, as though the contract had not been made.

The injured party may rescind the contract by giving notice to the other party. However, this is not always necessary as any act indicating repudiation, e.g., notifying the authorities, may suffice.

### Bars to Rescission

Rescission is an equitable remedy and is awarded at the discretion of the Court. The injured party may lose the right to rescind in the following four circumstances:

1. *Affirmation of the contract*: The injured party will affirm the contract if, with full knowledge of the misrepresentation and of their right to rescind, they expressly State that they intend to continue with the contract, or if they do an act from which the intention may be implied. In *Long* v. *Lloyd*[99], the defendant advertised for sale a lorry as being in 'exceptional condition' and he told the plaintiff purchaser that it did 11 miles to the gallon and, after a trial run, all that was wrong with the vehicle. The plaintiff purchased the lorry and, two days later, on a short run, further faults developed and the plaintiff noticed that it did only about 5 miles to the gallon. That evening, he reported these things to the defendant and the plaintiff accepted the defendant's offer to pay for some of the repairs. The next day the lorry set out on a longer journey and broke down. The plaintiff wrote to the defendant asking for the return of his money. The lorry had not been in a roadworthy condition, but the defendant's representations concerning it had been honestly made. The Court of Appeal held that the plaintiff was not entitled to rescission of the contract as he had finally accepted the lorry before he had purported to rescind. The second journey amounted to affirmation of the contract.
2. *Lapse of time*: If the injured party does not take action to rescind within a reasonable time, the right will be lost.

   Where the misrepresentation is fraudulent, time runs from the time when the fraud was, or with reasonable diligence, could have been discovered. In the case of non-fraudulent misrepresentation, time runs from the date of the contract, not the date of discovery of the misrepresentation. In *Leaf* v. *International Galleries*[100], the plaintiff bought a painting after an innocent misrepresentation was made to him that it was by 'J. Constable'. He did not discover this until five years later and claimed rescission immediately. The Court of Appeal held that the plaintiff had lost his right to rescind after such a period of time. His only remedy after that length of time was for damages only, a claim which he had not brought before the Court.
3. *Restitution in integrum impossible*: The injured party will lose the right to rescind if substantial restoration is impossible, i.e., if the parties cannot be restored to their original position. Where a lease of a mine which had been entered into as a result of a misrepresentation could not be rescinded as there

[99] [1958] 1 WLR 753.

[100] [1950] 2 KB 86.

had been considerable extraction of minerals since the date of the contract.[101] Precise restoration is not required and the remedy is still available if substantial restoration is possible. Thus, deterioration in the value or condition of property is not a bar to rescission.[102]

4. ***Third party acquires rights***: If a third party acquires rights in property, in good faith and for value, the misrepresentee will lose their right to rescind.[103] Thus, if A obtains goods from B by misrepresentation and sells the goods to C, who takes in good faith, B cannot later rescind when he discovers the misrepresentation in order to recover the goods from C.

### Section 19: Voidability of agreements without free consent

When consent to an agreement is caused by coercion, fraud or misrepresentation, the agreement is a contract voidable at the option of the party whose consent was so caused.

A party to a contract whose consent was caused by fraud or misrepresentation, may, if he thinks fit, insist that the contract shall be performed, and that he shall be put in the position in which he would have been if the representations made had been true.

***Exception***: If such consent was caused by misrepresentation or by silence, fraudulent within the meaning of Section 17, the contract, nevertheless, is not voidable, if the party whose consent was so caused had the means of discovering the truth with ordinary diligence.

***Explanation***: A fraud or misrepresentation which did not cause the consent to a contract of the party on whom such fraud was practiced, or to whom such misrepresentation was made, does not render a contract voidable.

### Illustrations

(a) A, intending to deceive B, falsely represents that five hundred *maunds* of indigo are made annually at A's factory, and thereby induces B to buy the factory. The contract is voidable at the option of B.

(b) A, by a misrepresentation, leads B erroneously to believe that, five hundred *maunds* of indigo are made annually at A's factory. B examines the accounts of the factory, which show that only four hundred *maunds* of indigo have been made. After this B buys the factory. The contract is not voidable on account of A's misrepresentation.

(c) A fraudulently informs B that A's estate is free from incumbrance. B thereupon buys the estate. The estate is subject to a mortgage. B may either avoid the contract, or may insist on its being carried out and the mortgage debt redeemed.

(d) B, having discovered a vein of ore on the estate of A, adopts means to conceal, and does conceal, the existence of the ore from A. Through A's ignorance B is

[101] *Vigers* v. *Pike*, (1842) 8 CI & F 562.

[102] *Armstrong* v. *Jackson*, [1917] 2 KB 822.

[103] See, *Phillips* v. *Brooks*, [1919] 2 KB 243 under mistake.

enabled to buy the estate at an under-value. The contract is voidable at the option of A.

(e) A is entitled to succeed to an estate at the death of B; B dies: C, having received intelligence of B's death, prevents the intelligence reaching A1 and thus induces A to sell him his interest in the estate. The sale is voidable at the option of A.

In *Mithoolal Nayak* v. *Life Insurance Corporation of India*[104], three conditions for the application of the insurance contract are to be complied with as per second part of Sec. 45 of the Insurance Act, 1938. They are as follows:

1. The statement must be on a material matter or must suppress facts which it was material to disclose.
2. The suppression must be fraudulently made by the policy holder.
3. The policy holder must have known at the time of making the statement that it was false or that it suppressed facts which it was material to disclose.

Where the policy holder, who had been treated, a few months before he submitted a proposal for the insurance of his life with the insurance company by a physician of repute for certain serious ailments as anemia, shortness of breath and asthma, not only failed to disclose in his answers to the questions put to him by the insurance company that he suffered from those ailments but he made a false statement to the effect that he had not been treated by any doctor for any such serious ailment. The Supreme Court held that as per the standard laid down in Sec. 17 of the Contract Act, the policy holder was clearly guilty of a fraudulent suppression of material facts when he made his statements, which he must have known were deliberately false and hence, the policy issued to him relying on those statements was vitiated. Further, the Court observed that the principle underlying the Explanation to Sec. 19 of the Contract Act is that a false representation, whether fraudulent or innocent, is irrelevant if it has not induced the party to whom it is made to act upon it by entering into a contract. That principle did not apply in the instant case. The terms of the policy made it clear that the averments made as to the state of health of the insured in the proposal form and the personal statement were the basis of the contract between the parties and the circumstance that the policy holder had taken pains to falsify or conceal that he had been treated for a serious ailment by a physician only a few months before the policy was taken showed that the falsification or concealment had an important bearing in obtaining the other party's consent. A man who has so acted cannot afterwards turn round and say, *"It could have made no difference if you had known the truth."* In the circumstances, no advantage could be taken of the Explanation to Sec. 19 of the Contract Act.

## Section 19A: Power to set aside contract induced by undue influence

When consent to an agreement is caused by undue influence, the agreement is a contract voidable at the option of the party whose consent was so caused.

Any such contract may be set aside either absolutely or, if the party who was entitled to avoid it has received any benefit there under, upon such terms and conditions as to the Court may seem just.

[104] AIR 1962 SC 814.

### Illustrations

(a) A's son has forged B's name to a promissory note. B, under threat of prosecuting A's son, obtains a bond from A for the amount of the forged note. If B sues on this bond, the Court may set the bond aside.

(b) A, a money-lender, advances ₹100 to B, an agriculturist, and, by undue influence, induces B to execute a bond for ₹200 with interest at 6% per month. The Court may set the bond aside; ordering B to repay the ₹100 with such interest as may seem just.

### Section 20: Agreement void where both parties are under mistake as to matter of fact

Where both the parties to an agreement are under a mistake as to a matter of fact essential to the agreement, the agreement is void.

*Explanation*: An erroneous opinion as to the value of the thing which forms the subject-matter of the agreement is not to be deemed a mistake as to a matter of fact.

### Illustrations

(a) A agrees to sell to B a specific cargo of goods supposed to be on its way from England to Bombay. It turns out that, before the day of the bargain, the ship conveying the cargo had been cast away and the goods lost. Neither party was aware of the facts. The agreement is void.

(b) A agrees to buy from B a certain horse. It turns out that the horse was dead at the time of the bargain, though neither party was aware of the fact. The agreement is void.

(c) A, being entitled to an estate for the life of B, agrees to sell it to C. B was dead at the time of the agreement, but both parties were ignorant of the fact. The agreement is void.

An agreement would be void if both the parties to the agreement were under a mistake as to a matter of fact essential to the agreement. The mistake has to be mutual and in order that the agreement would be treated as void, both the parties must be shown to be suffering from mistake of fact. Unilateral mistake is outside the scope of this section. The other requirement is that the mistake, apart from being mutual, should be in respect of a matter which is essential to the agreement. Where the parties to an agreement to sell land were not ad idem with respect to the unit of measuring land inasmuch as while the seller intended to sell the land in terms of "kanals", the plaintiff intended to purchase it in terms of "bighas", the "mistake" with which the parties were suffering, cannot be said to be not related to a matter essential to the agreement. In such a case, the dispute is not with regard to the unit of measurement only. Since these units relate to the area of the land, it is really a dispute with regard to the area of the land which was the subject-matter of agreement for sale, or, to put it differently, how much area of the land was agreed to be sold, is in dispute between the parties and it is with regard to the area of the land that the parties were suffering from a mutual mistake. The area of the land is as much essential to the agreement as the price which, incidentally, was to be calculated on the basis of the area. The remedies available under Secs. 73 and 74 of the Act for the breach of contract contemplate a valid and binding agreement between the parties. If the forfeiture clause is contained in an agreement which is void on account of the fact that the parties were not *ad idem* and were suffering from mistake of fact in respect of a matter which was essential to the contract, it cannot be enforced as the agreement itself is void under Sec. 20 of the Contract Act. A void agreement cannot be split up. None of the parties to the agreement can be permitted to seek enforcement of a part only of the contract through a Court of law. If the agreement is void, all its terms are void and none of the terms, except in certain known exceptions, especially where the clause is treated to constitute a separate and independent agreement, severable from the main agreement, can be enforced separately and independently.[105]

### Section 21: Effect of mistakes as to law

A contract is not voidable because it was caused by a mistake as to any law in force in India; but a mistake as to a law not in force in India has the same effect as a mistake of fact.

### Illustration

A and B make a contract grounded on the erroneous belief that a particular debt is barred by the Indian Law of Limitation: the contract is not voidable.

### Section 22: Contract caused by mistake of one party as to matter of fact

A contract is not voidable merely because it was caused by one of the parties to it being under a mistake as to a matter of fact.

Mistake may be of three types and they are as follows:

1. ***Mistake as to identity***: Mistake as to identity occurs when one person represents himself to be someone other than he really is. The following cases are discussed here for better understanding of application as to mistake of identity. The facts of *Cundy* v. *Linsay*[106] are as follows:

> Lindsay & Co. were manufacturers of linen handkerchiefs, amongst other things. They received correspondence from a rogue named Blenkarn. He had rented a room at 37, Wood Street, but purported to be 'Blenkiron & Co.', with premises on 123 Wood Street. Lindsay & Co. knew of a business named as 'Blenkiron & Co.', and knew them to be reputable and residing on the same road. Under this guise, and the rogue's signing of his letters as 'Blenkiron & Co.', Lindsay & Co. sold the rogue a large order of handkerchiefs. Blenkarn then sold the goods (250 dozen linen handkerchiefs) to an innocent third party, Cundy, who purchased the handkerchiefs on good faith. Lindsay & Co. sued the defendant for conversion of the goods.

The House of Lords held that Lindsay & Co. had meant to deal only with Blenkiron & Co. There could therefore have been no agreement or contract between them and the rogue.

[105] *Tarsem Singh* v. *Sukhminder Singh*, AIR 1998 SC 1400.

[106] (1878) 3 App Cas 459.

Accordingly, title did not pass to the rogue, and could not have passed to Cundy. They were forced to therefore return the goods. The House of Lords observed that to have a valid contract, there must be consensus of mind.

In *Phillips* v. *Brooks*[107], the facts were as follows:

A rogue named North purchased some items from the plaintiff's jewellers shop claiming to be Sir George Bullogh. He paid by cheque and persuaded the jewellers to allow him to take a ring immediately as he claimed it was his wive's birthday the following day. He gave the address of Sir George Bullogh and the jewellers checked the name matched the address in a directory. The rogue then pledged the ring with the defendant before the fraud was discovered and received £350. He then disappeared without a trace. The plaintiff brought an action against the defendant for conversion or its value.

The Court held that the contract was not void for mistake. Where the parties transact face to face, the law presumes they intend to deal with the person in front of them not the person they claim to be. The jewellers were unable to demonstrate that they would only have sold the ring to Sir George Bullogh.

The facts of *Ingram* v. *Little*[108] are as follows:

Two sisters Hilda and Elsie Ingram sold their car to a rogue calling himself Mr. Hutchinson. They agreed a price for cash, but when the rogue offered a cheque Elsie said the deal was off. She wanted cash or no sale. The rogue then gave them his full name and address and Hilda went to the post office, which was two minutes down the road, to check the details out. When she returned she informed Elsie that the details checked out and the sisters agreed to let Mr. Hutchinson take the car. The cheque was dishonoured and the car was sold on to Mr. Little. The sisters brought an action to recover the car.

It was held that the contract was void for mistake. The Court of Appeal held that the sisters only intended to deal with Mr. Hutchinson at the address given because they were not willing to offer a sale for payment by cheque from anyone else.

2. ***Mistake as to subject matter*:** Mistake as to subject matter may be in different kinds and they are as follows:

   (a) *Non-existent of subject matter*: This type of mistake happened in *Couturier* v. *Hastie*[109], The facts of the case are as follows:

The plaintiff merchants shipped a cargo of Indian corn and sent the bill of lading to their London agent, who employed the defendant to sell the cargo. On 15 May 1848, the defendant sold the cargo to Challender on credit. The vessel had sailed on 23 February but the cargo became so heated and fermented that it was unfit to be carried further and sold. On May 23 Challender gave the plaintiff notice that he repudiated the contract on the ground that at the time of the sale to him the cargo did not exist. The plaintiffs brought an action against the defendant (who was a del credere agent, i.e., guaranteed the performance of the contract) to recover the purchase price.

[107] (1919) 2 KB 243.

[108] (1961) 1QB 31.

[109] (1856) 5 HL Cas 673.

The Court held that it is a basic principle of every commercial transaction that at the time of contract, there would be something to sale and something to buy. But in this instant case, the goods had been already sold and thereafter the contract was made and hence the contract was *void ab initio*. Therefore, the plaintiffs could not recover. This judgment was affirmed by the House of Lords.

(b) *Mistake as to title*: The appropriate leading case as to mistake of title is *Cooper* v. *Phibbs*[110] and the facts of the case are as follows:

An uncle told his nephew, not intending to misrepresent anything, but being in fact in error, that he (the uncle) was entitled to a fishery. The nephew, after the uncle's death, acting in the belief of the truth of what the uncle had told him, entered into an agreement to rent the fishery from the uncle's daughters. However, the fishery actually belonged to the nephew himself.

The House of Lords held that the mistake was only such as to make the contract voidable. Lord Westbury said that if parties contract under a mutual mistake and misapprehension as to their relative and respective rights, the result is that that agreement is liable to be set aside as having proceeded upon a common mistake on such terms as the Court thought fit to impose; and it was so set aside. The House of Lords set the agreement aside on the terms that the defendant should have a lien on the fishery for such money as the defendant had expended on its improvements.

(c) *Different subject matter in mind*: Where the contracting parties have different subject matter in mind and they made the contract that may be due to mistake of fact, such contract would be void due to lack of true consent as defined under Sec. 13 of the Contract Act. *Raffles* v. *Wichelhaus*[111], which is popularly known as *Peerless* case, is a leading case on mutual mistake in the English law of contract. The case established that when both parties of a contract are mistaken as to an essential element of the contract, the Court will attempt to find a reasonable interpretation from the context of the agreement before it will void it. The facts of the case are as follows:

The plaintiff entered into a contract to sell "125 bales of Surat cotton, guarantied middling fair merchant's Dhollorah" to the defendant at the rate of 17¼ d. per pound. The contract specified that the cotton would be arriving in Liverpool on the ship Peerless from Bombay ("to arrive ex Peerless from Bombay"). It so happened that there were two ships named Peerless arriving from Bombay, one departing in October and another departing in December. The defendant, according to statements presented in Court, thought the contract was for cotton on the October ship while the plaintiff thought the contract was for the cotton on the December ship. When the December Peerless arrived, the plaintiff tried to deliver it; however, the defendant repudiated the agreement, saying that their contract was for the cotton on the October Peerless. The plaintiff sued for breach of contract, arguing that the date of the ship was not relevant and the only purpose of specifying the name of the ship is that in the contingency that the ship sunk en route, the contract could be voided.

[110] (1867) LR 2 HL 149.

[111] (1864) 2 H & C 906.

The issue before the Court was whether the defendant should be bound by the agreement to buy the cotton of the plaintiff's Peerless. Though Courts will strive to find a reasonable interpretation in order to preserve the agreement whenever possible, the Court in Raffles could not determine which ship named Peerless was intended in the contract. Consequently, as there was no consensus ad idem (as defendant alleged), the two parties did not agree to the same thing and there was no binding contract. Therefore, the defendants prevailed, and did not have to pay.

3. ***Mistake as to nature of promise***: If the mistake is common to both the contracting parties about the very nature of the promise, the contract would be declared as void.

## Section 23: What considerations and objects are lawful and what not

The consideration or object of an agreement is lawful, unless—

1. it is forbidden by law; or
2. is of such a nature that, if permitted, it would defeat the provisions of any law; or
3. is fraudulent; or
4. involves or implies injury to the person or property of another or;
5. the Court regards it as immoral or opposed to public policy.
6. In each of these cases, the consideration or object of an agreement is said to be unlawful. Every agreement of which the object or consideration is unlawful is void.

## Illustrations

(a) A agrees to sell his house to B for 10,000 rupees. Here B's promise to pay the sum of 10,000 rupees is the consideration for A's promise to sell the house, and A's promise to sell the house is the consideration for B's promise to pay the 10,000 rupees. These are lawful considerations.

(b) A promises to pay B 1,000 rupees at the end of six months, if C, who owes that sum to B, fails to pay it. B promises to grant time to C accordingly. Here the promise-of each party is the consideration for the promise of the other party and they are lawful considerations.

(c) A promises, for a certain sum paid to him by B, to make good to B the value of his ship if it is wrecked on a certain voyage. Here A's promise is the consideration for B's payment and B's payment is the consideration for A's promise and these are lawful considerations.

(d) A promises to maintain B's child and B promises to pay A 1,000 rupees yearly for the purpose. Here the promise of each party is the consideration for the promise of the 'other party. They are lawful considerations.

(e) A, B and C enter into an agreement for the division among them of gains acquired, or- to be acquired, by them by fraud. The agreement is void, as its object is unlawful.

(f) A promises to obtain for B an employment in the public service, and B promises to pay 1,000 rupees to A. The agreement is void, as the consideration for it is unlawful.

(g) A, being agent for a landed proprietor, agrees for money, without the knowledge of his principal, to obtain for B a lease of land belonging to his principal. The agreement between A and B is void as it implies a fraud by concealment, by A, on his principal.

(h) A promises B to drop a prosecution which he has instituted against B for robbery, and B promises to restore the value of the things taken. The agreement is void, as its object is unlawful.

(i) A's estate is sold for arrears of revenue under the provisions of an Act of the Legislature, by which the defaulter is prohibited from purchasing, the estate. B, upon an understanding with A, becomes the purchaser, and agrees to convey the estate to A upon receiving from him the price which B has paid. The agreement is void, as it renders the transaction, in effect a purchase by the defaulter, and would so defeat the object of the law.

(j) A, who is B's mukhtar, promises to exercise his influence, as such, with B in favour of C, and C promises to pay 1,000 rupees to A. The agreement is void, because it is immoral.

(k) A agrees to let her daughter to hire to B for concubine. The agreement is void, because it is immoral, though the letting may not be punishable under the Indian Penal Code. (45 of 1860)

Public policy or the policy of the law is an illusive concept; it has been described as "untrustworthy guide", "variable quality", "uncertain one", "unruly horse", etc. The primary duty of a Court of Law is to enforce a promise which the parties have made and to uphold the sanctity of contracts which form the basis of society, but in certain cases, the Court may relieve them of their duty on a rule founded on public policy; the doctrine of public policy is extended not only to harmful cases but also to harmful tendencies; this doctrine of public policy is only a branch of common law, and, just like any other branch of common law, it is governed by precedents; the principles have been crystallised under different heads and though it is permissible for Courts to expound an apply them to different situations, it should only be invoked in clear and incontestable cases of harm to the public; though the heads are not closed and though theoretically it may be permissible to evolve a new head under exceptional circumstances of a changing world, it is advisable in the interest of stability of society not to make any attempt to discover new heads in these days.[112]

Public policy is not capable of being given a precise definition. What is 'opposed to public policy' would be a matter depending upon the nature of the transaction. The pleadings of the parties and the materials brought on record would be relevant so as to enable the Court to judge the concept as to what is for public good or in the public interest or what would be injurious or harmful to the public good or the public interest at the relevant point of time as contra-distinguished from the policy of a particular Government.

[112] *Gherulal Parakh* v. *Mahadeodas Maiya*, AIR 1959 SC 781.

A law dealing with the rights of a citizen is required to be clear and unambiguous. Doctrine of public policy is contained in a branch of common law, it is governed by precedents. The principles have been crystallised under different heads and though it may be possible for the Courts to expound and apply them to different situations, it is trite that the said doctrine should not be taken recourse to in 'clear and incontestable cases of harm to the public though the heads are not closed and though theoretically it may be permissible to evolve a new head under exceptional circumstances of a changing world'. A contract being 'opposed to public policy' is a defence under Sec. 23 of the Indian Contract Act and the Courts, while deciding the validity of a contract, have to consider:

1. Pleadings in terms of Order 6 Rule 1 of the Code of Civil Procedure.
2. Statute governing the case.
3. Provisions of Parts III and IV of the Constitution of India.
4. Expert evidence, if any.
5. The materials brought on record of the case.
6. Other relevant factors, if any.

It becomes amply clear that it is not possible to define public policy with precision at any point of time. It is not for the Executive to fill these grey areas as the said power rests with the Judiciary. Whenever interpretation of the concept 'public policy' is required to be considered, it is for the Judiciary to do so and in doing so even the power of the judiciary is very limited. Even for the said purpose, the part dealing with public policy in Sec. 23 of the Contract Act is required to be construed in conjunction with other parts thereof.[113]

The Contract Act does not define the expression "public policy" or "opposed to public policy". From the very nature of things, the expressions "public policy", "opposed to public policy", or "contrary to public policy" are incapable of precise definition. Public policy, however, is not the policy of a particular Government. It connotes some matter which concerns the public good and the public interest. The concept of what is for the public good or in the public interest or what would be injurious or harmful to the public good or the public interest has varied from time to time. As new concepts take the place of old, transactions which were once considered against public policy are now being upheld by the Courts and similarly where there has been a well recognised head of policy, the Courts have not shirked from extending it to new transactions and changed circumstances and have at times not even flinched from inventing a new head of public policy. Practices which were considered perfectly normal at one time have today become obnoxious and oppressive to public conscience. If there is no head of public policy conscience and if there is no head of public policy which covers a case, then the Court must in consonance with public conscience and in keeping with public good and public interest declare such practice to be opposed to public policy. Above all, in deciding any case which may not be covered by authority, Courts have before them the beacon light of the Preamble to the Constitution. Lacking precedent, the Court can always be guided by that right and the principles underlying the Fundamental Rights and the Directive Principles enshrined in the Constitution.[114]

---

[113] *State of Rajasthan* v. *Basant Nahata*, AIR 2005 SC 3401.

[114] *Central Inland Water Transport Corporation Ltd.* v. *Brojo Nath Ganguly*, AIR 1986 SC 1571.

Section 23 of the Contract Act adumbrates that the consideration or object of an agreement is lawful unless it is forbidden by law; or is of such a nature that, if permitted, it would defeat the provision of any law; or is fraudulent, or involved or implied injury to the persons or property of another; or the Court regard it as immoral or opposed to public policy. In each of these cases, the consideration or object of an agreement is said to be unlawful. Every agreement of which the object or consideration is unlawful is void. The word 'object' would mean the purpose and design which is the object of the contract, if it is opposed to public policy which tends to defeat any provision of law or purpose of law, it becomes unlawful and thereby it is void under Sec. 23 of the Contract Act.

In *Manna Lal Khetan* v. *Kedar Nath Khetan*,[115] it has been observed by the Supreme Court that a contract is void if prohibited by statute under a penalty, even without express declaration that the contract is void, because such a penalty implies a prohibition. The above authorities lead to a conclusion that although for all practical purposes, illegal contracts and void contracts are taken at par with each other, nevertheless the distinction between the two is there. Illegality of a contract arises as a result of infraction, contravention or breach of any express or implied provisions of law properly so-called that is a constitutionally valid enactment made by the Legislature or of a subordinate legislation, i.e., rules, bye-laws, regulations or orders—or even usages and customs—having the force of law. On the other hand, the void contract is one which is declared as such by virtue of Secs. 23 to 30, etc. of the Contract Act or by a provision of any other enactment.

Under Sec. 23 of the Contract Act, the consideration or object of an agreement is lawful, unless it is opposed to public policy. Every agreement of which the object or consideration is unlawful is void. Hence there can be no doubt that an agreement to oust absolutely the jurisdiction of the Court will be unlawful and void being against the public policy. However, such will be the result only if it can be shown that the jurisdiction to which the parties have agreed to submit had nothing to do with the contract. If, on the other hand, it is found that the jurisdiction agreed would also be a proper jurisdiction in the matter of the contract, it could not be said that it outstayed the jurisdiction of the Court. In other words, where the parties to a contract agreed to submit the disputes arising from it to a particular jurisdiction which would otherwise also be a proper jurisdiction under the law their agreement to the extent they agreed not to submit to other jurisdictions cannot be said to be void as being against public policy. If, on the other hand, the jurisdiction they agreed to submit to would not otherwise be proper jurisdiction to decide disputes arising out of the contract, it must be declared void being against public policy. Section 28 also leads to the same conclusion. The principle of Private International Law that the parties should be bound by the jurisdiction clause to which they have agreed unless there is some reason to contrary is being applied to municipal contracts.

Where a brochure was issued by the Government of the State announcing its 'New Policy' declaring that incentive and concessions, one of them being refund of sales tax, would be available to those persons who set up selective large-scale industries in the specified area. Acting on its representative an industrialist met the Chief Minister personally and found that he was interested in encouraging the manufacturing unit the industrialist wanted to set up in the State. Therefore, the Manager of the industrialist

[115] AIR 1977 SC 536.

wrote a letter to the Chief Minister expressing willingness to set up the unit provided the concessions were made available to it. The Director of Industries (concerned officer) assured the industrialist that the concession as announced shall be available and further informed the industrialist that the Government was willing to consider such additional concession which the industrialist may require for implementation of the scheme and it was followed by exchange of correspondence and various meetings between the industrialist's representatives and officials of the Government. There was representation to the industrialist that it would be entitled to concession and incentives announced by the Government if it set up its unit in the prescribed area. In such a case, the letter seeking confirmation of availability of concessions was not counter-offer. But any agreement for refund of sales tax due under the Act to individual being contrary to public policy was void under Sec. 23 of the Contract Act. The constitutional requirements of levy of tax being for the welfare of the society and not for a specific individual the agreement or promise made by the Government was in contravention of public purpose and thus violative of public policy. No legal relationship could have arisen by operation of promissory *estoppel* as it was contrary both to the Constitution and the law. Realisation of tax through State mechanism for the sake of paying it to a private person directly or indirectly is impermissible under the constitutional scheme. The law does not permit it nor can equity countenance it. The scheme of refund of sales tax was thus incapable of being enforced in a Court of law.[116]

In *BCPP Mazdoor Sangh* v. *N.T.P.C.*[117], Services of employees recruited, trained, appointed by PSU (NTPC) and governed by service terms and conditions as applicable to NTPC employees cannot be transferred to a private concern on basis of a bi-partite agreement entered subsequently between NTPC and transferee-employer (BALCO) by giving the agreement a retrospective effect. Such agreement violates Sec. 23 of Contract Act as well as Art. 14 of Constitution. The clause in the appointment letters issued by NTPC provides that appointments were for a power plant owned by another PSU (BALCO) presently managed by NTPC. In case at a later date it is decided by BALCO to directly manage the Plant/Station or transfer its management to some other existing or new organisation then your post and your services will stand transferred to BALCO or such successor organisation as the case may be. The clause is illegal as at time of making appointments there was no agreement between NTPC and BALCO for making recruitment and appointment on behalf of BALCO for its BALCO Captive Power Plant. Undue influence was exercised by the management of NTPC on the unemployed candidates to execute undertakings for appointment. It was never disclosed to the candidates that their recruitment is exclusively for BALCO. In some of the appointment letters issued by NTPC, the terms and conditions of appointment are mentioned. It provides pay-scale of NTPC, allowances and HRA payable as per rules of NTPC and other facilities as admissible under the rules of NTPC. The appointment letter provides for initial appointment and posting to work at Korba and thereafter liable to be posted at the discretion of NTPC in other office/ project/Unit or in any other public sector undertakings in India or abroad. The aforesaid terms and conditions lead to an irresistible conclusion that NTPC was their employer in all purposes. The Government or its instrumentality cannot alter the conditions of service of its

[116] *Amrit Banaspati Co. Ltd.* v. *State of Punjab*, AIR 1992 SC 1075.

[117] AIR 2008 SC 336.

employees and any such alteration causing prejudice cannot be effected without affording opportunity of pre-decisional hearing to employees such change would amount to arbitrary and violative of Article 14. In the present case where employer has been changed, the employees are neither party to the agreement nor they have been heard before changing their service condition. Therefore, the action of the management is violative of Article 14 of the Constitution of India.

### Section 24: Agreement void, if considerations and objects unlawful in part

If any part of a single consideration for one or more objects, or anyone or any part of anyone of several considerations for a single object, is unlawful, the agreement is void.

### Illustration

A′ promises to superintend, on behalf of B, a legal manufacture of indigo, and an illegal traffic in other articles. B promises to pay to A a salary of 10,000 rupees a year. The agreement is void, the object of A's promise, and the consideration for B's promise, being in part unlawful.

### Section 25: Agreement without consideration, void, unless it is in writing and registered or is a promise to compensate for something done or is a promise to pay a debt barred by limitation law

An Agreement made without consideration is void, unless:

1. it is expressed in writing and registered under the law for the time being in force for the registration of documents, and is made on account of natural love and affection between parties standing in a, near relation to each other; or unless
2. it is a promise to compensate, wholly or in part, a person who has already voluntarily done something for the promisor, or something which the promisor was legally compellable to do; or unless
3. it is a promise, made in writing and signed by the person to be charged therewith, or by his agent generally or specially authorized in that behalf, to pay wholly or in part a debt of which the creditor might have enforced payment but for the law for the limitation of suits.

In any of these cases, such an agreement is a contract.

*Explanation* **1:** Nothing in this section shall affect the validity, as between the donor and donee, of any gift actually made.

*Explanation* **2:** An agreement to which the consent of the promisor is freely given is not void merely because the consideration is inadequate; but the inadequacy of the consideration may be taken into account by the Court in determining the question whether the consent of the promisor was freely given.

### Illustrations

(a) A promises, for no consideration, to give to B ₹1,000. This is a void agreement.

(b) A, for natural love and affection, promises to give his son, B, ₹1,000. A puts his promise to B into writing and registers it. This is a contract.

(c) A finds B's purse and gives it to him. B promises to give A ₹50. This is a contract.

(d) A supports B's infant son. B promises to pay A's expenses in so doing. This is a contract.

(e) A owes B ₹1,000, but the debt is barred by the Limitation Act. A signs a written promise to pay B ₹500 on account of the debt. This is a contract.

(f) A agrees to sell a horse worth ₹1,000 for ₹10. A's consent to the agreement was freely given. The agreement is a contract notwithstanding the inadequacy of the consideration.

(g) A agrees to sell a horse worth ₹1,000 for ₹10. A denies that his consent to the agreement was freely given.

The inadequacy of the consideration is a fact which the Court should take into account in considering whether or not A's consent was freely given.

An agreement alone does not make a valid contract which would be enforced by the Court of law. Both parties to the contract must provide consideration if they wish to sue on the contract. This means that each party to the contract must promise to give or do something for the other. Section 25 of the Contract Act specifically provides that an agreement made without consideration is void. So, consideration is a *sine qua non* for a valid contract. Section 2(d) of the Act defines consideration as follows:

> When, at the desire of the promisor, the promisee or any other person has done or abstained from doing, or does or abstains from doing, or promises to do or to abstain from doing, something, such act or abstinence or promise is called a consideration for the promise.

In 1875, in *Currie* v. *Misa*[118], the Court observed that consideration means some right, interest, profit or benefit accruing to one party, or some forbearance, detriment, loss or responsibility given, suffered or undertaken by the other.

The definition of consideration given by Sir Frederick Pollock has been approved by Lord Dunedin in *Dunlop* v. *Selfridge Ltd.*[119] and said that an act or forbearance of one party, or the promise thereof, is the price for which the promise of the other is bought, and the promise thus given for value is enforceable. Therefore consideration means something which is of some value in the eye of the law and it may be some benefit to the plaintiff or some detriment to the defendant.[120] Consideration may be the price of a promise, a return or *quid pro quo,* something of value received by the promise as inducement of the promise.[121]

## TYPES OF CONSIDERATION

Referring to the definition provided under Sec. 2 (d) of the Act, consideration may be of three kinds, such as:

118 (1875) LR 10 Exch 153.

119 [1915] AC 847.

120 *Thomas* v. *Thomas* (1842) 2 QB 851.

121 *Fazaluddin* v. *Panchanan Das,* AIR 1957 Cal 92.

1. Past consideration (has done or abstained from doing)
2. Present consideration (does or abstains from doing)
3. Future consideration (promises to do or to abstain from doing)

However, consideration may be either executory consideration or executed consideration.

## Executory Consideration

Consideration is called "executory" where there is an exchange of promises to perform acts in the future, e.g. a bilateral contract for the supply of goods whereby A promises to deliver goods to B at a future date and B promises to pay on delivery. If A does not deliver them, this is a breach of contract and B can sue. If A delivers the goods, his consideration then becomes executed.

## Executed Consideration

If one party makes a promise in exchange for an act by the other party, when that act is completed, it is executed consideration, e.g. in a unilateral contract where A offers ₹500 reward for the return of her lost handbag, if B finds the bag and returns it, B's consideration is executed.

### *No Consideration no Contract—Exceptions*

There are exceptions provided under Sec. 25 of the Act where consideration is not required and they are as follows:

1. Out of natural love and affection—Sec. 25(1)
2. Promise to compensate past voluntary service—Sec. 25(2)
3. Promise to pay time barred debt—Sec. 25(3)
4. Completed gift—Sec. 25, Explanation—1
5. Agency—Sec. 182
6. Guarantee—Sec. 127

## Section 26: Agreement in restraint of marriage void

Every agreement in restraint of the marriage of any person, other than a minor, is void.

## Section 27: Agreement in restraint of trade void

Every agreement, by which anyone is restrained from exercising a lawful profession, trade or business of any kind, is to that extent void.

*Exception 1*: Saving of agreement not to carry on business of which goodwill is sold: One who sells the goodwill of a business may agree with the buyer to refrain from carrying on a similar business, within specified local limits, so long as the buyer, or any person deriving title to the goodwill from him, carries on a like business therein, provided that such limits appear to the Court reasonable, regard being had to the nature of the business.

Section 27 of the Act is general in terms, and declares all agreements in restraint void *pro tanto*, except in the case specified in the exception. The question whether an agreement is void under Sec. 27 must be decided upon the wording of that section. There is nothing in the wording of Sec. 27 to suggest that the principle stated therein does not apply when the restraint is for a limited period only or is confined to a particular area. Such matters of partial restriction have effect only when the facts fall within the exception to the section. A contract, which has for its object a restraint of trade, is *prima facie* void. Section 27 of the Contract Act is general in terms and unless a particular contract can be distinctly brought within Exception 1, there is no escape from the prohibition. A contract in restraint of trade is one by which a party restricts his future liberty to carry on his trade, business or profession in such manner and with such persons as he chooses. A contract of this class is *prima facie* void, but it becomes binding upon proof that the restriction is justifiable in the circumstances as being reasonable from the point of view of the parties themselves and also to the community.

### *Negative Covenant*

A negative covenant is commonly used by businesses, particularly those that depend upon trade secrets for their success. An employer wants to ensure that a former employee will not disclose information, skills, customer lists, and personal relationships with clients acquired on the job to gain a better position with a competitor or to start his or her own business. An employer also wants to protect his or her business in the competitive marketplace against the use of the unique personal skills of a former employee. An employer can achieve these objectives by including a negative covenant in the employment contract. Such a provision specifies that the employee will not work for a competitor or start a competing business for a period of time after leaving the employer. The covenant must be reasonable in its scope and duration. It cannot bar the employee from working at all, anywhere, or for an unreasonable length of time.

A Court enforces a negative covenant by granting an injunction prohibiting the employee from working in a competitive enterprise as described in the covenant. It will do so only when necessary to protect the former employer's legitimate interests.

In *Niranjan Shankar Golikari* v. *Century Spinning and Manufacturing Co., Ltd.*,[122] the respondent company (Century Spinning and Manufacturing Co.) manufactures amongst other things tyre cord yarn at its plant at Kalyan known as the Century Rayon. Under an agreement, Algemene Kunstzijde Unie of Holland (hereinafter referred to as AKU) and Vereinigte Clanzstoff Fabrikan AG of West Germany (hereinafter referred to as VCF) agreed to transfer their technical know-how to the respondent company to be used exclusively for the respondent company's tyre cord yarn plant at Kalyan. Clause 4 of that agreement provided that:

> The Century Rayon should keep secret until the termination of the agreement and during three years thereafter all technical information, knowledge know-how experience, data and documents passed on by the said AKU and VCF and the Century Rayon should undertake to enter into corresponding, secrecy arrangements with its employees.

[122] AIR 1967 SC 1098.

The appellant, Niranjan Shankar, is appointed as Shift Supervisor and executes the said standard contract.

Clause 6 of the agreement provided:

> "The employee shall, during the period of his employment and any renewal thereof honesty, faithfully, diligently and efficiently to the utmost of his power and skill
>
> (a) * * * * *
>
> (b) devote the whole of his time and energy exclusively to the business and affairs of the company and shall not engage directly or indirectly in any business or serve whether as principal agent partner or employee or in any other capacity either full time or part time in any business whatsoever other than that of the company."

Clause 9 of the agreement provided:

> During the continuance of his employment as well as thereafter the employee shall keep confidential and prevent divulgence of any and all information, instruments, documents, etc., of the company that might come to his knowledge.

Clause 14 of the agreement provided:

> If the company were to close its business or curtail its activities due to circumstances beyond its control and if it found that it was no longer possible to employ the employee any further it should have option to terminate his services by giving him three months' notice or three months' salary in lieu thereof.

Clause 17 of the agreement provided:

> "In the event of the employee leaving, abandoning or resigning the service of the company in breach of the terms of the agreement before the expiry of the said period of five years he shall not directly or indirectly engage in or carry on of his own accord or in partnership with others the business at present being carried on by the company and he shall not serve in any capacity, whatsoever or be associated with any person, firm or company carrying on such business for the remainder of the said period and in addition pay to the company as liquidated damages an amount equal to the salaries the employee would have received during the period of six months thereafter and shall further reimburse to the company any amount that the company may have spent on the employee's training."

After the training period, the appellant resigned from the service which has not been accepted and he was asked to resume work with immediate effect. However, the appellant replied that he had already obtained another employment. It is clear from the evidence that he was negotiating with Rajasthan Rayon Company at Kotah, which was also manufacturing tyre cord yarn and got himself employed there at a higher salary than what he was getting from the respondent company. The respondent company thereupon filed a suit in the Court at Kalyan claiming *inter alia* an injunction restraining the appellant from serving in any capacity whatsoever or being associated with any person, firm or company including the said Rajasthan Rayon Company.

The Trial Court on a consideration of the evidence led by the parties held: (1) that the respondent company had established that the appellant had availed himself of the training imparted by the said AKU in relation to the manufacture of tyre cord, the yarn, the operation of the spinning machines and that he was made familiar with their know-how, secrets, techniques and information; (2) that his duties were not merely to supervise labour or to report deviations of temperature as alleged by him; (3) that the said agreement was not void or unenforceable; (4) that he committed breach of the said agreement; (5) that as a result of the said breach the respondent company suffered loss and inconvenience and was entitled to damages under Clause 17 and lastly that the company was entitled to an injunction. On these findings, the Trial Court passed the following order:

"1. The injunction is granted against the defendant and he is restrained from getting in the employ of or being engaged or connected as a Shift Supervison in the Manufacture of tyre cord yarn or as an employee under any title discharging substantially the same duties as a Shift Supervisor in Rajasthan Rayon, Kotah or any other company or firm or individual in any part of India for the term ending 15th March 1968.
2. The defendant is further restrained during the said period and, thereafter, from divulging any of the secrets, processes or information relating to the manufacture of tyre cord yarn by continuous spinning process obtained by him in the course of and as a result of his employment with the plaintiffs."

In the appeal filed by him in the High Court, the plea taken by him as to undue influence and coercion was given up. The High Court agreed with the Trial Court.

The counsel for the appellant raised the following three contentions before the Supreme Court:

1. That the said agreement constituted a restraint on trade and was therefore opposed to public policy,
2. That in order to be valid and enforceable the covenant in question should be reasonable in space and time and to the extent necessary to protect the employer's right of property, and
3. That the injection to enforce a negative stipulation can only be granted for the legitimate purpose of safeguarding the trade secretes of the employer. He argued that these conditions were lacking in the present case and therefore the respondent company was not entitled to the enforcement of' the said stipulation.

Section 27 of the Contract Act is not confined to restraint of trade in the ordinary meaning of the word "trade" and included restraints on the right of being employed. Where an agreement is challenged on the ground of its being a restraint of trade, the onus is upon the party supporting the contract to show that the restraint is reasonably necessary to protect his interests. Once this onus is discharged, the onus of showing that the restraint is nevertheless injurious to the public is upon the party attacking the contract.

The English Courts, however, have drawn a distinction between restraints applicable during the term of the contract of employment and those that apply after its cessation. A similar distinction has also been drawn by Courts in India and a restraint by which a person binds himself during the term of his agreement directly or indirectly not to take service with any other employer or be engaged by a third party has been held not to be void and not against Section 27 of the Contract Act. In *Brahmaputra Tea Co. Ltd.* v. *Scarth,*[123] the condition under which the covenantee was partially restrained from competing after the term of his engagement was over with his former employer was held to be bad but the condition by which he bound himself during the term of his agreement, not directly or indirectly, to compete with his employer was held good. At page 550 of the report, the Court observed that an agreement of service by which a person binds himself during the term of the agreement not to take service with anyone else, or directly or indirectly take part in, promote or aid any business in direct competition with that of his employer was not hit by Sec. 27 of the Contract Act.

An agreement of service contained both a positive covenant, viz., that the employee shall devote his whole-time attention to the service of the employers and also a negative covenant preventing the employee from working elsewhere during the term of the agreement. The Court held that such a negative covenant was enforced. The learned Judges observed that illustrations (c) and (d) to Sec. 57 of the Specific Relief Act in terms recognised such contracts and the existence of negative covenants therein and that therefore the contention that the existence of such a negative covenant in a service agreement made the agreement void on the ground that it was in restraint of trade and contrary to Sec. 27 of the Contract Act had no validity.[124]

The result of the above discussion is that considerations against restrictive covenants are different in cases where the restriction is to apply during the period after the termination of the contract than those in cases where it is to operate during the period of the contract. Negative covenants operating during the period of the contract of employment when the employee is bound to serve his employer exclusively are generally not regarded as restraint of trade and therefore do not fall under Sec. 27 of the Contract Act. A negative covenant that the employee would not engage himself in a trade or business or would not get himself employed by any other master for whom he would perform similar or substantially similar duties is not therefore a restraint of trade unless the contract as aforesaid is unconscionable or excessively harsh or unreasonable or one-sided. Accordingly, the Supreme Court held that the negative covenant in the present case restricted as it is to the period of employment and to work similar or substantially similar to the one carried on by the appellant when he was in the employ of the respondent company was reasonable and necessary for the protection of the company's interests and not such as the Court would refuse to enforce. There is, therefore, no validity in the contention that the negative covenant contained in Clause 17 amounted to a restraint of trade and therefore against public policy.

In *Superintendence Company of India (P) Ltd.* v. *Krishna Murgai,*[125] two substantial questions arose: (a) whether a post-service restrictive covenant in restraint of trade as contained in Clause (10) of the service agreement between the parties is void under Sec. 27 of the Indian Contract Act?, and (b) whether the said restrictive covenant, assuming it to be valid, is on its terms enforceable at the instance of the appellant company against the respondent?

[123] (1885) ILR 11 Cal 545.

[124] *Burn and Co. Ltd.* v. *Colin Mac Donald,* (1909) ILR 26 Cal 354.

[125] AIR 1980 SC 1717.

In the instant case, the appellant company carries on business as valuers and surveyors, undertaking inspection of quality, weighment, analysis, sampling of merchandise and commodities, cargoes, industrial products, machinery, textiles, etc. It has established a reputation and goodwill in its business by developing its own techniques for quality testing and control and possesses trade secrets in the form of these techniques and clientele. It has its head office at Calcutta and a branch at New Delhi and employs various persons as managers and in other capacities in Calcutta, New Delhi and other places. On 27 March, 1971, the respondent was employed by the appellant company as the Branch Manager of its New Delhi office on terms and conditions contained in the letter of appointment issued to him on the same date. Clause (10) of the terms and conditions of employment placed the respondent under a post-service restraint that he shall not serve any other competitive firm nor carry on business on his own in similar line as that of the appellant company for two years at the place of his last posting. Since it is vital, it is necessary to set out the said clause which runs as follows:

> Clause 10: That you will not be permitted to join any firm of our competitors or run a business of your own in similar lines directly and/or indirectly, for a period of two years at the place of your last posting after you leave the company.

On 24 November, 1978, the appellant company terminated the respondent's services with effect from 27 December, 1978. Thereafter, the respondent started his own business under the name and style of *"Superintendence and Surveillance Inspectorate of India"* at E-22, South Extension, New Delhi on lines identical with or substantially similar to that of the appellant company. On 19 April, 1979, the appellant company brought a suit in the Delhi High Court on its original side claiming ₹55,000 as damages on account of the breach of the aforesaid negative covenant contained in Clause (10) and for permanent injunction restraining the respondent by himself, his servants, agents or otherwise, from carrying on the said business or any other business on lines similar to that of the appellant company or associating or representing any competitors of the appellant company before the expiry of two years from 27 December, 1979. After filing the suit, the appellant company sought an interim injunction by way of enforcing the aforesaid negative covenant and a single Judge of the Delhi High Court initially granted an ad interim injunction on 29 April, 1979, which was confirmed by him on 25 May, 1979, after hearing the respondent. The learned single Judge took the view that the negative covenant, being in partial restraint of trade, was reasonable inasmuch as it was limited both in point of time (two years) and the area of operation (New Delhi which was his last posting) and, therefore, was not hit by Sec. 27 of the Contract Act. He also took the view that the negative covenant was enforceable as the expression "leave" in Clause (10) was not confined to voluntarily leaving of the service by the respondent but was wide enough to include termination of his services by the appellant company. On appeal by the respondent, a Division Bench of the High Court reversed the order of the learned single Judge on both the points and that is how the two questions indicated above came before the Supreme Court for consideration.

The Supreme Court interpreted the word "leave" in the context it has been drafted in Clause (10) of the service agreement and reading it along with all the other terms of employment and held that in the instant case, the word "leave" was intended by the parties to refer only to a case where the employee has voluntarily left the services of the appellant company of his own, and since here the respondent's services were terminated by the appellant company, the restrictive covenant contained in Clause (10) would be inapplicable and, therefore, not enforceable against the respondent at the instance of the appellant company. The counsel for the appellant company urged that the view taken by the Apex Court would lead to putting a premium upon a dishonest employee who by his own misdemeanour and misbehaviour may invite termination of his services. However, the Court said that the appellant company should have taken care to use appropriate language while incorporating such restrictive covenant so as to include *every case of cessation of employment arising from any reason whatsoever* and not used the expression "leave", which normally is synonymous to the expression "quit" and indicates voluntary act on the part of the employee.

In *Gujarat Bottling Co. Ltd., M/s.* v. *Coca Cola Company,*[126] the question that came before the Supreme Court for consideration was, whether exclusive dealing agreements hit Sec. 27 of the Contract Act. An agreement for grant of franchise by Coca Cola Co. to Gujarat Bottling Company (GBC) to manufacture, bottle, sell, and distribute beverages under trademarks held by the franchiser and where under contains a negative covenant by GBC not to manufacture, bottle, sell, deal or otherwise be concerned with the products, beverages of any other brands or trademarks/trade names during the subsistence of the agreement including the period of one year's notice. The Supreme Court observed that there is a growing trend to regulate distribution of goods and services through franchise agreements providing for grant of franchise by the franchiser on certain terms and conditions to the franchisee. Such agreements often incorporate a condition that the franchisee shall not deal with competing goods. Such a condition restricting the right of the franchisee to deal with competing goods is for facilitating the distribution of the goods of the franchiser and it cannot be regarded as in restraint of trade. The Court further observed that if the negative stipulation contained in the agreement is considered in the light of the observations made in *Esso Petroleum Co. Ltd.*[127] case, it will be found that the agreement for grant of franchise by Coca Cola to GBC to manufacture, bottle, sell and distribute the various beverages for which the trade marks were acquired by Coca Cola, is a commercial agreement whereunder both the parties have undertaken obligations for promoting the trade in beverages for their mutual benefit. The purpose of the said agreement is to promote the trade and the negative stipulation under challenge seeks to achieve the said purpose by requiring GBC to wholeheartedly apply to promoting the sale of the products of Coca Cola. In that context, it is also relevant to mention that the said negative stipulation operates only during the period the agreement is in operation because of the express use of the words *'during the subsistence of this agreement the period of one year as contemplated in* paragraph 21, of the agreement.' Accordingly, the Court held that the doctrine of restraint of trade is not attracted in cases where the restriction is to operate during the period the contract is subsisting and it applies in respect of a restriction which operates after the termination of the contract.

---

[126] AIR 1995 SC 2372.

[127] *Esso Petroleum Company Ltd.,* v. *Harper's Garage (Stourport) Ltd.,* (1967) 1 All ER 699.

In *Percept D'Mark (India) Pvt. Ltd.* v. *Zaheer Khan*,[128] Zaheer Khan, respondent No. 1, who was then the best fast bowler in the Indian Cricket Team and a rising star in the international world of cricket, entered into a promotion Agreement, with the appellant, *Percept D'Mark (India) Pvt. Ltd.*, where in the appellant was to act as the sole and exclusive agent to manage, market, render various consulting services, negotiate for, execute contracts on behalf of, render tax and other advice to, and generally manage diverse media affairs, endorsements, advertising and the like for respondent No. 1, during the term of the agreement. The term of the said agreement was for a period of three years commencing on 30 October, 2000 and ending on 29 October, 2003, unless extended by mutual consent of the appellant and respondent No. 1. The term of the contract came to an end on 29 October, 2003, as expressly stated by the appellant in the Arbitration Petition. Respondent No. 1, thereafter, entered into an agreement dated 22 November, 2003, with respondent No. 2, whereby respondent No. 2 became the agent for managing all media affairs of respondent No. 1 with effect from 1 December, 2003. The appellant filed a petition under Sec. 9 of the Arbitration and Conciliation Act, 1996 for enforcement of the agreement after its expiry, and contended that such enforcement of the expired agreement should be granted pending commencement and conclusion of arbitration proceedings by the appellant. The cause of action for filing the petition was the concluded agreement between respondent Nos. 1 and 2. An injunction was sought seeking to restrain respondent No. 1 from entering into any agreement/arrangement or acting upon any agreement/contract with respondent No. 2 or any third party without first performing and complying with Clause 31(b) of the said agreement. On the pleadings contained in the arbitration petition, there can be no escape from the conclusion that what the appellant sought to enforce was a negative covenant which, according to the appellant, survived the expiry of the agreement. This, as the High Court has rightly held, is impermissible as such a clause which is sought to be enforced after the term of the contract is *prima facie* void under Sec. 27 of the Contract Act. If the negative covenant or obligation under Clause 31(b) is sought to be enforced beyond the term, i.e., if it is enforced as against a contract entered into on 20 November, 2003, which came into effect on 1 December, 2003, then it constitutes an unlawful restriction on respondent No. 1's freedom to enter into fiduciary relationships with persons of his choice, and a compulsion on him to forcibly enter into a fresh contract with the appellant even though he has fully performed the previous contract, and is, therefore, a restraint of trade which is void under Sec. 27 of the Contract Act. Under Sec. 27 of the Contract Act, (a) a restrictive covenant extending beyond the term of the contract is void and not enforceable; (b) the doctrine of restraint of trade does not apply during the continuance of the contract for employment and it applied only when the contract comes to an end; and (c) this doctrine is not confined only to contracts of employment but is also applicable to all other contracts.

**Section 28: Agreements in restraint of legal proceedings void**

Every agreement:

(a) by which any party thereto is restricted absolutely from enforcing his rights under or in respect of any contract, by the usual legal proceedings in the ordinary tribunals, or which limits the time within which he may thus enforce his rights; or

[128] AIR 2006 SC 3426.

(b) which extinguishes the rights of any party thereto, or discharges any party thereto from any liability, under or in respect of any contract on the expiry of a specified period so as to restrict any party from enforcing his rights, is void to that extent.

***Exception 1*: *Saving of contract of refer to arbitration dispute that may arise*:** This section shall not render illegal a contract, by which two or more persons agree that any dispute which may arise between them in respect of any subject or class of subjects shall be recoverable in respect of the dispute so referred.

***Exception 2*: *Saving of contract to refer questions that have already arisen*:** Nor shall this section render, illegal any contract in writing, by which two or more persons agree to refer to arbitration any question between them which has already arisen, or affect any provision of any law in force for the time being as to references to arbitration.

The jurisdiction of the Court in the matter of a contract will depend on the place of the contract and the cause of action arising through connecting factors. In the matter of a contract, there may arise causes of action of various kinds. In a suit for damages for breach of contract, the cause of action consists of the making of the contract, and of its breach, so that the suit may be filed either at the place where the contract was made or at the place were it should have been performed and the breach occurred. The making of the contract is part of the cause of action. A suit on a contract, therefore, can be filed at the place where it was made. The determination of the place where the contract was made is part of the law of contract. But making of an offer on a particular place does not form cause of action in a suit for damages for breach of contract. Ordinarily, acceptance of an offer and its intimation result in a contract and hence a suit can be filed in a Court within whose jurisdiction the acceptance was communicated. The performance of a contract is part of cause of action and a suit in respect of the breach can always be filed at the place where the contract should have been performed or its performance completed. If the contract is to be performed at the place where it is made, the suit on the contract is to be filed there and nowhere else. In suits for agency actions, the cause of action arises at the place where the contract of agency was made or the place where actions are to be rendered and payment is to be made by the agent. Part of cause of action arises where money is expressly or impliedly payable under a contract. In cases of repudiation of a contract, the place where repudiation is received is the place where the suit would lie. If a contract is pleaded as part of the cause of action giving jurisdiction to the Court where the suit is filed and that contract is found to be invalid, such part of cause of the action disappears.[129]

In *Hakam Singh* v. *M/s. Gammon (India) Ltd.*,[130] the appellant agreed to do certain construction work for the respondent who had its principal place of business at Bombay on the terms and conditions of a written tender. Clause 13 of the agreement provided that notwithstanding the place where the work under the contract was to be executed, the contract shall be deemed to have been entered into by the parties at Bombay, and the Court in Bombay alone shall have jurisdiction to adjudicate upon. On dispute arising between the parties, the appellant submitted a petition to the Court at Varanasi. The respondent contended that in view of Clause 13 of the arbitration agreement, only the

---

[129] *A.B.C. Laminart Pvt. Ltd.* v. *A.P. Agencies, Salem*, AIR 1989 SC 1239.

[130] AIR 1971 SC 740.

Courts at Bombay had jurisdiction. The Trial Court also held that the entire cause of action had arisen at Varanasi and the parties could not by agreement confer jurisdiction on the Courts at Bombay which they did not otherwise possess. The High Court in revision held that the Courts at Bombay had jurisdiction under the general law and hence could entertain the petition and that in view of Clause 13 of the agreement, petition could not be entertained at Varanasi and directed the petition to be returned for presentation to the proper Court. On appeal therefrom, one of the questions that fell for consideration of the Apex Court was whether the Courts at Bombay alone had jurisdiction over the dispute. The jurisdiction of the Court in order to entertain a proceeding for filing a case is usually governed by the provisions of the Code of Civil Procedure. By the terms of Sec. 20(a) of the Code of Civil Procedure read with explanation 11 thereto, the respondent company which had its principal place of business at Bombay was liable to be sued at Bombay. It was held that it was not open to the parties to agreement to confer by their agreement jurisdiction on a Court which it did not possess under the Code. But where two Courts or more have under the Code of Civil Procedure jurisdiction to try suit or preceding an agreement between the parties that the dispute between them shall be tried in one of such Courts was not contrary to public policy and such an agreement did not contravene Sec. 28 of the Contract Act.

Thus, it is now a settled principle that where there may be two or more competent Courts which can entertain a suit consequent upon a part of the cause of action having arisen there within, if the parties to the contract agreed to vest jurisdiction in one such Court to try the dispute which might arise as between themselves, the agreement would be valid. If such a contract is clear, unambiguous and explicit and not vague, it is not hit by Secs. 23 and 28 of the Contract Act. When the Court has to decide the question of jurisdiction pursuant to an ouster clause, it is necessary to construe the ousting expression or clause properly. Often the stipulation is that the contract shall be deemed to have been made at a particular place. This would provide the connecting factor for jurisdiction to the Courts of that place in the matter of any dispute on or arising out of that contract. It would not, however, *ipso facto* take away jurisdiction of other Courts.

From the foregoing discussion, it can be reasonably deduced that where such an ouster clause occurs, it is pertinent to see whether there is ouster of jurisdiction of other Courts. When the clause is clear, unambiguous and specific accepted notions of contract would bind the parties and unless the absence of *ad idem* can be shown, the other Courts should avoid exercising jurisdiction. As regards construction of the ouster clause when words like 'alone', 'only', 'exclusive', and the like have been used, there may be no difficulty. Even without such words in appropriate cases the maxim *'expressio unius est exclusio alterius'* expression of one is the exclusion of another may be applied. What is an appropriate case shall depend on the facts of the case. In such a case, mention of one thing may imply exclusion of another. When certain jurisdiction is specified in a contract, an intention to exclude all others from its operation may in such cases be inferred. It has therefore to be properly construed.

An agreement which in effect seeks to curtail the period of limitation and prescribes a shorter period, than that prescribed by law would be void as offending Sec. 28 of the Contract Act. That is because such an agreement would seek to restrict party from enforcing his right in Court after the period prescribed under the agreement expires, even though the period prescribed by law for the enforcement of his right has yet not expired. But there could be agreements which do not seek to curtail the time for enforcement of the right but which provide for the forfeiture or waiver of the right itself if no action is commenced within the period stipulated by the agreement. Such a clause in the agreement would not fall within the mischief of Sec. 28 of the Act. To put it differently, curtailment of the period of limitation is not permissible in view of Sec. 28 but extinction of the right itself unless exercised within a specified time is permissible and can be enforced. If the policy of insurance provides that if a claim is made and rejected and no action is commenced within the time stated in the policy, the benefits flowing from the policy shall stand extinguished and any subsequent action would be time-barred. Such a clause would fall outside the scope of Sec. 28 of the Contract Act.[131]

Right of the parties to have recourse to legal action is not excluded by the agreement. The parties are only required to have their dispute/s adjudicated by having the same referred to arbitration. Merely because the arbitrators are situated in a foreign country cannot by itself be enough to nullify the arbitration agreement when the parties have with their eyes open willingly entered into the agreement. The instant case is clearly covered by Exception 1 to Sec. 28. Moreover, in this case the parties have willingly initiated arbitration proceedings on the disputes having arisen between them. They have appointed arbitrators, participated in arbitration proceedings and suffered an award. The plea that the parties between whom the dispute arose, are both Indian Parties and the contract which had the effect of compelling them to resort to arbitration by foreign arbitrators and thereby impliedly excluding the remedy available to them under the ordinary law of India should be held to be opposed to public policy was not raised either before or during arbitration proceedings, nor before the single Judge of the High Court in the objections filed before him, nor in the Letters Patent Appeal filed before the Division Bench. Such a plea would not be available to be raised by the appellant before the Supreme Court for the first time.[132]

## Section 29: Agreements void for uncertainty

Agreements, the meaning of which is not certain, or capable of being made certain, are void.

## Illustrations

(a) A agrees to sell to B "a hundred tons of oil". There is nothing whatever to show what kind of oil was intended. The agreement is void for uncertainty.

(b) A agrees to sell to B one hundred tons of oil of a 'specified' description, known as an article of commerce. There is no uncertainty here to make the agreement void.

(c) A, who is a dealer in cocoanut-oil only, agrees to sell to B "one hundred tons of oil". The nature of A's trade affords an indication of the meaning of the words, and A has entered into a contract for the sale of one hundred tons of cocoanut-oil.

---

[131] *National Insurance Co. Ltd.* v. *Sujir Ganesh Nayak and Co.*, AIR 1997 SC 2049.

[132] *Atlas Export Industries, M/s.* v. *M/s. Kotak and Company*, AIR 1999 SC 3286.

(d) A agrees to sell to B "all the grain in my granary at Ramnagar". There is no uncertainty here to make the agreement void.

(e) A agrees to sell B "one thousand maunds of rice at a price to be fixed by C". As the price is capable of being made certain, there is no uncertainty here to make the agreement void.

(f) A agrees to sell to B "my white horse for rupees five hundred or rupees one thousand". There is nothing to show which of the two prices was to be given. The agreement is void.

A contract must be construed in such a way that it must lead to a conclusion that the parties understood the meaning thereof. The terms of agreement cannot be vague or indefinite. No mechanism has been provided for interpretation of the terms of the contract. When a contract has been worked out, a fresh liability cannot be thrust upon a contracting party. It is settled that a definite price is an essential element of a binding agreement. Although a definite price need not be stated in the contract, assertion thereof either expressly or impliedly is imperative.[133]

In *Dhanrajamal Gobindram, M/s.* v. *M/s. Shamji Kalidas and Co.*,[134] where under Clause 6 of an agreement, the buyers were to obtain the import licence and to communicate the number thereof to the sellers not later than 20 February, 1958, and in the event of their failure to do so for any reason whatsoever, the sellers were entitled *"at their discretion"* either to carry over the goods or to ask the buyers to pay for the contracted goods and take delivery in British East Africa. By a subsequent letter, the sellers confirmed that *"if necessary"* they would carry over the contracted goods for two months, namely, March and April, subject to payment of charges. It was contended that the words *"if necessary"* were entirely vague and did not show, necessary for whom, when and why and held that the whole agreement was void for uncertainty.

### Section 30: Agreements by way of wager, void

Agreements by way of wager are void; and no suit shall be brought for recovering anything alleged to be won on any wager, or entrusted to any person to abide the result of any game or other uncertain event on which any wager is made.

***Exception in favour of certain prizes for horse-racing*:** This section shall not be deemed to render unlawful a subscription or contribution, or agreement to subscribe or contribute, made or entered into for or toward any plate, prize or sum of money, of the value or amount of five hundred rupees or upwards, to be awarded to the winner or winners of any horse-race.

***Section 294A of the Indian Penal Code not affected*:** Nothing in this section shall be deemed to legalize any transaction connected with horse-racing, to which the provisions of Section 294A of the Indian Penal Code apply.

[133] *Delhi Development Authority, N.D.* v. *Joint Action Committee, Allottee of SFS Flats*, AIR 2008 SC 1343.
[134] AIR 1961 SC 1285.

Section 30 does not define "wager". In *Gherulal Parakh* v. *Mahadeodas Maiya*,[135] the Supreme Court referred Anson's definition of "wager" as a promise to give money or money's worth upon the determination or ascertainment of an unascertained event. A classic definition is however available in the case of *Carlill* v. *Carbolic Smoke Ball Co.*, where the Court has categorically said that a wagering contract is one by which two persons, professing to hold opposite views touching the issue of a future uncertain[136] event, mutually agree that, dependent on the determination of that event, one shall win from the other, and that other shall pay or hand over to him, a sum of money or other stake; neither of the parties having any other interest in that contract than the sum or stake he will so win or lose, there being no other consideration for making of such contract by either of the parties. If either of the parties may win but cannot lose, or may lose but cannot win, it is not a wagering contract.

### *Essentials of wagering agreement*

1. ***Must be an uncertain event***: Uncertainty in the minds of the parties about the determination of the event in one way or other is necessary. A wager generally contemplates a future event; but it may even relate to an event which has already happened in the past, but the parties are not aware of its result or the time of its happening.
2. ***Equal chances of gain or loss to the parties***: There is no wager if there are no mutual chances of gain or loss, each party should stand to win or lose. If one party wins and there were not any chances of them losing, then in that case there is no wager. If winning or losing is completely based on skill, there will be no wager. It should be dependent on chance.
3. ***Neither party to have control over the event***: Neither party should have control over the happening of the event one way or the other.
4. ***No other interest in the event***: Neither party should have any interest in the happening of the event other than the sum or stake he will win or lose.

### *Effect of Wagering Contract*

Wagering agreement being void cannot be enforced in any Court of law. Though a wager is void and unenforceable, it is not forbidden by law and, therefore, the object of a collateral agreement is not unlawful under Sec. 23 of the Contract Act.

#### *Exceptions*

The following are exceptions:

1. Horse race
2. Crossword competitions and lottery

---

[135] AIR 1959 SC 781.

[136] (1892) 2 QB 484.

The Indian Penal Code Section 294A: Keeping lottery office reads as follows:

> Whoever keeps any office or place for the purpose of drawing any lottery not being a State lottery or a lottery authorised by the State Government, shall be punished with imprisonment of either description for a term which may extend to six months, or with fine, or with both.
>
> And whoever publishes any proposal to pay any sum, or to deliver any goods, or to do or forbear doing anything for the benefit of any person, on any event or contingency relative or applicable to the drawing of any ticket, lot, number or figure in any such lottery, shall be punished with fine which may extend to one thousand rupees.

# Chapter III Of Contingent Contracts

## Section 31: "Contingent contract" defined

A "contingent contract" is a contract to do or not to do something, if some event, collateral to such contract, does or does not happen.

### Illustration

A contracts to pay B ₹10,000 if B's house is burnt. This is a contingent contract.

Contingent contract is a contract which has to do or not to do something. For example, Krishna Contracts with Ram that he will give 1 crore rupees if rains fall on 31st December. It was held it is based on future whether it happens or may not happen. Insurance contracts provide the best example of contingent contracts.

### *Essential Elements of a Valid Contingent Contract*

1. There must be a valid contract.
2. The performance of the contract must be conditional.
3. The event must be future uncertain.
4. The event must be collateral to the contract.

## Section 32: Enforcement of contracts contingent on an event happening

Contingent contracts to do or not to do anything if an uncertain future event happens cannot be enforced by law unless and until that event has happened.

If the event becomes impossible, such contracts become void.

### Illustrations

(a) A makes a contract with B to buy B's horse if A survives C. This contract cannot be enforced by law unless and until C dies in A's lifetime.

(b) A makes a contract with B to sell a horse to B at a specified price, if C, to whom the horse has been offered, refuses to buy him. The contract cannot be enforced by law unless and until C refuses to buy the horse.

(c) A contracts to pay B a sum of money when B marries C. C dies without being married to B. The contract becomes void.

**Section 32 lays down two principles**

1. A contract to do an act on the happening of a future uncertain condition cannot be enforced unless and until that event happens.
2. If the happening of that event has become impossible, the contract becomes void.

### Section 33: Enforcement of contracts contingent on an event not happening

Contingent contracts to do or not to do anything if an uncertain future event does not happen can be enforced when the happening of that event becomes impossible, and not before.

### Illustration

A agrees to pay B a sum of money if a certain ship does not return. The ship is sunk. The contract can be enforced when the ship sinks.

### Section 34: When event on which contract is contingent to be deemed impossible, if it is the future conduct of a living person

If the future event on which a contract is contingent is the way in which a person will act at an unspecified time, the event shall be considered to become impossible when such person does anything which renders it impossible that he should so act within any definite time, or otherwise than under further contingencies.

A agrees to pay B a sum of money if B marries C. C marries D. The marriage of B to C must now be considered impossible, although it is possible that D may die and that C may afterwards marry B.

### Section 35: When contracts become void which are contingent on happening of specified event within fixed time

Contingent contracts to do or not to do anything if a specified uncertain event happens within a fixed time become void if, at the expiration of the time fixed, such event has not happened, or if, before the time fixed, such event becomes impossible.

**When contracts may be enforced which are contingent on specified event not happening within fixed time:** Contingent contracts to do or not to do anything if a specified uncertain event does not happen within a fixed time may be enforced by law when the time fixed has expired and such event has not happened or, before the time fixed has expired, if it becomes certain that such event will not happen.

### Illustrations

(a) A promises to pay B a sum of money if a certain ship returns within a year. The contract may be enforced if the ship returns within the year, and becomes void if the ship is burnt within the year.

(b) A promises to pay B a sum of money if a certain ship does not return within a year. The contract may be enforced if the ship does not return within the year, or is burnt within the year.

**Section 36: Agreement contingent on impossible event void**

Contingent agreements to do or not to do anything, if an impossible event happens, are void, whether the impossibility of the event is known or not to the parties to the agreement at the time when it is made.

**Illustrations**

(a) A agrees to pay B 1,000 rupees if two straight lines should enclose a space. The agreement is void.

(b) A agrees to pay B 1,000 rupees if B will marry A's daughter C. C was dead at the time of the agreement. The agreement is void.

## Chapter IV Of The Performance of Contracts

**(Contract which must be performed)**

**Section 37: Obligation of parties to contract**

The parties to a contract must either perform, or offer to perform, their respective promises, unless such performance is dispensed with or excused under the provisions of this Act, or of any other law.

Promises bind the representatives of the promisors in case of the death of such promisors before performance, unless a contrary intention appears from the contract.

**Illustrations**

(a) A promises to deliver goods to B on a certain day on payment of ₹1,000. A dies before that day. A's representatives are bound to deliver the goods to B, and B is bound to pay the ₹1,000 to A's representatives.

(b) A promises to paint a picture for B by a certain day, at a certain price. A dies before the day. The contract cannot be enforced either by A's representatives or by B.

The first para of Sec. 37 provides a statutory obligation on each party to the contract to perform his obligation, unless such performance is dispensed with or excused under the provisions of this Act, or of any other law. In the following situations, the parties to the contract may be excused or obligation to perform may be dispensed with—

1. Under Sec. 56 of the Contract Act, or/and;
2. Under Sec. 62 of the Contract Act, or/and;
3. Under Sec. 63 of the Contract Act.

As both the parties perform their respective contractual obligations as per the stipulations of the contract that they have made and therefore they are discharged from the contract. This is a simple way of discharge of contract.

## Section 38: Effect of refusal to accept offer of performance

Where a promisor has made an offer of performance to the promisee, and the offer has not been accepted, the promisor is not responsible for non-performance, nor does he thereby lose his rights under the contract.

Every such offer must fulfil the following conditions:—

(1) it must be unconditional;

(2) it must be made at a proper time and place, and under such circumstances that the person to whom it is made may have a reasonable opportunity of ascertaining that the person by whom it is made is able and willing there and then to do the whole of what he is bound by his promise to do;

(3) if the offer is an offer to deliver anything to the promisee, the promisee must have a reasonable opportunity of seeing that the thing offered is the thing which the promisor is bound by his promise to deliver.

An offer to one of several joint promisees has the same legal consequences as an offer to all of them.

### Illustration

A contracts to deliver to B at his warehouse, on the 1st March, 1873, 100 bales of cotton of a particular quality. In order to make an offer of a performance with the effect stated in this section, A must bring the cotton to B's warehouse, on the appointed day, under such circumstances that B may have a reasonable opportunity of satisfying himself that the thing offered is cotton of the quality contracted for, and that there are 100 bales.

## Section 39: Effect of refusal of party to perform promise wholly

When a party to a contract has refused to perform, or disabled himself from performing, his promise in its entirety, the promisee may put an end to the contract, unless he has signified, by words or conduct, his acquiescence in its continuance.

### Illustrations

(a) A, a singer, enters into a contract with B, the manager of a theatre, to sing at his theatre two nights in every week during the next two months, and B engages to pay her 100 rupees for each night's performance. On the sixth night A wilfully absents herself from the theatre. B is at liberty to put an end to the contract.

(b) A, a singer, enters into a contract with B, the manager of a theatre, to sing at his theatre two nights in every week during the next two months, and B engages to pay her at the rate of 100 rupees for each night. On the sixth night A wilfully absents herself. With the assent of B, A sings on the seventh night. B has signified his acquiescence in the continuance of the contract, and cannot now put an end to it, but is entitled to compensation for the damage sustained by him through A's failure to sing on the sixth night.

### Section 40: Person by whom promise is to be performed

If it appears from the nature of the case that it was the intention of the parties to any contract that any promise contained in it should be performed by the promisor himself, such promise must be performed by the promisor. In other cases, the promisor or his representatives may employ a competent person to perform it.

### Illustrations

(a) A promises to pay B a sum of money. A may perform this promise, either by personally paying the money to B or by causing it to be paid to B by another; and, if A dies before the time appointed for payment, his representatives must perform the promise, or employ some proper person to do so.

(b) A promises to paint a picture for B. A must perform this promise personally.

### Section 41: Effect of accepting performance from third person

When a promisee accepts performance of the promise from a third person, he cannot afterwards enforce it against the promisor.

### Section 42: Devolution of joint liabilities

When two or more persons have made a joint promise, then, unless a contrary intention appears by the contract, all such persons, during their joint lives, and, after the death of any of them, his representative jointly with the survivor or survivors, and, after the death of the last survivor, the representatives of all jointly, must fulfill the promise.

### Section 43: Anyone of joint promisors may be compelled to perform

When two or more persons make a joint promise, the promisee may, in the absence of express agreement to the contrary, compel any 1*[one or more] of such joint promisors, to perform the whole of the promise.

***Each promisor may compel contribution***: Each of two or more joint promisors may compel every other joint promisor to contribute equally with himself to the performance of the promise, unless a contrary intention appears from the contract.

***Sharing of loss by default in contribution***: If anyone of two or more joint promisors makes default in such contribution, the remaining joint promisors must bear the loss arising from such default in equal shares.

***Explanation***: Nothing in this section shall prevent a surety from recovering from his principal; payments made by the surety on behalf of the principal, or entitle the principal to recover anything from the surety on account of payments made by the principal.

### Illustrations

(a) A, B and C jointly promise to pay D 3,000 rupees. D may compel either A or B or C to pay him 3,000 rupees.

(b) A, B and C jointly promise to pay D the sum of 3,000 rupees. C is compelled to pay the whole. A is insolvent, but his assets are sufficient to pay one-half of his debts. C is entitled to receive 500 rupees from A's estate, and 1,250 rupees from B.

(c) A, B and C are under a joint promise to pay D 3,000 rupees. C is unable to pay anything, and A is compelled to pay the whole. A is entitled to receive 1,500 rupees from B.

(d) A, B and C are under a joint promise to pay D 3,000 rupees, A and B being only sureties for C. C fails to pay. A and B are compelled to pay the whole sum. They are entitled to recover it from C.

### Section 44: Effect of release of one joint promisor

Where two or more persons have made a joint promise, a release of one of such joint promisors by the promisee does not discharge the other joint promisor or joint promisors; neither does it free the joint promisors so released from responsibility to the other joint promisor or joint promisors.

### Section 45: Devolution of joint rights

When a person has made a promise to two or more persons jointly, then, unless a contrary intention appears from the contract, the right to claim performance rests, as between him and them, with them during their joint lives, and, after the death of any of them, with the representative of such deceased person jointly with the survivor or survivors, and, after the death of the last survivor, with the representatives of all jointly.

### Illustration

A, in consideration of 5,000 rupees, lent to him by B and C, promises B and C jointly to repay them that sum with interest on a day specified. B dies. The right to claim performance rests with B's representative jointly with C during C's life, and after the death of C with the representatives of B and C jointly.

## Time and Place for Performance

### Section 46: Time for performance of promise, when no application is to be made and no time is specified

Where, by the contract, a promisor is to perform his promise without application by the promisee, and no time for performance is specified, the engagement must be performed within a reasonable time.

***Explanation***: The question "what is a reasonable time" is, in each particular case, a question of fact.

**Section 47: Time and place for performance of promise, where time is specified and no application to be made**

When promise is to be performed on a certain day, and the promisor has undertaken to perform it without application by the promisee, the promisor may perform it at any time during the usual hours of business on such day and at the place at which the promise ought to be performed.

## Illustration

A promises to deliver goods at B's warehouse on the first January. On that day A brings the goods to B's warehouse, but after the usual hour for closing it, and they are not received. A has not performed his promise.

**Section 48: Application for performance on certain day to be at proper time and place**

When a promise is to be performed on a certain day, and the promisor has not undertaken to perform it without application by the promisee, it is the duty of the promisee to apply for performance at a proper place and within the usual hours of business.

*Explanation*: The question "what is a proper time and place" is, in each particular case, a question of fact.

**Section 49: Place for performance of promise, where no application to be made and no place fixed for performance**

When a promise is to be performed without application by the promisee, and no place is fixed for the performance of it, it is the duty of the promisor to apply to the promisee to appoint a reasonable place for the performance of the promise, and to perform it at such place.

## Illustration

A undertakes to deliver a thousand *maunds* of jute to B on a fixed day. A must apply to B to appoint a reasonable place for the purpose of receiving it, and must deliver it to him at such place.

**Section 50: Performance in manner or at time prescribed or sanctioned by promise**

The performance of any promise may be made in any manner, or at any time which the promisee prescribes or sanctions.

## Illustrations

(a) B owes A 2,000 rupees. A desires B to pay the amount to A's account with C, a banker. B, who also banks with C, orders the amount to be transferred from his account to A's credit, and this is done by C. Afterwards, and before A knows of the transfer, C fails. There has been a good payment by B.

(b) A and B are mutually indebted. A and B settle an account by setting off one item against another, and B pays A the balance found to be due from him upon such settlement. This amounts to a payment by A and B, respectively, of the sums which they owed to each other.

(c) A owes B 2,000 rupees. B accepts some of A's goods in reduction of the debt. The delivery of goods operates as a part payment.

(d) A desires B, who owes him ₹100, to send him a note for ₹100 by post. The debt is discharged as soon as B puts into the post a letter containing the note duly addressed to A.

## Performance of Reciprocal Promises

### Section 51: Promisor not bound to perform, unless reciprocal promisee ready and willing to perform

When a contract consists of reciprocal promises to be simultaneously performed, no promisor need perform his promise unless the promisee is ready and willing to perform his reciprocal promise.

#### Illustrations

(a) A and B contract that A shall deliver goods to B to be paid for by B on delivery.
A need not deliver the goods, unless B is ready and willing to pay for the goods on delivery.
B need not pay for the goods, unless A is ready and willing to deliver them on payment.

(b) A and B contract that A shall deliver goods to B at a price to be paid by instalments, the first instalment to be paid on delivery.
A need not deliver, unless B is ready and willing to pay the first instalment on delivery.
B need not pay the first instalment, unless A is ready and willing to deliver the goods on payment of the first instalment.

### Section 52: Order of performance of reciprocal promises

Where the order in which reciprocal promises are to be performed is expressly fixed by the contract, they shall be performed in that order; and, where the order is not expressly fixed by the contract, they shall be performed in that order which the nature of the transaction requires.

#### Illustrations

(a) A and B contract that A shall build a house for B at a fixed price. A's promise to build the house must be performed before B's promise to pay for it.

(b) A and B contract that A shall make over his stock-in-trade to B at a fixed price and B promises to give security for the payment of the money. A's promise need not be performed until the security is given, for the nature of the transaction requires that A should have security before he delivers up his stock.

**Section 53: Liability of party preventing event on which the contract is to take effect**

When a contract contains reciprocal promises, and one party to the contract prevents the other from performing his promise, the contract becomes voidable at the option of the party so prevented; and he is entitled to compensation from the other party for any loss which he may sustain in consequence of the non-performance of the contract.

**Illustration**

A and B contract that B shall execute certain work for A for a thousand rupees. B is ready and willing to execute the work accordingly, but A prevents him from doing so. The contract is voidable at the option of B; and, if he elects to rescind it, he is entitled to recover from A compensation for any loss which he has incurred by its non-performance.

**Section 54: Effect of default as to that promise which should be first performed, in contract consisting of reciprocal promises**

When a contract consists of reciprocal promises, such that one of them cannot be performed, or that its performance cannot be claimed till the other has been performed, and the promisor of the promise last mentioned fails to perform it, such promisor cannot claim the performance of the reciprocal promise, and must make compensation to the other party to the contract for any loss which such other party may sustain by the non-performance of the contract.

**Illustrations**

(a) A hires B's ship to take in and convey, from Calcutta to the Mauritius, a cargo to be provided by A, B receiving a certain freight for its conveyance. A does not provide any cargo for the ship. A cannot claim the performance of B's promise, and must make compensation to B for the loss which B sustains by the non-performance of the contract.

(b) A contracts with B to execute certain builder's work for a fixed price, B supplying the scaffolding and timber necessary for the work. B refuses to furnish any scaffolding or timber, and the work cannot be executed. A need not execute the work, and B is bound to make compensation to A for any loss caused to him by the non-performance of the contract.

(c) A contracts with B to deliver to him, at a specified price, certain merchandise on board a ship which cannot arrive for a month, and B engages to pay for the merchandise within a week from the date of the contract. B does not pay within the week. A's promise to deliver need not be performed, and B must make compensation.

(d) A promises B to sell him one hundred bales of merchandise, to be delivered next day, and B promises A to pay for them within a month. A does not deliver according to his promise. B's promise to pay need not be performed, and A must make compensation.

### Section 55: Effect of failure to perform at fixed time, in contract in which time is essential

When a party to a contract promises to do a certain thing at or before a specified time, or certain things at or before specified times, and fails to do any such thing at or before the specified time, the contract, or so much of it as has not been performed, becomes voidable at the option of the promisee, if the intention of the parties was that time should be of the essence of the contract.

***Effect of such failure when time is not essential*:** If it was not the intention of the parties that time should be of the essence of the contract, the contract does not become voidable by the failure to do such thing at or before the specified time; but the promisee is entitled to compensation from the promisor for any loss occasioned to him by such failure.

***Effect of acceptance of performance at time other than that agreed upon*:** If, in case of a contract voidable on account of the promisor's failure to perform his promise at the time agreed, the promisee accepts performance of such promise at any time other than that agreed, the promisee cannot claim compensation for any loss occasioned by the non-performance of the promise at the time agreed, unless, at the time of such acceptance he gives notice to the promisor of his intention to do so.

Time is always considered the essence of the contract in the following cases:

1. Where the parties have expressly agreed to treat it as the essence of the contract;
2. Where delay operates as an injury; and,
3. Where the nature and necessity of the contract require it to be so construed. Where time is of the essence of the contract and is extended, the extended date is also of the essence of the contract.[137]

Mere fixation of a period of delivery or a time in regard thereto does not by itself make the time as the essence of the contract, but the agreement shall have to be considered in its entirety and on proper appreciation of the intent and purport of the clauses incorporated therein. The State of facts and the relevant terms of the agreement ought to be noticed in its proper perspective so as to assess the intent of the parties. The Agreement must be read as a whole with corresponding obligations of the parties so as to ascertain the true intent of the parties. In the event the time is the essence of the contract, the question of their being any presumption or presumed extension or presumed acceptance of a renewed date would not arise. The extension, if any, should and ought to be categorical in nature rather than being vague or in the anvil of presumptions. In the event of the parties knowingly give a go-by to the stipulation as regards the time, the same may have two effects: (a) parties name a future specific date for delivery and (b) parties may also agree to the abandonment of the contract as regards (a) above, there must be a specific date within which delivery has to be effected and in the event there is no such specific date available in the course of conduct of the parties, then and in that event, the Courts are not left with any other conclusion but a finding that the parties themselves by their conduct have given a go-by to the original term of the contract as regards the time being the essence of the contract.

[137] *Orissa Textile Mills Ltd.* v. *M/s. Ganesh Das Ramkishun,* AIR 1961 PAT 107.

When the contract itself provides for extension of time, the same cannot be termed to be the essence of the contract and default, however, in such a case does not make the contract voidable either. It becomes voidable provided the matter in issue can be brought within the ambit of the first paragraph of Sec. 55 of the Act.[138]

Where time is "of the essence" of an obligation, Chitty on Contracts[139] states that a failure to perform by the stipulated time will entitle the innocent party to—

(a) terminate performance of the contract and thereby put an end to all the primary obligations of both parties remaining unperformed; and
(b) claim damages from the contract-breaker on the basis that he has committed a fundamental breach of the contract ('a breach going to the root of the contract') depriving the innocent party of the benefit of the contract ('damages for loss of the whole transaction').

In our country, the question of delay in performance of the contract is governed by Secs. 55 and 56 of the Indian Contract Act, 1872. If there is an abnormal rise in prices of material and labour, it may frustrate the contract and then the innocent party need not perform the contract. So also, if time is of the essence of the contract, failure of the employer to perform a mutual obligation would enable the contractor to avoid the contract as the contract becomes voidable at his option. If, instead of avoiding the contract, the contractor accepts the belated performance of reciprocal obligation on the part of the employer, the innocent party, i.e., the contractor, cannot claim compensation for any loss occasioned by the non-performance of the reciprocal promise by the employer at the time agreed, *"unless, at the time of such acceptance, he gives notice to the promisor of his intention to do so"*. Thus, it appears that under the Indian law, in spite of there being a contract between the parties whereunder the contractor has undertaken not to make any claim for delay in performance of the contract occasioned by an act of the employer, still a claim would be entertainable in one of the following situations: (i) if the contractor repudiates the contract exercising his right to do so under Sec. 55 of the Contract Act, (ii) the employer gives an extension of time either by entering into supplemental agreement or by making it clear that escalation of rates or compensation for delay would be permissible, (iii) if the contractor makes it clear that escalation of rates or compensation for delay shall have to be made by the employer and the employer accepts performance by the contractor in spite of delay and such notice by the contractor putting the employer on terms.[140]

### *Time—Whether Essence of Contract*

The different High Courts including the Supreme Court of India have formulated certain propositions when time would be considered as essence of the contract. However, the following propositions are only illustrative:

(i) The Bombay High Court held that the parties may make time of the essence either expressly in terms which unmistakably provide that they intended to do

[138] *Arosan Enterprises Ltd., M/s.* v. *Union of India*, AIR 1999 SC 3804.

[139] 28th Edn., 1999, at p. 1106, para 22.

[140] *State of Kerala* v. *M.A. Mathai*, AIR 2007 SC 1537.

so. Alternately, making of time as the essence of a contract may be inferred from the nature of the contract, the property or the surrounding circumstances.[141]

(ii) The Supreme Court of India held in *Arosan Enterprises Ltd.* v. *Union of India* that when the contract itself provides for extension of time, the same cannot be termed to be the essence of the contract and default, however, in such a case does not make the contract voidable.[142]

(iii) The Madras High Court held that the deferred clause indicated that time was not the essence of the contract.[143]

(iv) The Supreme Court in *Gomathinayagam Pillai* v. *Palaniswami Nadar* held that in a contract for the sale of land or immovable property, it would normally be presumed that time was not of the essence of the contract.[144]

### Section 56: Agreement to do impossible act

An agreement to do an act impossible in itself is void.

***Contract to do act afterwards becoming impossible or unlawful***: A contract to do an act which, after the contract is made, becomes impossible, or, by reason of some event which the promisor could not prevent, unlawful, becomes void when the act becomes impossible or unlawful.

***Compensation for loss through non-performance of act known to be impossible or unlawful***: Where one person has promised to do something which he knew, or, with reasonable diligence, might have known, and which the promisee did not know, to be impossible or unlawful, such promisor must make compensation to such promisee for any loss which such promisee sustains through the non-performance of the promise.

### Illustrations

(a) A agrees with B to discover treasure by magic. The agreement is void.

(b) A and B contract to marry each other. Before the time fixed for the marriage, A goes mad. The contract becomes void.

(c) A contracts to marry B, being already married to C, and being forbidden by the law to which he is subject to practise polygamy, A must make compensation to B for the loss caused to her by the non-performance of his promise.

(d) A contracts to take in cargo for B at a foreign port. A's Government afterwards declares war against the country in which the port is situated. The contract becomes void when war is declared.

(e) A contracts to act at a theatre for six months in consideration of a sum paid in advance by B. On several occasions A is too ill to act. The contract to act on those occasions becomes void.

---

[141] *Swarnam Ramchandran* v. *Aravacode Chakungal Jayapalan*, AIR 2000 Bom 410.

[142] AIR 1999 SC 3804.

[143] *Y.A. Kader* v. *Muthulakshmi Ammal*, AIR 1992 Mad 208.

[144] AIR 1967 SC 868.

The contracting parties while drafting an agreement usually incorporate a clause which is popularly known as *"force majeure"* in order to protect their interests if they are unable to perform their respective obligations due to certain reasons which are not contemplated while making the contract and those are beyond their control.

McCardie J. in *Lebeaupin* v. *Crispin*,[145] has given an account of what is meant by *"force majeure"*, with reference to its history. The expression *force majeure* is not a mere French version of the Latin expression *vis major*. It is undoubtedly a term of wider import. Difficulties have arisen in the past as to what could legitimately be included in *force majeure*. Judges have agreed that strikes, breakdown of machinery, which, though normally not included in *vis major*, are included in *force majeure*. *Force majeure* means to save the performing party who has agreed to perform but unable to perform his obligation due to certain unavoidable circumstances over which he has no control.

The word *'frustration'* has not been used in the Indian Contract Act. However, the principles on which the *'doctrine of frustration'* rest can be found in the Indian Law. The doctrine of frustration describes a situation where, after the conclusion of a contract, unforeseeable events occur, rendering the performance of that contract impossible. Under that doctrine, Courts have the power to discharge any contract that falls within its scope as *"frustrated"*, and its effect is that the parties are released from their contractual obligations.

Although various theories have been propounded by the judges and jurists in England regarding the juridical basis of the doctrine of frustration, yet the essential idea upon which the doctrine is based is that of impossibility of performance of the contract. In fact, impossibility and frustration are often used as interchangeable expressions.

## ORIGINS: PRINCIPLE OF ABSOLUTISM

Until the nineteenth century, the common law adopted a doctrine of absolute obligation to perform a contract. The rule of absolutism had been applied in *Paradine* v. *Jane*[146] where Paradine sued Jane for three years back rent, and Jane defended himself by asserting that he was not in possession of the land for the time in question because the land in question was under the control of military personnel. The Court, however, held that the parties had committed themselves to the lease, and if they had wanted to provide for the avoidance of liability in certain situations, they could have done so in the terms of the contract itself. Furthermore, the Court reasoned, if the lessee was to have the advantage of profiting from the use of the land, he should bear the losses which may occur from the use of the land as well.

The basic principle of frustration was formulated to avoid the harshness as caused in the *Paradine* case under the absolute obligation doctrine. The doctrine of frustration operates in situations where it is established that due to subsequent change in circumstances, the contract is rendered impossible to perform, or it has become deprived of its commercial purpose by an event not due to the act or default of either party. Lord Sumner considered the doctrine of frustration, formulating it as a *"device by which the rules as to absolute contracts*

145 1920–2 KB 714.

146 (1647) Aleyn 26.

*are reconciled with a special exception which justice demands".*[147] Section 56 of the Indian Contract Act relates to performance of contracts and it purports to deal with one class of circumstances under which performance of a contract is excused or dispensed with on the ground of the contract being void.

The first paragraph of Sec. 56 lays down the law in the same way as in English Law. It speaks of something which is impossible inherently or by its very nature, and no one can obviously be directed to perform such an act. The second paragraph enunciates the law relating to discharge of contract by reason of supervening impossibility or illegality of the act agreed to be done. In other words, Sec. 56 can be divided into two parts so far as impossibility is concerned. The first part relates to 'initial impossibility' because the first para of Sec. 56 provides that *'an agreement to do an act impossible in itself is void'* whereas the second part relates to 'subsequent impossibility' because the second para of Sec. 56 provides that *'a contract to do an act which after the contract is made, becomes impossible'*.

It is clear that the word *'impossible'* used in Sec. 56 of the Contract Act has not been used in the sense of physical or literal impossibility. The performance of an act may not be literally impossible but it may be impracticable and useless from the point of view of the object and purpose which the parties had in view; and if an untoward event or change of circumstances totally upsets the very foundation upon which the parties rested their bargain, it can very well be said that the promisor finds it impossible to do the act which he promised to do.

Lord Loreburn has rightly remarked in *Tamplin Steamship Co. Ltd.* v. *Anglo-Mexican Petroleum Products Co. Ltd.*[148] that the parties would be excused if substantially the whole contract becomes impossible of performance, or in other words, *'impracticable'* by some cause for which neither was responsible. It has been observed that the doctrine of frustration is only a special case of the discharge of contract by an impossibility of performance arising after the contract was made.[149]

The Supreme Court in *Satyabrata Ghose* v. *Mugneeram Bangur and Co.*[150] held that the doctrine of frustration is really an aspect or part of the law of discharge of contract by reason of supervening impossibility or illegality of the act agreed to be done and hence comes within the purview of Sec. 56 of the Indian Contract Act. It would be incorrect to say that Sec. 56 of the Contract Act applies only to cases of physical impossibility and that where this section is not applicable, recourse can be had to the principles of English law on the subject of frustration. The Court further observed that Sec. 56 of the Contract Act provides exhaustive propositions and therefore it is not permissible to import the principles of English law while deciding the cases relating to impossibility. The decisions of the English Courts possess only a persuasive value and may be helpful in showing how the Courts in England have decided cases under circumstances similar to those which have come before Indian Courts.

There can be no doubt that a man may by an absolute contract bind himself to perform which subsequently however becomes impossible, or to pay damages for the

[147] *Hirji Mulji* v. *Cheong Yue Steamship Co. Ltd.*, [1926] AC 497.

[148] 1916–2 AC 297.

[149] *Joseph Constantine Steamship Lime Limited* v. *Imperial Smelting Corporation Ltd.*, 1942–AC 154.

[150] AIR 1954 SC 44.

non-performance and this interpretation is to be placed upon an unqualified undertaking, where the event which causes the impossibility was or might have been anticipated and guarded against in the contract, or where the impossibility arises from the act or default of the promissor. But where the event is of such a character that it cannot reasonably be supposed to have been in the contemplation of the contracting parties when the contract was made, they will not be held bound by general words which, though large enough to include, were not used with reference to the possibility of the particular contingency which afterwards happened. It is on this principle that the act of God is, in some cases, said to excuse the breach of a contract. The Latin maxim referred to in the English judgment *"lex non cogit ad impossibilia"* also expressed as *"impotentia excusat legem"* in common English acceptation means, the law does not compel a man to do that which he cannot possibly perform.[151]

## Factors Causing Impossibility for Performance

The doctrine of frustration or impossibility of performance is applicable to a variety of situations and therefore it is not possible to lay down an exhaustive list of situations where the doctrine would be applied. Following grounds are earmarked after considering various case laws where the doctrine has been applied or pleaded.

### *Destruction of the subject matter*

The doctrine of frustration would be applied if the subject matter of a contract is destroyed due to no fault of either of the parties. In *Taylor* v. *Caldwell*,[152] the defendants Caldwell & Bishop owned Surrey Gardens & Music Hall, and agreed to rent it out to the plaintiffs, Taylor & Lewis, at the rate of £100/day. The plaintiffs had planned to use the music hall for four concerts for four different dates during the summer of 1861, and had intended to provide a variety of extravagant entertainments, including a singing performance by Sims Reeves. According to the contract the parties had signed, the defendants were to provide most of the performers. The plaintiffs were to receive the gate receipts and advertise for these events. Then, on 11 June, 1861, a week before the concert was to be given, the music hall burned to the ground. The plaintiffs sued the music hall owners for breach of contract for failing to rent the music hall.

Blackburn, J., began his opinion by stating that the agreement between the parties was a contract, despite their use of the term 'lease'. His Lordship reasoned that the rule of absolute liability set forth in the *Paradine* case only applied to positive, definite contracts, not to those in which there was an express or implied condition underlying the contract. The Court further reasoned that the continued existence of the Music Hall in Surrey Gardens was an implied condition essential for the fulfilment of the contract. The destruction of the music hall was the fault of neither party, and rendered the performance of the contract by either party impossible. His Lordship cited to the Civil code of France and the Roman law for the proposition that when the existence of a particular thing is essential to a contract, and the thing is destroyed by no fault of the either party, the parties to the contract are freed from contractual obligation.

---

[151] *I.F.C.I. Ltd.* v. *Cannanore Spg. and Wvg. Mills Ltd.*, AIR 2002 SC 1841.

[152] 3 B. & S. 826, 122 Eng. Rep. 309.

Blackburn J stated:

> "The principle seems to us to be that, in contracts in which the performance depends on the continued existence of a given person or thing, a condition is implied that the impossibility of performance arising from the perishing of the person or thing shall excuse the performance."

### *Personal incapacity*

Personal incapacity where the personality or skill of one of the parties is significant may frustrate the contract. In *Condor* v. *Barron Knights Ltd.*,[153] Edward Lottian Condor, a talented drummer, was contracted to play seven nights per week with the Barron Knights pop group, when he had a minor nervous breakdown. He was advised by a doctor that to continue the demanding schedule might well lead to a major breakdown, and therefore the contract was held to be frustrated. In *Robinson* v. *Davison*[154] a contract was made between the plaintiff and the defendant's wife, who was an eminent pianist that she should play the piano at a concert to be given by the plaintiff on a specified day. On the morning of the day in question, she informed the plaintiff that she was too ill to attend the concert. The concert had to be postponed and the plaintiff lost a sum of money. The plaintiff filed a case against the defendant for compensation as it amounts to breach of contract which was not accepted by the Court. The Court held that as she was unfit to play which was clearly subject to the condition of her being well enough to perform she may be thereby excused.

### *Non-occurrence of a specified event*

The non-occurrence of a specified event may frustrate the contract. In *Krell* v. *Henry*,[155] Henry hired a room from Krell for two days, to be used as a position from which to view the coronation procession of Edward VII, but the contract itself made no reference to that intended use. The King's illness caused a postponement of the procession. It was held that Henry was excused from paying the rent for the room. The holding of the procession on the dates planned was regarded by both parties as basic to enforcement of the contract. However, in *Herne Bay Steamboat Co.* v. *Hutton*,[156] Herne Bay agreed to hire a steamboat to Hutton for a period of two days for the purpose of taking passengers to Spithead to cruise round the fleet and see the naval review on the occasion of Edward VII's coronation. The review was cancelled, but the boat could have been used to cruise round the assembled fleet. It was held that the contract was not frustrated. The holding of the naval review was not the only event upon which the intended use of the boat was dependent. The other object of the contract was to cruise round the fleet, and this remained capable of fulfilment.

### *Interference by the Government or Legislature*

There may be a situation where the parties are not in a position to perform their obligation due to change of Government policy or change of law. When the contract was made it was

[153] [1966] 1 WLR 87.

[154] [1871] LR 6 Exch 269.

[155] [1903] 2 KB 740.

[156] [1903] 2 KB 683.

fine and parties to the contract were ready to perform their obligation as per the terms and conditions of the contract. But due to change of policy of the Government, the contract cannot be performed, if done, it may be illegal and therefore doctrine of frustration may be applied and Sec. 56 of the Act may be attracted.

Interference by the Government may frustrate a contract. In *Metropolitan Water Board* v. *Dick Kerr*,[157] Kerr agreed to build a reservoir for the Water Board within six years but after two years, Kerr was required by a wartime statute to stop the work immediately, thereby Kerr had to sell his plant. The contract was held to be frustrated due to interference by the Government. In *Satyabrata Ghose* v. *Mugneeram Bangur and Co.*,[158] the defendant company started a scheme for the development of a particular land into a housing colony. The plaintiff was allotted a plot on payment of earnest money. The company undertook to construct the roads and drains necessary for making the land suitable for building and residential purposes. But before anything could be done, a considerable portion of the land was requisitioned by the State during the Second World War for military purposes.

In these circumstances, the company decided to treat the agreement for sale as cancelled and provided an option of taking back the earnest money within one month from the receipt of the letter. There was an offer made in the alternative that in case the purchaser refused to treat the contract as cancelled, he could, if he liked, complete the conveyance within one month from the receipt of the letter by paying the balance of the consideration money and take the land in the condition in which it existed at that time, the company undertaking to construct the roads and the drains, as circumstances might permit, after the termination of the war. However, the letter ended by saying that in the event of the not accepting either of the two alternatives, the agreement would be deemed to be cancelled and thereby the earnest money would stand forfeited. The Court observed as follows:

> "If there was a definite time limit agreed to by the parties within which the construction work was to be finished, it could be said with perfect propriety that delay for an indefinite period would make the performance of the contract impossible within the specified time and this would seriously affect the object and purpose of the venture. But when there is no time limit whatsoever in the contract, nor even an understanding between the parties on that point and when during the war the parties could naturally anticipate restrictions of various kinds which would make the carrying on of these operations more tardy and difficult than time of peace, we do not think that the order of requisition affected the fundamental basis upon which the agreement rested or struck at the root of the adventure."[159]

Therefore, the Court held that Sec. 56 cannot be attracted and it would be beyond the purview of the application of doctrine of frustration.

### *Due to war—Suez Canal Case*

There may be a situation where both the contracting parties agreed to perform their respective obligations but after making the contract, it may not be possible for the parties

[157] [1918] AC 119.

[158] AIR 1954 SC 44.

[159] *Id* at pp. 49–50 per B.K. MUKHERJEA, J.

to perform it that they had mutually agreed due to war or war like situation. In a famous case, popularly known as *Suez Canal*[160] case, the appellants agreed to sell ground nuts to the respondents from Sudan to Hamburg in Nov./Dec. 1956. However, on 2 November, the Suez Canal was closed and remained closed for five months. The price of the nuts had been calculated on the basis of shipment via Suez Canal which was the normal and usual route, though there was no term in the contract designating it the exclusive route. The appellants refused to perform the contract. The House of Lords held that there was no frustration; it was still possible to ship the nuts via the Cape of Good Hope, a journey some 3,000 miles longer.

Here the Court has observed that if there are more than one ways of performing a contract and due to war or war like situations cuts off only one of them, the party cannot take the plea of frustration and thereby he would be excused to perform. Furthermore, he cannot take the plea of inconvenience, commercial hardship or expensive.

### *Supervening illegality*

A contract may become frustrated if it later becomes illegal. In *Denny, Mott & Dickinson* v. *James Fraser*,[161] a contract for the sale and purchase of timber contained an option to purchase a timber yard held to be illegal by a wartime control order passed by the Government. One party wanted to exercise the option. It was held that the order had frustrated the contract so, the option could not be exercised. Similarly, in *Re Shipton, Anderson and Harrison Brother*,[162] a contract was concluded between the parties for the sale of wheat lying in a warehouse. The Government requisitioned the wheat, in pursuance of wartime emergency regulations for the control of food supplies, before it had been delivered, and also before ownership in the goods had passed to the buyer under the terms of the contract. It was held that the seller was excused from further performance of the contract as it was now impossible to deliver the goods due to the Government's lawful requisition.

### *Application of Lease Property*

In *Raja Dhruv Dev Chand* v. *Raja Harmohinder Singh*,[163] the question that came before the Supreme Court for consideration was, whether Sec. 56 would be applied to lease property. The Court held that by its express terms, Sec. 56 of the Contract Act does not apply to cases in which there is a completed transfer. A covenant under a lease to do an act which after the contract is made becomes impossible or by reason of some event which the promisor could not prevent, unlawful, becomes void when the act becomes impossible or unlawful. But on that account the transfer of property resulting from the lease granted by the lessor to the lessee is not declared void. Under a lease of land, there is a transfer of right to enjoy that land. If any material part of the property be wholly destroyed or rendered substantially and permanently unfit for the purpose for which it was let out, because of fire, tempest, flood, violence of an army or a mob, or other irresistible force,

160 *Tsakiroglou & Co. Ltd.* v. *Noblee & Thorl GMBH* [1962] AC 93.

161 [1944] AC 265.

162 [1915] 3 KB 676.

163 AIR 1968 SC 1024.

the lease may, at the option of the lessee, be avoided. This rule is incorporated in Sec. 108 (e) of the Transfer of Property Act and applies to leases of land.

## Limitations of the Doctrine

1. The doctrine of frustration must be applied within very narrow limits.[164]
2. The doctrine of frustration was not lightly to be invoked to relieve contracting parties of the normal consequences of imprudent commercial bargains.[165]
3. The doctrine of frustration cannot override express contractual provision for the frustrating event.
4. The mere increase in expense or loss of profit is not a ground for frustration.[166]
5. Frustration must not be self-induced.[167]

## Effects of Frustration

If any contract falls within the purview of Sec. 56, by default Sec. 65 would be applied. The contract either may be initial impossibility or may be subsequent impossibility and would be void as per Sec. 56 of the Act (See Sec. 65 of the Contract Act).

## Section 57: Reciprocal promise to do things legal, and also other things illegal

Where persons reciprocally promise, firstly, to do certain things which are legal, and, secondly, under specified circumstances to do certain other things which are illegal, the first set of promises is a contract, but the second is a void agreement.

## Illustration

A and B agree that A shall sell B a house for 10,000 rupees, but that, if B uses it as a gambling house, he shall pay A 50,000 rupees for it.

The first set of reciprocal promises, namely, to sell the house and to pay 10,000 rupees for it, is a contract.

The second set is for an unlawful object, namely, that B may use the house as a gambling house, and is a void agreement.

Section 57 of the Contract Act applies to cases where two of promises are distinct. When the void part of an agreement can be properly separated from the rest, the latter does not become invalid. The ready-forward transaction consists of two parts. In the ready leg, there is a purchase or sale of securities at a stated price which is executed on payment of consideration for the spot delivery of the security certificates together with transfer forms. The full and absolute ownership of the title in securities vests in the purchaser, the entire property in the security passing immediately upon such delivery and payment. The seller is divested of all the rights, title and interests in the said securities. The forward leg

---

164 *Tsakiroglou & Co. Ltd.* v. *Noblee & Thorl GMBH* [1962] AC 93.

165 *Pioneer Shipping* v. *BTP Tioxide* [1982] AC 724.

166 *Davis Contractors* v. *Fareham UDC* [1956] AC 696.

167 *Maritime National Fish* v. *Ocean Trawlers* [1935] AC 524.

is to be performed at a later date on the stated price being paid. The securities are to be delivered back when the title in interest therein would pass to the original seller. It is clear that such a ready-forward transaction consists of a set of reciprocal promises. The first set of promises was fully executed, but the second set remained executory. Section 57 of the Contract Act would thus be attracted to the present case, the effect of which would be that the first set of promises would constitute a binding contract but the second or the forward leg would be void and unforceable. Neither the object nor the consideration of the ready leg is illegal, unlawful, or prohibited under Sec. 23 of the Contract Act. The forward leg is neither the consideration nor the object for entering into the ready leg. At best, it may be that the forward leg provided the parties with the motive for entering into the contract but that would not affect the severability of the forward leg, which alone is declared illegal under the Securities Control Regulation Act. What the notification issued under Sec. 16 was to prohibit the entering into of a forward contract, i.e., sale at a future date for a fixed price. It expressly permitted sale of securities by spot delivery which, in the present case, is represented by the ready leg. It is only the future sale or the resale of the securities at a later date which the notification did not permit. This later part of the agreement could not have been entered into and is clearly severable and cannot affect the transfer of the title which had already taken place at the time of the execution of the ready leg.[168]

### Section 58: Alternative promise, one branch being illegal

In the case of an alternative promise, one branch of which is legal and the other illegal, the legal branch alone can be enforced.

#### Illustration

A and B agree that A shall pay B 1,000 rupees for which B shall afterwards deliver to A either rice or smuggled opium.

This is a valid contract to deliver rice, and a void agreement as to the opium.

## Appropriation of Payments

### Section 59: Application of payment where debt to be discharged is indicated

Where a debtor, owing several distinct debts to one person, makes a payment to him, either with express intimation, or under circumstances implying that the payment is to be applied to the discharge of some particular debt, the payment, if accepted, must be applied accordingly.

#### Illustrations

(a) A owes B, among other debts, 1,000 rupees upon a promissory note which falls due on the' first June. He owes B no other debt of that amount. On the first June A pays to B 1,000 rupees. The payment is to be applied to the discharge of the promissory note.

[168] *B.O.I. Finance Ltd.* v. *Custodian*, AIR 1997 SC 1952.

(b) A owes to B, among other debts, the sum of 567 rupees. B writes to A and demands payment' of this sum A sends to B 567 rupees. This payment is to be applied to the discharge of the debt of which B had demanded payment.

### Section 60: Application of payment where debt to be discharged is not indicated

Where the debtor has omitted to intimate and there are no other circumstances, indicating to which debt the payment is to be applied, the creditor may apply it at his discretion to any lawful debt Actually due and payable to him from the debtor, whether its recovery is or is not barred by the law in force for the time being as to the limitation of suits.

### Section 61: Application of payment where neither party appropriates

Where neither party makes any appropriation, the payment shall be applied in discharge of the debts in order of time, whether they are or are not barred by the law in force for the time being as to the limitation of suits. If the debts are of equal standing, the payment shall be applied in discharge of each proportionably.

In *I.C.D.S. Ltd., M/s.* v. *Smithaben H. Patel,*[169] there are three questions required to be answered in this appeal and they are as follows:

1. Whether a judgment debtor has any option or right to make the payment of the decretal amount in the manner he likes unilaterally?
2. Whether the mere acceptance of such amount by the creditor can be held to be agreeing to the conditions put by the judgment debtor while satisfying the decree?
3. Whether a debtor can unilaterally insist upon the payment of the decretal amount in liquidation of the principal amount in the first instance notwithstanding his liability to pay the interest and costs?

A perusal of Sec. 59 would clearly indicate that it refers to several distinct debts payable by a person and not to the various heads of one debt. The principal and interest due on a single debt or decree passed on such debt carrying subsequent interest cannot be held to be several distinct debts. A Full Bench of the Lahore High Court in *Jia Ram* v. *Sulakhan Mal,*[170] dealt with the scope of Sec. 59 to Sec. 61 of the Indian Contract Act and held:

"Sections 59 to 61 Contract Act embodies the general rules as to appropriation of payments in cases where a debtor owes several distinct debts to one person and voluntarily makes payment to him. They do not deal with cases in which principal and interest are due on a single debt, or where a decree has been passed on such a debt, carrying interest on the sum adjudged to be due on the decree. These sections are based upon the rule of English Law well settled since (1816) 1 Mer 608: 14 RR 166 Clayton's case, that where a debtor, owing several distinct debts to one person, makes a payment to him intimating that the payment is to be applied in discharge of particular debt, the creditor, if he accepts the payment, must apply it accordingly. If, however, the debtor

[169] AIR 1999 SC 1036.

[170] AIR 1941 Lahore 386.

has omitted to intimate and there are no circumstances indicating to which debt the payment is to be applied the creditor may, at his discretion, apply it to any debt actually due and payable to him by the debtor at the time. In case neither party makes the appropriation, the payment is to be applied in discharge of the debts in order of time; and if the debts are of equal standing the payment is made in the discharge of each of them proportionately. It will be seen that these rules have no application to a case in which only one debt is due and at the time of payment, besides the principal sum secured, interest has also accrued due".[171]

The Supreme Court observed in this instant case that the judgment of the Lahore High Court is based upon sound principle and has kept in mind the intention of the Legislature in enacting Secs. 59 to 61 of the Act. The Apex Court does not agree with the learned counsel of the respondents that Sec. 60 of the Contract Act has to be read independently excluding the provisions of Sec. 59. Accepting such an argument would amount to doing violence to the language employed in the section and the purpose sought to be achieved by it. Besides, it would also be contradictory in terms. Section 60, if applied independently, cannot be held to be conferring any right upon the judgment debtor as it confers a discretion in favour of the creditor to apply such deposited amount to any lawful debt actually due and payable by the debtor when such debtor omits to intimate the discharge of the debt in the manner envisaged under Sec. 59. Further, the Court is of opinion that Secs. 59 and 60 of the Contract Act would be applicable only in pre-decretal stage and not thereafter. Post-decretal payments have to be made either in terms of the decree or in accordance with the agreement arrived at between the parties though on the general principles as mentioned in Secs. 59 and 60 of the Contract Act. As and when such an agreement either express or implied is relied upon, the burden of proving it would always be upon its propounder. The judgment debtors, in the instant case, are proved to have failed in discharging such an onus. There does not appear to be any obligation on the decree holder to intimate the judgment debtor that the amount paid to him had not been accepted in the manner specified by him in the letter accompanying the payment. Insisting upon such a course would result in unnecessary burden upon the financial institutions and conferment of unwanted unilateral discretion in favour of the defaulters. Acceptance of the plea that the amount paid first should be adjusted in the principal amount would not only be against the provisions of law but against public policy as well. To provide security, continuity and certainty in business transaction, the Legislature has been making specific provisions in that regard which may be found in various provisions of the Negotiable Instruments Act or Order 37, Code of Civil Procedure and other statutory provisions.

The Supreme Court held that the general rule of appropriation of payments towards a decretal amount is that such an amount is to be adjusted firstly strictly in accordance with the directions contained in the decree and in the absence of such direction, adjustments be made firstly in payment of interest and costs and thereafter in payment of the principal amount. Such a principle is, however, subject to one exception, i.e., that the parties may agree to the adjustment of the payment in any other manner despite the decree. As and when such an agreement is pleaded, the onus of proving is always upon the person pleading the agreement contrary to the general rule or the terms of the decree schedule.

---

[171] Paragraph quoted in *I.C.D.S. Ltd., M/s.* v. *Smithaben H. Patel*, AIR 1999 SC 1036.

The provisions of Secs. 59 to 61 of the Contract Act are applicable in cases where a debtor owes several distinct debts to one person and do not deal with cases in which the principal and interest are due on a single debt.

The normal rule in the case of a debt due with interest is that any payment made by the debtor is in the first instance to be applied towards satisfaction of interest and thereafter to the principal.[172]

## Contracts which Need not be Performed

### Section 62: Effect of novation, rescission, and alteration of contract

If the parties to a contract agree to substitute a new contract for it, or to rescind or alter it, the original contract need not be performed.

### Illustrations

(a) A owes money to B under a contract. It is agreed between A, B and C that B shall thenceforth accept C as his debtor, instead of A. The old debt of A to B is at an end, and a new debt from C to B has been contracted.

(b) A owes B 10,000 rupees. A enters into an arrangement with B, and gives B a mortgage of his (A's) estate for 5,000 rupees in place of the debt of 10,000 rupees. This is a new contract and extinguishes the old.

(c) A owes B 1,000 rupees under a contract. B owes C 1,000 rupees. B orders A to credit C with 1,000 rupees in his books, but C does not assent to the arrangement. B still owes C 1,000 rupees, and no new contract has been entered into.

### *Novation*

One of the essential requirements of 'novation', as contemplated by Sec. 62, is that there should be complete substitution of a new contract in place of the old. It is in that situation that the original contract need not be performed. Substitution of a new contract in place of the old contract which would have the effect of rescinding or completely altering the terms of the original contract has to be by agreement between the parties. A substituted contract should rescind or alter or extinguish the previous contract. But if the terms of the two contracts are inconsistent and they cannot stand together, the subsequent contract cannot be said to be in substitution of the earlier contract.[173]

Novation may be of two kinds:

1. *Substitution of parties or change of parties*: The first illustration to Sec. 62 is a case of novation by change of parties. Concurrence of all parties is required.
2. *Substitution of new agreement by same parties*: When both the parties agree to substitute a new contract for it, the original contract is discharged and need not

[172] *Meghraj* v. *Bayabai*. AIR 1970 SC 161.

[173] *Lata Construction* v. *Dr. Rameshchandra Ramniklal Shah*, AIR 2000 SC 380.

be performed. Novation of this kind is possible before breach of contract and not after breach of the contract.

### *Rescission*

Rescission must be distinguished from termination of the contract. 'Termination' occurs during the running of a contract and the contract just stops so that rights and liabilities in the future no longer apply. Accrued rights and liabilities (those that have already fallen due before the terminating event) are perfectly enforceable.

This is to be contrasted with 'rescission' where the contract is treated as if it had never been. It is a prerequisite of rescission that it must be possible to go back to the situation before the contract was made. It is logically impossible to sue for breach of a contract that is successfully rescinded.

Remember, rescission is the remedy available when something has gone wrong during the negotiations for the contract, such as misrepresentation or misleading conduct, unconscionable dealing, undue influence, duress or mistake. Termination is the remedy available where either the contract has been frustrated or one party has committed a breach which is so serious that it justifies the other party putting an end to the contract by terminating it.

Having said all this, it must be pointed out that the usage of these two terms (termination and rescission) is often muddled. Judges quite frequently talk of rescission when they mean termination.

### *Alteration*

The word *"alteration"* incorporated in Sec. 62 of the Contract Act does not mean that any alteration made in the contract would attract the effect of Sec. 62 and thereby the party concerned need not perform his obligation made in the contract. The author is of opinion that it should be read as "material alteration" where the right of one of the contracting parties would be extinguished and such alteration would be detrimental to him and his rights.

The Supreme Court in *Loonkaran Sethia* v. *Ivan E. John*[174] explained the meaning of 'material alteration' as follows:

> A material alteration, is one which varies the rights, liabilities, or legal position of the parties as ascertained by the deed in its original State, or otherwise varies the legal effect of the instrument as originally expressed or reduces to certainty some provision which was originally unascertained and as such void, or which may otherwise prejudice the party bound by the deed as originally executed.

The following alterations are material alterations which will make the instrument void:

1. Altering the date of the instrument
2. Altering the amount payable on the instrument
3. Altering time or place of payment
4. Addition of place of payment without the acceptor's assent.

---

[174] AIR 1977 SC 336.

Alterations permitted are:

1. Completing an inchoate instrument
2. Converting blank endorsements into endorsements in full
3. Crossing of cheques
4. Qualified acceptance
5. Alteration made with consent of the parties
6. Alteration made to carry out common intention of all the original parties; for example date of instruments is altered with the consent of parties
7. Alteration of any note on the margin of the instruments
8. Alteration though material if made before the issue of the instrument
9. Alteration made for purpose of correcting mistake.[175]

Section 87 of the Negotiable Instruments Act, 1881 provides the effect of material alteration which reads as follows:

> Any material alteration of a negotiable instrument renders the same void as against anyone who is a party thereto at the time of making such alteration and does not consent thereto, unless it was made in order to carry out the common intention of the original parties.

## Section 63: Promisee may dispense with or remit performance of promise

Every promisee may dispense with or remit, wholly or in part, the performance of the promise made to him, or may extend the time for such performance, or may accept instead of it any satisfaction which he thinks fit.

### Illustrations

(a) A promises to paint a picture for B. B afterwards forbids him to do so. A is no longer bound to perform the promise.

(b) A owes B 5,000 rupees. A pays to B, and B accepts, in satisfaction of the whole debt, 2,000 rupees paid at the time and place at which the 5,000 rupees were payable. The whole debt is discharged.

(c) A owes B 5,000 rupees. C pays to B 1,000 rupees, and B accepts them, in satisfaction of his claim on A. This payment is a discharge of the whole claim.

(d) A owes B, under a contract, a sum of money, the amount of which has not been ascertained. A' without ascertaining the amount, gives to B, and B, in satisfaction thereof, accepts, the sum of 2,000 rupees. This is a discharge of the whole debt, whatever may be its amount.

(e) A owes B 2,000 rupees, and is also indebted to other creditors. A makes an arrangement with his creditors, including B, to pay them a composition of eight annas in the rupee upon their respective demands. Payment to B of 1,000 rupees is a discharge of B's demand.

---

[175] http://www.citeman.com/10679-instances-of-material-alteration.html#ixzz1w34T2xDC

After reading Sec. 63 along with illustrations to Sec. 63, this section may be looked from three angles as follows:

1. ***Remit or dispense with (Waiver), wholly or in part***: In *Lala Kapurchand Godha* v. *Mir Nawab Himayatalikhan Azamjah*,[176] the defendant, the Prince of Berar, had executed in 1937, a promissory note in favour of the plaintiff for a sum of 13 lacs and odd rupees due on account of purchase of jewellery from the plaintiff. After the Military occupation of Hyderabad, the Princes Debt Settlement Committee set up by the Military Governor decided that the plaintiff should be paid a sum of ₹20 lacs in full satisfaction of his claim of ₹27 lacs under the note. The Government also made it clear that unless full satisfaction was recorded, payment would not be made. The plaintiff, after some protests, agreed to accept the sum of ₹20 lacs in full satisfaction of his claim and dully discharged the promissory note by endorsement of full satisfaction and received the payment. He then brought a suit against the defendant for recovery of the balance of ₹7 lacs. The Court held that the case was completely covered by Sec. 63 of the Contract Act and illustration (c) thereof and the plaintiff having accepted payment from a third person, viz. the Government in full satisfaction of their claim was not entitled to sue the defendant for the balance in view of Sec. 41 of the Contract Act.

   To *"dispense with"* means that the party entitled to claim performance may waive it. Waiver means abandonment of a right which normally everybody is at liberty to waive. A waver is nothing unless it amounts to a release. It signifies nothing more than an intention not to insist upon the right. It may be deduced from acquiescence or may be implied.[177]

   In 2011, the Supreme Court in *R.L. Kalathia Co.* v. *State of Gujarat*[178] has formulated the following principles in case *"No Due Certificate"*, or *"No-claim Certificate"* has been issued by one of the contracting parties to the opposite party before receiving the payment.

   1. Merely because the contractor has issued "No Due Certificate", if there is acceptable claim, the Court cannot reject the same on the ground of issuance of "No Due Certificate".
   2. Inasmuch as it is common that unless a discharge certificate is given in advance by the contractor, payment of bills are generally delayed, hence such a clause in the contract would not be an absolute bar to a contractor raising claims which are genuine at a later date even after submission of such "No-claim Certificate".
   3. Even after execution of full and final discharge voucher/receipt by one of the parties, if the said party is able to establish that he is entitled to further amount for which he is having adequate materials, he is not barred from claiming such amount merely because of acceptance of the final bill by mentioning "without prejudice" or by issuing "No Due Certificate".

[176] AIR 1963 SC 250.

[177] *Waman Shriniwas Kini* v. *Ratilal Bhagwandas and Co.*, AIR 1959 SC 689.

[178] AIR 2011 SC 754.

2. *Extension of time*: Section 63 permits a party to extend the time of performance but it should be always mutual, not unilateral. Consent of the other contracting party is required.
3. *Accord and satisfaction*: The accord and satisfaction discharges the causes of action for breaches of contract already committed. Where the accord and satisfaction is by substituted agreement, it is a question of construction of that agreement whether it also extinguishes all pre-existing rights and obligations and totally discharges the original contract.[179] The accord is an agreement made after breach. The liability arising out of breach may be discharged by accord and satisfaction.

## Section 64: Consequences of rescission of voidable contract

When a person at whose option a contract is voidable rescinds it, the other party thereto need not perform any promise therein contained in which he is promisor. The party rescinding a voidable contract shall, if he have received any benefit there under from another party to such contract, restore such benefit, so far as may be, to the person from whom it was received.

## Section 65: Obligation of person who has received advantage under void agreement, or contract that becomes void

When an agreement is discovered to be void, or when a contract becomes void, any person who has received any advantage under such agreement or contract is bound to restore it, or to make compensation for it to the person from whom he received it.

### Illustrations

(a) A pays B 1,000 rupees in consideration of B's promising to marry C, A's daughter. C is dead at the time of the promise. The agreement is void, but B must repay A the 1,000 rupees.

(b) A contracts with B to deliver to him 250 maunds of rice before the first of May. A delivers 130 *maunds* only before that day, and none after. B retains the 130 *maunds* after the first of May. He is bound to pay A for them.

(c) A, a singer, contracts with B, the manager of a theatre, to sing at his theatre for two nights in every week during the next two months, and B engages to pay her a hundred rupees for each night's performance. On the sixth night, A wilfully absents herself from the theatre, and B, in consequence, rescinds the contract. B must pay A for the five nights on which she had sung.

(d) A contracts to sing for B at a concert for 1,000 rupees, which are paid in advance. A is too ill to sing. A is not bound to make compensation, to B for the loss of the profits which B would have made if A had been able to sing, but must refund to B the 1,000 rupees paid in advance.

---

[179] AIR 1953 CAL 642.

Section 65 is based on equitable doctrine and provides for the restitution of any benefit received under a void agreement or contract. It cannot be said that the obligation to restitute arising under Sec. 65 would apply to a situation where the agreement is *"discovered to be void"* or where the contract *"becomes void"* and not to an agreement which is void from its inception. It may often be that the parties may realise, after having entered into the agreement or after having signed the contract, that one of the matters which was essential to the agreement, was not understood by them in the same sense and that both of them were carrying totally different impressions of that matter at the time of entering into the agreement or executing the document. Such realisations would have the effect of invalidating the agreement under Sec. 20 of the Act. On such realisations, it can be legitimately said that the agreement was *"discovered to be void"*. The words *"discovered to be void"*, therefore, comprehend a situation in which the parties were suffering from a mistake of fact from the very beginning but had not realised, at the time of entering into the agreement or signing of the document, that they were suffering from any such mistake and had, therefore, acted bona fide on such agreement. The agreement in such a case would be void from its inception, though discovered to be so at a much later stage.

Section 65 categorically provides that if some benefits have been passed to the other contracting party under a contract and it is discovered to be void or due to some supervening acts, it becomes void, the person who has received any benefit thereof must have to restore it. Thus, Sec. 65 is having no application to a contract where parties knew at the time of making that the contract is void.

Section 65 deals with two aspects: (a) agreements, and (b) contracts. The distinction between them is apparent from Sec. 2 of the Contract Act. By Clause (e), every promise and every set of promises forming the consideration for each other is an agreement, and by Clause (h) an agreement enforceable by law is a contract. Section 65, therefore, deals with (a) agreement enforceable by law, and (b) with agreements not so enforceable. By Clause (g), an agreement not enforceable by law is said to be void. An agreement, therefore, discovered to be void is one discovered to be not enforceable by law, and, on the language of Sec. 65 would include an agreement that was void in that sense from its inception as distinct from a contract that becomes void.[180]

Section 65 makes a distinction between an agreement and a contract. According to Sec. 2 of the Contract Act, an agreement which is enforceable by law is a contract and an agreement which is not enforceable by law is said to be void. Therefore, when the earlier part of Sec. 65 speaks of an agreement being discovered to be void, it means that the agreement is not enforceable and is, therefore, not a contract. It means that it was void. It may be that the parties or one of the parties to the agreement may not have, when they entered into the agreement, known that the agreement was in law not enforceable. They might have come to know later that the agreement was not enforceable. The second part of the section refers to a contract becoming void. That refers to a case where an agreement which was originally enforceable and was, therefore, a contract, becomes void due to subsequent happenings. In both these cases, any person who has received any advantage under such agreement or contract is bound to restore such advantage, or to make compensation for it to the person from whom he received it. But where even at the

[180] *Thakurain Harnath Kuar* v. *Thakur Indar Bahadur Singh*, AIR 1922 PC 403.

time when the agreement is entered into both the parties knew that it was not lawful and, therefore, void, there was no contract but only an agreement and it is not a case where it is discovered to be void subsequently. Nor is it a case of the contract becoming void due to subsequent happenings. Therefore, Sec. 65 of the Contract Act would not be applied. Where a mining lease in favour of the plaintiff was contrary to the provisions of the Mines and Minerals (Regulations and Development) Act 1948 and the Mineral Concession Rules (1949) and void *ab initio* and there was proof to show that the plaintiff could not have been in ignorance of the legal position, it was held that this was not a case to which Sec. 65 applied and the plaintiff was not entitled to claim refund of the sum paid in pursuance of the lease, under that provision.[181]

In *State of Rajasthan* v. *Associated Stone Industries (Kotah) Ltd.*[182], the State granted monopoly rights to the grantee to quarry stones and later on the agreement was discovered to be void or became void. The measure of the compensation payable to the grantor should be the reasonable royalty which the State would have otherwise received from the grantee. In addition, the grantee would also be liable to pay compensation for the exclusive rights granted to him. But it could not be said that the grantee was bound to restore the net profits earned by it during the relevant period to the State. It was not as if all that the Company did was to excavate stone. The grantee in order to market the excavated stone had to carry on various other activities besides extracting stone from the quarries, such as, polishing, plastering, flooring, painting, cementing, etc. Therefore, the net profits realised by the grantee as a result of all its various business activities could never be the measure of the compensation to be awarded under Sec. 65 of the Contract Act. It is not as if Sec. 65 of the Contract Act works in one direction only. If one party to the contract is asked to disgorge the advantage received by him under a void contract, the other party to the void contract may ask him to restore the advantage received by him. The restoration of advantage and the payment of compensation would necessarily be mutual.

## Section 66: Mode of communicating or revoking rescission of voidable contract

The rescission of a voidable contract may be communicated or revoked in the same manner, and subject to the same rules, as apply to the communication or revocation of a proposal.

## Section 67: Effect of neglect of promisee to afford promisor reasonable facilities for performance

If any promisee neglects or refuses to afford the promisor reasonable facilities for the performance of his promise, the promisor is excused by such neglect or refusal as to any non-performance caused thereby.

### Illustration

A contracts with B to repair B's house.

B neglects or refuses to point out to A the places in which his house requires repair.

A is excused for the nonperformance of the contract if it is caused by such neglector refusal.

---

[181] *Kuju Collieries Ltd.* v. *Jharkhand Mines Ltd.*, AIR 1974 SC 1892.

[182] AIR 1985 SC 466.

# Chapter V Of Certain Relations Resembling Those Created by Contract

## QUASI CONTRACT

Quasi-contract is a term used in the civil law. A quasi-contract is the act of a person, permitted by law, by which he obligates himself towards another, or by which another binds himself to him, without any agreement between them.

By the Civil Code of Louisiana, quasi-contracts are defined to be "the lawful and purely voluntary acts of a man, from which there results any obligation whatever to a third person, and sometime a reciprocal obligation between the parties." In contracts, it is the consent of the contracting parties which produces the obligation; in quasi-contracts no consent is required, and the obligation arises from the law or natural equity, on the facts of the case. These acts are called quasi-contracts, because, without being contracts, they bind the parties as contracts do.

*'Quasi'* means *'almost'* or *'apparently but not really'* or *'as if it were'*. This term is used when one subject resembles another in certain characteristics, but there are intrinsic differences between the two. *'Quasi-contract'* is not a 'contract'. It is an obligation which law created in the absence of any agreement. It is based on equity. Quasi-contracts are essentially situations in which one party has an obligation to another party not on the ground of a prior agreement. In Roman law, such an obligation would arise, for example, if a person incurred expense in protecting another's property in an emergency without his knowledge, the obligation to compensate him was said to be *'quasi ex contractu'*. Another kind of case was the obligation to return something if it was paid to you by someone who mistakenly believed that he owed it to you. Quasi-contract was a restricted category in Roman law of miscellaneous cases, where there was obviously an obligation but which did not rise from a contract: it was *'like a contract,'* though not actually a contract.

### Principle of Quasi-contract

In *Moses* v. *Macferlan*[183], Lord Mansfield, who is considered to be the founding father of the theory of unjust enrichment, said that the principle of quasi-contracts is based on the principle of unjust enrichment. It is a general principle that one person should not be permitted unjustly to enrich himself at the expense of another, but should be required to make restitution of or for property or benefits received, retained or appropriated, where it is just and equitable that such restitution be made, and where such action involves no violation or frustration of law or opposition to public policy, either directly or indirectly.[184] Unjust enrichment of a person occurs when he has and retains money or benefits which in justice and equity belong to another.[185]

---

183 (1760) 2 Burr 1005.

184 *Tulalip Shores, Inc.* v. *Mortland*, 9 Wash.App. 271, 511 P.2d 1402, 1404.

185 *L & A Drywall, Inc.* v. *Whitmore Const. Co., Inc.*, Utah, 608 P.2d 626, 630.

Three elements must be established in order to sustain a claim based on unjust enrichment and they are as follows:

1. A benefit conferred upon the defendant by the plaintiff;
2. An appreciation or knowledge by the defendant of the benefit; and
3. The acceptance or retention by the defendant of the benefit under such circumstances as to make it inequitable for the defendant to retain the benefit without the payment of its value.[186]

The Supreme Court in *Mahabir Kishore* v. *State of M.P.*[187] provided the following three ingredients for constituting unjust enrichment and observed:

> The principle of unjust enrichment requires: first, that the defendant has been 'enriched' by the receipt of a "benefit", secondly, that this enrichment is "at the expense of the plaintiff"; and thirdly; that the retention of the enrichment be unjust. This justifies restitution. Enrichment may take the form of direct advantage to the recipient's wealth such as by the receipt of money or indirect one for instance where inevitable expense has been saved.[188]

A quasi-contract is not a contract but it is based on equity. It is an obligation which is created by law in the absence of any agreement. Since there are certain terms resembling those of a contract, it is said to be a quasi-contract. The Indian Contract Act avoids the word quasi-contract but it does not mean that the Indian Contract law does not deal with the situation which is created under the quasi-contract principles. Chapter V of the Indian Contract Act deals with such situations under the heading of *"Of certain relations resembling those created by contract."* Sections 68 to 72 provide for five kinds of quasi contractual obligations.

### Section 68: Claim for necessaries supplied to person incapable of contracting, or on his account

If a person, incapable of entering into a contract, or anyone whom he is legally bound to support, is supplied by another, person with necessaries suited to his condition in life, the person who has furnished such supplies is entitled to be reimbursed from the property of such incapable person.

### Illustrations

(a) A supplies B, a lunatic, with necessaries suitable to his condition in life. A is entitled to be reimbursed from B's property.

(b) A supplies the wife and children of B, a lunatic, with necessaries suitable to their condition in life. A is entitled to be reimbursed from B's property.

---

186 *Everhart* v. *Miles*, 47 Md.App. 131, 136, 422 A.2d 28.

187 AIR 1990 SC 313.

188 *Id.* at pp. 317–318 per Saikia, J.

The persons who are not competent to make the contract including a minor are obliged to pay for goods or services provided such person that are *'necessary'* to maintain them in their station in life. The word *'necessary'* has not been defined under the Act and possibly it cannot be provided any precise meaning which would be applicable to all circumstances. Thus, 'what is necessary' is a relative fact to be determined with reference to the standard of living of a person in question. In *Nash* v. *Inman*,[189] a tailor sued a minor to whom he had supplied clothes, including 11 fancy waistcoats. It was decided that, as the minor was an undergraduate at Cambridge University at the time, the clothes were suitable according to the minor's station in life. Unfortunately for the tailor, however, it was further decided that they were not necessary, as he already had sufficient clothing. Minors are only under a legal obligation to pay for things necessary for their maintenance although even then they will only be required to pay a reasonable price for any necessaries purchased. So, no contact was enforceable.

"Necessaries" are those things without which a person cannot reasonably exist and include food, clothing, lodging, education or training in a trade and essential services. The "condition of life" of the minor means his social status and his wealth.

In *Chapel* v. *Cooper*,[190] the Court provided the meaning and scope of the term *"necessaries"* that without which an individual cannot reasonably exist, for example food, lodging and the like. For the proper cultivation of the mind of an individual, it is necessary for him to have some amounts of instruction in art or trade, or intellectual, moral and religious education. The 'necessary' of an individual is bound to vary from person to person. His clothes may be fine or coarse according to his rank; his education may vary according to his family status; and the medicines would depend on the illness with which he was afflicted. Thus, articles of *mere* luxury are always excluded, though luxurious articles of utility in some cases may be allowed.

An infant, like a lunatic, is incapable of making a contract of purchase in strict sense of the word; but if a man satisfies the needs of the infant or lunatic by supplying to him necessaries, the law will imply an obligation to repay him for the services so rendered, and will enforce that obligation against the estate of the infant or lunatic. The consequence is that the basis of the action is hardly contract. The real foundation is an obligation which the law imposes on the infant to make a fair payment in respect of the needs satisfied. In other words, the obligation arises *re* and not *consensus*. According to this section, therefore, the person entering into the contract must be a person who understands what he is doing and is able to form a rational judgment as to whether what he is about to do is to his interest or not. The crucial point, therefore, is to find out whether he is entering into the contract after he has understood it and he decided to enter into that contract after forming a rational judgment in regard to his interest. It does not necessarily mean that a man must be suffering from lunacy to disable him from entering into a contract. A person may to all appearances behave in a normal fashion, but, at the same time, he may be incapable of forming a judgment of his own, as to whether the act he is about to do is to his interest or not. In the present case, (he) was incapable of exercising his own judgment.

189 (1908) KB 1.

190 (1844) 13 M and W 252.

### Section 69: Reimbursement of person paying money due by another, in payment of which he is interested

A person who is interested in the payment of money which another is bound by law to pay, and who therefore pays it, is entitled to be reimbursed by the other.

#### Illustration

B holds land in Bengal, on a lease granted by A, the zamindar. The revenue payable by A to the Government being in arrear, his land is advertised for sale by the Government. Under the revenue law, the consequence of such sale will be the annulment of B's lease. B, to prevent the sale and the consequent annulment of his own lease, pays to the Government the sum due from A. A is bound to make good to B the amount so paid.

Section 69 would be invoked if the following conditions are satisfied:

1. The person making the payment should be interested in making the payment in order to protect his own interest.
2. The payment should not be a voluntary payment. It should be such that there should be some legal force.
3. The person making the payment should not be bound by law to pay.
4. The payment should be made to another person and not to himself.
5. The payment must be one which the other party was bound by law to pay.

### Section 70: Obligation of person enjoying benefit of non-gratuitous act

Where a person lawfully does anything for another person, or delivers anything to him, not intending to do so gratuitously, and such other person enjoys the benefit thereof, the latter is bound to make compensation to the former in respect of, or to restore, the thing so done or delivered.

#### Illustrations

(a) A, a tradesman, leaves goods at B's house by mistake. B treats the goods as his own. He is bound to pay A for them.

(b) A saves B's property from fire. A is not entitled to compensation from B, if the circumstances show that he intended to act gratuitously.

In *State of W.B.* v. *M/s. B.K. Mondal and Sons,*[191] the Supreme Court discussed two important issues: (a) application of Sec. 70; and (b) application of Sec. 70 to the Government. The case in hand reveals the following facts:

This appeal by special leave arises out of a suit filed by the respondent B.K. Mondal and Sons against the appellant the State of West Bengal claiming a sum of ₹19,325 for works done by it for the appellant. This claim was made out in two ways. It was alleged that the works in question had been done by the respondent in terms of a contract entered into between the parties and as such the appellant was liable to pay the amount due for

[191] AIR 1962 SC 779.

the said works. In the alternative it was alleged that if the contract in question was invalid, then the respondent's claim fell under Sec. 70 of the Indian Contract Act. The respondent had lawfully done such works not intending to act gratuitously in that behalf and the appellant had enjoyed the benefit thereof.

The Court after referring to Sec. 70 of the Act, observed that it is plain that three conditions must be satisfied before this section can be invoked. The *first* condition is that a person should lawfully do something for another person or deliver something to him. The *second* condition is that in doing the said thing or delivering the said thing, he must not intend to act gratuitously; and the *third* is that the other person for whom something is done or to whom something is delivered must enjoy the benefit thereof. When these conditions are satisfied, Sec. 70 imposes upon the latter person the liability to make compensation to the former in respect of, or to restore, the thing so done or delivered. In appreciating the scope and effect of the provisions of this section, it would be useful to illustrate how this Section would operate. If a person delivers something to another, it would be open to the latter person to refuse to accept the thing or to return it; in that case, Sec. 70 would not come into operation. Similarly, if a person does something for another, it would be open to the latter person not to accept what has been done by the former; in that case again Sec. 70 would not apply. In other words, the person said to be made liable under Sec. 70 always has the option not to accept the thing or to return it. It is only where he voluntarily accepts the thing or enjoys the work done that the liability under Sec. 70 arises. Taking the facts in the instant case, the Court held that after the respondent constructed the warehouse, for instance, it was open to the appellant to refuse to accept the said warehouse, and to have the benefit of it. It could have called upon the respondent to demolish the said warehouse and take away the materials used by it in constructing it; but, if the appellant accepted the said warehouse' and used it and enjoyed its benefit, then different considerations come into play and Sec. 70 can be invoked.

Section 70 occurs in Chapter V, which deals with *'certain relations resembling those created by contract'*. In other words, this chapter does not deal with the rights or liabilities accruing from the contract. It deals with the rights and liabilities accruing from relations which resemble those created by contract. That being so, reverting to the facts of the present case once again, after the respondent constructed the warehouse it would not be open to the respondent to compel the appellant to accept it because what the respondent has done is not in pursuance of the norms of any valid contract and the respondent in making the construction took the risk of the rejection of the work by the appellant. Therefore, in cases falling under Sec. 70, the person doing something for another or delivering something to another cannot sue for the specific performance of the contract nor ask for damages for the breach of the contract for the simple reason that there is no contract between him and the other person for whom he does something or to whom he delivers something. All that Sec. 70 provides is that if the goods delivered are accepted or the work done is voluntarily enjoyed, then the liability to pay compensation for the enjoyment of the said goods or the acceptance of the said work arises. Thus, where a claim for compensation is made by one person against another under Sec. 70, it is not on the basis of any subsisting contract between the parties; it is on the basis of the fact that something was done by the party for another and the said work so done has been voluntarily accepted by the other party. That broadly stated is the effect of the conditions prescribed by Sec. 70.

It is of course true that between the person claiming compensation and the person against whom it is claimed, some lawful relationship must subsist, for that is the implication of the use of the word "lawfully" in Sec. 70. But the said lawful relationship arises not because the party claiming compensation has done something for the party against whom the compensation is claimed but because what has been done by the former has been accepted and enjoyed by the latter.

In respect to question whether Sec. 70 would be applied to the Government, the Court held that in regard to the claim made against the Government of a State under Sec. 70, it may be that in many cases the work done or the goods delivered are the result of a request made by some officer or other on behalf of the said Government. In such a case, the request may be ineffective or invalid for the reason that the officer making the request was not authorised under Sec. 175(3) of the Government of India Act, 1935 or, if the said officer was authorised to make the said request, the request becomes inoperative because it was not followed up by a contract executed in the manner prescribed by Sec. 175(3). In either case the thing has been delivered or the work has been done without a contract and that brings in Sec. 70. A request is thus not an element of Sec. 70 at all though the existence of an invalid request may not make Sec. 70 inapplicable. An invalid request in law is no request at all, and so the conduct of the parties has to be judged on the basis that there was no subsisting contract between them at the material time.

In the present case, there has been no dispute about the amount of compensation but normally a claim for compensation made under Sec. 70 may not mean the same thing as a claim for damages for breach of contract if a contract was subsisting between the parties. Thus considered it would, we think, not be reasonable to suggest that in recognising the claim for compensation under Sec. 70 we are either directly or indirectly nullifying the effect of Sec. 175(3) of the Act or treating as valid a contract which is invalid. The fields covered by the two provisions are separate and distinct; Sec. 175(3) deals with contracts and provides how they should be made. Section 70 deals with cases where there is no valid contract and provides for compensation to be paid in a case where the three requisite conditions prescribed by the Court, as said above, are satisfied.

Accordingly, the Court observed as follows:

> It is well-known that in the functioning of the vast organisation represented by a modern State Government officers have invariably to enter into a variety of contracts which are often of a petty nature. Sometimes they may have to act in emergency, and on many occasions, in the pursuit of the welfare policy of the State Government officers may have to enter into contract orally or through correspondence without strictly complying with the provisions of S. 175(3) of the Act. If, in all these cases, what is done in pursuance of the contracts is for the benefit of the Government and for their use and enjoyment and is otherwise legitimate and proper S. 70 would step in and support a claim for compensation made by the contracting parties notwithstanding the fact that the contracts had not been made as required by S. 175(3).[192]

In *Mulamchand* v. *State of Madhya Pradesh*,[193] the contract between the appellant and the State Government was held to be void as it was entered into in contravention of the provisions

[192] *Id* at pp. 788–789 per Gajendragadkar, J.

[193] AIR 1968 SC 1218.

of the Government of India Act, 1935. The appellant, however, sued for return of his deposit and for the goods supplied and services rendered. The Supreme Court held that Sec. 70 of the Indian Contract Act can be invoked by the aggrieved party if the following conditions are satisfied:

1. The first condition is that a person should lawfully do something for another person or deliver something to him;
2. The second condition is that in doing the said thing or delivering the said thing he must not intend to act gratuitously; and
3. The third condition is that the other person for whom something is done or to whom something is delivered must enjoy the benefit thereof.

If these conditions are satisfied, Sec. 70 imposes upon the latter person the liability to make compensation to the former in respect of, or to restore, the thing so done or delivered. The important point to notice is that in a case falling under Sec. 70, the person doing something for another or delivering something to another cannot sue for the specific performance of the contract, nor ask for damages for the breach of the contract, for the simple reason that there is no contract between him and the other person for whom he does something or to whom he delivers something. So where a claim for compensation is made by one person against another under Sec. 70, it is not on the basis of any subsisting contract between the parties but on a different kind of obligation. The juristic basis of the obligation in such a case is not founded upon any contract or tort but upon a third category of law, namely, quasi-contract or restitution.

### Section 71: Responsibility of finder of goods

A person who finds goods belonging to another, and takes them into his custody, is subject to the same responsibility as a bailee.

### Section 72: Liability of person to whom money is paid or thing delivered by mistake or under coercion

A person to whom money has been paid, or anything delivered, by mistake or under coercion, must repay or return it.

### Illustrations

(a) A and B jointly owe 100 rupees to C. A alone pays the amount to C, and B, not knowing this fact, pays 100 rupees over again to C. C is bound to repay the amount to B.

(b) A railway company refuses to deliver up certain goods to the consignee, except upon the payment of an illegal charge for carriage. The consignee pays the sum charged in order to obtain the goods. He is entitled to recover so much of the charge as was illegally excessive.

The term *"mistake"* used in Sec. 72 of the Contract Act has been used without any qualification or limitation whatever and comprises within its scope a mistake of law as well as a mistake of fact. There is no warrant for ascribing any limited meaning to the word 'mistake' as has been used therein. There is no conflict between the provisions of Sec. 72, on the one hand, and Secs. 21 and 22 of the Contract Act on the other. The true principle is that if one party under a mistake, whether of fact or law, pays to party money which is not due by contract or otherwise that money must be repaid. The mistake lies in thinking that the money paid was due when in fact it was not due and that mistake, if established, entitles the party paying the money to recover it back from the party receiving the same.[194] The Supreme Court in *Dhanyalakshmi Rice Mills* v. *Commissioner of Civil Supplies*[195] discussed the application of Sec. 72 in details. The facts of the case are as follows:

The Government of Andhra Pradesh introduces a scheme known as "Incentive Export Scheme". Under that scheme all millers who delivered 50% of their purchases to the Food Corpn. of India towards mill levy were eligible for export under the Scheme. By an order dated 22 July, 1968, pursuant to the representation of the millers for export of rice outside the block but within the State, the Government of Andhra Pradesh passed orders that permits for export of rice would be issued subject to the fulfilment of their commitments and that administrative charge administrative charge of ₹2.50 per quintal of rice would be collected from the millers before the issue of permits. The Appellants applied for and obtained permits by fulfilling the two principal considerations. Subsequently, they applied to the Government to refund the amount paid as administrative surcharge as they had paid it under mistake of law and that the latter had no right to collect it in the petitions they contended that the respondents Government had no right to collect any administrative surcharge, and, therefore, the amount should be refunded. The Appellants alleged that they made the payments under mistake of law. The High Court held that the levy of administrative surcharges was not backed by valid legislative sanction but it, however, held that the appellants were not entitled to any relief on three grounds. First, the administrative surcharges were paid voluntarily by the appellants. Second, the Court would not be justified in exercising discretion in favour of the appellants who voluntarily paid the administrative charges, obtained the permits, and derived considerable profits therefrom. Third, there was undue delay in claiming the refund.

The Supreme Court observed that Sec. 72 of the Contract Act states that a person to whom money has been paid, or anything delivered by mistake or under coercion, must repay or return it. The mistake is material only as far as it leads to payment being made without consideration. The Court has said that the true principle is that if one party under a mistake of law pays money to another which is not due by contract or otherwise, that is to be repaid. When there is a clear and unambiguous position of law which entitles a party to the relief claimed by him, equitable considerations are not imported. A contract entered into under a mistake of law both parties falls under Sec. 21 of the Contract Act and not Sec. 72. If a mistake of law had led to the formation of a contract, Sec. 21 enacts that that contract is not for that reason voidable. If money is paid under that contract, it cannot be said that the money was paid under mistake of law; it was paid because it was due under a valid contract, if it had not been paid, payment could have been enforced. In the present case, the respondents do not support the demand for administrative charges either as a tax

[194] *Sales Tax Officer, Banaras* v. *Kanhaiya Lal Makund Lal Saraf*, AIR 1959 SC 135.

[195] AIR 1976 SC 2243.

or as a fee but as a term and condition, of permit and as a term of agreement between the parties for the maintenance and supervision expenses for the scheme for export permits of rice from one block to another within the State or outside the State. Accordingly, the appeal was dismissed.

There is no doubt that Sec. 72 of the Contract Act provides that a person to whom money has been paid or anything delivered by mistake or under coercion must repay or return it. That section in our opinion will only apply when we are dealing with a case of two persons, one paying the money and the other receiving the money on behalf of the person paying it. In such a case, if the payment is made by mistake the person receiving the money must return it. But Sec. 72 in our opinion has no application to a case where money is paid by a person to a bank with instructions that it should be deposited in the account of a third person who is a constituent of the bank. As soon as the money is so deposited in the account of the third person, who is a constituent of the bank, the money becomes the money of the constituent, and it is not open to the bank in such circumstances to reverse the entry of credit made in the account of the constituent and in effect pay back the money to the person who had deposited it, even though it might have been deposited by mistake.

As soon as the money is credited into the account of the constituent, even though the person paying it may have paid it by mistake, it becomes the money of the constituent, and the bank cannot pay it back to the person who paid it to the account of the constituent on his representation that it was paid by mistake, without obtaining the consent of the constituent.[196]

## Section 72 and the Law of Limitation

Section 17(1)(c) of the Limitation Act, 1963, provides that in the case of a suit for relief on the ground of mistake, the period of limitation does not begin to run until the plaintiff had discovered the mistake or could, with reasonable diligence, have discovered it. In a case where payment has been made under a mistake of law as contrasted with a mistake of fact, generally the mistake becomes known to the party only when a Court makes a declaration as to the invalidity of the law. Though a party could, with reasonable diligence, discover a mistake of fact even before a Court makes a pronouncement, it is seldom that a person can, even with reasonable diligence, discover a mistake of law before a judgment adjudging the validity of the law. It is thus a settled law that in a suit for refund of money paid by mistake of law, Sec. 72 of the Contract Act is applicable and the period of limitation is three years as prescribed by Art. 113 of the Schedule to the Indian Limitation Act, 1963 and the provisions of Sec. 17(1)(c) of that Act will be applicable so that the period will begin to run from the date of knowledge of the particular law, where under the money was paid, being declared void; and this could be the date of the judgment of a competent Court declaring that law void.[197] Section 72 is based upon and incorporates a rule of equity. In such a situation, equitable consideration cannot be ruled out while applying Sec. 72.

---

[196] *Jammu and Kashmir Bank Ltd.* v. *Attar-Ul-Nisa*, AIR 1967 SC 540.

[197] *Mahabir Kishore* v. *State of M.P.*, AIR 1990 SC 313.

## QUANTUM MERUIT

The expression *quantum meruit* means "the amount he deserves" or "what the job is worth". Essentially, *quantum meruit* is an action for payment of the reasonable value of services performed. It is used in various circumstances where the Court awards a money payment that is not determined, subject to what is said below, by reference to a contract. Put in the converse, a claim on a *quantum meruit* cannot arise if there is an existing contract on foot between the parties to pay an agreed sum. By and large, contractors incline to the view that a *quantum meruit* claim is the "holy grail" of claims because they can recover all their costs, overheads and profits; it is sometimes thought of as "cost-plus".

In essence, *quantum meruit* claims are based on the law of restitution; specifically, *quantum meruit* claims flow from the principle of unjust enrichment. To establish unjust enrichment, three elements must be present and they are as follows.

*Firstly,* the principal must have been enriched by the receipt of a "benefit". *Secondly,* that benefit must have been gained "at the contractor's expense". And, *thirdly,* it would be "unjust" in the circumstances to allow the principal to retain the benefit. Needless to say, there is a good deal of law involved in questions of "benefit", "contractor's expense", and "unjust".

### How it Arises?

In a *quantum meruit* claim, the Court awards a money payment that is not determined by reference to a contract. Most often, this arises where there has been a contract but it has been frustrated, made void, terminated, or is otherwise unenforceable. That is not to say, however, that a *quantum meruit* claim cannot be made where there is a contract on foot. In this regard, *quantum meruit* claims can be made in the following cases:

1. ***Contract but price not fixed***: There is a contract but no price is fixed by that contract. Where a contractor does work under an express or implied contract, and the contract fixes no price or pricing mechanism for that work, the contractor is entitled to be paid a reasonable sum for his labour and for the materials he has supplied.[198]
2. ***Quasi-contract***: This may arise where, for example, a contractor agrees to start work on site while still negotiating with the principal as to, at least, the essential terms of the contract. Those negotiations subsequently fail. Generally, the cases support the proposition that, in such circumstances, the principal has an obligation to pay a reasonable sum for the work done.[199] Predictably, however, it does not apply to all cases of failed contracts.

   In an English case from 1995,[200] for instance, the following circumstances led the Court to conclude that there was no such obligation to pay a reasonable sum:
   
   (i) The negotiations were entered into on express terms that each party was free to withdraw from negotiations at any time;

[198] *Powell* v. *Braun* [1954] 1 All ER 484.

[199] *Trollope & Colls Ltd.* v. *Atomic Power Constructions Ltd.* [1963] 1WLR 333.

[200] *Regalian Properties* v. *London Docklands Development Corporation* [1995] 1 WLR 212.

(ii) The negotiations were explicitly said to be "subject to contract";

(iii) The *quantum meruit* that was being sought had been incurred by the contractor for the purpose of putting the contractor in a good position to win the ultimate contract; it had not been incurred by way of performance under the terms of the anticipated contract; and

(iv) The principal had received no "benefit".

In practice, this type of *quantum meruit* is frequently constrained by letters of intent that often limit the amount a contractor can recover in the event the contract negotiations fail.

3. ***Work outside a contract***: Where there is a contract for specific work but the contractor does work outside the contract at the principal's request, the contractor is entitled to be paid a reasonable sum for that work. Implied contract[201] forms the basis of this entitlement.

4. ***Work under a void, unenforceable or terminated contract***: Where there is a contract but it is void, either for uncertainty[202] or for any other reason,[203] or where the contract is rendered unenforceable by operation of statute,[204] or where the contract has been repudiated by the principal,[205] the contractor may be entitled to claim on a *quantum meruit* for the work or services. In practical terms, this category is the most common, and it is also this category that causes some grief because contractors sometime wrongly assume that a *quantum meruit* claim automatically follows when a principal has repudiated the contract.

Repudiation of the contract by the principal—that is, the principal renounces liability under the contract, or shows an intention no longer to be bound by the contract, or shows an intention only to perform the contract in a particular way that is at odds with the contractual terms does not, in and of itself, bring a contract to an end. If, in fact, the principal indicates that he is no longer ready, willing and able to perform the contract in accordance with its terms, the contractor must elect to terminate the contract. The contractor has to elect between continuing the performance of his contractual obligations or accepting the principal's repudiation and bringing the contract to an end. Only if the contractor chooses the latter, may he then sue, and if the suit is successful, he must also elect between damages assessed on a *quantum meruit* or contractual damages.

The elements of a quantum meruit claim are:

(a) It is one thing to establish that a contractor may be entitled to make a *quantum meruit* claim; it is quite another to determine the extent of the entitlement. As it is mentioned earlier, contractors might like to think that *quantum meruit* is a kind of "holy grail" or "panacea" entitling them to all their costs plus an allowance for profit. However, in reality, it is somewhat different.

[201] *Thorn* v. *London Corp*. (1876) 1 App.Cas. 120, HL.

[202] *Bevelon Investments Pty. Ltd.* v. *Kingsley Air Conditioning Pty. Ltd.*, (1971) 1 ACLR 24.

[203] *Craven-Ellis* v. *Canons Ltd*. [1936] 2 KB 403.

[204] *Pavey and Matthews Pty. Ltd.* v. *Paul* (1987) 162 CLR 221.

[205] *Kane Constructions* v. *Sopov*, [2005] VSC 237.

(b) The basic reason for this is that Courts have not provided clear guidelines to assist in determining a "reasonable sum" that has to be provided to the contractor. Although it is clear that the contractor ought to be paid a fair commercial rate for the work done in all the relevant circumstances.[206] However, the essential problem remains the lack of precision in deciding what is reasonable in the circumstances. What might be reasonable for the principal is unlikely to be so for the contractor, and vice versa. For instance, a principal will want to limit his liability—if he is liable at all to the contractor's actual or tender costs.[207] The contractor, on the other hand, may want the reasonable sum to reflect the value of the work to the principal.[208] At other times, the contractor might take the view that actual costs plus an allowance for profit and overheads, should form the basis of a reasonable sum while the principal might adopt the view that what is reasonable should be determined by reference to the failed contract.

Some difficult questions arise and, unfortunately, there are few straightforward answers:

(i) Who should have the benefit if the contractor has managed to secure his resources (subcontractors, labour, materials and so on) at an especially low price? That is, should the principal have to pay less than a fair commercial rate in such circumstances?

(ii) If there has been a contract which, for whatever reason, is now void, unenforceable or terminated, should the contractor be limited to the amount of the contract price? The importance of this is most evident in the context of a losing contract; that is, where the value of the work (assessed at a fair commercial rate) far exceeds what the contractual amount the principal was obliged to pay. For instance, in a 1933 Californian case,[209] a contractor had been engaged in the construction of a dam and, near completion, the principal breached the contract in such a way that the contractor was justified in terminating the contract, and did terminate the contract. The Court eventually awarded the contractor on the *quantum meruit* claim more than 10 times his outstanding contractual entitlement.

(iii) Even the question of whether a contractor should be entitled to profit is not clear cut. The generally accepted industry position appears to be that a contractor should, in the normal course of a *quantum meruit* claim, be entitled to some measure of profit. However, a recent decision in the Victorian Supreme Court[210] casts considerable doubt on even this. Though the contractor had claimed a 10% margin for profit and overhead as part of his *quantum meruit* claim, the judge declined to award that part of it; she took the view that a margin should form no part of a *quantum meruit* claim.

---

[206] *Greenmast Shipping* v. *Jean Lion*, [1986] 2 Lloyd's Rep. 277.

[207] This was the position adopted in *Sanjay Lachhani* v. *Destination Canada (UK) Ltd.* (1997) 13 Const LJ 279.

[208] *Costain Civil Engineering* v. *Zanen Dredging* (1996) 85 BLR 77.

[209] *Boomer* v. *Muir* 24 P 2d 570 (Cal App 1933).

[210] *Kane* v. *Sopov* [2005] VSC 237.

### Concluding Words

1. *Quantum meruit* claims are based on the law of restitution and flow from the principles of unjust enrichment.
2. They can arise in certain circumstances: where there is a contract but no price has been fixed by that contract; quasi-contract, such as work carried out prior to contractual terms being settled, work done outside the scope of a contract; and, importantly, work under a void, unenforceable, or terminated contract.
3. Where a contract has been repudiated by the principal, a contractor must elect to accept the repudiation and terminate the contract before commencing proceedings.
4. Though contractors often think of *quantum meruit* as a cost-plus "holy grail", the reality is that Courts have not provided clear guidelines about what may be recovered under the broad heading of a "reasonable sum" determined by reference to a fair commercial rate.
5. Accordingly, the peculiar facts of any particular case are likely to have a greater influence on the outcome of a case than are anything else. Sometimes contractors have done very well out of a *quantum meruit* claim; sometimes the results have been less than might have been expected or desired.

## Chapter VI Of the Consequences of Breach of Contract

### Section 73: Compensation for loss or damage caused by breach of contract

When a contract has been broken, the party who suffers by such breach is entitled to receive, from the party who has broken the contract, compensation for any loss or damage caused to him thereby, which naturally arose in the usual course of things from such breach, or which the parties knew, when they made the contract, to be likely to result from the breach of it.

Such compensation is not to be given for any remote and indirect loss or damage sustained by reason of the breach.

***Compensation for failure to discharge obligation resembling those created by contract***: When an obligation resembling those created by contract has been incurred and has not been discharged, any person injured by the failure to discharge it is entitled to receive the same compensation from the party in default, as if such person had contracted to discharge it and had broken his contract.

***Explanation***: In estimating the loss or damage arising from a breach of contract, the means which existed of remedying the inconvenience caused-by the non-performance of the contract must be taken into account.

### Illustrations

(a) A contracts to sell and deliver 50 *maunds* of saltpetre to B, at a certain price to be paid on delivery. A breaks his promise. B is entitled to receive from A, by way of compensation, the sum, if any, by which the contract price falls short of the price for which B might have obtained 50 *maunds* of saltpetre of like quality at the time when the saltpetre ought to have been delivered.

(b) A hires B's ship to go to Bombay, and there take on board, on the first of January, a cargo which A is to provide and to bring it to Calcutta, the freight to be paid when earned. B's ship does not go to Bombay, but A has opportunities of procuring suitable conveyance for the cargo upon terms as advantageous as those on which he had chartered the ship. A avails himself of those opportunities, but is put to trouble and expense in doing so. A is entitled to receive compensation from B in respect of such trouble and expense.

(c) A contracts to buy of B, at a stated price, 50 maunds of rice, no time being fixed for delivery. A afterwards informs B that he will not accept the rice if tendered to him. B is entitled to receive from A, by way of compensation, the amount, if any, by which the contract price exceeds that which B can obtain for the rice at the time when A informs B that he will not accept it.

(d) A contracts to buy B's ship for 60,000 rupees, but breaks his promise. A must pay to B, by way of compensation, the excess, if any, of the contract price over the price which B can obtain for the ship at the time of the breach of promise.

(e) A, the owner of a boat, contracts with B to take a cargo of jute to Mirzapur, for sale at that place, starting on a specified day. The boat, owing to some avoidable cause, does not start at the time appointed, whereby the arrival of the cargo at Mirzapur is delayed beyond the time when it would have arrived if the boat had sailed according to the contract. After that date, and before the arrival of the cargo, the price of jute falls. The measure of the compensation payable to B by A is the difference between the price which B could have obtained for the cargo at Mirzapur at the time when it would have arrived if forwarded in due course, and its market price at the time when it actually arrived.

(f) A contracts to repair B's house in a certain manner, and receives payment in advance. A repairs the house, but not according to contract. B is entitled to recover from A the cost of making the repairs conform to the contract.

(g) A contracts to let his ship to B for a year, from the first of January, for a certain price. Freights rise, and, on the first of January, the hire obtainable for the ship is higher than the contract price. A breaks his promise. He must pay to B, by way of compensation, a sum equal to the difference between the contract price and the price for which B could hire a similar ship for a year on and from the first of January.

(h) A contracts to supply B with a certain quantity of iron at a fixed price, being a higher price than that for which A could procure and deliver the iron. B wrongfully refuses to receive the iron. B must pay to A, by way of compensation, the difference between the contract price of the iron and the sum for which A could have obtained and delivered it.

(i) A delivers to B, a common carrier, a machine, to be conveyed, without delay, to A's mill informing B that his mill is stopped for want of the machine. B unreasonably delays the delivery of the machine, and A, in consequence, loses a profitable contract with the Government. A is entitled to receive from B, by way of compensation, the average amount of profit which would have been made by the working of the Mill during the time that delivery of it was delayed, but not the loss sustained through the loss of the Government contract.

(j) A, having contracted with B to supply B with 1,000 tons of iron at 100 rupees a ton, to be delivered at a stated time, contracts with C for the purchase of 1,000 tons of iron at 180 rupees a ton, telling C that he does so for the purpose of performing his contract with B. C fails to perform his contract with A, who cannot procure other iron, and B, in consequence, rescinds the contract. C must pay to A 20,000 rupees, being the profit which A would have made by the performance of his contract with B.

(k) A contracts with B to make and deliver to B, by a fixed day, for a specified price, a certain piece of machinery. A does not deliver the piece of machinery at the time specified, and in consequence of this, B is obliged to procure another at a higher price than that which he was to have paid to A, and is prevented from performing a contract which B had made with a third person at the time of his contract with A (but which had not been then communicated to A), and is compelled to make compensation for breach of that contract. A must pay to B, by way of compensation, the difference between the contract price 47 of the piece of machinery and the sum paid by B for another, but not the sum paid by B to the third person by way of compensation. .

(l) A, a builder, contracts to erect and finish a house by the first of January, in order that B may give possession of it at that time to C, to whom B has contracted to let it. A is informed of the contract between B and C. A builds the house so badly that, before the first of January, it falls down and has to be re-built by B, who, in consequence, loses the rent which he was to have received from C, and is obliged to make compensation to C for the breach of his contract. A must make compensation to B for the cost of rebuilding the house, for the rent lost, and for the compensation made to C.

(m) A sells certain merchandise to B, warranting it to be of a particular quality, and B, in reliance upon this warranty, sells it to C with a similar warranty. The goods prove to be not according to the warranty, and B becomes liable to pay C a sum of money by way of compensation. B is entitled to be reimbursed this sum by A.

(n) A contracts to pay a sum of money to B on a day specified. A does not pay the money on that day; B, in consequence of not receiving the money on that day, is unable to pay his debts, and is totally ruined. A is not liable to make good to B anything except the principal sum he contracted to pay, together with interest up to 'the day of payment'.

(o) A contracts to deliver 50 *maunds* of saltpetre to B on the first of January, at a certain price. B afterwards, before the first of January, contracts to sell the saltpetre to C at a price higher than the market price of the first of January. A breaks his promise. In estimating the compensation payable by A to B, the market price of the first of January, and not the profit which would have arisen to B from the sale to C, is to be taken into account.

(p) A contracts to sell and deliver 500 bales of cotton to B on a fixed day. A knows nothing of B's mode of conducting his business. A breaks his promise, and B, having no cotton, is obliged to close his mill. A is not responsible to B for the loss caused to B by the closing of the mill.

(q) A contracts to sell and deliver to B, on the first of January, certain cloth which B intends to manufacture into caps of a particular kind, for which there is no demand, except at that season. The cloth is not delivered till after the appointed time, and too late to be used that year in making caps. B is entitled to receive from A, by way of compensation, the difference between the contract price of the cloth and its market price at the time of delivery, but not the profits which he expected to obtain by making caps, nor the expenses which he has been put to in making preparation for the manufacture.

(r) A, a ship-owner, contracts with B to convey him from Calcutta to Sydney in A's ship, sailing on the first of January, and B pays to A, by way of deposit, one-half of his passage-money. The ship does not sail on the first of January, and B, after being in consequence detained in Calcutta for some time and thereby put to some expense, proceeds to Sydney in another vessel, and, in consequence, arriving too late in Sydney, loses a sum of money. A is liable to repay to B his deposit with interest, and the expense to which he is put by his detention in Calcutta, and the excess, if any, of the passage-money paid for the second ship over that agreed upon for the first, but not the sum of money which B lost by arriving in Sydney too late.

Section 73 of the Contract Act incorporates two principles or two rules of *Hardley v. Baxendale*[211] case which was decided in 1854. The facts of the case are as follows:

The plaintiff, Hadley, operated a mill. The crankshaft of the mill broke, thus forcing the mill to shut down. Hadley contracted with the defendant, Baxendale, to deliver the crankshaft to engineers for repair by a certain date. Baxendale failed to deliver on the date in question, causing Hadley to lose some business. Hadley sued for the profits he lost due to Baxendale's late delivery, and the jury awarded Hadley damages of £25. Baxendale appealed, contending that he did not know that Hadley would suffer any particular damage by reason of the late delivery. The question raised by the appeal in this case was whether a defendant in a breach of contract case could be held liable for damages that the defendant was not aware would be incurred from a breach of the contract.

The Court said no to allowing Hadley to recover lost profits in this case, holding that Baxendale could only be held liable for losses that were generally foreseeable, or if Hadley had mentioned his special circumstances in advance. The mere fact that a party is sending something to be repaired does not indicate that they would lose profits if it was not delivered on time. The Court suggested various other circumstances under where Hadley could have entered into this contract which would not have presented such dire circumstances, and noted that where special circumstances do exist, provisions can be

[211] (1854) 9 Exch. 341.

made in the contract voluntarily entered into by the parties to impose extra damages for a breach.

In this case, however, the Court stated that the loss of profits here cannot reasonably be considered such a consequence of the breach of contract as could have been fairly and reasonably contemplated by both the parties when they made this contract.

The *Hardley* case prescribed two rules which are very much incorporated in Sec. 73 of the Act. The compensation would be awarded for any loss or damage:

1. Arising naturally in the usual course of things from the breach, or
2. Which the parties knew at the time of making the contract as likely to result from the breach.

Section 73 further prescribes that compensation would not be awarded for any loss suffered by the contracting party due to breach where the losses are having no direct bearing to such breach which is popularly known as remote and indirect loss. Section 73 covers unliquidated damages. The Supreme Court in its judgement has held that in a suit for damages for breach of contract (under Sec. 73), the plaintiff has not only to establish that alleged breach of contract, but he has further to establish that he has discharged the statutory duty cast upon him by the explanation of Sec. 73 of the Act. The statutory duty which is required to be discharged is to take all reasonable steps to mitigate the loss consequent upon the breach of contract.[212]

An interesting and important issue relating to consequence of breach of a bond executed by a student in favour of the State Government for pursuing his studies in U.S.A. at Government expense came before the Supreme Court for consideration in *M. Sham Singh* v. *State of Mysore*.[213] The facts may be shortly stated:

On 11 September, 1946, Mr. Singh applied to the State Government for an overseas scholarship and the same was sanctioned in his favour. The appellant, Mr. Singh, was required to execute a bond which he did on 2 July, 1947. In the bond it was stated *inter alia* that the scholar had to accept and be bound by all the conditions specified in the rules contained in the annexure to the Government proceedings mentioned therein. Clauses 3 and 4 of said rule are reproduced below:

> Clause 3 of Rule: That on the completion of such study or research course, the scholar shall return to the Mysore State, and if and when called upon to do so, serve the Government for a period of not less than five years, on such salary as Government may, in their sole discretion fix, provided that, if within six months after his return to Bangalore, Mysore State, Government do not find employment for him they shall be deemed to have waived their right to claim his services as aforesaid and the scholar shall, thereafter, be at liberty to seek employment elsewhere."
>
> Clause 4 of Rule: That in case the scholar fails to fulfil any of the first two conditions herein set forth or specified in the aforesaid rules he shall refund to Government the amounts received by him as scholarship, passage money and all other amounts that may be advanced to him upto the date of his return to the Mysore State in connection with the aforesaid course of study or research with such interest not exceeding 5% per annum as Government may, at their option, fix and demand. But if he fails to fulfil the third condition, viz., joining duty under and serving

212 *Murlidhar Chiranjilal, M/s.* v. *M/s. Harishchandra Dwarkadas*, AIR 1962 SC 366.

213 AIR 1972 SC 2440.

the Government for a period of five years, after the completion of the terms of scholarship or deputation he shall pay on the aggregate amount to be refunded as aforesaid, enhanced interest at 9% per annum, instead of 5% as mentioned above and a penalty of not less than one year's salary for each period of deputation (strike off the latter condition in the case of scholarship holders).

After completing the formalities, the appellant left for U.S.A. He joined the Polytechnic Institute of Brooklyn, New York in September 1949 for obtaining a diploma from that Institute in Electrical Engineering. On 25 July, 1949, by a letter, the Education Secretary, Embassy of India in U.S.A., wrote to the Chief Secretary, Government of Mysore conveying the request of the appellant that he be permitted to stay on for practical training with the General Electric Company for one year at his own expense beyond September 30, 1949. The Education Secretary supported this request with the comments that the training would be very valuable, the General Electric Company being well known. This request was duly granted by means of a cable Ext. P. 9, which was followed by a letter from the Secretary to the Government of Mysore, Education Department, and Bangalore intimating that the appellant had been permitted to undergo practical training for one year from 30 September, 1949 at his own expense.

The appellant completed his studies at the Polytechnic Institute of Brooklyn, New York in September 1949 and obtained the diploma from that Institute on 14 June, 1950. On 6 July, 1950 he returned to Bengalore and wrote a letter dated 18 July, 1950 to the Government of Mysore saying that he had returned from the United States after the completion of his studies there. On 29 November, 1950, the appellant addressed a letter to the Mysore Government saying that he be permitted to return to the United States to complete his training which he had interrupted on account of the news of the ill-health of his mother to see whom he had to return to India. The appellant assured the Mysore Government that he would place his services at its disposal on his return to India. The appellant made it clear that he would be going to the United States on his own without seeking any financial assistance from the Government. The Government acceded to the request of the appellant. In its order Ext. P-4, it is stated "In the circumstances Sri M. Sham Singh is permitted to return to U.S.A. for the continuance of his studies, at his own cost, subject to the condition that he should serve the Government of Mysore for a period of 5 years after his return". The appellant left India on 27 February, 1951. It appears that he never returned to India thereafter and continued to stay in the United States after taking up employment as Director of the Tourist Office at San Francisco.

The State of Mysore filed a suit against the appellant for recovery of ₹40,000 for breach of the conditions of the bond which had been executed by him. It was pleaded in the suit that owing to the breach of the conditions of the bond, the appellant was liable to refund all the monies advanced to him together with interest. The total amount, after calculation of interest, which was due from the appellant, came to over ₹62,000 but the claim was limited to ₹40,000 only. In the written statement, it was pleaded by the appellant that when he was permitted by the Mysore Government by its order dated 28 February, 1951 to return to the United States, the previous contract was discharged and ceased to be enforceable. In any event, it was asserted, that the suit was for breach of the terms of the bond which was for ₹16,000 only and the appellant was not liable to pay any amount exceeding that sum.

In appeal, the High Court, after considering all the facts and circumstances, came to the conclusion that when the appellant returned to Bangalore on 6 July, 1950, he had not abandoned the idea of completing the course of training with the General Electric Company. He had come only because of the illness of his mother who died a little before his arrival. Although he had submitted a report to the State Government with regard to his arrival at Bangalore on 18 July, 1950, his letter dated 27 November, 1950, was consistent with the original agreement which had already taken place between the parties that he should complete the course of training with the General Electric Company by staying for a period of one year at his own expense. It was observed by the High Court that the State Government having sent a scholar and having incurred an expenditure of about ₹35,000 for his training could not have refused his request for overstay for a period of one year particularly when such a stay did not entail any financial burden on the State Government. The High Court observed that it is regrettable that having secured the benefits of foreign technical education at the cost of the State exchequer, Mr. Singh has been adopting an attitude in the suit, in utter disregard of his legal and moral obligations under the scholarship bond.

The Supreme Court held that it is difficult to understand and appreciate how the Government should be deemed to have waived the right to claim the services of the appellant in terms of Clause 3 of the bond when by mutual consent it had been agreed that the appellant could stay for one year after he had completed his study at the Polytechnic Institute of Brookyn for getting practical training with the General Electric Company. The High Court is quite right in saying that when the appellant came to Bangalore in July 1950, he did not do so for the purpose of staying at Bangalore and accepting any employment which might be offered to him. He had to come as he admitted in his own letters, on account of domestic reasons. He wanted to go back and finish that period of training with the General Electric Company. He sought permission in that behalf and was allowed to return to the United States for that purpose. The Court is unable to see how in these circumstances the Government was bound to offer him any employment within a period of six months from 18 July, 1950. By writing the letter dated 27 November, 1950 the appellant had unequivocally indicated his desire to finish the training with the General Electric Company. He had made no suggestion and given no hint that he was waiting for the offer of any employment. The period of six months was to expire on 18 January, 1951 whereas the letter dated 27 November, 1950 was written well before that date. The mere fact that he left after the expiry of the period of six months would not show that he had returned to Bangalore and was waiting for any employment being offered to him within six months of his arrival in terms of the bond. It is significant that in the letter dated 27 November, 1950, he had reiterated his assurance that he would place his services at the disposal of the Government on his return provided a suitable position was available. This shows that he was fully conscious of what the true legal position was. Instead of returning to India, the appellant chose to take up a job at San Franciso. Surely the Mysore Government had not expended all the amount in question on the studies of the appellant to enable him to seek employment on his own without first placing his services at the disposal of the Mysore Government which he was legally bound to do under the terms of the bond and the subsequent mutual agreement between the parties. Therefore, the appeal fails and is dismissed with costs.

### Section 74: Compensation for breach of contract where penalty stipulated for

When a contract has been broken, if a sum is named in the contract as the amount to be paid in case of such breach, or if the contract contains any other stipulation by way of penalty, the party complaining of the breach is entitled, whether or not actual damage or loss is proved to have been caused thereby, to receive from the party who has broken the contract reasonable compensation not exceeding the amount so named or, as the case may be, the penalty stipulated for.

*Explanation*: A stipulation for increased interest from the date of default may be a stipulation by way of penalty.

*Exception*: When any person enters into any bail-bond, recognizance or other instrument of the same nature, or, under the provisions of any law, or under the orders of the Central Government or of any State Government, gives any bond for the performance of any public duty or act in which the public are interested, he shall be liable, upon breach of the condition of any such instrument, to pay the whole sum mentioned therein.

*Explanation*: A person who enters into a contract with Government does not necessarily thereby undertake any public duty or promise to do an act in which the public are interested.

### Illustrations

(a) A contracts with B to pay B ₹1,000, if he fails to pay B ₹500 on a given day. A fails to pay B ₹500 on that day. B is entitled to (recover from A such compensation, not exceeding ₹1,000, as the Court considers reasonable.

(b) A contracts with B that, if A practices as a surgeon within Calcutta, he will pay B ₹5,000. A practises as a surgeon in Calcutta. B is entitled to such compensation, not exceeding ₹5,000, as the Court considers reasonable.

(c) A gives a recognizance binding him in a penalty of ₹500 to appear in Court on a certain day. He forfeits his recognizance. He is liable to pay the whole penalty.

(d) A gives B a bond for the repayment of ₹1,000 with interest at 12% at the end of six months, with a stipulation that, in case of default, interest shall be payable at the rate of 75% from the date of default. This is a stipulation by way of penalty, and B is only entitled to recover from A such compensation as the Court considers reasonable.

(e) A, who owes money to B a money-lender, undertakes to repay him by delivering to him 10 maunds of grain on a certain date, and stipulates that, in the event of his not delivering the stipulated amount by the stipulated date, he shall be liable to deliver 20 maunds. This is a stipulation by way of penalty, and B is only entitled to reasonable compensation in case of breach.

(f) A undertakes to repay B a loan of ₹1,000 by five equal monthly instalments, with a stipulation that in default of payment of any instalment, the whole shall become due. This stipulation is not by way of penalty, and the contract may be enforced according to its terms.

(g) A borrows ₹100 from B and gives him a bond for ₹200 payable by five yearly installments of ₹40, with a stipulation that, in default of payment of any installment, the whole shall become due. This is a stipulation by way of penalty.

Section 74 is clearly an attempt to eliminate the somewhat elaborate refinements made under the English common law in distinguishing between stipulations providing for payment of liquidated damages and stipulations in the nature of penalty. Under the common law, a genuine pre-estimate of damages by mutual agreement is regarded as a stipulation naming liquidated damages and binding between the parties, a stipulation in a contract in terrorem is a penalty and the Court refuses to enforce it, awarding to the aggrieved party only reasonable compensation. The Indian Legislature has sought to cut across the web of rules and presumptions under the English common law, by enacting a uniform principle applicable to all stipulations naming amounts to be paid in case of breach, and stipulations by way of penalty.

Section 74 of the Indian Contract Act deals with the measure of damages in two classes of cases; (i) where the contract names a sum to be paid in case of breach and (ii) where the contract contains any other stipulation by way of penalty. The measure of damages in the case of breach of a stipulation by way of penalty is by Sec. 74 reasonable compensation not exceeding the penalty stipulated for. In assessing damages, the Court has, subject to the limit of the penalty stipulated, jurisdiction to award such compensation as it deems reasonable having regard to all the circumstances of the case. Jurisdiction of the Court to award compensation in case of breach of contract is unqualified except as to the maximum stipulated, but compensation has to be reasonable, and that imposes upon the Court duty to award compensation according to settled principles. Section 74 undoubtedly says that the aggrieved party is entitled to receive compensation from the party who has broken the contract whether or not actual damage or loss is proved to have been caused by the breach. Thereby it merely dispenses with proof of *"actual loss or damage"*; it does not justify the award of compensation when in consequence of the breach no legal injury at all has resulted because compensation for breach of contract can be awarded to make good loss or damage which naturally arose in the usual course of things, or which the parties knew when they made the contract, to be likely to result from the breach.

In *Fateh Chand* v. *Balkishan Dass*,[214] the question that came before the Supreme Court was, whether in a contract for sale of the immovable property provided for forfeiture of ₹25,000 in consequence of the default by the vendee and therefore Sec. 74 would be invoked. It was urged that Sec. 74 deals in terms with the right to receive from the party who has broken the contract reasonable compensation and not the right to forfeit what has already been received by the party aggrieved. There is however no warrant for the assumption made by some of the High Courts in India, that Sec. 74 applies only to cases where the aggrieved party is seeking to receive some amount on breach of contract and not to cases where upon breach of contract an amount received under the contract is sought to be forfeited. The Court in this instant case interpreted the expression *"the contract contains any other stipulation by of penalty"* and held that Sec. 74 may be applied to every covenant involving a penalty whether it is for payment on breach of contract of money

[214] AIR 1963 SC 1405.

or delivery of property in future, or for forfeiture of right to money or other property already delivered. Duty not to enforce the penalty clause but only to award reasonable compensation is statutorily imposed upon Courts by Sec. 74. In all cases, therefore, where there is a stipulation in the nature of penalty for forfeiture of an amount deposited pursuant to the terms of contract which expressly provides for forfeiture, the Court has jurisdiction to award such sum only as it considers reasonable, but not exceeding the amount specified in the contact as liable to forfeiture.

Section 74 emphasises that in case of breach of contract, the party complaining of the breach is entitled to receive reasonable compensation whether or not actual loss is proved to have been caused by such breach. Therefore, the emphasis is on reasonable compensation. If the compensation named in the contract is by way of penalty, consideration would be different and the party is only entitled to reasonable compensation for the loss suffered. But if the compensation named in the contract for such breach is genuine pre-estimate of loss which the parties knew when they made the contract to be likely to result from the breach of it, there is no question of proving such loss or such party is not required to lead evidence to prove actual loss suffered by him. Burden is on the other party to lead evidence for proving that no loss is likely to occur by such breach.[215]

In *Oil and Natural Gas Corpn. Ltd.* v. *SAW Pipes Ltd.*,[216] where the supplier delayed the delivery of casting pipes for which delay took place in deployment of rigs, and on that basis actual production of gas from platform B-121 had to be changed. It is undoubtedly true that the witness has stated that redeployment plan was made keeping in mind several constraints including shortage of casing pipes. Arbitral Tribunal, therefore, took into consideration the aforesaid statement volunteered by the witness that shortage of casing pipes was only one of the several reasons and not the only reason which led to change in deployment of plan or redeployment of rigs Trident-II platform B-121. The Tribunal therefore held that ONGC was not entitled to retain the compensation. However, the Supreme Court held that it would be difficult to prove exact loss or damage which the parties suffer because of the breach thereof. In such a situation, if the parties have pre-estimated such loss after clear understanding, it would be totally unjustified to arrive at the conclusion that party who has committed breach of the contract is not liable to pay compensation. It would be against the specific provisions of Sec. 73 and Sec. 74 of the Indian Contract Act. There was nothing on record that compensation contemplated by the parties was in any way unreasonable. It has been specifically mentioned that it was an agreed genuine pre-estimate of damages duly agreed by the parties. It was also mentioned that the liquidated damages are not by way of penalty. It was also provided in the contract that such damages are to be recovered by the purchaser from the bills for payment of the cost of material submitted by the contractor. No evidence is led by the claimant to establish that stipulated condition was by way of penalty or the compensation contemplated was, in any way, unreasonable. There was no reason for the Tribunal not to rely upon the clear and unambiguous terms of agreement stipulating pre-estimate damages because of delay in supply of goods. Further, while extending the time for delivery of the goods, the respondent was informed that it would be required to pay stipulated damages.

[215] *Oil and Natural Gas Corpn. Ltd.* v. *SAW Pipes Ltd.*, AIR 2003 SC 2629.

[216] AIR 2003 SC 2629.

The Supreme Court, while analysing both Sec. 73 and Sec. 74 of the Contract Act, observed as follows:

1. Terms of the contract are required to be taken into consideration before arriving at the conclusion whether the party claiming damages is entitled to the same.
2. If the terms are clear and unambiguous stipulating the liquidated damages in case of the breach of the contract unless it is held that such estimate of damages/ compensation is unreasonable or is by way of penalty, party who has committed the breach is required to pay such compensation and that is what is provided in Sec. 73 of the Contract Act.
3. Section 74 is to be read along with Sec. 73 and, therefore, in every case of breach of contract, the person aggrieved by the breach is not required to prove actual loss or damage suffered by him before he can claim a decree. The Court is competent to award reasonable compensation in case of breach even if no actual damage is proved to have been in consequences of the breach of a contract.
4. In some contracts, it would be impossible for the Court to assess the compensation arising from breach and if the compensation contemplated is not by way of penalty or unreasonable, the Court can award the same if it is genuine pre-estimate by the parties as the measure of reasonable compensation.

The remedies available under Sec. 73 and Sec. 74 for the breach of contract contemplate a valid and binding agreement between the parties. If the forfeiture clause is contained in an agreement which is void on account of the fact that the parties were not ad idem and were suffering from mistake of fact in respect of a matter which was essential to the contract, it cannot be enforced as the agreement itself is void under Sec. 20 of the Contract Act. A void agreement cannot be split up. None of the parties to the agreement can be permitted to seek enforcement of a part only of the contract through a Court of law. If the agreement is void, all its terms are void and none of the terms, except in certain known exceptions, especially where the clause is treated to constitute a separate and independent agreement, severable from the main agreement, can be enforced separately and independently.[217]

### *Liquidated Damages and Penalty*

In a contract, the parties may name a sum to be payable in the event of breach. If such sum is a genuine pre-estimate of loss it is termed liquidated damages, and if it bears no reflection on the loss suffered, it is termed a penalty. Courts are reluctant to enforce penalty clauses and in such cases the sum stipulated is normally reduced. Generally, the sum fixed upon will be considered either liquidated damages or a penalty according to the intent of the parties. The use of the words 'penalty', 'forfeiture', or 'liquidated damages', will not be decisive of the question if the instrument, taken as a whole, discloses a different intent.

### *The Position in England*

It is stated in a standard work that the specification of damages by the parties does not exclude the rule that damages for loss are expected to compensate for actual loss suffered.

[217] *Tarsem Singh* v. *Sukhminder Singh*, AIR 1998 SC 1400.

The major distinction between English and Indian law upon the point is that under English law, penalties are irrecoverable. In case of a penal clause, damages will be assessed in the usual way, and the plaintiff may even recover a sum greater than the stipulated amount.

Some rules for determining the true nature of the sum stipulated were laid down by Lord Dunedin in *Dunlop Pneumatic Tyre Co. Ltd.* v. *New Garage and Motor Co. Ltd.*[218]

(i) The sum will be a penalty if it is extravagant and unconscionable compared to greatest loss that could conceivably be proved to have followed from the breach;

(ii) The clause will be penal if the breach entails not paying a sum of money and the amount to be paid as damages exceeds the sum which ought to have been paid;

(iii) There is a presumption that the sum named is a penalty, when a single lump sum is made payable in cases of all breaches, irrespective of their nature or magnitude; and

(iv) It is no obstacle to a sum being treated as liquidated damages that the consequences of the breach are such as to make precise pre-estimation impossibility.

(iv) To assist this task of construction various tests have been suggested, which if applicable to the case under consideration, may prove helpful, or even inclusive. Such tests being:

   (a) It will be held to be a penalty if the sum stipulated is extravagant and unconscionable in amount in comparison with the greatest loss that could conceivably be proved to have followed from the breach.

   (b) It will be a penalty when a single lump sum is made payable by way of compensation, on the occurrence of one or more or all of several events, some of which may occasion serious and others but trifling damage.

   (c) It will be a penalty if the sum mentioned in the contract to be paid in case of breach is greater than the sum which ought to have been paid.

However, even under English law, a liquidated damages clause will result in the plaintiff recovering the stipulated sum without being required to prove damage and irrespective of any actual damage, even when actual damage is demonstrably smaller than the stipulated sum.

## Position in India

Statutory codification in India resulted in the elimination of one distinction between liquidated damages and penalties as observed in English law. As per Sec. 74 of the Indian Contract Act, 1872, irrespective of whether the stipulation is by way of liquidated damages or penalty, the Court is entitled to award reasonable compensation, not exceeding the amount named in the contract. As already pointed out, under English law only penalties may be reduced to reasonable compensation.

[218] (1915) AC 79.

The Act also provides illustrations of what may be considered penalties 75% interest in case of default on a bond normally carrying 12% interest, doubling the amount to be delivered.

### *Purposes of Provision of Liquidated Damages*

(a) It facilitates calculation of risks.

(b) It alleviates the difficulties and expenses of proving actual damage or loss and facilitates recovery of damages.

(c) It avoids the difficulties in assessment, even where the consequences of breach are ascertainable. It avoids the risk of under compensation.

(d) It gives the promisee an assurance that he may safely rely on the fulfilment of the promise.

### *Contractual agreement—whether penal in nature?*

The question whether a particular stipulation in a contractual agreement is in the nature of a penalty has to be determined by the Court against the background of various relevant factors, such as the character of the transaction and its special nature, if any, the relative situation of the parties, the rights and obligations accruing from such a transaction under the general law and the intention of the parties in incorporating in the contract the particular stipulation which is contended to be penal in nature. If on such a comprehensive consideration, the Court finds that the real purpose for which the stipulation was incorporated in the contract was that by reason of its burdensome or oppressive character it may operate in terrorem over the promisor so as to drive him to fulfil the contract, then the provision will be held to be one by way of penalty. Where a contract provides for payment of money in instalments and contains also a stipulation that on default being committed in paying any of the instalments the whole sum shall become payable at once and held that the stipulation is nothing but penalty.[219]

## Section 75: Party rightfully rescinding contract, entitled to compensation

A person who rightfully rescinds a contract is entitled to compensation for any damage which he has sustained through the non-fulfilment of the contract.

### Illustration

A, a singer, contracts with B, the manager of a theatre, to sing at his theatre for two nights. In every week during the next two months, and B engages to pay her 100 rupees for each night's performance. On the sixth night, A wilfully absents herself from the theatre, and B, in consequence, rescinds the contract. B is entitled to claim compensation for the damage which he has sustained through the non-fulfilment of the contract.

---

[219] *K.P. Subbarama Sastri* v. *K.S. Raghavan*, AIR 1987 SC 1257.

# Chapter VIII Of Indemnity and Guarantee

## Section 124: "Contract of indemnity" defined

A contract by which one party promises to save the other from loss caused to him by the contract of the promisor himself, or by the conduct of any other person, is called a "contract of indemnity".

### Illustration

A contracts to indemnify B against the consequences of any proceedings which C may take against B in respect of a certain sum of 200 rupees. This is a contract of indemnity.

This section is not so difficult to understand if we can relate it to day-to-day practice. Suppose someone is hired by a newspaper to write articles for them as a freelancer and there would be a contract between the writer and the newspaper company where there would be an indemnity clause so that if anyone writes something against a very important person and that person files a suit against the newspaper for defamatory material, the newspaper can show the indemnity clause that the article writer signed, protecting them from any form of loss caused due to his conduct. Then, the onus of fighting the defamation suit becomes the writer's responsibility. The indemnity clause is usually incorporated in all business contracts. A person who promises to bear the loss is known as indemnifier and the person whose loss is covered is known as indemnified. These types of contracts are mainly formed between insurance companies and their customers.

A contract of indemnity is a contract by which one party promises to save the other from loss caused to him by the conduct of any other person as contemplated in Sec. 124 of the Indian Contract Act. Therefore, it is found that Sec. 124 does not cover the loss caused by events, like fire, cyclone, earthquake, etc. or accidents which do not depend upon the conduct of the indemnifier or any other person.

Indemnity, as per English Law, is a promise to save another harmless from the loss caused as a result of a transaction entered into at the instance of the promisor. It is not necessary under English law that the loss be due to the conduct of a person; the loss could be caused by accidents or forces beyond one's control. Thus, the scope of application under English law of indemnity is wider.

A contract of indemnity either may be express or implied depending upon the circumstances of the case. There are certain provisions in the Contract Act where we can find out the cases of implied indemnity and they are as follows:

1. Section 69 of the Contract Act provides that if a person who is interested in payment of money which another is bound by law to pay and therefore pays it, he is entitled to be indemnified. For example, if the contractor is not paying the wages to the contract labour, the principal employer is bound to pay and recover the money from the contractor.
2. Section 145 provides for right of a surety to claim indemnity from the principal debtor for all sums which he has rightfully paid towards the guarantee.

3. Section 222 provides for liability of the principal to indemnify the agent in respect of all amounts paid by him during the lawful exercise of his authority.

   Indemnity being a contract and regulated under the Contract Act, all necessary pre requisites required to have a valid and enforceable contract must be present.

### *Insurance and principle of indemnity*

A contract of insurance may be defined as a contract by which a person promises to indemnify other, for a consideration called premium, against losses that might happen as a result of the perils or events against which insurance is taken. Thus, is a contract by which the assurer promises to indemnify the insured in case of the happening of the event against which the insurance was taken. It is a normal contract. All the general provisions apply to it. Thus, the requirement of Sec. 10 of the Indian Contract Act also applies and is to be fulfilled.

All types of contracts, except life and personal accident insurance, are contract of indemnity. According to them, the insurer undertakes to indemnify the insured against a loss of the subject matter of insurance due to insured cause. In life insurance, the question of loss, and therefore of its indemnification, does not arise because the loss of life cannot be estimated in terms of money. The principle of indemnity is based on the idea that the assured in the case of loss only shall be compensated against the actual total loss. But if no event happens, the insured has not to receive any amount, so in this case the premium paid by him becomes the profit of the insurer.

### Section 125: Rights of indemnity-holder when sued

The promisee in a contract of indemnity, acting within the scope of his authority, is entitled to recover from the promisor:

1. all damages which he may be compelled to pay in any suit in respect of any matter to which the promise to indemnify applies;
2. all costs which he may be compelled to pay in any such suit, if in bringing of defending it, he did not contravene the orders of the promisor, and acted as it would have been prudent for him to act in the absence of any contract of indemnity, or if the promisor authorised him to bring or defend the suit;
3. all sums which he may have paid under the terms of any compromise of any such suit, if the compromise was not contract to the orders of the promisor, and was one which it would have been prudent for the promisee to make in the absence of any contract of indemnity, or if the promisor authorised him to compromise the suit.

Section 125 deals with the rights of the indemnity-holder and it provides that the promisee in a contract of indemnity, acting within the scope of his authority, is entitled to recover from the promisor damages which he may be compelled to pay in any suit in respect of any matter to which the promise to indemnify applies. It also provides for the indemnity-holder's right to recover costs and other sums as mentioned in sub-sections (2) and (3) of Sec. 125. It is true that, if Sec. 125 is literally construed, the right of the indemnity-holder to sue the promisee under a contract of indemnity would arise only after the indemnity-holder has incurred damages. Sub-section (1) of Sec. 125 provides for a decree for damages and such a decree can be passed only if and after the indemnity-holder has had to incur damages by being compelled to discharge an obligation in respect of which a contract of indemnity has been executed in his favour. But the provisions contained in Sec. 125 is cannot be regarded as an exhaustive statement of the law applicable to contracts of indemnity. If Sec. 125 treated as an exhaustive statement of the law, it would obviously lead to unreasonable consequences. The object of obtaining a contract of indemnity is to protect the indemnity-holder from a claim made by a third party against him. If it is held that despite such a contract of indemnity the indemnity-holder cannot make a claim against the indemnifier unless and until he suffers damage, it might, in a sense, defeat the object of the contract of indemnity itself. That is why it has been held, following equitable principles, that a contract to indemnify does not mean a contract merely to reimburse in respect of monies paid, but it also means in a derivative sense the liability of the indemnifier to save the indemnity-holder from a claim by a third party in respect of which the contract of indemnity has been made. On this view, an indemnity-holder is entitled to sue the indemnifier even before he has incurred any damage, provided of course the indemnity-holder is able to satisfy the Court about the existence of a clear enforceable claim against him and is able to show that it is in respect of such a clear enforceable claim that a contract of indemnity has been executed.[220]

In order to support the above statement, we may refer to the decision of Mr. Justice Chagla, in *Gajanan Moreshwar* v. *Moreshwar Madan*[221] where His Lordship discussed the scope of Secs. 124 and 125 and accordingly observed that Sec. 124 deals only with one particular kind of indemnity which arises from a promise made by the indemnifier to save the indemnified from the loss caused to him by the conduct of the indemnifier himself or by the conduct of any other person; but that it does not deal with those classes of cases where the indemnity arises from loss caused by events or accidents which do not or may not depend upon the conduct of the indemnifier or any other person. In other words, according to the learned Judge, Sec. 124 does not exhaustively deal with all classes and kinds of contracts of indemnity. Similarly, Sec. 125 deals only with the rights of the indemnity-holder in the event of being sued, and it is by no means exhaustive of the rights of the indemnity-holder who has other rights besides those mentioned in the section.

### Right of the indemnity-holder

An indemnity-holder (i.e., indemnified) acting within the scope of his authority is entitled to the following rights:

1. ***Right to recover damages***— He is entitled to recover all damages which he might have been compelled to pay in any suit in respect of any matter covered by the contract.
2. ***Right to recover costs***— He is entitled to recover all costs incidental to the institution and defending of the suit.

[220] *Khetarpal* v. *Madhukar Pictures*, AIR 1956 Bom 106.

[221] AIR 1942 Bom 302.

3. ***Right to recover sums paid under compromise***—He is entitled to recover all amounts which he had paid under the terms of the compromise of such suit. However, the compensation must not be against the directions of the indemnifier. It must be prudent and authorised by the indemnifier.
4. ***Right to sue for specific performance***—He is entitled to sue for specific performance if he has incurred absolute liability and the contract covers such liability.

## Section 126: 'Contract of guarantee', 'surety', 'principal-debtor' and 'creditor'

A "contract of guarantee" is a contract to perform the promise, or discharge the liability, of a third person in case of his default. The person who gives the guarantee is called the "surety", the person in respect of whose default the guarantee is given is called the "principal debtor", and the person to whom the guarantee is given is called the "creditor". A guarantee may be either oral or written.

Under Sec. 126 of the Act, a contract of guarantee is defined as "a contract to perform the promise, or discharge the liability of a third person in case of his default." This type of contract is formed mainly to facilitate borrowing and lending money.

Three parties are involved in this type of contract and they are, surety: is the person by whom the guarantee is given; principal debtor: is the person from whom the assurance is given; and creditor: is the person to whom the guarantee is given.

### *Differences between Contract of Indemnity and Guarantee*

A few important distinctions between a contract of indemnity and a contract of guarantee are as follows:

**Number of parties:** In a contract of indemnity only two parties are involved, whereas in a contract of guarantee, three parties are involved.

**Purpose:** A contract of indemnity is formed to provide compensation of loss. A contract of guarantee is formed to give assurance to the creditor in lieu for his money.

**Nature of liability:** In a contract of indemnity, the indemnifier is the sole person who is held liable. In a contract of guarantee, the liability is shared by the surety and the principal debtor. The principal debtor owes the primary liability and the surety owes the secondary liability.

A promise to be primarily and independently liable for another person's conduct may amount to a contract of indemnity. A contract of guarantee requires concurrence of three persons—the principal debtor, the surety and the creditor—the surety undertaking an obligation at the request express or implied of the principal debtor. The obligation of the surety depends substantially on the principal debtor's default; under a contract of indemnity, liability arises from the loss caused to the promisee by the conduct of the promisor himself or by the conduct of another person.[222]

[222] *Punjab National Bank Ltd.* v. *Bikram Cotton Mills Ltd.*, AIR 1970 SC 1973.

## Section 127: Consideration for guarantee

Anything done, or any promise made, for the benefit of the principal debtor, may be a sufficient consideration to the surety for giving the guarantee.

### Illustrations

(a) B requests A to sell and deliver to him goods on credit. A agrees to do so, provided C will guarantee the payment of the price of the goods. C promises to guarantee the payment in consideration of A's promise to deliver the goods. This is a sufficient consideration for C's promise.

(b) A sells and delivers goods to B. C afterwards requests A to forbear to sue B for the debt for a year, and promises that, if he does so, C will pay for them in default of payment by B. A agrees to forbear as requested. This is a sufficient consideration for C's promise.

(c) A sells and delivers goods to B. C afterwards, without consideration, agrees to pay for them in default of B. The agreement is void.

## Section 128: Surety's liability

The liability of the surety is co-extensive with that of the principal debtor, unless it is otherwise provided by the contract.

### Illustration

A guarantees to B the payment of a bill of exchange by C, the acceptor. The bill is dishonoured by C. A is liable, not only for the amount of the bill, but also for any interest and charges which may have become due on it.

The liability of the sureties is co-extensive with that of the principal debtor. Consequently, the creditor can proceed against the principal debtor or against the sureties, unless it is otherwise provided in the contract. The same should also be the principle with regard to the rights and liabilities between co-sureties as well. A co-surety cannot insist that the creditor should proceed either against the principal debtor or against other sureties before proceeding against him.[223]

Under Sec. 128, save as provided in the contract, the liability of the surety is co-extensive with that of the principal debtor. The surety thus becomes liable to pay the entire amount. His liability is immediate. It is not deferred until the creditor exhausts his remedies against the principal debtor. In the absence of some special equity, the surety has no right to restrain an action against the him by the creditor on the ground that the principal is solvent or that the creditor may have relief against the principal in some other proceedings. Likewise, where the creditor has obtained a decree against the surety and the principal, the surety has no right to restrain execution against him until the creditor has exhausted his remedies against the principal.[224]

[223] *Kerala State Financial Enterprises Ltd.* v. *C.J. Thampi*, AIR 2000 Ker 36.

[224] *Bank of Bihar Ltd.* v. *Dr. Damodar Prasad*, AIR 1969 SC 297.

## Section 129: 'Continuing guarantee'

A guarantee which extends to a series of transaction, is called a "continuing guarantee".

### Illustrations

(a) *A*, in consideration that *B* will employ *C* in collecting the rents of *B's* zamindari, promises *B* to be responsible, to the amount of 5,000 rupees, for the due collection and payment by *C* of those rents. This is a continuing guarantee.

(b) *A* guarantees payment to *B*, a tea-dealer, to the amount of £100, for any tea he may from time to time supply to *C*. *B* supplies *C* with tea of above the value of £100, and *C* pays *B* for it. Afterwards, *B* supplies *C* with tea of the value of £200. *C* fails to pay. The guarantee given by *A* was a continuing guarantee, and he is accordingly liable to *B* to the extent of £100.

(c) *A* guarantees payment to *B* of the price of five sacks of flour to be delivered by *B* to *C* and to be paid for in a month. *B* delivers five sacks to *C*. *C* pays for them. Afterwards *B* delivers four sacks to *C*, which *C* does not pay for. The guarantee given by *A* was not a continuing guarantee, and accordingly he is not liable for the price of the four sacks.

A guarantor's liability depends upon the terms of his contract. A 'continuing guarantee' is different from an ordinary guarantee. There is also a difference between a guarantee which stipulates that the guarantor is liable to pay only on a demand by the creditor, and a guarantee which does not contain such a condition. Further, depending on the terms of the guarantee, the liability of a guarantor may be limited to a particular sum, instead of the liability being to the same extent as that of the principal debtor. The liability to pay may arise, on the principal debtor and the guarantor, at the same time or at different points of time. A claim may be even time-barred against the principal debtor, but still enforceable against the guarantor. The parties may agree that the liability of a guarantor shall arise at a later point of time than that of the principal debtor.[225]

The surety has given a continuing guarantee, limited in amount, to secure the floating balance which may from time to time be due from the principal debtor to the creditor; the guarantee is *prima facie* to be construed as being part only of the debt. A continuing guarantee may even be for the fixed period. It is well settled that the guarantor cannot be made liable beyond the terms of the agreements.[226]

## Section 130: Revocation of continuing guarantee

A continuing guarantee may at any time be revoked by the surety, as to future transactions, by notice to the creditor.

### Illustrations

(a) A, in consideration of B's discounting, at, A's request, bills of exchange for C, guarantees to B, for twelve months, the due payment of all such bills to the extent

[225] *Syndicate Bank* v. *Channaveerappa Beleri*, AIR 2006 SC 1874.

[226] *Aditya Narayan Chouresia* v. *Bank of India*, AIR 2000 Pat 222.

of 5,000 rupees. B discounts bills for C to the extent of 2,000 rupees. Afterwards, at the end of three months, A revokes the guarantee. This revocation discharges A from all liability to B for any subsequent discount. But A is liable to B for the 2,000 rupees, on default of C.

(b) A guarantees to B, to the extent of 10,000 rupees, that C shall pay all the bills that B shall draw upon him. B draws upon C, C accepts the bill. A gives notice of revocation. C dishonours the bill at maturity. A is liable upon his guarantee.

In *Sita Ram Gupta* v. *Punjab National Bank*[227], the only question that was raised on behalf of the appellant was that in view of the statutory provision under Sec. 130 of the Indian Contract Act, whether the High Court was justified in holding that the appellant who was a guarantor of the loan advanced to the defendant nos. 1 to 4 was liable to pay the decretal amount on the ground that the appellant had revoked the guarantee before such loan was actually paid to the defendant Nos. 1 to 4 and long before the suit was filed by the bank against the defendants for recovery of such loan.

Before dealing with the question as stated above, it is essential to have a look the agreement where the guarantor specifically agreed to:

> The Guarantors hereby declare that this guarantee shall be a continuing guarantee and shall not be considered as cancelled or in any way affected by the fact that at any time the said accounts may show no liability against the Borrower or may even show a credit in his favour but shall continue to be guarantee and remain in operation in respect of all subsequent transactions.

Keeping the agreement of guarantee as stated above, the fact of the present case is that the guarantee issued by the appellant to the Bank was subsequently cancelled by his letter dated 31 July, 1980 written to the Manager of the Bank and in that view of the matter, the appellant sought to substantiate his case that since his guarantee had stood revoked before the loan was in fact taken by the defendants from the bank. The contention of the appellant was that in view of Sec. 130 of the Act, he was not liable to pay the loan taken by the defendants in respect of which the appellant was a guarantor. The trial Court dismissed the suit against the appellant and in appeal by the Bank, the High Court had reversed the decree passed by the trial Court and granted decree in favour of the Bank. It was also an admitted fact that subsequent to the revocation of guarantee by the appellant, there were transactions in respect of the loan between the defendant and the bank. The suit was filed for recovery of loan by the Bank against the appellant as well as the other defendants.

The learned counsel appearing for the appellant, relying on Sec. 130 of the Act, sought to argue that in view of the fact that Sec. 130 clearly provides for revocation of a continuing guarantee as to future transactions by notice to the creditor and as in the present case, the guarantee was revoked long before the loan was given and the suit filed, the appellant was not liable to pay the decretal amount to the Bank. Accordingly, he submitted that the High Court was not justified in reversing the judgment of the trial Court and in decreeing the suit against the appellant.

[227] AIR 2008 SC 2416.

The Supreme Court held that there cannot be any dispute that the appellant had clearly agreed that the guarantee that he had entered into with the Bank was a continuing guarantee and the same was to continue and remain in operation for all subsequent transactions. Having entered into the agreement in the manner indicated above, it was, therefore, not open to the appellant to turn around and say that in view of Sec. 130 of the Act, since the guarantee was revoked before the loan was advanced to defendants, he was not liable to pay the decretal amount as a guarantor to the Bank as his guarantee had already stood revoked. The Court further observed that in view of the nature of guarantee entered into by the appellant with the Bank, the statutory provision under Sec. 130 of the Act shall not come to his help.

### Section 131: Revocation of continuing guarantee by surety's death

The death of the surety operates, in the absence of any contract to the contrary, as a revocation of a continuing guarantee, so far as regards future transactions.

### Section 132: Liability of two persons, primarily liable, not affected by arrangement between them that one shall be surety on other's default

Where two persons contract with third person to undertake a certain liability, and also contract with each other that one of them shall be liable only on the default of the other, the third person not being a party to such contract the liability of each of such two persons to the third person under the first contract is not affected by the existence of the second contract, although such third person may have been aware of its existence.

### Illustration

*A* and *B* make a joint and several promissory note to *C*. *A* makes it, in fact, as surety for *B*, and *C* knows this at the time when the note is made. The fact that *A*, to the knowledge of *C*, made the note as surety for *B*, is no answer to a suit by *C* against *A* upon the note.

### Section 133: Discharge of surety by variance in terms of contract

Any variance made without the surety's consent, in the terms of the contract between the principal debtor and the creditor, discharges the surety as to transactions subsequent to the variance.

### Illustrations

(a) A becomes surety to C for B's conduct as manager in C's bank. Afterwards, B and C contract, without A's consent, that B's salary shall be raised, and that he shall become liable for one-fourth of the losses on overdrafts. B allows a customer to over-draw, and the bank loses a sum of money.

A is discharged from his suretyship by the variance made without his consent, and is not liable to make good this loss.

(b) A guarantees C against the misconduct of B in an office to which B is appointed by C, and of which the duties are defined by an Act of the Legislature. By a subsequent Act, the nature of the office is materially altered. Afterwards, B misconducts himself. A is discharged by the change from future liability under his guarantee, though the misconduct of B is in respect of a duty not affected by the later Act.

(c) C agrees to appoint B as his clerk to sell goods at a yearly salary, upon A's becoming surety to C for B's duly accounting for moneys received by him as such clerk. Afterwards, without A's knowledge or consent, C and B agree that B should be paid by a commission on the goods sold by him and not by a fixed salary. A is not liable for subsequent misconduct of B.

(d) A gives to C a continuing guarantee to the extent of 3,000 rupees for any oil supplied by C to B on credit. Afterwards B becomes embarrassed, and, without the knowledge of A, B and C contract that C shall continue to supply B with oil for ready money, and that the payments shall be applied to the then, existing debts between B and C. A is not liable on his guarantee for any goods supplied after this new arrangement.

(e) C contracts to lend B 5,000 rupees on the 1st March. A guarantees repayment. C pays the 5,000 rupees to B on the 1st January; A is discharged from his liability, as the contract has been varied, inasmuch as C might sue B for the money before the first of March.

## Section 134: Discharge of surety by release or discharge of principal debtor

The surety is discharged by any contract between the creditor and the principal debtor, by which the principal debtor is released, or by any act or omission of the creditor, the legal consequence of which is the discharge of the principal debtor.

### Illustrations

(a) A gives a guarantee to C for goods to be supplied by C to B. C supplies goods to B, and afterwards B becomes embarrassed and contracts with his creditors (including C) to assign to them his property in consideration of their releasing him from their demands. Here B is released from his debt by the contract with C, and A is discharged from his suretyship.

(b) A contracts with B to grow a crop of indigo on A's land and to deliver it to B at a fixed rate, and C guarantees A's performance of this contract. B diverts a stream of water which is necessary for irrigation of A's land, and thereby prevents him from raising the indigo. C is no longer liable on his guarantee.

(c) A contracts with B for a fixed price to build a house for B within a stipulated time, B supplying the necessary timber. C guarantees A's performance of the contract. B omits to supply the timber. C is discharged from his suretyship.

Under Sec. 128 of the Contract Act, the liability of the surety is co-extensive with that of the principal debtor unless it is otherwise provided by the contract. A surety is no doubt discharged under Sec. 134 of the Act by any contract between the creditor and the principal debtor by which the principal debtor is released or by any act or omission of the creditor, the legal consequence of which is the discharge of the principal debtor. But a discharge which the principal debtor may secure by operation of law in bankruptcy (or in liquidation proceedings in the case of a company) does not absolve the surety of his liability.[228]

## Section 135: Discharge of surety when creditor compounds with, gives time to, or agrees not to sue, principal debtor

A contract between the creditor and the principal debtor, by which the creditor makes a composition with, or promises to give time, or not to sue, the principal debtor, discharges the surety, unless the surety assents to such contract.

The reason why an agreement to give time discharges the surety is because if after making such an agreement the creditor were to sue the surety, the latter would at once be turned on the principal debtor in breach of the agreement to given time so that the effect of such an agreement is to prevent the surety from either requiring the creditor to call upon the principal debtor to pay off the debt or himself having off the debt, and then suing the principal debtor, thereby causing prejudice to the surety.[229]

The agreement between a creditor Bank and the principal debtor provided that the latter should be responsible for the quality and quantity of goods pledged with the Bank and also for the correctness of the statements and returns furnished to the Bank from time to time. The goods pledged were further declared and agreed to be not actually weighed or valued in order to verify the returns furnished by the debtor. When on one occasion the Bank on actual weighment found some deficit in the quantity of goods, it granted some time for the principal debtor to make up the deficiency. It is held that the Bank's act of giving time to the principal debtor considered in the light of the above terms in the agreement did not tantamount to giving of time within the meaning of Sec. 135 of the Contract Act so as could exonerate the surety.[230]

## Section 136: Surety not discharged when agreement made with third person to give time to, or agree not to sue, principal debtor

Where a contract to give time to the principal debtor is made by the creditor with a third person, and not with the principal debtor, the surety is not discharged.

### Illustration

*C*, the holder of an overdue bill of exchange drawn by *A* as surety for *B*, and accepted by *B*, contracts with *M* to give to *B*. *A* is not discharged.

## Section 137: Creditor's forbearance to sue does not discharge surety

Mere forbearance on the part of the creditor to sue the principal debtor or to enforce any other remedy against him, does not, in the absence of any provision in the guarantee to the contrary, discharge the surety.

[228] *M.S.E.B., Bombay* v. *Official Liquidator, H.C., Ernakulam*, AIR 1982 SC 1497.
[229] *Rouse* v. *Bradford Banking Co.*, 1894-2 Ch 32 CA at p. 75. per A L. Smith, L J.
[230] *Amrit Lal Goverdhan Lalan* v. *State Bank of Travancore*, AIR 1968 SC 1432.

### Illustration

*B* owes to *C* a debt guaranteed by *A*. The debt becomes payable. *C* does not sue *B* for a year after the debt has become payable. *A* is not discharged from his suretyship.

### Section 138: Release of one co-surety does not discharge others

Where there are co-sureties, a release by the creditor of one of them does not discharge the others neither does set free the surety so released from his responsibility to the other sureties.

The liability of the sureties under the law is joint and several. If a creditor seeks to enforce the surety bond against some only of the joint sureties, the other sureties will not on that account be discharged, nor will release by the creditor of one of them discharge the other vide Secs. 137 and 138 of the Contract Act. But the fact that the surety bond is enforceable against each surety severally, and that it is open to the creditor to release one or more of the joint sureties, does not alter the true character of an adjudication of the Court when proceedings are commenced to enforce the covenants of the bond against all the sureties. We are not concerned in this appeal with the privilege which a creditor may exercise, but with the effect of an adjudication which the Court has made in a proceeding to enforce the covenant of the Bond. The mere fact that the obligation arising under a covenant may be enforced severally against all the covenantors does not make the liability of each covenantor distinct. It is true that in enforcement of the claim of the decree holder, the properties belonging to the sureties individually may be sold separately. But that is because the liability arises under distinct transactions.[231]

### Section 139: Discharge of surety by creditor's act or omission impairing surety's eventual remedy

If the creditor does any act which is inconsistent with the right of the surety, or omits to do any act which his duty to the surety requires him to do, and the eventual remedy of the surety himself against the principal debtor is thereby impaired, the surety is discharged.

### Illustrations

(a) B contracts to build a ship for C for a given sum, to be paid by instalments as the work reaches certain stages. A becomes surety to C for B's due performance of the contract. C, without the knowledge of A, prepays to B the last two instalments. A is discharged by this prepayment.

(b) C lends money to B on the security of a joint and several promissory note made in C's favour by B, and by A as surety for B, together with a bill of sale of B's furniture, which gives power to C to sell the furniture, and apply the proceeds in discharge of the note. Subsequently, C sells the furniture, but, owing to his misconduct and wilful negligence, only a small price is realised. A is discharged from liability on the note.

[231] *Chand* v. *M/s. Jagdish Pershad Kishan Chand*, AIR 1966 SC 1427.

(c) A puts M as apprentice to B, and gives a guarantee to B for M's fidelity. B promises on his part that he will at least once a month, see M make up the cash. B omits to see this done as promised, and M embezzles. A is not liable to B on his guarantee.

### Section 140: Rights of surety on payment or performance

Where a guaranteed debt has become due, or default of the principal debtor to perform a guaranteed duty has taken place, the surety upon payment or performance of all that he is liable for, is invested with all the rights which the creditor had against the principal debtor.

This section embodies the general rule of equity which provides that the surety would be entitled to every remedy which the creditor has against the principal debtor; to enforce every security and all means of payment, to stand in the place of the creditor, not only through the medium of contract, but even by means of securities entered into without the knowledge of the surety having a right to have those securities transferred to him, though there was no stipulation for that; and to avail himself of all those securities against the debtor. This right of a surety also stands not upon contract, but upon a principle of natural justice. The language of the section which employs the words *"is invested with all the rights which the creditor had against the principal debtor"* makes it plain that even without the necessity of a transfer, the law vests those rights in the surety.

### Section 141: Surety's right to benefit of creditor's securities

A surety is entitled to the benefit of every security which the creditor has against the principal debtor at the time when the contract of suretyship entered into, whether the surety knows of the existence of such security or not; and if the creditor loses, or without the consent of the existence of such security or not; and if the creditor loses, or without the consent of the surety, parts with such security, the surety, the surety is discharged to the extent of the value of the security.

### Illustrations

(a) C, advances to B, his tenant, 2,000 rupees on the guarantee of A. C has also a further security for the 2,000 rupees by a mortgage of B's furniture. C, cancels the mortgage. B becomes insolvent and C sues A on his guarantee. A is discharged from liability to the amount of the value of the furniture.

(b) C, a creditor, whose advance to B is secured by a decree, receives also a guarantee for that advance from A. C afterwards takes B's goods in execution under the decree, and then, without the knowledge of A, withdraws the execution. A is discharged.

(c) A, as surety for B, makes a bond jointly with B to C, to secure a loan from C to B. Afterwards, C obtains from B a further security for the same debt. Subsequently, C gives up the further security. A is not discharged.

The Supreme Court in *State of Madhya Pradesh* v. *Kaluram*[232] observed that the expression *"security"* in this section is not used in any technical sense; it includes all rights which the creditor has against the property at the date of the contract. The surely is entitled on payment of the debt or performance of all that he is liable for to the benefit of the rights of the creditor against the principal debtor which arise out of the transaction which gives rise to the right or liability. The surety is therefore on payment of the amount due by the principal debtor entitled to be put in the same position in which the creditor stood in relation to the principal debtor. If the creditor has lost or parted with the security without the consent of the surety, the latter is by the express provision contained in Sec. 141 discharged to the extent of the value of the security lost or parted with.

The expression *'if creditor loses security in S. 141 means'* and implies a voluntary act by reason whereof the creditor loses the security and which thus tantamounts to be without the consent of the surety. The expression *'or'* in between the words *'creditor loses'* and *'without the consent of the surety'* and the coma read in its proper sphere after the word *'loses'* and surety stands out to be significant since the same qualifies only the later part of the second limb, namely, parting with such security. The expression *'creditor loses'* cannot mean and imply an involuntary act but by reason of an act which is attributable to the creditor. The second alternative, parting with security without the knowledge of the surety is a contra situation but affords a meaning to the words used in the first para, to wit, *'the creditor loses'*. Section 141 would lose its efficacy and the Act would render itself totally nugatory if the expression is held as contemplating both voluntary and involuntary acts of the creditor. A definite volition is required to come within the ambit of Sec. 141. The heading of Sec. 141 also lends, though not normally a part of the statutory provision, assistance in interpreting the statutory intent since heading always serves as a guide to depict the intention. The contract of guarantee, though not a contract regarding a primary transaction, it is an independent transaction containing independent and reciprocal obligations. It is on principal to principal basis and by reason wherefore the Statute has provided both the creditor and the guarantor some relief as specified in Secs. 130–141 of the Contract Act. Section 141 thus involves an issue of a deliberate action on the part of the creditor and not a mere fortuitous situation beyond the control of the creditor.[233]

In a case where a Bank has given cash credit facility to a businessman to the tune of ₹75,000 as against two securities offered by him, namely, (1) the pledge of goods to be kept under lock and key under supervision of the Bank and (ii) personal guarantee of the surety. The pledge and the personal guarantee were not two independent transactions but they formed part and parcel of one composite transaction. The surety himself agreed to give personal guarantee on the specific understanding and with the full knowledge of the Bank that the principal debtor was offering another security, namely, pledge of goods. The surety in good faith contracted to offer personal guarantee on the clear understanding that the principal debtor has offered security by way of pledge of goods and the goods were to be in the custody of the creditor Bank. It was concurrently found that the Bank was utterly negligent with regard to the safe keeping and handling of pledged goods and the security of pledged goods was lost on account of the negligence of the Bank. It is held in

[232] AIR 1967 SC 1105.

[233] *I. F. C. I. Ltd.* v. *Cannanore Spg. and Wvg. Mills Ltd.*, AIR 2002 SC 1841.

the circumstances that Sec. 141 would be attracted. Section 141 comprehends a situation where the debtor has offered more than one security, one of which is the personal guarantee of the surety. Even if the surety of personal guarantee is not aware of any other security offered by the principal debtor, yet once the right of the surety against the principal debtor is impaired by any action or inaction which implies negligence appearing from lack of supervision undertaken in the contract, the surety would be discharged under the combined operation of Secs. 139 and 141 of the Act. In any event, if the creditor loses or without the consent of the surety parts with the security, the surety is discharged to the extent of the security lost as provided by Sec. 141.

### Section 142: Guarantee obtained by misrepresentation, invalid

Any guarantee which has been obtained by means of misrepresentation made by the creditor, or with his knowledge and assent, concerning a material part of the transaction, is invalid.

### Section 143: Guarantee obtained by concealment, invalid

Any guarantee which the creditor has obtained by means of keeping silence as to material circumstances is invalid.

#### Illustrations

(a) A engages B as clerk to collect money for him. B fails to account for some of his receipts, and A in consequence calls upon him to furnish security for his duly accounting. C gives his guarantee for B's duly accounting. A does not acquaint C with B's previous conduct. B afterwards makes default. The guarantee is invalid.

(b) A guarantees to C payment for iron to be supplied by him to B to the amount of 2,000 tons. B and C have privately agreed that B should pay five rupees per ton beyond the market price, such excess to be applied in liquidation of an old debt. This agreement is concealed from A. A is not liable as a surety.

### Section 144: Guarantee on contract that creditor shall not act on it until co-surety joins

Where a person gives a guarantee upon a contract that the creditor shall not act upon it until another person has jointed in it as co-surety, the guarantee is not valid that other person does not join.

### Section 145: Implied promise to indemnify surety

In every contract of guarantee there is an implied promise by the principal debtor to indemnify the surety, and the surety is entitled to recover from the principal debtor whatever sum he has rightfully paid under the guarantee, but no sums which he has paid wrongfully.

### Illustrations

(a) B is indebted to C, and A is surety for the debt. C demands payment from A, and on his refusal sues him for the amount. A defends the suit, having reasonable grounds for doing so, but he is compelled to pay the amount of debt with costs. He can recover from B the amount paid by him for costs, as well as the principal debt.

(b) C lends B a sum of money, and A, at the request of B, accepts a bill of exchange drawn by B upon A to secure the amount. C, the holder of the bill, demands payment of it from A, and, on A's refusal to pay, sues him upon the bill. A, not having reasonable grounds for so doing, defends the suit, and has to pay the amount of the bill and costs. He can recover from B the amount of the bill, but not the sum paid for costs, as there was no real ground for defending the action.

(c) A guarantees to C, to the extent of 2,000 rupees, payment for rice to be supplied by C to B. C supplies to B rice to a less amount than 2,000 rupees, but obtains from A payment of the sum of 2,000 rupees in respect of the rice supplied. A cannot recover from B more than the price of the rice actually supplied.

### Section 146: Co-surety liable to contribute equally

Where two or more persons are co-sureties for the same debt or duty, either jointly or severally, and whether under the same or different contract, and whether with or without the knowledge of each other the co-sureties, in the absence of any contract to the contrary, are liable, as between themselves, to pay each an equal share of the whole debt, or of that part of it which remains unpaid by the principal debtor.

### Illustrations

(a) A, B and C are sureties to D for the sum of 3,000 rupees lent to E. E makes default in payment. A, B and C are liable, as between themselves, to pay 1,000 rupees each.

(b) A, B and C are sureties to D for the sum of 1,000 rupees lent to E, and there is a contract between A, B and C that A is to be responsible to the extent of one-quarter, B to the extent of one-quarter, and C to the extent of one-half. E makes default in payment. As between the sureties, A is liable to pay 250 rupees, B 250 rupees, and C 500 rupees.

### Section 147: Liability of co-sureties bound in different sums

Co-sureties who are bound in different sums are liable to pay equally as far as the limits of their respective obligations permit.

### Illustrations

(a) A, B and C, as sureties for D, enter into three several bonds, each in a different penalty, namely, A in the penalty of 10,000 rupees, B in that of 20,000 rupees,

C in that of 40,000 rupees, conditioned for D's duly accounting to E. D makes default to the extent of 30,000 rupees. A, B and C are liable to pay 10,000 rupees.

(b) A, B and C, as sureties for D, enter into three several bonds, each in a different penalty, namely, A in the penalty of 10,000 rupees, B in that of 20,000 rupees, C in that of 40,000 rupees, conditioned for D's duly accounting to E. D makes default to the extent of 40,000 rupees. A is liable to pay 10,000 rupees, and B and C 15,000 rupees each.

(c) A, B and C, as sureties for D, enter into three several bonds, each in a different penalty, namely, A in the penalty of 10,000 rupees, B in that of 20,000 rupees, C in that of 40,000 rupees, conditioned for D's duly accounting to E. D makes default to the extent of 70,000 rupees. A, B and C have to pay the full penalty of his bond.

# Chapter IX Of Bailment

The term *bailment* is derived from the French word *bailor*, which means "to deliver". It is generally considered to be a contractual relationship since the bailor and the bailee, either expressly or impliedly, bind themselves to act according to particular terms. The bailee receives only control or possession of the property while the bailor retains the ownership interests in it. During the specific period a bailment exists, the bailee's interest in the property is superior to that of all others, including the bailor, unless the bailee violates some terms of the agreement. Once the purpose for which the property has been delivered has been accomplished, the property will be returned to the bailor or otherwise disposed of pursuant to the bailor's directions.

A bailment is not the same as a sale, which is an intentional transfer of ownership of personal property in exchange for something of value. A bailment involves only a transfer of possession or custody, not of ownership. A rental or lease of personal property might be a bailment, depending upon the agreement of the parties. A bailment is created when a parking garage attendant, the bailee, is given the keys to a motor vehicle by its owner, the bailor. The owner, in addition to renting the space, has transferred possession and control of the vehicle by relinquishing its keys to the attendant. If the keys were not made available and the vehicle was locked, the arrangement would be strictly a rental or lease, since there was no transfer of possession. Delivery of property for repair or safekeeping is also typical situations in which a bailment is created. Post Office may be considered as the bailee in the case of VPP articles.[234]

Bailment is a common type of business arrangement. In its simplest form, it is an arrangement between a person (a bailor) who owns or lawfully possesses goods and another person (a bailee) who is given possession of the goods for a specific purpose. Many business activities involve the transfer of possession of goods. For example, the storage of goods or equipment in a warehouse by a business is a bailment transaction because the ownership of the goods remains with the business and the warehouse operator holds the goods for the owner but does not have title to the goods. Similarly, where goods are

[234] *Commissioner of Income Tax, Delhi* v. *M/s P.M. Rathod and Co.*, AIR 1959 SC 1394.

shipped by a common carrier, such as a highway truck transport company, the carrier of the goods has possession of them only as a bailee. The carrier is responsible for the goods until they are delivered to the person or business named as the receiver. Other examples of business transactions that include a bailment would be transactions that require goods to be left with repair services, such as motor vehicle repair garages, jewellery shops, and appliance repair facilities.

Bailment is the process of placing personal property or goods in the temporary custody or control of another. The custodian or holder of the property, who's responsible for the safe keeping and return of the property, is know as the bailee. The person who delivers or transfers the property to the bailee is known as the bailor. For a bailment to be valid, the bailee must have actual physical control of the property with the intent to possess it. The bailee is generally not entitled to the use of the property while it's in his possession. A bailor can demand to have the property returned to him at any time.

## Section 148: "Bailment", "bailor" and "bailee" defined

A "bailment" is the delivery of goods by one person to another for some purpose, upon a contract that they shall, when the purpose is accomplished, be returned or otherwise disposed of according to the direction of the person delivering them. The person delivering the goods is called the "bailor". The person to whom they are delivered is called the "bailee".

***Explanation*:** If a person already in possession of the goods of other contracts hold them as a bailee, he thereby becomes the bailee, and the owner becomes the bailor of such goods, although they may not have been delivered by way of bailment.

### *Essential Features*

The definition of bailment as stated above prescribes three essential elements to constitute a contract of bailment and they are as follows:

**(1)** ***Delivery of goods*:** Here the delivery of goods means delivery of possession of goods. Delivery of possession for this purpose must be distinguished from mere custody. One who has custody without possession of goods is not a bailee. In *Ultzen* v. *Nicolls*[235], the plaintiff went to a restaurant for dining and when he entered the room, the waiter took his coat and hung it on a hook behind him. When the plaintiff arose to leave, the coat was gone. It was held that the waiter voluntarily took the responsibility of keeping the coat while the customer was dining and was thus a bailee. Therefore, he was liable to return it.

For instance, if the plaintiff had instructed the waiter where and how the coat should be kept, perhaps, the result would have been altogether different. In *Kaliaperumal Pillai* v. *Visalakshmi*,[236] a woman gave some gold to a jeweller to make jewellery. Every evening she used to take the unfinished jewels, put them in a box, lock the box and take the keys of the box with her while leaving the box at the goldsmith. One morning, when she opened the box the gold was gone. It was held that, in the night, the possession of the gold was not

[235] (1894) 1 QB 92.

[236] AIR 1938 Mad 32.

with the jeweler but with the plaintiff because she locked the box and kept the keys with her. The Madras High Court held that leaving the box in a room in the defendant's house and the plaintiff herself taking the key does not amount to delivery within the meaning of Sec. 149 of the Act which reads as follows:

> Delivery to bailee how made. The delivery to the bailee may be made by doing anything which has the effect of putting the goods in the possession of the intended bailee or of any person authorised to hold them on his behalf.

Referring to explanation attached to Sec. 148, which reads:

***Explanation***: If a person already in possession of the goods of another contract to hold them as a bailee, he thereby becomes the bailee, and the owner becomes the bailor of such goods, although they may not have been delivered by way of bailment.

Therefore, it may be safely said that delivery of possession may be of two types:

(1) Actual delivery

(2) Constructive delivery

Delivery is an act that shows the person's intention to transfer ownership—if the goods are physically given to the person buying them, then that is actual delivery. Constructive delevery takes place where there is no change of physical possession, goods remaining where they are. For example, delivery of a railway receipt or bill of lading amounts to constructive delivery. Where a person pledged cinema projector with the bank but the bank allowed him to keep the projector so as to keep the cinema hall running, the Andhra Pradesh High Court held that this was constructive delivery because something was done that changed the legal possession of the projector even though the physical possession was with the person, the legal possession with the bank.[237] A question that arose before the Supreme Court for consideration in *N.R. Srinivasa Iyer* v. *New India Assurance Co. Ltd. Madras*[238] was whether it would be deemed to be delivery under Sec. 148 of the Act and thereby the insurance company would be considered as bailee while shifting a damaged car for repair to the nearest garage. The Court held that there is an explanation appended to Sec. 148 which provides that if a person already in possession of the goods of another contracts to hold them as a bailee, he thereby becomes the bailee, and the owner becomes the bailor of such goods, although they may not have been delivered by way of bailment. Section 149 provides that the delivery to the bailee may be made by doing anything which has the effect of putting the goods in the possession of the intended bailee or of any person authorised to hold them on his behalf. The Court further held that once the damaged car was taken by the insurance company the company became the bailee and the garage would be considered as sub-bailee.

**(2)** ***Delivery should be upon contract***: In bailment, the delivery of goods is upon a contract and once the purpose is accomplished, such goods shall be returned to the bailor. In other words, there cannot be a bailment even if the possession of the goods is obtained by someone other than the contract. The Allahabad High Court has rightly decided in

[237] *Bank of Chittor* v. *Narsimbulu* , AIR 1966 AP 163.

[238] AIR 1983 SC 899.

*Ram Gulam* v. *Govt. of UP*[239] where the plaintiff's ornaments were seized by police on the suspicion that they were stolen. The ornaments were later on stolen from the custody of the police and the plaintiff sued the Government for returning the ornaments. It was held that the goods were not given to the police under any contract and thus there was no bailment.

The decision in the *Ram Gulam's* case was criticised and, finally, the Supreme Court in *State of Gujarat* v. *Memon Mahomed Haji Hasan*[240] held that bailment can happen even without an explicit contract. In this case, certain motor vehicles were seized by the State under the Sea Customs Act, which were then damaged. The Court held that the Government was indeed the bailee and the State was responsible for proper care of the goods. The Court observed as follows:

> "Bailment is dealt with by the Contract Act only in cases where it arises from a contract but it is not correct to say that there cannot be a bailment without an enforceable contract."[241]

**(3)** ***Delivery should be upon some purpose*:** In contract of bailment where the goods are delivered from one person to another, it should be upon some purpose. Once the purpose of the bailment has been completed, the bailee usually must return the property to the bailor, or account for it, depending upon the terms of the contract. If, through no fault of his or her own, the return of the property is delayed or becomes impossible—for example, when it is lost during the course of the bailment or when a hurricane blows the property into the ocean—the bailee will not be held liable for non-delivery on demand. In all other situations, however, the bailee will be responsible for the Tort of conversion for unjustifiable failure to redeliver the property as well as its unauthorised use.

### Types of bailment

There are three types of bailment:

(1) ***For the benefit of the bailor and the bailee*:** A bailment for the mutual benefit of the parties is created when there is an exchange of performances between the parties. A bailment for the repair of an item is a bailment for mutual benefit when the bailee receives a fee in exchange for his or her work.

(2) ***For the sole benefit of the bailor*:** A bailor receives the sole benefit from a bailment when a bailee acts gratuitously—for example, if a restaurant, a bailee, provides an attended coatroom free of charge to its customers, the bailors. By virtue of the terms of the bailment, the bailee agrees to act without any expectation of compensation.

(3) ***For the sole benefit of the bailee*:** A bailment is created for the sole benefit of the bailee when both parties agree the property temporarily in the bailee's custody is to be used to his or her own advantage without giving anything to the bailor in return. The loan of a book from a library is a bailment for the sole benefit of the bailee.

[239] AIR 1950 All 206.

[240] AIR 1967 SC 1885.

[241] *Id* at p. 1888 per Shelat, J.

## Section 149: Delivery to bailee how made

The delivery to be bailee may be made by doing anything which has the effect of putting the goods in the possession of the intended bailee or of any person authorised to hold them on his behalf.

## Section 150: Bailor's duty to disclose faults in goods bailed

The bailor is bound to disclose to the bailee faults in the goods bailed, of which the bailor is aware, and which materially interfere with the use of them, or expose the bailee to extraordinary risk; and if he does not make such disclosure, he is responsible for damage arising to the bailee directly from such faults.

If the goods are bailed for hire, the bailor is responsible for such damage, whether he was or was not aware of the existence of such faults in the goods bailed.

### Illustrations

(a) A lends a horse, which he knows to be vicious, to B. He does not disclose the fact that the horse is vicious. The horse runs away. B is thrown and injured. A is responsible to B for damage sustained.

(b) A hires a carriage of B. The carriage is unsafe, though B is not aware of it, and A is injured. B is responsible to A for the injury.

## Section 151: Care to be taken by bailee

In all cases of bailment the bailee is bound to take as much care of the goods bailed to him as a man of ordinary prudence would, under similar circumstances, take of his own goods of the same bulk, quantity and value as the goods bailed.

Section 151 prescribes a uniform standard of care for all cases of bailment. In *Blount* v. *War Office*,[242] where a house belonging to the plaintiff was requisitioned by the War Office and he was allowed to keep his certain articles in a room of the house, which he locked. The troops who occupied the house were not well controlled and broke into the room causing damage and theft of the articles. It was held that War office did not take care of the house as an owner would and held the War Office liable for the loss.

However, the bailee would not be held responsible, in the absence of any special contract, for the loss, destruction or deterioration of the thing bailed, if he has taken the amount of care of it as described in Sec. 151 of the Act. It is not possible to lay down the standard of care the bailee has to take. It would be decided and will vary from case to case. However, it is very much clear that the bailee has to take reasonable care of the goods as a man of ordinary prudence would take of his own goods under the similar circumstances. If the bailee can prove that he has taken reasonable care that he requires to take, he may not be held liable for the loss of goods bailed. In *Jain & Son* v. *Comeron*[243] the plaintiff stayed in a hotel and kept his belonging in his room which was stolen. The hotel was held liable because they did not take care of its security as an owner would.

[242] (1953) 1 All ER 1071.

[243] AIR 1922 All 735.

### Section 152: Bailee when not liable for loss, etc., of thing bailed

The bailee, in the absence of any special contract, is not responsible for the loss, destruction or deterioration of the thing bailed, if he has taken the amount of care of it described in Section 151.

The phrase *"in the absence of any special contract"* as incorporated in Sec. 152 of the Act does not mean that the bailee would be allowed to either exclude or reduce the amount of taking reasonable care of the goods bailed to him by making any contract with the bailor which would nullify the obligation cast on the bailee under Sec. 151 of the Act. Thus, we may derive that Sec. 152 is enhancing the standard of reasonable care as mentioned in Sec. 151 rather than limiting the standard of reasonable care as prescribed under Sec. 151.

In *Cochin Port Trust* v. *Associated Cotton Traders Ltd.*,[244] imported cotton bales are delivered to the Port Trust and the Port Trust stores them in its warehouse as a bailee of the goods; the Port Trust is bound to take as much care of the goods as a man of ordinary prudence would under similar circumstances, take of his own goods of the same bulk, quality or value as of the goods lost. When fire breaks out in the premises under the control of the bailee, he alone will be in a position to explain the cause of the fire. It is a fact especially within his knowledge and therefore, under Sec. 106 of the Evidence Act, the burden of proving of that fact will be upon him. Similarly burden of proving that he had taken all reasonable precautions which an ordinary man of prudence would take is also on him. The plaintiff may show that the bailee has failed to place before the Court all materials available to him under Sec. 106 of the Evidence Act and ask the Court to presume that if produced, such documents may go against the bailee. He may also show that on the materials produced, it could be seen that the bailee has not taken as much care as is required under law.

### Section 153: Termination of bailment by bailee's act inconsistent with conditions

A contract of bailment is voidable at the option of the bailor, if the bailee does any act with regard to the goods bailed, inconsistent with the conditions of the bailment.

#### Illustration

A lets to B, for hire, a horse for his own riding. B drives the horse in his carriage. This is, at the option of A, a termination of the bailment.

### Section 154: Liability of bailee making unauthorised use of goods bailed

If the bailee makes any use of the goods bailed which is not according to the conditions of the bailment; he is liable to make compensation to the bailor for any damage arising to the goods from or during such use of them.

#### Illustrations

(a) A lends a horse to B for his own riding only. B allows C, a member of his family, to ride the horse. C rides with care, but the horse accidentally falls and is injured. B is liable to make compensation to A for the injury done to the horse.

---

[244] AIR 1983 KERALA 154.

(b) A hires a horse in Calcutta from B expressly to march to Banaras. A rides with due care, but marches to Cuttack instead. The horse accidentally falls and is injured. A is liable to make compensation to B for the injury to the horse.

### Section 155: Effect of mixture with bailor's consent, of his goods with bailee's

If the bailee, with the consent of the bailor, mixes the goods of the bailor with his own goods, the bailor and the bailee shall have an interest, in proportion to their respective shares, in the mixture thus produced.

### Section 156: Effect of mixture, without bailor's consent, when the goods can be separated

If the bailee, without the consent of the bailor, mixes the goods of the bailor with his own goods and the goods can be separated or divided, the property in the goods remains in the parties respectively; but the bailee is bound to bear the expense of separation or division, and any damage arising from the mixture.

### Illustration

A bails 100 bales of cotton marked with a particular mark to B. B, without A's consent, mixes the 100 bales with other bales of his own, bearing a different mark; A is entitled to have his 100 bales returned, and B is bound to bear all the expense incurred in the separation of the bales, and any other incidental damage.

### Section 157: Effect of mixture, without bailor's consent, when the goods cannot be separated

If the bailee, without the consent of the bailor, mixes the foods of the bailor with his own goods in such a manner that it is impossible to separate the goods bailed from the other goods, and deliver them back, the bailor is entitled to be compensated by the bailee for the loss of the goods.

### Illustration

A bails a barrel of Cape flour worth ₹45 to B. B, without A's consent, mixes the flour with country flour of his own, worth only ₹25 a barrel. B must compensate A for the loss of his flour.

### Section 158: Repayment, by bailor, of necessary expenses

Where, by the conditions of the bailment, the goods are to be kept or to be carried, or to have work done upon them by the bailee for the bailor, and the bailee is to receive no remuneration, the bailor shall repay to the bailee the necessary expenses incurred by him for the purpose of the bailment.

### Section 159: Restoration of goods lent gratuitously

The lender of a thing for use may at any time require its return, if the loan was gratuitous, even though he lent it for a specified time or purpose. But if, on the faith of such loan made for a specified time or purpose, the borrower has acted in such a manner that the return of the thing lent before the time agreed upon would cause him losses exceeding the benefit actually derived by him from the loan, the lender must, if he compels the return. Indemnify the borrower for the amount in which the loss so occasioned exceeds the benefits so derived.

### Section 160: Return of goods bailed, on expiration of time or accomplishment of purpose

It is the duty of the bailee to return, or deliver according to the bailor's directions, the goods bailed, without demand, as soon as the time for which they were bailed has expired, or the purpose for which they were bailed has been accomplished.

### Section 161: Bailee's responsibility when goods are not duly returned

If by the fault of the bailee, the goods are not returned, delivered or tendered at the proper time, he is responsible to the bailor for any loss, destruction or deterioration of the goods from that time.

For example, in *Shaw & Co.* v. *Symmons & Sons,*[245] where the plaintiff gave certain books to the defendant to be bound and the defendant bound them but did not return them within reasonable time. Subsequently, the books were burnt in an accidental fire. The defendants were held liable for the loss of books.

### Section 162: Termination of gratuitous bailment by death

A gratuitous bailment is terminated by the death either of the bailor or of the bailee.

### Section 163: Bailer entitled to increase or profit from goods bailed

In the absence of any contract to the contrary, the bailee is bound to deliver to the bailer, or according to his directions, any increase or profit which may have accrued from the goods bailed.

### Illustration

A leaves a cow in the custody of B to be taken care of. The cow has a calf. B is bound to deliver the calf as well as the cow to A.

### Section 164: Bailor's responsibility to bailee

The bailor is responsible to the bailee for any loss which by bailee may sustain the reason that the bailor was not entitled to make the bailment, or to receive back the goods, or to give directions, respecting them.

### Section 165: Bailment by several joint owners

If several joint owners of goods bail them, the bailee may deliver them back to, or according to the directions of, one joint owner without the consent of all in the absence of any agreement to the contrary.

245 (1917) 1 KB 799.

### Section 166: Bailee not responsible on redelivery to bailor without title

If the bailor has no title to the goods, and the bailee, in good faith, delivers them back to, or according to the directions of the bailor, the bailee is not responsible to the owner in respect of such delivery.

### Section 167: Right of third person claiming goods bailed

If a person, other than the bailor, claims goods bailed, he may apply to the court to stop delivery of the goods to the bailor, and to decide the title to the goods.

### Section 168: Right to finder of goods; may sue for specific reward offered

The finder of goods has no right to sue the owner for compensation for trouble and expense, voluntary incurred by him to preserve the goods and to find out the owner; but he may retain the goods against the owner until he receives such compensation; and where the owner has offered a specific reward for the return of goods lost, the finder may sue for such reward, and may retain the goods until he receives it.

### Section 169: When finder of thing commonly on sale may sell it

When thing which is commonly the subject of sale is lost, if the owner cannot with reasonable diligence be found, or if he refuses, upon demand, to pay the lawful charges of the finder, the finder may sell it:

(1) when the thing is in danger of perishing or of losing the greater part of its value, or

(2) when the lawful charges of the finder, in respect of the thing found, amount to two-thirds of its value.

### Section 170: Bailee's particular lien

Where the bailee has, in accordance with the purpose of the bailment, rendered any service involving the exercise of labour or skill in respect of the goods bailed he has, in the absence of a contract to the contrary, a right to retain such goods until he receives due remuneration for the services he has rendered in respect of them.

### Illustrations

(a) A delivers a rough diamond to B, a jeweller, to be cut and polished, which is accordingly done. B is entitled to retain the stone till he is paid for the services he has rendered.

(b) A gives cloth to B, a tailor, to make into a coat. B promises A to deliver the coat as soon as it is finished, and to give a three months' credit for the price. B is not entitled to retain the coat until he is paid.

### Section 171: General lien of bankers, factors, wharfingers, attorneys and policy brokers

Bankers, factors, wharfingers, attorneys of a High Court and policy brokers may, in the absence of a contract to the contrary, retain as a security for a general balance of account, any goods bailed to them; but no other persons have a right to retain, as a security for such balance, goods bailed to them, unless there is an express contract to that effect.

Lien is the right to retain the lawful possession of the property of another until the owner fulfills a legal duty to the person holding the property, such as the payment of lawful charges for work done on the property. The 'right of lien' may be defined as a right of a person to retain the possession of any property of some other person until the charges due to the person in possession are paid. The bailee's lien may be of two types:

(1) Particular lien
(2) General lien.

General lien means right to retain the goods not only for demands arising out of the goods retained but for a general balance of account in favour of certain persons. Particular lien, on the other hand, means the right to retain the particular goods in respect of which the claim is due.

Right to general lien is a privilege and is specially conferred by Sec. 171 of the Act on certain kinds of bailees only and they are as follows:

(a) Bankers
(b) Factors
(c) Wharfingers
(d) Attorney of High Courts
(e) Policy brokers

***Bankers lien*:** So far as the legal requirements are concerned, there is no need of any special agreement, written or oral, to create the right of lien, but it arises only by operation of law for, under the Indian Law, such an agreement is implied by the terms of Sec. 171 of the Indian Contract Act, 1872 so long as the same is not expressly excluded. In order that the lien should arise, the following requirements are to be fulfilled:

(i) The property must come into the hands of the banker in the capacity as a banker in the ordinary course of business;
(ii) There should be no entrustment for a special purpose which would be inconsistent with the lien;
(iii) The possession of the property must be lawfully obtained in the capacity as a banker; and
(iv) There should be no agreement inconsistent with the lien.

A banker's lien on negotiable securities has been judicially defined as "an implied pledge." A banker has, in the absence of agreement to the contrary, a lien on all bills received from a customer in the ordinary course of banking business in respect of any balance that may be due from such customer. By mercantile custom the banker has a general lien over all forms of commercial paper deposited by or on behalf of a customer in the ordinary course of banking business. The custom does not extend to valuables lodged for the purpose of safe custody and may in any event be displaced by either an express contract or circumstances which show an implied agreement inconsistent with the lien. The lien is applicable to negotiable instruments which are remitted to the banker from the customer for the purpose of collection. When collection has been made, the process may be used by the banker in reduction of the customer's debit balance unless otherwise earmarked.

Apart from any specific security, the banker can look to his general lien as a protection against loss on loan or overdraft or other credit facility. The general lien of bankers is part of law merchant and judicially recognised as such. Bankers most undoubtedly have a general lien on all securities deposited with them as bankers by a customer, unless there be an express contract, or circumstances that show an implied contract, inconsistent with lien.

The above passages go to show that by mercantile system, the Bank has a general lien over all forms of securities or negotiable instruments deposited by or on behalf of the customer in the ordinary course of banking business and that the general lien is a valuable right of the banker judicially recognised and in the absence of an agreement to the contrary, a Banker has a general lien over such securities or bills received from a customer in the ordinary course of banking business and has a right to use the proceeds in respect of any balance that may be due from the customer by way of reduction of customer's debit balance. Such a lien is also applicable to negotiable instruments including FDRs which are remitted to the Bank by the customer for the purpose of collection. There is no gainsaying that such a lien extends to FDRs also which are deposited by the customer.[246]

The following principles govern banker's lien:

(1) It has been held in *Chettinad Mercantile Bank Ltd.* v. *P.L.A. Pichammai Achi*[247] that banker's lien can be exercised in respect of any of the securities held by the bank. The bank has a lien over these securities and it could hold them against the amount due by the customer.

(2) It is necessary that the ownership of a thing, which is in possession of the bank, must be with the customer and held by the bank as a security otherwise the bank can exercise no right of lien.[248]

(3) A bank may not be able to exercise any right of lien over the money deposited by the customer in as much as by itself becomes the owner of the money deposited, but still it has the right to adjust such amounts against any debts due to from the customer. The purpose of lien in such cases is attained by the application of the principle of set off.

(4) The banker's lien is subject to any contract to the contrary and one alleging it must prove the existence of such a contract.

(5) The bank gets a general lien in respect of all securities of the customer including negotiable instruments and FDRs, but only to the extent to which the customer is liable. If the bank fails to return the balance, and the customer suffers a loss thereby, the bank will be liable to pay damages to the customer. In the present case, the Court has based its decision on the principle that in order to invoke

246 *Syndicate Bank* v. *Vijay Kumar*, AIR 1992 SC 1066.

247 AIR 1945 Mad. 445.

248 *PNB Ltd.* v. *Arura Mal Durga Dass and another*, AIR 1960 Pun.632.

a lien by the bank, there should exist mutuality between the bank and the customer, i.e., when they mutually exist between the same parties and between them in the same capacity. Retaining the customer's properties beyond his liability is unauthorised and would attract liability to the bank for damages.[249]

**Section 172: "Pledge", "Pawnor", and "Pawnee" defined**

The bailment of goods as security for payment of a debt or performance of a promise is called "pledge". The bailor is in this case called "pawnor". The bailee is called "pawnee".

**Section 173: Pawnee's right of retainer**

The pawnee may retain the goods pledged, not only for payment of the debt or the performance of the promise, but for the interests of the debt, and all necessary expenses incurred by him in respect to the possession or for the preservation of the goods pledged.

**Section 174: Pawnee not to retain for debt or promise other than for which goods pledged: Presumption in case of subsequent advances**

The pawnee shall not, in the absence of a contract to that effect, retain the goods pledged for any debt or promise of other than the debtor promise for which they are pledged; but such contract, in the absence of anything to the contrary, shall be presumed in regard to subsequent advances made by the pawnee.

**Section 175: Pawnee's right as to extraordinary expenses incurred**

The pawnee is entitled to receive from the pawnor extraordinary expenses incurred by him for the preservation of the goods pledged.

**Section 176: Pawnee's right where pawnor makes default**

If the pawnor makes default in payment of the debt, or performance, at the stipulated time, or the promise, in respect of which the goods were pledged, the pawnee may bring a suit against the pawnor upon the debt or promise, and retain the goods pledged as a collateral security; or he may sell the thing pledged, on giving the pawnor reasonable notice of the sale.

If the proceeds of such sale are less than the amount due in respect of the debt or promise, the pawnor is still liable to pay the balance. If the proceeds of the sale are greater than the amount so due, the pawnee shall pay over the surplus to the pawnor.

It is the discretion of the pawnee to sell the goods in case the pawnor makes default but if the pawnee does not exercise that discretion, no blame can be put on the pawenee and the pawnee has the right to bring a suit for recovery of the debt and retain the goods pledged as collateral security; *State Bank of India* v. *Smt. Neela Ashok Naik*, AIR 2000 Bom 151.

[249] *City Union Bank Ltd.* v. *Thangarajan*, (2003)46 SCL 237 (Mad).

## Section 177: Defaulting pawnor's right to redeem

If a time is stipulated for the payment of the debt, or performance of the promise, for which the pledge is made, and the pawnor makes default in payment of the debt or performance of the promise at the stipulated time, he may redeem the goods pledged at any subsequent time before the actual sale of them; but he must, in that case, pay, in addition, any expenses which have arisen from his default.

## Section 178: Pledge by mercantile agent

Where a mercantile agent is, with the consent of the owner, in possession of goods or the documents of title to goods, any pledge made by him, when acting in the ordinary course of business of a mercantile agent, shall be as valid as if he were expressly authorised by the owner of the goods to make the same; provided that the pawnee acts in good faith and has not at the time of the pledge notice that the pawnor has not authority to pledge.

*Explanation*: In this section, the expression "mercantile agent" and "documents of title" shall have the meanings assigned to them in the Indian Sale of Goods Act, 1930 (3 of 1930).

## Section 178A: Pledge by person in possession under voidable contract

When the pawnor has obtained possession of the other goods pledged by him under a contract voidable under Section 19 or Section 19A, but the contract has not been rescinded at the time of the pledge, the pawnee acquires a good title to the goods, provided he acts in good faith and without notice of the pawnor's defect of title.

## Section 179: Pledge where pawnor has only a limited interest

Where a person pledges goods in which he has only a limited interest, the pledge is valid to the extent of that interest.

## Section 180: Suit by bailor or bailee against wrong-doer

If a third person wrongfully deprives the bailee of the use or possession of the goods bailed, or does them any injury, the bailee is entitled to use such remedies as the owner might have used in the like case if no bailment had been made; and either the bailor or the bailee may bring a suit against a third person for such deprivation or injury.

## Section 181: Apportionment of relief or compensation obtained by such suits

Whatever is obtained by way of relief or compensation in any such suit shall, as between the bailor and the bailee, be dealt with according to their respective interests.

# Chapter X Agency

Agency law is concerned with "principal"-"agent" relationship; a relationship in which one person has legal authority to act for another. Such relationships arise from explicit appointment, or by implication. The relationships are generally associated with the law of agency. The Indian Contract Act, 1872 deals with the law of agency which runs from Sec. 182 to Sec. 238.

The law of agency is based on the Latin maxim *"Qui facit per alium, facit per se"*, which means "he who acts through another is deemed in law to do it himself". Agency, in its legal sense, nearly always relates to commercial or contractual dealings.

Agency is a relationship which exists between two legal persons (the principal and the agent) in which the function of the agent is to form a contract between his principal and a third party. Partners, company directors, factors, brokers and commercial agents act as agents. Agency is a very important feature of modern commercial life.

There are numerous examples of agency relationships in daily life. Directors act as agents of the company. Factor or a mercantile agent is a person whose job is to sell or buy goods on behalf of another person. An example would be a motor dealer who sales the product on behalf of the owner. Auctioneers are agents who are authorised to sell property at an auction on behalf of the seller. Brokers may operate in many trades. Insurance brokers or agents duly appointed or authorised by the Insurance Company to receive the premium are a good example of this relationship.

## Section 182: "Agent" and "principal" defined

An "agent" is a person employed to do any act for another, or to represent another in dealing with third persons. The person for whom such act is done, or who is so represented, is called the "principal".

The concept of agency has been discussed in *Krishna* v. *Ganapathi*[250] as follows:

> "In legal phraseology, every person who acts for another is not an agent. A domestic servant renders to his master a personal service; a person may till another's field or tend his flocks or work in his shop or factory or mine or may be employed upon his roads or ways; one may act for another in aiding in the performance of his legal or contractual obligations to third persons, as when he serves a public carrier, warehouse-man or innkeeper in performance of the latter's duties to the public. In none of these capacities he is an "agent" within the above meaning as he is not acting for another in dealings with third persons. It is only when he acts as representative of the other in business negotiations, that is to say, in the creation, modification, or termination of contractual obligations between that other and the third persons, that he is an "agent." Representation of another in business negotiations with third persons so as to bind such other by his own acts as if they were done by the former is of the essence of the relation of agency and the distinguishing feature between an "agent" and other persons who act for another."[251]

Therefore, it may be stated that an agency is a contract of employment for the purpose of bringing another in legal relation with a third party or, in other words, the contract between

[250] AIR 1955 MADRAS 648.

[251] *Id* at p. 651 per RAMASWAMI, J.

the principal and the agent is primarily a contract of employment to bring him into legal relation with a third party or to contract such business as may be going on between him and the third party. An agent is thus a person either actually or by law held to be authorised and employed by any person to bring him into contractual or other legal relations with a third party. He is a representative vested with authority, real or ostensible, to create voluntary primary obligations for his principal by making promises or representations to third persons calculated to induce them to change their legal relations. Representative character and derivative authority may briefly be said to be the distinguishing features of an agent.

The Allahabad High Court has suggested the true test of existence of agency in *Loon Karan* v. *John and Co.*[252] The Court observed that the Court must examine the true nature of the agreement and the subsequent dealings between the parties, and then decide whether it established a relationship of agency under the law. It is common experience that the word 'agent' is frequently used to describe a relationship which is not an agency in law. In several cases, a person described as an agent in the agreement or his letter of appointment was held to be not an agent according to law. Agency depends on true nature of relationship. In order to ascertain whether the relation of agency exists, the true nature of the agreement or the exact circumstances of the relationship between the alleged principal and the agent will be regarded and if it is found that such agreement in substance contemplates the alleged agent acting on his own behalf, and not as an agent in the agreement, the relation of agency will not have arisen.

In order to establish whether a person is an agent of someone, it is not necessary that the word "agent" is used. In other words, the word by agent in the contract cannot be held to have the effect of making one agent, who, in fact, may not be an agent.

Section 182 of the Contract Act defines an agent as *"a person employed to do any act for another or to represent another in dealings with third person."* The section defines a principal as *"the person for whom such act is done or who is so represented."* According to this definition, an agent never acts on his own behalf but always on behalf of another. He either represents his principal in any transaction or dealing with a third person, or performs any act for the principal. In either case, the act of the agent will be deemed in law to be not own but of the principal. The crucial test of the status of an agent is that his acts bind the plaintiff.

The distinction between a servant and an agent is indicated in Powell's Law of Agency and Halsbury's Law of England which is cited by the Supreme Court in *Lakshiminarayan Ram Gopal and Son Ltd.* v. *Govt. of Hyderabad*.[253]

(a) A servant is a person who not only receives instructions from his master but is subject to his master's right to control the manner in which he carries out those instructions. An agent receives his principal's instructions but is generally free to carry out those instructions according to his own discretion.

(b) Generally a master can tell his servant what to do and how to do it. Generally a principal cannot tell his agent how to carry out his instructions. A servant is under more complete control than an agent.

[252] AIR 1967 ALLAHABAD 308.

[253] AIR 1954 SC 364.

(c) A servant acts under the direct control and supervision of his master, and is bound to conform to all reasonable orders given to him in the course of his work; an agent, on the other hand, is entirely independent of any control or interference and merely undertakes to produce a specified result, employing his own means to produce that result.

(d) A servant is having no authority to make contracts on behalf of his master. Generally, the purpose of employing an agent is to authorise him to make contracts on behalf of his principal.

(e) An agent is paid by commission upon affecting the result which he has been instructed by his principal to achieve. Generally, a servant is paid by wages or salary.

(f) A servant works for a single master whereas an agent may work for many.

## Section 183: Who may employ agent

Any person who is of the age of majority according to the law to which he is subject, and who is of sound mind, may employ an agent.

## Section 184: Who may be an agent

As between the principal and third persons, any person may become an agent, but no person who is not of the age of majority and sound mind can become an agent, so as to be responsible to the principal according to the provisions in that behalf herein contained.

## Section 185: Consideration not necessary

No consideration is necessary to create an agency.

## Section 186: Agent's authority may be expressed or implied

The authority of an agent may be expressed or implied.

## Section 187: Definitions of express and implied

An authority is said to be express when it is given by words spoken or written. An authority is said to be implied when it is to be inferred from the circumstances of the case; and things spoken or written, or the ordinary course of dealing, may be accounted circumstances of the case.

### Illustration

*A* owns a shop in Serampor, living himself in Calcutta, and visiting the shop occasionally. The shop is managed by *B*, and he is in the habit of ordering goods from *C* in the name of *A* for the purposes of the shop, and of paying for them out of *A's* funds with *A's* knowledge. *B* has an implied authority from *A* to order goods from *C* in the name of *A* for the purposes of the shop.

## Section 188: Extent of agent's authority

An agent, having an authority to do an act, has authority do every lawful thing which is necessary in order to do such act.

An agent having an authority to carry on a business has authority to do every lawful thing necessary for the purpose, or usually done in the course, of conducting such business.

### Illustrations

(a) *A* is employed by *B*, residing in London, to recover at Bombay a debt due to *B*. *A* may adopt any legal process necessary for the purpose of recovering the debt, and may give a valid discharge for the same.

(b) *A* constitutes *B* his agent to carry on his business of a ship-builder. *B* may purchase timber and other materials, and hire workmen, for the purpose of carrying on the business.

## Section 189: Agent's authority in an emergency

An agent has authority, in an emergency, to do all such acts for the purpose of protecting his principal from loss as would be done by a person of ordinary prudence, in his own case, under similar circumstances.

### Illustrations

(a) An agent for sale may have goods repaired if it be necessary.

(b) *A* consigns provisions to *B* at Calcutta, with directions to send them immediately to *C*, at Cuttack. *B* may sell the provisions at Calcutta, if they will not bear the journey to Cuttack without spoiling.

## Section 190: When agent cannot delegate

An agent cannot lawful employ another to perform acts which he has expressly or impliedly undertaken to perform personally, unless by the ordinary custom of trade a sub-agent may, or, from the nature of agency, a sub-agent must, be employed.

## Section 191: "Sub-agent" defined

A "sub-agent" is a person employed by, and acting under the control of, the original agent in the business of the agency.

## Section 192: Representation of principal by sub-agent properly appointed

Where a sub-agent is properly appointed, the principal is, so far as regards third persons, represented by the sub-agent, and is bound by and responsible for his acts, as if he were an agent originally appointed by the principal.

***Agent's responsibility for sub-agent***: The agent is responsible to the principal for the acts of the sub-agent.

***Sub-agent's responsibility:*** The sub-agent is responsible for his acts to the agent, but not to the principal, except in cases of fraud, or wilful wrong.

### Section 193: Agent's responsibility for sub-agent appointed without authority

Where an agent, without having authority to do so, has appointed a person to act as a sub-agent, the agent stands towards such person in the relation of a principal to an agent, and is responsible for his act both to the principal and to third person; the principal is not represented by or responsible for the acts of the person so employed, nor is that person responsible to the principal.

### Section 194: Relation between principal and person duly appointed by agent to act in business of agency

Where an agent, holding an express or implied authority to name another person to act for the principal in the business of the agency, has named another person accordingly, such person is not a sub-agent, but an agent of the principal for such part of the business of the agency as is entrusted to him.

### Illustrations

(a) *A* directs *B*, his solicitor, to sell his estate by auction, and to employ an auctioneer for the purpose. *B* names C, an auctioneer, to conduct the sale. C is not a sub-agent, but is *A's* agent for the conduct of the sale.

(b) *A* authorises *B*, a merchant in Calcutta, to recover the moneys due to *A* from C & *Co. B* instructs *D*, a solicitor, to take legal proceedings against *C* & *Co.* for the recovery of the money. *D* is not a sub-agent, but is solicitor for *A*.

### Section 195: Agent's duty in naming such person

In selecting such agent for his principal, an agent is bound to exercise the same amount of discretion as a man of ordinary prudence would exercise in his own case; and, if he does this, he is not responsible to the principal for the acts of negligence of the agent so selected.

### Illustrations

(a) *A* instructs *B*, a merchant, to buy a ship for him. *B* employs a ship-surveyor of good reputation to choose a ship for *A*. The surveyor makes the choice negligently and the ship turns out to be unseaworthy and is lost. *B* is not, but the surveyor is, responsible to *A*.

(b) *A* consigns goods to *B*, a merchant, for sale. *B*, in due course, employs an auctioneer in good credit to sell the goods of *A*, and allows the auctioneer to receive the proceeds of the sale. The auctioneer afterwards becomes insolvent without having accounted for the proceeds. *B* is not responsible to *A* for the proceeds.

## Ratification

### Section 196: Right of person as to acts done for him without his authority—effect of ratification

Where acts are done by one person on behalf of another, but without his knowledge or authority, he may elect to ratify or to disown such acts. If he ratifies them, the same effects will follow as if they had been performed by his authority.

### Section 197: Ratification may be expressed or implied

Ratification may be expressed or may be implied in the conduct of the person on whose behalf the acts are done.

### Illustrations

(a) A, without authority, buys goods for B. Afterwards B sells them to C on his own account; B's conduct implies a ratification of the purchase made for him by A.

(b) A, without B's authority, lends B's money to C. Afterwards B accepts interest on the money from C. B's conduct implies a ratification of the loan.

### Section 198: Knowledge requisite for valid ratification

No valid ratification can be made by a person whose knowledge of the facts of the case is materially defective.

### Section 199: Effect of ratifying unauthorised act forming part of a transaction

A person ratifying any unauthorised act done on his behalf ratifies the whole of the transaction of which such act formed a part.

### Section 200: Ratification of unauthorised act cannot injure third person

An act done by one person on behalf of another, without such other person's authority, which, if done with authority, would have the effect of subjecting a third person to damages, or of terminating any right or interest of a third person cannot, by ratification, be made to have such effect.

### Illustrations

(a) *A*, not being authorised thereto by *B*, demands, on behalf of *B*, the delivery of a chattel, the property of *B*, from *C* who is in possession of it. This demand cannot be ratified by *B*, so as to make *C* liable for damages for his refusal to deliver.

(b) *A* holds a lease from *B*, terminable on three months' notice. *C*, an unauthorised person, gives notice of termination to *A*. The notice cannot be ratified by *B*, so as to be binding on *A*.

***Ratification-apparent Authority (ratification by estoppel)*:** This type of authority is sometimes referred to as ostensible authority, and relates to an application of the doctrine of estoppel. It arises when a principal, whether by words or actions, creates the implication that the agent is entitled to act on his/her behalf, when in fact no such authority exists. An agent acting within this apparent authority will bind the principal to a third party despite the fact that he or she has no authority to act.

In *Spiro* v. *Lintern*,[254] the wife was asked by her husband to employ an estate agent to sell his house. The agents found a buyer and, acting on the wife's instructions, a contract of sale was signed. Although the husband did not authorise the sale, he had taken no action when he discovered the facts. He later tried to deny a valid contract existed and the Court estopped him from doing so.

***Agency by ratification*:** If an appointed agent enters into a contract without the authority of his/her principal or if a person having no authority to act as an agent purports to act in such a capacity, the principal may still adopt the contract. If the principal does ratify, the agreement, then the principal will be bound by it whether it is to her/his detriment or benefit. Ratification is a powerful doctrine because it acts retrospectively so that the authority of the agent is backdated to the moment at which the act was performed by the agent.[255]

## Revocation of Authority

### Section 201: Termination of agency

An agency is terminated by the principal revoking his authority, or by the agent renouncing the business of the agency; or by the business of the agency being completed; or by either the principal or agent dying or becoming of unsound mind; or by the principal being adjudicated an insolvent under the provisions of any Act for the time being in force for the relief of insolvent debtors.

### Section 202: Termination of agency, where agent has an interest in subject-matter

Where the agent has himself an interest in the property which forms the subject-matter of the agency, the agency cannot, in the absence of an express contract, be terminated to the prejudice of such interest.

### Illustrations

(a) A gives authority to B to sell A's land, and to pay himself, out of the proceeds, the debts due to him from A. A cannot revoke this authority, nor can it be terminated by his insanity or death.

(b) A consigns 1,000 bales of cotton to B, who has made advances to him on such cotton, and desires B to sell the cotton, and to repay himself out of the price the

---

[254] [1973] 3 All ER 319.

[255] See *Bolton Partners* v. *Lambert* (1889) 41 Ch D 295.

amount of his own advances. A cannot revoke this authority, nor is it terminated by his insanity or death.

**Section 203: When principal may revoke agent's authority**

The principal may, save as is otherwise provided by the last preceding section, revoke the authority given to his agent at any time before the authority has been exercised, so as to bind the principal.

**Section 204: Revocation where authority has been partly exercised**

The principal cannot revoke the authority given to his agent after the authority has been partly exercised so far as regards such acts and obligations as arise from acts already done in the agency.

**Illustrations**

(a) A authorises B to buy 1,000 bales of cotton on account of A and to pay for it out of A's moneys remaining in B's hands. B buys 1,000 bales of cotton in his own name, so as to make himself personally liable for the price. A cannot revoke B's authority so far as regards payment for the cotton.

(b) A authorises B to buy 1,000 bales of cotton on account of A, and to pay for it out of A's money remaining in B's hands. B buys 1,000 bales of cotton in A's name, and so as not to render himself personally liable for the price. A can revoke B's authority to pay for the cotton.

**Section 205: Compensation for revocation by principal, or renunciation by agent**

Where there is an express or implied contract that the agency should be continued for any period of time, the principal must make compensation to the agent, or the agent to the principal, as the case may be, for any previous revocation or renunciation of the agency without sufficient cause.

**Section 206: Notice of revocation or renunciation**

Reasonable notice must be given of such revocation or renunciation, otherwise the damage thereby resulting to the principal or the agent, as the case may be, must be made good to the one by the other.

**Section 207: Revocation and renunciation may be expressed or implied**

Revocation or renunciation may be expressed or may be implied in the conduct of that principal or agent respectively.

**Illustration**

*A* empowers *B* to let *A's* house. Afterwards *A* lets it himself. This is an implied revocation of *B's* authority.

### Section 208: When termination of agent's authority takes effect as to agent, and as to third persons

The termination of the authority of an agent does not, so far as regards the agent, take effect before it becomes known to him, or, so far as regards third persons, before it becomes known to them.

#### Illustrations

(a) *A* directs *B* to sell goods for him, and agrees to give *B* five per cent commission on the price fetched by the goods. *A* afterwards by letter, revokes *B's* authority. *B* after the letter is sent, but before he receives it, sells the goods for 100 rupees. The sale is binding on *A* and *B* is entitled to five rupees as his commission.

(b) *A*, at Madras, by letter directs *B* to sell for him some cotton lying in a warehouse in Bombay, and afterwards, by letter revokes his authority to sell, and directs *B* to send the cotton to Madras. *B* after receiving the second letter, enters into a contract with *C*, who knows of the first letter, but not of the second for the sale to him of the cotton. *C* pays *B* the money, with which *B* absconds. *C's* payment is good as against *A*.

(c) *A* directs *B*, his agent, to pay certain money to *C*. *A* dies, and *D* takes out probate to his will. *B*, after *A's* death, but before hearing of it, pays the money to *C*. The payment is good as against *D*, the executor.

### Section 209: Agent's duty on termination of agency by principal's death or insanity

When an agency is terminated by the principal dying or becoming of unsound mind, the agent is bound to take on behalf of the representative, of his late principal, all reasonable steps for the protection and reservation of the interests entrusted to him.

### Section 210: Termination of sub-agent's authority

The termination of the authority of an agent causes the termination (subject to the rules herein contained regarding the termination of an agent's authority) of the authority of all sub-agents appointed by him.

## Agent's Duty to Principal

### Section 211: Agent's duty in conducting principal's business

An agent is bound to conduct the business of his principal according to the directions given by the principal, or in the absence of any such directions according to the customs which prevails in doing business of the same kind at the place where the agent conducts such business. When the agent acts otherwise, if any loss be sustained, he must make it good to his principal and if any profit accrues, he must account for it.

### Illustrations

(a) A, an agent engaged in carrying on for B a business, in which it is the custom to invest from time to time, at interest, the moneys which may be in hand, on its to make such investments. A must make good to B the interest usually obtained by such investments.

(b) B, a broker in whose business it is not the custom to sell on credit, sells goods of A on credit to C, whose credit at the time was very high. C, before payment, becomes insolvent. B must make good the loss to A.

## Section 212: Skill and diligence required from agent

An agent is bound to conduct the business of the agency with as much skill as is generally possessed by persons engaged in similar business unless the principal has notice of his want of skill. The agent is always bound to act with reasonable diligence, and to use such skill as he possesses; and to make compensation to his principal in respect of the direct consequences of his own neglect, want of skill, or misconduct, but not in respect of loss or damage which are indirectly or remotely caused by such neglect, want of skill, or misconduct.

### Illustrations

(a) A, a merchant in Calcutta, has an agent, B, in London, to whom a sum of money is paid on A's account, with orders to remit. B retains the money for a considerable time. A, in consequence of not receiving the money, becomes insolvent. B is liable for the money and interest, from the day on which it ought to have been paid, according to the usual rate, and for any further direct loss—as, e.g., by variation of rate of exchange—but not further.

(b) A, an agent for the sale of goods, having authority to sell on credit, sells to B on credit, without making the proper and usual enquiries as to the solvency of B. B at the time of such sale is insolvent. A must make compensation to his principal in respect of any loss thereby sustained.

(c) A, an insurance-broker employed by B to effect an insurance on a ship, omits to see that the usual clauses are inserted in the policy. The ship is afterwards lost. In consequence of the omission of the clauses nothing can be recovered from the underwriters. A is bound to make good the loss to B.

(d) A, a merchant in England, directs B, his agent at Bombay, who accepts the agency, to send him 100 bales of cotton by a certain ship. B, having it in his power to send the cotton, omits to do so. The ship arrives safely in England. Soon after her arrival the price of cotton rises. B is bound to make good to A the profit which he might have made by the 100 bales of cotton at the time of ship arrived, but not any profit he might have made by the subsequent rise.

## Section 213: Agent's accounts

An agent is bound to render proper accounts to his principal on demand.

### Section 214: Agent's duty to communicate with principal

It is the duty of an agent in case of difficulty, to use all reasonable diligence in communicating with his principal, and in seeking to obtain his instructions.

### Section 215: Right of principal when agent deals, on his own account, in business of agency without principal's consent

If an agent deals on his own account in the business of the agency, without first obtaining the consent of his principal and acquainting him with all material circumstances which have come to his own knowledge on the subject, the principal may repudiate the transaction, if the case shows, either that any material fact has been dishonestly concealed from him by the agent, or that the dealings of the agent have been disadvantageous to him.

### Illustrations

(a) A directs B to sell A's estate. B buys the estate for himself in the name of C. A, on discovering that B has bought the estate for himself, may repudiate the sale, if he can show that B has dishonestly concealed any material fact, or that the sale has been disadvantageous to him.

(b) A directs B to sell A's estate. B, on looking over the estate before selling it, finds a mine on the estate which is unknown to A. B informs A that he wishes to buy the estate for himself, but conceals the discovery of the mine. A allows B to buy, in ignorance of the existence of the mine. A, on discovering that B knew of the mine at the time he bought the estate, may either repudiate or adopt the sale at his option.

### Section 216: Principal's right to benefit gained by agent dealing on his own account in business of agency

If an agent, without the knowledge of his principal, deals in the business of the agency on his own account instead of on account to his principal, the principal is entitled to claim from the agent any benefit which may have resulted to him from the transaction.

### Illustration

*A* directs *B*, his agent, to buy a certain house for him. *B* tells *A* it cannot be bought, and buys the house for himself. *A* may, on discovering that *B* has bought the house, compel him to sell it to *A* at the price he gave for it.

### Section 217: Agent's right of retainer out of sums received on principal's account

An agent may retain, out of any sums received on account of the principal in the business of the agency, all moneys due to himself in respect of advances made or expenses properly incurred by him in conducting such business, and also such remuneration as may be payable to him for acting as agent.

### Section 218: Agent's duty to pay sums received for principal

Subject to such deductions, the agent is bound to pay to his principal all sums received on his account.

### Section 219: When agent's remuneration becomes due

In the absence of any special contract, payment for the performance of any act is not due to the agent until the completion of such act; but an agent may detain moneys received by him on account of goods sold, although the whole of the goods consigned to him for sale may not have been sold, or although the sale may not be actually complete.

### Section 220: Agent not entitled to remuneration for business misconducted

An agent who is guilty of misconduct in the business of the agency, is not entitled to any remuneration in respect of that part of the business which he has misconducted.

### Illustrations

(a) *A* employs *B* to recover 1,00,000 rupees from *C*, and to lay it out on good security, *B* recovers the 1,00,000 rupees and lays out 90,000 rupees on good security, but lays out 10,000 rupees on security which he ought to have known to be bad, whereby *A* loses 2,000 rupees. *B* is entitled to remuneration for recovering the 1,00,000 rupees and for investing the 90,000 rupees. He is not entitled to any remuneration for investing the 10,000 rupees, and he must make good the 2,000 rupees to *B*.

(b) *A* employs *B* to recover 1,000 rupees from *C*. Through *B's* misconduct the money is not recovered. *B* is entitled to no remuneration for his services, and must make good the loss.

### Section 221: Agent's lien on principal's property

In the absence of any contract to the contrary, an agent is entitled to retain goods, papers, and other property, whether movable or immovable of the principal received by him, until the amount due to himself for commission, disbursements and services in respect of the same has been paid or accounted for to him.

## Principal's Duty to Agent

### Section 222: Agent to be indemnified against consequences of lawful acts

The employer of an agent is bound to indemnify him against the consequences of all lawful acts done by such agent in exercise of the authority conferred upon him.

### Illustrations

(a) B, at Singapure, under instructions from A of Calcutta, contracts with C to deliver certain goods to him. A does not send the goods to B, and C sues B for breach of contract. B informs A of the suit, and A authorises him to defend the suit. B defends the suit, and is compelled to pay damages and costs, and incurs expenses. A is liable to B for such damages, costs and expenses.

(b) B, a broker at Calcutta, by the orders of A, a merchant there, contracts with C for the purchase of 10 casks of oil for A. Afterwards A refuses to receive the oil, and C sues B. B informs A, who repudiates the contract altogether. B defends, but unsuccessfully, and has to pay damages and costs and incurs expenses. A is liable to B for such damages, costs and expenses.

### Section 223: Agent to be indemnified against consequences of acts done in good faith

Where one person employs another to do an act, and the agent does the act in good faith, the employer is liable to indemnify the agent against the consequences of that act, though it may cause an injury to the rights of third persons.

### Illustrations

(a) *A*, a decree-holder and entitled to execution of *B's* goods requires the officer of the Court to seize certain goods, representing them to be the goods of *B*. The officer seizes the goods, and is sued by *C*, the true owner of the goods. *A* is liable to indemnify the officer for the sum which he is compelled to pay to *C*, in consequence of obeying *A's* directions.

(b) *B*, at the request of *A*, sells goods in the possession of *A*, but which *A* had no right to dispose of. *B* does not know this, and hands over the proceeds of the sale to *A*. Afterwards *C*, the true owner of the goods, sues *B* and recovers the value of the goods and costs. *A* is liable to indemnify *B* for what he has been compelled to pay to *C*, and for *B's* own expenses.

### Section 224: Non-liability of employer of agent to do a criminal act

Where one person employees another to do an act which is criminal, the employer is not liable to the agent, either upon an express or an implied promise to indemnify him against the consequences of that act.

### Illustrations

(a) *A* employs *B* to beat *C*, and agrees to indemnify him against all consequences of the act. *B* thereupon beats *C*, and has to pay damages to *C* for so doing. *A* is not liable to indemnify *B* for those damages.

(b) *B*, the proprietor of a newspaper, publishes, at *A's* request, a libel upon *C* in the paper, and *A* agrees to indemnify *B* against the consequences of the publication, and all costs and damages of any action in respect thereof. *B* is sued by *C* and has to pay damages, and also incurs expenses. *A* is not liable to *B* upon the indemnity.

### Section 225: Compensation to agent for injury caused by principal's neglect

The principal must make compensation to his agent in respect of injury caused to such agent by the principal's neglect or want of skill.

### Illustration

*A* employs *B* as a bricklayer in building a house, and puts up the scaffolding himself. The scaffolding is unskilfully put up, and *B* is in consequence hurt. *A* must make compensation to *B*.

## Effect of Agency on Contracts with Third Persons

### Section 226: Enforcement and consequences of agent's contract

Contracts entered into through an agent, and obligations arising from acts done by an agent, may be enforced in the same manner, and will have the same legal consequences as if the contracts had been entered into and the acts done by the principal in person.

### Illustrations

(a) *A* buys goods from *B*, knowing that he is an agent for their sale, but not knowing who is the principal. *B's* principal is the person entitled to claim from *A* the price of the goods, and *A* cannot, in a suit by the principal, set-off against that claim a debt due to himself from *B*.

(b) *A*, being *B's* agent, with authority to receive money on his behalf, receives from *C* a sum of money due to *B*. *C* is discharged of his obligation to pay the sum in question to *B*.

### Section 227: Principal how far bound, when agent exceeds authority

When an agent does more than he is authorised to do, and when the part of what he does, which is within his authority, can be separated from the part which is beyond his authority, so much only of what he does as is within his authority is binding as between him and his principal.

### Illustration

*A*, being owner of a ship and cargo, authorizes *B* to procure an insurance for 4,000 rupees on the ship. *B* procures a policy for 4,000 rupees on the ship, and another for the like sum on the cargo. *A* is bound to pay the premium for the policy on the ship, but not the premium for the policy on the cargo.

### Section 228: Principal not bound when excess of agent's authority is not separable

Where an agent does more than he is authorised to do, and what he does beyond the scope of his authority cannot be separated from what is within it, the principal is not bound to recognise the transaction.

### Illustration

*A*, authorizes *B* to buy 500 sheep for him. *B* buys 500 sheep and 200 lambs for one sum of 6,000 rupees. *A* may repudiate the whole transaction.

### Section 229: Consequences of notice given to agent

Any notice given to or information obtained by the agent, provided it be given or obtained in the course of the business transacted by him for the principal, shall, as between the principal and third parties, have the same legal consequences as if it had been given to or obtained by the principal.

#### Illustrations

(a) *A* is employed by *B* to buy from *C* certain goods, of which *C* is the apparent owner, and buys them accordingly. In the course of the treaty for the sale, *A* learns that the goods really belonged to *D*, but *B* is ignorant of that fact. *B* is not entitled to set-off a debt owing to him from *C* against the price of the goods.

(b) *A* is employed by *B* to buy from *C* goods of which *C* is the apparent owner. *A* was, before he was so employed, a servant of *C*, and then learnt that the goods really belonged to *D*, but *B* is ignorant of that fact. In spite of the knowledge of his agent, *B* may set-off against the price of the goods a debt owing to him from *C*.

### Section 230: Agent cannot personally enforce, nor be bound by, contracts on behalf of principal

In the absence of any contract to that effect an agent cannot personally enforce contracts entered into by him on behalf of his principal, nor is he personally bound by them.

Presumption of contract to the contrary: Such a contract shall be presumed to exits in the following cases:

(1) Where the contract is made by an agent for the sale or purchase of goods for a merchant resident abroad;

(2) Where agent does not disclose the name of his principal;

(3) Where the principal, though disclosed, cannot be sued.

### Section 231: Right of parties to a contract made by agent not disclosed

If an agent makes a contract with a person who neither, knows, nor has reason to suspect, that he is an agent, his principal may require the performance of the contract; but the other contracting party has, as against the principal, the same right as he would have had as against if the agent had been the principal.

If the principal discloses himself before the contract is completed, the other contracting party may refuse to fulfil the contract, if he can show that, if he had known who was the principal in the contract, or if he had known that the agent was not a principal, he would not have entered into the contract.

### Section 232: Performance of contract with agent supposed to be principal

Where one man makes a contract with another, neither knowing nor having reasonable ground to suspect that the other is an agent, the principal, if he requires the performance of the contract, can only obtain such performance subject to the right and obligations subsisting between the agent and the other party of the contract.

### Illustration

*A*, who owes 500 rupees to *B*, sells 1,000 rupees worth of rice to *B*. *A* is acting as agent for *C* in the transaction, but *B* has no knowledge nor reasonable ground of suspicion that such is the case. *C* cannot compel *B* to take the rice without allowing him to set-off *A's* debt.

### Section 233: Right of person dealing with agent personally liable

In cases where the agent is personally liable, a person dealing with him may hold either him or his principal, or both of them, liable.

### Illustration

*A* enters into a contract with *B* to sell him 100 bales of cotton, and afterwards discovers that *B* was acting as agent for *C*. *A* may sue either *B* or *C*, or both, for the price of the cotton.

### Section 234: Consequence of inducing agent or principal to act on belief that principal or agent will be held exclusively liable

When a person who has made a contract with an agent induces the agent to act upon the belief that the principal only will be held liable, or induces the principal to act upon the belief that the agent only will be held liable, he cannot afterwards hold liable that agent or principal respectively.

### Section 235: Liability of pretended agent

A person untruly representing himself to be the authorised agent of another, and thereby including a third person to deal with him as such agent, is liable, if his alleged employer does not ratify his acts, to make compensation to the other in respect of any loss or damage which he has incurred by so dealing.

### Section 236: Person falsely contracting as agent, not entitled to performance

A person with whom a contract has been entered into in the character of agent, is not entitled to require the performance of it, if he was in reality acting, not as agent, but on his own account.

### Section 237: Liability of principal inducing belief that agent's unauthorised acts were authorised

When an agent has, without authority, done acts or incurred obligations to third person on behalf of his principal, the principal is bound by such acts or obligations, if he has by his word or conduct induced such third person to believe that such acts and obligations were within the scope of the agent's authority.

## Illustrations

(a) A consigns goods to B for sale, and gives him instructions not to sell under a fixed price. C, being ignorant of B's instructions, enters into a contract with B to buy the goods at a price lower than the reserved price. A is bound by the contract.

(b) A entrusts B with negotiable instruments endorsed in blank. B sells them to C in violation of private orders from A. The sale is good.

## Section 238: Effect, on agreement, of misrepresentation or fraud by agent

Misrepresentation made or frauds committed, by agents acting in the course of their business for their principals, have the same effect on agreements made by such agents as if such misrepresentations or frauds had been made or committed by the principals; but misrepresentations made, or frauds committed, by agents, in matters which do not fall within their authority, do not affect their principals.

## Illustrations

(a) *A*, being *B's* agent for the sale of goods, induces C to buy them by a misrepresentation, which he was not authorised by *B* to make. The contract is voidable, as between *B* and *C*, at the option of *C*.

(b) *A*, the captain of *B's* ship, signs bills of lading without having received on board the goods mentioned therein. The bills of lading are void as between *B* and the pretended consignor.

# 2

# The Sale of Goods Act, 1930

## INTRODUCTION

Till 1930, transactions relating to the sale and purchase of goods were regulated by the Indian Contract Act, 1872. In 1930, Secs. 76 to 123 of the Indian Contract Act, 1872 were repealed and a separate Act, called 'The Sale of Goods Act, 1930' was passed. It came into force on 1 July, 1930 but with effect from 22 September, 1963, the word 'Indian' was removed.

The object of The Sale of Goods Act is as follows:

An Act to define and amend the law relating to the sale of goods

WHEREAS it is expedient to define and amend the law relating to the sale of goods;

It is hereby enacted as follows.

According to Sec. 3, the provisions of The Indian Contract Act, 1872 still continue to apply to contracts for the sale of goods except where 'The Sale of Goods Act, 1930' provides for the contrary.

## ACT IN A NUTSHELL

The Sale of Goods Act runs for 66 sections, divided into seven chapters. Chapter I deals with short title, extent and commencement, definitions, and application of the Indian Contract Act, 1872. Chapter II deals with formation of the contract of sale in general and in particular, formalities of the contract, subject matter of contract, price, meaning and effect of conditions and warranties, implied undertaking as to title and principle of *caveat emptor*. Chapter III deals with the effect of the contract with special reference to transfer of property as between seller and buyer. More specifically, Sec. 27 of the Act provides the meaning and application of international principle, namely, *nemo dat quod non habet* and its exception. Chapter IV deals with performance of the contract with special reference to the duties of the seller and the buyer, instalment delivery, contract involving sea routes;

for example, CIF, FOB, Ex-Ship Contract. Chapter V deals with the right of the unpaid seller against the goods. This chapter may be considered as one of the important chapters as it provides the rights of the unpaid seller in case the buyer becomes insolvent or the buyer refuses to receive the goods already delivered to him. Chapter VI provides remedy in case of breach of contract. Chapter VII, entitled as miscellaneous which runs from Sec. 62 to Sec. 66, specifically deals with auction sale and saving clause.

## Chapter I Preliminary

### Section 1: Short title, extent and commencement

(1) This Act may be called the Sale of Goods Act, 1930.

(2) It extends to the whole of India except the State of Jammu and Kashmir.

(3) It shall come into force on the lst day of July, 1930.

The contracts for sale of goods are subject to the general principles of the law relating to contracts, i.e., the Indian Contact Act. A contract for sale of goods has, however, certain peculiar features, such as transfer of ownership of the goods, delivery of goods, rights and duties of the buyer and the seller, remedies for breach of contract, conditions and warranties implied under a contract for sale of goods, etc. These peculiarities are the subject matter of the provisions of the Sale of Goods Act, 1930.

### Section 2: Definitions

In this Act, unless there is anything repugnant in the subject of context,—

(1) **buyer** means a person who buys or agrees to buy goods;

(2) **delivery** means voluntary transfer of possession from one person to another;

(3) goods are said to be in a **delivered state** when they are in such State that the buyer would under the contract be bound to take delivery of them;

(4) **document of title to goods** includes bill of lading dock-warrant, warehouse keeper's certificate, wharfingers' certificate, railway receipt, multimodal transport document, warrant or order for the delivery of goods and any other document used in the ordinary course of business as proof of the possession or control of goods or authorising or purporting to authorise, either by endorsement or by delivery, the possessor of the document to transfer or receive goods thereby represented;

(5) **fault** means wrongful act or default;

(6) **future goods** means goods to be manufactured or produced or acquired by the seller after making of the contract of sale;

(7) **goods** means every kind of moveable property other than actionable claims and money; and includes stock and shares, growing crops, grass, and things attached to or forming part of the land which are agreed to be severed before sale or under the contract of sale;

The question came before the Supreme Court in *State of Kerala* v. *Prabhavathy Thankamma*[1] for consideration was whether a lottery ticket would be considered as goods defined in the Sale of Goods Act. The Court held that a lottery ticket has no value in itself. It is a mere piece of paper. Its value lies in the fact that it represents a chance or a right to a conditional benefit of winning a prize of a greater value than the consideration paid for the transfer of that chance. It is nothing more than a token or evidence of this right. The question is what is this right which the ticket represents? There can be no doubt that on purchasing a lottery ticket, the purchaser would have a claim to a conditional interest in the prize money which is not in the purchaser's possession. The right would fall squarely within the definition of an *actionable claim* and would therefore be excluded from the definition of *'goods'* under the Sale of Goods Act.

(8) A person is said to be **insolvent** who has ceased to pay his debts in the ordinary course of business, or cannot pay his debts as they become due, whether he has committed an act of insolvency or not;

(9) **mercantile agent** means a mercantile agent having in the customary course of business as such agent authority either to sell goods, or to consign goods for the purposes of sale, or to buy goods, or to raise money on the security of goods;

(10) **price** means the money consideration for a sale of goods;

The presence of money consideration is, therefore, an essential element in a transaction of sale. If the consideration is not money but some other valuable consideration, it may be an exchange or barter but not a sale. Both under the Sale of Goods Act and the Transfer of Property Act, sale is a transfer of property in the goods or of the ownership in immovable property for a money consideration. But in exchange, there is a reciprocated transfer of interest in the immovable property, the corresponding transfer of interest in the movable property being denoted by the word 'barter'. The difference between a sale and an exchange is this that in the former the price is paid in money, while in the latter, it is paid in goods by way of barter.[2]

(11) **property** means the general property in goods, and not merely a special property;

(12) **quality of goods** includes their State or condition;

(13) **seller** means a person who sells or agrees to sell goods;

(14) **specific goods** means goods identified and agreed upon at the time a contract of sale is made; and

(15) expressions used but not defined in this Act and defined in the Indian Contract Act, 1872, have the meaning assigned to them in that act.

## Section 3: Application of provisions of Act 9 of 1872

The unrepealed provisions of the Indian Contract Act, 1872, save insofar as they are inconsistent with the express provisions of this Act, shall continue to apply to contracts for the sale of goods.

[1] AIR 2009 SC (Supp) 2831.

[2] *Commissioner of Income-tax, A.P.* v. *M/s. Motors and General Stores (P) Ltd.*, AIR 1968 SC 200.

# Chapter II Formation of the Contract of Sale

## Section 4: Sale and agreement to sell

(1) A contract of sale of goods is a contract whereby the seller transfers or agrees to transfer the property in goods to the buyer for a price. There may be a contract of sale between one part-owner and another.

(2) A contract of sale may be absolute or conditional.

(3) Whereunder a contract of sale the property in the goods is transferred from the seller to the buyer, the contract is called a sale, but where the transfer of the property in the goods is to take place at a future time or subject to some condition thereafter to be fulfilled, the contract is called an agreement to sell.

(4) An agreement to sell becomes a sale when the time elapses or the conditions are fulfilled subject to which the property in the goods is to be transferred.

### Sale

According to Sec. 4(1) of the Sale of Goods Act, 1930, "contract of sale of goods is a contract whereby the seller transfers or agrees to transfer the property in goods to the buyer for a price." 'Contract of sale' is a generic term which includes both sale and an agreement to sell.

### *Hire purchase*

A hire purchase agreement is a contract of bailment coupled with an option to purchase, that is, the owner lets out the goods on hire and undertakes to sell it to the hirer on his making a certain number of payments.

There are two types of hire purchase agreements:

1. The parties may agree that the goods are leased to the hirer for a fee, but the hirer does not undertake an obligation to buy or only has an option to buy the goods.
2. On the other hand, the parties may agree that the hirer has an obligation to buy the goods but the property in the goods is not to pass to the hirer until all instalments of the agreed price are paid.

The first kind of contract is a hire purchase agreement outside the Sale of Goods Act. However, the second is an agreement to sell because 'the transfer of the property is to take place at a future time.' The Supreme Court has rightly observed in *Sundaram Finance Ltd.* v. *State of Kerala*[3] that the sum and substance of hire purchase agreement is twofold. One, the owner under the hire purchase agreement enters into a transaction of hiring out the goods on the terms and conditions mentioned in the agreement and the option to purchase exercisable by the hirer on payment of all the instalments of hire arises when the instalments are paid and not until then. There is no agreement to buy goods, the hirer being under no obligation to buy but has an option to return the goods or to become its owner by payment in full of the agreed hire purchase instalments and the price for exercising the

[3] AIR 1966 SC 1178.

option. The Apex Court further observed in *K.L. Johar and Co.* v. *Dy. Commercial Tax Officer*,[4] that a hire purchase agreement, as its very nature implies, has two aspects. There is first an aspect of bailment of the goods subjected to the hire purchase agreement, and secondly, an element of sale which fructifies when the option to purchase, which is usually a term of hire purchase agreements, is exercised by the intending purchaser. The distinguishing feature of a typical hire purchase agreement therefore is that the property does not pass when the agreement is made but only passes when the option is finally exercised after complying with all the terms of the agreement.

The major points of distinction between the two transactions are given below:

| Sale | Hire purchase |
|---|---|
| 1. The property is transferred but possession may be transferred immediately or postponed. | 1. The property is not transferred, only possession is transferred. |
| 2. The buyer becomes the owner of the goods and he has to take the risk of ownership. | 2. The hire purchaser is only a bailee, ownership remains with the seller. |
| 3. The buyer is bound to purchase the goods. and the seller can sue the buyer for price. | 3. The hirer is not bound to purchase the goods; the seller cannot sue for price. |
| 4. The buyer can sell the goods to a third party. | 4. The hirer has no authority to sell. |
| 5. If the buyer fails to pay, the seller cannot recover the goods in the buyer's possession. | 5. If instalments are not paid, he can resume possession. |

If in an agreement the person taking the goods has an option to terminate the agreement at any time before the transfer of ownership of goods, it will be an agreement of hire purchase. If, in an agreement, the person taking the goods has no option to terminate the agreement, it will be a contract of sale even if the price is payable in instalments.[5]

The basis of distinction between sale and hire purchase is given below:

| Basis of distinction | Sale | Hire purchase agreement |
|---|---|---|
| **1. Regulating law** | All contracts of sale are governed by the Sale of Goods Act, 1930. | The hire purchase agreements are governed by Hire Purchase Act, 1972. |
| **2. Nature of contract** | It is a contract of sale. | It is an agreement of hiring and hence an agreement to sell. |
| **3. Possession of goods** | Possession of goods need not necessarily be transferred immediately. | Possession of goods is necessarily transferred immediately. |
| **4. Transfer of ownership of goods** | Ownership of goods is transferred immediately. | Ownership of goods is transferred on the payment of the last instalment when the option to purchase is exercised. |

*(contd...)*

[4] AIR 1965 SC 1082.

[5] *Lee* v. *Butler*, 1893 2 Q.B. 318.

| Basis of distinction | Sale | Hire purchase agreement |
|---|---|---|
| **5. Right to terminate** | The buyer has no right to terminate the contract of sale. | The hirer has the right to terminate the agreement at any time before the ownership is transferred. |
| **6. Right to repossess the goods** | The seller has no right to repossess the goods. He can sue for price. | The hire-vendor has a right to repossess the goods if the hirer defaults. |
| **7. Transfer of good title to third party** | The buyer can transfer a good title to third party because ownership of goods has been transferred. | The hirer cannot transfer a good title to third party because the ownership of goods has not been transferred. |
| **8. Compulsion as to be in writing** | A contract of sale need not necessarily be in writing. | The hire purchase agreement must be in writing. |
| **9. Benefits of implied conditions and warranties under the Sale of Goods Act, 1930** | The benefits of implied conditions and warranties are available. | The benefits of implied conditions and warranties are not available. |
| **10. Sales tax** | In case of sale of taxable goods, sales tax is levied. | In case of hire of even taxable goods, sales tax is not levied. |

To constitute a valid sale, the following elements must be present:

1. ***Proper parties:*** It is a general rule of contract that all persons in the contract must be competent to make a contract. Here, the person may be a legal person like company and the company may be either a buyer or a seller.
2. ***A thing which is the object of the contract:*** There must be a thing which is the object of the sale and such thing must exist at the time of making a contract. If the thing sold at the time of the sale had ceased to exist it is clear that there can be no sale. For example, X wants to sell his house which is situated at Bangalore to Y and neither of the parties is aware that the house which is the object of the contract has collapsed due to earthquake. It would be held that there is no contract because there is nothing to be sold.
3. ***A price agreed upon:*** To constitute a sale, there must be a price which would be agreed between the parties. However, a sale may be valid if the price for the goods sold would be determined by a third person.
   The price must have the three following qualities:
   (a) It must be an actual price.
   (b) It must be certain or capable of being rendered certain.
   (c) It must consist of a sum of money.
4. ***The consent of the contracting parties:*** The consent of the contracting parties, which is of the essence of a sale, consists in the agreement of the will of the

seller to sell a certain thing to the buyer, for a certain price, and in the will of the buyer, to purchase the same thing for the price. This consent may be shown

(a) By an express agreement

(b) By all implied agreement.

Both parties must agree upon the same object of the sale; if, therefore, one gives consent to buy one thing, and the other to sell another, there is no sale. Both parties must agree as to the same price, for if the seller intends to sell for a greater sum than the buyer intends to give, there is no mutual consent; but if the case were reversed, and the seller intended to sell for a less price than the buyer intended to give, the sale would be good for the lesser sum.

Sale may be either absolute or conditional. An absolute sale is one made and completed without any condition whatever. A conditional sale is one which depends for its validity upon the fulfilment of some condition.

### *Sale vis-a-vis Agreement to Sell*

The distinction between a sale and an agreement to sell is drawn in the provisions of the Sale of Goods Act as follows:

"Where under a contract of sale the property in the goods is transferred from the seller to the buyer, the contract is called a sale; but where the transfer of the property in the goods is to take place at a future time or subject to some condition thereafter to be fulfilled, the contract is called an agreement to sell." An agreement to sell becomes a sale when the time elapses or the conditions are fulfilled subject to which the property in the goods is to be transferred.

The distinction between an agreement to sell and a sale is fundamental. The former is a contract pure and simple. At the time of the contract, the property in the goods does not pass, but the buyer acquires a right in *'personem'* to the transfer of the property upon the happening of an event or the fulfilment of a condition. A sale, on the other hand, is more than a contract. Its effect is to transfer to the buyer forthwith a right in *'rem'*—the property in the goods. Under an agreement to sell, the seller remains the owner until the agreement to sell becomes a sale, but under a sale the buyer becomes the owner forthwith. An agreement to sell and a sale are sometimes referred to as an executory contract of sale and an executed contract of sale, respectively.

(a) A contract of sale of goods is a contract by which the seller transfers or agrees to transfer property in goods to the buyer for a money consideration, called the price.

(b) There may be a contract of sale between one part owner and another.

(c) A contract of sale may be absolute or conditional.

(d) If, under a contract of sale, the property in the goods is transferred from the seller to the buyer, the contract is called a sale.

(e) If the transfer of the property in the goods is to take place at a future time or subject to a condition to be fulfilled after the transfer of the property in the goods, the contract is called an agreement to sell.

(f) An agreement to sell becomes a sale when the time elapses at which, or the conditions are fulfilled subject to which, the property in the goods is to be transferred.

The basis of distinction between sale and agreement to sell is given below:

| Basis of Distinction | Sale | Agreement to Sell |
|---|---|---|
| **1. Nature of contract** | Executed. | Executory |
| **2. Transfer of property** | Transfer takes place immediately. | Transfer is to take place at a future date or subject to the fulfilment of some condition. |
| **3. Nature of rights of buyer** | *Jus in rem* (right against property). The buyer gets a right to enjoy the goods against the whole world including the seller. | *Jus in personem* (right against the person) the buyer does not get such right to enjoy the goods. |
| **4. Rights of buyer in case of breach** | Recovery of goods, specific performance. | Damages |
| **5. Risk of loss** | Buyer's | Seller's |
| **6. Rights of seller in case of breach** | Suit for the price of goods. | Damages |
| **7. Right to resell** | Not available | May resale but liable for damages. |
| **8. Insolvency of seller** | The buyer can recover goods. | If price already paid, proportionate amount can be recovered. |
| **9. Insolvency of buyer** | If price is not paid, proportionate amount can be recovered; delivery of goods can be demanded. | The seller can refuse delivery unless full price is paid. |

## Section 5: Contract of sale how made

(1) A contract of sale is made by an offer to buy or sell goods for a price and the acceptance of such offer. The contract may provide for the immediate delivery of the goods or immediate payment of the price of both, or for the delivery or payment by installments, or that the delivery or payment or both shall be postponed.

(2) Subject to the provisions of any law for the time being in force, a contract of sale may be made in writing or by word of mouth, or partly in writing and partly by word of mouth or may be implied from the conduct of the parties.

According to Sec. 5 of the Sale of Goods Act, a contract of sale is made by an offer to buy or sell goods for a price and the acceptance of such offer. It may be oral or in writing or may even be inferred from the conduct of the parties, but it must of necessity originate in offer and acceptance. When the seller had offered to transfer his goods on payment of some price at a future date, in order to make it a binding contract that price must be accepted or agreed to by the intending purchaser. The mere fact that the latter had made an offer for purchase of goods does not render the contract complete by the acceptance of that offer even though it may be for a price which was not contained in the original offer. The price quoted will constitute a counter offer which must be accepted to develop into a contract. The requirements of a valid contract are varied. They are not satisfied if the offer to buy or sell unaccompanied by the quotation of price is accepted. There must be acceptance both of the purchase and of the price at which it is to be purchased.[6]

All the essential elements of a valid contract as specified under Sec. 10 of the Indian Contract Act, 1872 must also be present since a contract of sale is a special type of a contract. For example, an agreement to sell smuggled gold is not valid since its object is unlawful.

### *Seller and buyer*

There must be a seller as well as a buyer. 'Buyer' means a person who buys or agrees to buy goods [Sec. 2(1)]. 'Seller' means a person who sells or agrees to sell goods [Sec. 2(13)]. A person cannot be a seller as well as a buyer as a person cannot buy his own goods. That is why distribution of goods among partners on account of dissolution of a firm does not amount to a sale of goods because the partners are joint-owners and they cannot be both sellers and buyers. However, one part owner may be a seller and another part owner may be a buyer. Where a person's goods are sold under an execution decree, a bankrupt may also buy his own goods from his trustee.

### *Transfer of property*

Property means the general property in goods, and not merely a special property [Sec. 2(11)]. General property in goods means ownership of the goods. Special property in goods means possession of goods. Thus, there must be *either* a transfer of ownership of goods *or* an agreement to transfer the ownership of goods. The ownership may transfer either immediately on completion of sale or sometime in the future in an agreement to sell.

### *Goods*

There must be some goods. 'Goods' means every kind of movable property other than actionable claims and money and includes stocks and shares, growing crops, grass and things attached to or forming part of the land which are agreed to be severed before sale or under the contract of sale [Sec. 2(7)]. It may be noted that the contract relating to actionable claims, immovable property and services are not covered by this Act.

***Notes:***

1. The 'actionable claims' mean a claim which can be enforced through the Courts of Law, e.g. a debt due from one person to another is an actionable claim.
2. The 'money' here means the legal tender (i.e., currency of the country) and not old coins.

[6] *Alapati R.G.K. and Co.* v. *J. Ramanujam*, AIR 1961 ANDHRA PRADESH 408.

### *Price*

There must be a price. Price here means the money consideration for a sale of goods [Sec. 2(10)]. When the consideration is only goods, it amounts to a 'barter' and not sale. When there is no consideration, it amounts to a gift and not sale. However, the consideration may be partly in money and partly in goods because the law does not prohibit this as such.

### *Formalities of a contract of sale*

In connection with the formalities of a contract of sale, the provisions of Sec. 5 specifically provide only for the following three matters:

1. Offer and acceptance—A contract of sale is made by an offer to buy or sell the goods for a price and acceptance of such offer.
2. Delivery and payment—The contract of sale may provide for any of the following combinations:

| Option | Delivery | Payment |
|---|---|---|
| I | Immediate | Immediate |
| II | Immediate | By instalments |
| III | Immediate | At some future date |
| IV | By instalments | By instalments |
| V | By instalments | Immediate |
| VI | By instalments | At some future date |
| VII | At some future date | At some future date |
| VIII | At some future date | Immediate |
| IX | At some future date | By instalments |

3. Express or Implied—A contract of sale may be made express or implied by the conduct of the parties. If express, then it could be in writing, by word of mouth or partly in writing and partly by word of mouth.

It may be noted that an offer by word of mouth may be accepted in writing and an offer in writing may be accepted by word of mouth.

### Section 6: Existing or future goods

(1) The goods which form the subject of a contract of sale may be either existing goods, owned or possessed by the seller, or future goods.

(2) There may be a contract for the sale of goods the acquisition of which by the seller depends upon a contingency which may or may not happen.

(3) Where by a contract of sale the seller purports to effect a present sale of future goods, the contract operates as an agreement to sell the goods.

## Section 7: Goods perishing before making of contract

Where there is a contract for the sale of specific goods, the contract is void if the goods without the knowledge of the seller have, at the time when the contract was made, perished or become so damaged as no longer to answer to their description in the contract.

Where in a contract for sale of specific goods, at the time of making the contract, the goods, without knowledge of the seller, have perished or become so damaged as no longer to answer to their description in the contract, the contract shall become null and void. This is based on the rule of impossibility of performance. Since the subject matter of the contract, which is one of its essential ingredients, itself is destroyed, the contract cannot be carried out.

'Perishing of goods' includes not only complete destruction of the goods when the seller has been irretrievably deprived by the goods or when the goods have been stolen or have in some other way been lost and are untraceable, but also when the goods become unmerchantable, i.e., when the goods have lost their commercial value.

## Section 8: Goods perishing before sale but after agreement to sell

Where there is an agreement to sell specific goods, and subsequently the goods without any fault on the part of the seller or buyer perish or become so damaged as no longer to answer to their description in the agreement before the risk passes to the buyer, the agreement is thereby avoided.

Where in an agreement to sell specific goods, if subsequently the goods, without any fault on the part of the seller of buyer, perish or become so damaged as no longer answer to their description in the agreement, the agreement shall become void, provided the goods are perished before the ownership and risk passes to the buyer. This rule is based on the ground of impossibility of performance. If the title to the goods has already passed to the buyer, he must pay for the goods though the same cannot be delivered.

### *Possible causes of perishing of goods*

1. Physical destruction of goods
2. Damage of goods in such a manner that they lose their commercial value
3. Loss of goods by theft
4. Lawful acquisition of goods by Government.

### *Effect of perishing of goods*

**(1)** ***Goods perishing before formation of the contract***: Where specific goods form the subject matter of the contract of sale (both actual sale and an agreement to sell) and they perish without the knowledge of the seller at or before the time of contract, the contract is void. This provision is made either on the ground of mutual mistake as to matter of fact essential to agreement, or on the ground of impossibility of performance, both of which render the contract *void ab initio*.

In *Couturier* v. *Hastie*,[7] the plaintiff merchants shipped a cargo of Indian corn and sent the bill of lading to their London agent, who employed the defendant to sell the cargo. On 15 May 1848, the defendant sold the cargo to Challender on credit. The vessel had sailed on 23 February but the cargo became so heated and fermented that it was unfit to be carried further and sold. On May 23, Challender gave the plaintiff notice that he repudiated the contract on the ground that at the time of the sale to him, the cargo did not exist. The plaintiffs brought an action against the defendant (who was a *del credere* agent, i.e., guaranteed the performance of the contract) to recover the purchase price. Martin B ruled that the contract imported that, at the time of sale, the corn was in existence as such and capable of delivery, and that, as it had been sold, the plaintiffs could not recover. This judgment was affirmed by the House of Lords.

**(2)** ***Goods perishing before the sale but after the agreement to sell:*** Where there is an agreement to sell specific goods[8] and subsequently the goods, without any fault on the part of the seller or buyer perish before the risk passes to the buyer, the agreement is thereby avoided, i.e., sales becomes void and both parties are excused from performance. This is based on supervening impossibility.

If only part of the goods to be sold perish, the contract is void if the goods are indivisible or treated as such. In case the contract is divisible, perishing of goods rule applies to the extent of goods perished and is valid or upheld in case of the goods considered appropriate for sale.

It is to be noted that if fault of either party causes the destruction of the goods, then the party in default is liable for non-delivery or to pay for goods as the case may be. Again, if the risk has passed to the buyer, he must pay for the goods, though undelivered.

It is void under the following conditions:

(a) Agreement to sell specific goods.

(b) The goods must have perished or become so damaged as no longer to answer to their description in the contract of sale, before making of the contract.

(c) There must be no fault of the buyer or the seller.

(d) The risk must not have passed to the buyer, i.e., the goods must have perished before the agreement to sell becomes sale.

In *Elphick* v. *Barnes*,[9] a horse was taken on approval basis for eight days and the horse was found to be dead on the third day through no fault of the buyer and therefore it was held that the transaction had not become a sale when the horse died and so an action for price would not hold.

In *Howell* v. *Coupland*,[10] the contract was made in March, 1872 for the delivery of 200 ton potatoes the following autumn. In August the crop was destroyed by potato blight. The buyer accepted the 80 tons actually harvested and sued for non-delivery of the remainder. The Court of Appeal unanimously held that there was an implied term that both parties were excused in such a situation.

[7] 1852, 5 H.L.C. 673, 23 R.C. 204.

[8] "Identified and agreed upon at the time the contract of sale is made."

[9] 5 C.P.D. 321 (1880).

[10] (1876) 1 QBD 258.

**(3)** ***Effect of perishing of future goods:*** Section 8 provides that where there is an agreement to sell specific goods, and subsequently the goods without any fault on the part of the seller or buyer perish or become so damaged as no longer to answer to their description in the agreement before the risk passes to the buyer, the agreement is thereby avoided.

## Section 9: Ascertainment of price

(1) The price in a contract of sale may be fixed by the contract or may be left to be fixed in manner thereby agreed or may be determined by the course of dealing between the parties.

(2) Where the price is not determined in accordance with the foregoing provisions, the buyer shall pay the seller a reasonable price. What is a reasonable price is a question of fact dependent on the circumstances of each particular case.

Section 4, read with Sec. 2(10) of the Sale of Goods Act, 1930, requires that the contract of sale must provide for the payment of money as a consideration for the transfer of goods, or to put it differently, that a price must be paid. But Sec. 9 of the 1930 Act allows the parties not to fix the price at the time of the transfer and to leave the determination of the amount of consideration to a later date. An agreement which provides for the future fixation of price either by the parties themselves or by a third party is capable of being made certain and is not invalid as provided under Sec. 29 of the Contract Act, 1872 (See Illustration (e)). In view of such clear statutory provisions, the Supreme Court held that such a contract is void for uncertainly because the price was not fixed, is unacceptable.[11]

Section 29 of the Contract Act, 1872:

Illustration (e) A agrees to sell to B one thousand *maunds* of rice at a price to be decided by C. As the price capable of being made certain, there is no uncertainty here to make the agreement void.

## Section 10: Agreement to sell at valuation

(1) Where there is an agreement to sell goods on the terms that the price is to be fixed by the valuation of a third party and such third party cannot or does not make such valuation, the agreement is thereby avoided;

Provided that, if the goods or any part thereof have been delivered to, and appropriated by, the buyer, he shall pay a reasonable price therefor.

(2) Where such third party is prevented from making the valuation by the fault of the seller or buyer, the party not in fault may maintain a suit for damages against the party in fault.

[11] *M.S. Madhusoodhanan* v. *Kerala Kaumudi Pvt. Ltd.*, AIR 2004 SC 909.

# Chapter III Conditions and Warranties

## Section 11: Stipulations as to time

Unless a different intention appears from the terms of the contract, stipulations as to time of payment are not deemed to be of the essence of a contract of sale. Whether any other stipulation as to time is of the essence of the contract or not depends on the terms of the contract.

## Section 12: Condition and warranty

(1) A stipulation in a contract of sale with reference to goods which are the subject thereof may be a condition or a warranty.
(2) A condition is a stipulation essential to the main purpose of the contract, the breach of which gives rise to a right to treat the contract as repudiated.
(3) A warranty is a stipulation collateral to the main purpose of the contract, the breach of which gives rise to a claim for damages but not to a right to reject the goods and treat the contract as repudiated.
(4) Whether a stipulation in a contract of sale is a condition or a warranty depends in each case on the construction of the contract. A stipulation may be a condition, though called a warranty in the contract.

### *Meaning of stipulation [Sec. 12(1)]*

A stipulation is nothing but terms and conditions in a contract of sale which may be either a condition or warranty. It is often very difficult to decide whether the stipulation in a contract of sale would be a condition or warranty. One has to look at the substantive part of the contract of sale and to read the buyer's mind.[12]

### *Meaning of condition [Sec. 12(2)]*

A stipulation which is essential to the main purpose of the contract of sale and if the main purpose is not satisfied, it may lead to breach of contract which gives the aggrieved party a right to terminate the contract. In *Baldry* v. *Marshall,*[13] the plaintiff asked the defendants, who were motor dealers, to supply a car that would be suitable for touring purposes. The defendants recommended a *Bugatti,* which the plaintiff bought. The written contract excluded the defendant's liability for any *"guarantee or warranty, statutory or otherwise"*. The car turned out to be unsuitable for the plaintiff's purposes, so he rejected it and sued to recover what he had paid.

The Court of Appeal held that the requirement that the car be suitable for touring was a condition. Since the clause did not exclude liability for breach of a condition, the plaintiff was not bound by it.

---

[12] *Bentsen* v. *Taylor*, (1893) 2 Q.B. 274.
[13] (1925) 1KB 260.

### *Meaning of warranty [Sec. 12(3)]*

A stipulation is collateral to the main purpose of the contract, and the breach of which gives the aggrieved party a right to claim damages but not a right to reject goods and to terminate the contract.

A warranty is an express or implied statement of something which the party undertakes shall be part of a contract, and, though part of the contract, yet collateral to the express object of it. A "condition" is not defined in the statute. A condition is a term which is "of the essence" of the contract or, in other words, which is "regarded by the parties as a vital term going to the root of the contract."

The basis of distinction between condition and warranty is given below:

| Basis of Distinction | Condition | Warranty |
|---|---|---|
| **Essential collateral** | It is a stipulation which is essential to the main purpose of the contract. | It is a stipulation which is only collateral to the main purpose of the contract. |
| **Right in case of breach** | The aggrieved party can terminate the contract. | The aggrieved party can claim damages but cannot terminate the contract. |
| **Treatment** | A breach of condition can be treated as a breach of warranty. For example, a buyer may like to retain the goods and claim only damages. | A breach of warranty cannot be treated as a breach of condition. |

### Section 13: When condition to be treated as warranty

(1) Where a contract of sale is subject to any condition to be fulfilled by the seller, the buyer may waive the condition or elect to treat the breach of the condition as a breach of warranty and not as a ground for treating the contract as repudiated.

(2) Where a contract of sale is not severable and the buyer has accepted the goods or part thereof, the breach of any condition to be fulfilled by the seller can only be treated as a breach of warranty and not as a ground for rejecting the goods and treating the contract as repudiated, unless there is a term of the contract, express or implied, to that effect.

(3) Nothing in this section shall affect the case of any condition or warranty fulfilment of which is excused by law by reason of impossibility or otherwise.

### Section 14: Implied undertaking as to title, etc.

In a contract of sale, unless the circumstances of the contract are such as to show a different intention there is—

(a) an implied condition on the part of the seller that, in the case of a sale, he has a right to sell the goods and that, in the case of an agreement to sell, he will have a right to sell the goods at the time when the property is to pass;

(b) an implied warranty that the buyer shall have and enjoy quiet possession of the goods;

(c) an implied warranty that the goods shall be free from any charge or encumbrance in favour of any third party not declared or known to the buyer before or at the time when the contract is made.

In a contract of sale, unless the circumstances of the contract are such as to show a different intention, there is:

(1) An implied condition on the part of the seller that in the case of a sale the seller has a right to sell the goods, and that in the case of an agreement to sell the seller will have a right to sell the goods at the time when the property is to pass.

In *Rowland* v. *Divall,*[14] the plaintiff bought a motor car from the defendant and used it for several months. It then appeared that the defendant had had no title to it, and the plaintiff was compelled to surrender it to the true owner. The plaintiff sued the defendant to recover the purchase money that he had paid, as a total failure of consideration. It was held that notwithstanding that he had had the use of the car, the consideration had totally failed, and he was entitled to get the purchase money back. The use of the car that he had had was no part of the consideration that he had contracted for, which was the property in and lawful possession of the car, whereas what he got was an unlawful which exposed him to the risk of an action at the suit of the true owner.

(2) An implied warranty that the buyer shall have and enjoy quiet possession of the goods.

In every contract of sale, unless there is a contrary intention, there is an implied warranty that the buyer shall have and enjoy quiet possession of the goods. If the buyer's right to possession and enjoyment of the goods is in any way disturbed as consequences of the seller's defective title, the buyer may sue the seller for damages for breach of this warranty.

In *Niblett Limited* v. *Confectioners' Materials Co. Ltd.,*[15] the Confectioners' sold 3,000 tins of condensed milk to Niblett. The documents did not show which brand of condensed milk was. Therefore, Confectioners' argued that under an oral contract, it would be one of three brands—"Freedom", "Tucson", and "Nissley". Confectioners' delivered 2,000 cases of "Freedom" and then 1,000 tins of "Nissley". In November, Niblett received a letter from Nestle, stating that "Nissley" imitated the Nestle trademark and asked Niblett not to sell it. It also threatened to take proceedings against Niblett. Niblett signed an undertaking not to sell, advertise or offer for sale the "Nissley" condensed milk. They then unsuccessfully asked Confectioners' to take it back and unsuccessfully applied for an export license for it. The Court found that there was a clear breach of the Act because Confectioners' had no right to sell the goods as they were, and Niblett had never enjoyed quiet possession.

(3) An implied warranty that the goods shall be free from any charge or encumbrance in favour of any third party not declared or known to the buyer before or at the time when the contract is made.

[14] (1923) 2 KB 500.

[15] (1921) 3 KB 387.

The buyer is entitled to a further warranty that the goods shall be free from any charge or encumbrance in favour of any third party not declared or known to buyer before or at the time when the contract is made. If the buyer is required to discharge the amount of the encumbrance, it shall be a breach of this warranty and the buyer shall be entitled to damages for the same.

### *Exclusion of implied terms and conditions [Sec. 62]*

Where any right, duty or liability would arise under a contract of sale by implication of law, it may be negated or varied by express agreement or by the course of dealing between the parties, or by usage, if the usage is such as to bind both parties to the contract.

### Section 15: Sale by description

Where there is a contract for the sale of goods by description, there is an implied condition that the goods shall correspond with the description; and, if the sale is by sample as well as by description, it is not sufficient that the bulk of the goods corresponds with the sample if the goods do not also correspond with the description.

In a contract for the sale of goods by description, there is an implied condition that the goods must correspond with the description. Situations that would fall under this category include:

(1) Where the buyer has never seen the goods and buys them only on the basis of description given by the seller. In *Varley* v. *Whipp,*[16] the defendant agreed to buy a reaping machine which the defendant had never seen, but which the plaintiff seller stated to have been 'new the previous year and used very little'. On discovering that the machine did not comply with this description, the defendant returned the reaper to the plaintiff. The Court ruled in favour of the defendant and held that there was indeed a breach.

(2) Where the buyer has seen the goods but he buys them only on the basis of description given by the seller. In *Nicholson and Venn* v. *Smith Marriott,*[17] table linen was sold at an auction as being the property of King Charles I, although it was in fact Georgian; the main ground though was for breach of contract (misdescription).

(3) Where the method of packing has been described. In *Moore & Co.* v. *Landauer & Co.,*[18] the contract was for the sale of 3,100 cases of Australian canned fruit packed 30 tins to a case. Some cases were delivered with less than 30 tins to a case, some with more. The total number of tins delivered met the contract requirement. No loss resulted for failure to meet the contract description, yet the buyer was held entitled to rescind simply because it was not as per the description, in particular defective packing of goods.

---

[16] (1900) 1 QB.

[17] (1947) 177 L.T. 189.

[18] (1921) 2KB 519.

If the goods do not correspond with the description given while at the time of entering into the contract though they may suit the purpose of the buyer, the buyer has the right to reject the goods and the seller cannot take a plea that the goods suit the purpose of the buyer. In *Arcos* v. *Ranaasan & Sons,*[19] a delivery of staves which were nine-sixteenths of an inch thick instead of half an inch thick, as required by the contract, was a breach of description. There was strict application of implied condition of conformity with description, even when goods may be fit for the buyer's purpose.

### *Sale by description as well as sample [Sec. 15]*

When the sale takes place on the basis of both sample and description, the goods must correspond with both, the sample, and the description. It is not enough for one of the two alone to be fulfilled. In *Nichol* v. *Godts,*[20] Nichol showed samples of oil to Godts. He described the oil as: 'Foreign refined rape oil, warranted only equal to samples'. Godts entered into a written contract to buy 33 tons. The oil corresponded with the sample, but not the description. It was a mixture of rape and hemp oil. Godts refused to accept or pay and Nichol sued for payment which was not upheld by the Court.

### Section 16: Implied conditions as to quality or fitness

Subject to the provisions of this Act and of any other law for the time being in force, there is no implied warranty or condition as to the quality or fitness for any particular purpose of goods supplied under a contract of sale, except as follows:—

(1) Where the buyer, expressly or by implication, makes known to the seller the particular purpose for which the goods are required, so as to show that the buyer relies on the seller's skill or judgment, and the goods are of a description which it is in the course of the seller's business to supply (whether he is the manufacturer or producer or not), there is an implied condition that the goods shall be reasonably fit for such purpose:

Provided that, in the case of a contract for the sale of a specified article under its patent or other trade name, there is no implied condition as its fitness for any particular purpose.

(2) Where goods are bought by description from a seller who deals in goods of that description (whether he is the manufacturer or producer or not), there is an implied condition that the goods shall be of merchantable quality;

Provided that, if the buyer has examined the goods, there shall be no implied condition as regards defects which such examination ought to have revealed.

(3) An implied warranty or condition as to quality or fitness for a particular purpose may be annexed by the usage of trade.

(4) An express warranty or condition does not negative a warranty or condition implied by this Act unless inconsistent therewith.

[19] (1933) A.C. 470 102.

[20] (1854) 156 ER 410.

Section 16 is an exception to the rule of *'caveat emptor'*. The rule of *'caveat emptor'* applies whenever the buyer voluntarily chooses what he buys. But it does not mean that the buyer should 'take chance' but it means he should 'take care'. The most important exceptions to the rule of *'caveat emptor'* are the implied condition of fitness for a particular purpose and the merchantableness of the product. When a man sells an article, he thereby warrants that it is merchantable, i.e., it is fit for some purpose and if he sells it for some particular purpose, he thereby warrants it for that purpose.

Section 16(1) of the Sale of Goods Act deals with the implied conditions as to the quality or fitness of the articles sold.

In order to attract Sec. 16, it has to be proved that the buyer expressly or by implication had made known to the seller the particular purpose for which the goods were purchased. Ext. A13 letter sent by the 2nd respondent coupled with the invoice showing the sale of the sheets with accessories for the roofing would indicate that the purpose of purchase of the semi-corrugated asbestos sheets was for roofing and that had been disclosed too. Moreover, corrugated asbestos sheets are mainly used for roofing of buildings for protecting the building from sun and rain and it is not being used for a variety of purposes. The leak proof of the asbestos sheets is the essential quality of the sheets and only if it is leak proof, it can be said to be fit for the purpose for which it is purchased. The evidence would further reveal that the plaintiff wanted Everest asbestos sheets and Everest asbestos sheets had the reputation regarding its quality. Thus, the plaintiff was trusting the judgment or the skill of the 1st defendant, the manufacturer, or the dealer and thus there was an implied term of warranty that the articles would be reasonably fit for the purpose to which it was applied. The evidence would further reveal that the asbestos sheets supplied by the 2nd defendant had manufacturing defect and thereby it was leaking during rainy season. The report would further reveal that fissures were there on the sheets and that could be due to defective curing also. As the article was purchased for a specific purpose and it was disclosed to the seller, sub-section (1) of Sec. 16 would be attracted and there was an implied warranty as to the quality of the articles sold that it was fit for the purpose for which it was sold.[21] Where a layman purchases a watch of a particular make from a reputed firm which exclusively deals in such watches, the sale is governed by exception (1) to Sec. 16 of the Sale of Goods Act because in such a case, the purpose is only the common purpose and not any special purpose, the seller knows it, and the purchaser, being only a layman, relies on the seller's skill or judgment. Further, such transaction being a sale by description from a dealer who deals in goods of that description, exception (2) to Sec. 16 also applies. The plaintiff purchased a watch of a particular make from the defendant company which was the exclusive dealer for watches of that make. Along with the watch a guaranteed certificate was issued which provided a guarantee for one year unless unfairly used or damaged by accident. The watch, on being found to be defective, was returned to the seller for repairs twice or thrice but it was given back without any improvement in it. The plaintiff filed a suit for the refund of the price or its replacement. The defendant denied liability contending that the guarantee covered only free servicing. The Court held that on construction of the guarantee clause that it included the replacement also and the sale was governed by exceptions (1) and (2) to Sec. 16, the defendant was liable for breach

[21] *Eternit Everest Ltd.* v. *C.G. Abraham,* AIR 2003 KERALA 273.

of warranty under the Sale of Goods Act and was bound to replace the watch or refund its price.[22]

Section 16(1) of the Act, as is well known, engrafts an exception on the general maxim *caveat emptor*. It is also clear on an analysis of Sec. 16(1) that three conditions have to be satisfied before a buyer can invoke the implied condition that the goods supplied shall be reasonably fit for a particular purpose. The three conditions are as follows:

1. The buyer, expressly or by implication, makes known to the seller the particular purpose for which the goods are required.
2. This "making known" to the seller of the purpose would show that the buyer relies on the seller's skill or judgment.
3. The goods are of a description which it is in the course of the seller's business to supply.

This question as to the applicability of Sec. 16(1) of the Act therefore involves an investigation into a mixed question of law and fact. In other words, the Court has to find as a fact whether these three conditions which have been set out above for the applicability of Sec. 16(1) are satisfied. If they are satisfied, the Court is to draw the conclusion that in law it amounts to "implied warranty" as provided in that sub-section. From this, it necessarily follows that any buyer who is seeking to invoke the protection granted to it by Sec. 16(1) of the Act must allege and prove that the three conditions which are necessary for its application have in fact been satisfied.[23]

Section 16 deals with the implied conditions as to quality or fitness of goods for a particular purpose. No distinction appears to have been drawn in the section between contracts for the sale of specific as distinguished from those for the sale of unascertained goods. Exception 1 (Sec. 16(1)) applies where the buyer requires the goods for a particular purpose, where the buyer expressly or by implication makes known to the seller that particular purpose, where it is shown that the buyer relies on the seller's skill or judgment and where the seller's usual course of business is to sell such goods, whether he is the actual producer or not. Where all these essential facts exist, there is an implied condition that the goods shall be reasonably fit for such purpose. The buyer in our case did rely on the skill or judgment of the seller. This is not a case where he had inspected the goods and bought them on his own judgment. In this case, the buyer purchased the radio-set with some specified purpose. It could easily be said that the vendor sold this radio-set for that specified purpose. It has, therefore, to be of a certain quality. If it is not of that quality and if it is not fit for such purpose, then the law implies a promise from the vendor that he will supply to the purchaser an article of that quality and reasonably fit for the purpose for which it is required. The seller's liability in such cases to supply goods that are reasonably fit is an absolute one.

It is not necessary that the buyer should expressly or by implication make known to the seller a particular purpose. The words *"by implication"* in Sec. 16(1) clearly indicate that the communication of the purpose to the seller need not be expressed in words. It may be inferred from the description of the goods given by the buyer to the seller or

[22] *Raghava Menon* v. *Kuttappan Nair*, AIR 1962 KERALA 318.

[23] *Bengal Corporation* v. *Commrs. for the Port of Calcutta*, AIR 1971 CALCUTTA 357.

from the circumstances of the case. The buyer, however, must rely on the seller's skill or judgment. In this particular case, it does appear that the plaintiff naturally had relied on the radio set which he had purchased from the defendants. In the instant case, defendant No. 2 was a firm which was supplying radios in the ordinary course of their business. In fact they were supplying the goods manufactured by defendant No. 1. Therefore, the buyer naturally should expect goods which were fit enough for the purpose for which he was buying. We have seen that the radio set started giving the plaintiff trouble almost about two months after he purchased it. In this view of the matter, therefore, it appears to me that the case of the plaintiff could even come within the purview of Sec. 16(1). It could also come within the purview of Sec. 16(2). This sub-section embodies also an exception recognised at common law to the maxim "caveat emptor". If a dealer deals with certain goods of a particular description, and if the buyer purchases the same, then there would be an implied condition that the goods shall be of the merchantable quality. If, however, the buyer had examined the goods, then there shall be no implied condition as regards defects which such examination ought to have revealed. In other words, in the case of goods sold of a particular description by a seller who deals in such goods, he is always, in the absence of agreement to the contrary, responsible for the latent defects in the goods which render them unmerchantable, whether the buyer examined them or not, and for all such defects, whether latent or discoverable, on examination in cases where the buyer has not in fact examined the goods. Where the buyer, however, gets an opportunity of inspection but examines the goods superficially, he cannot complain of defects which a reasonable and more thorough examination ought to have revealed.[24]

The Sale of Goods Act does not give any definition of the word 'merchantable', yet the word has by long use become a term of art in commercial law. Merchantable quality means that the goods comply with the description in the contract so that to a purchaser buying goods of that description, the goods would be good tender. Goods are of merchantable quality if they are of such a quality and in such a condition that a reasonable man, acting reasonably, would, after a full examination, accept them under the circumstances of the case in performance of the offer to buy them, whether he buys for his own use or to sell again.

Goods cease to be merchantable because of defects rendering them unfit for the purpose for which they are usually sold. Merchantability is fulfilled when the goods do not differ from the normal quality of the described goods including, under the term quality, the State or condition as required by the contract. The goods should be immediately saleable under the description by which they are known in the market.

Section 16 of the Act, however, divides all such defects into two kinds, often called patent and latent defects. Patent defects are those which can be found on examination by a person of ordinary prudence with the exercise of due care and attention. Latent defects are those which cannot be discovered on such examination. There is an implied condition on the seller's part that the goods are free from latent defects. Whether a defect is latent or patent will depend on the nature of the goods and the nature of the defect and the extent of examination needed for its discovery. It is a question of fact in each case.[25]

---

[24] *R.S. Thakur* v. *H.G.E. Corporation*, AIR 1971 BOMBAY 97.

[25] *Sorabji H. Joshi and Co.* v. *V.M. Ismail*, AIR 1960 MADRAS 520.

In every contract to supply goods of a specified description, which the buyer had no opportunity to inspect, the goods must not only answer the description but must be saleable or merchantable under that description. Those two conditions, namely (i) answering the description in the contract, and (ii) merchantable quality are embodied in Secs. 15 and 16 of the Sale of Goods Act. Under Sec. 15, if there is a contract for the sale of goods by description, there is an implied condition that the goods shall correspond with the description. Under Sec. 16(2), there is a further implied condition where there had been no previous inspection by the buyer that the goods are of merchantable quality. The effect of these two definitions is to give a right or an occasion to the buyer to reject the goods in case what was tendered did not answer the description or was not of merchantable quality. The passing of property in the goods is not the test as to the applicability of this right. If the goods do not conform to the description, there is no performance of the contract at all. If the goods are not of the merchantable quality, the thing for which the buyer bargained for was not given. In either case, the default of the seller goes to the root of the transaction and therefore the occasion would arise to the buyer to reject the goods and sue for the price if he had paid the price.[26]

**Section 17: Sale by sample**

(1) A contract of sale is a contract for sale by sample where there is a term in the contract, express or implied, to that effect.

(2) In the case of a contract for sale by sample there is an implied condition—

(a) that the bulk shall correspond with the sample in quality;

(b) that the buyer shall have a reasonable opportunity of comparing the bulk with the sample;

(c) that the goods shall be free from any defect, rendering them unmerchantable, which would not be apparent on reasonable examination of the sample.

Sale by sample is subject to the following conditions:

1. The goods must correspond with the sample in quality;
2. The buyer must have a reasonable opportunity of comparing the bulk with the sample; and
3. The goods must be free from any defect which renders them unmerchantable and which would not be apparent on reasonable examination of the sample. Such defects are called latent defects and are discovered when the goods are put to use. It may be noted that the seller cannot be held responsible for apparent or liable defects which could be easily discovered by an ordinary prudent person.

## Chapter IV Effects of the Contract

**Section 18: Goods must be ascertained**

Where there is a contract for the sale of unascertained goods, no property in the goods is transferred to the buyer unless and until the goods are ascertained.

[26] *National Traders* v. *Hindustan Soap Works,* AIR 1959 MADRAS 112.

Section 18 of the Sale of Goods Act, 1930, provides that where there is a contract for the sale of unascertained goods, no property in the goods is transferred to the buyer unless and until the goods are ascertained. Even though there was a concluded contract for the sale of waste coal ash, the goods were not identified or specific as defined by Sec. 2(14). According to the terms of the contract, the defendants were to supply waste coal ash as and when the same was discharged from the bunkers of the Power House. In substance the contract was for the sale of unascertained goods; therefore, no property in the goods could pass to the appellant till the goods were ascertained by appropriation which in this case did not take place at all.[27]

### Section 19: Property passes when intended to pass

(1) Where there is a contract for the sale of specific or ascertained goods, the property in them is transferred to the buyer at such time as the parties to the contract intend it to be transferred.

(2) For the purpose of ascertaining the intention of the parties regard shall be had to the terms of the contract, the conduct of the parties and the circumstances of the case.

(3) Unless a different intention appears, the rules contained in Sections 20 to 24 are rules for ascertaining the intention of the parties as to the time at which the property in the goods is to pass to the buyer.

Section 19 attempts to give effect to the elementary principle of the Law of Contract that the parties may fix the time when the property in the goods shall be treated to have passed. It may be the time of delivery, or the time of payment of price or even the time of the making of contract. It all depends upon the intention of the parties. It is, therefore, the duty of the Court to ascertain the intention of the parties and in doing so, they have to be guided by the principles laid down in Sec. 19(2) which provides that for ascertaining the intention of the parties, regards shall be had to the terms of the contract, the conduct of the parties and the circumstances of the case.

Section 19 indicates that in the case of unconditional contract of sale in respect of specified goods in a deliverable state, the property in the goods passes to the buyer at such time as the parties intend it to be transferred. Section 19(3) provides that Secs. 20 to 24 contain the rules for ascertaining the intention of the parties as to the time at which the property in the goods shall be treated to have passed to the buyer. Both Secs. 19 and 20 apply to the sale of *"specific"* or *"ascertained"* goods.

### Section 20: Specific goods in a deliverable state

Where there is an unconditional contract for the sale of specific goods in a deliverable state, the property in the goods passes to the buyer when the contract is made, and it is immaterial whether the time of payment of the price or the time of delivery of the goods, or both, is postponed.

Section 20, which contains the first rule for ascertaining the intention of the parties, provides that where there is an unconditional contract for the sale of *"specific goods"* in

---

[27] *Tej Singh* v. *State*, AIR 1981 ALLAHABAD 103.

a *"deliverable state"*, the property in the goods passes to the buyer when the contract is made. This indicates that as soon as a contract is made in respect of specific goods which are in a deliverable state, the title in the goods passes to the purchaser. The passing of the title is not dependent upon the payment of price or the time of delivery of the goods. If the time for payment of price or the time for delivery of goods, or both, is postponed, it would not affect the passing of the title in the goods so purchased.

In order to apply Sec. 20, two conditions have to be fulfilled: (i) the contract of sale is for specific goods which are in a deliverable state; and (ii) the contract is an unconditional contract. If these two conditions are satisfied, Sec. 20 becomes applicable immediately and it is at this stage that it has to be seen whether there is anything either in the terms of the contract or in the conduct of the parties or in the circumstances of the case which indicates a contrary intention. This exercise has to be done to give effect to the opening words, namely, *"Unless a different intention appears"* occurring in Sec. 19(3). The intention of the parties would be the decisive factor as to when the property in goods passes to the purchaser. If the contract is silent, intention has to be gathered from the conduct and circumstances of the case.[28]

In the instant case, the goods which were the subject matter of sale were ascertained goods. They were also in a deliverable state. On the order being placed by the respondent, the seller in the State of Kerala, loaded the goods on the lorry and dispatched the same to Hyderabad. It is at this stage that the conduct of the parties becomes extremely relevant. It was one of the terms of the contract between the parties that the seller would not be liable for any future loss of goods and that the goods were being dispatched at the risk of the respondent. The respondent had also obtained insurance of the goods and had paid the policy premium. He, therefore, intended the goods to be treated as his own so that if there was any loss of goods in transit, he could validly claim the insurance money. The weighment of the goods at Hyderabad or the collection of documents from the bank or payment of price through the bank at Hyderbad were immaterial, inasmuch as the property in the goods had already passed at Kerala and it was not dependent upon the payment of price or the delivery of goods to the respondent.

The Supreme Court is of the opinion that having regard to the evidence on record which indicated that on the order placed by the respondent, the stocks were loaded into the trucks for dispatch to Hyderabad with the clear stipulation that the dispatch was at the risk of the purchaser and that the seller had no liability with regard to any future losses and that the stock was insured and the insurance premium was paid by the respondent, the sale took place in the State of Kerala and not at Hyderabad.

In *Digamber Pershad Kirti Prasad, M/s.* v. *State of U.P.*,[29] the auction in favour of the purchaser was approved by the Conservator of Forest, and the purchaser started felling the trees and the timber was collected at a central point for transportation, the contract was concluded and the purchaser cannot refuse to pay the purchase price on the ground that the contract was frustrated because the timber was destroyed in the fire. The agreement was not subjected to any future condition of the full payment having been made, but the agreement became a concluded contract when the auction was accepted by the competent

---

[28] *Agricultural Market Committee* v. *Shalimar Chemical Works Ltd.*, AIR 1997 SC 2502.

[29] AIR 1996 ALLAHABAD 1.

authority, possession of the trees to be felled by the purchaser was given and when he started felling the trees. Moreover, Sec. 20 would apply even if the payment of price was postponed. Section 20 states that where there is an unconditional contract for the sale of specific goods in a deliverable state, the property in the goods passes to the buyer when the contract is made and it is immaterial whether the time of payment of the price or the time of delivery of goods or both are postponed. In the instant case, the trees contracted to be severed were not only ascertained and duly identified, but they were actually felled and timber was sawn and collected at the central point and, therefore, the timber, when it was sawn and collected at the central point, was in a deliverable state within the meaning of Sec. 20 of the Act and contract not being conditional one, both the ingredients of Sec. 20 existed and the property in the goods can be held to have passed right at the stage when the purchaser took possession of the trees and felled them and when the timber was sawn and collected at the central point, from where that was to be transported through the check post upon full payment having been made. Simply because full payment was not made and the timber was not actually removed, it cannot be said that the property in the goods was not transferred.

Moreover, according to Sec. 26, the risk remains with the seller until the property in the goods is transferred to the buyer. But this rule is subject to the agreement made between the parties. It means that the parties are free to make an agreement contrary to this rule, meaning thereby the parties can agree that risk will pass to the buyer even before the property in the goods is transferred from the seller to the buyer, and according to one of the conditions of the contract in question, after 30 days from the date of acceptance of the contract or from the date of commencement of work under the contract, whichever is earlier, the buyer will be fully responsible for the damage caused to the goods.

### Section 21: Specific goods to be put into a deliverable state

Where there is a contract for the sale of specific goods and the seller is bound to do something to the goods for the purpose of putting them into a deliverable state, the property does not pass until such thing is done and the buyer has notice thereof.

### Section 22: Specific goods in a deliverable state, when the seller has to do anything thereto in order to ascertain price

Where there is a contract for the sale of specific goods in a deliverable state, but the seller is bound to weigh, measure, test or do some other act or thing with reference to the goods for the purpose of ascertaining the price, the property does not pass until such act or thing is done and the buyer has notice thereof.

### Section 23: Sale of unascertained goods and appropriation

(1) Where there is a contract for the sale of unascertained or future goods by description and goods of that description and in a deliverable state are unconditionally appropriated to the contract, either by the seller with the assent of the buyer or by the buyer with the assent of the seller, the property in the goods thereupon passes to the buyer. Such assent may be expressed or implied and may be given either before or after the appropriation is made.

(2) ***Delivery to carrier:*** Where, in pursuance of the contract, the seller delivers the goods to the buyer or to a carrier or other bailee (whether named by the buyer or not) for the purpose of transmission to the buyer, and does not reserve the right of disposal, he is deemed to have unconditionally appropriated the goods to the contract.

Section 23 of the Indian Sale of Goods Act lays down that where there is a contract for the sale of unascertained or future goods by description and goods of that description and in a deliverable state are unconditionally appropriated to the contract, either by the seller with the assent of the buyer or by the buyer with the assent of the seller, the property in the goods thereupon passes to the buyer. The requirement of the section is not only that there shall be appropriation of the goods to the contract but that such appropriation must be made unconditionally. This is further elaborated by Section 25 which provides that where there is a contract for the sale of specific goods or where goods are subsequently appropriated to the contract, the seller may, by the terms of the contract or appropriation, reserve the right of disposal of the goods until certain conditions are fulfilled. *'Prima facie'* such delivery of the goods to the buyer and the passing of the risk in respect of the goods from the seller to the buyer are strong indications as to the passing also of the property in the goods to the buyer but they are not decisive and may be negatived, for under Sec. 25 the seller may yet reserve to himself the right of disposal of goods until the fulfilment of certain conditions and thereby prevent the passing of property in the goods from him to the buyer.[30]

Section 23(1) is wholly independent of Sec. 23(2). Section 23(1) does not contemplate unconditional appropriation in pursuance of a contract; it refers to unconditional appropriation with the assent of the parties, whereas, in Sec. 23(2), it is the delivery to a carrier in pursuance of a contract which operates as an unconditional appropriation, and is, therefore, deemed to be unconditional appropriation. Where, therefore, a party relies upon what must be deemed to be an unconditional appropriation within the meaning of Sec. 23(2), he cannot be allowed to say that it was also, without more, an unconditional appropriation within the meaning of Sec. 23(1). Even where there is an unconditional appropriation within the meaning of sub-sections. (1) and (2) of Sec. 23, the question whether the seller intends to transfer the property in goods still persists and in ascertaining that intention regard must be had to the terms of the contract, the conduct of the parties, and the circumstances of the case, as laid down in Sec. 19(2).

Where a contract of sale contemplates delivery to the buyer in Calcutta, the seller, in making over the goods to a carrier in Assam, merely acts in execution of the contract as to the carriage of goods and not as to their delivery and the act of the seller cannot be deemed to be unconditional appropriation within the meaning of Sec. 23(2). In a given contract, there cannot be two distinct deliveries. Delivery in pursuance of the contract as to delivery may be made in different stages, but it is nevertheless one delivery made in different stages in pursuance of the contract as to delivery. The mere making over of the goods to a carrier for transmission to the buyer in pursuance of the contract as to carriage of the goods, as distinct from delivery cannot be regarded as delivery in pursuance of the contract.[31]

---

[30] *Commr. of Income-tax, Madras* v. *Mysore Chromite Ltd.*, AIR 1955 SC 98.

[31] *Ramniwas* v. *Commr. of Taxes*, AIR 1952 ASSAM 178.

The consignor has got a right to institute a suit against Railways for loss, damage or non-delivery of goods in transit entrusted to it for delivery to the consignee unless the consignee actually takes the delivery at the destination. This rule, however, is subject to the well-established exception contained in Secs. 23 and 39 of the Sale of Goods Act. To put it in a different way, the terms of the contract of sale have to be considered and whether they indicate that the moment the seller entrusts the goods to the carrier, the ownership in the goods vested in the buyer and the carrier is presumed not only to be the buyer's agent but to have assented to the appropriation to the contract of goods so delivered.

In *Union of India* v. *M/s. Indian and Overseas Trading Co.*,[32] the plaintiff received an order for supply of 44 cases of Indian Dressed Bristles from a foreign company. In pursuance of the said order, the plaintiff entrusted to the Railway Administration at Kanpur Central Goods Shed, 44 Cases of Indian Dressed Bristles, for carnage to Bombay, and the said consignment was consigned to the Chartered Bank, which was the beneficiary of the plaintiff at Kanpur and the endorsed consignees were M/S 'A' Company at Bombay who were the shipping agents of the said plaintiff. While in transit, the wagon in which the 44 cases was in transit was pilfered on its way to Bombay and on delivery being taken by the plaintiffs' shipping agents, the consignment was short delivered by six cases and a shortage certificate was issued by Railway Administration. The plaintiff, on account of shortage made a claim under Sec. 78B of the Railways Act, 1890. It was alleged that the suit was not maintainable at the instance of the plaintiff, who was the seller. But the Court held that in the facts and circumstances that the title in the goods sent by the disputed consignment vested in the seller, plaintiff and therefore the suit filed by the plaintiff was maintainable. Consequently, the decree directing recovery of the said damages in favour of the plaintiff confirmed.

### Section 24: Goods sent on approval or "on sale or return"

When goods are delivered to the buyer on approval or "on sale or return" or other similar terms, the property therein passes to the buyer—

(a) when he signifies his approval or acceptance to the seller or does any other act adopting the transaction;

(b) if he does not signify his approval or acceptance to the seller but retains the goods without giving notice of rejection, then, if a time has been fixed for the return of the goods, on the expiration of such time, and, if no time has been fixed, on the expiration of a reasonable time.

### Section 25: Reservation of right of disposal

(1) Where there is a contract for the sale of specific goods or where goods are subsequently appropriated to the contract, the seller may, by the terms of the contract or appropriation, reserve the right of disposal of the goods until certain conditions are fulfilled. In such case, notwithstanding the delivery of the goods to a buyer, or to a carrier or other bailee for the purpose of transmission to the

[32] AIR 1987 ALLAHABAD 196.

buyer, the property in the goods does not pass to the buyer until the conditions imposed by the seller are fulfilled.

(2) Where goods are shipped or delivered to a railway administration for carriage by railway and by the bill of lading or railway receipt, as the case may be, the goods are deliverable to the order of the seller or his agent, the seller is *prima facie* deemed to reserve right of disposal.

(3) Where the seller of goods draws on the buyer for the price and transmits to the buyer the bill of exchange together with the bill of lading or, as the case may be, the railway receipt, to secure acceptance or payment of the bill of exchange, the buyer is bound to return the bill of lading or the railway receipt if he does not honour the bill of exchange; and, if he wrongfully retains the bill lading or the railway receipt, the property in the goods does not pass to him.

***Explanation:*** In this section, the expressions "railway" and "railway administration" shall have the meanings respectively assigned to them under the Indian Railways Act, 1890.

### Section 26: Risk *prima facie* passes with property

Unless otherwise agreed, the goods remain at the seller's risk until the property therein is transferred to the buyer, but when the property therein is transferred to the buyer, the goods are at the buyer's risk whether delivery has been made or not:

Provided that, where delivery has been delayed through the fault of either buyer or seller, the goods are at the risk of the party in fault as regards any loss which might not have occurred but for such fault:

Provided also that nothing in this section shall affect the duties or liabilities of either seller or buyer as a bailee of the goods of the other party.

It is clear from the provisions of Sec. 26 that the second proviso applies to a case where the seller or the buyer holds the goods in the capacity of a bailee either under a contract of bailment or under circumstances which give rise to the relationship of bailor and bailee. The second proviso means that the operation of the provisions of Sec. 26 is excluded when the buyer or the seller happens to hold the goods in the character of a bailee.[33]

## Chapter V Transfer of Title

### Section 27: Sale by person not the owner

Subject to the provisions of this Act and of any other law for the time being in force, where goods are sold by a person who is not the owner thereof and who does not sell them under the authority or with the consent of the owner, the buyer acquires no better title to the goods than the seller had, unless the owner of the goods is by his conduct precluded from denying the seller's authority to sell:

Provided that where a mercantile agent is, with the consent of the owner, in possession of the goods or of a document of title to the goods, any sale made by him, when acting

[33] *Hanutmal Bhutoria* v. *Dominion of India*, AIR 1961 CALCUTTA 54.

in the ordinary course of business of a mercantile agent, shall be as valid as if he were expressly authorised by the owner of the goods to make the same; provided that the buyer acts in good faith and has not at the time of the contract of sale notice that the seller has no authority to sell.

### *Nemo dat quod non habet*—"no one can give that, which one does not have"[34]

There are numerous circumstances where goods are sold by someone who is not their true owner and the question whether such a non-owner might be able to transfer good title in those goods to a buyer subsequently arises. It is natural to advocate that this should be impossible in that only a true owner should be capable of voluntarily transferring such a good title. However, as far as the bona fide purchaser is concerned, is there any solution which he is able to seek to protect his own interests? In most cases on sales by a non-owner, the law has to choose between rigorously upholding the rights of the owner to his property, on the one hand, and protecting the interests of the purchaser who buys in good faith and for value, on the other.

A basic principle of the common law, *nemo dat quod non habet* states that no one can transfer to another person that which he does not have himself. This principle can be restated in common terms applicable to this case, i.e., no seller of goods can transfer a better title to a purchaser than he himself has.

Section 27 of the Act prescribes the rule of *nemo dat quod non habet* as well as exception to the rule. The intention of enacting this provision is to protect the innocent buyer who has acted in good faith.

### *Sale by a person not the owner*

In *Cundy* v. *Lindsay*[35], a rogue called Blenkarn, impersonating a well-known firm named Blenkiron which carried on business in the same street, ordered a quantity of linen by post from Lindsay & Co. in Belfast. When the linen arrived, Blenkarn sold part of it to Messrs Cundy, who bought it in good faith and without knowledge of Blenkarn's fraud. The first contract was held to be void (in modern terms, on ground of mistake of identity), so that no title in the linen passed to Blenkarn. It followed that he could not confer any title on Cundy, who were consequently liable to Lindsay & Co. in conversion.

Section 27 provides that subject to the provisions of this Act and of any other law for the time being in force, where goods are sold by a person who is not the owner thereof and who does not sell them under the authority or with the consent of the owner, the buyer acquires no better title to the goods than the seller had, unless the owner of the goods is by his conduct precluded from denying the seller's authority to sell, i.e., *estoppel* by conduct.

### *Estoppel*

1. The true owner intentionally or negligently represents that the seller is entitled to sell the goods.

[34] http://privatelaw.com.cn.

[35] (1878) 3 App. Cas. 459.

2. The innocent buyer acts in reliance on the representation.
3. The innocent buyer buys the goods.

It has become a basic norm of *estoppel* by conduct that where the owner merely permits another to have possession of goods or documents of title, he is not *estopped* from denying other's authority to sell.

### *Estoppel by Negligence*

It is really possible for the owner to be negligent and make the seller appear as an owner or having authority to sell goods. However, the level of negligence has to be considered carefully. As a general rule, a duty of care has to be shown by the buyer when he asserts that the original owner is negligent indeed. As in the law of tort, there can be no negligence unless there is a duty to take care. It is really possible for the owner to be negligent and make the seller appear as an owner or having authority to sell goods. However, the level of negligence has to be considered carefully. As a general rule, a duty of care has to be shown by the buyer when he asserts that the original owner is negligent indeed. As in the law of tort, there can be no negligence unless there is a duty to take care.

In *Mercantile Credit Co.* v. *Hamblin,*[36] Mrs. Hamblin wished to raise money using her Jaguar car as security. For reasons of convenience, she decided to go through an apparently respectable car dealer called Phelan. She signed three blank forms, the first proposal was offering to take her Jaguar on hire purchase from Mercantile Credit, the second was a receipt acknowledging that the car had been delivered to her and that the car was insured, and the third was a banker's order for payment of the instalments to Mercantile Credit. Phelan said that he would enquire about how much he could get for the car and report back to her over the telephone. He also gave her a blank cheque, which he said she could fill after he told her the appropriate amount. Things went wrong when Phelan filled the forms signed by Hamblin. He sent them to Mercantile Credit along with a further form claiming to be the owner of the car and offered to sell it to the finance company. The finance company would then let it on hire purchase to Hamblin. Phelan obtained £800 for the Jaguar and absconded leaving Hamblin to pay the hire purchase on the car who in turn refused to do so. Mercantile Credit argued that Hamblin was estopped by her conduct in signing the blank forms from asserting her ownership.

### *Essentials to be Estopped by Negligence*

1. The defendant owed the claimant a duty of care.
2. The defendant breached the duty of care.
3. The claimant suffered damage as a result of the breach.

Following are the exceptions:

1. Owner's conduct indicates that the seller had authority to sell.
   Example—The owner is present when the sale is taking place, etc.

[36] (1965) 2 QB 242; (1964) 1 WLR 423.

2. ***Unauthorised sale by mercantile agent [Sec. 59(1)]:*** The basic principle of "estoppel by conduct" applies 'where a mercantile agent, with the consent of the owner, in possession of goods or of the documents of title to goods, any sale, pledge, or other disposition of the goods, made by him when acting in the ordinary course of business of a mercantile agent, shall, subject to the provisions of this Act, be as valid as if he were expressly authorised by the owner of the goods to make the same; provided that the person taking under the disposition acts in good faith, and has not at the time of the disposition notice that the person making the disposition has not authority to make the same and the same is for a consideration'.
3. ***Sale by one of joint owners [Sec. 28]:*** This provides that if one of several joint owners of goods has the sole possession of the goods by permission of the co-owners, the property in the goods is transferred to any person who buys them from such joint owner in good faith and does not, at the time of the contract of sale, notice that the seller has no authority to sell.
4. ***Sale by person in possession under voidable contract [Sec. 29]:*** If possession is obtained under a contract voidable under Sec. 19 (consent by fraud or misrepresentation) or 19A (undue influence) of the Contract Act but the aggrieved party has not avoided the contract before passing the possession to third party and the said third party gets the valid title provided that he purchased the goods in good faith and without knowledge of the seller's defect of title.

   *Note*: Applicable only to voidable and not void contract as the latter gives no good title.
5. ***Seller in possession after sale [Sec. 30(1)]:*** The seller in possession of goods after the sale can pass on good title if the subsequent transferee receives the goods in good faith and for consideration.
6. ***Buyer in possession after sale [Sec. 30(2)]:*** If the goods are transferred but the property in goods has not been transferred, the buyer can still pass on good title if the subsequent transferee receives in good faith and for consideration.

   *Note*: Does not apply to hire purchase or lease as goods have neither been bought nor "agreed to buy".
7. ***Resale by unpaid seller [Sec. 54(3)]:*** An unpaid seller exercises his right of lien or stoppage in transit re-sells the goods, the buyer acquires a good title against the original buyer despite no notice of re-sale being given to the original buyer.
8. ***Exception under the Negotiable Instruments Act:*** A holder in due course gets good title in the negotiable instrument if he takes the instrument in good faith for consideration, before it is payable or reaches maturity.
9. ***Exception under the Contract Act:*** The buyer gets good title despite the seller having no title. Section 169 empowers the finder of goods to sale goods if they are in danger of perishing or lawful charges of the finder amount to two-thirds of the value of goods found. Section 176 enables the pawnee to sale goods after giving notice if the pawnor defaults in payment of debt or performance.
10. The receiver/liquidator in the case of insolvency/of company and by permission from the Court/NCLT, as the case may be, can sell goods even if he has no title giving the buyer a title equivalent to that of the original owner.

11. *Sale by bank/FI under Securitisation Act:* In case of default in payment by the borrower of principal or interest, possession and eventual sale is allowed by the lender.

**Section 28: Sale by one of joint owners**

If one of several joint owners of goods has the sole possession of them by permission of the co-owners, the property in the goods is transferred to any person who buys them of such joint owner in good faith and has not at the time of the contract of sale notice that the seller has not authority to sell.

**Section 29: Sale by person in possession under voidable contract**

When the seller of goods has obtained possession thereof under a contract voidable under Section 19 or Section 19A of the Indian Contract Act, 1872, but the contract has not rescinded at the time of the sale, the buyer acquires a good title to the goods, provided he buys them in good faith and without notice of the seller's defect of title.

**Section 30: Seller or buyer in possession after sale**

(1) Where a person, having sold goods continues or is in possession of the goods or of the documents of title to the goods, the delivery or transfer by that person or by a mercantile agent acting for him of the goods or documents of title under any sale, pledge or other disposition thereof to any person receiving the same in good faith and without notice of the previous sale shall have the same effect as if the person making the delivery or transfer were expressly authorised by the owner of the goods to make the same.

(2) Where a person, having bought or agreed to buy goods, obtains with the consent of the seller, possession of the goods or the documents of title to the goods, the delivery or transfer by that person or by a mercantile agent acting for him, of the goods or documents of title under any sale, pledge or other disposition thereof to any person receiving the same in good faith and without notice of any lien or other right of the original seller in respect of the goods shall have effect as if such lien or right did not exist.

It is elementary that no title can be transferred unless the transferor had title therein. A transfer by a person without title cannot give any title to the transferee. This rule, if rigidly adhered to in the case of transfer of movable property, may lead to serious inconvenience and injustice. In the case of movables, normally title is transferred by delivery. Law does not require either a deed or its registration for the purpose of effecting transfer of title in movables. An innocent purchaser who paid good money bona fide from a seller in actual physical possession of the goods may find that he had acquired no title to the property because his vendor had no title to convey. More important than this was the need of commerce. It was contended by the merchants that unless the rigidity of the rule is relaxed, trade and commerce would be seriously hampered. The rigidity of the rule has therefore been relaxed, and Sec. 27 to Sec. 30 of the Sale of Goods Act have been enacted whereby a transferee of goods acquires good title in the goods though his transferor had no title to convey. These sections lay down under what circumstances a person without title could convey good title to the buyer in certain circumstances. A seller in possession but without title is deemed in law competent to pass good title even though he had no title himself and no authority from the owner to pass title.

Section 30(1) does not require that the seller must be in actual physical possession of the goods. It is enough that he should have such control over the goods as to transfer possession by making over a document of title. The section refers to possession not merely of goods but also of documents of title of goods. Possession of documents of title to goods is equated to possession of goods. Possession of documents of title enables the holder of the document to transfer title and possession by endorsement and delivery of the documents of title to goods. The words *'other disposition'* must be construed *ejusdem generis*—that is of the same *generis* as 'sale or pledge', i.e., transfer of property or right to property for consideration. In any event, transfer contemplated by the section must include some property right in the movables, and hypothecatee gets no such property right in the movables. Even if the word "transfer" is construed to be referable to goods and not to documents of title in goods, Sec. 30(1) is not applicable to hypothecation of goods by the seller in possession.[37]

## Chapter VI Performance of the Contract

### Section 31: Duties of seller and buyer

It is the duty of the seller to deliver the goods and of the buyer to accept and pay for them, in accordance with the terms of the contract of sale.

### Section 32: Payment and delivery are concurrent conditions

Unless otherwise agreed, delivery of the goods and payment of the price are concurrent conditions, that is to say, the seller shall be ready and willing to give possession of the goods to the buyer in exchange for the price, and the buyer shall be ready and willing to pay the price in exchange for possession of the goods.

The delivery of goods and payment of price are concurrent. Referring to Sec. 32 of the Act further, it may be said that the seller shall be ready and willing to give possession of the goods to the buyer in exchange for the price and the buyer shall be ready and willing to pay the price in exchange for possession of the goods. Here again, *'exchange'* is synonymous with *'concurrent'* appearing in the earlier portion of Sec. 32. It is, therefore, clear that unless there is a consensus ad idem between the contracting parties in a contract of sale of goods regarding payment of price, it would be difficult to expect either the buyer to purchase or the seller to supply the goods under it. Section 64-A is a special provision in the Sale of Goods Act which provides for a specified contingency. In contracts of sale of goods, if during the working or performance of the same, customs or excise duty or tax on the sale or purchase of goods is imposed by any law for the time being in force, then, if such an imposition takes effect, Sec. 64-A (a) provides that the seller may add so

---

37 *Pramatha Nath* v. *Probirendra* , AIR 1966 CALCUTTA 405.

much of such increase to the contract price as will be equivalent to the amount paid or payable in respect of such tax or increase of tax and he shall be entitled to be paid and to sue for and recover such addition. This statutory entitlement vested in the seller to claim the increase in excise duty, as in the instant case, in case such a duty takes effect during the course of the working of the contract is, a right which is *per se* enforceable. Of course, there may be a contract to the contrary. So long as there is none, the force of this section could compel the seller to demand as of right the payment of such levy or increase in levy in excise duty and add the same to the contract price and ask for its payment. The compendium of the initial contract price and the tax or the duty or the increase in the excise duty would automatically become the agreed price between the parties. Such payment of price and delivery of goods are concurrent conditions and one is an exchange for the other. As per Sec. 32 of the Sale of Goods Act, any attempt on the part of the buyer to avoid such a statutory obligation would entitle the seller not to perform his reciprocal concurrent obligation of delivering the goods.[38]

### Section 33: Delivery

Delivery of goods sold may be made by doing anything which the parties agree shall be treated as delivery or which has the effect of putting the goods in the possession of the buyer or of any person authorised to hold them on his behalf.

### Section 34: Effect of part delivery

A delivery of part of goods, in progress of the delivery of the whole has the same effect, for the purpose of passing the property in such goods, as a delivery of the whole; but a delivery of part of the goods, with an intention of severing it from the whole, does not operate as a delivery of the remainder.

### Section 35: Buyer to apply for delivery

Apart from any express contract, the seller of goods is not bound to deliver them until the buyer applies for delivery.

The language of Sec. 35 clearly indicates that the provision is intended for the benefit of the seller. The seller may, if he chooses, deliver the goods without any application in that behalf by the buyer. But he is also entitled to wait until the buyer applies for delivery unless he has contracted himself out of this right. An "express contract" means the reciprocal promises contained in the words of the contract or resulting from a true construction of them and excludes stipulations which may arise out of any usage or custom or which may be inferred from the conduct or course of dealings between the parties. Section 35 imports into all contracts of sale of goods, a term that the seller is not bound to deliver the goods until the buyer applies for delivery, which may be negatived only by the actual words used in the bargain between them or a true construction of those words.

In A. *Ramamoorthy* v. *P. Satyanarayana*,[39] the plaintiff entered into contracts with the defendants to buy gunnies. The contracts were for the sale of goods by description and were executory. Although the time and place of delivery were fixed, payment was stipulated

[38] *N. Sundareswaran* v. *Krishna Refineries*, AIR 1977 MADRAS 109.

[39] AIR 1958 ANDHRA PRADESH 550.

against delivery order. At the end of the contracts, the plaintiff passed to the defendants a "stop-loss" letter, under which the plaintiff agreed to accept damages in lieu of delivery. The plaintiff, without applying for delivery, sued the defendants for damages for non-delivery. It was held that the contracts could by no means be construed as relieving the plaintiff of his obligation to apply for delivery. As the plaintiff admittedly did not apply for delivery, he had no cause of action for claiming damages. The defendants were not bound to deliver until the plaintiff made an effective application for delivery and in the absence of any such application they could not be held liable for non-delivery.

Section 35 says that apart from any express contract, the seller of goods is not bound to deliver them until the buyer applies for delivery. It would, therefore, follow that unless there is a contract to the contrary to relieve the buyer from the obligation to apply for delivery, or unless there is a trade usage or custom which expressly relieves the buyer from the statutory obligation, the seller is not bound to deliver. Therefore, if the seller can establish that there was no demand for the delivery of the goods, there can be no question of breach of contract if he fails to deliver goods and the buyer can have no cause of action as against the seller.[40]

## Section 36: Rules as to delivery

(1) Whether it is for the buyer to take possession of the goods or for the seller to send them to the buyer is a question depending in each case on the contract, express or implied, between the parties. Apart from any such contract, goods sold are to be delivered at the place at which they are at the time of the sale, and goods agreed to be sold are to be delivered at the place at which they are at the time of the agreement to sell, if not then in existence, at the place at which they are manufactured or produced.

(2) Where under the contract of sale the seller is bound to send the goods to the buyer, but no time for sending them is fixed, the seller is bound to send them within a reasonable time.

(3) Where the goods at the time of sale are in the possession of a third person, there is no delivery by seller to buyer unless and until such third person acknowledges to the buyer that he holds the goods on his behalf:

Provided that nothing in this section shall affect the operation of the issue or transfer of any document of title to goods.

(4) Demand or tender of delivery may be treated as ineffectual unless made at a reasonable hour. What is a reasonable hour is a question of fact.

(5) Unless otherwise agreed, the expenses of and incidental to putting the goods into a deliverable state shall be borne by the seller.

## Section 37: Delivery of wrong quantity

(1) Where the seller delivers to the buyer a quantity of goods less than he contracted to sell, the buyer may reject them, but if the buyer accepts the goods so delivered he shall pay for them at the contract rate.

---

[40] *H.M. Corpn.* v. *M. Venkateswarlu and Co.*, AIR 1959 ANDHRA PRADESH 545.

(2) Where the seller delivers to the buyer a quantity of goods larger than he contracted to sell the buyer may accept the goods included in the contract and reject the rest, or he may reject the whole. If the buyer accepts the whole of the goods so delivered, he shall pay for them at the contract rate.

(3) Where the seller delivers to the buyer the goods he contracted to sell mixed with goods of a different description not included in the contract, the buyer may accept the goods which are in accordance with the contract and reject the rest, or may reject the whole.

(4) The provisions of this section are subject to any usage of trade, special agreement of course of dealing between the parties.

**Section 38: Instalment deliveries**

(1) Unless otherwise agreed, the buyer of goods is not bound to accept delivery thereof by instalments.

(2) Where there is a contract for the sale of goods to be delivered by stated instalments which are to be separately paid for, and the seller makes no delivery or defective delivery in respect of one or more instalments, or the buyer neglects or refuses to take delivery of or pay for one or more instalments, it is a question in each case depending on the terms of the contract and the circumstances of the case, whether the breach of contract is a repudiation of the whole contract, or whether it is a severable breach giving rise to a claim for compensation, but not to a right to treat the whole contract as repudiated.

**Section 39: Delivery to carrier or wharfinger**

(1) Where, in pursuance of a contract of sale, the seller is authorised or required to send the goods to the buyer, delivery of the goods to a carrier, whether named by the buyer or not, for the purpose of transmission to the buyer, or delivery of the goods to a wharfinger for safe custody, is *prima facie* deemed to be a delivery of the goods to the buyer.

(2) Unless otherwise authorised by the buyer, the seller shall make such contract with the carrier or wharfinger on behalf of the buyer as may be reasonable having regard to the nature of the goods and the other circumstances of the case. If the seller omits so to do and the goods are lost or damaged in course of transit or whilst in the custody of the wharfinger, the buyer may decline to treat the delivery to the carrier or wharfinger as a delivery to himself or may hold the seller responsible in damages.

(3) Unless otherwise agreed, where goods are sent by the seller to the buyer by a route involving sea transit, in circumstances in which it is usual to insure, the seller shall give such notice to the buyer as may enable him to insure them during their sea transit and if the seller fails so to do, the goods shall be deemed to be at his risk during such sea transit.

The question as to the meaning of F.O.R. contract came for consideration in the case of *Girija Proshad Pal* v. *National Coal Co. Ltd.*[41]. The Court observed that the words F.O.R. are well-known words in commercial contracts. It qualifies the place of delivery, which the seller's liability is to place the goods free on the rail as the place of delivery. Once that is done, the risk belongs to the buyer. In a case, the seller delivered the goods in the railway wagons at Jodhpur for transmission to the buyer, the consignee, without reserving any right of disposal. The seller is deemed to have unconditionally appropriated the goods to the contract only under Sec. 26 of the Act; the goods remained at the seller's risk until the property therein is transferred to the buyer. In this connection, reference may be made to Sec. 39(1) of the said Act. Considering the aforesaid provisions of the Sale of Goods Act, 1930 as well as the terms and conditions of delivery, i.e., 'F.O.R. Jodhpur', the irresistible conclusion that follows is that the property in the goods together with the risk passed from the seller to the buyer, i.e., from the consignor to the consignee as soon as the goods were loaded in the railway wagons at Jodhpur as per the terms of delivery, i.e., F.O.R. Jodhpur. Therefore, the finding of the trial Court that the risk throughout remained with the appellant until the goods were actually delivered to the Commandant, C.O.D., Kanpur is wholly wrong and illegal.[42]

### *Contract involving sea route [Section 39(3)]*[43]

Goods in transit are a target for opportunists and thieves. Fire can break out almost anywhere. More rarely, road and rail accidents occur. Goods carried across water are subject to the predictable risks of loss or damage during the course of loading and of discharging, by sinking, stranding, by the ingress of water, by contamination by other goods, sweating and damage through shifting, etc. Perishable goods suffer if delayed. Some cargoes, especially bulk cargoes, suffer a measure of inevitable loss due (for example) to natural shrinkage or to the difficulties of accurately measuring or assessing their true weight on loading and discharge. Cargoes carried by air tend to suffer less damage but as non-perishable air cargo is often of high value, air cargoes are a magnet for thieves. International carriage can involve partial carriage by sea, road and rail with transshipment and consolidation for the purposes of making up full loads. Each operation increases the risk of goods going astray or becoming damaged. So how do sellers and buyers protect themselves? Who bears the risk?

The passing of risk in relation to **CIF** and **FOB** contracts concludes that neither option is preferable and that either type of contract brings with it its own difficulties.

CIF stands for 'Cost, Insurance, and Freight'. A CIF contract is a type of contract wherein the price includes cost, insurance and freight charges. Under a CIF contract, the seller is required to insure the goods, deliver them to the shipping company, arrange for their affreightment and send the bill of lading and insurance policy together with the invoice.

---

[41] AIR 1949 Cal 472.

[42] *Marwar Tent Factory, M/s.* v. *Union of India*, AIR 1990 SC 1753.

[43] Limited information available in the Indian context, have resorted to International Laws & Conventions on Sale of Goods.

FOB stands for 'Free on Board'. It is a trade term requiring the seller to deliver goods on board a vessel designated by the buyer. The seller fulfills his obligations to deliver when the goods have passed over the ship's rail. All subsequent expenses of freight, insurance, etc. are to be borne by the buyer.

It is difficult to define an FOB contract because there are many different variants. Devlin J explains the FOB contract as a "flexible instrument"[44].

The main obligations of the parties to an FOB contract were described judicially in *Wimble, Sons and Co.* v. *Rosenberg.*[45]

1. The seller must put on board ship goods which conform to the contract and must pay all charges in connection with loading.
2. The seller is not obliged to book shipping space in advance; the buyer must nominate the ship to carry the goods and notify the seller of the nomination in time to allow the seller to deliver the goods on board.
3. The costs of carriage are for the buyer's account.

However, the parties may, and frequently do, modify their obligations under any FOB contract. In particular, the relationship between seller, and buyer and carrier may vary according to the nature of the arrangements made. In *Pyrene and Co. Ltd.* v. *Scindia Steam Navigation Co. Ltd.*[46], Devlin J. recognised three situations:

1. B designates a ship on which S is required to load the goods. There is no prior contractual arrangement between B and the carrier. S delivers the goods to the ship and puts them on board in return for a bill of lading, either in his own name or showing B as consignor. In either case, S forwards the bill of lading to B and, according to Devlin J., S makes the contract of carriage and is a party to it. Devlin J. describes this as a classic FOB contract.
2. S may undertake additional duties. Under this type of FOB contract, S undertakes to arrange the carriage, and possibly insurance. S places the goods on board ship and receives a bill of lading in his own name, which he forwards to B in return for payment. S is clearly a party to the contract of carriage in this case, and the contract is very similar to a CIF contract; however, the contract price excludes carriage costs so that if they increase, B must pay extra.
3. Alternatively, B may take the contract of carriage in advance. In this case S puts the goods on board ship in exchange for a mate's receipt, which he forwards to S who uses it to obtain a bill of lading."

Passing of risk does not follow when passing of property occurs in an FOB contract. The general rule is applied to FOB contracts and risk *prima facie* passes with property so that risk normally passes to the buyer when the goods are put across the ship's rail. Thus, in *Pyrene & Co. Ltd.* v. *Scindia Steam Navigation Co. Ltd.*, the tender was at the seller's risk when it was dropped during loading prior to crossing the ship's rail.

---

[44] http://www.law-essays-uk.com/freeessays/CIF-and-FOB-contracts.php

[45] (1913) 3 KB 743.

[46] (1954) 2 QB 402.

Even in circumstances where property does not pass to the buyer on loading, risk normally will pass. This will apply even where goods shipped for the buyer form an unascertained part of a larger bulk; once the goods are shipped, the seller has fulfilled his obligation to deliver the goods and nothing remains to be done by him under the contract. The buyer has an insurable interest in the goods from the time of shipment. If the contract varies the seller's duties, it may therefore vary the point at which risk passes; for instance, if the contract is for the goods to be delivered "free on board stowed", the seller's duties are not complete until the goods are safely stowed, so that risk may not pass until this point.

Risk of loss may also remain with the seller by virtue of the provisions of Sec. 39 of the Sale of Goods Act. Sec. 39(3) provides that:

> Unless otherwise agreed, where goods are sent by the seller to the buyer by a route involving sea transit, under circumstances in which it is usual to insure, the seller must give such notice to the buyer as may enable him to insure them during their sea transit, and, if the seller fails to do so, the goods shall be deemed to be at his risk during such sea transit.

It has been argued that Sec. 39(3) can have no application to FOB sales because the contract requires the seller to deliver the goods "free on board" and delivery to a carrier is normally deemed to be delivery to the buyer.

In the alternative, risk may pass to the buyer prior to shipment. In *Cunningham* v. *Munro*,[47] it was suggested that if the goods deteriorate because of the buyer's delay in giving the seller shipping instructions, or because the buyer induces the seller to deliver goods to the port before the goods can be loaded, the buyer would be liable for such deterioration; he would be entitled to reject the goods for non-compliance with the implied conditions as to quality in the Sale of Goods Act, but would be liable to the seller in damages for the deterioration.

This section is further discussed and analysed in *Wimble, Sons & Co.* v. *Rosenberg*[48], in which it was held, by a majority of the Court, that sub-Section 3 applies to an FOB contract, and, by one judge, that if before the goods are shipped the buyer has all information necessary to enable him to insure, the seller is not obliged to give notice to the buyer of the shipment of the goods on a particular ship.

However, this section does not apply to a CIF contract entered into in time of peace, in as much as the contract itself provides for all the insurance that is contemplated or usual at the time when it is made, and the sub-section does not impose on the seller any new obligation to give notice to the buyer so as to enable him to insure against war risks, if, after the date of the contract, war becomes imminent.

The **CIF contract** is a cost, insurance and freight contract. As Lord Wright observed in 1940:

> It is a type of contract which is more widely and more frequently in use than any other contract used for the purposes of sea-borne commerce. Under a CIF contract the seller is required to arrange the carriage of the goods and their insurance in transit, and the cost of those arrangements is

[47] (1922) 28 Com Cas 42.

[48] (1913) 3 K.B. 743.

included in the contract price. The seller obtains a bill of lading and a policy of insurance and forwards them to the buyer, together with an invoice for the price, and the buyer pays on receipt of the documents.

The vendor on CIF terms is in the absence of any specific provision to the contrary, bound by his contract (i) to make out an invoice of the goods sold; (ii) to ship the goods at the port of shipment, unless the contract is in regard to goods already afloat; (iii) to procure on shipment a contract of affreightment under which goods will be delivered at the destination contemplated by the contract; (iv) to arrange for an insurance upon the terms current in the trade which will be available for the benefit of the buyer. The seller having procured the necessary documents is under an obligation to send them forward to the buyer, accompanied by an invoice showing the amount due from the buyer, within a reasonable time. He must make every reasonable exertion to send them forward as soon as possible after he has destined the goods to the buyer. If no place is named in the contract for the tender of the shipping documents, they must *prima facie* be tendered at the residence or place of business of the buyer. The buyer must be prepared to pay or accept the draft, as the case may be according to the terms of the contract of sale, within a reasonable time after the shipping documents are tendered to him. What is a reasonable time is a question of fact depending on the circumstances of that case. In ordinary cases, obviously, payment must be made promptly on the tender of the documents with the invoice. As the essential feature of a contract of sale CIF is that performance is satisfied by delivery of documents and not by the actual physical delivery of the goods, it follows that all that the buyer can call for is the delivery of the documents above mentioned. This represents the measure of the buyer's right and the extent of the vendor's duty. The buyer cannot refuse the documents and ask for the actual goods nor can the vendor withhold the documents and tender the goods they represent. It would, therefore, be seen that while it is the duty of a CIF seller to see that he is in a position to procure the necessary documents for tender which might entail an obligation to ensure that the export is possible, for otherwise the shipping documents cannot be obtained, there would not be necessarily any obligation on him to see that the buyer was in a position to clear the goods from the ship or clear them through the customs at the port of destination.[49]

The CIF has many advantages. The buyer has the advantage of knowing from the date of the contract the exact price he must pay to obtain the goods; the contract price includes freight and insurance. More importantly, the use of documents to perform the contract and represent the goods allows the parties to deal with the goods afloat. Thus, the buyer may resell the goods before they arrive. The use of documents facilitates the involvement of financial institutions: the documents can be transferred direct to the buyer's bank as security for the advance of the price and the bank will be willing to take up and hold documents where it would not be prepared to take possession of the goods themselves and, normally, where the payment is to be by the bankers' documentary credit, this is what happens. This, in turn, allows the seller to be assured of payment and to receive the goods. Indeed, he is assured of payment even if the goods are damaged or never arrive at all for he is entitled to be paid on presentation of the documents; the buyer is generally

[49] *Narayanaswami Chetti* v. *Soundararajan and Co.*, AIR 1958 MADRAS 43.

protected against such losses by the bill of lading, giving a contractual right against the carrier, and the policy of insurance, covering most accidental losses.

CIF contracts are an exception to the general rule which links the passing of risk to the passing of property. Whereas property under a CIF contract passes at the time the buyer pays and takes up the documents, the goods are deemed to be at the buyer's risk from the time of shipment. Where the seller ships goods for the buyer, risk passes at the time of shipment; where the contract is made after shipment, risk passes at the time of the contract but retrospectively, so that the goods are deemed to have been at the buyer's risk since the time of shipment. This might seem hard on the buyer, but in fact imposes little hardship. The buyer takes the benefit of the contract of carriage and policy of insurance and is therefore able to claim, either under the contract or the policy, in respect of most damages or losses from the time of shipment.

In the case of *Manbre Saccharine Co.* v. *Corn Products Co.*,[50] McCardie J defined the six stages at which loss or damage may occur during a CIF transaction:

1. Loss/deterioration after the buyer has paid the price is clearly for the buyer's account. The goods are the buyer's property and at his risk.
2. Loss/deterioration after the tender of documents is also for the buyer's account unless the buyer is entitled to reject the documents and throw the loss back to the seller.
3. If the goods are lost or deteriorate after the goods have been appropriated to the contract, the seller may still tender the documents; once goods have been appropriated to the contract, the seller is not entitled to tender any others.
4. If the goods are lost after shipment but before they have been appropriated to any particular contract, can the seller appropriate them to contract and require the buyer to pay? There are judicial dicta which suggest that he can appropriate on the lost cargo; the buyer is, after all, protected by the policy of insurance and contract of carriage against most losses.
5. Goods are lost after the contract is made but before shipment. Here the position is clear; the seller cannot ship any goods and so cannot fulfil his contract using the "lost" goods.
6. The goods are lost after shipment, but before the contract of sale: can the seller make a contract to sell lost goods? A contract to sell specific goods would be void in such a case, and a contract for unascertained goods from a designated source, as where the seller contracts to sell part of the cargo of a named vessel already lost, would be void for mistake at common law in such circumstances. Alternatively, the seller might be held impliedly to warrant the existence of the goods at the time of the contract; and if the seller knows of the loss, he may be held to have fraudulently misrepresented his belief in that the goods exist. If the goods exist at the time the contract is made but have already deteriorated, the position is equally unclear.

In conclusion, the following comparisons can be made between the two types of contracts. The first is that under an **FOB contract,** the buyer bears the risk of fluctuations

[50] (1919) 1 KB 198.

in freight rates and insurance premiums and secondly that a **CIF contract** will always be an export contract. The most salient point must be that since the seller makes the arrangements for carriage and insurance, the Sale of Goods cannot apply to CIF contracts, and it has been demonstrated that this can produce a degree of uncertainty in these contracts. However, to conclude in relation to risk, neither method is preferable, and it can be said that each type of contract bears with it its own risk.

Under an **ex-ship contract**, the seller has to deliver the goods to the buyer at the port of destination. In such contracts, the property in the goods does not pass until actual delivery. The goods are at the seller's risk during the voyage. It is, therefore, for the seller to insure the goods to protect his interest. The seller is to pay the freight, or otherwise release the ship owner's lien and to furnish the buyer with a delivery order or an effectual direction to the ship owner to deliver.

The following chart summarises the responsibilities of both the buyer and the seller for the international sales contracts discussed.[51]

| | FOB | CIF | ES |
|---|---|---|---|
| **Services** | **(Free Onboard Vessel)** | **(Cost, Insurance and Freight)** | **(Ex-Ship)** |
| Warehouse storage | Seller | Seller | Seller |
| Warehouse labour | Seller | Seller | Seller |
| Export packing | Seller | Seller | Seller |
| Loading charges | Seller | Seller | Seller |
| Inland freight | Seller | Seller | Seller |
| Terminal charges | Seller | Seller | Seller |
| Forwarder's fees | Buyer | Seller | Seller |
| Loading on vessel | Seller | Seller | Seller |
| Ocean/Air freight | Buyer | Seller | Seller |
| Charges on arrival at destination | Buyer | Buyer | Buyer |
| Duty, taxes and customs clearance | Buyer | Buyer | Buyer |
| Delivery to destination | Buyer | Buyer | Buyer |

## Section 40: Risk where goods are delivered at distant place

Where the seller of goods agrees to deliver them at his own risk at a place other than that where they are when sold, the buyer shall, nevertheless, unless otherwise agreed, take any risk of deterioration in the goods necessarily incident to the course of transit.

---

51 http://www.i-b-t.net/incoterms.html#EXW.

### Section 41: Buyer's right of examining the goods

(1) Where goods are delivered to the buyer which he has not previously examined, he is not deemed to have accepted them unless and until he has had a reasonable opportunity of examining them for the purpose of ascertaining whether they are in conformity with the contract.

(2) Unless otherwise agreed, when the seller tenders delivery of goods to the buyer, he is bound, on request, to afford the buyer a reasonable opportunity of examining the goods for the purpose of ascertaining whether they are in conformity with the contract.

Section 41 of the Act gives the buyer only a right of examining the goods. It does not give him a right to repudiate the contract. The right of inspection under Sec. 41 can only arise either when the consignee has taken delivery from the carrier or when it is tendered for delivery to the buyer. When the buyer is the consignee, the question of affording an opportunity could arise only after the consignee receives consignment. Where the seller is the consignee, it is his duty to take delivery of goods and give an opportunity to the buyer to inspect and examine the goods. It means that when the seller tenders the goods to the buyer, he is bound to afford an opportunity for inspection of goods.

A contract was entered into between the parties by means of telegrams for purchase of certain quantity of peas of particular variety deliverable FOR at the buyer's place. The seller dispatched the goods without the buyer examining them at dispatching station. The buyer had been intimated about the dispatch of Hundi and R.R. The buyer did not honour the Hundi and did not take delivery. The seller's agent went to the buyer's place, took delivery of goods and asked the buyer to examine the goods, but the buyer refused to examine them and take delivery.

The Court held that it was the bounden duty of the buyer to have received the goods, made the inspection and then if the goods are found to be of inferior quality, he could have sued for damages. Even though the seller afforded him an opportunity to examine the goods, he refused to do so. Under the circumstances, the buyer could not be heard to say that the goods were of an inferior quality. He could not repudiate the contract. The seller was entitled to recover damages from the buyer.[52]

Where, as provided *inter alia* by Sec. 42 of the Sale of Goods Act, the buyer does an act in relation to the sold goods which is inconsistent with the ownership of the seller, Sec. 42 must be treated as coming into operation notwithstanding that the reasonable opportunity of examining the goods has not expired. The construction which requires that Sec. 41 should be read as limiting the provisions of Sec. 42 so that the buyer is not, even in the events specified in Sec. 42, to be deemed to have accepted the goods unless he has had a reasonable opportunity of examining them for the purpose of ascertaining whether they are in conformity with the contract, is incorrect and deserves to be rejected. Section 42 is independent of Sec. 41 and must be given effect to whenever anyone of the acts specified in that section is done by the buyer irrespective of the question whether such act is done during the currency or after the expiration of the reasonable time for examination of the goods. The right of examination of the goods for the purpose of ascertaining whether

---

[52] *Dharampal and Co., Agra* v. *K.G. Ram Chandra Rao and Co.,* AIR 1980 ALLAHABAD 316.

they are in conformity with the contract is a right which is conferred on the buyer for the purpose of enabling him to decide whether to accept the goods or to reject them. But it is open to him to waive that right and he may choose to accept the goods without exercising that right. It will thus be seen that no conflict is created between Secs. 41 and 42 by reading Sec. 42 as independent of Sec. 41 and not limiting the provisions of Sec. 42 by Sec. 41.

The act of the buyer in selling and delivering a part of the goods to the sub-purchasers is an act in relation to the goods which is inconsistent with the ownership of the seller, and the buyer is, therefore, deemed to have accepted the goods by selling and delivering a part of the goods to the sub-purchasers. It is immaterial in such a case whether the act of selling and delivering a part of the goods to the sub-purchasers is done by the buyer before the reasonable opportunity of examining the goods has expired or is done by the buyer after the expiration of the reasonable time for examination of the goods. Hence, in such a case, the buyer is not entitled to reject the goods on the ground that the goods are not in conformity with the contract. If it is found that the seller has committed a breach of the condition precedent of the contract by delivering goods which are not of the contract description, the buyer is entitled to treat the breach of the condition as a breach of warranty on the part of the seller and to claim damages from him for the loss suffered by the buyer as a result of the breach committed by the seller.[53]

## Section 42: Acceptance

The buyer is deemed to have accepted the goods when he intimates to the seller that he has accepted them, or when the goods have been delivered to him and he does any act in relation to them which is inconsistent with the ownership of the seller, or when, after the lapse of a reasonable time, he retains the goods without intimating to the seller that he has rejected them.

Where in a contract for supply of software the defendant buyer had made substantial payment for initial supply and later raised grievance that subsequent supply was defective but said that the defect was not detected within a reasonable time, such goods shall be deemed to have been accepted by the buyer by virtue of Secs. 41, 42 of the Sale of Goods Act. Furthermore, by making substantial payments for the price of the goods the defendant can be said to have acted in a manner which would render it inconsistent for the plaintiff to still claim ownership thereon. On a careful reading of the Act, it appears that the intendment is generally that the price of the goods must be paid and if there is a subsequent defect (in contradistinction to a defect detected within a reasonable time of the delivery), the remedy that is envisaged is for the buyer to sue for damages. This is obviously impregnated with sound commonsense and business ethics. In the instant case, raising question pertaining to the suitability of the supply after one year is not reasonable. A triable issue does not arise because what was supplied by the plaintiff was what was ordered by the defendant; if it did not suit the latter's requirements, the plaintiff cannot be made responsible and liable. To judicially countenance complaints raised after several months would tantamount to violating the Legislature's intent of an expeditious disposal of commercial complaints.[54]

[53] *Mohanlal Manilal* v. *Firm Dhirubhai Bavajibhai*, AIR 1962 GUJARAT 56.

[54] *KLG Systel Ltd., M/s.* v. *M/s. Fujitsu ICIM Ltd.*, AIR 2001 DELHI 357.

**Section 43: Buyer not bound to return rejected goods**

Unless otherwise agreed, where goods are delivered to the buyer and he refuses to accept them, having the right so to do, he is not bound to return them to the seller, but it is sufficient if he intimates to the seller that he refuses to accept them.

**Section 44: Liability of buyer for neglecting or refusing delivery of goods**

When the seller is ready and willing to deliver the goods and requests the buyer to take delivery, and the buyer does not within a reasonable time after such request take delivery of the goods, he is liable to the seller for any loss occasioned by his neglect or refusal to take delivery and also for a reasonable charge for the care and custody of the goods:

Provided that nothing in this section shall affect the rights of the seller where the neglect or refusal of the buyer to take delivery amounts to a repudiation of the contract.

## Chapter VII Rights of Unpaid Seller against the Goods

**Section 45: "Unpaid seller" defined**

(1) The seller of goods is deemed to be an "unpaid seller" within the meaning of this Act—
  - (a) When the whole of the price has not been paid or tendered;
  - (b) When a bill of exchange or other negotiable instrument has been received as conditional payment, and the condition on which it was received has not been fulfilled by reason of the dishonour of the instrument or otherwise.

(2) In this Chapter, the term "seller" includes any person who is in the position of a seller, as, for instance, an agent of the seller to whom the bill of lading has been endorsed, or a consignor or agent who has himself paid, or is directly responsible for, the price.

Section 45(2) defines "seller" and such definition or meaning would be applicable only for Chapter –VII. Under this clause, an agent, who has himself paid, or is directly responsible for the price is included in the term "seller" within the meaning of the Indian Sale of Goods Act and he will, therefore, have all the rights of and the remedies available to an "unpaid seller" under the Act. In the present case, the defendant is directly responsible for the price and is definitely to be deemed to be an "unpaid seller". Then, what are his rights? Under Sec. 46(1)(a), he has a lien on the goods for the price while he is in possession of them and under Clause (1)(c) of Sec. 46, he has a right of resale as limited by the Act. Section 54(2) provides that the unpaid seller, who gives notice to the buyer of his intention to sell, may, if the buyer does not within a reasonable time pay or tender the price, resell the goods within a reasonable time and recover from the original buyer damages for any loss occasioned by his breach of contract, but the buyer shall not be entitled to any profit which may occur on the resale. These provisions of the Indian Sale of Goods Act make it clear that the defendant in the instant case is fully justified in selling the 400 pallas of cotton seeds when the plaintiff, in spite of repeated notices, failed to pay the balance of the price, or at least to pay such amount which would cover the risk which the defendant has taken, as the prices were falling. The defendant sold the goods only after giving reasonable notice to the plaintiff.[55]

### Section 46: Unpaid seller's rights

(1) Subject to the provisions of this Act and of any law for the time being in force, notwithstanding that the property in the goods may have passed to the buyer, the unpaid seller of goods, as such, has by implication of law—

(a) a lien on the goods for the price while he is in possession of them;

(b) in case of the insolvency of the buyer a right of stopping the goods in transit after he has parted with the possession of them;

(c) a right of re-sale as limited by this Act.

(2) Where the property in goods has not passed to the buyer, the unpaid seller has, in addition to his other remedies, a right of withholding delivery similar to and co-extensive with his rights of lien and stoppage in transit where the property has passed to the buyer.

The unpaid seller has the following rights subject to the provisions of this Act and of any law for the time being in force in India:

1. ***Right a lien on the goods:*** This is right is available to the unpaid seller if the goods are in his possession.
2. ***Right to stoppage in transit:*** Right to stoppage in transit may be exercised by the unpaid seller in case of the insolvency of the buyer. This right may be exercised when the unpaid seller lost the possession and goods are in transit.
3. A right of re-sale.

### Section 47: Seller's lien

(1) Subject to the provisions of this Act, the unpaid seller of goods who is in possession of them is entitled to retain possession of them until payment or tender of the price in the following cases, namely:—

(a) where the goods have been sold without any stipulation as to credit;

(b) where the goods have been sold on credit, but the term of credit has expired;

(c) where the buyer becomes insolvent.

(2) The seller may exercise his right of lien notwithstanding that he is in possession of the goods as agent or bailee for the buyer.

### Section 48: Part delivery

Where an unpaid seller has made part delivery of the goods, he may exercise his right of lien on the remainder, unless such part delivery has been made under such circumstances as to show an agreement to waive the lien.

[55] *Girdharilal, M/s.* v. *Jethmal,* AIR 1963 ANDHRA PRADESH 185.

### Section 49: Termination of lien

(1) The unpaid seller of goods loses his lien thereon—
   (a) when he delivers the goods to a carrier or other bailee for the purpose of transmission to the buyer without reserving the right of disposal of the goods;
   (b) when the buyer or his agent lawfully obtains possession of the goods;
   (c) by waiver thereof.

(2) The unpaid seller of goods, having a lien thereon, does not lose his lien by reason only that he has obtained a decree for the price of the goods.

Right of lien would be terminated in the following situations:
(a) Delivery to carrier
(b) Delivery to buyer
(c) Waiver
(d) Received price for the goods.

### Section 50: Right of stoppage in transit

Subject to the provisions of this Act, when the buyer of goods becomes insolvent, the unpaid seller who has parted with the possession of the goods has the right of stopping them in transit, that is to say, he may resume possession of the goods as long as they are in the course of transit and may retain them until payment or tender of the price.

### Section 51: Duration of transit

(1) Goods are deemed to be in course of transit from the time when they are delivered to a carrier or other bailee for the purpose of transmission to the buyer, until the buyer or his agent in that behalf takes delivery of them from such carrier or other bailee.
(2) If the buyer or his agent in that behalf obtains delivery of the goods before their arrival at the appointed destination, the transit is at an end.
(3) If, after the arrival of the goods at the appointed destination, the carrier or other bailee acknowledges to the buyer or his agent that he holds the goods on his behalf and continues in possession of them as bailee for the buyer or his agent, the transit is at an end and it is immaterial that a further destination for the goods may have been indicated by the buyer.
(4) If the goods are rejected by the buyer and the carrier or other bailee continues in possession of them, the transit is not deemed to be at an end, even if the seller has refused to receive them back.
(5) When goods are delivered to a ship chartered by the buyer, it is a question depending on the circumstances of the particular case, whether they are in the possession of the master as a carrier or as agent of the buyer.
(6) Where the carrier or other bailee wrongfully refuses to deliver the goods to the buyer or his agent in that behalf, the transit is deemed to be at an end.

(7) Where part delivery of the goods has been made to the buyer or his agent in that behalf, the remainder of the goods may be stopped in transit, unless such part delivery has been given in such circumstances as to show an agreement to give up possession of the whole of the goods.

In Sec. 51(1), delivery to the carrier and taking delivery from the carrier represent two different capacities of the carrier. As a result of the first mentioned delivery, which is for purposes of transmission, the carrier is an agent of the buyer, but while actually delivering to the buyer he is the agent of the seller. This distinction became necessary because the seller has a right, if unpaid and if the buyer has become insolvent, to retake the goods before they are actually delivered to the buyer or someone who is named as his agent, and on that ground it is only the actual delivery to the buyer or his agent that puts an end to the course of transit. But if all the rights of the seller have been merged in the buyer with the result that the seller has no longer any right either of lien or stoppage in transit or reclamation of the property, this distinction between constructive and actual delivery comes to an end.[56]

## Section 52: How stoppage in transit is effected

(1) The unpaid seller may exercise his right of stoppage in transit either by taking actual possession of the goods, or by giving notice of his claim to the carrier or other bailee in whose possession the goods are. Such notice may be given either to the person in actual possession of the goods or to his principal. In the latter case the notice, to be effectual, shall be given at such time and in such circumstances, that the principal, by the exercise of reasonable diligence, may communicate it to his servant or agent in time to prevent a delivery to the buyer.

(2) When notice of stoppage in transit is given by the seller to the carrier or other bailee in possession of the goods, he shall re-deliver the goods to, or according to the directions of, the seller. The expenses of such re-delivery shall be borne by the seller.

## Section 53: Effect of sub-sale or pledge by buyer

(1) Subject to the provisions of this Act, the unpaid seller's right of lien or stoppage in transit is not affected by any sale or other disposition of the goods which the buyer may have made, unless the seller has assented thereto:

Provided that where a document of title to goods has been issued or lawfully transferred to any person as buyer or owner of the goods, and that person transfers the document to a person who takes the document in good faith and for consideration, then, if such last mentioned transfer was by way of sale, the unpaid seller's right of lien or stoppage in transit is defeated, and, if such last mentioned transfer was by way of pledge or other disposition for value, the unpaid seller's right of lien or stoppage in transit can only be exercised subject to the rights of the transferee.

[56] *R.C. Society* v. *State of Andhra*, AIR 1961 ANDHRA PRADESH 86.

(2) Where the transfer is by way of pledge, the unpaid seller may require the pledgee to have the amount secured by the pledge satisfied in the first instance, as far as possible, out of any other goods or securities of the buyer in the hands of the pledgee and available against the buyer.

### Section 54: Sale not generally rescinded by lien or stoppage in transit

(1) Subject to the provisions of this section, a contract of sale is not rescinded by the mere exercise by an unpaid seller of his right of lien or stoppage in transit.

(2) Where the goods are of a perishable nature, or where the unpaid seller who has exercised his right of lien or stoppage in transit gives notice to the buyer of his intention to re-sell, the unpaid seller may, if the buyer does not within a reasonable time pay or tender the price, re-sell the goods within a reasonable time and recover from the original buyer damages for any loss occasioned by his breach of contract, but the buyer shall not be entitled to any profit which may occur on the re-sale. If such notice is not given, the unpaid seller shall not be entitled to recover such damages and the buyer shall be entitled to the profit, if any, on the re-sale.

(3) Where an unpaid seller who has exercised his right of lien or stoppage in transit re-sells the goods, the buyer acquires a good title thereto as against the original buyer, notwithstanding that no notice of the re-sale has been given to the original buyer.

(4) Where the seller expressly reserves a right of re-sale in case the buyer should make default, and, on the buyer making default, re-sells the goods, the original contract of sale is thereby rescinded, but without prejudice to any claim which the seller may have for damages.

In order to apply the provisions of Sec. 54(2), Sale of Goods Act, it is necessary (i) that the property in goods sold should have passed on to the buyer; (ii) that the goods sold should be in actual possession of the unpaid seller; (iii) that the buyer should have failed to pay or tender the price within reasonable time from being called upon to do so; and (iv) that the goods should be resold within reasonable time from the date of the notice.

The object of introducing the last sentence in Sec. 54(2) is obvious. If notice is given to the buyer, he can arrange for purchasers or can otherwise take steps to secure better price for his goods. But if the seller deprives him of this opportunity and sells the goods behind his back, he cannot saddle him with damages which, if he had been informed, he might have taken steps to avoid. The position, therefore, is that if Sec. 54 applies and the sale takes place without notice to the buyer, the seller cannot claim any damages from him. An unpaid seller has two rights, viz. a right of re-sale under Sec. 54(2) and an independent right under Sec. 55 to sue for the price of the goods. It is open to him not to sell the goods and to sue for the price leaving it to the purchaser to take delivery of the goods lying with him (the seller) at his own convenience. He has to sue, in that case, for the entire amount and not for the amount that, according to him, remains due to him after deducting the price fetched by the goods re-sold.[57] Section 54(2) does not permit an

[57] *Kalka Prasad, M/s.* v. *Harish Chandra*, AIR 1957 ALLAHABAD 25.

unpaid seller to exercise his right of re-sale without a notice. If the seller does it, he does it at his own peril. If he sells the goods, he must content himself with what the goods fetch and not ask for anything more. But as soon as the seller gives the notice, his right to re-sell arises, and if for any reason (such as, resale taking place after an unreasonable time of the giving of notice) the resale is not proper, it does not mean that the seller is deprived of the damages contemplated by Sec. 54(2). In such a case, the damages are to be ascertained not at the difference between what the re-sale realises and the price of the goods but the difference between what the Court holds should have been realised by a seller on a proper re-sale and the purchase price.[58]

Where the title to the goods has not passed and there is no clause in the agreement giving the seller a right to re-sell the goods and there is a breach of the contract, the seller can only claim the difference between the contract rate and the rate prevailing on the date of the breach. If, however, the title to the goods has passed, the seller is entitled to claim the difference between the contract price and the price realised at the re-sale, provided he has sold the goods within a reasonable time and after due notice. But the goods that were sold must be the goods that were meant for the buyer. He must establish that the goods that he re-sold were the goods which, so far as he was concerned, he had appropriated towards the contract and had intended to deliver to the buyer.[59]

Section 54(4) itself provides that though the original contract of sale is rescinded, that is without prejudice to the seller's claim to recover damages. It does not mean, therefore, that the contract in its entirety becomes non-existent or inoperative. The seller's right to recover damages is expressly saved by virtue of sub-sec. (4) of Sec. 54 and that must necessarily save the machinery which may be provided by the contract to settle the disputes, if any, regarding damages and for their being ascertained and assessed. Hence, where the contract for the sale of goods provides that all disputes in respect of the contract have to be referred to the arbitration of certain Association and gives the right to the unpaid seller to resell the goods in case of the buyer's default, and the seller resells the goods on the buyer's default, the machinery which is provided under the contract would not fall by virtue of sub-sec. (4) of Sec. 54 of the Sale of Goods Act in so far as the dispute as to damages claimed by the seller from the buyer is concerned.[60]

## Chapter VIII Suits for Breach of the Contract

### Section 55: Suit for price

(1) Where under a contract of sale the property in the goods has passed to the buyer and the buyer wrongfully neglects or refuses to pay for the goods according to the terms of the contract, the seller may sue him for the price of the goods.

(2) Where under a contract of sale the price is payable on a day certain irrespective of delivery and the buyer wrongfully neglects or refuses to pay such price, the

[58] *Hirji Bharmal, M/s.* v. *Bombay Cotton Ltd.*, AIR 1958 BOMBAY 411.

[59] *Moti Lal* v. *Mool Chand*, AIR 1952 ALLAHABAD 242.

[60] *Gulabchand Rawatmal, M/s.* v. *S.C. Mfg. Co.*, AIR 1959 BOMBAY 158.

seller may sue him for the price although the property in the goods has not passed and the goods have not been appropriated to the contract.

### Section 56: Damages for non-acceptance

Where the buyer wrongfully neglects or refuses to accept and pay for the goods, the seller may sue him for damages for non-acceptance.

### Section 57: Damages for non-delivery

Where the seller wrongfully neglects or refuses to deliver the goods to the buyer, the buyer may sue the seller for damages for non-delivery.

### Section 58: Specific performance

Subject to the provisions of Chapter II of the Specific Relief Act, 1877, in any suit for breach of contract to deliver specific or ascertained goods, the Court may, if it thinks fit, on the application of the plaintiff, by its decree direct that the contract shall be performed specifically, without giving the defendant the option of retaining the goods on payment of damages. The decree may be unconditional, or upon such terms and conditions as to damages, payment of the price or otherwise, as the Court may deem just, and the application of the plaintiff may be made at any time before the decree.

### Section 59: Remedy for breach of warranty

(1) Where there is a breach of warranty by the seller, or where the buyer elects or is compelled to treat any breach of a condition on the part of the seller as a breach of warranty, the buyer is not by reason only of such breach of warranty entitled to reject the goods; but he may—
   (a) set up against the seller the breach of warranty in diminution or extinction of the price, or
   (b) sue the seller for damages for breach of warranty.

(2) The fact that a buyer has set up a breach of warranty in diminution or extinction of the price does not prevent him from suing for the same breach of warranty if he has suffered further damage.

Remedies under Sec. 59 are not absolute and cannot be resorted to at any point or strategical point suitable to the buyer. He is duty bound to give notice of his intention. Its proper time, form and manner will, of course, depend upon the facts and circumstances of each case. To hold otherwise would amount to placing the seller in an awkward and indefinite position, which is not warranted either by law or by equity.

Where the buyer accepted major instalments of the goods supplied to it which did not strictly conform to the specifications given in the purchase order and the contract between the buyer and the supplier (slightly oversised M.S. Round bars in the instant case); consumed it for its own use, made payments of all bills but the payment of the last two bills was withheld on ground that there was breach of warranty since goods supplied were not as per specifications though notice of the buyer's intention to claim compensation for a breach of warranty or to set up the breach in diminution or extinction of price was not given and in any case, no evidence to that effect was adduced by the buyer, it was held that the buyer must be deemed to have voluntarily waived the condition as to size of the goods supplied. The buyer was fully aware of the so-called over size of the goods and yet did not reject the goods though specifically provided for in the contract, consumed the goods without giving any opportunity to the supplier to replace the same and even paid the price for major quantity. All this amounted to waiver. Section 59 comes into play only when the buyer does not waive the condition. That apart, in absence of any notice to the supplier, the buyer has failed to prove that it has, in fact, elected to treat the breach of condition as a breach of warranty as contemplated under Sec. 59. The buyer had also not adduced any proof of actual damages or its likelihood in future. Thus, the buyer was not entitled to withhold the payment of full price by invoking Sec. 59.[61]

If a buyer wants to buy an Electrolux or Refrigerator, he expects it to perform all the functions which machines of that character ordinarily perform. If, therefore, an Electrolux does not form ice but does the other thing which machines of this character usually do, it would be held that it is a defective machine and that if anybody sells a machine of that kind, there is a breach of a condition. If there is a breach of condition, the buyer undoubtedly would get the benefit provided under Sec. 59 of the Act to treat that breach of a condition as a breach of warranty and then proceed to seek the reliefs provided for in the section. The position, therefore, is that although it is quite true that there could not be an implied warranty in a case of this description, the purchaser could ask for damages on the basis of a breach of warranty by treating a breach of a condition as a breach of the former kind.[62]

### Section 60: Repudiation of contract before due date

Where either party to a contract of sale repudiates the contract before the date of delivery, the other may either treat the contract as subsisting and wait till the date of delivery, or he may treat the contract as rescinded and sue for damages for the breach.

### Section 61: Interest by way of damages and special damages

(1) Nothing in this Act shall affect the right of the seller or the buyer to recover interest or special damages in any case whereby law interest or special damages may be recoverable, or to recover the money paid where the consideration for the payment of it has failed.

(2) In the absence of a contract to the contrary, the Court may award interest at such rate as it thinks fit on the amount of the price—

   (a) to the seller in a suit by him for the amount of the price-from the date of the tender of the goods or from the date on which the price was payable;

   (b) to the buyer in a suit by him for the refund of the price in a case of a breach of the contract on the part of the seller-from the date on which the payment was made.

---

[61] *City and I.D. Corpn. of Maharashtra Ltd.* v. *Nagpur Steel and Alloys Pvt. Ltd.*, AIR 1992 BOMBAY 55.

[62] *E.W. Evans* v. *S. Benjamin*, AIR 1951 CALCUTTA 470.

# Chapter IX Miscellaneous

## Section 62: Exclusion of implied terms and conditions

Where any right, duty or liability would arise under a contract of sale by implication of law, it may be negatived or varied by express agreement or by the course of dealing between the parties, or by usage, if the usage is such as to bind both parties to the contract.

Ordinary measure of damages upon breach of the contract for sale of goods is the difference between the contract price and the market price on the date of breach. It is, however, open to the parties to lay down a different rule. It is quite possible for the business people to reach to an agreement that in the event of a seller failing to complete his contract, the purchaser shall not be entitled to ordinary remedy of law, but in lieu thereof, he shall, subject to certain allowances referred to in the terms of the contract, be entitled to retain only a sufficient portion of the purchase money to enable him to obtain from elsewhere the commodity, the subject matter of the contract, and that he must pay over any balance of purchase price to the vendor. In other words, it is open to the parties to the contract to agree for themselves to any special rights and obligations as they may please, such as providing for measure of damages in case of breach of the contract and specially exclude any of the terms and conditions which law attaches to the contract of sale of goods. In fact, Sec. 62 of the Sale of Goods Act is a statutory recognition of this right in the parties. Section 62 of the Sale of Goods Act clearly recognises the rights of the parties to vary the ordinary incidence of a contract by express terms of the contract of sale of goods between them.

Where a clause in a contract to supply material and equipment specially provides that in case of failure of the supplier to supply full quantity of agreed material and equipment, a right is reserved to the purchaser to purchase materials and equipment from the open market and to claim damages from the supplier, the right to claim damages under Sec. 73 of the Contract Act stands excluded and the purchaser cannot claim damages unless actually purchases the goods, not supplied by the contractors, from the open market after termination of the contract. Section 73 of the Contract Act is not applicablee when the purchaser has not actually purchased goods, not supplied by supplier, from open market, in view of the special provision of the said clause incorporated in the contract. As such the damages sought to be claimed by the purchaser on the basis of Sec. 73 cannot be awarded.

It is a well settled law that where loss in terms of money is prayed for, the party claiming compensation must prove such loss suffered by it. The concept of compensation is linked up with loss or damages that result from breach of contract and where no loss or damage is ensued, there would be no question of awarding compensation. Section 73 of the Contract Act does not give any cause of action unless and until damages are actually suffered, otherwise Sec. 73 will become nugatory and the party would be penalised though the other party suffered no loss. Thus, even under Sec. 73 of the Contract Act, the party claiming compensation is under an obligation to prove the loss suffered on account of breach of agreement by the opposite party. In a contract for supply of goods, the contractor failed to supply full quantity of agreed goods. The purchaser could not claim damages for breach of contract since he has failed to prove the quantum of loss actually suffered by him.[63]

---

[63] *M.S.E.B.* v. *Sterlite Industries (India) Ltd.*, AIR 2000 BOMBAY 204.

## Section 63: Reasonable time a question of fact

Where in this Act any reference is made to a reasonable time, the question what is reasonable time is a question of fact.

## Section 64: Auction sale

In the case of sale by auction—

(1) where goods are put up for sale in lots, each lot is *prima facie* deemed to be the subject of a separate contract of sale;

(2) the sale is complete when the auctioneer announces its completion by the fall of the hammer or in other customary manner; and, until such announcement is made, any bidder may retract his bid;

(3) a right to bid may be reserved expressly by or on behalf of the seller and, where such right is expressly so reserved, but not otherwise, the seller or anyone person on his behalf may, subject to the provisions hereinafter contained, bid at the auction;

(4) where the sale is not notified to be subject to a right to bid on behalf of the seller, it shall not be lawful for the seller to bid himself or to employ any person to bid at such sale, or for the auctioneer knowingly to take any bid from the seller or any such person; and any sale contravening this rule may be treated as fraudulent by the buyer;

(5) the sale may be notified to be subject to a reserved or upset price;

(6) if the seller makes use of pretended bidding to raise the price, the sale is voidable at the option of the buyer.

Two questions arose for determination in *Consolidated Coffee Ltd.* v. *Coffee Board, Bangalore*[64]: What is the true import of Sec. 64(2)? And whether Sec. 64 is subject to a contract to the contrary? Section 64(2) of the Sale of Goods Act does not deal with the question of the passing of the property in the goods sold at auction sale but instead it deals with the completion of the contract of sale. It is true that sub-section (2) says that "the sale is complete" when the auctioneer announces its completion by the fall of hammer or in other customary manner, but, the next following provision which says: "and until such announcement is made any bidder may retract his bid" suggests that what is complete at the fall of the hammer or the announcement of closure in other customary manner is that the contract for sale is complete. Section 64(2) of our Sale of Goods Act, being in *pari materia* with Sec. 58(2) of the English Sale of Goods Act, 1893, will have to be interpreted in the same manner and therefore, it does not deal with the question of passing of the property at auction sale but merely deals with completion of the contract of sale which takes place at the fall of the hammer or at the announcement of the close of the sale in other customary manner by the auctioneer. It would also be correct to say that if the auction sale of chattels is unconditional and is in respect of specific ascertained goods and nothing remains to be

[64] AIR 1980 SC 1468.

done to the goods for putting them in a condition ready for delivery, the property in the goods would pass to the purchaser upon the acceptance of the bid but that would not be because of Sec. 64(2) but because of Sec. 20 and such would not be the case if the goods sold thereat are non-specific or unascertained goods or the auction sale is conditional. At the auction sale, all that happens at the fall of hammer or at the announcement of the closure of the sale in other customary manner is that a contract of sale comes into existence and parties get into the relationship of a promisor and a promisee in an executory contract. Secondly, auction sales could be conditional or unconditional and if it is the latter, then by virtue of the goods being specific and in a deliverable State, the property in the goods knocked down passes at the fall of hammer by reason of the provision concerned relating to the passing of the property. Section 64(2) of the Sale of Goods Act has nothing to do with the aspect of the passing of the property at an auction sale and it is by virtue of goods being specific and in a deliverable State that under Sec. 20 the property in such goods passes to the buyer at the completion of the contract at the fall of hammer at such sale.

Section 64 of the Sale of Goods Act is subject to a contract to the contrary. In the first place, Sec. 64 occurs in Chapter VII which contains *"Miscellaneous"* provisions and Sec. 62 which occurs in the same Chapter clearly provides that where any right, duty or liability would arise under a contract of sale by implication of law, it may be negatived or varied by express agreement or by the course of dealing between the parties or by usage, if the usage is such as to bind both the parties to the contract. Ordinarily, the rights, duties and liabilities arising under a contract of sale by implication of law spoken of in Sec. 62 refer to the rights, duties and obligations referred to in Chapter III containing provisions which lay down rules as to transfer of property as between seller and buyer and transfer of title but there is no reason why Sec. 62 should not apply to rights, duties and obligations arising under Sec. 64 in regard to auction sales. In other words, Sec. 64 would be subject to Sec. 62. Moreover, there is intrinsic material in Sec. 64 itself which shows that the provisions thereof could be subject to a contract to the contrary. Sub-sections (1), (3), (4) and (5) of Sec. 64, if carefully scrutinised, also indicate that there could be a contract to the contrary. Moreover, once it is accepted that auction sales to which Sec. 64 applies could be unconditional or conditional and that the auctioneer can prescribe his own terms and conditions on the basis of which the property is exposed to sale by auction, it must be held that the acceptance of any bid as well as the passing of the property in the goods sold thereat would be governed by those terms and conditions.

The generality of law as contained in Sec. 64 of the Sale of Goods Act mentions that the sale is complete when the auctioneer announces its completion by the fall of the hammer and until such announcement is made any bidder may retract his bid. If before the fall of the hammer any bidder retracts his bid, the security amount may not be forfeited. If after the fall of the hammer the highest bid recalls his bid, the security may be liable to be forfeited. An indication that the auction is closed at the highest bid signifies an intention to finalise the contract on the last bid.[65]

65 *Zila Parishad, Muzaffarnagar* v. *Udai Veer Singh*, AIR 1989 ALLAHABAD 64.

**Section 64A: In contracts of sale, amount of increased or decreased taxes to be added or deducted**

(1) Unless a different intention appears from the terms of the contract, in the event of any tax of the nature described in sub-section (2) being imposed, increased, decreased or remitted in respect of any goods after the making of any contract for the sale or purchase of such goods without stipulation as to the payment of tax where tax was not chargeable at the time of the making of the contract, or for the sale or purchase of such good tax-paid where tax was chargeable at that time,—

(a) if such imposition or increase so takes effect that the tax or increased tax, as the case may be, or any part of such tax is paid or is payable, the seller may add so much to the contract price as will be equivalent to the amount paid or payable in respect of such tax or increase of tax, and he shall be entitled to be paid and to sue for and recover such addition; and

(b) if such decrease or remission so takes effect that the decreased tax only, or no tax, as the case may be, is paid or is payable, the buyer may deduct so much from the contract price as will be equivalent to the decrease of tax or remitted tax, and he shall not be liable to pay, or be sued for, or in respect of, such deduction.

(2) The provisions of sub-section (1) apply to the following taxes, namely:—

(a) any duty of customs or excise on goods;

(b) any tax on the sale or purchase of goods.

The purpose in enacting Sec. 64A of the Sale of Goods Act obviously was that increase or decrease in duty should be taken note of in the case of contracts concluded prior to the increase or decrease. In this view, no party should be made to unnecessarily gain or suffer on account of State action in increasing or decreasing duty.

The intention of the Legislature in enacting provisions of Sec. 64A ascertained by reading the section is that in the event of imposition of fresh duty, the seller should not suffer or bear such duty and in the event of decrease or remission of duty, the seller should not retain benefit of such remission or abolition of duty. The reason is that, as is well known, customs and/or export and/or excise duty are indirect taxes. The burden of the duty of customs or excise is always intended to be transferred to the consumers. It is for that reason that Sec. 64A (a) clearly provides that the seller may add to the price the increase for freshly imposed duty. Sub-section (b) is enacted to deprive the seller of the amount of the abolished or remitted duty by deduction thereof from the agreed price. The word "deduct" bears the dictionary meaning of "subtract" and/or "take off" and is more appropriate in regard to the calculation of the contract price due and payable under the contracts. It is not appropriate or possible to give to the words "deduct" and 'deduction' as contained in sub-section (b) a meaning which relates to the set of deduction to the physical act of deduction at the time of payment of price. The phrase "so much from the contract price" in has no relation to the physical act of payment of price. The word "deduct" in the context refers and relates to and means the right to subtract and/or take off the duty in the process of calculation of and arriving at the contract price.

In respect of such deduction, the liability to pay price is wiped off. When the phrase *"he shall not be liable to pay x x x such deduction"* is used in this sub-section, it means that the buyer shall not be liable to pay towards the contract price the amount "as will be equivalent to the decrease of duty or remitted duty". Obviously, the provisions of Sec. 64A are applicable only when the incidence of imposition, increase, remission, or abolition of duty is connected with and related to the goods of a particular contract for sale of goods between a seller and a buyer.[66]

## Section 65: [Repeal] Rep. by the Repealing Act, 1938 (1 of 1938), with Section 2 and Schedule

## Section 66: Savings

(1) Nothing in this Act or in any repeal effected thereby shall affect or be deemed to affect—

(a) any right, title interest, obligation or liability already acquired, accrued or incurred before the commencement of this Act, or

(b) any legal proceedings or remedy in respect of any such right, title, interest, obligation or liability, or

(c) anything done or suffered before the commencement of this Act, or

(d) any enactment relating to the sale of goods which is not expressly repealed by this Act, or

(e) any rule of law not inconsistent with this Act.

(2) The rules of insolvency relating to contracts for the sale of goods shall continue to apply thereto, notwithstanding anything contained in this Act.

(3) The provisions of this Act relating to contracts of sale do not apply to any transaction in the form of a contract of sale which is intended to operate by way of mortgage, pledge, charge or other security.

[66] *Central H.I. Trading Co.* v. *Pitty Bros.*, AIR 1962 BOMBAY 222.

# 3

# The Consumer Protection Act, 2019

## INTRODUCTION

The industrial revolution and the development in international trade and commerce has led to the vast expansion of business and trade, as a result of which a variety of consumer goods have appeared in the market to cater to the needs of the consumers and a host of services have been made available to the consumers such as insurance, transport, electricity, housing, entertainment, finance, and banking. A well-organized sector of manufacturers and traders with better knowledge of markets has come into existence, thereby affecting the relationship between the traders and the consumers making the principle of consumer sovereignty almost inapplicable. The advertisements of goods and services in television, newspapers and magazines influence the demand for the same by the consumers though there may be Manufacturing defects or imperfections or shortcomings in the quality, quantity and the purity of the goods or there may be deficiency in the services rendered. In addition, the production of the same item by many firms has led the consumers, who have little time to select, to think before they can purchase the best. For the welfare of the public, the glut of adulterated and sub-standard Articles in the market has to be checked. In spite of various provisions providing protection to the consumer and providing for stringent Action against adulterated and sub-standard Articles in the different enactments, like, the Code of Civil Procedure, 1908, the Indian Contract Act, 1872, the Sale of Goods Act, 1930, the Indian Penal Code, 1860, the Standards of Weights and Measures Act, 1976, and the Motor Vehicles Act, 1988, very little could be achieved in the field of consumers protection. Though the Monopolies and Restrictive Trade Practices Act, 1969 and the Prevention of Food Adulteration Act, 1954 provided relief to the consumers, yet it became necessary to protect the consumers from the exploitation and to save them from adulteration and sub-standard goods and services, and to safeguard the interests of the consumers.[1]

[1] http://himachal.nic.in/food/cpa1986.htm.

In order to provide for better protection of the interests of the consumer, the Secretary General of United Nations submitted draft guidelines to the Economic and Social Council (UNESCO) in 1983 after good number of consultations with Governments and international organizations. After extensive discussions and negotiations among Governments on the scope and content of the guidelines, the General assembly of the United Nations adopted the guidelines for consumer protection by consensus on 9th April 1985 (General Assembly Resolution No. 39/248). The guidelines issued are placed under four heads, viz., objectives, general principles, guidelines, and international co-operation. The aforesaid guidelines provide the following objectives:

(a) To assist countries in achieving or maintaining adequate protection for their population as consumers.

(b) To facilitate production and distribution patterns responsive to the needs and desires of consumers.

(c) To encourage high levels of ethical conduct for those engaged in the production and distribution of goods and services to consumers.

(d) To assist countries in curbing abusive business practices by all enterprises at the national and international levels which adversely affect consumers.

(e) To facilitate the development of independent consumer groups.

(f) To further international co-operation in the field of consumer protection.

(g) To encourage the development of market conditions which provide consumers with greater choice at lower prices.[2]

In order to provide better protection of the interest of the consumers, the Consumer Protection Act, 1986, was passed by the Parliament. The 1986 Act is repealed in 2019 and the Consumer Protection Act, 2019 came into force with effect from 20th July 2020.

***Note:*** The Consumer Protection Act, 1986 was repealed in 2019. However, few important definitions and provisions are *pari materia* to that of 1986 Act. Hence, the interpretation and the decision of the Supreme Court prior to 2019 shall be applicable to 2019 Act as well.

## PREAMBLE

The Preamble to the Act provides that an Act to provide for protection of the interests of consumers and for the said purpose, to establish authorities for timely and effective administration and settlement of consumers' disputes and for matters connected therewith or incidental thereto.

The preamble to the Act can afford useful assistance to ascertain the legislative intention; it was enacted to provide for the protection of the interest of consumers. The use of the word 'protection' furnishes key to the minds of the makers of the Act. Various definitions and provisions which elaborately attempt to achieve this objective have to be construed in this light without departing from the settled view that a preamble cannot

[2] *Laxmi Engineering Works* v. *P.S.G. Industrial Institute*, AIR 1995 SC 1428.

control the otherwise plain meaning of a provision. In fact, the law meets the long-felt necessity of protecting the common man from such wrongs for which the remedy under ordinary law for various reasons has become illusory.

## SALIENT FEATURES OF THE ACT

The salient features of the Act are summed up as under:

1. The Act applies to all goods and services unless specifically exempted by the Central Government.
2. It covers all the sectors whether private, public, or cooperative.
3. The provisions of the Act are compensatory in nature.
4. It enshrines the following rights of consumers—
   (a) right to be protected against the marketing of goods and services which are hazardous to life and property.
   (b) right to be informed about the quality, quantity, potency, purity, standard and price of goods or services so as to protect the consumer against unfair trade practices.
   (c) right to be assured, wherever possible, access to a variety of goods and services at competitive prices.
   (d) right to be heard and to be assured that consumers' interests will receive due consideration at appropriate forums.
   (e) right to seek redressal against unfair trade practices, and unscrupulous exploitation of consumers.
   (f) right to consumer education.
5. The Act envisages the establishment of Consumer Protection Councils at the Central and State levels, whose main objectives will be to promote and protect the rights of the consumers.

## OBJECTIVES OF THE ACT

CONSUMER PROTECTION ACT, 2019 (CPA, hereafter) is a milestone in the history of socio-economic legislation in the country. It is one of the most progressive and comprehensive pieces of Legislation enacted for the protection of consumers. It was enacted after an in-depth study of consumer protection laws in a number of countries and in consultation with the representatives of consumers, trade and industry and extensive discussions within the Government. The main objective of the Act is to provide for better protection of consumers. Unlike existing laws which are punitive or preventive in nature, the provisions of this Act are compensatory in nature. The Act is intended to provide simple, speedy, and inexpensive redressal to the consumers' grievances, and relief of a specific nature and award of compensation wherever appropriate to the consumer. The Act has been amended in 1993, 2002 and recently in 2019, both to extend its coverage and scope and to enhance the powers of the redressal machinery.

The Supreme Court categorically attached the importance of the Act and observed in *Lucknow Development Authority* v. *M.K. Gupta*,[3] that this Act attempts to remove the helplessness of a consumer which he faces against powerful business, described as 'a network of rackets' or a society in which, 'producers have secured power' to 'rob the rest'. The Consumer Protection Act is one of the benevolent pieces of Legislation intended to protect a large body of consumers from exploitation. The Act, therefore, provides for an alternative system of consumer justice by summary trial.[4]

## CONSTITUTIONALITY OF THE ACT

The basic question involved in the batch of appeals and the writ petitions is the constitutionality of the Consumer Protection Act, 1986 filed by Vishwabharathi House Building Co-operative Society arising out of a judgment and order passed by a Division Bench of the High Court of Karnataka upholding the *vires* of the Consumer Protection Act, 1986. The state of Karnataka has filed the appeal being against the judgment and order of the Karnataka High Court questioning certain observations made therein as regards interpretation of Sec. 25 of the Act, and others filed the writ petitions under Article 32 of the Constitution of India questioning the constitutionality of the Act before the Supreme Court in *State of Karnataka* v. *Vishwabarathi House Building Co-op. Society*.[5]

The contentions on behalf of appellants' petitioners are as under:

1. The Parliament is not empowered to establish hierarchy of Courts like the District Fora, State Commission, and the National Commission parallel to the hierarchy of Courts established under the Constitution, namely, District Courts, High Courts and Supreme Court in the absence of a suitable amendment made in the Constitution of India in terms of Article 368 thereof.
2. Such a hierarchy of Consumer Courts established under the Act would result in conflict of decisions with the hierarchy of Courts established under the Constitution dealing with similar matters.
3. The Parliament having regard to the provisions of Articles 323-A and 323-B of the Constitution of India could not enact the Act by establishing forums which are substitutes of the Civil Courts including the High Court. The provisions of the said Act strike at the independence of the judiciary.
4. As the Act does not contain any provision to transfer a case from one Consumer Court to another and, furthermore, the forum and the Commissions having no power to pass interim orders, the functioning thereof is unworkable.
5. The Parliament can only establish Courts which may deal with special subjects specified thereof but not a Court which will run parallel to Civil Courts.

The legislative competence of the Parliament and the State Legislatures respectively to provide for creation of Courts and Tribunals as envisaged in different lists contained in the VIIth Schedule of the Constitution of India are as under:

[3] AIR 1994 SC 787.

[4] *Charan Singh v. Healing Touch Hospital and others*, AIR 2000 SC 3138.

[5] AIR 2003 SC 1043.

**Item 77 of List I of the Seventh Schedule:** Constitution, organisation, jurisdiction, and powers of the Supreme Court (including contempt of such Court), and the fees taken therein; persons entitled to practice before the Supreme Court.

**Item 78 of List I of the Seventh Schedule:** Constitution and organisation (including vacations) of the High Courts except provisions as to officers and servants of high Courts; persons entitled to practice before the High Courts.

**Item 79 of List I of the Seventh Schedule:** Extension of the jurisdiction of a High Court to and exclusion of the jurisdiction of a High Court from any Union Territory.

**Item 95 of List I of the Seventh Schedule:** Jurisdiction and powers of all Courts, except the Supreme Court with respect to any of the matters in this List: admiralty jurisdiction.

**Item 11A of List III of the Seventh Schedule:** Administration of justice; constitution and organisation of all Courts, except the Supreme Court and the High Courts.

**Item 46 of List III of the Seventh Schedule:** Jurisdiction and powers of all Courts, except the Supreme Court, with respect to any of the matters in this List.

A bare perusal of the aforementioned provisions does not leave any iota of doubt as regards the legislative competence of the Parliament to provide for the creation of special Courts and tribunals. Administration of justice, constitution, and organization of all Courts, except the Supreme Court and the high Courts, is squarely covered by entry 11A of List III of the Constitution of India.

The Court further held that by virtue of Clause 2 of Article 246 of the Constitution, the Parliament has the requisite power to make laws with respect to the constitution of organization of all Courts except the Supreme Court and the High Court. In view of the constitutional Scheme relating to legislative competence of the Parliament and State Legislature, there cannot be any doubt or dispute that the Parliament has the requisite legislative competence to enact the Consumer Protection Act.

The question as regards legislative competence of the Parliament to create such special Tribunals as also the effect of Articles 323-A and 323-B of the Constitution is no longer *res integra* having regard to the recent decision of the Supreme Court in *Union of India* v. *Delhi High Court Bar Association*.[6]

## ACT IN A NUTSHELL

The Act runs into 107 provisions and is divided into 8 chapters. Chapter I deals with the applicability of the Act and provides a dictionary (definition) so that we can know the meaning of different concepts. Chapter II runs from Sec. 3 to Sec. 9 and deals with the establishment of different types of Consumer Protection Councils and their objectives, such as Central Consumer Council, State Consumer Council and District Consumer Council. This chapter specifically provides the objectives of such councils, and they are as follows:

1. The right to be protected against the marketing of goods and services which are hazardous to life and property.

[6] (2002) 4 SCC 275.

2. The right to be informed about the quality, quantity, potency, purity, standard and price of goods or services, as the case may be so as to protect the consumer against unfair trade practices.
3. The right to be assured, wherever possible, access to a variety of goods and services at competitive prices.
4. The right to be heard and to be assured that consumer interests will receive due consideration at appropriate forums.
5. The right to seek redressal against unfair trade practices or restrictive trade practices or unscrupulous exploitation of consumers.
6. The right to consumer education.

Chapter III deals with Establishment of a Central Consumer Protection Authority and the procedure, qualification, appointment of Commissioner and other officers. It runs from Sec. 10 to Sec. 27. Chapter IV, named as Consumer Disputes Redressal Commission runs from Sec. 28 to Sec. 73. This Chapter deals with the establishment of different consumer redressal commissions and their function, power, and procedures of making complaints. Chapter V, which runs from Sec. 74 to Sec. 81, deals with mediation between parties. Chapter VI deals with Product Liability and runs from Sec. 82 to Sec. 87. Chapter VII prescribes offences and penalties, which run from Sec. 88 to Sec. 93. Chapter VIII named as Miscellaneous that runs from Sec. 88 to Sec. 107.

# Chapter I Preliminary

## Section 1: Short title, extent, commencement and application

(1) This Act may be called the Consumer Protection Act, 2019.

(2) It extends to the whole of India except the State of Jammu and Kashmir.

(3) It shall come into force on such date as the Central Government may, by notification, appoint and different dates may be appointed for different States and for different provisions of this Act and any reference in any such provision to the commencement of this Act shall be construed as a reference to the coming into force of that provision.

(4) Save as otherwise expressly provided by the Central Government, by notification, this Act shall apply to all goods and services.

## Section 2: Definitions

In this Act, unless the context otherwise requires, —

(1) **"Advertisement"** means any audio or visual publicity, representation, endorsement or pronouncement made by means of light, sound, smoke, gas, print, electronic media, internet or website and includes any notice, circular, label, wrapper, invoice or such other documents.

(2) **"Appropriate laboratory"** means a laboratory or an organisation—

(i) recognised by the Central Government; or

(ii) recognised by a State Government, subject to such guidelines as may be issued by the Central Government in this behalf; or

(iii) established by or under any law for the time being in force, which is maintained, financed or aided by the Central Government or a State Government for carrying out analysis or test of any goods with a view to determining whether such goods suffer from any defect;

(3) **"Branch office"** means—

(i) any office or place of work described as a branch by the establishment; or

(ii) any establishment carrying on either the same or substantially the same activity carried on by the head office of the establishment;

(4) **"Central Authority"** means the Central Consumer Protection Authority established under Section 10;

(5) **"Complainant"** means—

(i) a consumer; or

(ii) any voluntary consumer association registered under any law for the time being in force; or

(iii) the Central Government or any State Government; or

(iv) the Central Authority; or

(v) one or more consumers, where there are numerous consumers having the same interest; or

(vi) in case of death of a consumer, his legal heir or legal representative; or

(vii) in case of a consumer being a minor, his parent or legal guardian;

(6) **"Complaint"** means any allegation in writing, made by a complainant for obtaining any relief provided by or under this Act, that—

(i) an unfair contract or unfair trade practice or a restrictive trade practice has been adopted by any trader or service provider;

(ii) the goods bought by him or agreed to be bought by him suffer from one or more defects;

(iii) the services hired or availed of or agreed to be hired or availed of by him suffer from any deficiency;

(iv) a trader or a service provider, as the case may be, has charged for the goods or for the services mentioned in the complaint, a price in excess of the price—

(a) fixed by or under any law for the time being in force; or

(b) displayed on the goods or any package containing such goods; or

(c) displayed on the price list exhibited by him by or under any law for the time being in force; or

(d) agreed between the parties;

(v) the goods, which are hazardous to life and safety when used, are being offered for sale to the public—

(a) in contravention of standards relating to safety of such goods as required to be complied with, by or under any law for the time being in force;

(b) where the trader knows that the goods so offered are unsafe to the public;

(vi) the services which are hazardous or likely to be hazardous to life and safety of the public when used, are being offered by a person who provides any service and who knows it to be injurious to life and safety;

(vii) a claim for product liability action lies against the product manufacturer, product seller or product service provider, as the case may be;

(7) **"Consumer"** means any person who—

(i) buys any goods for a consideration which has been paid or promised or partly paid and partly promised, or under any system of deferred payment and includes any user of such goods other than the person who buys such goods for consideration paid or promised or partly paid or partly promised, or under any system of deferred payment, when such use is made with the approval of such person, but does not include a person who obtains such goods for resale or for any commercial purpose; or

(ii) hires or avails of any service for a consideration which has been paid or promised or partly paid and partly promised, or under any system of deferred payment and includes any beneficiary of such service other than the person who hires or avails of the services for consideration paid or promised, or partly paid and partly promised, or under any system of deferred payment when such services are availed of with the approval of the first mentioned person, but does not include a person who avails of such service for any commercial purpose.

***Explanation:*** For the purposes of this clause,—

(a) the expression "commercial purpose" does not include use by a person of goods bought and used by him exclusively for the purpose of earning his livelihood, by means of self-employment.

(b) the expressions "buys any goods" and "hires or avails any services" includes offline or online transactions through electronic means or by teleshopping or direct selling or multi-level marketing.

## WHO IS A CONSUMER?

All of us are consumers of goods and services. For the purpose of the CPA, the word *'consumer'* has been defined separately for *'goods'* and *'services'*.

1. For the purpose of *'goods'*, a consumer means a person belonging to the following categories:

(a) One who buys or agrees to buy any goods for a consideration which has been paid or promised or partly paid and partly promised or under any system of deferred payment.

(b) It includes any user of such goods other than the person who actually buys goods, and such use is made with the approval of the purchaser.

***Note:*** a person is not a consumer if he purchases goods for commercial or resale purposes. However, the word *'commercial'* does not include use by consumer of goods bought and used by him exclusively for the purpose of earning his livelihood, by means of self-employment.

2. For the purpose of *'services'*, a *'consumer'* means a person belonging to the following categories:

(a) One who hires or avails of any service or services for a consideration which has been paid or promised or partly paid and partly promised or under any system of deferred payment.

(b) It includes any beneficiary of such service other than the one who actually hires or avails of the service for consideration and such services are availed with the approval of such person.

***Note:*** a person is not a consumer who avails such service for any commercial purpose.

The consumer, as the term implies, is the one who consumes. He is the one who purchases goods for private use or consumption. The meaning of the word 'consumer' can be broadly stated as to include anyone who consumes goods or services at the end of the chain of production. The comprehensive definition provided in the Act aims at covering every man who pays money as the price or cost of goods and services. The consumer deserves to get what he pays for in real quantity and true quality. In every society, the consumer remains the center of gravity of all business and industrial Activity. He needs protection from the manufacturer, producer, supplier, wholesaler, and retailer.[7]

Thus, the definition of consumer covers:

(1) One who buys goods for consideration for personal use.
(2) One who uses such goods with permission or approval of buyer of goods.
(3) One who obtains goods on hire purchase or lease.
(4) One who hires or avails of any services for consideration.
(5) One who uses the services with the permission of the person who has hired the services.
(6) One who obtains services on deferred payment basis—i.e., hire purchase or lease.
(7) One who buys goods or avails services exclusively for the purpose of earning his livelihood as self-employment.

The definition of 'consumer' may be divided into two parts. The first part deals with goods and the second with services. Both parts first declare the meaning of goods and

[7] *Morgan Stanley Mutual Fund* v. *Kartick Das*, (1994) 4 SCC 225.

services by use of wide expressions. Their ambit is further enlarged by use of the inclusive clause. For instance, it is not only the purchaser of goods or hirer of services but even those who use the goods or who are beneficiaries of services with approval of the person who purchased the goods or who hired services are included in the definition of 'consumer'.

In *Spring Meadows Hospital* v. *Harjol Ahluwalia*[8], the following questions arose before the Supreme Court for its consideration:

(1) The minor child being the patient who was admitted into the hospital for treatment, can the parents of the child be considered to be consumers so as to claim compensation under the provisions of the CPA?

(2) Is the Commission under the Act entitled to award compensation to the parents for mental agony in view of the powers of the Commission under the Act?

(3) Even if the child as well as the parents of the child would come under the definition of the 'Consumer', whether compensation can be awarded in favour of both the consumers and compensation can be awarded only to the beneficiary of the services rendered, who in the present case would be the child who was admitted into the hospital?

Before discussing the aforesaid issues, it is felt necessary to reveal the facts of the case. A complaint petition was filed by minor Harjol Ahluwalia through his parents before the Commission alleging that the minor was being treated at a Nursing home in Noida in December 1993. As there was no improvement in his health, the said minor was taken to M/s. Spring Meadows hospital. In the hospital, the patient was examined by the senior Consultant Pediatricians, Dr. Promila Bhutani and on the advice of the said doctor, the patient was admitted as an in-patient in the hospital. The doctor made the diagnosis that the patient was suffering from typhoid and intimated the parents that medicines have been prescribed for the treatment of typhoid fever. On the 30 of December 1993 at 9.00 a.m., a nurse of the hospital asked the father of the minor patient to get the injection, Inj Lariago, to be administered intravenously to the minor patient. The father of the minor child purchased the medicine, which was prescribed, and the nurse injected the same to the minor patient. The patient, immediately on being injected, collapsed while still in the lap of his mother. It was further alleged that before administering the injection, the nurse had not done any sensitive test to find out whether there would be any adverse reaction on the patient.

Seeing the minor child collapse, the parents immediately called for help and the resident doctor attended to the patient. The doctor told the parents that the child had suffered a cardiac arrest and then, by manually pumping the chest, the doctor attempted to revive the heartbeat. The hospital authorities then summoned an anaesthetist, who arrived within half an hour and then started a procedure of manual respiration by applying the oxygen cylinder and manual respirator. Though the child was kept alive on the manual ventilator, the condition of the child did not show any sign of improvement.

On the advice of the doctor, the parents admitted the child in the Paediatric Intensive Care Unit of the All-India Institute of Medical Science (AIIMS) on 3 January 1994. In the Institute, the doctors examined the minor child thoroughly and informed the parents that

[8] AIR 1998 SC 1801.

the child is critical and even if he would survive, he would live only in a vegetative state as irreparable damage had been caused to his brain and there was no chance of revival of the damaged parts. The minor was then kept in the Paediatric Intensive Care Unit of the AIIMS till 24 January 1994 and was thereafter discharged after informing the parents that no useful purpose would be served by keeping the minor child in the hospital.

The complainant alleged that the child, on account of negligence and deficiency on the part of the hospital authorities, suffered irreparable damage and could survive only as a mere vegetative and accordingly claimed compensation to the tune of 28 lacs. The Commission determined the quantum of compensation and awarded 12.5 lacs as compensation to the minor patient. In addition to the aforesaid sum of 12.5 lacs, the Commission also awarded 5 lacs as compensation to be paid to the parents of the minor child for the acute mental agony that has been caused to the parents by reason of their only son having been reduced to a vegetative state requiring lifelong care and attention. The hospital challenged the decision of the Commission before the Apex Court.

The Supreme Court held that a *'consumer'* would mean a person who hires or avails of any services and includes any beneficiary of such services other than the person who hires or avails of the services. When a young child is taken to a hospital by his parents and the child is treated by the doctor, the parents would come within the definition of consumer having hired the services and the young child would also become a consumer under the inclusive definition of being a beneficiary of such services. The definition clause being wide enough to include not only the person who hires the services but also the beneficiary of such services, accordingly, both the parents of the child and the child would be consumers within the meaning of the definition of consumer provided under the Act.

An important question of law that arose before the Supreme Court in *Regional Provident Fund Commissioner* v. *Shiv Kumar Joshi*[9] was, whether the provisions of the CPA can be invoked against the Provident Fund Commissioner by a member of the employees' Provident Fund Scheme? It has to be ascertained as to whether any such member is a *'consumer'* and the duty performed by the Provident Fund Commissioner under the relevant Scheme is a *'service'* within the meaning of the Act. If it is held that such a member is the *'consumer'* and the facilities provided are *'services'*, it has to be further considered as to whether the delayed payment of the provident fund to a member-employee amounts to deficiency of service under the Act.

The Supreme Court held that the provisions of the CPA can be invoked against the Provident Fund Commissioner by a member of the employees' Provident Fund Scheme as such member is a *'consumer'* and the duty performed by the Provident Fund Commissioner under the relevant Scheme is a 'service' within the meaning of the Act.

In 2010, the question that came before the Supreme Court in *Bihar School Examination Board* v. *Suresh Prasad Sinha*[10] was whether the School Examination Board would be considered as *'service provider'* and the student would be a *'consumer'* defined in the CPA.

The Supreme Court observed that in the course of conduct of the examination, or evaluation of answer-scripts, or furnishing of mark-sheets or certificates, there may be some negligence, omission, or deficiency, does not convert the Board into a service-provider for

[9] AIR 2000 SC 331.

[10] AIR 2010 SC 93.

a consideration, nor convert the examinee into a consumer who can make a complaint under the Act. Accordingly, the Court held that the Board is not a *'service provider'* and a student who takes an examination is not a *'consumer'* and consequently, a complaint under the Act will not be maintainable against the Board.

## Commercial Purpose

The phrase *'commercial purpose'* has been used in both the parts of the definition including explanation. It needs to be interpreted in the right perspective as it excludes the buyer from the purview of the Act and thereby, he is not entitled to file any complaint whatsoever. a person who buys goods for resale or commercial purposes is specifically excluded from the definition of *'consumer'*. The Supreme Court of India in *Laxmi Engineering Works* v. *P.S.G. Industrial Institute*[11] has elaborately discussed the meaning of the phrase *'commercial purpose'* and its implication and observed that since the cases of resale have been separately referred to, it becomes obvious that the words *'for any commercial purpose'* are intended to cover cases other than those of resale of the goods concerned. The words *'for any commercial purpose'* are wide enough to take in all cases where goods are purchased for being used in any Activity directly intended to generate profit.

The intention of the Parliament is to exclude from the scope of the expression *'consumer'* any person who buys goods for the purpose of their being used in any activity engaged on a large scale for the purpose of making profit. As already indicated, since resale of goods has been separately and specifically mentioned in the earlier portion of the definition clause, the words *'for any commercial purpose'* must be understood as covering cases other than those of resale of goods. It is thus obvious that the Parliament wanted to exclude from the scope of the definition not merely persons who obtain goods for resale but also those who purchase goods with a view to using such goods for carrying on any activity on a large scale for the purpose of earning profit. On this interpretation of the definition, persons buying goods either for resale or for use in large-scale profit-making activity will not be *'consumer'* entitled to protection under the Act. It is obvious that the Parliament intended to restrict the benefits of the Act to ordinary consumers purchasing goods either for their own consumption or even for use in some small venture which they may have embarked upon in order to make a living as distinct from large-scale manufacturing or processing activity carried on for profit.

Both the parts of the definition of *'consumer'* provided under the Act have to be interpreted harmoniously. The interpretation of the words *'commercial purpose'* must be logical and equitable so as to avoid patent anomalies and inconsistencies in the application of the law. Viewed in this background, the various tests for determining whether the goods have been purchased for a commercial purpose would be as follows:

1. The goods are not for immediate final consumption but there is only transfer of goods, i.e., resale.
2. There should be a direct nexus between the purchase of goods and the profit or loss from their further disposal. Such a direct nexus is absent when the goods or services are converted for producing other goods or services. After conversion,

[11] AIR 1995 SC 1428.

there is no direct nexus between the kind of goods purchased and the kind of goods sold.

3. There is a nexus of form and kind between the goods purchased and the goods sold. Such a direct nexus of form and kind ceases when the goods undergo transformation or conversion.

In brief, the immediate purpose as distinct from the ultimate purpose of purchase, the sale in the same form or after conversion and a direct nexus with profit or loss would be the determinants of the character of a transaction to ascertain whether it is of a *'commercial purpose'* or not. Thus, buyers of goods or commodities for *'self-consumption'* would be consumers as defined in the Act. However, the purpose for which a person has bought goods is a *'commercial purpose'* within the meaning of the definition of the expression *'consumer'* in provided in the Act is always a question of fact to be decided on the facts and circumstances of each case.[12]

In *Kalpavruksha Charitable Trust* v. *Toshniwal Brothers (Bombay) Pvt. Ltd.*,[13] it was held that a charitable trust is not a consumer if it has purchased machinery for its Diagnostic Centre, when only 10% patients are provided free service and charges are levied on the remaining patients. Thus, the use is for *'commercial purpose'* and hence it is not *'consumer'*.

(8) **"Consumer dispute"** means a dispute where the person against whom a complaint has been made, denies or disputes the allegations contained in the complaint;

(9) **"Consumer rights"** includes, —

(i) the right to be protected against the marketing of goods, products or services which are hazardous to life and property;

(ii) the right to be informed about the quality, quantity, potency, purity, standard and price of goods, products or services, as the case may be, so as to protect the consumer against unfair trade practices;

(iii) the right to be assured, wherever possible, access to a variety of goods, products or services at competitive prices;

(iv) the right to be heard and to be assured that consumer's interests will receive due consideration at appropriate fora;

(v) the right to seek redressal against unfair trade practice or restrictive trade practices or unscrupulous exploitation of consumers; and

(vi) the right to consumer awareness;

(10) **"Defect"** means any fault, imperfection or shortcoming in the quality, quantity, potency, purity or standard which is required to be maintained by or under any law for the time being in force or under any contract, express or implied or as is claimed by the trader in any manner whatsoever in relation to any goods or product and the expression "defective" shall be construed accordingly;

---

[12] *Kalpavruksha Charitable Trust* v. *Toshniwal Brothers (Bombay) Pvt. Ltd.*, AIR 1999 SC 3356.

[13] AIR 1999 SC 3356.

(11) **"Deficiency"** means any fault, imperfection, shortcoming or inadequacy in the quality, nature and manner of performance which is required to be maintained by or under any law for the time being in force or has been undertaken to be performed by a person in pursuance of a contract or otherwise in relation to any service and includes—

(i) any act of negligence or omission or commission by such person which causes loss or injury to the consumer; and

(ii) deliberate withholding of relevant information by such person to the consumer;

Mere loss or injury is not enough to award any compensation. It shall be coupled with negligence. The consumer shall be compensated for any loss or injury suffered by him due to the negligence of the opposite party. Section 39(1)(d) specifically reads as follows:

*"To pay such amount as may be awarded by it as compensation to the consumer for any loss or injury suffered by the consumer due to the negligence of the opposite party."*

Each word used in Section 39(1)(d) is of wide connotation and is fully comprehended both in common and legal sense. Negligence is the absence of reasonable or prudent care which a reasonable person is expected to observe in a given set of circumstances. But the negligence for which a consumer can claim to be compensated under this sub-section must cause some loss or injury to him. Loss is a generic term. It signifies some detriment or deprivation or damage. Injury too means any damage or wrong. It means *'invasion of any legally protected interest of another'*. Thus, the provisions of Sec. 39(1)(d) are attracted if the person from whom damages are claimed is found to have acted negligently and such negligence must result in some loss to the person claiming damages. In other words, loss, or injury, if any, must flow from negligence. Mere loss or injury without negligence is not contemplated by this Section.[14]

The Supreme Court in *Ravneet Singh Bagga* v. *KLM Royal Dutch Airlines*[15] has further held that deficiency of service requires proof of willful fault, imperfection, shortcoming, or inadequacy in quality, nature and manner of performance which is required to be performed in pursuance of contract or otherwise in relation to service. The burden of proving deficiency is on the party who alleges it. If a person who has rendered the service has taken all reasonable care and precaution and his action was in good faith, it cannot be said that there is any deficiency of service.

(12) **"Design",** in relation to a product, means the intended or known physical and material characteristics of such product and includes any intended or known formulation or content of such product and the usual result of the intended manufacturing or other process used to produce such product;

(13) **"Direct selling"** means marketing, distribution and sale of goods or provision of services through a network of sellers, other than through a permanent retail location;

[14] *Consumer Unity and Trust Society, Jaipur* v. *Chairman and Managing Director, Bank of Baroda, Calcutta*, (1995) 2 SCC 150

[15] (2000) 1 SCC 66.

(14) **"Director-General"** means the Director-General appointed under sub-section (2) of Section 15;

(15) **"District Commission"** means a District Consumer Disputes Redressal Commission established under sub-section (1) of Section 28;

(16) **"E-commerce"** means buying or selling of goods or services including digital products over digital or electronic network;

(17) **"Electronic service provider"** means a person who provides technologies or processes to enable a product seller to engage in advertising or selling goods or services to a consumer and includes any online marketplace or online auction sites;

(18) **"Endorsement"**, in relation to an advertisement, means—

(i) any message, verbal statement, demonstration; or

(ii) depiction of the name, signature, likeness or other identifiable personal characteristics of an individual; or

(iii) depiction of the name or seal of any institution or organisation, which makes the consumer to believe that it reflects the opinion, finding or experience of the person making such endorsement;

(19) **"Establishment"** includes an advertising agency, commission agent, manufacturing, trading or any other commercial agency which carries on any business, trade or profession or any work in connection with or incidental or ancillary to any commercial activity, trade or profession, or such other class or classes of persons including public utility entities in the manner as may be prescribed;

(20) **"Express warranty"** means any material statement, affirmation of fact, promise or description relating to a product or service warranting that it conforms to such material statement, affirmation, promise or description and includes any sample or model of a product warranting that the whole of such product conforms to such sample or model;

(21) **"Goods"** means every kind of movable property and includes "food" as defined in clause (j) of sub-section (1) of Section 3 of the Food Safety and Standards Act, 2006; (34 of 2006);

(22) **"Harm"**, in relation to a product liability, includes—

(i) damage to any property, other than the product itself;

(ii) personal injury, illness or death;

(iii) mental agony or emotional distress attendant to personal injury or illness or damage to property; or

(iv) any loss of consortium or services or other loss resulting from a harm referred to in sub-clause (i) or sub-clause (ii) or sub-clause (iii),

But shall not include any harm caused to a product itself or any damage to the property on account of breach of warranty conditions or any commercial or economic loss, including any direct, incidental or consequential loss relating thereto;

(23) **"Injury"** means any harm whatever illegally caused to any person, in body, mind or property;

(24) **"Manufacturer"** means a person who—

(i) makes any goods or parts thereof; or

(ii) assembles any goods or parts thereof made by others; or

(iii) puts or causes to be put his own mark on any goods made by any other person;

(25) **"Mediation"** means the process by which a mediator mediates the consumer disputes;

(26) **"Mediator"** means a mediator referred to in Section 75;

(27) **"Member"** includes the President and a member of the National Commission or a State Commission or a District Commission, as the case may be;

(28) **"Misleading advertisement"** in relation to any product or service, means an advertisement, which—

(i) falsely describes such product or service; or

(ii) gives a false guarantee to, or is likely to mislead the consumers as to the nature, substance, quantity or quality of such product or service; or

(iii) conveys an express or implied representation which, if made by the manufacturer or seller or service provider thereof, would constitute an unfair trade practice; or

(iv) deliberately conceals important information;

(29) **"National Commission"** means the National Consumer Disputes Redressal Commission established under sub-section (1) of Section 53;

(30) **"Notification"** means a notification published in the Official Gazette and the term "notify" shall be construed accordingly;

(31) **"Person"** includes—

(i) an individual;

(ii) a firm whether registered or not;

(iii) a Hindu undivided family;

(iv) a co-operative society;

(v) an association of persons whether registered under the Societies Registration Act, 1860 (21 of 1860) or not;

(vi) any corporation, company or a body of individuals whether incorporated or not;

(vii) any artificial juridical person, not falling within any of the preceding sub-clauses;

(32) **"Prescribed"** means prescribed by rules made by the Central Government, or, as the case may be, the State Government;

(33) **"Product"** means any article or goods or substance or raw material or any extended cycle of such product, which may be in gaseous, liquid, or solid state

possessing intrinsic value which is capable of delivery either as wholly assembled or as a component part and is produced for introduction to trade or commerce, but does not include human tissues, blood, blood products and organs;

(34) **"Product liability"** means the responsibility of a product manufacturer or product seller, of any product or service, to compensate for any harm caused to a consumer by such defective product manufactured or sold or by deficiency in services relating thereto;

(35) **"Product liability action"** means a complaint filed by a person before a District Commission or State Commission or National Commission, as the case may be, for claiming compensation for the harm caused to him;

(36) **"Product manufacturer"** means a person who—

(i) makes any product or parts thereof; or

(ii) assembles parts thereof made by others; or

(iii) puts or causes to be put his own mark on any products made by any other person; or

(iv) makes a product and sells, distributes, leases, installs, prepares, packages, labels, markets, repairs, maintains such product or is otherwise involved in placing such product for commercial purpose; or

(v) designs, produces, fabricates, constructs or re-manufactures any product before its sale; or

(vi) being a product seller of a product, is also a manufacturer of such product;

(37) **"Product seller"**, in relation to a product, means a person who, in the course of business, imports, sells, distributes, leases, installs, prepares, packages, labels, markets, repairs, maintains, or otherwise is involved in placing such product for commercial purpose and includes—

(i) a manufacturer who is also a product seller; or

(ii) a service provider;

But does not include—

(a) a seller of immovable property, unless such person is engaged in the sale of constructed house or in the construction of homes or flats;

(b) a provider of professional services in any transaction in which, the sale or use of a product is only incidental thereto, but furnishing of opinion, skill or services being the essence of such transaction;

(c) a person who—

(i) acts only in a financial capacity with respect to the sale of the product;

(ii) is not a manufacturer, wholesaler, distributor, retailer, direct seller or an electronic service provider;

(iii) leases a product, without having a reasonable opportunity to inspect and discover defects in the product, under a lease arrangement in which the selection, possession, maintenance, and operation of the product are controlled by a person other than the lessor;

(38) **"Product service provider"**, in relation to a product, means a person who provides any service in respect of such product;

(39) **"Regulations"** means the regulations made by the National Commission, or as the case may be, the Central Authority;

(40) **"Regulator"** means a body, or any authority established under any other law for the time being in force;

(41) **"Restrictive trade practice"** means a trade practice which tends to bring about manipulation of price or its conditions of delivery or to affect flow of supplies in the market relating to goods or services in such a manner as to impose on the consumers unjustified costs or restrictions and shall include—

(i) delay beyond the period agreed to by a trader in supply of such goods or in providing the services which has led or is likely to lead to rise in the price;

(ii) any trade practice which requires a consumer to buy, hire or avail of any goods or, as the case may be, services as condition precedent for buying, hiring or availing of other goods or services;

(42) **"Service"** means service of any description which is made available to potential users and includes, but not limited to, the provision of facilities in connection with banking, financing, insurance, transport, processing, supply of electrical or other energy, telecom, boarding or lodging or both, housing construction, entertainment, amusement or the purveying of news or other information, but does not include the rendering of any service free of charge or under a contract of personal service;

A consumer can file a complaint if he is not provided with the services that are required. Therefore, deficiency of service is one of the crucial aspects of the Act. The author thinks it proper to deal with both the concepts, i.e., *'service'* and *'deficiency'* in detail with the help of decided cases of the Supreme Court.

A complaint can be lodged against the service provider if there is a deficiency in service, or if he charges higher prices or provides services which are hazardous or where the service provider followed unfair or restrictive trade practice. Hence, it is necessary to understand the meaning of *'service'* and *'deficiency'*.

The definition of *'service' provided* in the Act can be split up into three parts as follows:

1. Main part
2. Inclusive part
3. Exclusive part

The main part is explanatory in nature and defines service to mean service of any description which is made available to the potential users. The inclusive part expressly includes the provision of facilities in connection with banking, financing, insurance, transport, processing, supply of electrical or other energy, telecom, boarding or lodging or both, housing construction, entertainment, amusement or the purveying of news or other information. The exclusive part excludes from the ambit of the definition if the service is rendered free of charge under a contract of personal service.[16] The Supreme Court has observed in *Lucknow Development Authority* v. *M.K. Gupta*,[17] that the main clause itself is very wide. It applies to any service made available to potential users. The words *'any'* and *'potential'* are significant. Both are of wide amplitude. The dictionary meaning of the word *'any'* means one or some or all. In Black's Law Dictionary, it is explained thus: the word *'any'* has a diversity of meaning and may be employed to indicate *'all'* or *'every'* as well as *'some'* or *'one'* and its meaning in a given statute depends upon the context and the subject-matter of the statute. The use of the word *'any'* in the context it has been used in the definition indicates that it has been used in a wide sense extending from one to all. The other word *'potential'* is again very wide. In Oxford Dictionary, it is defined as 'capable of coming into being, possibility'. In Black's Law Dictionary, it is defined are 'existing in possibility'. In other words, a service which is not only extended to actual users but those who are capable of using it are covered in the definition. The clause is thus very wide and extends to any or all actual or potential users.

Referring to the inclusive part of the definition, it can be said that the inclusive clause succeeded in widening its scope but not exhausting the services which could be covered in the earlier part. So, any service except when it is free of charge or under constraint of personal service is included in it. The words 'but not limited to', further clarify that any type of service, whether mentioned in the definition or not, can be brought within the ambit of the definition. The services mentioned in the definition, like banking, financing, insurance, transport, processing, supply of electrical or other energy, board or lodging or both, housing construction, entertainment, amusement or the purveying of news or other information, are only illustrative, not exhaustive.

## Contract of Service and Contract for Service

Contracts of personal services are excluded from the ambit of the definition of service. The Supreme Court has discussed about the distinction between a *'contract of service'* and a *'contract for services'* in *Dharangadhara Chemical Words Ltd.* v. *State of Saurashtra*,[18] and held that a *'contract for services'* implies a contract whereby one party undertakes to render services, e.g. professional or technical services, to or for another in the performance of which he is not subject to detailed direction and control but exercises professional or technical skill and uses his own knowledge and discretion. A *'contract of service'* implies relationship of master and servant and involves an obligation to obey orders in the work to be performed.[19]

The Parliament has deliberately chosen the expression *'contract of service'* instead of the expression *'contract for services'* in the exclusive part of the definition of *'service'* provided in Sec. 2(42). The reason is that an employer cannot be regarded as a consumer in respect of the services rendered by his employees in pursuance of a contract of employment. It is, no doubt, true that the relationship between a medical practitioner and a patient carries

[16] *Indian Medical Association* v. *V.P. Shantha*, AIR 1996 SC 550.

[17] (1994) 1 SCC 243.

[18] AIR 1957 SC 264.

[19] *See also Simmons* v. *Heath Laundry Co.*, (1990) 1 KB 543.

within it certain degree of mutual confidence and trust and, therefore, the services rendered by the medical practitioner can be regarded as services of personal nature, but since there is no relationship of master and servant between the doctor and the patient, the contract between the medical practitioner and his patient cannot be treated as a contract of personal service but is a contract for services and the service rendered by the medical practitioner to his patient under such a contract is not covered by the exclusionary part of the definition of 'service' contained in Sec. 2(42) of the Act.[20]

## SERVICES MARKETING

There may be many cases where the provisions of deficient services involve liability for breach of contract between the consumer and the provider, or for tort of negligence in general. But now, the CPA provides an additional dispensation to the consumer who suffers on account of negligence or deficiency in service. Now, the consumer aggrieved by any negligence or deficiency in any such services is entitled to seek his remedy before the Consumer Forum designed for speedy justice with less or no expense. The author thinks it proper to discuss some of the aspects of deficiency of services in the services sectors and these are as follows.

### Medical Services

The duties which a doctor owes to his patient are clear. A person who is ready to give medical advice and treatment impliedly undertakes that he possesses the skill and knowledge for the purpose. Such a person, when consulted by a patient, owes him certain duties, viz., a duty of care in deciding whether to undertake the case, a duty of care in deciding what treatment to give or a duty of care in the administration of that treatment. A breach of any of those duties gives a right of action for negligence to the patient. The practitioner must bring to his task a reasonable degree of skill and knowledge and must exercise a reasonable degree of care. Neither the very highest nor a very low degree of care and competence judged in the light of the particular circumstances of each case is what the law requires. The doctor, no doubt, has discretion in choosing treatment which he proposes to give to the patient and such discretion is relatively ampler in cases of emergency.[21]

There was a controversy in regard to application of the CPA to the medical practitioner or, in other words, whether the service provided by the doctors would be brought within the meaning of definition of *'service'* provided in the Act. It was contented before the Supreme Court in *Indian Medical Association* v. *V.P. Shantha*[22] that if medical practitioners are brought within the ambit of the CPA, the consequences would be that the medical practitioner may refuse to attend to the patients and there would be no safeguard against frivolous and vexatious complaints and consequent blackmail. The Court refused to accept such apprehension and held that medical practitioners fall within the substantive law

[20] *Indian Medical Association* v. *V.P. Shantha*, AIR 1996 SC 550.

[21] *Laxman Balkrishna Joshi* v. *Dr. Trimbak Bapu Godbole*, AIR 1969 SC 128.

[22] AIR 1996 SC 550.

governing claim for compensation on the ground of negligence and the principles which apply to the determination of such a claim before the Civil Court would equally apply to Consumer Disputes redressal agencies under the CPA.

The Supreme Court evolved some guidelines and they are as follows:

1. Service rendered to a patient by a medical practitioner (except where the doctor renders service free of charge to every patient or under a contract of personal service), by way of consultation diagnosis and treatment, both medical and surgical, would fall within the ambit of *'service'* as defined under the CPA.
2. The fact that medical practitioners belong to the medical profession and are subject to the disciplinary control of the Medial Council of India and/or State Medical Councils constituted under the provisions of the Indian Medical Council Act would not exclude the service rendered by them from the ambit of the Act.
3. A *'contract of personal service'* has to be distinguished from a *'contract for personal services*. In the absence of a relationship of master and servant between the patient and the medical practitioners, the service rendered by a medical practitioner to the patient cannot be regarded as service rendered under a *'contract of personal service'*. Such service is service rendered under a *'contract for personal services'* and is not covered by exclusionary clause of the definition of *'service'* contained in the Act.
4.. The expression *'contract of personal service'* provided in the definition of *'service'* cannot be confined to contract for employment of domestic servants only and the said expression would include the employment of medical officer for the purpose of rendering medical service to the employer. The service rendered by a medical officer to his employer under the contract of employment would be outside the purview of *'service'* as defined in the Act.
5. Service rendered free of charge by a medical practitioner attached to a hospital/ nursing home or a medical officer employed in a hospital/Nursing home where such services are rendered free of charge of everybody, would not be *'service'* as defined in the Act. The payment of a token amount for registration purpose only at the hospital/nursing home would not alter the position.
6. Service rendered at a non-government hospital/nursing home where no charge whatsoever is made from any person availing the service and all patients (rich and poor) are given free service, is outside the purview of the expression *'service'* as defined in the Act. The payment of a token amount for registration purpose only at the hospital/nursing home would not alter the position.
7. Service rendered at a non-government hospital/nursing home where charges are required to be paid by the persons availing such services falls within the purview of the expression *'service'* as defined in the Act.
8. Service rendered at a non-government hospital/nursing home where charges are required to be paid by persons who are in a position to pay and persons who cannot afford to pay are rendered service free of charge would fall within the ambit of the expression *'service'* as defined in the Act irrespective of the fact that the service is rendered free of charge to persons who are not in a position

to pay for such services. Free service would also be *'service'* and the recipient a *'consumer'* under the Act.

9. Service rendered at a government hospital/health Centre/dispensary where no charge whatsoever is made from any person availing the services and all patients (rich and poor) are given free service, is outside the purview of the expression *'service'* as defined in the Act. The payment of a token amount for registration purpose only at the hospital/nursing home would not alter the position.
10. Service rendered at a government hospital/health Centre/dispensary where services are rendered on payment of charges and also rendered free of charge to other persons availing such services would fall within the ambit of the expression *'service'* as defined the Act irrespective of the fact that service is rendered free of charge to persons who do not pay for such service. Free service would also be *'service'* and the recipient a *'consumer'* under the Act.
11. Service rendered by a medical practitioner or hospital/nursing home cannot be regarded as service rendered free of charge, if the person availing the service has taken an insurance policy for medical care where under the charges for consultation diagnosis and medical treatment are borne by the insurance company and such service would fall within the ambit of *'service'* as defined in the Act.
12. Similarly, where, as a part of the conditions of service, the employer bears the expenses of medical treatment of an employee and his family members dependent on him, the service rendered to such an employee and his family members by a medical practitioner or a hospital/nursing home would not be free of charge and would constitute *'service'* under the Act.

The charge of professional negligence on a medical person is a serious one as it affects his professional status and reputation and as such the burden of proof would be more onerous. A doctor cannot be held negligent only because something has gone wrong. He also cannot be held liable for mischance or misadventure or for an error of judgment in making a choice when two options are available. The mistake in diagnosis is not necessarily a negligent diagnosis. Even under the law of tort, medical practitioners can only be held liable in respect of an erroneous diagnosis if his error is so palpably wrong as to prove by itself that it was negligently arrived at or it was the product of absence of reasonable skill and care on his part regard being held to the ordinary level of skill in the profession. For fastening criminal liability, a very high degree of such negligence is required to be proved. Death is the ultimate result of all serious ailments, and the doctors are there to save the victims from such ailments. The experience and expertise of a doctor are utilized for the recovery. But it is not expected that in case of all ailments, the doctor can give guarantee of cure.

For establishing medical negligence or deficiency in service, the Courts would determine the following:

(i) No guarantee is given by any doctor or surgeon that the patient will be cured.
(ii) The doctor, however, must undertake a fair, reasonable and competent degree of skill, which may not be the highest skill.
(iii) Adoption of one of the modes of treatment, if there are many, and treating the patient with due care and caution would not constitute any negligence.

(iv) Failure to act in accordance with the standard, reasonable, competent medical means at the time would not constitute negligence. However, a medical practitioner must exercise the reasonable degree of care and skill and knowledge which he possesses. Failure to use due skill in diagnosis with the result that wrong treatment is given would be negligence.

(v) In a complicated case, the Court would be slow in contributing negligence on the part of the doctor, if he is performing his duties to the best of his ability.[23]

A contention has also been raised in the *Indian Medical Association* case that even in the government hospitals/health centers/dispensaries where services are rendered free of charge to all the patients, the provision of the Act shall apply because the expenses of running the said hospitals are met by appropriation from the Consolidated Fund, which is raised from the taxes paid by the tax payers. The Supreme Court referred its earlier decision where it has been held that the essential characteristics of a tax are that:

(i) It is imposed under statutory power without the taxpayer's consent and the payment is enforced by law;

(ii) It is an imposition made for public purpose without reference to any special benefit to be conferred on the payer of the tax; and

(iii) It is part of the common burden and the quantum of imposition upon the taxpayer depends generally upon his capacity to pay.[24]

Accordingly, the Court held that the tax paid by the person availing the service at a government hospital cannot be treated as a consideration or charge for the service rendered at the said hospital and such service, though rendered free of charge, does not cease to be so because the person availing the service happens to be a tax payer.

### *Compensation for negligence*

Section 39(1)(d) of the Consumer Protection Act, 2019 reads:

*to pay such amount as may be awarded by it as compensation to the consumer for any loss or injury suffered by the consumer due to the negligence of the opposite party.*

The consumer would be entitled to compensation only after proving the negligence of the opposite party. In other words, compensation is coupled with negligence and the burden of proof of negligence of the opposite party lies on the consumer.

The question may arise at what point of time can one say that the medical practitioner is negligent in his duty and what amount of care he needs to take.

> "I myself would prefer to put it this way a doctor is not guilty of negligence if he has acted in accordance with a practice accepted as proper by a responsible body of medical men skilled in that particular art. Putting it the other way round, a doctor is not negligent, if he is acting in accordance with such a practice, merely because there is a body of opinion that takes a contrary view."[25]

[23] *Malay Kumar Ganguly* v. *Sukumar Mukherjee*, AIR 2010 SC 1162.

[24] *See The Commr. Hindu Religious Endowments, Madras* v. *Sri Lakshmindra Thirtha Swamiar of Sri Shirur Mutt*, AIR 1954 SC 282 at p. 295 per B.K. Mukherjea, J.

[25] *Bolam* v. *Friem Hospital Management Committee*, (1957) 2 All. ER 118.

This is the legal position of the standard of care required by a doctor. A doctor will not be guilty of negligence if he has acted in accordance with the practice accepted as proper by a responsible body of medical men skilled in that particular art and if he has acted in accordance with such practice merely, because there is a body of opinion that takes a contrary view will not make him liable for negligence.

The Supreme Court in *Achutrao Haribhau Khodwa* v. *State of Maharashtra*[26] had occasion to examine the test for determining negligence of reasonable skill, knowledge, and care in the matter of performing his duties by a medical practitioner. The Court observed that the duties which a doctor owes to his patient are clear. A person who holds himself out ready to give medical advice and treatment impliedly undertakes that he possesses the skill and knowledge for the purpose. Such a person, when consulted by a patient, owes him certain duties, viz., a duty of care in deciding whether to undertake the case, the duty of care in deciding whether treatment to give or a duty of care in the administration of that treatment. A breach of any of those duties gives a right of Action for negligence to the patient. The practitioner must bring to his task a reasonable degree of skill and knowledge and must exercise a reasonable degree of care. Neither the very highest nor a very low degree of care and competence judged in the light of the particular circumstances of each case is what the law requires. The Supreme Court in *Laxman Balakrishnan Joshi* v. *Dr. Trimbak Bapu Godbole*[27] held the same opinion in regard to duty of a doctor as in the *Achutrao Haribhau Khodwa* case.

*Vinitha Ashok* v. *Lakshmi Hospital*[28] reveals an unfortunate case of a woman losing her uterus—vital organ of regeneration—consequent upon an ectopic pregnancy in the cervical canal, which reason is seriously challenged, but denied equally seriously by the other side. Vinitha Ashok filed a complaint before the National Consumer Disputes Redressal Commission, New Delhi for compensation on the ground of negligence on the part of the respondents in the matter of removal of her uterus. The Commission held that the appellant has not proved negligence on the part of the respondents and dismissed the claim. Hence, it was an appeal before the Apex Court.

Facts leading to the said complaint are as follows:

The appellant gave birth to a son on 6 June 1989 after caeasarean operation. On or about 3 February 1990, having suspected that she was pregnant again, she and her husband went to Lakshmi Hospital for consultation. The appellant was examined by Dr. Santha Warriar, respondent No. 2. On examination, respondent No. 2 informed the appellant that she was pregnant, and it was decided to terminate the pregnancy for which 10 February 1990 was fixed. On 9 February 1990, lamineria tent was inserted when the appellant went to the hospital. On 10 February 1990, the appellant went to the hospital at about 8.30 a.m. Dr. Santha Warriar, respondent No. 2, took the appellant to the labor room. At about 10 O'clock, Dr. Soma Latha, respondent No. 3, informed the appellant's husband that the appellant was bleeding profusely and, therefore, they decided to conduct an operation. She also informed the appellant's husband that the appellant was in a very serious condition,

[26] (1996) 2 SCC 634.

[27] (1969) 1 SCR 206.

[28] AIR 2001 SC 3914.

and it was better to inform her near relatives. At about 4 O'clock, the operation was over, and the appellant's relatives were informed that she was better but under sedation. Dr. Santha Warriar informed the appellant's husband that it was a case of Cervical Pregnancy and her uterus had been removed. The appellant was discharged from the hospital on 22 February 1990.

The appellant complained that the respondents had not acted with due care and caution required of medical professionals in diagnosing the problem, in taking care to prevent the problem, in the performance of their duties and lack of necessary facilities and infrastructure at the hospital. The appellant pleaded that the procedure was unnecessarily done on her which led to other problems resulting in loss of uterus at a very young age. This complaint is resisted by the respondents contending that they have not been negligent to any extent either in diagnosing the appellant's condition or in administering the required treatment.

Basing on different experts' opinion, the Supreme Court held that:

> "... even if there is difference of opinion amongst the experts on the procedure adopted by a doctor, but a procedure which is commonly in practice in an area if adopted by a doctor, it cannot be said that there is negligence on his part."[29]

### *Compensation to both consumer and beneficiary*

The relationship between the doctor and the patient is not always equally balanced. The attitude of a patient is poised between trust in the learning of another and the general distress of one who is in a state of uncertainty, and, such ambivalence naturally leads to a sense of inferiority, and, it is, therefore, the function of medical ethics to ensure that the superiority of the doctor is not abused in any manner. It is a great mistake to think that doctors and hospitals are easy targets for dissatisfied patients. It is indeed very difficult to raise an action of negligence. Not only there are practical difficulties in linking the injury sustained with the medical treatment, but also, it is still more difficult to establish the standard of care in medical negligence of which a complaint can be made. All these factors together with the sheer expense of bringing a legal action and the denial of legal aid to all but the poorest operate to limit medical litigation in this country. With the emergence of the CPA, no doubt, in some cases patients have been able to establish the negligence of the doctors rendering service and in taking compensation thereof but the same is very few in number. In recent days, there has been increasing pressure on hospital facilities, falling standard of professional competence, and, in addition to all, the ever-increasing complexity of therapeutic and diagnostic methods and all these together are responsible for medical negligence.

Very often, in a claim for compensation arising out of medical negligence, a plea is taken that it is a case of bona fide mistake which under certain circumstances may be excusable, but, a mistake which would tantamount to negligence cannot be pardoned. In *Spring Meadows Hospital* v. *Harjol Ahluwalia*[30] (fact of the case already discussed), the

29 Id. at p. 3920 per Rajendrababu, J.

30 AIR 1998 SC 1801.

Supreme Court held that the definition of *'consumer'* is wide enough to include not only the person who hires or avails services but also the beneficiary of such services other than the person who hires or avails services. If a child is admitted and treated in a hospital by doctor, then such child, as well as his parents would be *'consumer.'* Awarding compensation to both of them for the injury each one of them has sustained is proper.

### *Unsuccessful sterilization operation*

In India, where the population is increasing by the tick of every second on the clock and the Government had taken up the family planning as an important program for the implementation of which it had created mass awakening for the use of various devices including sterilization operation. The doctor, as also the state, must be held responsible in damages if the sterilization operation performed by him is a failure on account of his negligence, which is directly responsible for another birth in the family, creating additional economic burden on the person who had chosen to be operated upon for sterilization. Negligence is a tort, i.e., civil wrong. Every doctor who enters the medical profession has a duty to act with a reasonable degree of care and skill. This is what is known as *'implied undertaking'* by a member of the medical profession that he would use a fair, reasonable, and competent degree of skill. Where a person is guilty of negligence *per se*, no further proof is required. The Medical Officers entrusted with the implementation of the Family Planning Program cannot, by their negligent acts in not performing the complete sterilization operation, sabotage the scheme of national importance.

In *State of Haryana* v. *Santra,*[31] the respondent had undergone a sterilization operation at the General Hospital, as she already had seven children and wanted to take advantage of the scheme of sterilization launched by the State Government. She underwent the sterilization operation, and she was issued a certificate that her operation was successful. She was assured that she would not conceive a child in future. But, as the luck would have it, she conceived and ultimately gave birth to a female child. The respondent was a poor lady who already had seven children. She was already under considerable monetary burden. The unwanted child (girl) born to her has created additional burden for her on account of the negligence of the doctor who performed sterilization operation upon her, and, therefore, she is clearly entitled to claim full damages from the State Government as well as doctor to enable her to bring up the child at least till she attains puberty. Damages for the birth of an unwanted child may not be of any value for those who are affluent but those who live below the poverty line or who belong to the labour class earning their livelihood on daily basis by taking up the job of an ordinary labour, cannot be denied the claim for damages on account of medical negligence.

### *Homoeopathic Doctor Prescribing Allopathic Medicines*

In *Poonam Verma* v. *Ashwin Patel,*[32] respondent No. 1 was awarded a Diploma in Homoeopathic Medicine and Surgery on the basis of which he was registered as a Medical Practitioner in 1983.

[31] AIR 2000 SC 1888.

[32] AIR 1996 SC 2111.

Pramod Verma, husband of the appellant, complained of fever which was examined at his residence by respondent No. 1 (Dr. Ashwin Patel). He prescribed allopathic drugs for viral fever and thereafter, for typhoid fever. When the condition of Pramod Verma deteriorated, he was shifted to Sanjivani Maternity and General Nursing Home of Dr. Rajeev Warty (respondent No. 2) as an indoor patient. This was done on the advice of respondent No. 1. Verma received treatment there till the evening of 14 July 1982. Thereafter, he was transferred to the Hinduja Hospital in an unconscious state. After about four and a half hours of admission, he died.

The Supreme Court held that the respondent-doctor in the instant case was registered as a medical practitioner which required him to practice homoeopathy only. He was under a statutory duty not to enter the field of any other system of medicine. Since he trespassed into a prohibited field and prescribed the allopathic medicine, he would be liable to be prosecuted under Sec. 15(3) of the Indian Medical Council Act, 1956. His conduct amounted to an actionable negligence particularly as the duty of care indicated by the apex Court in *Laxman Balkrishna Joshi* v. *Dr. Trimbak Bapu Godbole*[33] was breached by him on all counts indicated therein. The Court made the following observations in the *Laxman Balkrishna Joshi* case:

> "The duties which a doctor owes to his patient are clear. A person who holds himself out ready to give medical advice and treatment impliedly undertakes that he is possessed of skill and knowledge for the purpose. Such a person when consulted by a patient owes him certain duties, viz., a duty of care in deciding whether to undertake the case, a duty of care in deciding what treatment to give or a duty of care in the administration of that treatment. A breach of any of those duties gives a right of Action for negligence to the patient. The practitioner must bring to his task a reasonable degree of skill and knowledge and must exercise a reasonable degree of care. Neither the very highest nor a very low degree of care and competence judged in the light of the particular circumstances of each case is what the law requires (of Halsbury's Laws of England, 3rd ed. vol. 26 p. 17). The doctor no doubt has discretion in choosing treatment which he proposes to give to the patient and such discretion is relatively ampler in cases of emergency."[34]

Thus, the claim of the claimant was decreed against the doctor for a sum of 3 lakhs. The Medical Council of India was directed to initiate appropriate proceeding against the doctor under Sec. 15(3) for his having practiced in allopathic system of medicine without being registered with the Medical Council of India or the State Medical Council as also without having the requisite qualification as required.

### *Medical negligence*

In *Jacob Mathew* v. *State of Punjab*,[35] a three-Judge Bench considered the question whether charges could be framed against the appellant under Sec. 304A read with Sec. 34 of the IPC on the allegation of negligence. The three-Judge Bench highlighted the jurisprudential distinction between civil and criminal liability in cases of medical negligence, considered various facets of negligence by professionals and laid down several propositions including the followings:

[33] AIR 1969 SC 128.

[34] Id. at pp. 131–132 per Shelat, J.

[35] AIR 2005 SC 3180.

1. Negligence is the breach of a duty caused by omission to do something which a reasonable man guided by those considerations which ordinarily regulate the conduct of human affairs would do, or doing something which a prudent and reasonable man would not do. Negligence becomes actionable on account of injury resulting from the act or omission amounting to negligence attributable to the person sued. The essential components of negligence are three: "duty", "breach" and "resulting damage." [(a) a legal duty to exercise due care on the part of the party complained of towards the party complaining the former's conduct within the scope of the duty; (b) breach of the said duty; and (c) consequential damage.]
2. Negligence in the context of the medical profession necessarily calls for a treatment with a difference. To infer rashness or negligence on the part of a professional, in particular a doctor, additional considerations apply. A case of occupational negligence is different from one of professional negligence. A simple lack of care, an error of judgment or an accident is not a case of negligence on the part of a medical professional. If a doctor follows a practice acceptable to the medical profession of that day, he cannot be held liable for negligence merely because a better alternative course or method of treatment was also available. Similarly, when the charge of negligence arises out of failure to use some particular equipment, the charge would fail, if the equipment was not generally available at that particular time (that is, the time of the incident) at which it is suggested it should have been used.
3. A professional may be held liable for negligence on one of the two findings, that is, either he was not possessed of the requisite skill which he professed to have possessed, or he did not exercise, with reasonable competence in the given case, the skill which he did possess.
4. The test for determining medical negligence as laid down in the *Bolam* case, WLR at p. 586 holds good in its applicability in India. The ratio of the Bolam's case is that it is enough for the defendant to show that the standard of care and the skill attained was that of the ordinary competent medical practitioner exercising an ordinary degree of professional skill. The fact that the respondent charged with negligence acted in accordance with the general and approved practice is enough to clear him of the charge. Two things are pertinent to be noted.

   *Firstly*, the standard of care, when assessing the practice as adopted, is judged in the light of knowledge available at the time (of the incident), and not at the date of trial.

   *Secondly*, when the charge of negligence arises out of failure to use some particular equipment, the charge would fail if the equipment was not generally available at that point of time on which it is suggested as should have been used.
5. The jurisprudential concept of negligence differs in civil and criminal law. What may be negligence in civil law may not necessarily be negligence in criminal law. For negligence to amount to an offence, the element of *mens rea* must be shown to exist. For an act to amount to criminal negligence, the degree of negligence should be much higher, i.e., gross or of a very high degree. Negligence which

is neither gross nor of a higher degree may provide a ground for action in civil law but cannot form the basis for prosecution.

6. The word *'gross'* has not been used in Sec. 304A of the IPC, yet it is settled that in criminal law negligence or recklessness, to be so held, must be of such a high degree as to be *'gross'*. The expression *'rash or negligent act'* as occurring in Sec. 304A of the IPC has to be read as qualified by the word *'grossly'*.
7. To prosecute a medical professional for negligence under criminal law it must be shown that the accused did something or failed to do something which in the given facts and circumstances no medical professional in his ordinary senses and prudence would have done or failed to do. The hazard taken by the accused doctor should be of such a nature that the injury which resulted was most likely imminent.
8. *Res ipsa loquitur* (the thing speaks for itself) is only a rule of evidence and operates in the domain of civil law especially in cases of torts and helps in determining the onus of proof in actions relating to negligence. It cannot be pressed in service for determining *per se* the liability for negligence within the domain of criminal law. *Res ipsa loquitur* has, if at all, a limited application in trial on a charge of criminal negligence.[36]

In *Martin F. D'Souza* v. *Mohd. Ishfaq*,[37] a two-Judge Bench referred to the judgment in *Jacob Mathew's* case and proceeded to equate a criminal complaint against the doctor or the hospital with a complaint filed under the CPA. The Court categorically held as follows:

> "We, therefore, direct that whenever a complaint is received against a doctor or hospital by the Consumer Fora (whether District, State or National) or by the Criminal Court then before issuing notice to the doctor or hospital against whom the complaint was made the Consumer Forum or the Criminal Court should first refer the matter to a competent doctor or committee of doctors, specialized in the field relating to which the medical negligence is attributed, and only after that doctor or committee reports that there is a *prima facie* case of medical negligence should notice be then issued to the doctor/hospital concerned. This is necessary to avoid harassment to doctors who may not be ultimately found to be negligent. We further warn the police officials not to arrest or harass doctors unless the Facts clearly come within the parameters laid down in Jacob Mathew case (AIR 2005 SC 3180), otherwise the policemen will themselves have to face legal Action."[38]

### Concluding Remark: (Author's View)

In *V. Kishan Rao* v. *Nikhil Super Specialty Hospital and another*,[39] the Supreme Court noted that the proposition laid down in *Martin D'Souza's* case is contrary to the three-Judge Bench judgment in *Jacob Mathew's* case and observed that the directions in *D'souza* are not consistent with the law laid down by the larger Bench in the *Mathew* case. In the *Mathew*

[36] *See Jacob Mathew* v. *State of Punjab*, AIR 2005 SC 3180.

[37] AIR 2009 SC 2049.

[38] Id at p. 2065 per Markandey Katju, J.

[39] AIR 2010 SCW 4252.

case, the direction for consulting the opinion of another doctor before proceeding with criminal investigation was confined only in cases of criminal complaint and not in respect of cases before the Consumer Fora. The reason why the larger Bench in the *Mathew* case did not equate between the two is obvious in view of the jurisprudential and conceptual difference between cases of negligence in civil and criminal matters.

## Banking Services

Banking is a commercial function. Banking means acceptance, for the purposes of lending or investment of deposit of money from the public, repayable on demand or otherwise.[40] The CPA to protect consumers of such services rendered by the banks. Banks provide or render service/facility to their customers or even non-customers. They render facilities/services such as remittances, accepting deposits, providing lockers, facility for discounting of cheques, collection of cheques, issue of bank drafts, etc. In *Vimal Chandra Grover* v. *Bank of India*,[41] the Apex Court held that banking is business transaction between banks and customers. Such customers are consumers within the meaning of definition provided under the CPA hence CPA shall be applicable.

In *Standard Chartered Bank Ltd.* v. *Dr. B.N. Raman*,[42] the respondent who was a non-resident Indian placed with the bank US$ 5000 in FCNR (Foreign Currency Non-Resident) account for 63 months at 9% p.a. The deposit was to mature on 17 November 1984. The appellant confirmed the deposit. The deposit receipt is annexed to the paper book. In 1984, the Reserve Bank of India (RBI) allowed the banks to keep FCNR for six years. Interest on such deposits was increased from 9% to 13% p.a. According to the respondent, in June 1984, intimation was given to the appellant to reinvest the entire amount in the FCNR account on maturity for a further period of six years at 13% p.a. In 1986, the respondent visited India. He attended the branch office of the bank. The respondent claims that he was assured by the bank that everything was in order and that US$ 7939.56 was lying in the FCNR account of which amount stood reinvested at 13% p.a. for six years maturing on 17 November 1990. The respondent alleged that in September 1990, he requested the bank to reinvest the entire amount in his FCNR account for a further period of three years. This was to be done on the maturity of his deposit on 17 November 1990. In January 1992, as stated above, the respondent returned to India. He enquired about the status of his deposits. He did not get any response. He made a complaint in writing on 5 January 1992 and on 14 January 1992. On 7 September 1992, he received a letter from the bank stating that no outstanding amount was there in his name in the FCNR account. By letter dated 15 October 1992, the appellant stated that from their records it is seen that the said deposit was prematurely withdrawn on 22 November 1979. The respondent herein denied the fact of premature withdrawal of the deposit. He complained to RBI. On 19 April 1993 the bank stated that the deposit was withdrawn prematurely not on 22 November 1979 but on 23 November 1979. A copy of the sale/purchase register was also enclosed by the bank to show that the deposits were withdrawn on 23 November 1979. Ultimately, on 28 September 1994 the respondent preferred a complaint under the CPA before the State Commission.

[40] See, Sec. 5(b) of the Banking regulation Act, 1949.

[41] AIR 2000 SC 2181.

[42] AIR 2006 SC 2810.

The State Commission came to the conclusion that the respondent had deposited US $ 5000 on 17 august, 1979 carrying 9% interest and maturing on 17 November, 1984; that the receipt was retained in Safe Custody; that there was no record to show that the said amount was prematurely withdrawn; that there was no evidence regarding destruction of the records on completion of eight years and since the initial deposit of US$ 5000 on 17 July, 1979 stood established the decree, as prayed for, was granted by the state Commission. Aggrieved by the decision of the State Commission, the appellant herein went in appeal to the National Commission under the CPA. The findings of the State Commission were confirmed. The appeal was accordingly dismissed. Hence, this civil appeal came before the Supreme Court for consideration.

The Supreme Court observed that the burden is on the complainant to show the rate of exchange prevalent on the above stated dates in order to assist the Court to arrive at the indicative prices. This has not been done in the present case. Neither the State Commission nor the National Commission has examined this question regarding selection of the appropriate date, the appropriate rate of exchange on that particular date as also the rate of interest which the appellant was required to pay. Therefore, the Court partly allowed the appeal and remitted the matter to the State Commission to pass the decree in favour of the respondent herein in accordance with law.

In *Synco Industries* v. *State Bank of Bikaner & Jaipur*,[43] the appellants moved the National Commission alleging that the respondents had been guilty of deficiency in service that they had, without good reason, frozen the sanctioned working facilities of the appellant without prior intimation. The appellant asked for damages in the sum of rupees fifteen crores and an additional sum of 60 lacs to cover the cost of travelling, man-days lost, and other expenses incurred by the appellant in pursuing the matter with the respondents. The National Commission dismissed the complaint and held that it was not a fit case to be tried under the CPA. However, the complainant was at liberty to go to the Civil Court or any other forum if he so desired. Against this order of dismissal of the complaint, the appellant filed an appeal before the Supreme Court. The Supreme Court held that given the nature of the claim in the complaint and the prayer for damages in the sum of rupees fifteen crores and for an additional sum of 60 lacs for covering the cost of travelling and other expenses incurred by the appellant, it is obvious that detailed evidence would have to be led, both to prove the claim and thereafter, to prove the damages and expenses. It is, therefore, in any event, not an appropriate case to be heard and disposed of in a summary fashion. The National Commission was right in giving the appellant liberty to move the Civil Court. This was an appropriate claim for a Civil Court to decide and, obviously, was not filed before a Civil Court to start with because before the Consumer Forum, any figure in damages can be claimed without having to pay Court fees. This, in that sense, was an abuse of the process of Consumer Forum.

In *Pradeep Kumar Jain* v. *Citibank*,[44] the appellant borrowed money after making certain initial payments for the purchase of a car from the bank. He obtained the car a policy of insurance from the Oriental Insurance Company covering the period from 21 January 1989 to 20 January 1990 and the policy was endorsed to indicate that the subject of hire-

[43] AIR 2002 SC 568.

[44] AIR 1999 SC 3119.

purchase would be payable by the bank. The appellant issued 36 cheques in favour of the bank towards monthly instalments to pay off the entire loan. He also issued two cheques in favour of the Oriental Insurance Company Limited towards insurance premium for two years beyond 20 January 1990. The appellant claimed that in view of the assurance given by the bank that they would take policies for subsequent two years beyond 21 January 1990, the two cheques had been issued by him and the policy was automatically renewed in the name of the appellant. The appellant took delivery of the car on 8 March 1989. On 15 August 1990, when the appellant was driving the car along with five inmates, he met with an accident on the Delhi-Jaipur National highway. Not only his car damaged, but all occupants of the car sustained injuries and, later on, they succumbed to the same. The appellant was under a shock for quite some time and on 5 June 1991, instructed the bank not to honour the cheques towards instalments, to get the claim settled from the insurance company and to provide particulars of insurance for the period from 21 January 1990 to 20 January 1991. The bank did not reply. The appellant claimed that the bank had grievously neglected its duty in insuring the vehicle. The appellant made a claim before the National Commission covering the loss of the car as well as damages payable towards those who died in the accident. The Court held that mere payment of premium could not result in an automatic renewal of the policy. In the circumstances, the appellant also had certain duties to discharge in the matter of obtaining insurance policy and could not merely put the blame on the first respondent and accordingly the appeal was dismissed.

### *Strike in Bank*

In *Consumer Unity and Trust Society, Jaipur* v. *Chairman and Managing Director, Bank of Baroda, Calcutta*,[45] the employees of the respondent Bank resorted to illegal strike which continued for 54 days. In complaint filed before the National Commission, it was urged that the Bank was liable to pay various amounts to the customers like interest on overdrafts accounts to be reimbursed at lending rate during the period the account was not operative; interest at the lending rate on the negotiable instruments held in suspense during this period to be reimbursed to the customers, etc. This Court referred to the definitions of *'service'* and *'deficiency'* provided in the Act and said that the expression *'any deficiency'* widens the ambit of service and extends it to any service and even though the depositors were deprived of the service of the Bank, but the deficiency did not arise due to one of the reasons mentioned in Clause (g). This is how the Court considered the question. The Court observed that the shortcoming in the service by the Bank did not arise due to failure on the part of the Bank in performing its duty or discharging its obligations as required by law. Since the depositors were prevented to avail of the services of the Bank not because of any deficiency on the part of the Bank but due to strike resorted to by the employees who almost physically prevented the Bank from functioning, the failure of the Bank to render service could not be held to give rise to claim for recovery of any amount under the Act.

"to pay such amount as may be awarded by it as compensation to the consumer for any loss or injury suffered by the consumer due to the negligence of the opposite party."

[45] (1995) 2 SCC 150.

## Real Estates

### *Non delivery of flats in time*

In *Lata Construction* v. *Rameshchandra Ramniklal Shah,*[46] the respondents approached the Commission with the complaint that the appellants, Lata Construction, had promised, under a written agreement, dated 27 January 1987 to provide a flat to them, but had failed to do so and, therefore, they were guilty of *'deficiency in service'*. It was indicated in the complaint that the respondents, who were at that time in Libya, had entered into an agreement dated 27 January 1987 with Lata Construction, which stipulated that the appellants would develop, construct and hand over possession of flat situated in a building named 'Madhusudan', in Vile Parle, Bombay. In June 1988, when the respondents returned from Libya, they requested the appellants to deliver the possession of the flat to them as the construction of the building was complete, but the appellants refused to accept the final payment and deliver possession on the plea that the building was still under construction, particularly as the electricity, plumbing, tiling, and fencing work was in progress. The appellants, however, assured the respondents that as and when the building would be completed in all respects, they would accept the balance amount of sale consideration and deliver possession to them. In April 1990, when the respondents again came back from Libya on a short visit to India and visited the building, they found that the flat was locked and outside the main door of the flat, a name plate of 'Indira Joshi' had been put up. The respondents returned from Libya in January 1991 and when they demanded the possession of the flat, the appellants expressed their inability to give possession of the flat to the respondents in compliance of the agreement, dated 27 January 1987. The appellants, however, entered into a fresh agreement with the respondents on 23 February 1991 agreeing to pay to the respondents a sum of ₹ 9,51,000 in lieu of the flat in three instalments on or before 30 May, 1991 as under:

1. ₹ 3,00,000 on or before 20 March 1991
2. ₹ 3,00,000 on or before 20 April 1991
3. ₹ 3,51,000 on or before 30 May 1991

The respondents had entered into a fresh agreement with the appellants without prejudice to their rights under the earlier agreement dated 27 January 1987. Since the appellants did not honour the commitments under both the agreements, the respondents approached the National Commission which decreed the claim of the respondents for a sum of ₹ 9,51,000 together with interest at the rate of 18% p.a. with effect from 23 February 1991 till the date of payment. Another sum of ₹ 1 lac was allowed as compensation for pain and suffering undergone by the respondents. The Commission also allowed a sum of ₹ 10,000 to the respondents as costs of the proceedings. The Supreme Court upheld the decision of the National Commission.

---

[46] AIR 2000 SC 380.

### *Interest paid for delayed service*

In *Haryana Urban Development Authority* v. *Rajnish Chander Sharda*,[47] in view of inordinate delay in allotment of plot, the Supreme Court upheld the decision of the National Commission and, accordingly, directed the appellant, Haryana Urban Development authority, to pay interest at the rate of 18% p.a. on the amounts that had been deposited by the respondent, from time-to-time from 1979 onwards till a new plot was allotted to him and possession thereof was delivered.

However, the Supreme Court in *Ghaziabad Development Authority* v. *Balbir Singh*[48] observed that the power and duty to award compensation does not mean that irrespective of facts of the case, interest can be awarded in all matters at a uniform rate of 18% p.a. What is being awarded is compensation, i.e., recompense for the loss or injury. It therefore necessarily has to be based on a finding of loss or injury and has to correlate with the amount of loss or injury. Thus, the Forum or the Commission must determine that there has been deficiency in service and/or misfeasance in public office that has resulted in loss or injury. No hard and fast rules can be laid down. However, a few examples would be where an allotment is made, price is received/paid but possession is not given within the period set out in the brochure. The Commission/Forum would then need to determine the loss. Loss could be determined on the basis of loss of rent which could have been earned if possession was given and the premises let out or if the consumer has had to stay in rented premises, then on the basis of rent actually paid by him. Along with recompensing the loss, the Commission/Forum may also compensate for harassment/injury both mental and physical. Similarly, compensation can be given if after allotment is made, there has been cancellation of scheme without any justifiable cause. Compensation cannot be the same in all cases irrespective of the type of loss or injury suffered by the consumer. The National Forum has been awarding interest at a flat rate of 18% p.a. irrespective of the facts of each case, which is not reasonable. The award of compensation must be under different separate heads and must vary from case to case, depending on the facts of each case. It is clear that in all these cases, interest is being awarded as and by way of compensation/damages. Whilst so awarding, it must be shown that there is a relationship between the amount awarded and the default/unjustifiable delay/harassment. It is thus necessary that there be separate awards under each such head with reasons why such an award is justified. However, the principle that interest must be granted at the current rate of interest is only applicable where the proceedings are for recovery of debt or damages. They apply where a refund of an amount is being claimed and the direction is to refund amounts with interest. The principles which govern grants of interest do not apply to grants of compensation. For this reason, also, it becomes necessary to consider facts and award damage/compensation under various heads. Normally in cases of refund, interest will be payable from the date the monies were deposited with the body till they are returned either by payment to that party or deposited in Court. In cases where compensation is directed to be paid, the Commission/Forum must direct payment within a particular period and further direct that if payment is not made within that time, the authority will also pay interest. Such interest must be based on the current rate of interest.

---

47 AIR 2000 SC 3573.

48 AIR 2004 SC 2141.

Now-a-days, consumers are aware that interest is being awarded for belated delivery of possession/non-delivery of possession and unscrupulous consumer may, on one pretext or the other, deliberately avoid taking possession with an intention to earn more interest. In a recent case,[49] the allottee was offered possession but the allottee did not take possession nor furnished any reply to the offer of possession. He filed a complaint before the District Forum and, ultimately, possession was delivered to him. In such a situation, if there is no reply filed by the allottee assigning the reasons for not being able to take possession, the rate of interest would be reckoned from the date the amount is deposited to the date the offer for possession is made by the body. Similarly, if the allottee replies to the offer stating thereunder the reason for not taking over the possession, as offered by the body, and the reason assigned is reasonably acceptable, the Commission may then examine the reasons assigned by the allottee and may pass necessary order. But in the instant case, there is nothing on record to show that the allottee has replied to the letter of offer. This being the position, the allottee would not be entitled to the interest from the date of offer of possession till possession was delivered.

In 2010, the Supreme Court categorically held in *Punjab Urban Planning and Development Authority* v. *Daya Singh*[50] that if it is found that delay was on account of the order passed by the High Court, directing the parties to maintain *status quo* on the question of possession of plots in question, the question of payment of interest for such delayed possession given to the respective respondents in respect of their plots may not arise at all.

### Compensation for harassment, mental agony, or oppression

The CPA has a wide reach, and the Commission has jurisdiction even in cases of service rendered by statutory and public authorities. Such authorities become liable to compensate for misfeasance in public office, i.e., an Act which is oppressive or capricious or arbitrary or negligent provided loss or injury is suffered by a citizen. The word *'compensation'* has a very wide connotation. It may constitute actual loss or expected loss and may extend to compensation for physical, mental, or even national sufferings, insult or injury or loss. The CPA enables a consumer to claim and empower the Commission to redress any injustice done. The Commission or the Forum is entitled to award not only the value of goods or services but also to compensate a consumer for injustice suffered by him. The Commission/Forum must determine that such sufferance is due to *mala fide* or capricious or oppressive Act. It can then determine the amount for which the authority is liable to compensate the consumer for his sufferance due to misfeasance in public office by the officers.

The consumer must not be made to run from pillar to post. Where there has been capricious or arbitrary or negligent exercise or non-exercise of power by an officer of the authority, the Commission/Forum has a statutory obligation to award compensation. If the Commission/Forum is satisfied that a complainant is entitled to compensation for loss or injury or for harassment or mental agony or oppression, then, after recording a finding, it

[49] *Ghaziabad Development Authority* v. *Balbir Singh*, AIR 2005 SC 1206. See also *Haryana Urban Development Authority* v. *Jeewan Asha Garg*, AIR 2005 SC 1397; *Haryana Urban Development Authority* v. *Dheer Singh Bhatti*, AIR 2005 SC 1472; *Haryana Urban Development Authority* v. *Dropadi Devi*, AIR 2005 SC 1487.

[50] AIR 2010 SC 486.

must direct the authority to pay compensation and then also direct recovery from those found responsible for such unpardonable behaviour.[51]

In *Lucknow Development Authority* v. *M.K. Gupta*,[52] the appellant, Lucknow Development authority, with a view to easing the acute housing problem in the city of Lucknow, undertook development of land and formed plots of different categories/sizes and constructed dwelling units for people belonging to different income groups. After the construction was complete, the authority invited applications from people desirous of purchasing plots or dwelling houses. The respondent applied on the prescribed form for registration for allotment of a flat in the category of Middle-Income Group (M.I.G.) in Gomti Nagar Scheme in Lucknow on a cash-down basis. Since the number of applicants was more, the authority decided to draw lots in which flat No. II/75 in Vinay Khand-II was allotted to the respondent on 26 April 1988. He deposited a sum of ₹ 6,132 on 2 July 1988 and a sum of ₹ 1,09,975 on 29 July 1988. Since the entire payment was made in July 1988, the flat was registered on 18 August 1988. Thereafter, the appellant, Lucknow Development Authority, in a letter, dated 23 August 1988, directed executive engineer to hand over the possession of the flat to the respondent. This information was given to him on 30 November 1988, yet the flat was not delivered as the construction work was not complete. The respondent approached the authority, but no steps were taken nor were possessions handed over. Consequently, he filed a complaint alleging that even after the payment of the entire amount in respect of cash-down scheme, the appellant was not handing over possession nor they were completing the formalities and the work was still incomplete.

The State Commission directed the appellant to pay 12% annual simple interest upon the deposit made by the respondent. The appellant was further directed to hand over possession of the flat without delay after completing construction work up to June 1990. The Commission further directed that if it was not possible for the appellant to complete the construction, then it should hand over possession of the flat to the respondent by 5 April 1990 after determining the deficiencies and the estimated cost of such deficient construction shall be refunded to the respondent latest by 20 April 1990. The appellant, instead of complying with the order, approached the National Commission and raised the question of jurisdiction. However, it was overruled, and the appeal was dismissed. But the cross-appeal of the respondent was allowed and it was directed that since the architect of the appellant had estimated in October 1989, the cost of completing construction at ₹ 44,615, the appellant shall pay the same to the respondent. The Commission further held that the action of the appellant amounted to harassment, mental torture, and agony to the respondent, and therefore, it directed the appellant to pay a sum of ₹ 10,000 as compensation.

The Supreme Court upheld the decision of the National Commission and observed that today the issue is not only of award of compensation but who should bear the brunt. The concept of authority and power exercised by public functionaries has many dimensions. It has undergone tremendous change with the passage of time and change in socio-economic outlook. The authority empowered to function under a statute while exercising power discharges public duty. It has to act to subserve general welfare and

[51] *Ghaziabad Development Authority* v. *Balbir Singh*, AIR 2004 SC 2141.

[52] AIR 1994 SC 787.

common good. In discharging this duty honestly and bona fide, loss may accrue to any person. And he may claim compensation which may in circumstances be payable. But where the duty is performed capriciously or the exercise of power results in harassment and agony then the responsibility to pay the loss determined should be whose? In a modern society, no authority can arrogate to itself the power to act in a manner which is arbitrary. It is unfortunate that matters which require immediate attention linger on and the man in the street is made to run from one end to other with no result. Accordingly, the Court held as follows:

> "Even in ordinary matters a common man who has neither the political backing nor the financial strength to match the inaction in public oriented departments gets frustrated and it erodes the credibility in the system. Public administration, no doubt involves a vast amount of administrative discretion which shields the action of administrative authority. But where it is found that exercise of discretion was mala fide, and the complainant is entitled to compensation for mental and physical harassment then the officer can no more claim to be under protective cover. When a citizen seeks to recover compensation from a public authority in respect of injuries suffered by him for capricious exercise of power and the National Commission finds it duly proved then it has a statutory obligation to award the same? It was never more necessary than today when even social obligations are regulated by grant of statutory powers. The tests of permissive form of grant are over. It is now imperative and implicit in the exercise of power that it should be for the sake of society. When the Court directs payment of damages or compensation against the state the ultimate sufferer is the common man. It is the taxpayers' money which is paid for inaction of those who are entrusted under the Act to discharge their duties in accordance with law. It is, therefore, necessary that the Commission when it is satisfied that a complainant is entitled to compensation for harassment or mental agony or oppression, which finding of course should be recorded carefully on material and convincing circumstances and not lightly, then it should further direct the department concerned to pay the amount to the complainant from the public fund 'immediately but to recover the same from those who are found responsible for such unpardonable behaviour by dividing it proportionately where there are more than one functionaries."[53]

### *No deficiency if no mala fides*[53]

In *Haryana Urban Development Authority* v. *Smt. Nalini Aggarwal*,[54] a notification was issued calling for the applications for allotment of houses and the respondents had applied on 20 April 1993. The last date for making applications was 31 May 1993. After the necessary steps were taken, scrutiny was made; lots were drawn on 7 June 1994. Since the respondents remained unsuccessful in the lots, the earnest money deposited by them was refunded on 20 July 1994 within one month.

The question, therefore, was: whether the unsuccessful applicants would be entitled to payment of interest for the period from the date of deposit till the date of refund? One of the conditions imposed in the notification inviting applications for allotment was that:

> *'No interest shall be payable on the money of the applicant for the period for which the same is lying with the authority.'*

---

[53] Id. at pp. 799–800 per R.M. Sahai, J.

[54] AIR 1997 SC 2582.

The Supreme Court observed that having accepted the above conditions while applying for allotment, the respondents were not entitled to the payment of interest for the period during which the deposit was lying with the authority. It was true that there was an interlude of around one year between the date of calling applications and the date of draw of lots. It was obvious that the drawing of lots was delayed due to administrative exigencies and not on account of any *mala fide* action of any individual. Therefore, the respondent was not allowed to get any interest.

## Goods carrier Services

In *Patel Roadways Ltd.* v. *Birla Yamaha Ltd.*,[55] the core question that came before the Supreme Court for consideration was whether Sec. 9 of the Carriers Act, 1865, would be applicable to a proceeding under the Consumer Protection Act.

Section 9 of the Carriers Act, 1865 reads:

> *"In any suit brought against a common carrier for the loss, damage, or non-delivery of "goods (including containers, pallets or similar Article of transport used to consolidate goods) entrusted to him for carriage, it shall not be necessary for the plaintiff to prove that such loss, damage or non-delivery was owing to the negligence or criminal act of the carrier, his servants or agents."*

The respondent Birla Yamaha Ltd. booked 237 consignments containing 267 generator sets at Ghaziabad in the State of UP, with the appellant-Patel Roadways Limited for transportation. The freight charges were duly paid by the consignor to the carrier. The goods booked by the respondent were destroyed in a fire which took place in the warehouse of the appellant shortly after booking of the consignments. The respondent claimed ₹ 56,00,799 along with interest. The said sum comprised ₹ 50,78,231 as cost of 267 generator sets, ₹ 22,568 as freight charges and ₹ 5 lacs as general and special damages on account of harassment and undue loss of time. It was alleged in the complaint, *inter alia*, that the carrier having accepted the responsibility of transportation of the consignments and safe delivery of goods, failed to deliver the same. Thus, there was deficiency in the service to be rendered by the appellant as carrier.

The Commission rejected the claim of ₹ 5 lacs towards general and special damages. The Commission in its order placed reliance on the provision of Sec. 9 of the Carriers Act, 1865, to hold that the appellant was deficient in the performance of service as a common carrier, as the goods entrusted had not been at all delivered in accordance with the contract of carriage. The Commission held that Sec. 9 relieves the complainant from the burden of showing that the loss or non-delivery was owing to any negligence or criminal act; and that the loss of the goods sent was *prima facie* evidence of negligence. Feeling aggrieved by the said order, the appellant preferred to appeal under CPA.

The Supreme Court observed that the liability of a common carrier under the Carriers Act is that of an insurer. This position is made further clear by the provision in Sec. 9, in which, it is specifically laid down that in case of claim of damage or loss to or deterioration of goods entrusted to a carrier, it is not necessary for the plaintiff to establish negligence. Even assuming that the general principle in cases of tortious liability is that the party

[55] AIR 2000 SC 1461.

who alleges negligence against the other must prove the same, the said principle has no application to a case covered under the Carriers Act. This is also the position notwithstanding a special contract between the parties. These principles have held the field over a considerable length of time and have been crystallized into an accepted position of law.

The Court further observed that the principle regarding the liability of a carrier contained in Sec. 9 of the Carriers Act, namely, that the liability of a carrier is that of an insurer and that in case of loss or damage to goods entrusted to the carrier, the plaintiff need not prove negligence. Therefore, the Court held that the consumer dispute redressal agencies, i.e., District Forums, State Commissions and the National Commission are vested with powers of adjudication of all types of consumer disputes including claims for loss or damage to goods entrusted to a carrier for transportation and, accordingly, the appeal was dismissed.

However, in *Arvind Mills Ltd.* v. *M/s. Associated Roadways*,[56] the Supreme Court held that the remedies under the CPA are in addition to and not in derogation of any other law, does not mean that the rights under the Carriers Act can be exercised, except in accordance with the manner provided under the Act. Secs. 9 and 10 of the Carriers Act form an integral scheme by which a common carrier is fastened with liability irrespective of proof of negligence. Merely because the procedure under the CPA is summary in nature, does not in any way warrant the abrogation of the requirement to serve notice under Sec. 10 of the Carriers Act before fastening any liability under that Act on the carriers.

The Supreme Court in *Economic Transport Organization* v. *Dharwad Distt. Khadi Gramudyog Sangh*[57] relied on the *Patel Roadways Ltd.*, case and held that the principle underlying Sec. 9 of the Carriers Act relating to burden of proof is a principle of common law and has been incorporated in Sec. 9 of the Act. The burden of proof shifted to the carriers by the application of the legal presumption under the common law. The principles laid down in CPA need to be understood in that manner. Therefore, it is held that it is for the carrier to prove absence of negligence.

In *Nath Bros.* v. *Best Roadways Ltd.*,[58] it was held that the liability to whom goods are entrusted for carriage is that of an insurer and absolute in terms. So long as the goods are in the custody of a carrier, it is the duty of the carrier to take due care as he would have taken of his own goods, and he would be liable if any loss or damage is caused to the goods on account of his own negligence or criminal act or that of his agent and servants. This would be so even if goods are carried *at the owner's risk*. The *'owner's risk'* is understood in the sense that the carrier would not be liable for damage or loss to the goods if it was not caused on account of the carrier's own negligence or the negligence of his servants and agents. The expression *'owner's risk'* does not exempt a carrier from his own negligence or the negligence of his servants or agents. The carrier can escape his liability only if loss or damage was due to an act of God or enemy State.

## Insurance

It is the fundamental principle of insurance law that utmost good faith must be observed by the contracting parties and good faith forbids either party from non-disclosure of the facts

[56] AIR 2004 SC 5147.

[57] AIR 2000 SC 1635.

[58] 2000 AIR SCW 2116.

which the parties know. The insured has a duty to disclose and similarly it is the duty of the insurance company and its agents to disclose all material facts in their knowledge since obligation of good faith applies to both equally. In a case where the terms and conditions of the standard policy wherein the exclusion clause was included, were neither a part of the contract of insurance nor disclosed to the insured, the insurer cannot claim the benefit of the said exclusion clause.[59]

An important question arose in *L.I.C. of India* v. *Anuradha*[60] before the Supreme Court for consideration as to presumption of death of a person whose whereabouts was known to his family members and later they came to know that the person, whose whereabouts was known, has taken life insurance and paid some money in respect of his premium.

The Court observed that the law as to presumption of death remains the same whether in Common Law of England or in the statutory provisions contained in Secs. 107 and 108 of the Indian Evidence Act, 1872. In the scheme of the Evidence Act, though Secs. 107 and 108 are drafted as two Sections, in effect, Sec. 108 is an exception to the rule enacted in Sec. 107. The human life shown to be in existence at a given point of time, which according to Sec. 107 ought to be a point within 30 years calculated backwards from the date when the question arises, is presumed to continue to be living. The rule is subject to a proviso or exception as contained in Sec. 108. If the persons, who would have naturally and in the ordinary course of human affairs heard of the person in question, have not so heard of him for seven years, the presumption raised under Sec. 107 ceases to operate. Sec. 107 has the effect of shifting the burden of proving that the person is dead on him who affirms the fact. Sec. 108, subject to its applicability being attracted, has the effect of shifting the burden of proof back on the one who asserts the fact of that person being alive. The presumption raised under Sec. 108 is a limited presumption confined only to presuming the *factum* of death of the person whose life or death is in issue. Though it will be presumed that the person is dead, there is no presumption as to the date or time of death. There is no presumption as to the facts and circumstances under which the person may have died. The presumption as to death by reference to Sec. 108 would arise only on lapse of seven years and would not by applying any logic or reasoning be permitted to be raised on expiry of 6 years and 364 days or at any time short of it. An occasion for raising the presumption would arise only when the question is raised in a Court, Tribunal or before an authority that is called upon to decide as to whether a person is alive or dead. So long as the dispute is not raised before any Forum and in any legal proceedings, the occasion for raising the presumption does not arise. If an issue may arise as to the date or time of death, the same shall have to be determined on evidence direct or circumstantial and not by assumption or presumption. The burden of proof would lie on the person who makes assertion of death having taken place at a given date or time in order to succeed in his claim. Rarely it may be permissible to proceed on premise that the death had occurred on any given date before which the period of seven years absence was shown to have elapsed. The Court, in the instant case, held that a policy lapses because of non-payment of premium

---

59 *Modern Insulators Ltd., M/s.* v. *Oriental Insurance Co. Ltd.*, AIR 2000 SC 1014.

60 AIR 2004 SC 2070.

until the claim is made and therefore the claimant is only entitled to the paid-up value of the policy. However, the Court made the following observations:

> "Unfortunately, some of the regions or states in India are insurgency afflicted. The life has become uncertain there. People live constantly under fear of death. Uncertainty of life has been accepted as a normal course of living. The Life Insurance Corporation, as a social welfare institution, more so when life insurance has been nationalized and the service is not available in private sector, should think of devising a policy available in insurgency afflicted regions which would take care of the assured and his family members in such areas. When the assured suddenly disappears or ceases to be traceable, may be the beneficiaries or nominees do not even know that the deceased had an insured policy. They may not be aware if the insurance premiums have been paid or have remained not paid and what were the due dates and other obligations to be performed by the assured to keep the policy alive. Insurance policies with terms and conditions suited to the requirements of people inhabiting insurgency or militancy affected areas need to be devised and propagated."[61]

In *Life Insurance Corporation of India* v. *S. Sindhu*,[62] the short question that arose for consideration in this appeal before the Supreme Court was, whether in the case of a lapsed life insurance policy, the LIC while paying the reduced sum payable by treating it as a paid-up policy is liable to pay interest in regard to premiums paid from the respective dates of payment of premiums to date of settlement.

The facts of this instant case reveal the following information:

That a policy of insurance dated 11 March 1994 for an assured sum of ₹ 5 lacs with risk commencing from 4 December 1993 was issued in regard to the life of K. Thankachan under the 'money-back policy' scheme for a period of 20 years. The premium payable was ₹ 8,306 every quarter. The conditions of the policy made it clear that the policy will be in force only if the premiums were paid regularly, every quarter, and that if the premium was not paid before the expiry of the grace period provided, the policy will lapse. K. Thankachan paid the premiums till 4 June 1994 and did not pay the premiums thereafter. In August 1996, he opted for revival of the policy by paying the arrears of premium from 4 September 1994 to 4 June 1996 with interest. Accordingly, the policy was revived, and he paid the premium till 4 December 1996. Thereafter, the policy again lapsed from 4 March 1997 as premium was not paid. K. Thankachan died on 5 December 1997 and his widow/nominee (the respondent herein) made a claim for payment of the amount under the policy, by letter dated 1 January 1968.

Condition No. 4 of the policy reads as follows:

> "4. Non-forfeiture regulations: If, after at least three full years premiums have been paid in respect of this Policy, any subsequent premium be not duly paid this policy shall not be wholly void but shall subsist as a paid-up policy for a reduced sum payable on the Date of Maturity or at the Life assured's prior death provided the paid-up sum assured is not less than ₹ 250. The amount of paid-up assurance for integral number of years' premiums paid will be calculated as per Table given below. The policy so reduced shall thereafter be free from all liability for payment of within mentioned premium but shall not be entitled to participate in future profits. The existing bonus additions, if any, will remain attached to the reduced paid-up policy."

---

[61] Id. at p. 2075 per R. C. Lahoti, J.

[62] AIR 2006 SC 2366.

The Supreme Court examined whether award of interest can be sustained in any manner. It is now well-settled that interest prior to the date of suit/claim can be awarded in the following circumstances:

1. Where the contract provides for payment of interest; or
2. Where a statute applicable to the transaction/liability, provides for payment of interest; or
3. Where interest is payable as per the provisions of the Interest Act, 1978.

Dealing with question No. 1, the Court observed that the insurance policy provides that if the premium is not paid (after regularly paying premiums for a period of three full years), the policy shall subsist only as a paid-up policy for a reduced sum payable on the date of maturity or at the prior death of the life assured. It does not provide for payment of interest on the premiums paid. In fact, the operative portion of the policy specifically provides that no interest will be paid. Payment of interest on the premium amounts, from the respective dates of remittance of premiums, is alien to the concept of life insurance. In this case, the assured died on 5 December 1997 prior to the date of maturity. Therefore, the reduced sum as a paid-up policy became due and payable without any interest on 5 December 1997. The claim was settled by payment of ₹ 1,13,750 on 26 March 1998, within three months from the date of intimation of death. Therefore, under the contract, no interest is payable by LIC.

Answering question No. 2, the Court observed that where a statute provides for payment of interest, such interest will have to be paid in accordance with the provisions of such statute. Admittedly, there is no enactment, or rules made under any enactment, either relating to contracts in general or insurance in particular, which provides for payment of interest in regard to amount payable under such a policy.

Before answering question No. 3, it is required to have a look at the objectives of the Interest Act, 1978 and relevant provisions dealing directly or indirectly with the issue in question. The provisions of the Interest Act, 1978 deal with payment of interest up to the date of suit/claim. The Act was enacted to consolidate and amend the law relating to the allowance of interest in certain cases. The objects and reasons state that the Act was enacted to prescribe the general law of interest in a comprehensive and precise manner, which becomes applicable in the absence of any contractual or statutory provision specifically dealing with interest. Sub-section (1) of Sec. 3 of the Act provides that in any proceedings for the recovery of any debt for damages, or in any proceedings in which a claim for interest in respect of any debt or damages already paid is made, the Court may, if it thinks fit, allow interest to the person entitled to the debt or damages or to the person making such claim, as the case may be, at a rate not exceeding the current rate of interest, for the whole or part of the following period, that is to say,—

(a) If the proceedings relate to a debt payable by virtue of a written instrument at a certain time, then, from the date when the debt is payable to the date of institution of the proceedings.

(b) If the proceedings do not relate to any such debt, then, from the date mentioned in that regard in a written notice given by the person entitled or the person making the claim to the person liable that interest will be claimed, to the date of institution of the proceedings.

Sub-section (3) of Sec. 3 makes it clear that nothing in Sec. 3 shall apply in relation to any debt or damages upon which interest is payable as of right, by virtue of any agreement, or any debt or damagés upon which payment of interest is barred, by virtue of an express agreement. Clause (a) of Sec. 2 of the Act defines 'Court' as including a Tribunal and an Arbitrator. Clause (c) of Sec. 2 defines 'debt' as any liability for an ascertained sum of money and includes a debt payable in kind but does not include a judgment debt; and Clause (b) defines 'current rate of interest'. Sub-section (1) of Sec. 4 of the Act provides that notwithstanding anything contained in Sec. 3, interest shall be payable in all cases in which it is payable by virtue of any enactment or other rule of law or usage having the force of law. Sub-section (2) of Sec. 4 provides that notwithstanding what is stated in Sec. 3 or Sec. 4(1) of the Act, in the cases of money deposited as security for performance of an obligation, interest is payable from the date of deposit; and in the case of money payable by virtue of a fiduciary relationship, money/property obtained/retained by fraud and money due as dower/maintenance, interest is payable from the date of cause of action.

The Court, while answering to question No. 3, held that a claim for interest on the amounts of premium paid, from the respective dates of payment of premium to date of settlement of claim, does not find support from any of the provisions of the Act and accordingly allow this appeal and hold that the LIC is not liable to pay any interest on the sum of ₹ 1,13,750.

## Postal Service

In 2011, the Supreme Court in *A.D. Thirukoil, Palani* v. *Director General of Post Offices, Department of Posts*[63] made the following suggestions to the Post Offices dealing with various accounts of deposits:

(i) Whether it is metropolitan or rural area, persons dealing with public money or those who are in charge of accepting deposits to be conversant with all the details relating to types of deposits, period, rate of interest, eligibility criteria, etc. for availing benefits under different schemes.

(ii) It is desirable to exhibit all these details in vernacular language in a conspicuous place to facilitate the persons who intend to invest/deposit money.

(iii) That if the Central Governments issues any notification/instructions regarding change in the interest rate or any other aspect with regard to deposits, the decision taken shall be immediately passed on to all the authorities concerned by using latest technology methods, i.e., by fax, e-mail, or any other form of communication so that they are kept updated of the latest developments.

(iv) If there is any change in different types of schemes, it must be brought to the notice of the subordinate staff of the post offices dealing with deposits in order to ensure that correct procedures are followed, and correct information is given to the public.

(43) **"Spurious goods"** means such goods which are falsely claimed to be genuine;

---

[63] AIR 2011 SC 2604.

(44) **"State Commission"** means a State Consumer Disputes Redressal Commission established under sub-section (1) of Section 42;

(45) **"Trader"**, in relation to any goods, means a person who sells or distributes any goods for sale and includes the manufacturer thereof, and where such goods are sold or distributed in package form, includes the packer thereof;

(46) **"Unfair contract"** means a contract between a manufacturer or trader or service provider on one hand, and a consumer on the other, having such terms which cause significant change in the rights of such consumer, including the following, namely:—

(i) requiring manifestly excessive security deposits to be given by a consumer for the performance of contractual obligations; or

(ii) imposing any penalty on the consumer, for the breach of contract thereof which is wholly disproportionate to the loss occurred due to such breach to the other party to the contract; or (iii) refusing to accept early repayment of debts on payment of applicable penalty; or

(iii) entitling a party to the contract to terminate such contract unilaterally, without reasonable cause; or

(iv) permitting or has the effect of permitting one party to assign the contract to the detriment of the other party who is a consumer, without his consent; or

(v) imposing on the consumer any unreasonable charge, obligation or condition which puts such consumer to disadvantage;

An unfair contract typically refers to a contractual agreement that contains terms or conditions that give one party an unjust advantage over the other. Unfair contracts may exploit imbalances in bargaining power, lack of transparency, or unequal access to information.

The CPA provides protection to the consumers from unfair contracts. The one of the objects of CPA to ensure the contracts are fair, reasonable, and that both parties have a clear understanding of the terms and conditions. In the law of contract unfair contract terms may be considered unenforceable or subject to legal remedies.

Unfair contract terms can take various forms, such as terms that are excessively one-sided, terms that are hidden in complex language or fine print, or terms that exploit the vulnerability of one party. Common examples include terms that allow one party to unilaterally change the terms of the contract, excessively limit one party's rights, or impose disproportionately high penalties.

The definition of unfair contract provided in the CPA is to protect the interest of consumer and sub-clause (i) to (vi) are only examples or illustrative. The CPA is designed to safeguard the rights and interests of consumers in their transactions with businesses. Unfair contracts are often addressed within the framework of consumer protection laws, which may include provisions specifically targeting unfair contract terms. Here are some key points regarding the relationship between consumer protection laws and unfair contracts:

1. *Unfair Contract Terms*: There are few provisions under the CPA declare certain contract terms as unfair or unreasonable. These provisions are intended to prevent businesses from taking advantage of consumers by imposing terms that create a significant imbalance in the parties' rights and obligations.

2. *Standard Form Contracts*: Consumer protection laws often focus on standard form contracts, which are pre-drafted agreements where consumers have little or no opportunity to negotiate terms. In such contracts, there may be clauses that are considered unfair, and consumer protection laws may empower authorities to declare those terms void or unenforceable.
3. *Transparency and Plain Language*: Consumer protection laws may require businesses to use clear and understandable language in their contracts, ensuring that consumers can easily comprehend the terms and conditions. Clarity helps prevent unfair surprises and ensures that consumers are fully informed before entering into an agreement.
4. *Prohibited Practices*: Consumer protection laws typically prohibit certain unfair practices, such as deceptive advertising, false claims, and aggressive sales tactics. These provisions aim to protect consumers from being misled or coerced into accepting unfair contract terms.
5. *Remedies and Enforcement*: Consumer protection laws often provide remedies for consumers who have been subjected to unfair contracts. These remedies may include the right to void unfair terms, seek compensation for damages, or pursue other legal actions. Enforcement agencies may have the authority to investigate and act against businesses that violate consumer protection laws.

It's essential for consumers to be aware of their rights under local consumer protection laws and to carefully review contracts before entering into agreements. If a consumer believes that a contract term is unfair or violates consumer protection laws, seeking legal advice or reporting the issue to relevant authorities may be appropriate. Keep in mind that specific details and provisions can vary between different jurisdictions and their respective consumer protection laws.

(47) **"Unfair trade practice"** means a trade practice which, for the purpose of promoting the sale, use or supply of any goods or for the provision of any service, adopts any unfair method or unfair or deceptive practice including any of the following practices, namely:—

(i) making any statement, whether orally or in writing or by visible representation including by means of electronic record, which—

(a) falsely represents that the goods are of a particular standard, quality, quantity, grade, composition, style or model;

(b) falsely represents that the services are of a particular standard, quality or grade;

(c) falsely represents any re-built, second-hand, renovated, reconditioned or old goods as new goods;

(d) represents that the goods or services have sponsorship, approval, performance, characteristics, accessories, uses or benefits which such goods or services do not have;

(e) represents that the seller or the supplier has a sponsorship or approval or affiliation which such seller or supplier does not have;

(f) makes a false or misleading representation concerning the need for, or the usefulness of, any goods or services;

(g) gives to the public any warranty or guarantee of the performance, efficacy, or length of life of a product or of any goods that is not based on an adequate or proper test thereof:

Provided that where a defence is raised to the effect that such warranty or guarantee is based on adequate or proper test, the burden of proof of such defence shall lie on the person raising such defence;

(h) makes to the public a representation in a form that purports to be—

(A) a warranty or guarantee of a product or of any goods or services; or

(B) a promise to replace, maintain or repair an article or any part thereof or to repeat or continue a service until it has achieved a specified result, if such purported warranty or guarantee or promise is materially misleading or if there is no reasonable prospect that such warranty, guarantee or promise will be carried out;

(i) materially misleads the public concerning the price at which a product or like products or goods or services, have been or are, ordinarily sold or provided, and, for this purpose, a representation as to price shall be deemed to refer to the price at which the product or goods or services has or have been sold by sellers or provided by suppliers generally in the relevant market unless it is clearly specified to be the price at which the product has been sold or services have been provided by the person by whom or on whose behalf the representation is made;

(j) gives false or misleading facts disparaging the goods, services or trade of another person.

*Explanation*: For the purposes of this sub-clause, a statement that is,—

(A) expressed on an article offered or displayed for sale, or on its wrapper or container; or

(B) expressed on anything attached to, inserted in, or accompanying, an article offered or displayed for sale, or on anything on which the article is mounted for display or sale; or

(C) contained in or on anything that is sold, sent, delivered, transmitted or in any other manner whatsoever made available to a member of the public, shall be deemed to be a statement made to the public by, and only by, the person who had caused the statement to be so expressed, made or contained;

(ii) permitting the publication of any advertisement, whether in any newspaper or otherwise, including by way of electronic record, for the sale or supply at a bargain price of goods or services that are not intended to be offered for sale or supply at the bargain price, or for a period that is, and in quantities that are, reasonable, having regard to the nature of the market in which the business is carried on, the nature and size of business, and the nature of the advertisement.

*Explanation*: For the purpose of this sub-clause, "bargain price" means,—

(A) a price that is stated in any advertisement to be a bargain price, by reference to an ordinary price or otherwise; or

(B) a price that a person who reads, hears or sees the advertisement, would reasonably understand to be a bargain price having regard to the prices at which the product advertised or like products are ordinarily sold;

(iii) permitting—

(a) the offering of gifts, prizes or other items with the intention of not providing them as offered or creating impression that something is being given or offered free of charge when it is fully or partly covered by the amount charged, in the transaction as a whole;

(b) the conduct of any contest, lottery, game of chance or skill, for the purpose of promoting, directly or indirectly, the sale, use or supply of any product or any business interest, except such contest, lottery, game of chance or skill as may be prescribed;

(c) withholding from the participants of any scheme offering gifts, prizes or other items free of charge on its closure, the information about final results of the scheme.

*Explanation*: For the purpose of this sub-clause, the participants of a scheme shall be deemed to have been informed of the final results of the scheme where such results are within a reasonable time published, prominently in the same newspaper in which the scheme was originally advertised;

(iv) permitting the sale or supply of goods intended to be used, or are of a kind likely to be used by consumers, knowing or having reason to believe that the goods do not comply with the standards prescribed by the competent authority relating to performance, composition, contents, design, constructions, finishing or packaging as are necessary to prevent or reduce the risk of injury to the person using the goods;

(v) permitting the hoarding or destruction of goods, or refusal to sell the goods or to make them available for sale or to provide any service, if such hoarding or destruction or refusal raises or tends to raise or is intended to raise, the cost of those or other similar goods or services;

(vi) manufacturing of spurious goods or offering such goods for sale or adopting deceptive practices in the provision of services;

(vii) not issuing bill or cash memo or receipt for the goods sold or services rendered in such manner as may be prescribed;

(viii) refusing, after selling goods or rendering services, to take back or withdraw defective goods or to withdraw or discontinue deficient services and to refund the consideration thereof, if paid, within the period stipulated in the bill or cash memo or receipt or in the absence of such stipulation, within a period of thirty days;

(ix) disclosing to other person any personal information given in confidence by the consumer unless such disclosure is made in accordance with the provisions of any law for the time being in force.

In *Maruti Suzuki India Ltd.* v. *Rajiv Kumar Loomba*,[64] the grievance of the complainant (Rajiv Kumar Loomba) was that he was being overcharged for a catalytic converter which he neither demanded nor was it actually fitted in his car purchased from the appellant (Maruti Suzuki). The Supreme Court held that the complaint filed by the respondent is justified as the aforesaid act amounts to an unfair trade practice as defined in the CPA. Further the Court observed that the definition in Sec. 2(1)(r) is an inclusive one and is not exhaustive of sub-clauses (i) to (x) therein.

## Chapter II Consumer Protection Councils

### Section 3: Central consumer protection council

(1) The Central Government shall, by notification, establish with effect from such date as it may specify in that notification, the Central Consumer Protection Council to be known as the Central Council.

(2) The Central Council shall be an advisory council and consist of the following members, namely:—

(a) the Minister-in-charge of the Department of Consumer Affairs in the Central Government, who shall be the Chairperson; and

(b) such number of other official or non-official members representing such interests as may be prescribed.

### Section 4: Procedure for meetings of central council

(1) The Central Council shall meet as and when necessary, but at least one meeting of the Council shall be held every year.

(2) The Central Council shall meet at such time and place as the Chairperson may think fit and shall observe such procedure in regard to the transaction of its business as may be prescribed.

### Section 5: Objects of central council

The objects of the Central Council shall be to render advice on promotion and protection of the consumers' rights under this Act.

### Section 6: State consumer protection councils

(1) Every State Government shall, by notification, establish with effect from such date as it may specify in such notification, a State Consumer Protection Council for such State to be known as the State Council.

[64] AIR 2010 SC 3141.

(2) The State Council shall be an advisory council and consist of the following members, namely:—

(a) the Minister-in-charge of Consumer Affairs in the State Government who shall be the Chairperson;

(b) such number of other official or non-official members representing such interests as may be prescribed;

(c) such number of other official or non-official members, not exceeding ten, as may be nominated by the Central Government.

(3) The State Council shall meet as and when necessary but not less than two meetings shall be held every year.

(4) The State Council shall meet at such time and place as the Chairperson may think fit and shall observe such procedure in regard to the transaction of its business, as may be prescribed.

### Section 7: Objects of state council

The objects of every State Council shall be to render advice on promotion and protection of consumer rights under this Act within the State.

### Section 8: District consumer protection council

(1) The State Government shall, by notification, establish for every District with effect from such date as it may specify in such notification, a District Consumer Protection Council to be known as the District Council.

(2) The District Council shall be an advisory council and consist of the following members, namely:—

(a) the Collector of the district (by whatever name called), who shall be the Chairperson; and

(b) such number of other official and non-official members representing such interests as may be prescribed.

(3) The District Council shall meet as and when necessary but not less than two meetings shall be held every year.

(4) The District Council shall meet at such time and place within the district as the Chairperson may think fit and shall observe such procedure in regard to the transaction of its business as may be prescribed.

### Section 9: Objects of district council

The objects of every District Council shall be to render advice on promotion and protection of consumer rights under this Act within the district.

## Chapter III Central Consumer Protection Authority

### Section 10: Establishment of Central Consumer Protection Authority

(1) The Central Government shall, by notification, establish with effect from such date as it may specify in that notification, a Central Consumer Protection Authority

to be known as the Central Authority to regulate matters relating to violation of rights of consumers, unfair trade practices and false or misleading advertisements which are prejudicial to the interests of public and consumers and to promote, protect and enforce the rights of consumers as a class.

(2) The Central Authority shall consist of a Chief Commissioner and such number of other Commissioners as may be prescribed, to be appointed by the Central Government to exercise the powers and discharge the functions under this Act.

(3) The headquarters of the Central Authority shall be at such place in the National Capital Region of Delhi, and it shall have regional and other offices in any other place in India as the Central Government may decide.

## Section 11: Qualifications, method of recruitment, etc., of Chief Commissioner and Commissioners

The Central Government may, by notification, make rules to provide for the qualifications for appointment, method of recruitment, procedure for appointment, term of office, salaries and allowances, resignation, removal and other terms and conditions of the service of the Chief Commissioner and Commissioners of the Central Authority.

## Section 12: Vacancy, etc., not to invalidate proceedings of Central Authority

No act or proceeding of the Central Authority shall be invalid merely by reason of—

(a) any vacancy in, or any defect in the constitution of, the Central Authority; or

(b) any defect in the appointment of a person acting as the Chief Commissioner or as a Commissioner; or

(c) any irregularity in the procedure of the Central Authority not affecting the merits of the case.

## Section 13: Appointment of officers, experts, professionals and other employees of Central Authority

(1) The Central Government shall provide the Central Authority such number of officers and other employees as it considers necessary for the efficient performance of its functions under this Act.

(2) The salaries and allowances payable to, and the other terms and conditions of service of, the officers and other employees of the Central Authority appointed under this Act shall be such as may be prescribed.

(3) The Central Authority may engage, in accordance with the procedure specified by regulations, such number of experts and professionals of integrity and ability, who have special knowledge and experience in the areas of consumer rights and welfare, consumer policy, law, medicine, food safety, health, engineering, product safety, commerce, economics, public affairs or administration, as it deems necessary to assist it in the discharge of its functions under this Act.

### Section 14: Procedure of Central Authority

(1) The Central Authority shall regulate the procedure for transaction of its business and allocation of its business amongst the Chief Commissioner and Commissioners as may be specified by regulations.

(2) The Chief Commissioner shall have the powers of general superintendence, direction and control in respect of all administrative matters of the Central Authority:

Provided that the Chief Commissioner may delegate such of his powers relating to administrative matters of the Central Authority, as he may think fit, to any Commissioner (including Commissioner of a regional office) or any other officer of the Central Authority.

### Section 15: Investigation Wing

(1) The Central Authority shall have an Investigation Wing headed by a Director-General for the purpose of conducting inquiry or investigation under this Act as may be directed by the Central Authority.

(2) The Central Government may appoint a Director-General and such number of Additional Director-General, Director, Joint Director, Deputy Director and Assistant Director, from amongst persons who have experience in investigation and possess such qualifications, in such manner, as may be prescribed.

(3) Every Additional Director-General, Director, Joint Director, Deputy Director and Assistant Director shall exercise his powers, and discharge his functions, subject to the general control, supervision and direction of the Director-General.

(4) The Director-General may delegate all or any of his powers to the Additional Director-General or Director, Joint Director or Deputy Director or Assistant Director, as the case may be, while conducting inquiries or investigations under this Act.

(5) The inquiries or the investigations made by the Director-General shall be submitted to the Central Authority in such form, in such manner and within such time, as may be specified by regulations.

### Section 16: Power of District Collector

The District Collector (by whatever name called) may, on a complaint or on a reference made to him by the Central Authority or the Commissioner of a regional office, inquire into or investigate complaints regarding violation of rights of consumers as a class, on matters relating to violations of consumer rights, unfair trade practices and false or misleading advertisements, within his jurisdiction and submit his report to the Central Authority or to the Commissioner of a regional office, as the case may be.

### Section 17: Complaints to authorities

A complaint relating to violation of consumer rights or unfair trade practices or false or misleading advertisements which are prejudicial to the interests of consumers as a class, may be forwarded either in writing or in electronic mode, to anyone of the authorities, namely, the District Collector or the Commissioner of regional office or the Central Authority.

**Section 18: Powers and functions of Central Authority**

(1) The Central Authority shall—

(a) protect, promote and enforce the rights of consumers as a class, and prevent violation of consumers rights under this Act;

(b) prevent unfair trade practices and ensure that no person engages himself in unfair trade practices;

(c) ensure that no false or misleading advertisement is made of any goods or services which contravenes the provisions of this Act or the rules or regulations made thereunder;

(d) ensure that no person takes part in the publication of any advertisement which is false or misleading.

(2) Without prejudice to the generality of the provisions contained in sub-section (1), the Central Authority may, for any of the purposes aforesaid,—

(a) inquire or cause an inquiry or investigation to be made into violations of consumer rights or unfair trade practices, either *suo motu* or on a complaint received or on the directions from the Central Government;

(b) file complaints before the District Commission, the State Commission or the National Commission, as the case may be, under this Act;

(c) intervene in any proceedings before the District Commission or the State Commission or the National Commission, as the case may be, in respect of any allegation of violation of consumer rights or unfair trade practices;

(d) review the matters relating to, and the factors inhibiting enjoyment of, consumer rights, including safeguards provided for the protection of consumers under any other law for the time being in force and recommend appropriate remedial measures for their effective implementation;

(e) recommend adoption of international covenants and best international practices on consumer rights to ensure effective enforcement of consumer rights;

(f) undertake and promote research in the field of consumer rights;

(g) spread and promote awareness on consumer rights;

(h) encourage non-Governmental organisations and other institutions working in the field of consumer rights to co-operate and work with consumer protection agencies;

(i) mandate the use of unique and universal goods identifiers in such goods, as may be necessary, to prevent unfair trade practices and to protect consumers' interest;

(j) issue safety notices to alert consumers against dangerous or hazardous or unsafe goods or services;

(k) advise the Ministries and Departments of the Central and State Governments on consumer welfare measures;

(l) issue necessary guidelines to prevent unfair trade practices and protect consumers' interest.

**Section 19: Power of Central Authority to refer matter for Investigation or to other Regulator**

(1) The Central Authority may, after receiving any information or complaint or directions from the Central Government or of its own motion, conduct or cause to be conducted a preliminary inquiry as to whether there exists a *prima facie* case of violation of consumer rights or any unfair trade practice or any false or misleading advertisement, by any person, which is prejudicial to the public interest or to the interests of consumers and if it is satisfied that there exists a *prima facie* case, it shall cause investigation to be made by the Director General or by the District Collector.

(2) Where, after preliminary inquiry, the Central Authority is of the opinion that the matter is to be dealt with by a Regulator established under any other law for the time being in force, it may refer such matter to the concerned Regulator along with its report.

(3) For the purposes of investigation under sub-section (1), the Central Authority, the Director General or the District Collector may call upon a person referred to in sub-section (1) and also direct him to produce any document or record in his possession.

**Section 20: Power of Central Authority to recall goods, etc.**

Where the Central Authority is satisfied on the basis of investigation that there is sufficient evidence to show violation of consumer rights or unfair trade practice by a person, it may pass such order as may be necessary, including—

(a) recalling of goods or withdrawal of services which are dangerous, hazardous or unsafe;

(b) reimbursement of the prices of goods or services so recalled to purchasers of such goods or services; and

(c) discontinuation of practices which are unfair and prejudicial to consumers' interest:

Provided that the Central Authority shall give the person an opportunity of being heard before passing an order under this section.

**Section 21: Power of Central Authority to issue directions and penalties against false or misleading advertisements**

(1) Where the Central Authority is satisfied after investigation that any advertisement is false or misleading and is prejudicial to the interest of any consumer or is in contravention of consumer rights, it may, by order, issue directions to the

concerned trader or manufacturer or endorser or advertiser or publisher, as the case may be, to discontinue such advertisement or to modify the same in such manner and within such time as may be specified in that order.

(2) Notwithstanding the order passed under sub-section (1), if the Central Authority is of the opinion that it is necessary to impose a penalty in respect of such false or misleading advertisement, by a manufacturer or an endorser, it may, by order, impose on manufacturer or endorser a penalty which may extend to ten lakh rupees:

Provided that the Central Authority may, for every subsequent contravention by a manufacturer or endorser, impose a penalty which may extend to fifty lakh rupees.

(3) Notwithstanding any order under sub-sections (1) and (2), where the Central Authority deems it necessary, it may, by order, prohibit the endorser of a false or misleading advertisement from making endorsement of any product or service for a period which may extend to one year.

Provided that the Central Authority may, for every subsequent contravention, prohibit such endorser from making endorsement in respect of any product or service for a period which may extend to three years.

(4) Where the Central Authority is satisfied after investigation that any person is found to publish, or is a party to the publication of, a misleading advertisement, it may impose on such person a penalty which may extend to ten lakh rupees.

(5) No endorser shall be liable to a penalty under sub-sections (2) and (3) if he has exercised due diligence to verify the veracity of the claims made in the advertisement regarding the product or service being endorsed by him.

(6) No person shall be liable to such penalty if he proves that he had published or arranged for the publication of such advertisement in the ordinary course of his business:

Provided that no such defence shall be available to such person if he had previous knowledge of the order passed by the Central Authority for withdrawal or modification of such advertisement.

(7) While determining the penalty under this section, regard shall be had to the following, namely:—

(a) the population and the area impacted or affected by such offence;

(b) the frequency and duration of such offence;

(c) the vulnerability of the class of persons likely to be adversely affected by such offence; and

(d) the gross revenue from the sales effected by virtue of such offence.

(8) The Central Authority shall give the person an opportunity of being heard before an order under this section is passed.

## Section 22: Search and Seizure

(1) For the purpose of conducting an investigation after preliminary inquiry under sub-section (1) of Section 19, the Director-General or any other officer authorised

by him in this behalf, or the District Collector, as the case may be, may, if he has any reason to believe that any person has violated any consumer rights or committed unfair trade practice or causes any false or misleading advertisement to be made, shall,—

(a) enter at any reasonable time into any such premises and search for any document or record or article or any other form of evidence and seize such document, record, article or such evidence;

(b) make a note or an inventory of such record or article; or

(c) require any person to produce any record, register or other document or article.

(2) The provisions of the Code of Criminal Procedure, 1973, relating to search and seizure shall apply, as far as may be, for search and seizure under this Act.

(3) Every document, record or article seized under clause (a) of sub-section (1) or produced under clause (c) of that sub-section shall be returned to the person, from whom they were seized or who produced the same, within a period of twenty days of the date of such seizure or production, as the case may be, after copies thereof or extracts therefrom certified by that person, in such manner as may be prescribed, have been taken.

(4) Where any article seized under sub-section (1) are subject to speedy or natural decay, the Director-General or such other officer may dispose of the article in such manner as may be prescribed.

(5) In the case of articles other than the articles referred to in sub-section (4), provisions contained in clause (c) of sub-section (2) of Section 38 shall *mutatis mutandis* apply in relation to analysis or tests.

**Section 23: Designation of any statutory authority or body to function as Central Authority**

The Central Government may, if it considers necessary, by notification, designate any statutory authority or body to exercise the powers and perform the functions of the Central Authority referred to in Section 10.

**Section 24: Appeal**

A person aggrieved by any order passed by the Central Authority under Sections 20 and 21 may file an appeal to the National Commission within a period of thirty days from the date of receipt of such order.

**Section 25: Grants by Central Government**

The Central Government may, after due appropriation made by Parliament by law in this behalf, make to the Central Authority grants of such sums of money as that Government may think fit for being utilised for the purposes of this Act.

**Section 26: Accounts and Audit**

(1) The Central Authority shall maintain proper accounts and other relevant records and prepare an annual statement of accounts in such form and manner as may

be prescribed in consultation with the Comptroller and Auditor-General of India.

(2) The accounts of the Central Authority shall be audited by the Comptroller and Auditor-General of India at such intervals as may be specified by him and any expenditure incurred in connection with such audit shall be payable by the Central Authority to the Comptroller and Auditor-General of India.

(3) The Comptroller and Auditor-General of India or any other person appointed by him in connection with the audit of the accounts of the Central Authority shall have the same rights, privileges and authority in connection with such audit as the Comptroller and Auditor-General of India generally has, in connection with the audit of the Government accounts and, in particular, shall have the right to demand the production of books, accounts, connected vouchers and other documents and papers and to inspect any of the offices of the Central Authority.

(4) The accounts of the Central Authority as certified by the Comptroller and Auditor-General of India or any other person appointed by him in this behalf together with the audit report thereon shall be forwarded annually to the Central Government which shall cause the same to be laid before each House of Parliament.

### Section 27: Furnishing of annual reports, etc.

(1) The Central Authority shall prepare once in every year, in such form, manner and at such time as may be prescribed, an annual report giving full account of its activities during the previous year and such other reports and returns, as may be directed, and copies of such report and returns shall be forwarded to the Central Government.

(2) A copy of the annual report received under sub-section (1) shall be laid, as soon as may be after it is received, before each House of Parliament.

## Chapter IV Consumer Disputes Redressal Commission

### Section 28: Establishment of District Consumer Disputes Redressal Commission

(1) The State Government shall, by notification, establish a District Consumer Disputes Redressal Commission, to be known as the District Commission, in each district of the State:

Provided that the State Government may, if it deems fit, establish more than one District Commission in a district.

(2) Each District Commission shall consist of—

(a) a President; and

(b) not less than two and not more than such number of members as may be prescribed, in consultation with the Central Government.

## COMMENTS

**Judicial authority:** Consumer forum is a 'judicial authority'- *Morgan Securities P Ltd.* v. *Modi Rubber Ltd.* (2007) 73 SCL 219 (SC).

### Section 29: Qualifications, etc., of President and members of District Commission

The Central Government may, by notification, make rules to provide for the qualifications, method of recruitment, procedure for appointment, term of office, resignation and removal of the President and members of the District Commission.

### Section 30: Salaries, allowances and other terms and conditions of service of President and members of District Commission

The State Government may, by notification, make rules to provide for salaries and allowances and other terms and conditions of service of the President, and members of the District Commission.

### Section 31: Transitional provision

Any person appointed as President or, as the case may be, a member of the District Commission immediately before the commencement of this Act shall hold office as such as President or, as the case may be, as member till the completion of his term for which he has been appointed.

### Section 32: Vacancy in office of member of District Commission

If, at any time, there is a vacancy in the office of the President or member of a District Commission, the State Government may, by notification, direct—

(a) any other District Commission specified in that notification to exercise the jurisdiction in respect of that district also; or

(b) the President or a member of any other District Commission specified in that notification to exercise the powers and discharge the functions of the President or member of that District Commission also.

### Section 33: Officers and other employees of District Commission

(1) The State Government shall provide the District Commission with such officers and other employees as may be required to assist the District Commission in the discharge of its functions.

(2) The officers and other employees of the District Commission shall discharge their functions under the general superintendence of the President of the District Commission.

(3) The salaries and allowances payable to, and the other terms and conditions of service of, the officers and other employees of the District Commission shall be such as may be prescribed.

## Section 34: Jurisdiction of District Commission

(1) Subject to the other provisions of this Act, the District Commission shall have jurisdiction to entertain complaints where the value of the goods or services paid as consideration does not exceed one crore rupees:

Provided that where the Central Government deems it necessary so to do, it may prescribe such other value, as it deems fit.

(2) A complaint shall be instituted in a District Commission within the local limits of whose jurisdiction,—

(a) the opposite party or each of the opposite parties, where there are more than one, at the time of the institution of the complaint, ordinarily resides or carries on business or has a branch office or personally works for gain; or

(b) any of the opposite parties, where there are more than one, at the time of the institution of the complaint, actually and voluntarily resides, or carries on business or has a branch office, or personally works for gain, provided that in such case the permission of the District Commission is given; or

(c) the cause of action, wholly or in part, arises; or

(d) the complainant resides or personally works for gain.

(3) The District Commission shall ordinarily function in the district headquarters and may perform its functions at such other place in the district, as the State Government may, in consultation with the State Commission, notify in the Official Gazette from time to time.

## Section 35: Manner in which complaint shall be made

(1) A complaint, in relation to any goods sold or delivered or agreed to be sold or delivered or any service provided or agreed to be provided, may be filed with a District Commission by—

(a) the consumer,—

(i) to whom such goods are sold or delivered or agreed to be sold or delivered or such service is provided or agreed to be provided; or

(ii) who alleges unfair trade practice in respect of such goods or service;

(b) any recognised consumer association, whether the consumer to whom such goods are sold or delivered or agreed to be sold or delivered or such service is provided or agreed to be provided, or who alleges unfair trade practice in respect of such goods or service, is a member of such association or not;

(c) one or more consumers, where there are numerous consumers having the same interest, with the permission of the District Commission, on behalf of, or for the benefit of, all consumers so interested; or

(d) the Central Government, the Central Authority or the State Government, as the case may be:

Provided that the complaint under this sub-section may be filed electronically in such manner as may be prescribed.

*Explanation*: For the purposes of this sub-section, "recognised consumer association" means any voluntary consumer association registered under any law for the time being in force.

(2) Every complaint filed under sub-section (1) shall be accompanied with such fee and payable in such manner, including electronic form, as may be prescribed.

## Section 36: Proceedings before District Commission

(1) Every proceeding before the District Commission shall be conducted by the President of that Commission and at least one member thereof, sitting together:

Provided that where a member, for any reason, is unable to conduct a proceeding till it is completed, the President and the other member shall continue the proceeding from the stage at which it was last heard by the previous member.

(2) On receipt of a complaint made under Section 35, the District Commission may, by order, admit the complaint for being proceeded with or reject the same:

Provided that a complaint shall not be rejected under this section unless an opportunity of being heard has been given to the complainant:

Provided further that the admissibility of the complaint shall ordinarily be decided within twenty-one days from the date on which the complaint was filed.

(3) Where the District Commission does not decide the issue of admissibility of the complaint within the period so specified, it shall be deemed to have been admitted.

## Section 37: Reference to Mediation

(1) At the first hearing of the complaint after its admission, or at any later stage, if it appears to the District Commission that there exists elements of a settlement which may be acceptable to the parties, except in such cases as may be prescribed, it may direct the parties to give in writing, within five days, consent to have their dispute settled by mediation in accordance with the provisions of Chapter V.

(2) Where the parties agree for settlement by mediation and give their consent in writing, the District Commission shall, within five days of receipt of such consent, refer the matter for mediation, and in such case, the provisions of Chapter V, relating to mediation, shall apply.

## Section 38: Procedure on admission of complaint

(1) The District Commission shall, on admission of a complaint, or in respect of cases referred for mediation on failure of settlement by mediation, proceed with such complaint.

(2) Where the complaint relates to any goods, the District Commission shall,—

(a) refer a copy of the admitted complaint, within twenty-one days from the date of its admission to the opposite party mentioned in the complaint directing him to give his version of the case within a period of thirty days or such extended period not exceeding fifteen days as may be granted by it;

(b) if the opposite party on receipt of a complaint referred to him under clause (a) denies or disputes the allegations contained in the complaint, or omits or fails to take any action to represent his case within the time given by the District Commission, proceed to settle the consumer dispute in the manner specified in clauses (c) to (g);

(c) if the complaint alleges a defect in the goods which cannot be determined without proper analysis or test of the goods, obtain a sample of the goods from the complainant, seal it and authenticate it in the manner as may be prescribed and refer the sample so sealed to the appropriate laboratory along with a direction that such laboratory to make an analysis or test, whichever may be necessary, with a view to finding out whether such goods suffer from any defect alleged in the complaint or from any other defect and to report its findings thereon to the District Commission within a period of forty-five days of the receipt of the reference or within such extended period as may be granted by it;

(d) before any sample of the goods is referred to any appropriate laboratory under clause (c), require the complainant to deposit to the credit of the Commission such fees as may be specified, for payment to the appropriate laboratory for carrying out the necessary analysis or test in relation to the goods in question;

(e) remit the amount deposited to its credit under clause (d) to the appropriate laboratory to enable it to carry out the analysis or test mentioned in clause (c) and on receipt of the report from the appropriate laboratory, it shall forward a copy of the report along with such remarks as it may feel appropriate to the opposite party;

(f) if any of the parties disputes the correctness of the findings of the appropriate laboratory, or disputes the correctness of the methods of analysis or test adopted by the appropriate laboratory, require the opposite party or the complainant to submit in writing his objections with regard to the report made by the appropriate laboratory;

(g) give a reasonable opportunity to the complainant as well as the opposite party of being heard as to the correctness or otherwise of the report made by the appropriate laboratory and also as to the objection made in relation thereto under clause (f) and issue an appropriate order under Section 39.

(3) The District Commission shall, if the complaint admitted by it under sub-section (2) of Section 36 relates to goods in respect of which the procedure specified in sub-section (2) cannot be followed, or if the complaint relates to any services,—

(a) refer a copy of such complaint to the opposite party directing him to give his version of the case within a period of thirty days or such extended period not exceeding fifteen days as may be granted by the District Commission;

(b) if the opposite party, on receipt of a copy of the complaint, referred to him under clause (a) denies or disputes the allegations contained in the complaint, or omits or fails to take any action to represent his case within the time given by the District Commission, it shall proceed to settle the consumer dispute—

(i) on the basis of evidence brought to its notice by the complainant and the opposite party, if the opposite party denies or disputes the allegations contained in the complaint, or

(ii) *ex parte* on the basis of evidence brought to its notice by the complainant, where the opposite party omits or fails to take any action to represent his case within the time given by the Commission;

(c) decide the complaint on merits if the complainant fails to appear on the date of hearing.

(4) For the purposes of sub-sections (2) and (3), the District Commission may, by order, require an electronic service provider to provide such information, documents or records, as may be specified in that order.

(5) No proceedings complying with the procedure laid down in sub-sections (1) and (2) shall be called in question in any court on the ground that the principles of natural justice have not been complied with.

(6) Every complaint shall be heard by the District Commission on the basis of affidavit and documentary evidence placed on record:

Provided that where an application is made for hearing or for examination of parties in person or through video conferencing, the District Commission may, on sufficient cause being shown, and after recording its reasons in writing, allow the same.

(7) Every complaint shall be disposed of as expeditiously as possible and endeavour shall be made to decide the complaint within a period of three months from the date of receipt of notice by opposite party where the complaint does not require analysis or testing of commodities and within five months if it requires analysis or testing of commodities:

Provided that no adjournment shall ordinarily be granted by the District Commission unless sufficient cause is shown and the reasons for grant of adjournment have been recorded in writing by the Commission:

Provided further that the District Commission shall make such orders as to the costs occasioned by the adjournment as may be specified by regulations:

Provided also that in the event of a complaint being disposed of after the period so specified, the District Commission shall record in writing, the reasons for the same at the time of disposing of the said complaint.

(8) Where during the pendency of any proceeding before the District Commission, if it appears necessary, it may pass such interim order as is just and proper in the facts and circumstances of the case.

(9) For the purposes of this section, the District Commission shall have the same powers as are vested in a civil court under the Code of Civil Procedure, 1908 while trying a suit in respect of the following matters, namely:—

(a) the summoning and enforcing the attendance of any defendant or witness and examining the witness on oath;

(b) requiring the discovery and production of any document or other material object as evidence;

(c) receiving of evidence on affidavits;

(d) the requisitioning of the report of the concerned analysis or test from the appropriate laboratory or from any other relevant source;

(e) issuing of commissions for the examination of any witness, or document; and

(f) any other matter which may be prescribed by the Central Government.

(10) Every proceeding before the District Commission shall be deemed to be a judicial proceeding within the meaning of Section 193 and 228 of the Indian Penal Code, and the District Commission shall be deemed to be a criminal court for the purposes of Section 195 and Chapter XXVI of the Code of Criminal Procedure, 1973.

(11) Where the complainant is a consumer referred to in sub-clause (v) of clause (5) of Section 2, the provisions of Order I Rule 8 of the First Schedule to the Code of Civil Procedure, 1908 shall apply subject to the modification that every reference therein to a suit or decree shall be construed as a reference to a complaint or the order of the District Commission thereon.

(12) In the event of death of a complainant who is a consumer or of the opposite party against whom the complaint has been filed, the provisions of Order XXII of the First Schedule to the Code of Civil Procedure, 1908 shall apply subject to the modification that every reference therein to the plaintiff and the defendant shall be construed as reference to a complainant or the opposite party, as the case may be.

## Section 39: Findings of District Commission

(1) Where the District Commission is satisfied that the goods complained against suffer from any of the defects specified in the complaint or that any of the allegations contained in the complaint about the services or any unfair trade practices, or claims for compensation under product liability are proved, it shall issue an order to the opposite party directing him to do one or more of the following, namely:—

(a) to remove the defect pointed out by the appropriate laboratory from the goods in question;

(b) to replace the goods with new goods of similar description which shall be free from any defect;

(c) to return to the complainant the price, or, as the case may be, the charges paid by the complainant along with such interest on such price or charges as may be decided;

(d) to pay such amount as may be awarded by it as compensation to the consumer for any loss or injury suffered by the consumer due to the negligence of the opposite party:

Provided that the District Commission shall have the power to grant punitive damages in such circumstances as it deems fit;

(e) to pay such amount as may be awarded by it as compensation in a product liability action under Chapter VI;

(f) to remove the defects in goods or deficiencies in the services in question;

(g) to discontinue the unfair trade practice or restrictive trade practice and not to repeat them;

(h) not to offer the hazardous or unsafe goods for sale;

(i) to withdraw the hazardous goods from being offered for sale;

(j) to cease manufacture of hazardous goods and to desist from offering services which are hazardous in nature;

(k) to pay such sum as may be determined by it, if it is of the opinion that loss or injury has been suffered by a large number of consumers who are not identifiable conveniently:

Provided that the minimum amount of sum so payable shall not be less than twenty-five per cent of the value of such defective goods sold or service provided, as the case may be, to such consumers;

(l) to issue corrective advertisement to neutralise the effect of misleading advertisement at the cost of the opposite party responsible for issuing such misleading advertisement;

(m) to provide for adequate costs to parties; and

(n) to cease and desist from issuing any misleading advertisement.

(2) Any amount obtained under sub-section (1) shall be credited to such fund and utilised in such manner as may be prescribed.

(3) In any proceeding conducted by the President and a member and if they differ on any point or points, they shall state the point or points on which they differ and refer the same to another member for hearing on such point or points and the opinion of the majority shall be the order of the District Commission:

Provided that the other member shall give his opinion on such point or points referred to him within a period of one month from the date of such reference.

(4) Every order made by the District Commission under sub-section (1) shall be signed by the President and the member who conducted the proceeding:

Provided that where the order is made as per majority opinion under sub-section (3), such order shall also be signed by the other member.

### Section 40: Review by District Commission in certain cases

The District Commission shall have the power to review any of the order passed by it if there is an error apparent on the face of the record, either of its own motion or on an application made by any of the parties within thirty days of such order.

### Section 41: Appeal against order of District Commission

Any person aggrieved by an order made by the District Commission may prefer an appeal against such order to the State Commission on the grounds of facts or law within a period of forty-five days from the date of the order, in such form and manner, as may be prescribed:

Provided that the State Commission may entertain an appeal after the expiry of the said period of forty-five days, if it is satisfied that there was sufficient cause for not filing it within that period:

Provided further that no appeal by a person, who is required to pay any amount in terms of an order of the District Commission, shall be entertained by the State Commission unless the appellant has deposited fifty per cent of that amount in the manner as may be prescribed:

Provided also that no appeal shall lie from any order passed under sub-section (1) of Section 81 by the District Commission pursuant to a settlement by mediation under Section 80.

## Section 42: Establishment of State Consumer Disputes Redressal Commission

(1) The State Government shall, by notification, establish a State Consumer Disputes Redressal Commission, to be known as the State Commission, in the State.

(2) The State Commission shall ordinarily function at the State capital and perform its functions at such other places as the State Government may in consultation with the State Commission notify in the Official Gazette:

Provided that the State Government may, by notification, establish regional benches of the State Commission, at such places, as it deems fit.

(3) Each State Commission shall consist of—

(a) a President; and

(b) not less than four or not more than such number of members as may be prescribed in consultation with the Central Government.

## Section 43: Qualifications, etc., of President and members of State Commission

The Central Government may, by notification, make rules to provide for the qualification for appointment, method of recruitment, procedure of appointment, term of office, resignation and removal of the President and members of the State Commission.

## Section 44: Salaries, allowances and other terms and conditions of service of President and members of State Commission

The State Government may, by notification, make rules to provide for salaries and allowances and other terms and conditions of service of the President and members of the State Commission.

## Section 45: Transitional provision

Any person appointed as President or, as the case may be, a member of the State Commission immediately before the commencement of this Act shall hold office as such, as President or member, as the case may be, till the completion of his term.

## Section 46: Officers and employees of State Commission

(1) The State Government shall determine the nature and categories of the officers and other employees required to assist the State Commission in the discharge of

its functions and provide the Commission with such officers and other employees as it may think fit.

(2) The officers and other employees of the State Commission shall discharge their functions under the general superintendence of the President.

(3) The salaries and allowances payable to and the other terms and conditions of service of, the officers and other employees of the State Commission shall be such as may be prescribed.

**Section 47: Jurisdiction of State Commission**

(1) Subject to the other provisions of this Act, the State Commission shall have jurisdiction—

(a) to entertain—

(i) complaints where the value of the goods or services paid as consideration, exceeds rupees one crore, but does not exceed rupees ten crore:

Provided that where the Central Government deems it necessary so to do, it may prescribe such other value, as it deems fit;

(ii) complaints against unfair contracts, where the value of goods or services paid as consideration does not exceed ten crore rupees;

(iii) appeals against the orders of any District Commission within the State; and

(b) to call for the records and pass appropriate orders in any consumer dispute which is pending before or has been decided by any District Commission within the State, where it appears to the State Commission that such District Commission has exercised a jurisdiction not vested in it by law, or has failed to exercise a jurisdiction so vested or has acted in exercise of its jurisdiction illegally or with material irregularity.

(2) The jurisdiction, powers and authority of the State Commission may be exercised by Benches thereof, and a Bench may be constituted by the President with one or more members as the President may deem fit:

Provided that the senior-most member shall preside over the Bench.

(3) Where the members of a Bench differ in opinion on any point, the points shall be decided according to the opinion of the majority, if there is a majority, but if the members are equally divided, they shall state the point or points on which they differ, and make a reference to the President who shall either hear the point or points himself or refer the case for hearing on such point or points by one or more of the other members and such point or points shall be decided according to the opinion of the majority of the members who have heard the case, including those who first heard it:

Provided that the President or the other members, as the case may be, shall give opinion on the point or points so referred within a period of one month from the date of such reference.

(4) A complaint shall be instituted in a State Commission within the limits of whose jurisdiction,—

(a) the opposite party or each of the opposite parties, where there are more than one, at the time of the institution of the complaint, ordinarily resides or carries on business or has a branch office or personally works for gain; or
(b) any of the opposite parties, where there are more than one, at the time of the institution of the complaint, actually and voluntarily resides, or carries on business or has a branch office or personally works for gain, provided in such case, the permission of the State Commission is given; or
(c) the cause of action, wholly or in part, arises; or
(d) the complainant resides or personally works for gain.

The State Commission is having the following Jurisdictions:

1. ***Pecuniary jurisdiction:*** The state Commission is established in each State, and it has jurisdiction to entertain complaints where the value of goods or services and the compensation, if any, claimed exceeds ₹ 1,00,00,000 (one crore) but does not exceed ₹ 10,00,00,000 (Ten crore).
2. ***Territorial jurisdiction:*** The State Commission shall ordinarily function in the State Capital but may perform its functions at such other place as the State Government may, in consultation with the State Commission, notify in the official Gazette, from time to time, which is otherwise known as regional benches.

   A complaint shall be instituted in a State Commission with the limits of whose jurisdiction—
   - The opposite party resides or
   - Carries on his business or works for gain or
   - Where the cause of Action arises.
   - The complainant resides or personally works for gain.
3. ***Appellate jurisdiction [Sec. 41]:*** Any person aggrieved by an order made by the District Commission may prefer an appeal against such order to the state Commission within a period of Forty-Five days from the date of the order. However, the State Commission may entertain an appeal after the expiry of the said period of Forty-Five days if it is satisfied that there was sufficient cause for delay. Such appeal shall not be entertained by the State Commission unless the appellant has deposited fifty per cent of that amount which is required to pay any amount in terms of an order of the District Forum.
4. ***Revisional jurisdiction [Sec. 47 (1)(b)]:*** The State Commission shall have jurisdiction to call for the records and pass an appropriate orders in any consumer dispute which is pending before or has been decided by any District Forum within the State, where it appears to the State Commission that such District Forum has exercised a jurisdiction not vested in it by law, or has failed to exercise a jurisdiction so vested or has acted in exercise of its jurisdiction illegally or with material irregularity.
5. ***Review [Sec. 50]:*** The State Commission shall have the power to review any of the orders passed by it if there is an error apparent on the face of the record, either of its own motion or on an application made by any of the parties within thirty days of such order.

**Section 48: Transfer of cases**

On the application of the complainant or of its own motion, the State Commission may, at any stage of the proceeding, transfer any complaint pending before a District Commission to another District Commission within the State if the interest of justice so requires.

**Section 49: Procedure applicable to State Commission**

(1) The provisions relating to complaints under Sections 35, 36, 37, 38 and 39 shall, with such modifications as may be necessary, be applicable to the disposal of complaints by the State Commission.

(2) Without prejudice to the provisions of sub-section (1), the State Commission may also declare any terms of contract, which is unfair to any consumer, to be null and void.

**Section 50: Review by State Commission in certain cases**

The State Commission shall have the power to review any of the order passed by it if there is an error apparent on the face of the record, either of its own motion or on an application made by any of the parties within thirty days of such order.

**Section 51: Appeal to National Commission**

(1) Any person aggrieved by an order made by the State Commission in exercise of its powers conferred by sub-clause (i) or (ii) of clause (a) of sub-section (1) of Section 47 may prefer an appeal against such order to the National Commission within a period of thirty days from the date of the order in such form and manner as may be prescribed:

Provided that the National Commission shall not entertain the appeal after the expiry of the said period of thirty days unless it is satisfied that there was sufficient cause for not filing it within that period:

Provided further that no appeal by a person, who is required to pay any amount in terms of an order of the State Commission, shall be entertained by the National Commission unless the appellant has deposited fifty per cent of that amount in the manner as may be prescribed.

(2) Save as otherwise expressly provided under this Act or by any other law for the time being in force, an appeal shall lie to the National Commission from any order passed in appeal by any State Commission, if the National Commission is satisfied that the case involves a substantial question of law.

(3) In an appeal involving a question of law, the memorandum of appeal shall precisely state the substantial question of law involved in the appeal.

(4) Where the National Commission is satisfied that a substantial question of law is involved in any case, it shall formulate that question and hear the appeal on that question:

Provided that nothing in this sub-section shall be deemed to take away or abridge the power of the National Commission to hear, for reasons to be recorded in writing, the appeal on any other substantial question of law, if it is satisfied that the case involves such question of law.

(5) An appeal may lie to the National Commission under this section from an order passed *ex parte* by the State Commission.

**Section 52: Hearing of appeal**

An appeal filed before the State Commission or the National Commission, as the case may be, shall be heard as expeditiously as possible and every endeavour shall be made to dispose of the appeal within a period of ninety days from the date of its admission:

Provided that no adjournment shall ordinarily be granted by the State Commission or the National Commission, as the case may be, unless sufficient cause is shown and the reasons for grant of adjournment have been recorded in writing by such Commission:

Provided further that the State Commission or the National Commission, as the case may be, shall make such orders as to the costs occasioned by the adjournment, as may be specified by regulations:

Provided also that in the event of an appeal being disposed of after the period so specified, the State Commission or the National Commission, as the case may be, shall record in writing the reasons for the same at the time of disposing of the said appeal.

**Section 53: Establishment of National Consumer Disputes Redressal Commission**

(1) The Central Government shall, by notification, establish a National Consumer Disputes Redressal Commission, to be known as the National Commission.

(2) The National Commission shall ordinarily function at the National Capital Region and perform its functions at such other places as the Central Government may in consultation with the National Commission notify in the Official Gazette:

Provided that the Central Government may, by notification, establish regional Benches of the National Commission, at such places, as it deems fit.

**Section 54: Composition of National Commission**

The National Commission shall consist of—

(a) a President; and

(b) not less than four and not more than such number of members as may be prescribed.

**Section 55: Qualifications, etc., of President and members of National Commission**

(1) The Central Government may, by notification, make rules to provide for qualifications, appointment, term of office, salaries and allowances, resignation, removal and other terms and conditions of service of the President and members of the National Commission:

Provided that the President and members of the National Commission shall hold office for such term as specified in the rules made by the Central Government but not exceeding five years from the date on which he enters upon his office and shall be eligible for re-appointment:

Provided further that no President or members shall hold office as such after he has attained such age as specified in the rules made by the Central Government which shall not exceed,—

(a) in the case of the President, the age of seventy years;

(b) in the case of any other member, the age of sixty-seven years.

(2) Neither the salary and allowances nor the other terms and conditions of service of President and members of the National Commission shall be varied to his disadvantage after his appointment.

## Section 56: Transitional provision

The President and every other member appointed immediately before the commencement of Section 177 of the Finance Act, 2017 shall continue to be governed by the provisions of the Consumer Protection Act, 1986 and the rules made thereunder as if this Act had not come into force.

## Section 57: Other officers and employees of National Commission

(1) The Central Government shall provide, in consultation with the President of the National Commission, such number of officers and other employees to assist the National Commission in the discharge of its functions as it may think fit.

(2) The officers and other employees of the National Commission shall discharge their functions under the general superintendence of the President of the National Commission.

(3) The salaries and allowances payable to, and the other terms and conditions of service of, the officers and other employees of the National Commission shall be such as may be prescribed.

## Section 58: Jurisdiction of National Commission

(1) Subject to the other provisions of this Act, the National Commission shall have jurisdiction—

(a) to entertain—

(i) complaints where the value of the goods or services paid as consideration exceeds rupees ten crore:

Provided that where the Central Government deems it necessary so to do, it may prescribe such other value, as it deems fit;

(ii) complaints against unfair contracts, where the value of goods or services paid as consideration exceeds ten crore rupees;

(iii) appeals against the orders of any State Commission;

(iv) appeals against the orders of the Central Authority; and

(b) to call for the records and pass appropriate orders in any consumer dispute which is pending before or has been decided by any State Commission where it appears to the National Commission that such State Commission has exercised a jurisdiction not vested in it by law, or has failed to exercise a jurisdiction so vested, or has acted in the exercise of its jurisdiction illegally or with material irregularity.

(2) The jurisdiction, powers and authority of the National Commission may be exercised by Benches thereof and a Bench may be constituted by the President with one or more members as he may deem fit:

Provided that the senior-most member of the Bench shall preside over the Bench.

(3) Where the members of a Bench differ in opinion on any point, the points shall be decided according to the opinion of the majority, if there is a majority, but if the members are equally divided, they shall state the point or points on which they differ, and make a reference to the President who shall either hear the point or points himself or refer the case for hearing on such point or points by one or more of the other members and such point or points shall be decided according to the opinion of the majority of the members who have heard the case, including those who first heard it:

Provided that the President or the other member, as the case may be, shall give opinion on the point or points so referred within a period of two months from the date of such reference.

The National commission is having the following jurisdiction:

(1) ***Pecuniary jurisdiction:*** The National Commission has jurisdiction to entertain complaints where the value of goods or services and the compensation, if any, claimed exceeds ₹ 10 crore (Ten crore).

(2) ***Territorial jurisdiction:*** The territorial jurisdiction of the National Commission is whole of India.

(3) ***Appellate jurisdiction [Sec. 51]:*** Any person aggrieved by an order made by the state Commission may prefer an appeal against such order to the National Commission within a period of thirty days from the date of the order. However, the National Commission may entertain an appeal after the expiry of the said period of thirty days if it is satisfied that there was sufficient cause for not filing it within that period. such appeal shall not be entertained by the National Commission unless the appellant has deposited fifty per cent of that amount or thirty-five thousand rupees, whichever is less which is required to pay any amount in terms of an order of the state Commission.

(4) ***Revisional jurisdiction [Sec. 58(1)(b)]:*** The National Commission shall have jurisdiction to call for the records and pass appropriate orders in any consumer dispute which is pending before or has been decided by any state Commission where it appears to the National Commission that such state Commission has exercised a jurisdiction not vested in it by law, or has failed to exercise a jurisdiction so vested, or has Acted in the exercise of its jurisdiction illegally or with material irregularity.

(5) ***Review jurisdiction [Sec 60]:*** The National Commission shall have the power to review any order made by it, when there is an error apparent on the face of record.

In *General Manager, Telecom* v. *M. Krishnan*[65], the dispute in this case was regarding non-payment of telephone bill for the telephone connection provided to the respondent and for the said non-payment of the bill, the telephone connection was disconnected. aggrieved against the said disconnection, the respondent filed a complaint before the District Consumer Disputes redressal Forum, Kozhikode. The Consumer Forum allowed the complaint and directed the appellant herein to re-connect the telephone connection to the respondent No. 1 and pay compensation of `5,000 with interest @ 12% p.a. from the date of filing of the complaint. aggrieved against the order of the Consumer Forum, the appellant filed a writ petition before the High Court of Kerala challenging the jurisdiction of the Consumer Forum. A learned single Judge of the High Court dismissed the writ petition. Thereafter, the appellant filed a writ appeal before the Division Bench of the High Court. The Division Bench felt that the matter required consideration by a larger Bench and hence the matter was placed before the Full Bench. By the impugned order, the Full Bench of the High Court has dismissed the writ appeal. Hence, the appellant is before the Supreme Court by special leave.

The Supreme Court observed that when there is a special remedy provided in Sec. 7B of the Indian Telegraph Act regarding disputes in respect of telephone bills, then the remedy under the Consumer Protection Act is by implication barred. Section 7B of the Telegraph Act reads as under:

Sec. 7B. Arbitration of Disputes:—

(1) except as otherwise expressly provided in this Act, if any dispute concerning any telegraph line, appliance or apparatus arises between the telegraph authority and the person or whose benefit the line, appliance or apparatus is, or has been provided, the dispute shall be determined by arbitration and shall, for the purpose of such determination, be referred to an arbitrator appointed by the Central Government either specifically for the determination of that dispute or generally for the determination of disputes under this section.

(2) The award of the arbitrator appointed under sub-section (1) shall be conclusive between the parties to the dispute and shall not be questioned in any Court.

The Court accordingly held that it is well settled that the special law overrides the general law. The Telegraph Act being a special Act shall override the Consumer Protection Act.

### Section 59: Procedure applicable to National Commission

(1) The provisions relating to complaints under Sections 35, 36, 37, 38 and 39 shall, with such modifications as may be considered necessary, be applicable to the disposal of complaints by the National Commission.

(2) Without prejudice to sub-section (1), the National Commission may also declare any terms of contract which is unfair to any consumer to be null and void.

[65] AIR 2010 SC 90.

**Section 60: Review by National Commission in certain cases**

The National Commission shall have the power to review any of the order passed by it if there is an error apparent on the face of the record, either of its own motion or on an application made by any of the parties within thirty days of such order.

**Section 61: Power to set aside *ex parte* orders**

Where an order is passed by the National Commission *ex parte*, the aggrieved party may make an application to the Commission for setting aside such order.

**Section 62: Transfer of cases**

On the application of the complainant or of its own motion, the National Commission may, at any stage of the proceeding, in the interest of justice, transfer any complaint pending before the District Commission of one State to a District Commission of another State or before one State Commission to another State Commission.

**Section 63: Vacancy in office of President of National Commission**

When the office of President of the National Commission is vacant or a person occupying such office is, by reason of absence or otherwise, unable to perform the duties of his office, these shall be performed by the senior-most member of the National Commission:

Provided that where a retired Judge of a High Court or a person who has been a Judicial Member is a member of the National Commission, such member or where the number of such members is more than one, the senior-most person amongst such members, shall preside over the National Commission in the absence of President of that Commission.

**Section 64: Vacancies or defects in appointment not to invalidate orders**

No act or proceeding of the District Commission, the State Commission or the National Commission shall be invalid by reason only of the existence of any vacancy amongst its members or any defect in the constitution thereof.

**Section 65: Service of notice, etc.**

(1) All notices, required by this Act to be served, shall be served by delivering or transmitting a copy thereof by registered post acknowledgment due addressed to opposite party against whom complaint is made or to the complainant by speed post or by such courier service, approved by the District Commission, the State Commission, or the National Commission, as the case may be, or by any other mode of transmission of documents including electronic means.

(2) Without prejudice to the provisions contained in sub-section (1), the notice required by this Act may be served on an electronic service provider at the address provided by it on the electronic platform from where it provides its services as such and for this purpose, the electronic service provider shall designate a nodal officer to accept and process such notices.

(3) When an acknowledgment or any other receipt purporting to be signed by the opposite party or his agent or, as the case may be, by the complainant is received

by the District Commission, the State Commission or the National Commission, as the case may be, or postal article containing the notice is received back by such District Commission, State Commission or the National Commission, with an endorsement purporting to have been made by a postal employee or by any person authorised by the courier service to the effect that the opposite party or his agent or complainant had refused to take delivery of the postal article containing the notice or had refused to accept the notice by any other means specified in sub-section (1) when tendered or transmitted to him, the District Commission or the State Commission or the National Commission, as the case may be, shall declare that the notice has been duly served on the opposite party or to the complainant, as the case may be:

Provided that where the notice was properly addressed, pre-paid and duly sent by registered post acknowledgment due, a declaration referred to in this sub-section shall be made notwithstanding the fact that the acknowledgment has been lost or misplaced, or for any other reason, has not been received by the District Commission, the State Commission, or the National Commission, as the case may be, within thirty days from the date of issue of notice.

(4) All notices required to be served on an opposite party or to complainant, as the case may be, shall be deemed to be sufficiently served, if addressed in the case of the opposite party, to the place where business or profession is carried on, and in case of the complainant, the place where such person actually and voluntarily resides.

### Section 66: Experts to assist National Commission or State Commission

Where the National Commission or the State Commission, as the case may be, on an application by a complainant or otherwise, is of the opinion that it involves the larger interest of consumers, it may direct any individual or organisation or expert to assist the National Commission or the State Commission, as the case may be.

### Section 67: Appeal against order of National Commission

Any person, aggrieved by an order made by the National Commission in exercise of its powers conferred by sub-clause (i) or (ii) of clause (a) of sub-section (1) of Section 58, may prefer an appeal against such order to the Supreme Court within a period of thirty days from the date of the order:

Provided that the Supreme Court may entertain an appeal after the expiry of the said period of thirty days if it is satisfied that there was sufficient cause for not filing it within that period:

Provided further that no appeal by a person who is required to pay any amount in terms of an order of the National Commission shall be entertained by the Supreme Court unless that person has deposited fifty per cent of that amount in the manner as may be prescribed.

### Section 68: Finality of orders

Every order of a District Commission or the State Commission or the National Commission, as the case may be, shall, if no appeal has been preferred against such order under the provisions of this Act, be final.

## Section 69: Limitation period

(1) The District Commission, the State Commission or the National Commission shall not admit a complaint unless it is filed within two years from the date on which the cause of action has arisen.

(2) Notwithstanding anything contained in sub-section (1), a complaint may be entertained after the period specified in sub-section (1), if the complainant satisfies the District Commission, the State Commission, or the National Commission, as the case may be, that he had sufficient cause for not filing the complaint within such period:

Provided that no such complaint shall be entertained unless the District Commission or the State Commission or the National Commission, as the case may be, records its reasons for condoning such delay.

## Section 70: Administrative Control

(1) The National Commission shall have the authority to lay down such adequate standards in consultation with the Central Government from time to time, for better protection of the interests of consumers and for that purpose, shall have administrative control over all the State Commissions in the following matters, namely:—

(a) monitoring performance of the State Commissions in terms of their disposal by calling for periodical returns regarding the institution, disposal and pendency of cases;

(b) investigating into any allegations against the President and members of a State Commission and submitting inquiry report to the State Government concerned along with copy endorsed to the Central Government for necessary action;

(c) issuance of instructions regarding adoption of uniform procedure in the hearing of matters, prior service of copies of documents produced by one party to the opposite parties, furnishing of english translation of judgments written in any language, speedy grant of copies of documents;

(d) overseeing the functioning of the State Commission or the District Commission either by way of inspection or by any other means, as the National Commission may like to order from time to time, to ensure that the objects and purposes of the Act are best served and the standards set by the National Commission are implemented without interfering with their quasi-judicial freedom.

(2) There shall be a monitoring cell to be constituted by the President of the National Commission to oversee the functioning of the State Commissions from the administrative point of view.

(3) The State Commission shall have administrative control over all the District Commissions within its jurisdiction in all matters referred to in sub-section (1).

(4) The National Commission and the State Commissions shall furnish to the Central Government periodically or as and when required, any information including the pendency of cases in such form and manner as may be prescribed.

(5) The State Commission shall furnish, periodically or as and when required to the State Government any information including pendency of cases in such form and manner as may be prescribed.

### Section 71: Enforcement of orders of District Commission, State Commission and National Commission

Every order made by a District Commission, State Commission or the National Commission shall be enforced by it in the same manner as if it were a decree made by a Court in a suit before it and the provisions of Order XXI of the First Schedule to the Code of Civil Procedure, 1908 shall, as far as may be, applicable, subject to the modification that every reference therein to the decree shall be construed as reference to the order made under this Act.

### Section 72: Penalty for non-compliance of order

(1) Whoever fails to comply with any order made by the District Commission or the State Commission or the National Commission, as the case may be, shall be punishable with imprisonment for a term which shall not be less than one month, but which may extend to three years, or with fine, which shall not be less than twenty-five thousand rupees, but which may extend to one lakh rupees, or with both.

(2) Notwithstanding anything contained in the Code of Criminal Procedure, 1973, the District Commission, the State Commission or the National Commission, as the case may be, shall have the power of a Judicial Magistrate of first class for the trial of offences under sub-section (1), and on conferment of such powers, the District Commission or the State Commission or the National Commission, as the case may be, shall be deemed to be a Judicial Magistrate of first class for the purposes of the Code of Criminal Procedure, 1973.

(3) Save as otherwise provided, the offences under sub-section (1) shall be tried summarily by the District Commission or the State Commission or the National Commission, as the case may be.

### Section 73: Appeal against order passed under Section 72

(1) Notwithstanding anything contained in the Code of Criminal Procedure, 1973, where an order is passed under sub-section (1) of Section 72, an appeal shall lie, both on facts and on law from—

(a) the order made by the District Commission to the State Commission;

(b) the order made by the State Commission to the National Commission; and

(c) the order made by the National Commission to the Supreme Court.

(2) Except as provided in sub-section (1), no appeal shall lie before any court, from any order of a District Commission or a State Commission or the National Commission, as the case may be.

(3) Every appeal under this section shall be preferred within a period of thirty days from the date of order of a District Commission or a State Commission or the National Commission, as the case may be:

Provided that the State Commission or the National Commission or the Supreme Court, as the case may be, may entertain an appeal after the expiry of the said period of thirty days, if it is satisfied that the appellant had sufficient cause for not preferring the appeal within the said period of thirty days.

# Chapter V Mediation

## Section 74: Establishment of consumer mediation cell

(1) The State Government shall establish, by notification, a consumer mediation cell to be attached to each of the District Commissions and the State Commissions of that State.

(2) The Central Government shall establish, by notification, a consumer mediation cell to be attached to the National Commission and each of the regional Benches.

(3) A consumer mediation cell shall consist of such persons as may be prescribed.

(4) Every consumer mediation cell shall maintain—

(a) a list of empanelled mediators;

(b) a list of cases handled by the cell;

(c) record of proceeding; and

(d) any other information as may be specified by regulations.

(5) Every consumer mediation cell shall submit a quarterly report to the District Commission, State Commission or the National Commission to which it is attached, in the manner specified by regulations.

## Section 75: Empanelment of mediators

(1) For the purpose of mediation, the National Commission or the State Commission or the District Commission, as the case may be, shall prepare a panel of the mediators to be maintained by the consumer mediation cell attached to it, on the recommendation of a selection committee consisting of the President and a member of that Commission.

(2) The qualifications and experience required for empanelment as mediator, the procedure for empanelment, the manner of training empanelled mediators, the fee payable to empanelled mediator, the terms and conditions for empanelment, the code of conduct for empanelled mediators, the grounds on which, and the manner in which, empanelled mediators shall be removed or empanelment shall be cancelled and other matters relating thereto, shall be such as may be specified by regulations.

(3) The panel of mediators prepared under sub-section (1) shall be valid for a period of five years, and the empanelled mediators shall be eligible to be considered for re-empanelment for another term, subject to such conditions as may be specified by regulations.

**Section 76: Nomination of mediators from panel**

The District Commission, the State Commission or the National Commission shall, while nominating any person from the panel of mediators referred to in Section 75, consider his suitability for resolving the consumer dispute involved.

**Section 77: Duty of mediator to disclose certain facts**

It shall be the duty of the mediator to disclose—

(a) any personal, professional or financial interest in the outcome of the consumer dispute;

(b) the circumstances which may give rise to a justifiable doubt as to his independence or impartiality; and

(c) such other facts as may be specified by regulations.

**Section 78: Replacement of mediator in certain cases**

Where the District Commission or the State Commission or the National Commission, as the case may be, is satisfied, on the information furnished by the mediator or on the information received from any other person including parties to the complaint and after hearing the mediator, it shall replace such mediator by another mediator.

**Section 79: Procedure for mediation**

(1) The mediation shall be held in the consumer mediation cell attached to the District Commission, the State Commission or the National Commission, as the case may be.

(2) Where a consumer dispute is referred for mediation by the District Commission or the State Commission or the National Commission, as the case may be, the mediator nominated by such Commission shall have regard to the rights and obligations of the parties, the usages of trade, if any, the circumstances giving rise to the consumer dispute and such other relevant factors, as he may deem necessary and shall be guided by the principles of natural justice while carrying out mediation.

(3) The mediator so nominated shall conduct mediation within such time and in such manner as may be specified by regulations.

**Section 80: Settlement through mediation**

(1) Pursuant to mediation, if an agreement is reached between the parties with respect to all of the issues involved in the consumer dispute or with respect to only some of the issues, the terms of such agreement shall be reduced to

writing accordingly and signed by the parties to such dispute or their authorised representatives.

(2) The mediator shall prepare a settlement report of the settlement and forward the signed agreement along with such report to the concerned Commission.

(3) Where no agreement is reached between the parties within the specified time or the mediator is of the opinion that settlement is not possible, he shall prepare his report accordingly and submit the same to the concerned Commission.

### Section 81: Recording settlement and passing of order

(1) The District Commission or the State Commission or the National Commission, as the case may be, shall, within seven days of the receipt of the settlement report, pass suitable order recording such settlement of consumer dispute and dispose of the matter accordingly.

(2) Where the consumer dispute is settled only in part, the District Commission or the State Commission or the National Commission, as the case may be, shall record settlement of the issues which have been so settled and continue to hear other issues involved in such consumer dispute.

(3) Where the consumer dispute could not be settled by mediation, the District Commission or the State Commission or the National Commission, as the case may be, shall continue to hear all the issues involved in such consumer dispute.

## Chapter VI Product Liability

### Section 82: Application of Chapter

This Chapter shall apply to every claim for compensation under a product liability action by a complainant for any harm caused by a defective product manufactured by a product manufacturer or serviced by a product service provider or sold by a product seller.

### Section 83: Product liability action

A product liability action may be brought by a complainant against a product manufacturer or a product service provider or a product seller, as the case may be, for any harm caused to him on account of a defective product.

### Section 84: Liability of product manufacturer

(1) A product manufacturer shall be liable in a product liability action, if—

(a) the product contains a manufacturing defect; or

(b) the product is defective in design; or

(c) there is a deviation from manufacturing specifications; or

(d) the product does not conform to the express warranty; or

(e) the product fails to contain adequate instructions of correct usage to prevent any harm or any warning regarding improper or incorrect usage.

(2) A product manufacturer shall be liable in a product liability action even if he proves that he was not negligent or fraudulent in making the express warranty of a product.

**Section 85: Liability of product service provider**

A product service provider shall be liable in a product liability action, if—

(a) the service provided by him was faulty or imperfect or deficient or inadequate in quality, nature or manner of performance which is required to be provided by or under any law for the time being in force, or pursuant to any contract or otherwise; or

(b) there was an act of omission or commission or negligence or conscious withholding any information which caused harm; or

(c) the service provider did not issue adequate instructions or warnings to prevent any harm; or

(d) the service did not conform to express warranty or the terms and conditions of the contract.

**Section 86: Liability of product sellers**

A product seller who is not a product manufacturer shall be liable in a product liability action, if—

(a) he has exercised substantial control over the designing, testing, manufacturing, packaging or labelling of a product that caused harm; or

(b) he has altered or modified the product and such alteration or modification was the substantial factor in causing the harm; or

(c) he has made an express warranty of a product independent of any express warranty made by a manufacturer and such product failed to conform to the express warranty made by the product seller which caused the harm; or

(d) the product has been sold by him and the identity of product manufacturer of such product is not known, or if known, the service of notice or process or warrant cannot be effected on him or he is not subject to the law which is in force in India or the order, if any, passed or to be passed cannot be enforced against him; or

(e) he failed to exercise reasonable care in assembling, inspecting or maintaining such product or he did not pass on the warnings or instructions of the product manufacturer regarding the dangers involved or proper usage of the product while selling such product and such failure was the proximate cause of the harm.

**Section 87: Exceptions to product liability action**

(1) A product liability action cannot be brought against the product seller if, at the time of harm, the product was misused, altered, or modified.

(2) In any product liability action based on the failure to provide adequate warnings or instructions, the product manufacturer shall not be liable, if—

(a) the product was purchased by an employer for use at the workplace and the product manufacturer had provided warnings or instructions to such employer;

(b) the product was sold as a component or material to be used in another product and necessary warnings or instructions were given by the product manufacturer to the purchaser of such component or material, but the harm was caused to the complainant by use of the end product in which such component or material was used;

(c) the product was one which was legally meant to be used or dispensed only by or under the supervision of an expert or a class of experts and the product manufacturer had employed reasonable means to give the warnings or instructions for usage of such product to such expert or class of experts; or

(d) the complainant, while using such product, was under the influence of alcohol or any prescription drug which had not been prescribed by a medical practitioner.

(3) A product manufacturer shall not be liable for failure to instruct or warn about a danger which is obvious or commonly known to the user or consumer of such product or which, such user or consumer, ought to have known, taking into account the characteristics of such product.

***Product Liability***

Before the 2019 CPA came into force, product liability claims were mostly based on the principle of negligence and strict liability under the Law of Torts and the principle of warranty under the Law of Contract to claim damages for product liabilities.

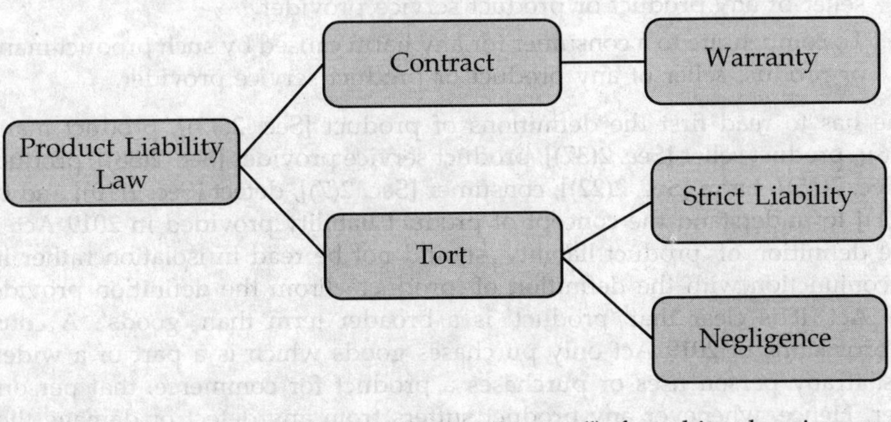


Earlier, the notion of *Caveat Emptor* ("Buyer Beware"), found its place in common law. As a result, the buyer of the product had to protect himself against defects in the goods. Thus, no remedy could be claimed against the seller of defective goods unless there was an express warranty or condition to that effect in the contract. However, after the commencement of

CPA, 2019, there is a statutory liability imposed on product manufacturers and product sellers for any defective product. Moreover, such liability is strict in nature as it can hold them liable just based on the defective product without the consumer having to prove actual negligence. It derives its base from the concept of *Caveat Venditor* which means that the "Seller must Beware" thereby making the seller liable for any harm caused by the product to the consumer.

Chapter VI of the 2019 Act entitled "Product Liability" introduced a new system of liability for injury caused by a defective product into Indian Consumer Law. This is a significant legislative change in the area of consumer protection in general and product liability in particular. This law provides a guarantee to protect the interest of consumers who were harmed by a defective product. This appears to be a step forward from the contract law principle of "Let the Buyer Beware" (*caveat emptor*) to "Let the Seller Beware" (*caveat venditor*).

> This Chapter runs from Secs. 82 to 87. In order to understand the newly codified concept of product liability and its consequences thereof, one has to read the provisions of this Act which are having direct and/or indirect relationship with product liability.

### *What is Product Liability?*

Sec. 2(34) "Product liability" means the responsibility of a product manufacturer or product seller, of any product or service, to compensate for any harm caused to a consumer by such defective product manufactured or sold or by deficiency in services relating thereto.

The definition of product liability may be looked from two aspects:

1. Who are having legal responsibility to provide no defect product and no deficiency services to the consumer. They are product manufacturer or product seller of any product or product service provider.
2. To compensate to a consumer for any harm caused by such product manufacturer or product seller of any product or product service provider.

One has to read first the definitions of product [Sec. 2(33)], product manufacturer [Sec. 2(36)], product seller [Sec. 2(37)], product service provider [Sec. 2(38)], product liability action [Sec. 2(35)], harm [Sec. 2(22)], consumer [Sec. 2(7)], defect [Sec. 2(10)] and deficiency [Sec. 2(11)] to understand the concept of product liability provided in 2019 Act.

The definition of 'product liability' should not be read in isolation rather it shall be read in conjunction with the definition of 'product'. From the definition provided under the 2019 Act, it is clear that 'product' is a broader term than 'goods'. A consumer as per the provisions of 2019 Act only purchases goods which is a part of a wider term of products. If any person uses or purchases a product for commerce, that person is not a consumer. Hence, whenever any product suffers from any defect or damage the product manufacturer or seller can be held liable by the consumer. Whereas "product liability" means the responsibility of a product manufacturer or product seller, of any product or service, to compensate for any harm caused to a consumer by such defective product manufactured or sold or by deficiency in services relating thereto. Thus, the scope of the doctrine of 'product liability', under the 2019 Act is limited to only consumer.

### *Harm*

In order to bring product liability action against the product manufacturer or product seller or product service provider, the consumer needs to prove that there is a harm caused to him. Hence, it is necessary to understand the meaning of 'harm' provided under the Act. Sec. 2(22) defines harm as follows:

"Harm", in relation to a product liability, includes—

(i) damage to any property, other than the product itself;
(ii) personal injury, illness, or death;
(iii) mental agony or emotional distress attendant to personal injury or illness or damage to property; or
(iv) any loss of consortium or services or other loss resulting from a harm referred to in sub-clause (i) or sub-clause (ii) or sub-clause (iii),

but shall not include any harm caused to a product itself or any damage to the property on account of breach of warranty conditions or any commercial or economic loss, including any direct, incidental, or consequential loss relating thereto;

### *Product liability action*

Sec. 2(35) defines product liability action as follows:

> Product liability action means a complaint filed by a person before a District Commission or State Commission or National Commission, as the case may be, for claiming compensation for the harm caused to him.

Further, Sec. 83 of the 2019 Act provides that;

> "a product liability action may be brought by a complainant against a product manufacturer or a product service provider or a product seller, as the case may be, for any harm caused to him on account of a defective product."

A careful observation of the provision provides that there shall be three essential ingredients to satisfy a product liability action against the respondent, i.e.,

(i) harm caused to the complainant;
(ii) the harm caused on account of a defective product; and
(iii) product manufacturer or product service provider of product seller should be held responsible for the defect in the product.

After reading Sec. 2(35) and Sec. 83 of the Act, it can be observed that the product liability action may be instituted against a product manufacturer or a product service provider or a product seller who may be jointly or severally liable for any harm caused to the consumer due to the defective product.

### *Exceptions to product liability action*

Sec. 87 of the 2019 Act specifically provides some exceptions under which a product liability action cannot be brought against product seller and product manufacturer and they are as follows:

1. A product liability action cannot be brought against the product seller if, at the time of harm, the product was misused, altered, or modified.
2. The product manufacturer shall not be liable on the failure to provide adequate warnings or instructions to the end used if the product was purchased by an employer for use at the workplace and the product manufacturer had provided warnings or instructions to such employer but not to the end user.
3. The product manufacturer shall not be liable on the failure to provide adequate warnings or instructions if the product was sold as a component or material to be used in another product and necessary warnings or instructions were given by the product manufacturer to the purchaser of such component or material, but the harm was caused to the complainant by use of the end product in which such component or material was used.
4. The product manufacturer shall not be liable on the failure to provide adequate warnings or instructions if the product was one which was legally meant to be used or dispensed only by or under the supervision of an expert or a class of experts and the product manufacturer had employed reasonable means to give the warnings or instructions for usage of such product to such expert or class of experts.
5. The product manufacturer shall not be liable on the failure to provide adequate warnings or instructions if the complainant, while using such product, was under the influence of alcohol or any prescription drug which had not been prescribed by a medical practitioner.
6. A product manufacturer shall not be liable for failure to instruct or warn about a danger which is obvious or commonly known to the user or consumer of such product or which, such user or consumer, ought to have known, taking into account the characteristics of such product.

## Chapter VII Offences and Penalties

### Section 88: Penalty for non-compliance of direction of Central Authority

Whoever fails to comply with any direction of the Central Authority under Sections 20 and 21, shall be punished with imprisonment for a term which may extend to six months or with fine which may extend to twenty lakh rupees, or with both.

### Section 89: Punishment for false or misleading advertisement

Any manufacturer or service provider who causes a false or misleading advertisement to be made which is prejudicial to the interest of consumers shall be punished with imprisonment for a term which may extend to two years and with fine which may extend to ten lakh rupees; and for every subsequent offence, be punished with imprisonment for a term which may extend to five years and with fine which may extend to fifty lakh rupees.

**Section 90: Punishment for manufacturing for sale or storing, selling or distributing or importing products containing adulterant**

(1) Whoever, by himself or by any other person on his behalf, manufactures for sale or stores or sells or distributes or imports any product containing an adulterant shall be punished, if such act—

(a) does not result in any injury to the consumer, with imprisonment for a term which may extend to six months and with fine which may extend to one lakh rupees;

(b) causing injury not amounting to grievous hurt to the consumer, with imprisonment for a term which may extend to one year and with fine which may extend to three lakh rupees;

(c) causing injury resulting in grievous hurt to the consumer, with imprisonment for a term which may extend to seven years and with fine which may extend to five lakh rupees; and

(d) results in the death of a consumer, with imprisonment for a term which shall not be less than seven years, but which may extend to imprisonment for life and with fine which shall not be less than ten lakh rupees.

(2) The offences under clauses (c) and (d) of sub-section (1) shall be cognizable and non-bailable.

(3) Notwithstanding the punishment under sub-section (1), the court may, in case of first conviction, suspend any licence issued to the person referred to in that sub-section, under any law for the time being in force, for a period up to two years, and in case of second or subsequent conviction, cancel the licence.

*Explanation:* For the purposes of this section,—

(a) "adulterant" means any material including extraneous matter which is employed or used for making a product unsafe;

(b) "grievous hurt" shall have the same meaning as assigned to it in Section 320 of the Indian Penal Code.

**Section 91: Punishment for manufacturing for sale or for storing or selling or distributing or importing spurious goods**

(1) Whoever, by himself or by any other person on his behalf, manufactures for sale or stores or sells or distributes or imports any spurious goods shall be punished, if such act—

(a) causing injury not amounting to grievous hurt to the consumer, with imprisonment for a term which may extend to one year and with fine which may extend to three lakh rupees;

(b) causing injury resulting in grievous hurt to the consumer, with imprisonment for a term which may extend to seven years and with fine which may extend to five lakh rupees;

(c) results in the death of a consumer, with imprisonment for a term which shall not be less than seven years but may extend to imprisonment for life and with fine which shall not be less than ten lakh rupees.

(2) The offences under clauses (b) and (c) of sub-section (1) shall be cognizable and non-bailable.

(3) Notwithstanding the punishment under sub-section (1), the court may, in case of first conviction, suspend any licence issued to the person referred to in that sub-section, under any law for the time being in force, for a period up to two years, and in case of second or subsequent conviction, cancel the licence.

**Section 92: Cognizance of offence by court**

No cognizance shall be taken by a competent court of any offence under Sections 88 and 89 except on a complaint filed by the Central Authority or any officer authorised by it in this behalf.

**Section 93: Vexatious search**

The Director General or any other officer, exercising powers under Section 22, who knows that there are no reasonable grounds for so doing, and yet—

(a) searches, or causes to be searched any premises; or

(b) seizes any record, register or other document or article,

shall, for every such offence, be punished with imprisonment for a term which may extend to one year, or with fine which may extend to ten thousand rupees or with both.

## Chapter VIII Miscellaneous

**Section 94: Measures to prevent unfair trade practices in e-commerce, direct selling, etc.**

For the purposes of preventing unfair trade practices in e-commerce, direct selling and also to protect the interest and rights of consumers, the Central Government may take such measures in the manner as may be prescribed.

**Section 95: Presidents, members, Chief Commissioner, Commissioner, and certain officers to be public servants**

The Presidents and members of the District Commission, the State Commission and the National Commission, and officers and other employees thereof, the Chief Commissioner and the Commissioner of the Central Authority, the Director General, the Additional Director General, the Director, the Joint Director, the Deputy Director and the Assistant Director and all other officers and employees of the Central Authority and other persons performing any duty under this Act, while acting or purporting to act in pursuance of any of the provisions of this Act, shall be deemed to be public servants within the meaning of Section 21 of the Indian Penal Code.

**Section 96: Compounding of offences**

(1) Any offence punishable under Sections 88 and 89, may, either before or after the institution of the prosecution, be compounded, on payment of such amount as may be prescribed:

Provided that no compounding of such offence shall be made without the leave of the court before which a complaint has been filed under Section 92:

Provided further that such sum shall not, in any case, exceed the maximum amount of the fine, which may be imposed under this Act for the offence so compounded.

(2) The Central Authority or any officer as may be specially authorised by him in this behalf, may compound offences under sub-section (1).

(3) Nothing in sub-section (1) shall apply to person who commits the same or similar offence, within a period of three years from the date on which the first offence, committed by him, was compounded.

*Explanation:* For the purposes of this sub-section, any second or subsequent offence committed after the expiry of a period of three years from the date on which the offence was previously compounded, shall be deemed to be a first offence.

(4) Where an offence has been compounded under sub-section (1), no proceeding or further proceeding, as the case may be, shall be taken against the offender in respect of the offence so compounded.

(5) The acceptance of the sum of money for compounding an offence in accordance with sub-section (1) by the Central Authority or an officer of the Central Authority empowered in this behalf shall be deemed to amount to an acquittal within the meaning of the Code of Criminal Procedure, 1973.

**Section 97: Manner of crediting penalty**

The penalty collected under Section 21 and the amount collected under Section 96 shall be credited to such fund as may be prescribed.

**Section 98: Protection of action taken in good faith**

No suit, prosecution or other legal proceeding shall lie against the Presidents and members of the District Commission, the State Commission and the National Commission, the Chief Commissioner, the Commissioner, any officer or employee and other person performing any duty under this Act, for any act which is in good faith done or intended to be done in pursuance of this Act or under any rule or order made thereunder.

**Section 99: Power to give directions by Central Government**

(1) Without prejudice to the foregoing provisions of this Act, the Central Authority, shall, in exercise of its powers or the performance of its functions under this Act,

be bound by such directions on questions of policy, as the Central Government may give in writing to it from time to time:

Provided that the Central Authority shall, as far as practicable, be given an opportunity to express its views before any direction is given under this sub-section.

(2) The decision of the Central Government whether a question is one of policy or not shall be final.

**Section 100: Act not in derogation of any other law**

The provisions of this Act shall be in addition to and not in derogation of the provisions of any other law for the time being in force.

**Section 101: Power of Central Government to make rules**

(1) The Central Government may, by notification, make rules for carrying out any of the provisions contained in this Act.

(2) Without prejudice to the generality of the foregoing power, such rules may provide for,—

(a) the other class or classes of persons including public utility entities under clause (19) of Section 2;

(b) the contest, lottery, game of chance or skill which are to be exempted under item (b) of sub-clause (iii) of clause (47) of Section 2;

(c) the manner of issuing bill or cash memo or receipt for goods sold or services rendered under sub-clause (vii) of clause (47) of Section 2;

(d) the number of other official or non-official members of the Central Council under clause (b) of sub-section (2) of Section 3;

(e) the time and place of meeting of Central Council and the procedure for the transaction of its business under sub-section (2) of Section 4;

(f) the number of Commissioners in the Central Authority under sub-section (2) of Section 10;

(g) the qualifications for appointment, method of recruitment, procedure of appointment, term of office, salaries and allowances, resignation, removal and other terms and conditions of service of the Chief Commissioner and other Commissioners of the Central Authority under Section 11;

(h) the salaries and allowances payable to, and the other terms and conditions of service of, the officers and other employees of the Central Authority under sub-section (2) of Section 13;

(i) the qualifications for appointment of Director General, Additional Director General, Director, Joint Director, Deputy Director and Assistant Director and the manner of appointment under sub-section (2) of Section 15;

(j) the manner of taking copies or extracts of document, record or article seized or produced before returning to the person under sub-section (3) of Section 22;

(k) the officer and the manner of disposing of articles which are subject to speedy or natural decay under sub-section (4) of Section 22;

(l) the form and manner for preparing annual statement of accounts by the Central Authority in consultation with the Comptroller and Auditor-General of India under sub-section (1) of Section 26;

(m) the form in which, and the time within which, an annual report, other reports and returns may be prepared by the Central Authority under sub-section (1) of Section 27;

(n) the qualifications for appointment, method of recruitment, procedure for appointment, term of office, resignation and removal of President and members of the District Commission under Section 29;

(o) the other value of goods and services in respect of which the District Commission shall have jurisdiction to entertain complaints under proviso to sub-section (1) of Section 34;

(p) the manner of electronically filing complaint under the proviso to sub-section (1) of Section 35;

(q) the fee, electronic form and the manner of payment of fee for filing complaint under sub-section (2) of Section 35;

(r) the cases which may not be referred for settlement by mediation under sub-section (1) of Section 37;

(s) the manner of authentication of goods sampled in case of the National Commission under clause (c) of sub-section (2) of Section 38;

(t) any other matter which may be prescribed under clause (f) of sub-section (9) of Section 38;

(u) the fund where the amount obtained may be credited and the manner of utilisation of such amount under sub-section (2) of Section 39;

(v) the form and the manner in which appeal may be preferred to the State Commission under Section 41;

(w) the qualifications for appointment, method of recruitment, procedure for appointment, term of office, resignation and removal of the President and members of the State Commission under Section 43;

(x) the other value of goods and services in respect of which the State Commission shall have jurisdiction under the proviso to sub-clause (i) of clause (a) of sub-section (1) of Section 47;

(y) the form and manner of filing appeal to the National Commission, and the manner of depositing fifty per cent of the amount before filing appeal, under sub-section (1) of Section 51;

(z) the number of members of the National Commission under clause (b) of Section 54;

(za) the qualifications, appointment, term of office, salaries and allowances, resignation, removal and other terms and conditions of service of the President and members of the National Commission under sub-section (1) of Section 55;

(zb) the salaries and allowances payable to, and other terms and conditions of service of, the officers and other employees of the National Commission under sub-section (3) of Section 57;

(zc) the other value of goods and services in respect of which the National Commission shall have jurisdiction under the proviso to sub-clause (i) of clause (a) of sub-section (1) of Section 58;

(zd) the manner of depositing fifty per cent of the amount under the second proviso to Section 67;

(ze) the form in which the National Commission and the State Commission shall furnish information to the Central Government under sub-section (4) of Section 70;

(zf) the persons in the consumer mediation cell under sub-section (3) of Section 74;

(zg) the measures to be taken by the Central Government to prevent unfair trade practices in e-commerce, direct selling under Section 94;

(zh) the amount for compounding offences under sub-section (1) of Section 96;

(zi) the fund to which the penalty and amount collected shall be credited under Section 97; and

(zj) any other matter which is to be, or may be, prescribed, or in respect of which provisions are to be, or may be, made by rules.

**Section 102: Power of State Government to make rules**

(1) The State Governments may, by notification, make rules for carrying out the provisions of this Act:

Provided that the Central Government may, frame model rules in respect of all or any of the matters with respect to which the State Government may make rules under this section, and where any such model rules have been framed in respect of any such matter, they shall apply to the State until the rules in respect of that matter is made by the State Government and while making any such rules, so far as is practicable, they shall conform to such model rules.

(2) In particular, and without prejudice to the generality of the foregoing power, such rules may provide for all or any of the following matters, namely:—

(a) the other class or classes of persons including public utility entities under clause (19) of Section 2;

(b) the contest, lottery, game of chance or skill which are to be exempted under item (b) of sub-clause (iii) of clause (47) of Section 2;

(c) the number of other official or non-official members of the State Council under clause (b) of sub-section (2) of Section 6;

(d) the time and place of meeting of the State Council and the procedure for the transaction of its business under sub-section (4) of Section 6;

(e) the number of other official and non-official members of District Council under clause (b) of sub-section (2) of Section 8;

(f) the time and place of meeting of the District Council and procedure for the transaction of its business under sub-section (4) of Section 8;

(g) the number of members of the District Commission under clause (b) of sub-section (2) of Section 28;

(h) the salaries and allowances payable to, and other terms and conditions of service of, the President and members of the District Commission under Section 30;

(i) the salaries and allowances payable to, and other terms and conditions of service of, the officers and other employees of the District Commission under sub-section (3) of Section 33;

(j) the manner of authentication of goods sampled by the State Commission and the District Commission under clause (c) of sub-section (2) of Section 38;

(k) the manner of depositing fifty per cent of the amount before filing appeal under second proviso to Section 41;

(l) the number of members of the State Commission under sub-section (3) of Section 42;

(m) the salaries and allowances payable to, and other terms and conditions of service of, the President and members of the State Commission under Section 44;

(n) the salaries and allowances payable to, and other terms and conditions of service of, the officers and other employees of the State Commission under sub-section (3) of Section 46;

(o) the form in which the State Commission shall furnish information to the State Government under sub-section (5) of Section 70;

(p) the persons in the consumer mediation cell under sub-section (3) of Section 74;

(q) any other matter which is to be, or may be prescribed, or in respect of which provisions are to be, or may be, made by rules.

**Section 103: Power of National Commission to make regulations**

(1) The National Commission may, with the previous approval of the Central Government, by notification, make regulations not inconsistent with this Act to provide for all matters for which provision is necessary or expedient for the purpose of giving effect to the provisions of this Act.

(2) In particular, and without prejudice to the generality of the foregoing power, such regulations may make provisions for—

(a) the costs for adjournment to be imposed by the District Commission under the second proviso to sub-section (7) of Section 38;

(b) the costs for adjournment to be imposed by the State Commission or the National Commission, as the case may be, under the second proviso to Section 52;

(c) the maintenance of any other information by the consumer mediation cell under sub-section (4) of Section 74;

(d) the manner of submission of quarterly report by consumer mediation cell to the District Commission, the State Commission or the National Commission under sub-section (5) of Section 74;

(e) the qualifications and experience required for empanelment as mediator, the procedure for empanelment, the manner of training empanelled mediators, the fee payable to empanelled mediator, the terms and conditions for empanelment, the code of conduct for empanelled mediators, the grounds on which, and the manner in which, empanelled mediators shall be removed or empanelment shall be cancelled and the other matters relating thereto under sub-section (2) of Section 75;

(f) the conditions for re-empanelment of mediators for another term under sub-section (3) of Section 75;

(g) the other facts to be disclosed by mediators under clause (c) of Section 77;

(h) the time within which, and the manner in which, mediation may be conducted under sub-section (3) of Section 79; and

(i) such other matter for which provision is to be, or may be, made by regulation.

## Section 104: Power of Central Authority to make regulations

(1) The Central Authority may, with the previous approval of the Central Government, by notification, make regulations not inconsistent with this Act, for the purpose of giving effect to the provisions of this Act.

(2) In particular, and without prejudice to the generality of the foregoing power, such regulations may provide for all or any of the following matters, namely:—

(a) the procedure for engaging experts and professionals and the number of such experts and professionals under sub-section (3) of Section 13;

(b) the procedure for transaction of business and the allocation of business of the Chief Commissioner and Commissioner under sub-section (1) of Section 14;

(c) the form, manner and time within which, inquiries or investigation made by the Director-General shall be submitted to the Central Authority under sub-section (5) of Section 15; and

(d) such other matter for which provision is to be, or may be, made by regulation.

## Section 105: Rules and regulations to be laid before each House of Parliament

(1) Every rule and every regulation made under this Act shall be laid, as soon as may be after it is made, before each House of Parliament, while it is in session, for a total period of thirty days which may be comprised in one session or in two or more successive sessions, and if, before the expiry of the session immediately following the session or the successive sessions aforesaid, both Houses agree in making any modification in the rule or regulation or both Houses agree that the rule or regulation shall thereafter have effect only in such modified form or be of no effect, as the case may be; so, however, that any such modification or annulment shall be without prejudice to the validity of anything previously done under that rule or regulation.

(2) Every rule made by a State Government under this Act shall be laid as soon as may be after it is made, before the State Legislature.

## Section 106: Power to remove difficulties

If any difficulty arises in giving effect to the provisions of this Act, the Central Government may, by order in the Official Gazette, make such provisions not inconsistent with the provisions of this Act as appear to it to be necessary or expedient for removing the difficulty:

Provided that no such order shall be made after the expiry of a period of two years from the commencement of this Act.

## Section 107: Repeal and savings

(1) The Consumer Protection Act, 1986, is hereby repealed.

(2) Notwithstanding such repeal, anything done or any action taken or purported to have been done or taken under the Act hereby repealed shall, insofar as it is not inconsistent with the provisions of this Act, be deemed to have been done or taken under the corresponding provisions of this Act.

(3) The mention of particular matters in sub-section (2) shall not be held to prejudice or affect the general application of Section 6 of the General Clauses Act, 1897 with regard to the effect of repeal.

# 4

# The Companies Act, 2013

## Chapter I Meaning and Features

### INTRODUCTION

The word 'company' is an amalgamation of two Latin words *'Com'* and *'Pains'*. The word *'Com'* means "with or together" and *'Pains'* means *"bread"*. Originally, it was referred to a group of persons who took their meals together. A company is nothing but a group of persons who have come together or who have contributed money for some common purpose either to earn profit or not.

In India, the Companies Act, 2013, is one of the most important legislations that empower the Central Government to regulate the formation, financing, functioning and winding-up of companies. The Act contains the mechanism for incorporation, issuance of prospectus, holding meetings, declaring dividends, preventing *mismanagement*, appointment of directors and powers, duties and liabilities of directors and other related aspects.

### DEFINITION OF A COMPANY

Company is a voluntary association of persons formed for the purpose of doing business having a distinct name and limited liability. It is a juristic person having a separate legal entity distinct from the members who constitute it, capable of rights and duties of its own and endowed with the potential of perpetual succession. Sec. 2(20) of the Companies Act, 2013, defines the company as "company" means a company incorporated under this Act or under any previous company law. Considering the definition of company provided under the Act, it can be said that Parliament is unable to provide the real meaning of the company rather provided the meaning of company in a circular form of definition. Therefore, it is suggested that to know the real meaning of 'company' we have to refer the definition or meaning provided by the House of Lords in a famous case *Salomon* v. *Salomon & Co.*[1] The House of Lords observed that a company is an artificial person created by law and having independent corporate existence.

In order to provide an appropriate definition of company many attempts were made by various authorities, some of them are as follows:—

Lord Justice Lindley—"A Company is an association of many persons who contribute money or monies worth to common stock and employed in some trade or business and who share the profit and loss arising there from it. The common stock so contributed is denoted in money and is the capital of the company. The persons who contribute to it or to whom it pertains are members. The proportion of capital to which each member is entitled is his share. The shares are always transferable although the right to transfer is often more or less restricted." Prof. Haney—"A company is an artificial person created by law, having separate entity, with a perpetual succession and common seal." Justice James—"Company means an association of person united for a common object"

## CHARACTERISTICS

A company registered under the Companies Act has the following characteristics:

1. **Separate Legal Entity:** Once the company is registered under the Companies Act, a company becomes a separate legal entity as compared to its members. The company is different and distinct from its members who have created the company. The company is identified by its own name. Its assets and liabilities are separate and distinct from those of its members. The company can buy and hold the property in its own name. The company is the owner of the company and all employees are appointed by the company and therefore it is said that the company is the employer. The company can enter into a contract and can sue and be sued.
2. **Incorporated Body:** A company must be incorporated or registered under the Companies Act. In the eye of law, the company is born once the certificate of incorporation is issued in the name of the company. In the case of a public company, the minimum number of members required is 7 and it is 2 in the case of a private company. But after the insertion of the concept of One Person Company under Sec. 2(62) of the Companies Act, 2013, now a single person can form a company.
3. **Artificial Legal Person:** A company is created with the sanction of law and is not itself a human being, it is therefore, called artificial legal person. Like a human being, the company enjoys the benefit provided under Article 14 of the Indian Constitution. Article 14 provides that the State shall not deny to any person equality before the law or the equal protection of the law within the territory of India which is popularly known as equality before law.

[1] (1897) AC 22.

4. **Perpetual Succession:** A company does not die or cease to exist unless it is specifically wound up or the object for which it was formed has been completed. Membership of a company may keep on changing from time to time but that does not affect life of the company. Death or insolvency of member does not affect the existence of the company. Therefore, it is rightly said that "men may come and men may go but I go for ever".
5. **Limited Liability:** The liability of the members of the company is limited to the extent of their share capital or contribution or promise (Guarantee) made to the company. There may be a situation where the financial institution is unable to recover the money from the company's assets because the liability of the company may be more than the assets of the company and in this situation also, the financial institution is having no right to recover the money from the members of the company as their liabilities are limited. This is the beauty of Corporate Law. On the other hand, partners of a partnership firm have unlimited liability, i.e., if the assets of the firm are not adequate to pay the liabilities of the firm, the creditors can force the partners to make good the deficit from their personal assets.
6. **Common Seal:** A company is an artificial person and does not have a physical presence. Therefore, it acts through its Board of Directors for carrying out its activities and entering into various agreements. Such contracts must be under the seal of the company. The common seal is the official signature of the company. The name of the company must be engraved on the common seal. Any document not bearing the seal of the company may not be accepted as authentic and may not have any legal force.
7. **Separate Property:** A company is a distinct legal entity. The company's property is its own. A member cannot claim to be owner of the company's property during the existence of the company.
8. **Capacity to Sue and being Sued:** Like a living human being a company can sue or be sued in its own name.
9. **Transferability of Shares:** Shares in a company are freely transferable, subject to certain conditions, such that no shareholder is permanently or necessarily wedded to a company. When a member transfers his shares to another person, the transferee steps into the shoes of the transferor and acquires all the rights of the transferor in respect of those shares.

## DISTINCTION BETWEEN COMPANY AND PARTNERSHIP

1. A partnership firm does not have a separate legal entity like a company. A company has a separate legal entity as soon as it is incorporated under law.
2. The liability of the partners is unlimited in the partnership firm. However, the liability of shareholders of a limited company is limited to the extent of unpaid share or to the tune of the unpaid amount guaranteed by the shareholder.
3. The property of the firm belongs to the partners and they are collectively entitled to it. In the case of a company, the property belongs to the company and not to its members.

4. A partner cannot transfer his shares in the partnership firm without the consent of all other partners. In the case of a company, shares may be transferred without the permission of other members, in absence of provision to the contrary in articles of association of the company.
5. The membership of a partnership must not exceed the limit of 50 members. A public company may have as many members as it desires subject to a minimum of 7 members. A private company cannot have more than 200 members.
6. There must be at least 2 members in order to form a partnership firm. The minimum number of members necessary for a public limited company is seven and two for a private limited company, except in case of one person Company.
7. In case of a partnership, 100% consensus is required for any decision. In case of a company, decision of the majority prevails.
8. On the death of any partner, the partnership is dissolved unless there is provision to the contrary. On the death of the shareholder the company's existence does not get affected.

## IS COMPANY A CITIZEN?

A company is a legal person but not a citizen either under the Constitution of India or under the Citizenship Act. In *State Trading Corporation of India Ltd.* v. *Commercial Tax Officer*,[2] the Supreme Court held that the State Trading Corporation, a company registered under the Indian Companies Act, 1956, is not a citizen within the meaning of Article 19 of the Constitution and cannot ask for the enforcement of fundamental rights granted to citizens under the said Article. The provisions of Part III of the Constitution makes it clear that the makers of the Constitution deliberately and advisedly made a clear distinction between fundamental rights available to 'any person' and those guaranteed to 'all citizens'. In other words, all citizens are persons but all persons are not citizens under the Constitution. Corporations may have nationality in accordance with the country of their incorporation, but that does not necessarily confer citizenship on them. Part II of the Constitution, when it deals with citizenship, that refers to natural persons only. This is further made absolutely clear by the Citizenship Act which deals with citizenship after the Constitution came into force and confines it only to natural persons. Part II & Part III of the Constitution are to be considered to know who should be the citizen of the country and both the parts suggest that a natural Person would be only a citizen of India. The fact that corporations may be nationals of the country for the purposes of international law will not make them citizens of this country for the purposes of municipal law or the Constitution. The word "citizen" used in Article 19 of the Constitution is not used in a different sense from that in which it is used in Part II of the Constitution. The State Trading Corporation cannot be regarded either by itself or by taking it as the aggregate of citizens, as a citizen for the purpose of enforcing rights under

[2] AIR 1963 SC 1811.

Article 19 of the Constitution. The nationality of a corporation is a different concept not to be confused with citizenship of natural persons. The State Trading Corporation is really a department of Government behind the corporate veil and it is not possible to pierce the veil of incorporation in India to determine the citizenship of the members and then to give the corporation the benefit of Article 19 of the Constitution by declaring the company as a citizen.

## LIFTING OF CORPORATE VEIL (LCV)

Once the company is registered under the Companies Act, a certificate of incorporation is issued and thereby the company acquires a special status and that may be an Independent Corporate Existence (ICE). The meaning of ICE is that the company is different to that of its members including promoters and directors. The principle of ICE was well discussing in 1897 in *Salomon* v. *Salomon & Company*.[3] The facts of the case are as follows:

Aron Salomon was a successful leather merchant who specialized in manufacturing leather boots. For many years he ran his business as a sole proprietor. By 1892, his sons had become interested in taking part in business. Salomon decided to incorporate his business as a Limited Liability Company, Salomon & Co. Ltd. At the time the legal requirement for incorporation was that at least seven persons subscribe as members of a company, i.e., as shareholders. The shareholders were Mr. Salomon, his wife, daughter and four sons. Two of his sons became directors; Mr. Salomon himself was managing director. Mr. Salomon owned 20,001 of the company's 20,007 shares—the remaining six were shared individually between the other six shareholders. Mr. Salomon sold his business to the new corporation for almost £39,000, of which £10,000 was a debt to him. He was thus simultaneously the company's principal shareholder and its principal creditor. When the company went into liquidation, the liquidator argued that the debentures used by Mr. Salomon as security for the debt were invalid, on the grounds of fraud. The judge, Vaughan Williams J. accepted this argument, ruling that since Mr. Salomon had created the company solely to transfer his business to it, the company was in reality his agent and he as principal was liable for debts to unsecured creditors. In appeal the Court of Appeal also ruled against Mr. Salomon and observed that Mr. Salomon incorporated a Limited Company only with a malafide motive and in fact the company was having no independent existence being it was controlled absolutely by Mr. Salomon.

The House of Lords unanimously overturned this decision, rejecting the arguments from agency and fraud. They held that once the company is registered it acquires a special status of independent corporate existence (ICE) which is distinct to that of its members. The Court is having no power to see who are controller of the company and who receives the profit or benefit of the company. Further the Court held that Mr. Salomon, who is a secured debenture-holder, should acquire the property to the extent of his interest and after realisation his dues if something would be left out, that may be shared among the unsecured debentures.

[3] (1897) AC 22.

## LIFTING THE CORPORATE VEIL IN INDIA (LIC V. ESCORTS)

The most important case, *LIC* v. *Escorts*[4] where the Supreme Court of India dealt with the issue of an independent legal personality and the removal of the veil. The case concerned a non-resident portfolio investment scheme that existed under the former Foreign Exchange Regulation Act, 1973 (FERA). The scheme allowed non-resident companies that were owned by or in which the beneficial interest vested in non-resident individuals of Indian nationality/origin was at least 60%, to invest in the shares of Indian companies.

First, the Supreme Court noted the Salomon judgment and held that it was firmly established that once a company has been incorporated, it has an independent and legal personality distinct from its members. It also noted that the corporate veil can only be lifted in certain exceptional circumstances, the corporate personality ignored and the individual members recognized for who they are. Finally, the Supreme Court held that the removal of the veil would be appropriate to a restricted degree, i.e., to ascertain the nationality or ethnicity of the shareholders, in the facts of this case and only to ascertain the ownership of the investment. The actual identity of each of them was not to be decided. Just because more than 60 per cent of the shares of foreign investor companies were held by a trust to which Mr Swraj Paul and his family members were beneficiaries, the companies could not deny the establishment of the scheme on the ground that the authorisation granted was unlawful. As such, the Court overlooked the fact that the identity of the shareholders may be generic, while acknowledging that each corporation has an individual legal entity, looking only at nationality to comply with the requirements of the scheme. The Supreme Court also took the chance to set out the basic conditions and values to adhere, and the specific situations under which a company's corporate veil could be pierced, i.e., to cast liability or responsibility for a company-led act. Such actions may include fraud or corruption, the avoidance of taxes or a charitable statute, or where related entities are inextricably connected as being, in fact, part of one concern and should, therefore, be regarded as such.

The Supreme Court of India in *State of U.P.* v. *Renu Sagar Power Company*[5] observed that the concept of lifting the corporate veil is a changing concept. The veil of corporate personality is more and more transparent in modern corporate jurisprudence. It is high time to rethink about the status of independent corporate existence in modern jurisprudence. Lifting the corporate veil is permissible but denying independent status of a company depends primarily on the realities of the situation.

The circumstances under which the Court may lift the corporate veil may be broadly be discussed under the following two heads:

(A) Under Judicial Interpretation, and

(B) Under Statutory Provisions.

[4] 1984 SCR (3) 643.

[5] AIR 1988 SC 1773.

**(A) Under Judicial Interpretation:** The LCV may be considered as an antithesis to the principle of ICE. The Courts may sometimes disregard the principle of ICE and pierce the corporate veil in order to reach the person behind the veil or reveal the true form and character of the concerned company. The rationale behind this is, probably that the law will not allow the corporate form to be misused or for the purposes which is set out in the statute. In those circumstances in which the court feels that the corporate form is being misused it will rip through the corporate veil and expose its true character and nature disregarding the Salomon principal as laid down by the House of Lords. The Court has applied the doctrine of LCV in the following grounds so far and these are only illustrative.

1. **Determination of character of a company:** It may be required for the betterment of the society or for security and sovereignty of the country to know the character of a company whether the company is controlled by enemy or a terrorist group. Therefore, it is essential to reject the principle of ICE and to apply the doctrine of LCV in order to lift the corporate veil and to ascertain its true character. In *Daimler Co. Ltd.* v. *Continental Tyre and Rubber Co. (Great Britain) Ltd.*[6] a company was registered in England in order to sell the tyres manufactured in Germany by a German Company. All the directors were Germans, resident in Germany. In other words, it may be said that the real control of the English Company was in German hands. During the First World War the English Company commenced an action to recover the trade debt. The question came before the Court for consideration whether an enemy company would be barred from maintaining the action.

   The Court held that a company incorporated under the Act is a legal entity, a creation of law with a status of ICE that the law confers. It is not a natural person with mind or conscience. Therefore, it can neither be loyal nor disloyal. It can neither be a friend nor enemy. But considering the facts of the case it can be considered as enemy because it is controlled by the enemy country. If a person knowingly deals with the company it may constitute nothing more than trading with enemy. Therefore, the company was not allowed to recover the debt at that juncture that is during war. The Court further held that if the company would be allowed to recover the debt during the war same money may be used against the country which would be in turn agaist the public policy.
2. **Fraud:** The Court will not allow Salomon's ICE principal which would be used as an engine of fraud. The classic case of the fraud is *Gilford Motor Company Ltd.* v. *Horne.*[7] Horne was managing director of Gilford Motors; his appointment was subject to a written agreement stating that he would not solicit customers for his own purposes either while he was managing director or after he left. Horne subsequently left Gilford and started up his own company in the name of his wife and solicited the customers of the company. Gilford sued for breach of the employment contract, Horne argue that the company had a separate legal identity and the clause only bound him personally, but not the company-owing to the separate legal identity as per the decision of Salomon case. The Court of Appeal

[6] [1916] 2 AC 307.

[7] [1933] 1 Ch 935.

was satisfied that the company was formed for the purpose of avoiding liability under the agreement and accordingly the Court held that the new company has its own separate legal identity after incorporation but if the company was formed as a device, a stratagem to allow Horne to evade the conditions of the agreement, the Court would not accept ICE and definitely would apply the doctrine of LCV.

3. **Tax Evasion:** If any company is incorporated only for tax evasion, the Court is having power to reject the principle of ICE. The best example would be the case of *Re Dinshwa Maneeckjee Petit*.[8] A wealthy man earning huge dividend formed four private companies. Income received was credited in the accounts of the company. But the company returned back the amount to that of wealthy man as a pretended loan. By this process the wealthy man divided the income into four parts thereby he was in apposition to reduce his tax liability. But the Court held that all four companies were incorporated only to avoid the tax and doing no other business and controlled by an individual hence the ICE status of such companies were rejected.
4. **Government Companies:** The assets and business of Burmah Shell, a private registered company, was acquired by the Central Govt. The employees of the company filed a writ petition against the company for their PF and other dues. The question came before the Supreme Court in *Som Prakash Rekhi* v. *Union of India*[9] that whether writ would be maintainable against the private company. The Constitution of India has provided that the writ would be maintainable only against the State defined under Article 12 of the Constitution. The Supreme Court in the instant case lifted the corporate veil and looked in to the nature and function of the company. The Court observed that the true owner of the company in question is State, the controller is State and it is nothing but an incarnation of State. Therefore, the Court held that writ would be maintainable in the instant case.

**(B) Under Statutory Provisions**

1. **False Information:** Sec. 7 of the Act prescribes that a declaration shall be made that all information submitted to ROC for incorporation of a company is true. But if it is found that the facts are not true or suppressed the material facts to obtain the certificate of incorporation fraudulently, then, the promoters, the first directors of the company, and the persons making declarations shall be liable for action under Sec. 447 of the Act. Provided the Tribunal also has the jurisdiction to take appropriate action on sufficient grounds where the Tribunal can pass an order for changes in the management of the company, remove the name of the company from the register of the companies, or direct the winding-up of the company.
2. **Criminal and Civil Liability for Misstatement in Prospectus:** Criminal and civil liability for misstatement in prospectus are provided under Sec. 34 and Sec. 35, respectively, under the Act. It states that if the prospectus of the company contains any misleading or untrue information that can confuse the public and cause

[8] AIR 1926 Bom 371.
[9] AIR 1981 SC 212.

damage based on such statements, then every person who knowingly issued such a prospectus will be held liable. Whereas under Sec. 36 of the Act, if any person knowingly induces any other person by making a false or fraudulent statement or concealing any facts for the investment of money by such person, then he will be liable for fraud under Sec. 447 of the Act.

3. **Repayment of Deposits:** When a company fails to repay the deposit or part thereof, or interest of such deposit within the time specified by the tribunal, then every officer of the company responsible for such default will be held liable under Sec. 74(3) of the Act.
4. **Strike off the Name of the Company from the Register of the Companies:** The Registrar of the Company has the power to strike off the name of the company from the Register of the Companies on the application of the company under Sect. 242(2) of the Act, provided that such company must extinguish all its liabilities and obligations before such application. The officers of the companies misuse the provision to avoid liabilities, defraud the creditors, or evade tax. In such circumstances, the officer in charge of the company will be jointly liable for the fraudulent application for removal of name under Sec. 251 of the Act.
5. **Defraud the Creditor or any other Person:** When the company is in the process of winding-up and it appears that the company carried out business to defraud the creditor or any other person, then on the application from the official liquidator, the company liquidator or the creditor, any officer of the company who intentionally tries to defraud shall be held personally liable by the National Company Law Tribunal as per Section 339 of the Act.

## Chapter II Kinds of Company

Companies can be classified under the following heads:

1. On the basis of formation
2. On the basis of liability
3. On the basis of membership
4. On the basis of domicile
5. On the basis of control
6. Other Companies (Not falling within 1 to 5 Category).

**1. On the basis of formation:**

(a) *Statutory company*: These companies are constituted by a special Act of Parliament or State Legislature. These companies are formed mainly with the intention to provide public services. Though primarily they are governed under that Special Act, still the Companies Act , 2013 will be applicable to them except where the said provisions are inconsistent with the provisions of the Act creating them (as Special Act prevails over General Act). Examples of these types of companies are Reserve Bank of India, Life Insurance Corporation of India, Industrial Financial Corporation of India, Delhi State Finance Corporation, etc.

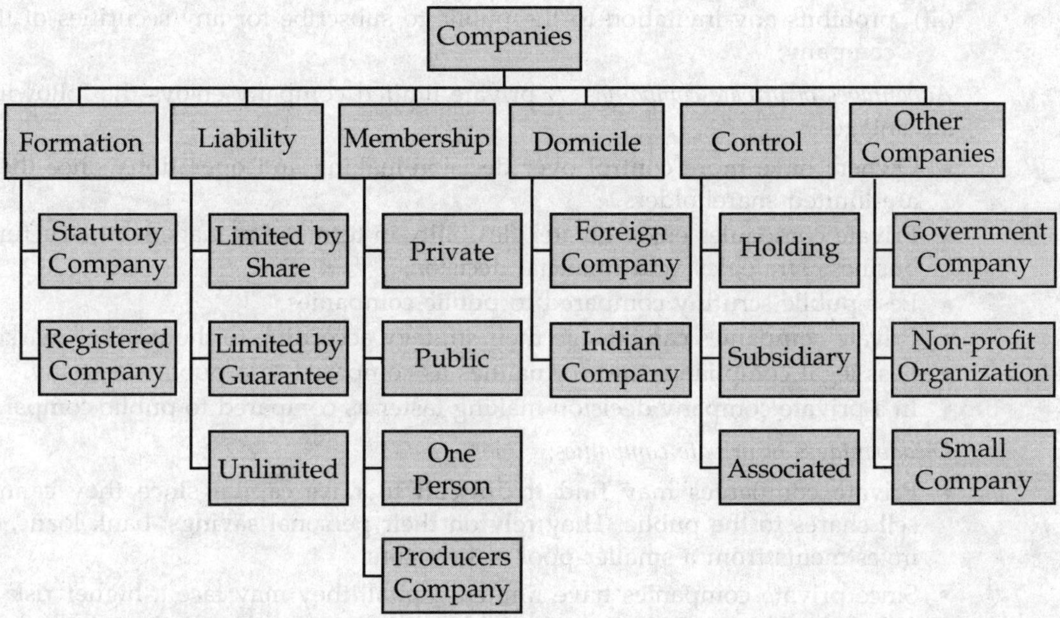


(b) *Registered company*: A company which is registered under the Companies Act, 2013 or earlier Companies Acts is called a Registered Company. The working of such companies is regulated by the provisions of the Companies Act.

**2. On the basis of liability:**

(a) *Company limited by shares*: In this case, the liability of members is limited to the amount of uncalled share capital. No member of company limited by the shares can be called upon to pay more than the face value of shares or so much of it as is remaining unpaid. Members have no liability in case of fully paid-up shares.

(b) *Company limited by the guarantee*: A company limited by guarantee means the members have undertaken the liability to the extent of their promise which would be paid at the time of liquidation if required. The liability of the members to pay the guaranteed amount arises only when the company has gone into liquidation and not when it is a going concern. A guaranteed company may be a company with share capital or without share capital.

(c) *Unlimited company*: The liability of members of an unlimited company is unlimited. Therefore, their liability is similar to that of the liability of the partners of a partnership firm.

**3. On the basis of membership:**

(a) *Private company*: Sec. 2(68) of the Companies Act, 2013 defines private company. Private company means a company having a minimum paid-up share capital as may be prescribed and which by its articles,—

(i) restricts the right to transfer its shares;

(ii) the number of its members—minimum two and maximum two hundred;

(iii) prohibits any invitation to the public to subscribe for any securities of the company;

*Advantages of private company*: A private limited company enjoys the following advantages:

- Owners have more control over decision-making and operations since there are limited shareholders.
- Private companies enjoy greater flexibility in terms of management structure, business strategies, and financial decisions.
- Less public scrutiny compared to public companies.
- Private companies can change their strategy according to the need of market.
- Less legal compliance and formalities as compared to a public company.
- In a private company decision making faster as compared to public company.

*Disadvantages of private companies*:

- Private companies may find it difficult to raise capital since they cannot sell shares to the public. They rely on their personal savings, bank loans, or investments from a smaller pool of investors.
- Since private companies have limited capital, they may face a higher risk of failure, especially during economic downturns or market disruptions.

(b) *Public company*: Sec. 2(71) of the Companies Act, 2013 defines public company. Public company means a company which—

(i) is not a private company;

(ii) has a minimum paid-up share capital as may be prescribed;

(iii) a public company must have a minimum of seven members, and there is no restriction on the maximum number of members;

(iv) issue shares and debentures;

(v) no restriction on transfer of shares;

*Advantages of a public company*:

- Public companies can easily raise funds by issuing shares to the public through the stock market. It facilitates the company to expand.
- Public companies are more visible; hence, they can offer better job opportunities and pay and thereby talented person to manage better the affairs of company.

*Disadvantages of public companies*:

- Public companies have many directors and managers. Decisions are made in meetings, which can take a long time.
- Public companies need to follow many rules and require many legal compliances. This will limit flexibility.
- Some investors might try to influence the company's decisions to serve their own interests; this can create conflicts and cause disruptions in managing the company affairs.

The major differences between public company and private company are as follows:

| | Basis | Public Company | Private company |
|---|---|---|---|
| 1. | Minimum number of members | Minimum number of members required to form a public company is seven | Minimum number of members required to form a private company is two |
| 2. | Maximum number of members | No limit on maximum number of members | Maximum number of members is 200 |
| 3. | Name | The word 'Limited' is used at the end of the company's name | The word 'Private Limited' is used at the end of the company's name |
| 4. | Commencement of business | It can start its business only after getting a certificate of commencement of business | It can start its business only after getting a certificate of commencement of business |
| 5. | Invitation to public | It invites public to subscribe to its shares | It cannot invite public to subscribe to its shares |
| 6. | Transfer of shares | There is no restriction on transfer of its shares | There is restriction on the transfer of its shares |
| 7. | Number of directors | It must have at least three directors | It must have at least two directors |

(c) *Producer company*: Sec. 378A(l) of the Companies Act, 2013 defines producers company as producer company means a body corporate having objects or activities specified in Sec. 378B of the Companies Act, 2013 and registered as Producer Company under 2013 Act or under the Companies Act, 1956.

Any ten or more individuals, each of them being a producer or any two or more Producer Institutions, or a combination of ten or more individuals and Producer Institutions, desirous of forming a Producer Company having its objects specified in Sec. 378B and otherwise complying with the requirements of XXIA of the Companies Act, 2013 and the provisions of the Companies Act, 2013 in respect of registration, may form an incorporated company as a Producer Company under the Companies Act, 2013.

*Objects of forming the Producer Company (Sec. 378B)*: The objects of the Producer Company shall relate to all or any of the following matters, namely:—

(i) production, harvesting, procurement, grading, pooling, handling, marketing, selling, export of primary produce of the Members or import of goods or services for their benefit: Provided that the Producer Company may carry on any of the activities specified in this clause either by itself or through other institution;

(ii) processing including preserving, drying, distilling, brewing, vinting, canning and packaging of produce of its Members;

(iii) manufacture, sale or supply of machinery, equipment or consumables mainly to its Members;

(iv) providing education on the mutual assistance principles to its Members and others;

(v) rendering technical services, consultancy services, training, research and development and all other activities for the promotion of the interests of its Members;

(vi) generation, transmission and distribution of power, revitalization of land and water resources, their use, conservation and communications relatable to primary produce;

(vii) insurance of producers or their primary produce;

(viii) promoting techniques of mutuality and mutual assistance;

(ix) welfare measures or facilities for the benefit of Members as may be decided by the Board;

(x) any other activity, ancillary or incidental to any of the activities referred to in clauses (i) to (ix) or other activities which may promote the principles of mutuality and mutual assistance amongst the Members in any other manner;

(xi) financing of procurement, processing, marketing, or other activities specified in clauses (i) to (x) which include extending of credit facilities or any other financial services to its Members.

(d) *One person company (OPC)*: Sec. 2(62) of the Companies Act, 2013 defines One Person Company. One Person Company means a company which has only one person as a member.

*Salient features of OPC*: The salient features of OPC are—

- OPC provides freedom that allows the professional skilled person to adopt the business of his choice.
- Personality driven passion and implementation of a business plan.
- The desire of the entrepreneurial person to take extra risk and willingness to take additional responsibility.
- Personal commitment to business is the sole idea of the person and close to his heart.
- It is run by individuals yet OPCs are a separate legal entity similar to that of any registered corporate.
- A One Person Company is incorporated as a private limited company.
- It must have only one member at any point of time and may have only one director.
- The member and nominee should be natural persons, Indian Citizens, and resident in India.
- One person cannot incorporate more than one OPC.

*Advantages of OPC*: Setting up an OPC is relatively easy and requires only one person to start.

- An OPC offers limited liability protection to its owner; accordingly, personal assets are not at risk in the case of business debts.

- The owner has complete control over the company without sharing decision-making power with anyone else.
- An OPC is seen as its own legal entity, separate from its owner. This makes it look more credible and makes it easier to get funding.
- Compared to bigger companies, OPCs usually have fewer legal rules to follow and less paperwork to deal with, making it simpler to run the business.
- Since there is only one owner, decisions can be made easily without needing to consult or get approval from others. This makes it easier to adapt to changes in the market.

*Disadvantages of OPC:*

- Only one person can own an OPC, which might cause difficulty in growing and getting investments compared to larger companies with multiple owners.
- OPCs are owned by just one person and have to deal with a lot of legal paperwork and rules, which can be more complicated compared to businesses.
- Some people might think OPCs are less stable or reliable than bigger companies with more owners.
- With just one owner, OPCs might find it hard to get enough money, expertise, or connections, making it tough for them to grow.
- If something happens to the owner, like if they get sick or pass away, it can be hard to figure out what to do with the OPC next, especially if there is no plan in place.
- Selling or giving away an OPC can be complicated and might scare off potential buyers or investors because of all the legal stuff involved.

**4. Company on the basis of domicile:**

(a) *Foreign company*: Sec. 2(42) of the Companies Act, 2013 defines foreign company. Foreign company means any company or body corporate incorporated outside India which,—

(i) has a place of business in India whether by itself or through an agent, physically or through electronic mode; and

(ii) conducts any business activity in India in any other manner.

Sec. 379 of the Act specifically provides that Sec. 380 to 386 (both inclusive) and Sec. 392 and 393 of the Companies Act, 2013 shall apply to all foreign company.

(b) *Indian company*: A company formed and registered in India is known as an Indian company.

**5. Companies on the basis of control:**

(a) *Holding company*: Sec. 2(46) of the Companies Act, 2013 defines a holding company as a holding company, in relation to one or more other companies, means a company of which such companies are subsidiary companies.

A holding company is a company that owns one or more other companies. These other companies are called subsidiary companies because they are controlled by the holding company. So, the holding company is like the parent company, and the subsidiaries are its smaller companies. Such a type of company, directly or indirectly, via another company, either holds more than half of the equity share capital of another company or controls the composition of the Board of Directors of another company. A company can become the holding company of another company in any of the following ways:

- by holding more than 50% of the issued equity capital of the company,
- by holding more than 50% of the voting rights in the company,
- by holding the right to appoint the majority of the directors of the company.

(b) *Subsidiary company*: A subsidiary company is a company that is both owned and controlled by another company. The owning company is called a parent company or a holding company. If a parent or holding company possesses complete ownership of another company, that company is referred to as a "wholly owned subsidiary." The holding company runs its own operations, while the subsidiary might engage in a related business. For example, the subsidiary might handle owning and managing the holding company's property assets to keep their liabilities separate.

Sec. 2(87) of the Companies Act defines subsidiary company.

Subsidiary company in relation to any other company (that is to say the holding company), means a company in which the holding company—

(i) controls the composition of the Board of Directors; or

(ii) exercises or controls more than one-half of the total share capital either at its own or together with one or more of its subsidiary companies.

A company shall be deemed to be a subsidiary company of the holding company even if the control is of another subsidiary company of the holding company. Furthermore, the composition of a company's Board of Directors shall be deemed to be controlled by another company if that other company by exercise of some power exercisable by it at its discretion can appoint or remove all or a majority of the directors.

(c) *Associated company*: Sec. 2(6) of the Companies Act, 2013 defines associated company as associate company, in relation to another company, means a company in which that other company has a significant influence, but which is not a subsidiary company of the company having such influence and includes a joint venture company.

For the purpose of above definition the expression 'significant influence' means control of at least twenty per cent of total voting power, or control of or participation in business decisions under an agreement and the expression 'joint venture' provided in the definition means a joint arrangement whereby the parties that have joint control of the arrangement have rights to the net assets of the arrangement.

Whereas per Sec. 2(27) defines the meaning of control. Control shall include the right to appoint majority of the directors or to control the management or policy decisions exercisable by a person or persons acting individually or in concert, directly or indirectly, including by virtue of their shareholding or management rights or shareholders agreements or voting agreements or in any other manner.

**6. Other Companies (Not falling within 1 To 5 Category):**

(a) *Government company*: Sec. 2(45) of the Companies Act, 2013 defines government company as— "Government company" means any company in which not less than 51% of the paid-up share capital is held by the Central Government, or by any State Government or Governments, or partly by the Central Government and partly by one or more State Governments and includes a company which is a subsidiary company of such a Government company. The term 'paid-up share capital' used in the definition of government company provided under Sec. 2(45) means:

As per Sec. 2(64) of the Companies Act, 2013 "paid-up share capital" means such aggregate amount of money credited as paid-up as is equivalent to the amount received as paid-up in respect of shares issued and also includes any amount credited as paid-up in respect of shares of the company but does not include any other amount received in respect of such shares, by whatever name called.

*Example of Government Companies*: ONGC, GAIL, NTPC, NPCIL, IOCL, HPCL, PGCIL, MCL, BEL, etc.

(b) *Non-profit organisation—Sec. 8 Company*: The Companies Act, 2013 recognised a non-profit organization as a company. The object of such company to promote social welfare, arts, commerce, education, charity, environmental protection, sports, science, and research. Unlike typical for-profit companies, a Section 8 company uses its profits and income to advance its objectives rather than distributing them as dividends. These companies are "Limited" company but exempt from using the term "Limited" in their name, reflecting their non-profit nature. Sec. 8 companies often enjoy certain exemptions and benefits under the Companies Act, Income Tax Act, and other regulations.

(c) *Small company*: Sec. 2(85) of the Companies Act, 2013 defines small company. Small company means a company other than a public company. There are two main conditions which determine a small company and they are as follows:

(i) Paid-up Share Capital does not exceed fifty lakh rupees or such higher amount as may be prescribed which shall not be more than ten crore rupees; and

(ii) Turnover as per profit and loss account for the immediately preceding financial year does not exceed two crore rupees or such higher amount as may be prescribed which shall not be more than one hundred crore rupees.

## Chapter III Registration and Incorporation

In order to obtain a certificate of registration of a companyone has to file an application to the Registrar of companies (ROC). The prescribed application form is available with the

ROC or may be available on line. The following documents are required to be attached as per Sec. 7 of the Companies Act, 2013 with the application form and they are as follows:

- the memorandum and articles of the company duly signed by all the subscribers to the memorandum A declaration;
- a declaration in the prescribed form by an advocate, a chartered accountant, cost accountant or company secretary in practice, who is engaged in the formation of the company, and by a person named in the articles as a director, manager, or secretary of the company, that all the requirements of this Act and the rules made thereunder in respect of registration of the company have been complied with;
- an affidavit from each of the subscribers to the memorandum and from persons first directors name in the article that he is not convicted of any offence in connection with the promotion, formation, or management of any company, or that he has not been found guilty of any fraud or misfeasance or of any breach of duty to any company during the preceding five years;
- an affidavit that all the documents filed with the Registrar for registration of the company is correct and complete and true to the best of his knowledge and belief;
- the address for correspondence till its registered office is established;
- the particulars of name, including surname or family name, residential address, nationality, and such other particulars of every subscriber to the memorandum along with proof of identity;
- the particulars of the persons mentioned in the articles as the first directors of the company, their names, including surnames or family names, the Director Identification Number, residential address, nationality, and such other particulars including proof of identity as may be prescribed.

## CERTIFICATE OF INCORPORATION

Once all the above documents have been filed and they are found to be in order, the ROC will issue a Certificate of Incorporation of the Company. This document is considered to be the birth certificate of the company and is proof of the existence of the company. Once the certificate of incorporation is issued, the company cannot cease its existence unless it is dissolved.

The Registrar shall allot to the company a corporate identity number, which shall be a distinct identity for the company and which shall also be included in the certificate. After the incorporation of a company, if it is proved that the company has been obtained certificate of incorporation by furnishing any false or incorrect information or representation or by suppressing any material fact or information in any of the documents or declaration filed or made for incorporating such company, or by any fraudulent action, the promoters, the persons named as the first directors of the company and the persons making declaration shall be liable for action under Sec. 447 of the Companies Act.

The Tribunal is empowered to take any action in the case of furnishing false or untrue information to obtain the certificate of incorporation and they are as follow:

- pass such orders, as it may think fit, for regulation of the management of the company including changes, if any, in its memorandum and articles, in public interest or in the interest of the company and its members and creditors; or
- direct that liability of the members shall be unlimited; or
- direct removal of the name of the company from the register of companies; or
- pass an order for the winding-up of the company; or
- pass such other orders as it may deem fit:

However, the Tribunal shall provide a reasonable opportunity of being heard in the matter; and the Tribunal shall take into consideration the transactions entered into by the company, including the obligations, if any, contracted or payment of any liability.

## EFFECT OF REGISTRATION

From the date of incorporation mentioned in the certificate of incorporation company enjoys following benefits:

- Company shall be a body corporate by the name suggested in MOA;
- Company is having perpetual succession;
- Company is having power to acquire, hold and dispose of property, both movable and immovable, tangible, and intangible by its name;
- Company can sue be sued by its name.

## PRE-INCORPORATION CONTRACT AND ITS CONSEQUENCES

There may be possibility that a contract may be made by the promoter on behalf of a company which is not duly incorporated. To make a valid contract there must be at least two persons who would give their free consent. But a contract is made before incorporation of a company which is nonexistent in the eye of law, hence the contract would be declared as null and void. In this situation, there would be two consequences and they are as follows:

(a) Company cannot be sued on pre-incorporation contract; and

(b) Company cannot sue on pre-incorporation contract.

## COMMENCEMENT OF BUSINESS (SEC. 10A)

The concept of a Certificate of 'Commencement of Business' was first introduced in the Companies Act, 1956, and it was reintroduced in the Companies Act, 2013 under Sec. 11 of the Act. The Companies (Amendment) Act, 2015, however, excluded (deleted) Sec. 11 with effect from May 29, 2015. Sec. 10A is inserted by the Companies (Amendment) Act, 2019 but came into effect on 02-11-2018 retrospectively. Companies can be classified into two groups based on when they started doing business and they are:—Companies with no share capital, both public and private, and, Companies with Share Capital, both public and private.

### Companies with no Share Capital, both public and private

A public company or a private limited company without share capital is not necessary to follow any other procedures and may begin operating immediately after receiving a certificate of incorporation from the Registrar of Companies.

### Companies with Share Capital, both public and private

All newly ( 02-11-2018 and thereafter) constituted Public and Private Companies with Share Capital will now be required to obtain a certificate of commencement of business from the concerned Registrar of Companies before commencing business or exercising borrowing rights, as per Section 10A of the Companies Act, 2013.

## WHO NEED TO FILE DECLARATION FOR COMMENCEMENT OF BUSINESS?

As per Sec. 10A of the Companies Act 2013, a company having share capital and registered on or after 2nd November 2018, is required to file a declaration for commencement of business before commencing any business or exercising any borrowing powers.

The following companies need to file the declaration for commencement of business:

1. Companies incorporated on or after 2nd November 2018 that have share capital.
2. Companies that have increased their authorized share capital after 2nd November 2018.
3. Companies that have converted from companies without share capital to companies with share capital after 2nd November 2018.

It is important to note that companies that do not have share capital are exempt from filing the declaration for commencement of business. Also, if a company has been incorporated before 2nd November 2018, it does not need to file the declaration for commencement of business.

## CONSEQUENCES OF NON-COMPLIANCE OF SECTION 10A

The consequences as provided in the Sec. 10A (2) and (3) of the Companies Act, 2013 are as follows:

1. That the company shall be liable to a penalty of ₹ 50,000 and every officer who is in default shall be liable to a penalty of ₹ 1000 for each day during which the default continues but not exceeding ₹ 100,000;
2. That the Registrar may initiate action for removal of name of company from the register of company where no declaration has been filed within period of 180 days and he has reasonable cause to believe that the company is not carrying on any business or operations.

# Chapter IV Memorandum of Association

## WHAT IS MEMORANDUM OF ASSOCIATION?

Memorandum of Association (MOA) is a document that regulates a company's external activities. It must be prepared and submitted to the ROC at the time of incorporation along with Articles of Association (AOA). MOA provides the proposed name of the company, and location of its registered office. It also states the proposed company's objectives, amount of authorized share capital, whether liability of its members is limited by shares or by guarantee. The MOA can be altered by the members by following the prescribed procedures. The MOA is a public document and may be inspected and it is available with ROC.

The memorandum contains the following important clauses:

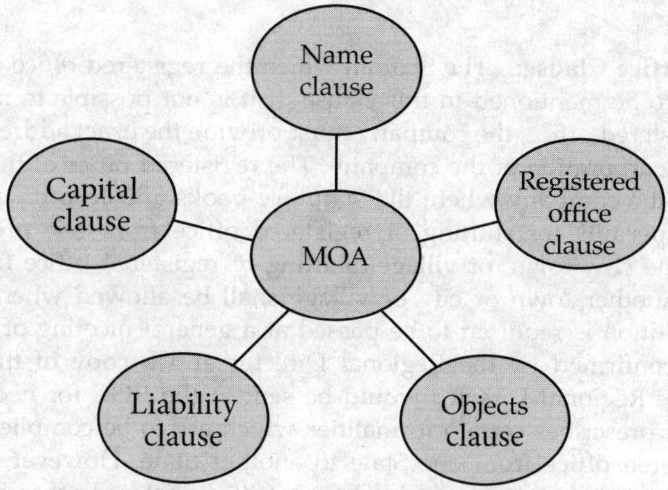


## CONTENTS OF MEMORANDUM

The memorandum of association of every company must contain the following clauses:

**(a) Name clause:** The company is identified by its name. The promoters or persons behind the formation of a company must take reasonable care and suggest the name of the proposed company in such a manner that the proposed name has not been previously used or registered. In this matter, the opinion of the Registrar of Trademarks may also be taken. In case an identical name has been proposed and accepted by the ROC, the existing company, in same name or identical name, has a right to apply for an injunction to restrain the newcomer from using a similar or identical name.

A public limited company must end with the word 'Limited' and a private limited company must end with the words 'Private Limited'. However, the word 'Limited' or 'Private Limited' is not required if a company is registered with charitable objects. The company cannot have a name, which in the opinion of the Central Government is undesirable. A company cannot use a name which is prohibited under the Names and Emblems (Prevention of Improper Use) Act, 1950, for example; the name, emblem, or official seal of the United Nations Organization; the name, emblem or official seal of the World Health Organization; the Indian National Flag; the name, emblem or official seal of the Government of India or of any State; the emblems of the St. John Ambulance Association (India), etc. The name of a company may be altered on obtaining prior approval of the Central Government for the altered name, passing a special resolution at a general meeting of the company to that effect and obtaining new certificate of incorporation signifying the changed name. The Companies Act, 2013, provides that the change of name shall not affect any rights or obligations of the company or render defective any legal proceedings by or against it; and any legal proceedings which might have been continued or commenced by or against the company by its former name may be continued by or against the company by its new name.

**(b) Registered Office Clause:** The State in which the registered office of company shall be situated needs to be mentioned in this clause. If it is not possible to mention the exact location of the registered office, the company must provide the exact address within 30 days from the date of incorporation of the company. The registered office of the company is the official address of the company where the statutory books and records must be normally be kept. The Act permits for shifting of registered office from one premise to another premise in the same city, town, or village. Shifting of registered office from one town or city or village to another town or city or village shall be allowed where it is prescribed that a special resolution is required to be passed at a general meeting of the shareholders which would be confirmed by the Regional Director and a copy of the resolution and confirmation of the Regional Director would be sent to the ROC for necessary change in the MOA. The Act prescribes certain formalities which are to be complied with in case of shifting the registered office from one State to another State. However, In *Re Mackinnon Mackenzie & Co.*[10] where a company decided to shift its registered office from West Bengal to Bombay was not allowed to shift on the ground of loss of revenue of the State. The facts of the case are as follows:

The petitioner, Mackinnon Mackenzie & Co. Private, Limited was incorporated on 30th March, 1951, under the provisions of the Indian Companies Act, 1913, as a public limited company. The company became a private limited company on and from 27th March, 1956, and the name of the company was changed to Mackinnon Mackenzie and Company Private Limited as from 16th June, 1961. The registered office of the company was situated at 16, Strand Road, Calcutta. By a special resolution of the company duly passed in accordance with Sec. 189 of the Companies Act, 1956, at a general meeting held on and November, 1965, at the registered office of the company after due notices as provided in the Act, it was unanimously resolved that the registered office of the company would be shifted to the State of Maharashtra. It is alleged in the petition that the directors and

[10] (1967) 37 Comp Cas 516.

shareholders of the company considered that it was necessary and desirable that, having regard to the business activities of the company, the registered office of the company should be transferred from Calcutta to Bombay and that such alteration would enable the company to carry on its business more efficiently and more economically. The contention on behalf of the State of West Bengal and the Registrar of Companies was that there would be loss of revenue to the State of West Bengal if shifting of registered office would be allowed. The Calcutta High Court refused to accept the contention and allowed to shift from West Bengal to Bombay and observed as follows:

> "The right of a State as such to appear in applications under Section 17 of the Companies Act,1956, does not flow from the provisions of the section. I am of opinion that there is no statutory right of the State as a State to intervene in applications under Section 17 of the Companies Act with regard to change of registered office. If notice has been directed by the court to the State, the State appears pursuant to the notice. If notice is given to secure whether revenues have been paid or not, the court in exercising its discretion sees that a company before removing its office from one State to another does not leave liabilities to the State undischarged. The court in making an order can impose terms to secure discharge of such liabilities. It is true that the decisions of the Orissa High Court have considered the contentions advanced by the State as to the possibility of loss of revenue and have held such matters to be relevant in the consideration of change of office. In my opinion, no hard and fast rule can be laid down that under no circumstance it is open to the State to contend that there may be loss of revenue. Suppose a large number of companies desire to change their registered office from one State to another, it may be open to the State to contend the possibility of disturbance in the economy of the State. In the ultimate analysis, the question of revenue, if it falls for consideration, is to be considered on the basis of the integrity of the Republic of India and not in a sectional and parochial manner. To hold that the possibility of loss of revenue is not only relevant but of persuasive force in regard to change of office from one State to another is to rob Section 17 of the Companies Act, 1956, of the statutory power conferred on a company to change its registered office and also to impose upon the statute a limitation with regard to change of office."[11]

In *Minerva Mills Ltd.* v. *Govt. of Maharastra*[12] Justice Ray of the Bombay High Court stated that the Company Law Board cannot refuse confirmation for change of registered office on the ground that it would cause loss to the general revenue of the State or that it will harm the State economy adversely. The loss to one State would be a gain to another and that is how it should be looked in to at the larger interest of nation as a whole.

**(c) Objects clause:** This clause is the most important clause of the company. It prescribes the activities which a company is authorized to carry on. The objects clause both defines and confines the powers of the company. Thus, it is a clause in a memorandum of association that describes the objectives for which the company is formed. If the company's activities fall outside the purview of its objectives mentioned in MOA, the action taken by the company would be declared as *ultra vires* (beyond its powers). The utility or importance of objects clause may be looked from three perspectives and they are as follows:

---

[11] Id at para 29 per A Ray, J.

[12] (1975) 45 Com Cas1 (Bom).

### *Utility of Objects Clause*

1. *Shareholder's point of view*: The shareholders buy the shares of a company and agree to part their money on the faith that their money would be utilized on that purpose, which are specified in the objects clause. The intention of shareholders is to receive good return (dividend) therefore the shareholders are more concerned about their money and the objects clause of MOA.
2. *Creditor's point of view*: The creditors give credit to the company on the faith that their money would be utilized only for the purposes of business specified in the objects clause.
3. *Public Interest*: The objects clause prevents diversification of company's affairs which are not connected with the business for which the company is incorporated. Any diversification from the initial business needs to be approved by the competent authority where the said authority will consider the public interest before approving the new plan or project for diversification.

## DOCTRINE OF THE ULTRA VIRES

After considering the utility and importance of objects clause of MOA, the author is of opinion that objects clause is nothing but LOC (line of control) for a company. It curtails the freedom of director to make a contract which would not fall within the ambit of objects clause. If the company steps out of LOC the action would be declared as *ultra vires*. *"Ultra"* means beyond, *"vires"* means powers. The implication of doctrine of *ultra vires* was discussed and applied first time in *Ashbury Railway Carriage and Iron Co. Ltd.* v. *Riche*[13] case. In this case, the objects of the company as stated in the objects clause of its memorandum, were

> 'to make and sell, or lend on hire railway carriages and wagons, and all kinds of railway plaint, fittings, machinery and rolling stock to carry on the business of mechanical engineers and general contractors to purchase and sell as merchants timber, coal, metal or other materials; and to buy and sell any materials on commissions or as agents.'

The directors of the company entered into a contract with Riche for financing a construction of a railway line in Belgium. The contract was ratified by all the members of the company, but later on it was repudiated by the company. Riche sued the company for breach of contract. The issue was whether the contract was valid and if not, whether it could be ratified by the members of the company.

The House of Lords unanimously held as follows that;

(a) The contract was beyond the objects clause as defined in the objects clause of its MOA and, therefore it was void, and

(b) The company had no capacity to ratify the contract.

---

[13] (1875) LR 7 HL 653.

In 1880, the House of Lords in *Attorney General* v. *Great Eastern Railway Co.*[14] affirmed the principle laid down in *Ashbury Railway* case but held that the doctrine of *'ultra vires'* ought to be reasonably and not unreasonably understood and applied and that whatever may be fairly regarded as incidental to the objects authorized ought not to be held as *'ultra vires'* unless it is expressly prohibited. The outcome of the decision would be as follows:

The company may do an act which is: (a) necessary for, or (b) incidental to, the attainment of its objects, or (c) which is otherwise authorized by the Act.

## Position in India

The doctrine has been affirmed by the Supreme Court of India in *A. Lakshmanaswami Mudaliar* v. *Life Insurance Corporation of India*[15] in 1963 where the Supreme Court observed that a company was competent to carry out its objects specified in the Memorandum of Association and could not travel beyond the objects. The Memorandum of Association must like any other document be construed according to accepted principles applicable to the interpretation of all legal documents and no rigid canon of construction was to be applied to such a document. Like any other judgement, it must be read fairly and its import derived from a reasonable interpretation of the language which it employed. Power to carry out an object, undoubtedly included power to carry out what was incidental or conducive to the attainment of that object, for such extension merely permitted something to be done which was connected with the objects to be attained, as being naturally conducive thereto. Undoubtedly the Memorandum of Association had to be read together with the Articles of Association, where the terms were ambiguous or silent. The Articles might explain the Memorandum but could not extend its scope.

The primary object of the Company was to carry on Life Insurance business in all its branches, and donations of the Company's funds for the benefit of a trust for charitable purposes was not incidental to or naturally conducive to that object. There was in fact no discernible connection between the donation and the objects of the Company. The trust had numerous objects one of which was undoubtedly to promote art, science, industrial, technical, or business knowledge including knowledge in banking, insurance, commerce and industry. There was no obligation upon the trustees to utilize the fund or any part thereof for promoting education in insurance, and even if the trustees utilized the fund for that purpose, it was problematic whether any such persons trained in insurance business and practice were likely to take up employment with the Company. Thus, the ultimate benefit which might result to the Company from the availability of personnel trained in insurance, if the trust utilized the fund for promoting education, insurance, practice and business was too indirect, to be regarded as incidental or naturally conducive to the objects of the Company. Therefore, the resolution donating the funds of the Company was not within the objects mentioned in the Memorandum of Association and on that account it was *ultra vires*.

Where a company did not act which was *ultra vires*, no legal relationship or effect ensued there from. Such an act was absolutely void and could not be ratified even if all the shareholders agreed. The payment made pursuant to the resolution was therefore

[14] (1880) 5AC 473.

[15] AIR 1963 SC 1185.

unauthorized and the trustees acquired no right to the amount paid by the Directors to the trust. As office bearers of the Company responsible for passing the resolution *ultra vires* the Company, they would be personally liable to make good the amount belonging to the Company which was unlawfully disbursed in pursuance of the resolution. The trustees as representing the trust had benefited from the payment. The amount was not disposed of before the Corporation demanded it from the trustees, and if with notice of the infirmity in the resolution, the trustees proceeded to deal with the fund to which the trust was not legitimately entitled, it would be open to the tribunal to direct the trustees personally to repay the amount received by them and to which they were not lawfully entitled.

Section 4 of the Companies Act, 2013, prescribes that the objects clause must mention and contain namely:

> The object for which the company is proposed to be incorporated and any matter considered necessary in furtherance thereof.

## Consequences of ultra vires transactions

If a company is involved with an *ultra vires* transaction the following consequences may be held and they are as follows:

1. *Injunction*: Where a company enters into an *ultra vires* transaction, the members of the company have an option to approach the Court and obtain an injunction order against such a transaction and thereby the Company would be restraint from proceeding with such *ultra vires* transaction.
2. *Personal liability of directors to the company*: It is the duty of the directors to see that the funds of the company are used only for legitimate business of the company. Consequently, if the funds of the company are used for a purpose which is not within the objects clause as specified in MOA, the directors will be personally liable to restore the money to the company.
3. *Personal liability of directors to third party*: The directors of a company are treated as agents of the company. The directors are authorized to make a contract on behalf of the company. It is the duty of the directors not to make any contract for which they are not authorized. In other words, the directors are authorized to make a contract if such transaction falls within the scope of the objects clause. Where the directors represents the third party that the contract entered into by them on behalf of the company is within the powers of the company while in reality the company has not such powers under its memorandum, the directors will personally be liable to the third party for his loss on account of the breach of warranty of authority. However, to make the directors personally liable for the loss to the third party, the following conditions must be satisfied and they are as follows:
   (a) There must be a representation of authority by the directors and such representation must be of fact, not of law.
   (b) There must be an inducement to the third party to make a contract with the company in respect of a matter beyond the memorandum or powers of the company.

(c) The third party must have acted on such inducement and thereby suffered some loss.

4. *Ultra vires Contracts*: An *ultra vires* contract is wholly void and of no legal effect. It is not only void but void *ab ignition* (from the very beginning) and therefore it cannot be *intra vires* (within power) either by *estoppel*, acquiescence or by ratification. An *ultra vires* contract is always *ultra vires* and in no circumstances it can be made as *intra vires*.
5. *Property acquired under ultra vires transaction*: Where the funds of a company are applied in purchasing some property, the company's right over that property will be protected even though the expenditure on such purchasing has been *ultra vires*.
6. *Ultra vires torts*: The law is not very much clear in respect to applicability of doctrine of *ultra vires* to torts. However, different authorities have different views and they are as follows:

(a) A company is allowed to do only those acts which are stated in the objects clause of its memorandum and, therefore, an act beyond the objects clause is not considered as an act of the company. Since the objects clause can never include the commission of wrongs, a company can never be liable in torts. In other words, a company will not be bound for a wrong committed by its servants or agents because their acts are beyond the scope of objectives clause of the company. However, this is not the present law on this point and in practice companies are made liable in torts.

(b) The second view is that the doctrine of *ultra vires* applies only to contract and property and never applies to tortuous or criminal liability.

(c) The third view is that a company may be held liable in torts provided that they are committed in the course of an activity, which is warranted by the objects clause of its memorandum. In other words, an act of the company's servants or agents beyond the objects clause is not an act of the company and therefore, the company cannot be held liable for the wrongs committed by its servants or agents in respect of an activity which is not covered by the objects clause of its memorandum.

But the correct rule is that a company may be held liable for torts committed in pursuance of its stated objects but should not be liable for acts entirely outside its objects. Thus, a company may be held liable for torts provided that the following conditions are satisfied and they are as follows:

(i) The tort has been committed by the officers or agents or directors or the servants of the company within the course of their employment, and

(ii) The tort has been committed in respect of or in pursuance of any activity which falls within the scope of the objects clause of its memorandum.

**Alteration of objects clause**

The companies Act, 2013, permits for alteration of objectives clause within certain permissible limits and they are as follows:

(a) to carry on its business more economically or more efficiently; or

(b) to attain its main purpose by new or improved means; or

(c) to enlarge or change the local area of its operations; or

(d) to carry on some business which under existing circumstances may conveniently or advantageously be combined with the business of the company; or

(e) to restrict or abandon any of the objects specified in the memorandum; or

(f) to sell or dispose of the whole or any part of the undertaking, or of any of the undertakings, of the company; or

(g) to amalgamate with any other company or body of persons.

**(d) Liability Clause:** Fourth among the Memorandum of Association clauses is the "Liability Clause". This clause mentions the kind of liability that the owners have towards the company. A company can either offer limited or unlimited liability to its owners. Further, if the liabilities are limited, they may be limited either by shares or guarantees. Clear information about the nature of liability must be clarified in the "Liability" clause of the MOA. Let's understand what each of these liabilities means.

1. **Limited by Shares:** The liability of each shareholder is limited to the unpaid amount of their individual subscribed capital, which is worth the amount of shares bought by them from the company.
2. **Limited by Guarantee:** The liability is limited by guarantee of the promoters. Each promoter guarantees an amount they will pay in the event of the company being wound while he is a member, or a year after he ceases to be a member. This amount will be used to pay off the debts and liabilities of the company that were accumulated while the promoter was a member, in addition to the charges and expenses of winding-up.
3. **Unlimited:** Unlimited Liability indicates that the shareholder's liability is unrestricted by any fixed amount. Additionally, their personal assets are at risk of loss during unprecedented circumstances like winding-up or debt recovery.

**(e) Capital Clause:** The capital clause serves the following purpose:

- The capital clause defines the company's share capital during the company registration process. Moreover, it defines the maximum capital the company can raise, i.e., its authorised capital or nominal capital;
- It sets the limit of capital and shares. The company cannot raise more capital or issue more shares than as mentioned in capital clause of MOA. In the event the company needs to raise more shares than the limit of your capital clause, the company needs to amend the capital clause;
- Lastly, it also defines the various types of shares that the company can have, its number and also the face value. Here, for public listed companies, it is mandatory to define the face value of their shares in the capital clause in MOA.

### Alteration of capital clause

There are five different types of alterations that the company may opt anyone of the procedures to alter the capital clause of MOA. These include:

- **Increase in authorised share capital:** It will allow the company to increase the limit of funds intends to raise for the company;
- **Consolidation of share capital:** Company can consolidate the shares of smaller denominations with the shares of larger denomination;
- **Conversion of share capital:** A company can either alter their stock into fully paid-up shares or convert their fully paid-up shares into stock;
- **Subdivision of share capital:** The company divides its existing number of shares into even smaller shares and increases the number of shares; and
- **Cancellation of share capital:** This alteration in the capital clause of memorandum of association is required when the company is desirous of reducing the number of its shares and share capital.

### Declaration Clause

The last paragraph of Memorandum of Association is the "Declaration of Association" This paragraph mentions the names of all the members/shareholders/promoters of a company along with their designations and shareholding in the company. This paragraph will be signed by all the shareholders in the presence of witnesses. The names, addresses, and occupations of all such witnesses must also be mentioned adjacent to the signatures of the shareholders. Finally, the shareholders declare their desire to form a company as per the provisions of the MOA and agree to subscribe to the number of shares mentioned adjacent to their names. Owing to their signatures in this paragraph, the document is legally binding on the shareholders.

## ALTERATION OF MEMORANDUM: (SECTION 13)

The MOA serves as a foundational framework for a company's incorporation, it is not static and can be subject to modifications under specific circumstances. The legal provisions regarding alterations in the clauses of Memorandum of Association are primarily governed by the Companies Act, 2013. Sec. 13 of the Act prescribes certain procedure which are required to be satisfied before altering any clause or clauses of Memorandum of Association. It stipulates that alterations must be in adherence to the provisions of the Companies Act and the Articles of Association (AOA). It emphasizes the following key aspects:

1. **Adherence to MOA & AOA:** Any alteration in the clauses of Memorandum of Association must confirm to the provisions outlined in both the Companies Act and AOA. The AOA specifies the internal rules and regulations governing the company, including the specific procedures for changing the MOA clauses.
2. **Special Resolution & Shareholder's Approval:** Changes in the Memorandum of Association clauses necessitate the passing of a special resolution by shareholders

during a general meeting. This resolution, approved by a two-third majority, lays the foundation for proposed alterations.

3. **Approval by Other Regulatory Authorities:** Certain substantial changes may require additional approval by other relevant regulatory authorities like the Tribunal, Regional Directors, State Governments, and Central Governments. The process of approval mentioned in the AOA must be followed diligently.
4. **Notice to Registrar:** Following the approval of alterations of MOA clauses by shareholders and applicable regulatory authorities, the company must promptly file the revised MOA with the Registrar of Companies (ROC), ensuring the updating of public records.

# Chapter V Articles of Association

The Articles of Association (AOA) are the rules, regulations, and byelaws for the internal management of the affairs of company. They are framed with the object of carrying out the aims and objects as set out in the memorandum of Association. They are as such subordinate to, and controlled by, the Memorandum of Association. The AOA is nothing but a contract between the company and its members and also between the members themselves that they shall abide by the rules and regulations of internal management of the company specified in the AOA. It specifies the rights and duties of the members and directors. The provisions of the AOA must not be inconsistent with the provisions of the MOA. In case of such inconsistency, the MOA will prevail.

## Definition under the Companies Act, 2013

Sec. 2(5) of the 2013 Act defines 'articles' as follows:

> "articles" means the articles of association of a company as originally framed or as altered from time to time or applied in pursuance of any previous company law or of this Act.

In a nutshell it can be said that AOA contain all the rules and regulations framed by the Directors of the company to govern the internal management and governance, which can also be altered from time to time.

## Model Forms of Article of Association (AOA)

As per the Companies Act of 2013, different model forms are prescribed under Schedule 1 of the 2013 Act for different types of companies; such as, companies limited by shares, companies limited by guarantee having a share capital, companies limited by guarantee not having a share capital, etc.

Schedule: I of the Companies Act, 2013 contains the model Articles under the forms in Tables F, G, H, I and J. The Companies of different natures are required to register the AOA using these forms:

| Tables in Schedule I | Details of the Forms |
|---|---|
| Table F | Form for the Articles of Association for a company limited by shares (as per Section 2 (22) of the Companies Act, 2013) |
| Table G | Form for the Articles of Association for a company limited by guarantee and having a share capital (as per Section 2 (21) of the Companies Act, 2013) |
| Table H | Form for the Articles of Association for a company limited by guarantee and not having a share capital |
| Table I | Form for the Articles of Association for an unlimited company and having share capital [as per Section 2 (92) of the Companies Act, 2013] |
| Table J | Form for the Articles of Association for an unlimited company and not having a share capital |

## Contents of Articles of Association (AOA)

Sec. 5 (2) of the Act read with Rules prescribed the matters which are required to be mentioned in the AOA and they are as follows:

- The extent to which 'Table A' of the Companies Act is applicable
- Management decisions
- Clause relating to adoption of preliminary contracts
- The different classes of shareholders
- The rights and duties of different classes of shareholders
- Appointment of Directors
- The powers and rights of Directors
- Borrowing powers of Directors
- The procedure of issuing share certificates and share warrants
- The voting of the Directors and Chairman
- The Dividend policy of the company
- The creation of reserves
- Confidentiality of the trade secrets and trade know-how of the company and penalty over their unauthorised disclosure
- The intellectual property valuations of the company
- The alteration of share capital
- Issue and transfer of shares
- Transmission clause relating to the transfer of title of share by insolvency, succession, death, etc.
- Forfeiture and surrender of shares
- The procedure for board meetings and for special resolutions that can be passed
- Arbitration clause in case of disputes
- Accounts and audits of a company
- Clause relating to the common seal of the company

- The winding-up procedure of a company, including the conditions required and the period of notice given to the members of the company.

These are some of the matters that are usually included in the AOA.

### Provisions for Entrenchment

In the contents of the AOA given above, certain contents or provisions are made as such to be harder to change, amend or alter, making them 'entrenched' in nature. Entrenchment means fortification or protection. The AOA can contain provisions for entrenchment for specific provisions. The provisions for entrenchment can ensure that the specified provisions are altered only if certain conditions or procedures are met or complied with.

Sec. 5(3) of the Companies Act, 2013 explicitly talks about 'entrenchment' clauses in AOA, stating that certain provisions in the AOA cannot be altered or amended by simply passing a special resolution but also require additional procedures, which would be covered later in the article. Section 5(4) further mentions that such entrenchment clauses can be introduced in the AOA only during:

1. The incorporation;
2. By bringing an amendment later to the provisions of the AOA through:
   - An agreement between all the members in case it is a private company.
   - Special resolution if it is a public company.

## ALTERATION OF AOA

Companies have wide powers under Sec. 14 of 2013 Act to alter their articles. Any restriction on the exercise of their powers will be invalid. Articles of association may be altered by a company by passing a special resolution to that effect. The altered articles will bind the members in the same way as did the original articles. The company must file with the ROC a copy of the altered AOA within 15 days from the date of such alteration.

### Limitations on power to alter Articles of Association (AOA)

- It is to be remembered that the AOA is subordinate to MOA and the Companies Act, hence, the altered AOA shall not be in contravention of the MOA or the Companies Act.
- The altered AOA cannot have a retrospective effect. In simpler terms, the alteration made in the AOA changing any of the rules made there under shall not be applicable to the time or situation before its alteration to avoid unfair treatment or arbitrary actions.
- The alteration cannot be in contravention with the order passed by the Tribunal under Sec. 242 of 2013 Act.
- The alteration to the AOA shall not be made which shall be in contravention of morality, public policy, or any of the laws of the Country. In addition to that, such alteration to the AOA should be made for the benefit of the company and not to solely fraud or suppress the minority shareholder.

- In the case of the conversion of a public company to a private one, no such alteration can be made without the approval of the Central Government. .
- The alteration in the AOA should not be used by the company to breach any contract or escape from the liability of a pre-existing contract.

## DOCTRINE OF CONSTRUCTIVE NOTICE

MOA and AOA are important and public documents kept with ROC which is available for the public to consult at the time of necessity. The doctrine of constructive notice explains that every person dealing with the company should have knowledge of the contents of AOA and MOA thereby he would be in a position to know about the company. Doctrine of constructive notice is based on presumption clause that a person who is dealing with the company must have read the AOA and MOA. Therefore, the doctrine protects the company against the outsider.

An important case in this regard is that of *Kotla Venkataswamy* v. *Ramamurthy*[16] where the AOA prescribed that all deed would be signed by managing director, secretary and working director whereas the plaintiff accepted a deed which was signed by secretary and working director. The Court observed that if the plaintiff could have consulted with AOA where it was specifically specified that the deed would be signed by three people the plaintiff would not have accepted the deed. The plaintiff might have acted in good faith and the money of the said plaintiff might have been applied to the purposes of the company but never the less the bond was declared as invalid.

## DOCTRINE OF INDOOR-MANAGEMENT

The doctrine of indoor management is an exception to the rule of constructive notice. Doctrine of constructive notice protects the company against the outsider whereas doctrine of indoor management protects the outsider against the company. The rule of constructive notice specifically deals with the external position of the company and therefore it follows that there is no notice to the outsider as to how the internal machineries are handled by the company's officer.

Every transaction in the business world has two aspects, namely, substantive and procedural. An outsider dealing with the company can only find out the substantive aspect by reading the memorandum and articles which are public documents available with ROC. A person who deals with the company may find out the procedural aspect after reading AOA but it is not possible for him to trace out whether such procedure has been followed or not. For example, AOA prescribes that a company may have borrowing powers by passing a resolution. An outsider can only know that the company can borrow the money but he cannot find out whether the resolution has in fact been passed or not. The outsiders dealing with the company are presumed to have read and understood the memorandum and articles and to see that the proposed dealing is not inconsistent therewith, but they are not bound to do more; they need not inquire into the regularity of

[16] AIR 1934 Mad 579.

the internal proceedings as required by the memorandum and articles. They can presume that all is being done regularly.

The doctrine of indoor management is also known as TURQUAND rule after *Royal British Bank* v. *Turquand*[17] case. In this case, the directors of a company had issued a bond to Turquand. They had the power under the articles to issue such bond provided they were authorized by a resolution passed by the shareholders at a general meeting of the company. But no such resolution was passed by the company. It was held that Turquand could recover the amount of the bond from the company on the ground that he was entitled to assume that the resolution was passed.

The rule is based on public convenience and justice because the internal procedure is not a matter of public knowledge. An outsider is presumed to know the constitution of a company, but not what may or may not have taken place within the doors that are closed to him.

The Turquand's rule has been approved by the Indian Court in *VarkeySouriar* v. *Keraleeya Banking Co. Ltd.*,[18] The Kerala High Court observed that it is no doubt that a company is regulated by a memorandum and articles and the persons dealing with the company are bound to read the registered documents which are kept with ROC and to see that the proposed dealing is not inconsistent therewith but they are not bound to do more. They need not enquire into the regularity of the internal proceedings, which is nothing but indoor management.

In 1957 the Allahabad High Court in *Lakshmi Ratan Cotton Mills Co., Ltd.* v. *J. K. Jute Mills Co., Ltd.*,[19] observed that creditor dealing with a trading company is required by law to be conversant with the terms of its Memorandum and Articles of Association and no more. If it is found that the transaction of loan into which the creditor is entering is not barred by the charter of the Company or its Articles of Association and could be entered into on behalf of the Company by the person negotiating it, then he is entitled to presume that all the formalities required in connection therewith have been complied with. If the transaction in question could be authorized by the passing of a resolution, such an act is a mere formality. A bona fide creditor, in the absence of any suspicious circumstances, is entitled to presume its existence. A transaction entered into by the borrowing company under such circumstances cannot be defeated merely on the ground that no such resolution was in fact passed. The passing of such a resolution is a mere matter of indoor or internal management and its absence, under such circumstances, cannot be used to defeat the just claim of a bona fide creditor. A creditor being an outsider or a third party and an innocent stranger, is entitled to proceed on the assumption of its existence; and is not expected to know what happens within the doors that are closed to him. Where the act is not 'ultra vires' the statute or the company such a creditor would be entitled to assume the apparent or ostensible authority of the agent to be a real or genuine one. He could assume that such a person had the power to represent the company, and if he in fact advanced the money on such assumption, he would be protected by the doctrine of internal management.

[17] (1856) 119 ER 886.

[18] AIR 1957 KER 97.

[19] AIR 1957 ALL 311.

### Exceptions to the doctrine of indoor management

The exceptions to the doctrine of indoor management are as under:

1. *Knowledge of irregularity*: When a person dealing with a company has actual knowledge of irregularity as regard to company's internal management, he cannot claim the protection under the rule of indoor management. There may be possibility, someone person may be a part of the internal procedure and therefore he cannot claim the benefit of indoor management because he is a party to such irregularity. In *Howard* v. *Patent Ivory Co.*[20], the directors had the authority under the articles to borrow only up to £1000 without the resolution of general meeting. For any amount beyond £1000, a resolution is required. But the directors borrowed £3500 from themselves without the concurrence of general meeting or shareholders. It was held that they had knowledge of internal irregularity and therefore they are not entitled to the protection of indoor management.
2. *Suspicion of irregularity*: Where a person dealing with a company may discover some irregularities and if he has not made any proper inquiries, he cannot claim the benefit of the rule of indoor management. The protection of Turquand rule is also not available where the circumstances surrounding the contract are so suspicious as to invite inquiry, and the outsider dealing with the company does not make proper inquiry. If, for example, an officer of a company purports to act outside the scope of his apparent authority, suspicion should arise and the outsider should make proper inquiry before entering into a contract with the company. *Anand Bihari Lal* v. *Dinshaw & Co.*[21], the plaintiff, in this case, accepted a transfer of a company's property from its accountant. Held, the transfer was void as such a transaction was apparently beyond the scope of the accountant's authority. The plaintiff should have seen the power of attorney executed in favour of the accountant by the company.
3. *Forgery*: The rule in Turquand's case does not apply where a person relies upon a document that turns out to be forged since nothing can validate forgery. A company can never be held bound for forgeries committed by its officers. The leading case on the point is that of *Ruben* v. *Great Fingall Consolidated Co.*[22], the secretary of a company issued a share certificate under the company's seal with his own signature and the signature of a director forged by him. Held, the share certificate was not binding on the company. The person who advanced money on the strength of this certificate was not entitled to be registered as holder of the shares.
4. *Representation through Articles*: This is the fourth exception of the *"Turquand Rule"*. *Lakshmi Ratan Lal Cotton Mills* v. *J.K. Jute Mills Co.*[23] explains the meaning and effect of a "delegation clause" which is generally included in the articles.

[20] (1888) 38 Ch.D 156.

[21] A.I.R 1942 Oudh 417.

[22] 1906 AC 439.

[23] AIR 1957 All 311

Here one G was director of the company. G was a director of the company with other managing agents also. The articles authorised directors to borrow money and also empowered them to delegate this power to any or more of them. G borrowed a sum of money from the plaintiffs for which the company refused to be bound on the ground that there was no resolution of the board delegating the powers to borrow to G. Yet the company was held bound by the loans.

Thus, the effect of a "delegation clause" is that a person who contracts with an individual director of a company, knowing that the board has power to delegate its authority to such an individual, may assume that the power of delegation has been exercised.

5. *Acts outside the scope of apparent authority*: If an officer of a company enters into a contract with a third party and if the act of the officer is beyond the scope of his authority, the company is not bound. In such a case, the plaintiff cannot claim the protection of the rule of indoor management simply because under the articles the power to do the act could have been delegated to him. The plaintiff can sue the company only if the power to act has in fact been delegated to the officer with whom he entered into the contract.

# Chapter VI Prospectus

A prospectus is a legal document that provides the details of a company and its financial history. It includes certain important facts about the company to help prospective investors to decide on whether to invest or not in a given company. Before investing money in any company, it is necessary for everyone to read the prospectus carefully. The Legislature, SEBI, stock exchanges, etc. play a very proactive role in this regard.

## Definition of prospectus: Sec. 2(70)

Sec. 2 (70) of Companies Act, 2013 defines the prospectus as follows:

> "prospectus" means any document described or issued as a prospectus and includes a red herring prospectus referred to in Section 32 or shelf prospectus referred to in Section 31 or any notice, circular, advertisement or other document inviting offers from the public for the subscription or purchase of any securities of a body corporate"

In short we can say that a prospectus is an invitation to offer to the public at large to take shares or debentures of the company or to deposit the money with the company. As the publication of a prospectus is too expensive, the company is also authorized to issue the prospectus in an abridged form. The public company which is listed is entitled to issue the prospectus to the public. Sec. 2 (52) of the Companies Act, 2013, defines listed company. Listed company means a company, the securities of which have been listed on any recognized stock exchange. A private company is prohibited under the Act to offer any invitation to the public to subscribe for any shares in, or debentures of, the company. If the promoters of a public company are confident to raise the money through their personal contacts, then the company need not issue the prospectus to the public.

## Objectives of prospectus

Prospectus is issued with the following broad objectives:

1. It informs the public about the company.
2. It provides terms and conditions of issue of shares or debentures of a company.
3. It induces the investors to invest in the shares and debentures of the company.
4. It describes the nature, extent, and future prospects of the company.

## Kinds of prospectus

In the business world corporate houses issue different types of documents to invite the public to invest the money in their company.

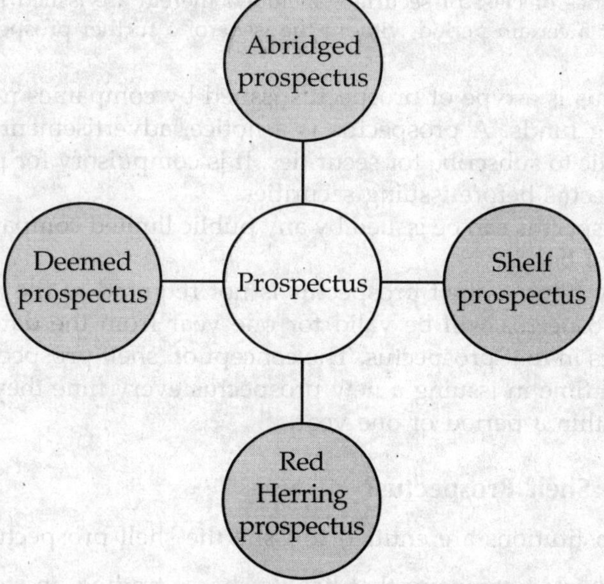


1. ***Abridge Prospectus:*** A prospectus usually runs into hundreds of pages in a single issue, which may prove to be a hectic task for investors to refer and understand. The investors may have limited knowledge and might not be competent enough to understand the intricate details mentioned in the prospectus. A solution to this problem is an abridged prospectus.

Section 2(1) of the Companies Act, 2013 defines an abridged prospectus means a memorandum containing such salient features of a prospectus as may be specified by the Securities and Exchange Board by making regulations in this behalf;

Further, Section 33 of the Act mandates for annexing an abridged prospectus along with form for application of purchase of securities. However, the proviso to sub-section (1) provides that this requirement may be dispensed with where the form of application was issued for:

- "in connection with a bona fide invitation to a person to enter into an underwriting agreement with respect to such securities; or
- in relation to securities which were not offered to the public."

Section 33(3) of the Act provides that if the company fails to comply with the provisions of abridged prospectus as discussed above, it shall be subjected to a penalty of up to ₹ 50,000 for every default.

2. *Shelf Prospectus: (Sec. 31 of 2013 Act):* The Explanation to Sec. 31 of 2013 Act provides the meaning of as follows:

> For the purposes of this section, the expression "shelf prospectus" means a prospectus in respect of which the securities or class of securities included therein are issued for subscription in one or more issues over a certain period without the issue of a further prospectus. Explanation—For the purposes of this section, the expression "shelf prospectus" means a prospectus in respect of which the securities or class of securities included therein are issued for subscription in one or more issues over a certain period without the issue of a further prospectus.

A shelf prospectus is a type of prospectus issued by companies making multiple issues of bonds for raising funds. A prospectus is a notice, advertisement or any other document inviting the public to subscribe for securities. It is compulsory for public limited companies to issue a prospectus before issuing securities.

A shelf prospectus can be issued by any public limited company raising funds through multiple issues of bonds.

A company filing a shelf prospectus is not required to file a fresh prospectus every time. A shelf prospectus will be valid for one year from the date of opening of the first issue of securities in that prospectus. The concept of 'shelf prospectus' will save company's expenditure and time in issuing a new prospectus every time they wish to issue securities to the public within a period of one year.

### Who can Issue Shelf Prospectus?

The following institutions are entitled to issue the shelf prospectus:

- A publicly listed company that has its shares trading on stock exchanges in India
- Public sector banks
- Non-banking financial corporations (NBFC)
- Public financial institution (the government owns 51% of shares of these companies)

### Conditions

These are the conditions that should be followed by a company opting to issue a shelf prospectus:

- The company's net worth should be more than ₹ 500 crores.
- The company distributed its profit during the preceding three years.
- A merchant banker should be appointed for the issue. The merchant banker must be registered with the SEBI.

- In case debentures are issued, a debenture trustee should be appointed.
- The company's directors or promoters should not have been faced with any regulatory action.
- The company should not have defaulted in repayment of deposits during the preceding three years.

3. ***Red-herring Prospectus (Sec. 32 of 2013 Act):*** The concept of "Red-herring Prospectus" has been introduced in the Companies Act in 2000. The Explanation of Sec. 32 of 2013 Act provides the meaning of "Red Herring Prospectus" that explains that it is a prospectus which does not have details of either price or number of shares being offered or the amount of issue.

Sec. 32 of 2013 Act contains the following provisions with respect to 'red herring prospectus':

(1) A company proposing to make an offer of securities may issue a red herring prospectus prior to the issue of a prospectus.

(2) A company proposing to issue a red herring prospectus shall file it with the Registrar at least three days prior to the opening of the subscription list and the offer.

(3) A red herring prospectus shall carry the same obligations as are applicable to a prospectus.

(4) Any variation between the red herring prospectus and a prospectus shall be highlighted as variations in the prospectus.

(5) Upon the closing of the offer of securities under this section, the prospectus stating therein:—

(a) the total capital raised, whether by way of debt or share capital,

(b) the closing price of the securities, and

(c) any other details that are not included in the red herring prospectus.

shall be filed with the Registrar and the Securities and Exchange Board.

A public company making an issue of securities may circulate information memorandum to the public prior to filing of a prospectus. A company that invites subscription by circulating an information memorandum has to file a prospectus prior to the opening of the subscription lists and the offer as a red-herring prospectus, at least three days before the opening of the offer. The information memorandum and red-herring prospectus shall carry the same obligations as are applicable in the case of a traditional prospectus. Any variation between the information memorandum and the red-herring prospectus shall be highlighted as variations by the issuing company.

Every variation as made and highlighted in accordance shall be individually intimated to the persons invited to subscribe to the issue of securities. If any advance has been received by way of cash or post-dated cheques, the company shall not en cash such subscription moneys or post-dated cheques, as the case may be, without having individually intimated the prospective subscribers of the variation and without having offered an opportunity to such prospective subscribers to withdraw their application and cancel their post-dated cheques or return of subscription paid as an advance.

4. ***Deemed Prospectus: Sec. 25:*** Sec. 25(1) of the Companies Act 2013 provides that any document used by a company to offer its securities to investors is deemed to be a prospectus, i.e., a deemed prospectus. This document constitutes an invitation to offer to the public without being the final prospectus. A deemed prospectus, as this name suggests, is deemed to be a company's prospectus. In simple terms, this is a detailed legal document which contains all information regarding stocks, shares, or securities that a company offers to public.

As mentioned in Sec. 25 (1) of the Company's Act, 2013, a deemed prospectus is a form of a prospectus. This idea of a deemed document is only relevant when a company intends to sell shares through an intermediary in order to avoid SEBI guideline compliance. These intermediaries can be an issuing agency or merchant bank.

## CONTENTS OF PROSPECTUS

For filing and issuing the prospectus of a public company, it must be signed and dated and contain all the following necessary information as stated under Sec. 26 of the Companies Act, 2013:

1. Name and other crucial information, such as the registered address of the office, its secretary, auditor, etc.;
2. The dates of issue, including the opening date and the closing date;
3. Undertakings of the Board of Directors regarding separate bank accounts for the purpose of keeping receipts of the issue;
4. Undertakings of the Board of Directors regarding the details of utilisation and non-utilisation of receipts of previous issues;
5. Consent of the directors, auditors, and bankers to the issue, and expert opinions;
6. The details of the resolution passed for the issue;
7. Procedure and time scheduled for the allotment of securities;
8. The capital structure of the company;
9. The objective of the issue;
10. The objective of the business and its location;
11. Particulars related to risk factors of the specific project, gestation period of the project, any pending legal action and other important details related to the project;
12. The amount is payable on the premium;
13. Details of directors, their remuneration and the extent of their interest in the company;
14. Reports for financial information such as auditor's report, report of profit and loss of the five financial years, business and transaction reports, statement of compliance with the provisions of the Act and any other report.

As per Sec. 26(4) of the Companies Act, 2013, the company issuing the prospectus has to deliver a copy of the prospectus, signed by every person whose name has been mentioned in the prospectus as a director of the company or the attorney of the director, to the Registrar on or before the date of publication.

The punishment for contravention of the mandatory provisions is provided under Section 26(9) of the Act, which includes a fine of not less than ₹ 50,000 extending up to ₹ 3,00,000. Any person knowingly participating in the issue of prospectus even after knowing that it is in contravention of the provisions shall be punished with imprisonment up to a term of 3 years, or a fine of more than ₹ 50,000 not exceeding ₹ 3,00,000.

## LIABILITY FOR MISSTATEMENTS UNDER COMPANY LAW

A prospectus is used by potential investors to gather information about the company. Thus, it is the duty of the company and its authorised persons to make true and correct statements in the prospectus. Generally, when false or incorrect information is added to the prospectus, it becomes a misstatement. Even an omission of important information amounts to a misstatement in a prospectus. Making a false or misleading statement thus entails certain liabilities. Under the Companies Act, 2013, there are two types of liability for misstatements in the prospectus.

### Civil Liability

Civil liability under the Companies Act, 2013 is provided under Sec. 35 of the Companies Act, 2013. It provides that where a person has subscribed to the securities of the company acting on any misstatement included in the prospectus and has consequently suffered any loss, the company and the persons authorising the issue of such prospectus are liable for such loss, provided that certain conditions are fulfilled. These conditions include:

1. Subscription to the securities acting upon the misstatement
2. Loss or damages due to such misstatement
3. Knowledge of the Defendant must be proved by the Plaintiff
4. Such misstatement must be material to the facts

If the above conditions are satisfied, the aggrieved person can claim remedies against the company as well as against the authorised personnel. The remedies include rescission of the contract, damages, and damages for the non-disclosure of material facts.

### Criminal Liability

Apart from the civil liability in case of misstatements, Sec. 34 of the Act also provides the liability of the authorised personnel for the misstatements in the prospectus. Criminal liability has been provided under Sec. 447 of the Act. In case of fraud on the aggrieved party (investor of the company), a criminal case can be filed against the following persons:

1. All the directors authorising the issue of the prospectus
2. All the proposed directors of the company
3. Each promoter
4. Any expert involved in the issue

Sec. 447 of the Act prescribes a minimum imprisonment of six months but not more than ten years, along with a fine which shall not be less than the amount of damages suffered but not more than three times of such amount. The proviso to the provision provides that in case the issue involves a public interest, the minimum term of imprisonment of the aforesaid persons shall be three years.

## REMEDIES UNDER CIVIL LAW

**(a)** ***Compensation:*** In *Derry* v. *Peek* (1889)14 AC 337 where the defendant railway company indicated in a company prospectus that its carriages would shortly be moved by steam power and not animal power as was then the case. The plaintiff purchased shares in the railway company based on the information contained in the prospectus. The railway company then failed to obtain the necessary government approval for steam power and the company dissolved. The plaintiff brought an action in deceit against the railway company for fraudulent misrepresentation. The House of Lords held that in order to establish a cause of action resulting in damages for misrepresentation, the statement must be fraudulent, or must be equivalent to being fraudulent, which will be the case if the statement is made recklessly, not caring whether it be true or false. The House of Lords observed that a statement made by a person honestly believed that to get the approval from the authority was only a procedure so the person concerned would not be exposed to an action in deceit. The House of Lords allowed the appeal and held the defendants not liable because they had honestly believed the statement to be true when they placed it in their prospectus.

The English Parliament passed the Director's Liability Act, 1890 just within a year of *Derry* v. *Peek* decision in order to mitigate the injustice caused in *Derry case* which was subsequently replaced by Sec. 43 of English Companies Act, 1948. Sec. 35 of the Companies Act, 2013, is the corresponding provision in the Indian Companies Act.

Sec. 35 of the Companies Act, 2013 makes certain persons liable to pay compensation to every person who subscribes for any shares or debentures on the faith of the prospectus for any loss or damage he may have suffered by reason of any untrue statement made in the prospectus. These would include directors of the company, promoters, or even the company. Thus, this section deals with the cases of misstatements of facts in a prospectus. It is immaterial for the purpose of this section whether the Director sees the prospectus or not; it is enough that he authorizes its issue. The effect of Sec. 35 provides a legal presumption against the director or promoter which helps out to establish liability against the directors in a common law action of deceit. Thus, this provision is an effective remedy to the deceived shareholders. This section is meant to tighten up the duties of directors and others who are in connection with the prospectus. So, this section provides statutory civil liability for 'untrue statement'.

### *Conditions for invoking Section 35 of the Companies Act, 2013*

(1) The company had issued a prospectus inviting persons to subscribe for its shares or debentures.

(2) An untrue statement was included in the prospectus.

(3) The person who is claiming for the compensation had subscribed for the shares or debentures offered by the prospectus.

(4) Such person has subscribed for the shares or debentures relying upon the untrue statement contained in the prospectus.

(5) Such person has sustained a loss or damage after having subscribed for the shares or debentures.

**(b)** ***Rescission of contract:*** The investor who buys a share in the company on the basis of the prospectus and latter finds out that the same was a misrepresentation, in that case he has the option of rescinding the contract. However, his option to rescind the contract would be lost in the following grounds and they are as follows:

(i) *By affirmation*: If the shareholder upholds the contract in spite of his full knowledge of misrepresentation he cannot afterwards rescind the contract. Affirmation may be express or implied.

(ii) *By Unreasonable delay*: The cardinal principle of equity is—delay defeats equity.

(iii) *By Commencement of Winding-up*: Shareholders would not be permitted to rescind the contract once the winding-up procedure has been initiated. The reason may be that the names of the shareholders are entered in the register of members and the register is *prima facie* evidence of membership. If they would be permitted to remove their names from the register the creditors would be seriously misled.

**(c)** ***Damages for Deceit:*** Deceit is a tort. It means fraud. False statements in a prospectus may also attract payment of damages under general law by the persons responsible for the issue. A person who has been induced to invest money in a company by fraudulent statement in a prospectus can recover damages for fraud under the 'Indian Contract Act' or the 'Law of Torts'.

# Chapter VII Share and Share Capital

## DEFINITION AND MEANING OF SHARE

Section 2(84) of the Companies Act, 2013 defines the term "share". Share means a share in the share capital of a company and includes stock. The Supreme Court in *Commissioner of Income-tax (Central) Calcutta* v. *Standard Vacuum Oil Co.*[24] held that a share is not a sum of money; it represents an interest measured by a sum of money and made up of diverse rights contained in the contract evidenced by the articles of association of the Company. Sec. 2(7) of the Sale of Goods Act recognized share as goods. Sec. 44 of the Companies Act, 2013, recognized share as movable property which provides that the shares or other interest of any member in a company shall be movable property, transferable in the manner provided by the articles of the company. The Madras High Court in *S. Viswanathan* v. *East India Distilleries and Sugar Factories Ltd.*[25] observed as follows:

[24] AIR 1966 SC 1393.

[25] AIR 1957 MADRAS 341.

> "A share is undoubtedly moveable property, but, it is not moveable property in the same way in which a bolt of cloth or bag of wheat is moveable property. Such commodities are not brought into existence by any legislative enactment; in fact, no legislative enactment by itself can call them into being. In origin and in nature they are independent of legislative volition, and in normal times there would be no special legislative rules governing their acquisition, transfer, or disposal. But a share in a company belongs to a totally different category of property. It is incorporeal in its nature, and it consists merely of a bundle of rights and obligations."[26]

### Meaning of share and share capital

A share is one unit into which the total share capital is divided. Share capital of the company can be explained as a fund or sum with which a company is formed to carry on the business and which is raised by the issue of shares. The amount collected by the company from the public towards its capital, collectively, is known as share capital and individually is known as share. Sec. 46 of the Companies Act, 2013, suggests that the share certificate shall be *prima facie* evidence of title.

### Stocks

Whenever a company plans to raise capital, it can issue stocks or try to borrow some money. They are the securities that represent a part of ownership in the company. Some stocks pay monthly, quarterly, or annual dividends, a portion of the issuing company's earnings. Whenever a company issues stocks, each unit of the stock is considered a share. Therefore, one stock share equals one unit of ownership in a given company. Shares are the owner of one particular company.

When an investor buys a company's stock, that person is not lending the company money but is buying a percentage of ownership in that company. In exchange for purchasing stocks in a given company, stockholders have a claim on part of its earnings and assets. Stockholders, stakeholders, and shareholders are all correct terms to refer to those who own stocks in a public company. Although the term shares generally refers to the stock units in a public company, it can also refer to other investments, like, mutual fund.

### Key Differences Between Stocks vs Shares

There are many differences between Stocks vs Shares. Let's look at the top differences between Stocks vs Shares below—

- Stocks are the collection of shares of multiple companies or are a collection of shares of a single company. Shares ascertain the smallest unit of ownership in a company. A stock is a collection of something or a collection of shares. Shares are a part of something bigger, i.e., stocks.
- Shares represent the proportion of ownership in the company, while stock is a simple aggregation of shares in a company.

[26] Id at p. 342 per Balakrishna Ayyar, J.

- When a company issues shares, it can do so at par, discount, or premium. The conversion of the shares of a member into one fund is known as stock. When a company lists its shares on the market, it converts them into stocks.

### Comparison between Stocks and Shares

**Meaning:** Stocks are the ownership of the company and companies, whereas, shares are the owner of one particular company.

**Denominations:** Two different stocks of a company may or may not have equal value, whereas, two different shares of a company can have the same value.

**Nominal Value:** In stock, there is no associated nominal value, whereas, a nominal value is associated with the share.

**Numeric value:** Stock does not have any such number, whereas, a share has a definite number known as a distinctive number.

**Paid-up value:** By nature, stocks are always fully paid-up. Whereas, shares are either fully paid-up or partly paid-up.

### Kinds of Shares

Section 43 of the Companies Act, 2013, provides that the share capital of a company limited by shares shall be of two kinds, namely:—

(a) equity share capital—
  (i) with voting right; or
  (ii) with differential rights as to dividend, voting or otherwise in accordance with such rules as may be prescribed; and

(b) preference share capital.

## EQUITY SHARE CAPITAL

Equity Share Capital is the funds generated by a company through issuing Equity shares (also known as ordinary shares). It consists of company shares that the owners decide to sell to individual investors and institutions in the stock market. The Equity Shareholders become stakeholders in the organisation, and these investors are eligible for both ownership and voting rights in the company to select their management.

### Features of Equity Shares:

- Equity Share Capital Remains with the organization, and the investors can claim it back only when the company winds up their operations. It is like a perpetual source of funding for the organization.
- They get a percentage of the company's profits, but only after preference shareholders get their dividend.

- The Equity Shareholders do not get a fixed rate of dividend. The dividend amount depends on the surfeit capital with the company after paying the preference shareholders.
- Equity shareholders get voting rights in the selection of the company's management.

## PREFERENCE SHARE CAPITAL

Preference Share Capital is the funds generated by a company through issuing preference shares (also known as Preference stock. Preference Shareholders have the first right to receive dividends even before equity shareholders). They are also part owners of the company, but they do not get any voting rights to select its management. They are entitled to a fixed rate of compensation every time the company decides to declare a dividend. They also have the right to claim repayment of capital if the company dissolves.

### Features of Preference Shares:

- Preference Shareholders have the first right to claim the company's assets whenever they decide to wind up their operations.
- Preference Shareholders have the first claim to their dividend.
- The Preference Shareholders get a fixed rate of dividend.
- Preference shareholders do not get voting rights in the selection of the company's management.
- Preference Shares have features of both debt and equity investment. They are also known as a hybrid security option for their investors.

### Differences between Equity Share Capital and Preference Share Capital:

The main differences between Equity Share Capital and Preference Share Capital are as follows:

| Preference Share Capital | Equity Share Capital |
|---|---|
| **Definition** | |
| Preference Share Capital is the funds that a company has generated by issuing preference shares. | Equity Share Capital is the funds that a company has generated by issuing Equity shares. |
| **Dividend Rate** | |
| The Dividend Rate in the case of Preference Share Capital is not changeable. | The Dividend Rate is changeable or fluctuating in the case of Equity Share Capital. |
| **Voting Rights** | |
| Preference Shareholders do not have any voting rights in the selection of the management. | Equity Shareholders have voting rights in the selection of the management. |
| **Participation in Management** | |
| Preference Shareholders do not have the right to participate in the management decisions. | Equity Shareholders have the right to participate in the management decisions. |

| Preference Share Capital | Equity Share Capital |
|---|---|
| **Claim to Assets of the Company** | |
| Preference Shareholders have a right to claim over the company's assets whenever they decide to wind-up their operations. | Equity Shareholders do not have any right to claim their assets whenever they decide to wind-up their operations. |
| **Preference in Paying Dividend** | |
| Preference shareholders get the first preference when the company pays a dividend. | Equity shareholders get second preference when the company pays a dividend. |
| **Types of Shares** | |
| The different types of Preference Shares are as follows:<br>• Cumulative Preference Shares<br>• Participating Preference Shares<br>• Redeemable Preference Shares<br>• Convertible Preference Shares<br>• Non-cumulative Preference Shares<br>• Non-participating Preference Shares<br>• Non-redeemable Preference Shares<br>• Non-convertible Preference Shares | The different types of Equity Shares are as follows:<br>• Authorised Share Capital<br>• Issued Share Capital<br>• Subscribed Share Capital<br>• Paid-up Share Capital<br>• Rights Share<br>• Bonus Share<br>• Sweat Equity Share |
| **Arrears of Dividend** | |
| Preference Shareholders are eligible to get arrears of unpaid dividends from previous years. They can get it along with the dividend of the current year, except for non-cumulative preference shares. | Equity Shareholders are not eligible to get arrears of unpaid dividends from previous years. |
| **Convertibility** | |
| Preference Shares are eligible to get converted into Equity Shares. | Equity Shares can never be eligible to get converted into Preference Shares. |
| **Risk** | |
| Preference Shareholders are at a lower risk compared to Equity Shareholders. | Equity Shareholders are at a higher risk compared to Preference Shareholders. |

**Preference shares may be classified according to the rights attached to them as follows:**

### *Cumulative and Non-cumulative Preference shares*

Cumulative preference shares enjoy the right to receive the dividend in arrears for the years in which company earned no profits or insufficient profits. In other words, dividend on these shares will go on accumulating until it is paid in full of arrears before any dividend is paid on equity shareholders. In case of non-cumulative preference shares dividend does not accumulate and therefore, no arrears of dividend would be paid in the year of profits. If company does not have any profits in a year, no dividend will be paid to non-cumulative preference shareholders.

### *Redeemable and Irredeemable Preference Shares*

Redeemable preference shares can be redeemed on or after a period fixed for redemption under the terms of issue or after giving a proper notice of redemption to preference shareholders. The Act, however, imposes certain restrictions for the redemption of preference shares. Irredeemable preference shares are those shares which cannot be redeemed during the lifetime of the company.

### *Convertible and Non-convertible Preference Shares*

Where the preference shareholders are given a right to covert their holding into ordinary shares, within a specified period of time, such shares as known as convertible preference shares. The holders of non-convertible preference shares have no such right of conversion.

### *Participating and Non-participating Preference Shares*

The holders of participating preference shares have a right to participate in the surplus profits of the company remained after paying dividend to the equity shareholders and preference shareholders at a fixed rate. The preference shares which do not have such right to participate in surplus profits, are known as non-participating preference shares.

## ISSUE OF SHARES AT DISCOUNT

Shares are said to be issued at a discount when they are issued at a price lower than the face value. For example, if a share of ₹ 10 is issued at ₹ 9, means, the share has been issued at discount. Sec. 53 of the Companies Act, 2013 prohibits on issue of shares at discount except Sweat Equity. Any share issued at discount other than Sweat Equity shall be void. However, a company may issue shares at a discount to its creditors when its debt is converted into shares in pursuance of any statutory resolution plan or debt restructuring scheme in accordance with any guidelines or directions or regulations specified by the Reserve Bank of India under the Reserve Bank of India Act, 1934 or the Banking (Regulation) Act, 1949.

The company and every officer who violates the provision of Sec. 53 of the Act, shall be liable to a penalty which may extend to an amount equal to the amount raised through the issue of shares at a discount or five lakh rupees, whichever is less, and the company shall also be liable to refund all monies received with interest at the rate of twelve per cent per annum from the date of issue of such shares to the persons to whom such shares have been issued.

## ISSUE OF SHARES AT A PREMIUM

A company may issue shares at a premium when it is able to sell them at a price more than at par or nominal value, irrespective of the fact whether the shares are listed on Stock Exchange or not. The rate of premium will be decided by the Board of Directors of a Company. Sec. 52 of the Companies Act, 2013 deals with the concept of share at a premium which provides that the premium cannot be treated as profit and as such the amount of premium is not available for distribution as dividend. Sec. 52 of the Act provides that where a company issue shares at a premium, whether for cash or otherwise, a sum equal to the aggregate amount of the premium received on those shares shall be transferred to a—securities premium account.

The securities premium account may be applied by the company—

(a) towards the issue of unissued shares of the company to the members of the company as fully paid bonus shares;
(b) in writing off the preliminary expenses of the company;
(c) in writing off the expenses of, or the commission paid or discount allowed on, any issue of shares or debentures of the company;
(d) in providing for the premium payable on the redemption of any redeemable preference shares or of any debentures of the company; or
(e) for the purchase of its own shares (buyback) or other securities.

## EMPLOYEE STOCK OPTION PLAN (ESOP)

Sec. 2(37) of the Companies Act, 2013, defines ESOP as follows:

> "employees' stock option" means the option given to the directors, officers, or employees of a company or of its holding company or subsidiary company or companies, if any, which gives such directors, officers or employees, the benefit or right to purchase, or to subscribe for, the shares of the company at a future date at a pre-determined price.

Employee Stock option plan or Employee Stock Ownership Plan (ESOP) is an employee benefit scheme that enables employees to own shares in the company. These shares are purchased by employees at price below market price, or in other words, a discounted price.

The purpose of providing ESOP is to make the employee more committed towards the company. In other words, ESOP motivates the employee to be committed towards the company for the long term and also take ownership of the company. If the employees are provided with a sense of ownership of the company by making them shareholders of the company, this will result in the employees focusing more on performing better for the company. However, in order to claim the benefits of the ESOP, the employees have to wait for a certain time period which is known as the vesting period. After the completion of the vesting period the employees can purchase the specified number of shares.

Sec. 62(1)(b) of the Companies Act, 2013, provides that where at any time, a company having a share capital proposes to increase its subscribed capital by the issue of further shares, such shares shall be offered to employees under a scheme of employees' stock option, subject to special resolution passed by company and subject to such conditions as may be prescribed.

### Benefits of ESOP

1. It acts as a source of motivation for employees who will be benefiting when the prices of the company shares rise in the market.

2. It helps to retain employees in the organisation.
3. Employees are benefited for the hard work they perform in trying times.
4. It helps in preventing a significant amount of cash outflow from the company.

## Types of ESOP

The following types of Employee Stock Option Plan (ESOP) are usually offered to an employee by the employer and they are as follows:

### *Employee Stock Purchase Plan (ESPP)*

An employee may purchase shares below the market price, generally fixed at a discounted price. The price and the date at which the employee may purchase the shares of the company is pre-determined by a plan term. This is known as the Employee Stock Purchase Plan (ESPP).

### *Employee Stock Option Scheme (ESOS)*

Under the Employee Stock Option Scheme, the employee is not under any obligation but has every right to exercise shares at a pre-determined price. The employee must ensure to complete a target or a specific tenure before vesting. Then, the employee may purchase the shares at the pre-determined price upon exercise.

### *Phantom Equity Plan (PEP) or Stock Appreciation Right (SAR)*

In a Phantom Equity Plan (PEP) or a Stock Appreciation Right (SAR), employees are offered shares of the company in theory, which the employee may obtain a cash value that is equal to the price appreciation over the grant price, once they achieve their vesting conditions.

### *Restricted Stock Award (RSA)*

An employee is offered shares in the company along, certain voting rights and is entitled to dividends if the employee meets the pre-set conditions by the employer. However, if the employee fails to meet such requirements, then the employee is no longer eligible to obtain the company's shares. The conditions set by the employer may depend on a particular tenure or may refer to a specific target. The Restricted Stock Award may be bought at a cost that is lesser than the market value. Typically, there are no costs attached to the stocks. In cases of such ESOPs, the employee owns the shares from the very first day and is eligible to receive a bonus and dividends during the vesting period.

### *Restricted Stock Unit (RSU)*

The Restricted Stock Unit is very similar to the Restricted Stock Award. However, the difference lies in the fact that the employee has no voting rights nor has a right to dividends. The employee may only exercise the shares granted by the employer once the pre-determined conditions are met. Restricted Stock Units do not get transferred immediately to the employee. However, the employee may be entitled to partial dividends in the future or under specific circumstances.

### Tax Implications

Generally, there are two tax implications for ESOPs. The first tax implication is when the employee exercises their right to purchase a company's shares. The second implication is when the employee is willing to sell their acquired shares.

#### *First Tax Implication*

When an employee chooses to exercise their option, the gain is added to their salary and is taxed by their employer. The value of the shares allotted for the employee is treated at an average value of the market value if the company is listed in India. When the company is not listed, then a certificate that estimates the market value of the allotted shares must be obtained from a merchant banker. Moreover, if an employee is offered shares of a listed foreign company, it is typically treated the same as an unlisted Indian company. Therefore, a certificate that estimates the market value of the allotted shares must be obtained from the merchant banker for this case as well.

#### *Second Tax Implication*

When an employee decides to sell their shares, they will be liable to capital gains taxes. The tax rate will depend on the duration the employee held on to their shares; accordingly, short-term, or long-term capital gain (LTCG) taxes will be applicable. Moreover, it also depends on the fact that if the shares held by the employee are listed or not in India to estimate their liability to taxes.

## BUYBACK OF SHARES

Buyback of share is the practice where companies decide to purchase their own share from their existing shareholders either through a tender offer or through an open market. In such a situation, the price of concerning shares is higher than the prevailing market price. When companies decide to opt for the open market mechanism to repurchase shares, they can do so through the secondary market. On the other hand, those who choose the tender offer can avail the same by submitting or tendering a portion of their shares within a given period. Alternatively, it can be looked at as a means to reward existing shareholders other than offering timely dividends.

Originally there was no provision for buyback of shares in the Companies Act, 1956. But there had been a persistent demand for buyback of own shares from the corporate sector. The Central Government approved the buyback of shares by companies and ordinance to this effect was issued by the President on 31st October, 1998. Thus, the provisions for buyback of shares were introduced w.e.f. 31-10-1998 in the Companies Act, 1956. Section 68 of the Companies Act, 2013 gives power to the company to purchase its own shares, that is buyback of share.

### Objectives/Advantages of Buyback

The following may be the objectives/advantages of buyback of shares:

(a) To increase promoters holding as the shares which are bought back are cancelled.

(b) To discourage others to make hostile bid to take over the company as the buyback will increase the promoters holding.

(c) To pay surplus cash to the shareholders when the company does not need it for the business.

(d) To reward the shareholders by buyback of shares at substantially higher price than market price.

### Restrictions

Sec. 68 of the Companies Act, 2013, provides certain restrictions for buying back of its own shares and they are as follows:

(a) the buyback is authorized by its articles;

(b) a special resolution has been passed at a general meeting of the company authorizing the buyback;

(c) the buyback is twenty-five per cent or less of the aggregate of paid-up capital and free reserves of the company;

(d) the ratio of the aggregate of secured and unsecured debts owed by the company after buyback is not more than twice the paid-up capital and its free reserves;

(e) all the shares or other specified securities for buyback are fully paid-up;

(f) the buyback of the shares or other specified securities listed on any recognized stock exchange is in accordance with the regulations made by the Securities and Exchange Board in this behalf.

## SWEAT EQUITY SHARES

The Promoters and employees who contribute to the formation of the company may like to get compensated against their hard work (Sweat) in the form of equity either discounted price or consideration other than cash. This is what term as sweat equity. It helps the business retain its brilliant human resources and also raise fund without availing debt. Sec. 2(88) of the Companies Act defines 'sweat equity shares' as equity shares issued by a company to its directors or employees at a discount or for consideration, other than cash, for providing their know-how or making available intellectual property rights or value additions, by whatever name called.

### Features of Sweat Equity Shares

Sweat equity shares have the following features:

1. Issued to employees, directors, or consultants who have contributed to the growth and development of the company.
2. Issued at a discounted price or for no consideration.
3. Can only be issued after the company has been incorporated for at least one year.

4. Cannot be issued for more than 15% of the existing paid-up share capital of the company.
5. Cannot be issued for more than ₹ 5 crores in a financial year.
6. Cannot be transferred or sold for a period of three years from the date of issue.
7. Must be held for a minimum period of three years from the date of issue.

### Conditions for Issuing Sweat Equity Shares

The issue of sweat equity shares is subject to certain conditions laid down by the Companies Act, 2013, and the Securities and Exchange Board of India (SEBI) regulations. Some of the conditions for issuing sweat equity shares are as follows:

- **Approval of the shareholders:** The issue of sweat equity shares must be approved by the shareholders of the company by way of a special resolution passed at a general meeting.
- **Limit on issue:** The total number of sweat equity shares issued by a company cannot exceed 15% of the paid-up share capital of the company at any time.
- **Lock-in period:** The sweat equity shares issued by a company must be locked-in for a minimum period of three years from the date of allotment.
- **Valuation:** The valuation of the sweat equity shares must be done by a registered valuer as per the guidelines laid down by SEBI.
- **Eligibility criteria:** The employees eligible for the issue of sweat equity shares must have contributed to the growth and success of the company in a significant manner.
- **Disclosure requirements:** The Company shall make adequate disclosure regarding the issue of sweat equity shares in its annual report and on its website.

## CLASSIFICATION OF SHARE CAPITAL

Share capital of a company can be classified into 5 ways which are as follows—

1. *Authorized or nominal share capital*: It is the share capital which the company is authorized to issue by its memorandum of association. It is the maximum amount up to which a company is authorized to issue shares to the public without altering the memorandum of association.
2. *Issued capital*: It is the nominal value of shares which are offered to the public for subscription through initial public offering.
3. *Subscribed capital*: It is the value of the shares taken up by the public through initial public offering; it will be equal to issued capital when all the shares offered to the public are taken by the public.
4. *Called up capital*: It is that part of the capital which has been called up. Sometimes company takes money in installments like 20% on application remaining after some time. It will be equal to subscribed capital if company takes all money at one go.
5. *Paid-up capital*: It is that part of the called-up capital which has been paid by the shareholders of the company.

## Share certificate and share warrant

### *Share Certificate*

A share certificate is a certificate issued to a member in his name by a company under its common seal specifying the number of shares held by him and the amount paid on each share. A share certificate is *prime facie* evidence of his title to the share. A share certificate once issued binds the company in two ways:

*Estoppel as to title*—It is a declaration by the company to the entire world that the person in whose name the certificate is made out and to whom it is given is a bona fide shareholder of the company. In other words, the company is stopped from denying its title to the shares.

*Estoppel as to payment*—If the certificate states that on each of the shares full amount has been paid, the company is stopped from alleging that they are not fully paid.

### *Share Warrant*

A share warrant is a negotiable instrument, issued by the public limited company only against fully paid-up shares. It is also termed as a document of title because the holder of the share warrant is entitled to the number of shares mentioned in it. There is no compulsion of the issue of share warrants by the company. Although if the public company wants to issue share warrants, then previous approval of the Central Government (CG) is required, along with that the issue of a share warrant must be authorized in the articles of association of the company.

The holder of the share warrant can take a share certificate only if he surrenders the share warrant and pays the required fee for the issue of share certificate. Thereafter, the company will cancel the warrant and issue a new share certificate to him as well as the company will enter his name as the member of the company, in the register of members, after which he will become a member of the company.

Generally, the holder of the share warrant is not the member of the company, but if the articles of association of the company provide it, then the bearer is deemed to be the member of the company.

## Distinction between Share Certificate and Share Warrant

1. Share certificate is registered evidence of title. Share warrant is a bearer document of title.
2. Share certificate is not a negotiable instrument. Share warrant is a negotiable instrument.
3. Both private and public Company can issue share certificate. Only public company can issue share warrant.
4. Issue of share certificate does not require approval of central Government where as issue of share warrant requires approval of central Government.
5. Holder of share certificate has full rights (voting, participation in management, etc.) in a company but holder of share warrant does not have has full rights in a company.

6. Share certificate is issued in respect of partly paid or fully paid shares but share warrant is issued in respect of only fully paid shares.

## ALLOTMENT OF SHARES

The term allotment has not been defined anywhere in the 2013 Act. Allotment means distribution of shares among those who have submitted written application. It is on allotment that shares come into existence. The meaning of the word "allotment" has been construed as an appropriation out of the previously unappropriated capital of a company. Allotment of shares means an appropriation of a certain number of shares to an applicant in response to his application for shares.

### General Principles regarding Allotment

With regard to the allotment of shares, the following general principles should be observed in addition to the statutory provisions:—

There should be a valid offer and acceptance for the allotment. The company invites for allotment to the public at large and the applicant submits his application for allotment and the company may accept or reject. Allotment of shares must be made within a reasonable time. An applicant may refuse to take shares if the allotment is made after a long time. The allotment should be absolute and unconditional. The allotment must be communicated. Posting of letter of allotment will be taken as a valid communication even if the letter is lost in transit or delayed in transit.

Sec. 39 of the Companies Act, 2013 prescribes certain procedure for allotment of securities by the company and they are as follows:

(1) No allotment of any securities of a company offered to the public for subscription shall be made unless the amount stated in the prospectus as the minimum amount has been subscribed and the sums payable on application for the amount so stated have been paid to and received by the company by cheque or other instrument.

(2) The amount payable on application on every security shall not be less than five per cent of the nominal amount of the security or such other percentage or amount, as may be specified by the SEBI.

(3) If the stated minimum amount has not been subscribed and the sum payable on application is not received within a period of thirty days from the date of issue of the prospectus, or such other period as may be specified by the SEBI, the amount received under shall be returned within such time and manner as may be prescribed.

(4) Whenever a company having a share capital makes any allotment of securities, it shall file with the Registrar a return of allotment in such manner as may be prescribed.

(5) In case of any default, the company and its officer who is in default shall be liable to a penalty, for each default, of one thousand rupees for each day during which such default continues or one lakh rupees, whichever is less.

### Minimum Subscription

A public limited company cannot make any allotment of shares unless minimum subscription as stated in the prospectus has been subscribed; sum payable on applications has been received in cash. Minimum subscription is the minimum amount, which in the opinion of directors, must be raised by the issue of shares to meet the preliminary expenditure of the company. The amount of minimum subscription must be stated in the prospectus. Shares allotted for consideration other than cash are not to be included towards minimum subscription.

### Calls and Forfeiture

#### *Meaning of Call*

A call is a demand made by the company in pursuance of AOA and resolution passed by the board to the shareholder either to pay the whole or part of the balance due on each class of share or shares allotted or held by him. A call may also be made by the liquidator in the course of winding-up of the company.

#### *Forfeiture of Shares*

If a shareholder fails to pay the allotment money and/or calls made on him, his shares are liable to be forfeited. Forfeiture of shares may be said to be the compulsory termination of membership by way of penalty for non-payment of allotment and/or any call money. The Companies Act does not contain any specific provisions regarding forfeiture. In fact, the power to forfeit shares must be contained in the Articles of the Company and the directors can forfeit the shares of a member only in pursuance of the authority given by the Articles. But the directors must follow certain procedures for forfeiting the shares. They have to give notice to the defaulting shareholder calling upon him to pay the amount due from him together with interest before a specified date (not being earlier than the expiry of 14 days from the date of service of the notice). This notice must state that if the shareholder fails to pay the amount along with interest that may be due within the specified date, the shares will be forfeited. If the payment is not received by the time, the directors meet to consider the forfeiture and they can proceed to forfeit the shares. The directors must pass a resolution for forfeiting the shares at a duly constituted meeting of the Board of directors and the defaulting shareholder should be informed about the forfeiture of his shares.

The effect of forfeiture of shares is that the defaulting shareholder loses all his rights in the shares and ceases to be a member. The name of the shareholder is removed from the Register of Members and the amount already paid by him is forfeited.

## Chapter VIII Shareholders and Members

There is a misconception that a person who holds the shares of a company, by-default, he becomes a member of that company. But this is not correct. Sec. 2(55) of the Companies Act, 2013 defines member.

## Definition of member

Sec. 2(55) of the Companies Act, 2013 defines member that in relation to a company member means:

(1) The subscribers of the memorandum of a company shall be deemed to have agreed to become members of the company, and on its registration, shall be entered as members in its register of members.

(2) Every other person who agrees in writing to become a member of a company and whose name is entered in the register of members of the company shall be a member of the company.

(3) Every person holding shares of a company and whose name is entered as beneficial owner in the records of the depository shall be deemed to be member of the concerned company.

Accordingly, there are two important elements, which must be satisfied before a person can acquire membership of a company, viz.

(i) written agreement to become a member; and

(ii) entry of the name of the person agreeing, in the register of members.

## Modes of acquiring membership

(1) *By subscribing to the memorandum*: Under the Company law the subscribers to the MOA are deemed to have agreed to become the members of the company. No application or allotment is required for them to become a member of the company.

(2) *By an application and allotment*: A person who applies for shares becomes a member when shares are allotted to him, a notice of allotment is issued to him and his name is entered on the register of members.

(3) *By transfer of shares*: A person can become a member by acquiring shares from an existing member and by having the transfer of shares registered in the books of the company, i.e., by getting his name entered in the register of members of the company.

(4) *By transmission of shares*: A person may become a member of a company by operation of law. On the death of a member, his executor or the person who is entitled under the law to succeed to his estate gets the rights to have the shares transmitted and registered in his name in the company's register of members.

## Who can become a member

Subject to the memorandum and articles of a company, any *"sui juris"* (a person who is competent to contract) can become a member of a company. However, it is important to note the following points in relation to certain organizations and persons:—

(a) *Company as a member of another company*: A company is a legal person and so is competent to contract. Therefore, it can become a member of any other company.

However, it must be authorised by its Memorandum of Association to invest in the shares of that company or any other company. A subsidiary company cannot become a member of its holding company. Also, a company cannot become a member of itself.

(b) *Partnership firm as a member*: A partnership firm is not a legal person and as such it cannot, in its own name, become a member of a company. However, its partners may become joint shareholders of a company and their names be entered in the register of members.

(c) *Foreigners as members*: A foreigner may take shares in an Indian company and become a member subject to the provisions of the Foreign Exchange Management Act, 1999, but in the event of war with his country, he becomes an alien enemy and his power of voting and his right to receive notices is suspended.

(d) *Minor as member*: A minor is wholly incompetent to enter into a contract and as such he cannot become a member of a company.

## Cessation of Membership

A person ceases to be a member of a company when his name is removed from its register of members, which may occur in any of the following situations:—

(a) He transfers his shares to another person and the shares are registered in the name of the transferee;
(b) His shares are forfeited by the company for non-payment of calls or on any other grounds provided in the AOA;
(c) He surrenders his shares to the company and the company accepts the surrender;
(d) His shares are sold by the company to enforce a lien, and buyer of these shares is registered as member;
(e) He dies and his legal representative or nominee gets his own name registered in the Register of members or sells shares to a third party who gets his name registered in the Register of members;
(f) He is adjudged insolvent;
(g) His redeemable preference shares are redeemed;
(h) His shares are bought-back;
(i) His shares are attached by the Court in satisfaction of a decree.

## Rights of Members

Once a person becomes a member, he is entitled to exercise all the rights of a member until he ceases to be a member in accordance of the provisions of the Act. The rights of member are:—

(1) A member can transfer his shares.
(2) A member is having right to have a share certificate issued to him in respect of his shares.
(3) A member is having right to vote on resolutions passed at meetings of the company.

(4) A member is having right to inspect the various registers of the company.

(5) A member is having right to requisition to have an extraordinary general meeting of the company.

(6) A member is having right to receive notice of general meetings and to attend and speak at general meetings.

(7) A member may appoint proxy and inspect proxy registers.

(8) To enjoy the profits of the company in the shape of dividend.

(9) To apply to the tribunal for relief in case of oppression of the minority shareholders.

(10) To apply to the tribunal for relief in case of *mismanagement*.

(11) To apply to the court for winding-up of the company.

(12) To share in the surplus on winding-up.

### Liability of Members

Liability of members depends on the nature of company. For example, if a company is registered with unlimited liability, the liability of every member of that company would be unlimited. If the company is limited by guarantee the liability of every member of that company would be to the extent of guaranteed amount specified in the MOA. If the company is registered with limited liability, every member of that company would be liable to the extent of their share capital.

### 'Member' and 'Shareholder'

A member is a person whose name appears on the Register of Members of the company where as a shareholder is a person who holds the shares of the company. A shareholder would continue to be shareholder if his name is not registered in the register of members. A member may be a member and he need not be a shareholder for example, in the case of companies limited by guarantee or unlimited companies, a member need not be a shareholder because such companies may not have a share capital.

### 'Member' and 'Contributory'

Sec. 2(26) of the Companies Act, 2013 defines contributory. Contributory means a person liable to contribute towards the assets of the company in the event of its wound up.

In the event of the winding-up of the company, member may be called upon to contribute towards the assets of the company. Accordingly, they are called as contributories. The term contributory and member are not inter changeable. Every member may be contributory whereas all contributories need not be members of the company.

## Chapter IX Debentures

Debentures are debt instruments issued by a company. Debenture-holders get interest on their debentures. They are creditors of the company. They do not get dividend. They are entitled to a fixed interest. Only shareholders get dividend.

Sec. 2 (30) of the Companies Act, 2013 define debenture as follows:

> "debenture" includes debenture stock, bonds or any other instrument of a company evidencing a debt, whether constituting a charge on the assets of the company or not.

Whereas Sec. 2 (35) of the Companies Act, 2013 further provided a meaning of debenture which includes an interim dividend also.

## CHARACTERISTICS OF A DEBENTURE

1. It is a written instrument.
2. It is an acknowledgement of the indebtedness of the company to its holder for the amount stated there in.
3. It provides for the payment fixed sum with interest of a specified rate for a specified time in spite of loss to the company. But this is not essential because a company may issue perpetual debentures.
4. It is generally secured by a charge, fixed, or floating on any part of the company's property or undertaking.

## KINDS OF DEBENTURES

1. *Secured Debentures*: Secured debentures provide an added of security for debenture-holders. These debentures are backed by specific assets or collateral of the issuing company. In case of default, the debenture-holders have the right to claim those assets to recover their investments.
2. *Unsecured Debentures*: Unlike secured debentures, unsecured debentures do not have specific collateral backing. Investors rely solely on the creditworthiness and reputation of the issuing company. While they may carry a higher risk, unsecured debentures often offer potentially higher returns.
3. *Convertible Debentures*: Convertible debentures allow investors to convert their debentures into equity shares of the issuing company. This allows investors to benefit from any potential appreciation in the company's value. It provides an opportunity to participate in the company's growth and potentially enjoy capital gains.
4. *Non-convertible Debentures*: Non-convertible debentures, as the name suggests, do not have the option for conversion into equity shares. These debentures offer a fixed return on investment and are preferred by investors seeking stability and regular income.
5. *Redeemable Debentures*: Redeemable debentures have a specified maturity date, upon which the issuing company must repay the principal amount to the debenture-holders. These debentures are suitable for investors who prefer a fixed-term investment with the assurance of capital repayment.

6. *Irredeemable Debentures*: Irredeemable or perpetual debentures do not have a specific maturity date. The issuing company is not obligated to repay the principal amount to debenture-holders. Instead, the interest payments continue indefinitely. Debenture-holder prefers this type of debentures who prefers long-term income.
7. *Registered Debentures*: Registered debentures are issued in the name of the debenture-holders, and the company maintains a register to record the ownership details. These debentures provide a clear record of ownership, allowing for ease of transfer and tracking of interests.
8. *Bearer Debentures*: Bearer debentures, on the other hand, are not registered in the name of any specific individual. They are negotiable instruments and can be transferred by mere delivery. Bearer debentures offer anonymity to the holders and facilitate easy transferability.

## DIFFERENCE BETWEEN SHARES AND DEBENTURES

1. *from capital point of view*: A share is a part of equity or preference share capital of a company. The holders of the shares may be described as part-owner of the company. A debenture is a part of loan capital of the company. The holder of a debenture is the creditor of the company.
2. *from interest/return of the parties' point of view*: The shareholders are interested on dividends which may vary from year to year. It is linked with profit whereas the debenture-holders are interested on interest which is usually fixed and the company compulsorily pays it at a fixed rate whether there are profits or losses.
3. *from charge on property point of view*: Shares do not create any charge on the assets of the company where as debentures may create a charge on the asset of the company.
4. *from redemption point of view*: Normally the share capital is not returned during the lifetime of the company where as the amount of debentures has to be returned after a stipulated period of time as per the conditions of issue.
5. *from discount on Issue or premium on issue point of view*: Shares can be issued at discount only when the conditions lay down in the Companies Act 2013 are fulfilled. But there are no restrictions on issue of debentures at a discount. The premium received on issue of shares can be utilized by the company subject to the conditions provided in the Companies Act, 2013. Premiums received on issue of debentures can be utilized by company in any manner it likes.
6. *from convertibility point of view*: Shares cannot be converted into debentures. Debentures can be converted into shares according to the conditions of issue of debentures.
7. *from control of companies' affairs point of view*: A shareholder has the right to control the affairs of the company by exercising his right to attend the general

meeting of the company and by exercising his voting right. A debenture-holder does not have any right to control the affairs of the company.

8. *from winding-up of companies' point of view*: At the time of winding-up the shareholders are paid their capital at the end. Debenture-holders have a priority as to return of amount received from them in the event of winding-up of the company.

## TYPES OF DEBENTURES

### From the Point of view of Security

*Secured and unsecured debentures*: Secured debentures are those debentures where a charge is created on the assets of the company for the purpose of payment in case of default. The charge may be fixed or floating. A fixed charge is created on a specific asset whereas a floating charge is created on the general assets of the company.

Unsecured debentures do not have a specific charge on the assets of the company. However, a floating charge may be created on these debentures by default. Normally, these kinds of debentures are not issued.

### From the Point of view of Tenure

*Redeemable Debentures and Irredeemable Debentures*: Redeemable debentures are those which are payable on the expiry of the specific period either in lump sum or in installments during the life time of the company. Debentures can be redeemed either at par or at premium. Irredeemable debentures are also known as perpetual debentures because the company does not undertake for the repayment of money borrowed by issuing such debentures. These debentures are repayable on the on winding-up of a company.

### From the Point of view of Convertibility

*Convertible Debentures and Non-convertible Debentures*: Debentures which are convertible into equity shares or in any other security either at the option of the company or the debenture-holders are called convertible debentures. The debentures which cannot be converted into shares or in any other securities are called non-convertible debentures. Most debentures issued by companies fell in this category.

## LEGAL FRAMEWORK OF ISSUING DEBENTURES AND REMEDIES

A company is not empowered to issue any debentures carrying any voting rights. Where debentures are issued by a company, the company shall create a debenture redemption reserve account out of the profits of the company available for payment of dividend and the amount credited to such account shall not be utilised by the company except for the redemption of debentures. As per Section 71(5) of the Companies Act, 2013 when a company wants to issue debentures to more than 500 members, then the company needs to execute a debenture trust deed appointing trustee to protect the interests of debenture-holders. A debenture trustee shall take steps to protect the interests of the debenture-holders and redress their grievances in accordance with such rules as may be prescribed.

### *Debenture Trustee and its Role*

A debenture trustee plays a crucial role in safeguarding the interests of debenture-holders. These trustees are appointed based on their expertise and qualifications, ensuring they possess the necessary knowledge to protect debenture-holders' rights. Acting as custodians, their primary duty is to ensure that the company fulfils its obligations towards the debenture-holders. They watch the proper utilization of funds raised through debentures, ensuring that the company uses them as intended. In addition, they are responsible for safeguarding the security or collateral provided against debentures. The presence of a debenture trustee brings an added layer of security and trust to debenture transactions. Investors can feel more confident knowing that an independent entity oversees the company's compliance and protects its interests.

### *Remedies*

Where at any time the debenture trustee comes to a conclusion that the assets of the company are insufficient or are likely to become in sufficient to discharge the principal amount as and when it becomes due, the debenture trustee may file a petition before the Tribunal and the Tribunal may, after hearing the company and any other person interested in the matter, by order, impose such restrictions on the incurring of any further liabilities by the company as the Tribunal may consider necessary in the interests of the debenture-holders. Where a company fails to redeem the debentures on the date of their maturity or fails to pay interest on the debentures when it is due, the Tribunal may, on the application of any or all of the debenture-holders, or debenture trustee and, after hearing the parties concerned, direct, by order, the company to redeem the debentures forth with on payment of principal and interest due thereon.

## DIFFERENCES BETWEEN SHAREHOLDERS AND DEBENTURE-HOLDERS

A shareholder invests the money in the company and therefore may be considered as the proprietor of the company. On the other hand, a debenture-holder is the creditor of the company. Moreover, shareholders have the right to attend general meetings that the company holds whereas the debenture-holder does not have such right. This, in turn, gives the shareholders the right to vote in the general meeting as well. Once again, as the debenture-holders are not allowed to attend the general meetings, the case of voting does not apply to them in the first place. Furthermore, a shareholder gets a share in the profit, which has a tendency to fluctuate. As for the debenture-holder, they get interest whose rate is fixed. Shares could be bought at discount, it is not the case with debentures, which could not be purchased at a discount rate. Lastly, shares could be bought back by a shareholder but a debenture-holder could not buy the debentures back.

# Chapter X Corporate Social Responsibility (CSR)

The main objective CSR activity is to give back the community because the corporates utilise space and resources. CSR activities adds value to the community by organizing activities that are essential for maintaining community standards. It is a self-regulating model that businesses have to comply with in order to become socially accountable to the company, its stakeholders and towards society. It is mandatory for every company to comply with the Companies Act, 2013. The objective of CSR provisions is to involve the corporates as partners in the social development process. Use of corporate innovations and management skills in the delivery of 'public goods' is at the core of CSR implementation by the companies. Therefore, CSR should not be interpreted as a source of financing the resource gaps in Government Schemes. However, the Board of the eligible company may undertake similar activities independently subject to fulfilment of Companies (CSR Policy) Rules, 2014.

Sec. 135 of the Companies Act, 2013 made mandatory for the company:

- A net worth of ₹ 500 crore or more,
- Or turnover of ₹ 1000 crore or more,
- Or net profit of ₹ 5 crore or more.

The companies fall under above stated category need to constitute a CSR committee of the Board. That committee shall be responsible for CSR activities.

## LEGAL COMPLIANCE

If the company falls under the criteria as mentioned above, the committee should consist of three or more directors including one independent director. If it is a listed company having at least one-third of total directors as independent directors with respect to sub-section (4) of Section 149, it shall have two or more directors. There are a number of mandatory legal requirements that a Company has to fulfil with respect to successfully operating a CSR activity as per law.

## CSR POLICY

As per the Sec. 135 of the Act, it is mandatory for the company to:

- Formulate a CSR policy mentioning all the activities which company would undertake.
- Recommend the amount that would be spent on the activities.
- It is mandatory for the company to spend at least 2% of the amount from the net profit.
- Monitor the policy on a timely basis.

## CSR ACTIVITIES AS PER SCHEDULE VII

Activities which may be included by companies in their Corporate Social Responsibility Policies relating to:

1. Eradicating hunger, poverty, and malnutrition, promoting health care including preventive health care and sanitation including contribution to the Swachh Bharat Kosh set-up by the Central Government for the promotion of sanitation and making available safe drinking water;
2. Promoting education, including special education and employment enhancing vocation skills especially among children, women, elderly, and the differently abled and livelihood enhancement projects;
3. Promoting gender equality, empowering women, setting up homes and hostels for women and orphans; setting up old age homes, day care centres and such other facilities for senior citizens and measures for reducing inequalities faced by socially and economically backward groups;
4. Ensuring environmental sustainability, ecological balance, protection of flora and fauna, animal welfare, agroforestry, conservation of natural resources and maintaining quality of soil, air and water including contribution to the Clean Ganga. Fund set-up by the Central Government for rejuvenation of river Ganga;
5. Protection of national heritage, art and culture including restoration of buildings and sites of historical importance and works of art; setting up public libraries; promotion and development of traditional art and handicrafts;
6. Measures for the benefit of armed forces veterans, war widows and their dependents;
7. Training to promote rural sports, nationally recognised sports, paralympic sports and Olympic sports;
8. Contribution to the Prime Minister's national relief fund or any other fund set up by the central govt. for socio-economic development and relief and welfare of the schedule caste, tribes, other backward classes, minorities, and women;
9. Contributions or funds provided to technology incubators located within academic institutions which are approved by the central govt.;
10. Rural development projects;
11. Slum area development;
12. Disaster management, including relief, rehabilitation, and reconstruction activities.

## ACTIVITIES DO NOT QUALIFY UNDER CSR ACTIVITY

The following activities are specifically excluded from being considered as eligible CSR activity:

(i) Activities undertaken in pursuance of normal course of business of the company;
(ii) Activities undertaken outside India, except for training of Indian sports personnel representing any State or Union Territory at national level or India at international level;
(iii) Contribution of any amount, directly or indirectly, to any political party;
(iv) Activities benefitting employees of the company as defined in Section 2(k) of the Code on Wages, 2019;

(v) Sponsorship activities for deriving marketing benefits for products/services;
(vi) Activities for fulfilling statutory obligations under any law in force in India.

## AMOUNT TO BE SPENT AND WHERE: AREA OF OPERATION OF CSR

Sec. 135 (5) of the Act provides that the Board ( CSR Committee ) of every company shall ensure that the company spends, in every financial year, at least two per cent of the average net profits of the company made during the three immediately preceding financial years, in pursuance of its Corporate Social Responsibility Policy:

Provided that the company shall give preference to the local area and areas around it where it operates, for spending the amount earmarked for Corporate Social Responsibility activities.

The first proviso to Sec. 135(5) of the Act provides that the company shall give preference to local areas and the areas around where it operates. Some activities in Schedule VII such as welfare activities for war widows, art and culture, and other similar activities, transcend geographical boundaries and are applicable across the country. With the advent of Information and Communication Technology (ICT) and emergence of new age businesses like e-commerce companies, process-outsourcing companies, and aggregator companies, it is becoming increasingly difficult to determine the local area of various activities. The spirit of the Act is to ensure that CSR initiatives are aligned with the national priorities and enhance engagement of the corporate sector towards achieving Sustainable Development Goals (SDGs). Thus, the preference to local area in the Act is only directory and not mandatory in nature and companies need to balance local area preference with national priorities.

## PENAL ACTION IN CASE OF DEFAULT/NON-COMPLIANCE

The non-compliance with regard the provisions regarding transfer of unspent amount is a civil wrong and shall attract the following penalties:

- Company: Twice the unspent amount required to be transferred to any fund included in Schedule VII of the Act or Unspent CSR Account, as the case may be, or one crore rupees, whichever is less.
- Every Officer in Default: 1/10th of the unspent amount required to be transferred to any fund included in Schedule VII of the Act or Unspent CSR Account, or two lakh rupees, whichever is less.
- In case of non-compliance with any other provisions of the section or rules, the provisions of Sec. 135(8) or general penalty under Sec. 450 of the Act will be applicable.
- As per Sec. 450, the company and every officer of the company who is in default or such other person shall be liable to a penalty of ten thousand rupees, and in case of continuing contravention, with a further penalty of one thousand rupees for each day after the first during which the contravention continues, subject to a maximum of two lakh rupees in case of a company and fifty thousand rupees in case of an officer who is in default.

# Chapter XI Directors

A company is an artificial person created by law and in fact it does not have any physical existence. It cannot act just like a human being. Therefore, it is required that its affairs would be managed by a living man or group of persons who have sufficient knowledge how to manage the corporate affairs. They are definitely professional man and they may be called as directors. The Companies Act is unable to define their position, however Sec. 2(34) of the Act defines a 'director' to mean a director appointed to the Board of a company. Sec. 149 of the Act provides that only an individual can be appointed as director. Thus, no body corporate, association or firm can be appointed director of a company. Sec. 149(1) of the Companies Act, 2013 requires that every company shall have a minimum number of three directors in the case of a public company, two directors in the case of a private company, and one director in the case of a One Person Company. A company can appoint maximum fifteen directors. A company may appoint more than fifteen directors after passing a special resolution in general meeting and approval of Central Government is not required. A period of one year has been provided to enable the companies to comply with this requirement.

Secs. 149 to 172 of the Companies Act, 2013 deals with the appointment of directors, remuneration of directors, disqualification of directors, vacation of office by directors, meeting of board of directors and other matters relating to directors.

## POSITION OF DIRECTORS

Considering the powers and liabilities of director under the Companies Act it is difficult to explain the position of a director in the corporate sector. It is said that a director of a company is neither an employee nor a servant to the company. They are professional people who were hired by the company to direct its affairs.

However in *Lee* v. *Lee's Air Farming Ltd.*[27] a director was working as a pilot and accordingly the Court held that a director may, however, work as an employee in different capacity.

### *Directors as agent*

In *Ferguson* v. *Wilson*[28], the Court clearly recognized that directors are agents of the company. The Court observed that the company can act only through directors. When the directors contract in the name, and on behalf of the company, it is the company which is liable on it and not the directors. The basic principle of law of agency can be applied to the directors and company. Company is the principal whereas the directors are merely agent of the company. What a company thinks the director does. The law of agency provides that the principal would not be held liable if the agent acts which are beyond his power. Same principle can be found in the case of *ultra vires* contract where the company would

[27] [1960] 3 All ER 420.

[28] (1866) 2 Ch App 77.

not be held liable but the director would be personally liable. The reason may be that the director acts beyond his power.

### *Directors as trustees*

A trustee is a person who is vested the legal ownership of the assets which he administered for the benefit of another or others. Directors are regarded as trustees of the company's assets because they manage the assets of the company and they work for the interest of the company and not for their own personal advantage.

In *York and North Midland Ry.* v. *Hudson,*[29] directors who had improperly dealt with funds of the company were held liable as trustees. The Court held that the directors are persons selected to manage the affairs of the company for the benefit of the shareholders; it is an office of trust, which, if they undertake, it is their duty to perform fully and entirely. They are no doubt trustees of assets which have come into their hands, or which are under their control. The Madras High Court in 1966 in *Ramaswamy Iyer* v. *Brahmayya & Co.*[30] held that the directors of a company are trustees for the company, and with reference to their power of applying funds of the company and for misuse of the power they could be rendered liable as trustees and on their death, cause of action survives against their legal representatives. But it is very much clear that directors are not trustee of the individual shareholder rather they are trustee of the company. In the real sense the directors are not trustees. A trustee is the legal owner of the trust property and contracts in his own name. On the other hand, director makes the contract on behalf of the company and he is not owner of the company. He is only a paid agent or officer of the company.

### *Director as organs of corporate body*

The organic theory of corporate life treats certain officials as organs of the company, for whose action the company is held liable just as a natural person is for the action of his limbs. Thus, the modern directors are more than mere agents or trustees. The Board is also correctly recognized to be a primary organ of the company. Directors represent the mind or will of the company and control what it does. The state of mind of directors is the state of mind of the company and is treated by law as such. The practical effects of these rules are that the directors' personal fault in the business of the company becomes the fault of the company provided that the directors act within their permissible limit.

Lord Denning stated in *H.L. Bolton (Engg.) Co. Ltd.* v. *T.J. Graham,*[31] as follows:

> A company may in many ways be likened to a human body. They have a brain and a nerve centre which controls what they do. They also have hands which hold the tools and act in accordance with directions from the centre. Some of the people in the company are mere servants and agents who are nothing more than hands to do the work and cannot be said to represent the mind or will. Others are directors and managers who represent the directing mind and will of the company, and control what they do. The state of mind of these managers is the state of mind of the company and is treated by the law as such.

[29] (1853) 16 Beav. 485.

[30] [1966] 1 Comp LJ 107.

[31] [1957] 1 QB 169

### *Director as an employee/officer*

Shareholders elect directors in a general meeting convened by the company. Once a director is elected, they have rights and powers granted to them by the law. These powers and rights cannot be revoked by the shareholders, and shareholders cannot interfere in the decision-making processes of the directors. Because directors possess these substantial powers and rights, they cannot be classified as employees of the company. Employees typically have limited authority and work under the direction of the employer without the ability to interfere in decision-making. Hence, the legal position of director can be considered as an employee.

In the case of *Re Lee Behrens & Co. Ltd.*,[32] it was established that shareholders elect representatives who then direct the company's affairs on their behalf, akin to acting in the capacity of agents. This ruling also clarified that directors are not employees or servants of the company. However, the Madras High Court, in the case of *R.R. Kothandaraman* v. *CIT* (1957), held that in the absence of specific legal constraints, directors can choose to enter into special contracts with the company to be considered employees. Directors are also regarded as officers in certain aspects of a company. They can be held accountable for penalties if they fail to comply with the law. To summarize the legal position of directors in a company, the statement of Jessel M.R. from *Forest of Dean Coal Mining Co., Re*[33] can be quoted: "Directors have sometimes been called trustees or commercial trustees, and sometimes they have been called managing partners.

It does not matter much what you call them as long as you understand the legal position of director in a company, which is that they are essentially businesspeople managing a trading entity for their own benefit and for the benefit of all the shareholders. They hold a fiduciary position with respect to the company, given their control overpowers and capital."

## NUMBER OF DIRECTORS

(1) Every public company shall have a minimum of three directors.

(2) Every private company shall have at least two directors.

(3) According to Sec. 151 of the Companies Act, 2013, every listed company may have one director elected by such small shareholders in such a manner and with such terms and conditions as may be prescribed. For the purpose of this section, "small shareholder" means a shareholder holding shares of nominal value of not more than twenty thousand rupees or such other sum as may be prescribed.

(4) No public company shall have more than fifteen directors, including additional directors, if any.

(5) No body corporate, association or firm shall be appointed as director of a company, and only an individual shall be so appointed.

[32] [1932] 2 Ch 46.

[33] [1878] 10 Ch. D. 450.

## APPOINTMENT OF DIRECTORS

### *First director*

"First directors" mean those directors who hold office from the date of incorporation of the company. Sec. 152 of the Act prescribes that subscriber of the memorandum, who are individuals, shall be deemed to be the directors of the company, until the directors are duly appointed. The idea behind of Sec. 152 is that as the office of a director is to some extent an office of trust, there should be somebody readily available who can be held responsible for the failure to carry out the trust. Therefore, Sec. 152 prescribes that immediately after the incorporation the subscribers of MOA would be deemed to be the directors.

### *Appointment by shareholders in General Meeting*

According to Sec. 152(6) of the Act, directors would be appointed by the company in general meetings. Generally, in a public company or a private company subsidiary of a public company, two-third of the total numbers of Directors are appointed by the shareholders and the remaining one-third is appointed in accordance with the manner prescribed in Articles failing which, the remaining one-third of the Directors must be appointed by the shareholders. The Articles of a public company or a private company subsidiary of a public company may provide for the retirement of all the Directors at every AGM.

### *Appointment by Board*

The power to appoint the directors is vested in the general meeting of the shareholders but the board may appoint the directors at least in two cases. Firstly, AOA may empower the board to appoint the directors and secondly, board is authorized under the Act to fill up the casual vacancy.

As per the provisions of the 2013 Act, the board has the power to appoint any person as director if he fulfils the requirements in a general meeting. As per Sec. 162 of the 2013 Act, the following directors can be appointed by the board, namely:

1. Additional director : Section 161(1)
2. Alternate director : Section 161(2)
3. Nominee director : Section 161(3)
4. To fill in vacancies of directors: Section 161(4)

### *Appointment by Central Government*

Sec. 167(3) of the Act empowers the Central Government to appoint directors in case of vacancy of directors in case of disqualification. Such directors shall hold office till the directors are appointed by the company in the general meeting.

In the famous case of, *Union of India* v. *Satyam Computer Services Ltd.*,[34] considering the larger public interest at stake and to create confidence in the minds of all those connected

[34] [2009] 89 SCL 393 (CLB).

with the company in any capacity and also to assure that regulatory/judicial mechanism in India is alive and active to take immediate and positive steps in case of needs, it was ordered that:

(i) The present board of directors stands suspended with immediate effect. None of the present directors shall represent himself to be a director of the company and shall also not exercise any powers as a director.

(ii) On the authority of this order, in the name and on behalf of this Board, the Central Government shall immediately constitute a fresh Board of the company with not more than 10 persons of eminence as directors. The Central Government may also designate one of them as the Chairman of the Board. This Board shall be entitled to exercise and discharge all powers vested in the Board by the Articles and the Act. The said constitution shall be notwithstanding anything contrary contained in the Articles, the Act, Listing Agreement, or any other law/regulations relating to the constitution of the board of a listed company. The said Board will continue till further orders.

### *Appointment by Tribunal*

The Tribunal has the power to appoint directors for the purpose of prevention of oppression and mismanagement under Sec. 242 of the Act.

## INDEPENDENT DIRECTOR

The provisions pertaining to the independent directors are laid down under Section 149(4) of the 2013 Act. It enumerates that at least one-third of the total number of directors in every listed company should be independent directors. However, as far as the public companies are concerned, the central government has the power to prescribe the minimum number of independent directors.

### *Who is an independent director?*

Sec. 149(6) of the 2013 Act provides for the definition of an independent director. It states that an independent director is a director other than a managing director, or a whole-time director, or a nominee director. It further lays down certain conditions which need to be complied with before nominating or selecting an independent director. The following points are to be considered:

1. A person with integrity who has the desired expertise and experience.
2. A person who has never been a promoter of the company, its subsidiary or any other holding company in the past or present.
3. A person who does not have a pecuniary relationship with the company, its subsidiary, or any other holding company, directors, or promoters.
4. A person whose relative or he himself does not hold any post of key managerial personnel. Further, he must also not be an employee of the company.

It is pertinent to note that every independent director is required to clarify and declare his independence at the very first board meeting and shall continue to do so every year at the first board meeting of every financial year. It is to be noted that an independent director holds the office of directorship for a period of five years. Also, an independent director can be reappointed, provided the same shall be done after the passing of a special resolution. However, an independent director can only hold office for two consecutive terms.

## WOMAN DIRECTOR

Every listed company shall appoint at least one-woman director within one year from the commencement of the second proviso to Sec. 149(1) of the Act. Every other public company having paid-up share capital of ₹ 100 crores or more or turnover of ₹ 300 crore or more as on the last date of latest audited financial statements, shall also appoint at least one-woman director within 1 years from the commencement of second proviso to Sec. 149(1) of the Act.

## REMOVAL OF DIRECTORS

1. *Removal by shareholders*: Sec. 169 of the Companies Act provides that a company may, by ordinary resolution, remove the director before expiration of his period of office. However, there are following directors who cannot be removed. An independent director, if re-appointed for second term, shall be removed by the company only by passing a special resolution by giving him a reasonable opportunity to be heard.
   (a) Sec. 169 is having no application in the case where directors are appointed by the Tribunal.
   (b) Sec. 169 is having no application in the case where a director appointed under the system of two-third proportional representation.
2. *Removal by Tribunal (Sec. 242)*: If any application is made to the Tribunal relating for relief in cases of oppression and mismanagement, the tribunal may remove the managing director, manager, or any directors of the company.

## DUTIES OF DIRECTORS

The duties of directors may be divided into two broad categories. They are (1) Statutory duties—Statutory duties are those duties which are prescribed under the Companies Act; (2) Other duties—which are prescribed by the common law principle.

1. ***Statutory Duties***
   (a) *To file return of allotment*: Sec. 39(4) of the Act requires a company having share capital to file with the Registrar, within a period of 30 days, a return of the allotments stating the specified particulars like the number and nominal amount of the shares comprised in the allotment, the names, addresses and occupations

of the allotees, and the amount, if any, paid or due and payable on each share. In case of failure to file the directors shall be liable as "officer in default", for each default, of ₹ 1000 per day till the default continues or on lakh rupee, whichever is less.

Sec. 2(60) of the Companies Act provides a list of persons who would be considered as "officer in default" and they are:—(a) the managing director or managing directors; (b) the whole-time director or whole-time directors; (c) the manager; and (d) the secretary.

(b) *Non-discloser of interest (Section 184)*: Sec. 184 of the Act casts an obligation on a director to disclose and provides that every director of a company who is in any way, whether directly or indirectly, concerned or interested in a contract or arrangement, or proposed contract or arrangement, entered into or to be entered into, by or on behalf of the company, shall disclose, the nature of his concern or interest at the first meeting of the Board of directors.

Every director who fails to comply with the aforesaid requirements as to disclosure of concern or interest shall be punishable with imprisonment for a term which may extend to one year or with fine, which shall not be less than ₹ 50,000/– but which may extend to ₹ 1 Lakh, with or both.

(c) *Not to participate where there is an interest (Sec. 166(4))*: Sec. 166(4) of the Act provides that no director of a company shall not involve in a situation in which he may have a direct or indirect interest that conflicts with the interest of the company.

(d) *To disclose receipt from transfer of property (Sec. 191)*: Sec. 191 of the Act prescribes that no director of a company shall, in connection with the transfer of the whole or any part of any undertaking or property of the company, receive any payment, by way of compensation for loss of office, or as consideration for retirement from office, or in connection with such loss or retirement—(a) from such company; or (b) from the transferee of such undertaking or property or from any other person, unless particulars with respect to the payment proposed to be made by such transferee or person (including the amount thereof) have been disclosed to the members of the company and the proposal has been approved by the company in general meeting. Where a director of a company receives payment of any amount in contravention of sub-section (1), the amount shall be deemed to have been received by him in trust for the company.

(e) *Duty to attend Board meeting [(Sec. 167(1)(b)]*: A number of powers of the company are exercised by the Board of directors in their meetings held from time to time. Although a director may not be able to attend all the meetings if he fails to attend all meetings for a period of twelve months whichever is longer, without permission of the Board, his office shall automatically fall vacant.

(f) *To convene statutory, Annual General meeting (AGM) and also extraordinary general meetings [Sections 96 and 100]*

(g) *To prepare and place at the AGM along with the balance sheet and profit and loss account a report on the company's affairs including the report of the Board of Directors (Sec. 134).*

(h) *To authenticate and approve the annual financial statement (Sec. 134).*

(i) *To appoint first auditor of the company (Sec. 139).*

(j) *To appoint cost auditor of the company (Sec. 148).*

(k) *To make a declaration of solvency in the case of Members voluntary winding-up (Sec. 305).*

**2.** ***Other Duties***

(a) *Duty of good faith*: It is the duty of the directors to act in the best interest of the company. Therefore, it is required that the directors must act: (a) in good faith, (b) with due care, and (c) with loyalty. The most general obligation of a director is the duty of acting in good faith. This requires a director to always discharge the responsibilities of the office of director honestly, conscientiously, and fairly. It also requires a director to make decisions for the corporation that are in the best interests of all the corporation's shareholders and not for the advantage or benefit of one group over another.

(b) *Duty of care*: Good faith alone is not the limit of a director's obligation to the company. In addition, directors are under an affirmative duty to direct and supervise the affairs of the company with diligence and care. In essence, the duty of responsible inquiry requires directors to diligently monitor and reasonably investigate the ongoing operations of the company. He would not be excused that he is not aware of the facts and situations if there is an allegation of *mismanagement* or fraud.

(c) *Duty not to delegate*: Directors are appointed by the shareholders because of their faith in their skill, competence, and integrity. Therefore, it is required that the basic duty and function which are supposed to be performed by the director alone need not be delegated. He is bound by the maxim *'delegatus non-potest delegare'*. However, he can delegate his duty in two cases. He can delegate if he authorized either by the Act or AOA; or due to business exigencies.

## POWERS OF DIRECTORS

(a) General Powers

(b) Special Powers

(c) Powers Exercised only at the Board Meeting

**(A)** ***General Powers***

Sec. 179 of the Act provides for general powers of the board of directors as follows:

The board of directors of a company shall be entitled to exercise all such powers, and to do all such acts and things, as the company is authorized to do. However, the board shall not exercise any power or do any act or thing which is by the MOA or AOA to be exercised by the company in the general meeting of the shareholders. It is interesting to note that if any regulation is made in the general meeting and such regulation shall not invalidate the valid action taken by the board prior to such regulation.

**(B)** ***Special Powers***

Sec. 179 of the Act provides that the board of directors of a company shall exercise the following powers on behalf of the company, and it shall do so only by means of resolutions passed at meetings of the Board:

The power:

(a) The power to make calls on shareholders in respect of money unpaid on their shares;

(b) The power to authorize the buyback under Sec. 68;

(c) The power to issue debentures;

(d) The power to borrow moneys otherwise than on debentures;

(e) The power to invest the funds of the company;

(f) The power to make loans;

(g) The power to approve financial statement and the Board's report;

(h) The power to diversify the business of the company;

(i) The power to approve amalgamation, merger, or reconstruction; and

(j) The power to take over a company or acquire a controlling or substantial stake in another company.

**(C)** ***Powers Exercised only at the Board Meeting***

(a) Filling casual vacancy (Sec. 161);

(b) Sanctioning a contract in which a director is interested (Sec. 188);

(c) Appoint additional directors (Sec. 203);

(d) Appoint alternate directors;

(e) Recommend rate of dividends;

(f) Power to make political contributions (Sec. 182);

(g) Power to give loan to or invest in any shares of any other body corporate (Sec. 186);

(h) Power to enter into any contract or arrangement with a related party (Sec. 188).

## RESTRICTIONS OF POWERS OF BOARD OF DIRECTORS

According to Sec. 180 of the Act, the Board of directors of a company cannot exercise the following powers without the consent of the shareholders by way of special resolution;

1. Sell, lease or otherwise dispose of the whole, or substantially the whole, of the undertaking of the company, or where the company owns more than one undertaking, of the whole, or substantially the whole, of any such undertaking.
2. Remit, or give time for the repayment of, any debt due by a director except in the case of renewal or continuance of an advance made by a banking company to its director in the ordinary course of business.
3. Invest, otherwise than in trust securities, the amount of compensation received by the company in respect of the compulsory acquisition of any such undertaking or of any premises or properties used for any such undertaking.

4. Borrow moneys, where the money to be borrowed, together with the moneys already borrowed by the company (apart from temporary loans obtained from the company's bankers in the ordinary course of business), will exceed the aggregate of the paid-up capital of the company and its free reserves.
5. Contribute to charitable and other funds not directly relating to the business of the company or to the welfare of its employees, any amounts the aggregate of which will, in any financial year, exceed five per cent of its average net profits during the three immediately preceding financial years (Sec. 181).

## LIABILITIES OF DIRECTORS

**1. Liability to the company:**

(a) ***Breach of fiduciary duty:*** Where a director acts dishonestly to the interest of the company, he will be held liable for breach of fiduciary duty. Most of the powers of directors are powers in trust and therefore should be exercised in the interest of the company and not in the interest of the directors or any section of members.

(b) ***Ultra vires acts:*** Directors are supposed to act within the parameters of the provisions of the Companies Act, Memorandum and Articles of Association, since these lay down the limits to the activities of the company and consequently to the powers of the Board of directors. Further, the powers of the directors may be limited in terms of specific restrictions contained in the Articles of Association. The directors shall be held personally liable for acts beyond the aforesaid limits, being *ultra vires* the company or the directors.

(c) ***Negligence:*** As long as the directors' act within their powers with reasonable skill and care as expected of them as prudent businessman, they discharge their duties to the company. But where they fail to exercise reasonable care, skill and diligence, they shall be deemed to have acted negligently in discharge of their duties and consequently shall be liable for any loss or damage resulting from.

(d) ***Mala fide acts:*** Directors are the trustee for the moneys and property of the company handled by them, as well as exercises of the powers vested in them. If they dishonestly or in a mala fide manner, exercise their powers and perform their duties, they will be liable for breach of trust and may be required to make good the loss or damage suffered by the company by reason of such mala fide acts. They are also accountable to the company for any secret profits they might have made in course of performance of duties on behalf of the company. Directors can also be held liable for their acts of misfeasance, i.e., misconduct or willful misuse of powers.

**2. Liability to third parties:**

**(A)** ***Prospectus***: The director would be personally liable if he fails to state any particular or particulars required as per the requirement of the Sec. 26 and Schedule II of the Act or provides any false information or suppress any material facts and thereby a third party sustains any damages. Sec. 35 of the Act considers it as a civil liability for misstatement in prospectus. Sec. 35 prescribes that where a prospectus invites persons to subscribe for shares in or debentures of a company, the following persons shall be liable to pay compensation to every person who has subscribed for securities of a company acting on any statement included, or the inclusion or omission of any matter, in the prospectus which is misleading and has sustained any loss or damage as a consequence thereof, the company and every person who—

(a) is a director of the company at the time of the issue of the prospectus;

(b) has authorised himself to be named and is named in the prospectus as a director of the company, or has agreed to become such director, either immediately or after an interval of time;

(c) is a promoter of the company;

(d) has authorised the issue of the prospectus; and

(e) An expert is a person who is not, and has not been, engaged or interested in the formation or promotion or management, of the company and has given his written consent to the issue of the prospectus and has not withdrawn such consent before the delivery of a copy of the prospectus to the Registrar for registration and a statement to that effect shall be included in the prospectus;

shall, without prejudice to any punishment to which any person may be liable under Section 36, be liable to pay compensation to every person who has sustained such loss or damage.

No person shall be liable under sub-section (1), if he proves—

(a) that, having consented to become a director of the company, he withdrew his consent before the issue of the prospectus, and that it was issued without his authority or consent; or

(b) that the prospectus was issued without his knowledge or consent, and that on becoming aware of its issue, he forthwith gave reasonable public notice that it was issued without his knowledge or consent.

In *Adams* v. *Thrift*[35] an action was brought by the plaintiff to recover compensation from a director of a company in respect of false statements incorporated in a prospectus. However, the director contended that the statements were prepared by the promoters and before issuing he enquired from one of them "Is everything perfectly alright" and the promoter said "of course, it is". The Court held that although the director honestly believes the statement to be true, he has no reasonable ground to do so. The Court said that the promoter is the very last person whose uncorroborated statement ought to be relied upon by an intending director as justification for saying that he has reasonable ground for belief. Accordingly, the director was held liable to the plaintiff.

**(B)** ***In the case of allotment:*** Directors may also incur personal liability for:

(i) *Irregular allotment*: Sec. 39 of the Act prohibits of allotment unless minimum subscription is received. Further it provides that the allotment shall not be made of any share capital of a company offered to the public for subscription unless the amount stated in the prospectus as the minimum amount not received by the

[35] (1915) 2 Ch 21.

company. If any director of a company knowingly contravenes above stipulation as prescribed under Sec. 39 with respect to allotment, he shall be liable to compensate the company and the allottee respectively for any loss, damages, or costs which the company or the allottee may have sustained or incurred thereby.

(ii) *Failure to repay application money*: If any amount is to be paid back to the applicant and it is not paid within the stipulated period as prescribed under the Act the directors of the company shall be jointly and severally liable to repay that money with interest on the expiry such stipulated period. However, a director shall not be liable if he proves that the default in repayment of money was not due to any misconduct or negligence on his part.

(iii) *Failure to repay application monies when application for listing of securities are not made or is refused.*

Sec. 40 of the Act requires that every company intending to offer shares or debentures to the public for subscription by the issue of a prospectus shall, before such issue, make an application to one or more recognised stock exchange for permission for the shares or debentures intending to be so offered to be dealt with in the stock exchange.

However, Sec. 40(5) provides that if a default is made, the company shall be punishable with a fine which shall not be less than five lakh rupees but which may extend to fifty lakh rupees and every officer of the company who is in default shall be punishable with imprisonment for a term which may extend to one year or with fine which shall not be less than fifty thousand rupees but which may extend to three lakh rupees, or with both.

**(C)** ***In the case of fraudulent trading:*** Directors may also be made personally liable for the debts or liabilities of a company by an order of the Tribunal under Sec. 339. Such an order shall be made by the Tribunal where the directors have been found guilty of fraudulent trading. Sec. 339(1) provides that if in the course of the winding-up of a company, it appears that any business of the company has been carried on, with intent to defraud creditors of the company or any other persons or for any fraudulent purpose, the Tribunal, on the application of the Official Liquidator, or the liquidator or any creditor or contributory of the company, may, if it thinks it proper so to do, declare that any persons who were knowingly parties to the carrying on of the business in the manner aforesaid shall be personally responsible, without any limitation of liability, for all or any of the debts or other liabilities of the company as the Tribunal may direct. Further, Sec. 339(3) provides that every person who was knowingly a party to the carrying on of the business in the manner aforesaid, shall be punishable with imprisonment, fine or both as per Sec. 447.

### 2. Criminal liability

Apart from the civil liability under that Act or under the common law, directors of a company may also incur criminal liability. Some of the provisions of the Companies Act, which make directors criminally liable, are as follows:

(i) Sec. 34 provides that any person who authorised the filing of prospectus or statement in lieu of prospectus shall be punishable with imprisonment, fine or both as per Section 447, if it is found that some or any untrue statements are incorporated therein. However, he would be exempted from such punishment provided that he proves either that such untrue statement was immaterial or that he had reasonable ground to believe and did up to the time of the filing of the prospectus or statement believe, that the statement was true.

(ii) Sec. 36 of the Act prescribes punishment for fraudulently inducing persons to invest money. It provides that any person who either by knowingly or recklessly making any statement, promise or forecast which is false, deceptive, or misleading or by any dishonest concealment of material facts, induces or attempts to induce another person to enter into any agreement for or with a view to acquiring, disposing of, subscribing for, or underwriting shares or debentures shall be punishable with imprisonment, fine or both as per Sec. 447.

(iii) Sec. 40 of the Act prescribes that the director may be punished with imprisonment for a term up to one year in case of failure to repay excess application money within the stipulated time prescribes in Sec. 40 of the Act.

(iv) Sec. 46 of the Act provides that if a company with intent to defraud renews a certificate or issues a duplicate thereof, the company shall be punishable with fine which shall not be less than five times the face value of the share involved in the issue of the duplicate certificate but which may extend to ten times the face value of such shares or rupees ten crores whichever is higher and every officer of the company who is in default shall be liable for action under Sec. 447.

(v) Sec. 164 of the Act prescribes penalty and imprisonment for a period of seven years or more and shall not be eligible to be appointed as a director in any company in case of undischarged insolvent acting as director.

(vi) Sec. 128 of the Act provides that it shall be the duty of every director, other officer or employee of the company to produce to the ROC and any other person authorized for inspection of all books of account and other books and papers of the company in his custody or control and to furnish him with any statement, information or explanation relating to the affairs of the company as the said person may require of him within such time and at such place as he may specify. If the director or other officer or employee does not assist or provide necessary documents or information required for inspection shall be punished with imprisonment for a term which may extend to one year or with fine which shall not be less than fifty thousand rupees but which may extend to five lakh rupees or with both.

(vii) Sec. 129 prescribes that a balance sheet and profit and loss account for that period shall be produced by the Board of directors of the company at every annual general meeting held in pursuance of Sec. 96 of the Act. In case of failure to do so a penalty and imprisonment has been prescribed by the Act which may extend up to one year or with fine which shall not be less than fifty thousand rupees but which may extend to five lakh rupees, or with both.

(viii) Sec. 222 of the Act imposes certain restrictions as well as prohibitions upon transfer of shares or debentures in certain cases. The director shall be punished up to with imprisonment for a term which may extend to six months or with fine which shall not be less than twenty-five thousand rupees but which may extend to five lakh rupees, or with both, if the director fails to honour such restrictions and prohibitions upon transfer of shares and debentures imposed by the Tribunal.

(ix) Sec. 182 of the Act prohibits and restricts for political contributions. It provides that no government company; and no other company which has been in existence for less than three financial years, shall contribute any amount or amounts, directly or indirectly to any political party; or for any political purpose to any person. However other companies not being a government company or a company existed more than three financial may contribute any amount or amounts, directly or indirectly to any political party or for any political purpose to any person. Further Section 182 stipulates that such contribution shall not be more than seven and a half per cent of its average net profits determined in accordance with the provision of Sec. 198 during the three immediately preceding financial years. If any director of a company contravenes the provision of Section 182, he shall be punished for a term which may extend to six months and with fine which may extend to five times the amount so contributed.

(x) Sec. 185 of the Act provides that no company makes any loan or gives any guarantee or provides any security in connection with a loan made without obtaining the previous approval of the Central Government. If the director contravenes the provision of Sec. 185, he shall be punished either with fine which may extend to twenty-five lakh rupees or with simple imprisonment for a term which may extend to six months, or both.

(xi) Sec. 184 of the Act provides that every director of a company who is in any way, whether directly or indirectly, concerned or interested in a contract or arrangement, or proposed contract or arrangement, entered into or to be entered into, by or on behalf of the company, shall disclose, the nature of his concern or interest at a meeting of the Board of directors or else he shall be punished with imprisonment for a term which may extend to one year or with fine which may extend to one lakh rupees, or both.

(xii) Sec. 243 of the Act provides that no managing or other director or manager whose agreement is so terminated or set aside shall act as the managing or other director or manager of the company for a period of five years from the date of the order terminating or setting aside the agreement without the leave of the Tribunal. Any person who knowingly acts as a managing or other director or manager of a company in contravention of the above stipulation shall be punishable with imprisonment for a term which may extent to six months, or with fine which may extend to five lakh rupees or with both.

(xiii) Sec. 305 of the Act requires a declaration of solvency in case of a proposal for voluntary winding-up. Any director of a company making a declaration without having reasonable grounds for the opinion that the company will be able to pay its debts in full within the period specified in the declaration shall be punishable with imprisonment for a term which may extend to three years, or with fine which may extend to three lakh rupees, or with both.

## MEETINGS OF DIRECTORS

A meeting of the Board of directors is an important forum in the working of companies. Several statutory prescriptions are incorporated in the Companies Act, 2013, to ensure that the actions approved by the Board are in the interest of the company and reflect the fiduciary nature of the duties of directors. Sec. 173 of the Act provides that every company, private or public, shall hold at least one meeting of the Board in a period of three months and four meetings in a year. But a company registered under Sec. 8 of the Companies Act has privilege that the Board or the Governing Body may meet at least once in six months.

### *Notice of meeting of the Board*

Section 173(3) of the Companies Act stipulates that a meeting of the Board of directors shall be held after giving notice. The notice shall be given in writing to every director in India and at his usual address in India. Notice shall be given reasonably in advance, say for seven days before the date of the meeting.

### *Time of holding Board Meetings*

Board meetings can be held during business hours or outside business hours. There is no restriction on that matter under the Act.

### *Place for holding Board Meeting*

Board meetings can be held at any place whether it is a company's registered office or head office or any other premises and whether or not it is within the same city, town, village or State in which the registered office of the company is situated. Board meeting can also be held at places other than these places including abroad.

### *Quorum of the Board Meeting*

In terms of the provisions of Sec. 174 of the Act, the quorum for a Board meeting shall be one-third of its total strength of directors who are in office or two directors whichever is higher. Any fraction arising in counting of one-third will be rounded off as one. For example, in a Board having seven directors, the quorum shall be three directors. It is also provided that where the interested directors exceed or equal two-third of the total strength, the number of remaining disinterested directors present at the meeting being not less than two shall be the quorum of that business of the meeting. This section also applies to a private company. Sec. 174(2) lays down only minimum number to from a quorum: the company by its articles can provide for a higher number as quorum.

### *Procedure where meeting adjourned for want of quorum*

If a meeting of the Board could not be held for want of quorum, then, unless the articles otherwise provide, the meeting shall automatically stand adjourned till the same day in the next week, at the same time and place, or if that day is a public holiday, till the next succeeding day which is not a public holiday, at the same time and place.

### *Time, day, and place for holding adjourned Board Meetings*

As per provisions of Sec. 174(4), if a Board meeting is adjourned for want of quorum then the adjourned meeting shall be held at the same day in the next week at the same time and place or if the day is a public holiday till the next succeeding day which is not a public holiday at the same time and place. Therefore, an adjourned meeting should be held only on a working day.

### *Directors cannot appoint a Proxy for Board Meetings*

The Companies Act provides that it is necessary for the directors to attend the Board meetings personally once in every quarter. Proxies are not allowed at Board meetings and directors are not allowed to appoint their representatives to attend the Board meetings and cast vote on their behalf.

### *Interested director not to participate or vote in Board's proceedings*

A director who is interested in any matter cannot participate or vote in connection with that matter. He will also not be considered for determining quorum for the meeting.

This provision is not applicable to:

1. A private company which is neither a subsidiary nor a holding company of a public company
2. A private company which is a subsidiary of a public company, in respect of any contract or arrangement entered into, or to be entered into, by the private company with the holding company thereof
3. Any contract of indemnity against any loss which the directors, or anyone or more of them, may suffer by reason of becoming or being sureties or a surety for the company
4. Any contract or arrangement entered into or to be entered into with a public company, or a private company which is a subsidiary of a public company, in which the interest of the director aforesaid consists solely (i) in his being a director of such company and the holder of not more than qualification or (ii) in his being a member holding not more than two per cent of its paid-up share capital
5. A public company, or a private company which is a subsidiary of a public company, in respect of which a notification by the Central Government is issued to the extent specified in the notification.

## REMUNERATION OF DIRECTORS

The remuneration payable to the directors of a company, including any managing or whole-time director shall be determined either by the AOA or by a special resolution passed by the company in general meeting. A director may receive remuneration by way of a fee for each meeting of the Board, or a committee thereof, attended by him. A director who is either in the whole-time employment of the company or a managing director may be paid remuneration either by way of a monthly, payment or at a specified percentage of the net profits of the company or partly by one way and partly by the other. Such remuneration cannot exceed five per cent of the net profits for one such director, and if there is more than one such director, ten per cent for all of them except with the approval of the Central Government.

The total managerial remuneration payable by a public company or a private company which is a subsidiary of a public company to its directors and its manager in any financial year must not exceed 11% of the net profits of the company calculated in accordance with the provisions of Secs. 197 and 198 of the Act. The above provisions pertaining to remuneration do not apply to a private company unless it is a subsidiary of a public company.

### *Director cannot to hold office or place of profit (Sec. 188)*

Except with the previous consent of the company accorded by a special resolution, no director of a company can hold any office or place of profit in that company. No partner or relative of such a director (i.e., a director holding an office or place of profit in the company), no firm in which such a director or relative is a partner, no private company of which such a director is a director or member, and no director, or manger of such a private company can hold any office or place of profit carrying monthly remuneration in excess of the prescribed amount.

If any office or place of profit under the company or a subsidiary thereof is held in contravention of the above provisions, the director, partner, relative, firm, private company or, manager shall be deemed to have vacated his office, with effect from the day following the date of general meeting mentioned above. Such person will also be liable to refund to the company any remuneration received, or the monetary equivalent of any perquisites or advantage enjoyed by him, in respect of such office or place of profit. The company will not be able to waive recovery of such amounts, except with the approval of the Central Government.

Any office or place in a company shall be deemed to be an office or place or profit under the company for these provisions:

(a) in case the office or place is held by a director, if the director holding it obtains from the company anything by way of remuneration over and above the remuneration to which he is entitled as such director, whether as salary, fees, commission, perquisites, the right to occupy free of rent any premises as a place of residence, or otherwise;

(b) in case the office or place is held by an individual other than a director or by any firm, private company, or other body corporate, if the individual, firm private company or body corporate holding it obtains from the company anything by way of remuneration whether as salary, fees, commission, perquisites, the right to occupy free of rent any premises as a place of residence, or otherwise.

None of the above provisions apply to a director appointed by the Central Government under Sec. 167(3) of the Companies Act, 2013.

# Chapter XII Meetings

A company is an artificial person created by law which is managed and supervised by human beings. Shareholders invest the money to receive dividend and debenture-holders provide loan to the company for a higher percentage of return. Various matters are discussed and decided by the shareholders in a meeting. Decisions are made usually according to the view of the majority of shareholders. Different policy decisions are taken place at the various meetings which may take place between members and between the directors. Therefore, the Companies Act, 2013, contains several provisions regarding meetings.

## REQUISITES OF A VALID MEETING

The following conditions must be satisfied for a meeting to be called a valid meeting:

1. It must be properly convened. The persons calling the meeting must be authorized to do so.
2. Proper and adequate notice must have been given to all those entitled to attend.
3. The meeting must be legally constituted. There must be a chairperson. The rules of quorum must be maintained and the provisions of the Companies Act, 2013 and the AOC must be complied with.
4. The business at the meeting must be validly transacted. The meeting must be conducted in accordance with the rules and regulations governing the meetings.

## KINDS OF MEETINGS

1. Shareholders' Meetings:
   (a) Annual General Meeting (AGM)
   (b) Extraordinary General Meeting (EGM)
   (c) Class Meeting
2. Board Meetings
3. Meetings of the Creditors

### Shareholders' Meetings

#### (A) Annual General Meeting (AGM) (Sec. 96): (Shareholders Meeting)

Shareholders or members exercise their rights for formulating the policy of the company. AGM is therefore known as an important institution for the protection of shareholders. The ultimate control of the company lies in the hands of shareholders and therefore it is required that without any fail they should come and attend the AGM. The shareholders review the work of the company and seek for clarifications. Important issues like appointment of directors, auditors, declaration of dividend, amendment to the MOA and other related matters are discussed. Resolutions are passed.

Every company other than a One Person Company shall hold a general meeting as its AGM in each year in addition to any other meetings. However, there shall not be a gap of more than fifteen months between two AGM. If any default is made in holding the AGM, the Tribunal may, on the application of any member of the company, direct the company to hold AGM. If a general meeting is held in pursuance of the direction of Tribunal, then such meeting shall be deemed to be an AGM of the company under the Act. The AGM must be held on a working day during business hours at the registered office of the company or at some other place within the city, town, or village in which the registered office of the company is situated.

### *Consequences of not Conducting an Annual General*

Failure to hold AGM can lead to several consequences, for example:

- **Tribunal Intervention:** The Tribunal has the authority to order the convening of an AGM under Section 97 of the Companies Act, 2013.
- **Financial Penalties:** If a company or any authorized person fails to conduct the AGM they may face monetary penalties. The Tribunal can impose a fine on the company and every officer found to be in default, with the fine amount extending to ₹ 1 lakh.
- **Continuing Default:** If the default continues beyond the initial penalty, the Tribunal may impose an additional fine of ₹ 5,000 per day for each day during which the default persists.

These consequences emphasize the importance of conducting AGMs in accordance with the statutory requirements and timelines as specified in the Companies Act 2013. Failure to do so can result in both financial penalties and legal intervention by the Tribunal.

### *Notice of Meeting*

A general meeting of a company may be called by giving not less than clear twenty-one days' notice either in writing or through electronic mode in such manner as may be prescribed. However, a general meeting may be called after giving a shorter notice if consent is given in writing or by electronic mode by not less than ninety-five per cent of the members entitled to vote at such meeting. Every notice of a meeting shall specify the place, date, day, and the hour of the meeting and shall contain a statement of the business to be transacted at such meeting. The notice of every meeting of the company shall be given to—

(a) every member of the company, legal representative of any deceased member or the assignee of an insolvent member;
(b) the auditor or auditors of the company; and
(c) every director of the company.

### Statement to be annexed to notice

A statement setting out the following material facts shall be attached with the notice:

(a) the nature of concern or interest, financial or otherwise, if any, in respect of each item of—
   (i) every director and the manager, if any;
   (ii) every other key managerial personnel; and
   (iii) relatives of the directors, managers, and other key managerial personnel.

(b) the consideration of financial statements and the reports of the Board of Directors and auditors—
   (i) the declaration of any dividend;
   (ii) the appointment of directors in place of those retiring;
   (iii) the appointment of, and the fixing of the remuneration of, the auditors;
   (iv) any other matter which deems fit for the interest of Company.

## CHAIRMAN

Unless the Articles of Association of the company otherwise provide, the members personally present at the meeting shall elect one of themselves to be the Chairman thereof on a show of hands. If a poll is demanded on the election of the Chairman, it shall be taken forthwith in accordance with the provisions of this Act and the Chairman elected on a show of hands shall continue to be the Chairman of the meeting until some other person is elected as Chairman as a result of the poll, and such other person shall be the Chairman for the rest of the meeting.

### *Duties of the Chairman*

Without a chairman, a meeting is incomplete. The chairman is the regulator of the meeting. His duties include the following:—

1. He must ensure that the meeting is properly convened and constituted, i.e., that proper notice has been given, that the required quorum is present, etc.
2. He must ensure that the provisions of the act and the articles in regard to the meeting and its procedures are observed.
3. He must ensure that business is taken in the order set out in agenda and no business which is not mentioned in the agenda is taken up unless agreed to by the members.
4. He must impartially regulate the proceedings of the meeting and maintain discipline at the meeting.
5. He may exercise his powers of adjournment of the meeting, should be in good faith feel that such a step is necessary. The chairman has the power to adjourn the meeting in case of indiscipline at the meeting. A chairman however does not have the power to stop or adjourn the meeting at his own will and pleasure. If he adjourns the meeting prematurely, the members present may decide to continue the meeting and elect another chairman and proceed with the business for which it was convened.

6. He must exercise his power to order a poll correctly and must order it to be taken when demanded properly.
7. He must exercise his casting vote bona fide in the interest of the company.

## Vote

Whenever an investor buys shares in the company he is entitled to certain rights. One such significant right is the right to vote on definite corporate matters. The voting right will be in the percentage of his shares in the paid-up equity share capital of the company. Therefore, if a shareholder owns 51% of the company's stake, he will have the right to exercise majority control over the company. Section 47 of the Company's Act 2013 bestows voting rights to the shareholders. This right incorporates the election of directors and recommendations for essential changes influencing the company.

The Chairman of the meeting shall take the voting by way of show hands at the first instance of any resolution. He is required to seek choice of the members present 'for' and then 'against' the resolution. The number of members voting for either side shall be counted and noted by the Chairman.

The following methods are adopted in the meeting of the company to know the opinion of the members for passing any resolution that proposed:

**(a)** *Voting by show of hands:* Sec. 107 of the Act prescribes that at any general meeting, a resolution put to the vote of the meeting shall be decided on a show of hands., if a poll or voting through electronic means is not demanded. A declaration by the Chairman of the meeting of the passing of a resolution by show of hands in the meeting of the company shall be conclusive evidence of the fact of passing of such resolution or otherwise.

**(b)** *Voting through electronic means:* Sec. 108 of the Act empowers the Central Government to prescribe the class or classes of companies and manner in which a member may exercise his right to vote by electronic means.

**(c)** *Postal ballot:* 'Postal Ballot' includes voting by shareholders by postal or electronic mode instead of voting personally by presenting for transacting businesses in a general meeting of the company.

Section 110 of the Companies Act, 2013 read with Rules 22 of Companies (Management and Administration) Rules, 2014 states about the provisions of Postal Ballot.

### *Items to be transacted through Postal Ballot:*

1. Alteration of the objects clause of the Memorandum.
2. Alteration of Articles of Association in relation to insertion or removal of provisions which are required to be included in the Articles of a company in order to constitute it a private company.
3. Change in place of Registered Office outside the local limits of any city, town, or village.
4. Change in objects for which a company has raised money from public through prospectus and still has any unutilized amount out of the money so raised.
5. Issue of shares with differential rights as to voting or dividend or otherwise.

6. Variation in the rights attached to a class of shares or debentures or other securities.
7. Buyback of shares by a company.
8. Appointment of a Director elected by Small Shareholders.
9. Sale of the whole or substantially the whole of an undertaking of a company or where the company owns more than one undertaking, of whole or substantially the whole of any of such undertakings.
10. Giving loans or extending guarantee or providing security in excess of the limit specified u/s 186.
11. Any other Resolution prescribed under any applicable law, rules or regulations.

***Items not to be transacted by means of Postal Ballot:***

1. Any item in the nature of Ordinary Business.
2. Any business in which directors or auditors have right to be heard at any meeting.

**(d)** *By Proxy:* The term 'proxy' is used in two ways under the Companies Act, 2013. The first refers to the individual appointed by a member to attend and vote in the meeting on his behalf as a representative. The other refers to the instrument/document by which such an individual is appointed as a proxy. The facility of proxy allows a member to vote in a meeting that he cannot attend due to any reason. The concept of proxy is extensively dealt with under Section 105 of the Companies Act, 2013. A proxy is an agent legally authorized to act on behalf of another party or a format that allows an investor to vote without being physically present at the meeting. Shareholders not attending a company's annual general meeting (AGM) may vote their shares by proxy by allowing someone else to cast votes on their behalf, or they may vote by mail. While proxy voting is often an option, management encourages shareholders to vote in person. If the shareholder cannot attend, voting by proxy is another option. For a person to act as a proxy for an individual, formal documentation may be required that outlines the extent to which the proxy can speak on the individual's behalf.

Any member of a company who is entitled to attend and vote at a meeting of the company shall be entitled to appoint another person as a proxy to attend and vote at the meeting on his behalf. A proxy need not be a member. A proxy shall be a Member in case of companies with charitable objects, etc. and not for profit registered under the specified provisions of the Act. A person appointed as proxy shall not have the right to give views on the agenda for which the meeting is conducted at the meeting. A proxy cannot vote on a show of hands. A proxy is not counted for quorum.

**(e)** *By Poll:* In case of dissatisfaction about the result of voting by show of hands a poll can be demanded. A poll may be ordered by the chairman of his own motion and he would be bound to order a poll when it is demanded in the following situations:

(a) in the case of a company having a share capital, by any member or members present in person or by proxy and holding shares in the company which confer a power to vote on the resolution not being less than one tenth of the total voting power in respect of the resolution, or on which an aggregate sum of not less than five lakh rupees has been paid-up.

(b) in the case of any other company, by any member or members present in person or by proxy and having not less than one tenth of the total voting power in respect of the resolution.

However, the demand for a poll may be withdrawn at any time by the person or persons who made the demand.

The Calcutta High Court in *Mahaliram* v. *Fort Gloster Manufacturing Company*[36] held that the Courts have evolved certain well-defined principles which regulate company meetings. *Primarily* the AOA and the company Statute provide the matrix of the Company Law on the point. *Secondly*, the Courts are generally reluctant to interfere with the decisions taken at company meetings, unless there is almost a manifest breach of the Articles or the Statute, because it is the company and not the Court which is responsible for its management. The Court is hardly a substitute for the company in this respect except in specified cases provided by Statute and these again are mostly cases where the company itself finds it difficult to manage its own affairs as in liquidation or schemes or where in public interest the Court has to interfere or sanction as in cases of fraud by the majority on the minority or cases of amalgamation or reduction. This is the rule of domestic forum applied to company jurisprudence. The third principle which the Courts have evolved as a corollary of the first two principles, is that '*prima facie*' the decision of the chairman at such company meetings is allowed to stand until it is proved to be in breach of the Articles or Statute. The burden of proving the chairman's decision to be wrong rests with the party challenging his decision and it is not for those who rely on his decision to bring evidence in the first instance, to show that the chairman was right. This is the rule of convenience and of practical wisdom. It is of great practical utility. The chairman by virtue of his position and the nature of his duties has to decide on the spot all emergent questions that arise at the meeting and it will be mere folly to reduce the *prima facie* authority of his verdict. The burden of holding and conducting company meetings and recording votes cast therein and for taking decisions at such meetings is the primary responsibility of the company's shareholders and their chosen directors and not of the High Court.

### *Quorum of AGM*

In the case of a private company, the quorum for AGM is two members present at the meeting. In the case of a public company, the quorum for AGM is five members present at the meeting if the number of members is within one thousand. Fifteen members present at the meeting if the number of members is more than one thousand but within five thousand. Thirty members present at the meeting if the number of members is more than five thousand.

In case the quorum for the meeting is not present within half an hour from the scheduled time, the meeting will be adjourned to the same day in the next week for the same time and at the same place.

[36] AIR 1955 Cal.132.

## RESOLUTIONS

Company decisions are usually taken through resolutions. Resolutions mean decisions taken at a meeting. A motion, with or without amendments is put to vote at a meeting. Once the motion is passed, it becomes a resolution. A valid resolution can be passed at a properly convened meeting with the required quorum. Resolutions are of two kinds, namely:

1. Ordinary resolution, and
2. Special resolution.

An ordinary resolution is one which can be passed by a simple majority, i.e., if the votes (including the casting vote, if any, of the chairman), at a general meeting cast by members entitled to vote in its favor are more than votes cast against it. Voting may be by way of a show of hands or by a poll.

A special resolution is one in regard to which is passed by a 75% majority only, i.e., the number of votes cast in favor of the resolution is at least three times the number of votes cast against it, either by a show of hands or on a poll in person or by proxy. The intention to propose a resolution as a special resolution must be specifically mentioned in the notice of the general meeting.

Special resolutions are needed to decide on important matters of the company. Examples where special resolutions are required are.

(a) Alteration of AOA while converting from Private Limited to Public Limited and vice versa
(b) To change the Registered office of the company outside the Local limits of the city, town, or village
(c) For Alteration of Memorandum of Association of the Company
(d) For Alteration of Article of Association of the Company
(e) Change in the Object Clause of Memorandum of Association of the Company
(f) To issue Global Depository Receipt in any Foreign Country
(g) Issue of Sweat Equity Shares (Except this share cannot be issued at discount)
(h) For issuing further shares to Employees of the Company under the scheme of Employee Stock Option Plan & to determine the terms of issuing Debentures convertible into shares
(i) Reduction of Share Capital
(j) Buyback of Shares
(k) To issue Debenture convertible into shares, wholly or partly
(l) Removal of Auditor appointed before expiry of his term
(m) Re-appointment of Independent Director for a further period of 5 years
(n) Restriction on power of Board
(o) Loans and Investment by the Company
(p) Appointment of persons aged 70 years or more as Managing Director, Whole Time Director, or Manager

(q) To apply to Central Government for conducting an investigation the affairs of the company.

(r) To apply to Fraud Investigation office for conducting investigation the affairs of the company.

(s) To make an application to Registrar for Striking off the name of Company Approval of Scheme of Merger and Amalgamation

(t) Winding-up of Company by Tribunal

**(B) Extraordinary General Meeting (EGM): (Sec. 100) (Shareholders Meeting)**

An extraordinary general meeting (EGM) refers to any shareholder meeting called by a company other than its scheduled AGM. The extraordinary general meeting is required to deal with urgent matters that come up between annual shareholders' meetings. An Extraordinary General Meeting (EGM) can be called by the members or shareholders of a company, but there are specific requirements outlined under Section 100 of the Companies Act, 2013. The Board may, whenever it deems fit, call an EGM of the company or the Board may call an EGM on the requisition of the members. Members who can request an EGM include those who hold at least 1/10th of paid-up capital of the company in case of companies having share capital, or members who hold at least 1/10th of total voting power of all the members in case of companies not having share capital. The Board shall hold such EGM within 21 days from the receipt of a valid requisition. If the Board fails to call the meeting within the stipulated period, the meeting may be called and held by the requisitionists themselves within 3 months from the date of requisition. Any reasonable expenses incurred by the requisitionists in calling a meeting shall be reimbursed to the requisitionists by the company and the sums so paid shall be deducted from any fee or other remuneration payable to the directors who were in default in calling the meeting in spite of proper requisition.

***Power of the Tribunal to call EGM: (Sec. 98)***

Sec. 98 of the Companies Act, 2013, empowers the Tribunal for calling of EGM if for any reason, the company could not call, hold, or conduct meeting. The Tribunal may order for a meeting of the company and hold or conduct it in such manner as it thinks fit. Sec. 98 provides that one member of the company present in person or by proxy shall be deemed to constitute a meeting. The Tribunal may do so either on its own motion or on the application of any director of the company or on the application of any member of the company who would be entitled to vote at the meeting.

**(C) Class Meeting: (Sec. 48)(Shareholders Meeting)**

Class meetings are meetings which are held by the holders of a particular class of shareholders that are normally called when it is proposed to vary the rights of that particular class of shares. Sec. 48 of the Act provides that where a share capital of the company is divided into different classes of shares, the rights attached to the shares of any class may be varied with the consent in writing of the holders of not less than three-fourth of the issued shares of that class or by means of a special resolution passed at a separate meeting of the holders of the issued shares of that class,—

(a) if provision with respect to such variation is contained in the memorandum or articles of the company; or

(b) in the absence of any such provision in the memorandum or articles, if such variation is not prohibited by the terms of issue of the shares of that class.

In case variation by one class of shareholders affects the rights of any other class of shareholders, the consent of three-fourths of such other class of shareholders shall also be obtained.

Where the holders of not less than ten per cent of the issued shares of a class did not consent to such variation or vote in favour of the special resolution for the variation, they may apply to the Tribunal to have the variation cancelled, and where any such application is made, the variation shall not have effect unless and until it is confirmed by the Tribunal. The decision of the Tribunal shall be binding on the shareholders. The company shall, within thirty days of the date of the order of the Tribunal, file a copy thereof with the Registrar.

## Board Meeting (Sec. 173)

Every company shall hold the first meeting of the Board of Directors within thirty days of the date of its incorporation and thereafter hold a minimum number of four meetings of its Board of Directors every year in such a manner that not more than one hundred and twenty days shall intervene between two consecutive meetings of the Board.

The participation of directors in a meeting of the Board may be either in person or through video conferencing or other audio-visual means, as may be prescribed, which are capable of recording and recognising the participation of the directors and of recording and storing the proceedings of such meetings along with date and time.

A meeting of the Board shall be called by giving not less than seven days' notice in writing to every director at his address registered with the company and such notice shall be sent by hand delivery or by post or by electronic means. However, a meeting of the Board may be called at shorter notice to transact urgent business subject to the condition that at least one independent director, if any, shall be present at the meeting. If the independent directors is not available in the meeting, decisions taken shall be circulated to all the directors and shall be final only on ratification thereof by at least one independent director, if any.

A One Person Company, small company and dormant company shall be deemed to have complied with the provisions of this section if at least one meeting of the Board of Directors has been conducted in each half of a calendar year and the gap between the two meetings is not less than ninety days. The provisions of Sec. 174 shall not apply to One Person Company in which there is only one director on its Board of Directors.

## Quorum for meetings of Board (Sec. 174)

The quorum for a meeting of the Board of Directors of a company shall be one third of its total strength or two directors, whichever is higher, and the participation of the directors by video conferencing or by other audio-visual means shall also be counted for the purposes of quorum.

Where a meeting of the Board could not be held for want of quorum, then, unless the articles of the company otherwise provide, the meeting shall automatically stand adjourned to the same day at the same time and place in the next week or if that day is a national holiday, till the next succeeding day, which is not a national holiday, at the same time and place.

## Meeting of Board: Passing of resolution by circulation (Sec. 175)

A company is a legal entity and it cannot function without the directors, hence there is Board of Directors. Board possesses the authority to exercise the company's powers, subject to the constraints outlined in the relevant laws, the company's memorandum and articles of association, and decisions made during general meetings of the company. The Board's periodic meetings serve as a platform for in-depth discussions on various matters, facilitating the collective wisdom of the Board in shaping the company's policies and operational decisions. However, there are instances where convening a formal Board meeting may be impractical, particularly when urgent decisions are essential. In such scenarios, the practice of passing resolutions by circulation is a valuable alternative, enabling the Board to address critical matters promptly without compromising the company's governance processes.

Therefore, Resolution by circulation provided under Sec. 175 of the Companies Act 2013 is indeed a useful option. At least one-third of the total directors of the company request that a circulated resolution should be decided at a meeting, the chairperson is obliged to put the resolution on the agenda for discussion at a Board meeting.

## Meetings of the Creditors (Sec. 230)

Where a compromise or arrangement is proposed between a company and its creditors or any class of them; the Tribunal may, on the application of the company or of any creditor order a meeting of the creditors or class of creditors, as the case may be, to be called, held, and conducted in such manner as the Tribunal directs. For the purpose of Sec. 230 of the Act, arrangement includes a re-organisation of the company's share capital by the consolidation of shares of different classes or by the division of shares into shares of different classes, or by both of those methods.

The company or any other person, by whom an application is made, shall disclose to the Tribunal by affidavit—

(a) all-material facts relating to the company, such as the latest financial position of the company, the latest auditor's report on the accounts of the company and the pendency of any investigation or proceedings against the company;

(b) reduction of share capital of the company, if any, included in the compromise or arrangement;

(c) any scheme of corporate debt restructuring consented to by not less than seventy-five per cent of the secured creditors in value, including—

    (i) a creditor's responsibility statement in the prescribed form;

    (ii) safeguards for the protection of other secured and unsecured creditors;

(iii) report by the auditor that the fund requirements of the company after the corporate debt restructuring as approved shall conform to the liquidity test based upon the estimates provided to them by the Board;

(iv) where the company proposes to adopt the corporate debt restructuring guidelines specified by the Reserve Bank of India, a statement to that effect; and

(v) a valuation report in respect of the shares and the property and all assets, tangible and intangible, movable, and immovable, of the company by a registered valuer.

Where a meeting is proposed to be called in pursuance of an order of the Tribunal, a notice of such meeting shall be sent to all the creditors or class of creditors of the company, individually at the address registered with the company which shall be accompanied by a statement disclosing the details of the compromise or arrangement, a copy of the valuation report, if any, and explaining their effect on creditors.

A notice shall provide that the persons to whom the notice is sent may vote in the meeting either themselves or through proxies or by postal ballot to the adoption of the compromise or arrangement within one month from the date of receipt of such notice:

The Tribunal shall provide for all or any of the following matters, namely:—

(a) where the compromise or arrangement provides for conversion of preference shares into equity shares, such preference shareholders shall be given an option to either obtain arrears of dividend in cash or accept equity shares equal to the value of the dividend payable;

(b) the protection of any class of creditors;

(c) if the compromise or arrangement results in the variation of the shareholders' rights, it shall be given effect to under the provisions of Sec. 48;

The order of the Tribunal shall be filed with the Registrar by the company within a period of thirty days of the receipt of the order. The Tribunal may dispense with calling of a meeting of creditor or class of creditors where such creditors or class of creditors, having at least ninety per cent value, agree and confirm, by way of affidavit, to the scheme of compromise or arrangement. However, no compromise or arrangement in respect of any buyback of securities under Sec. 230 shall be sanctioned by the Tribunal unless such buyback is in accordance with the provisions of Section 68. An aggrieved party may make an application to the Tribunal in the event of any grievances with respect to the takeover offer of companies other than listed companies in such manner as may be prescribed and the Tribunal may, on application, pass such order as it may deem fit.

## REGISTRATION OF RESOLUTIONS AND AGREEMENTS

All resolutions and agreements are to be registered with ROC within thirty days of the passing or making thereof as per Sec. 117 of the Act. If a company fails to file the resolution or the agreement before the expiry of the period specified under the Act, the company shall be punishable with fine which shall not be less than five lakh rupees but which may extend to twenty-five lakh rupees and every officer of the company who is in default, including liquidator of the company, if any, shall be punishable with fine which shall not be less than one lakh rupees but which may extend to five lakh rupees.

Following resolutions and agreements are to be registered with ROC—

(a) special resolutions;

(b) resolutions which have been agreed to by all the members of a company, but which, if not so agreed to, would not have been effective for their purpose unless they had been passed as special resolutions;

(c) any resolution of the Board of Directors of a company or agreement executed by a company, relating to the appointment, re-appointment or renewal of the appointment, or variation of the terms of appointment, of a managing director;

(d) resolutions or agreements which have been agreed to by any class of members but which, if not so agreed to, would not have been effective for their purpose unless they had been passed by a specified majority or otherwise in some particular manner; and all resolutions or agreements which effectively bind such class of members though not agreed to by all those members;

(e) resolutions requiring a company to be wound up voluntarily passed in pursuance of the Insolvency and Bankruptcy Code 2016;

(f) resolutions passed in pursuance of sub-section (3) of Section 179; and

(g) any other resolution or agreement as may be prescribed and placed in the public domain.

# Chapter XIII Majority Powers and Minority Rights

This chapter intends to discuss about the protection of minority shareholders in the corporate sectors. The majority shareholders always prefer that their decision should prevail in the administration of company and they do not like that minority shareholders should interfere in the company's administration. The aim of modern company law to strike a balance between the supremacy of majority shareholders and provides due protection to the minority shareholders and recognizes the rights of minority shareholders as well.

The Rule in *Foss* v. *Harbottle* is actually rule of majority supremacy. It means that once a resolution is passed by majority, it is binding on all the members including the minority shareholders. The Court will not interfere to protect the minority interest so long the directors' act within their power. This is based on the rational that each person impliedly consents to submit to the will of majority. In other words, it is a corollary to the rule that only the company can sue, which again translates to the wish of the majority.

## *FOSS* v. *HARBOTTLE*[37]

The basic principle relating to the administration of the company is that the Court will not, in general, intervene at the instance of shareholders in matters of internal administration,

[37] (1843) 67 ER 189.

and will not interfere with the management of a company by its directors, so long as they are acting within the power conferred on them under the Articles of Association.[38] The rule was laid down in 1843 where the facts of the case are as follows:

> Two minority shareholders initiated legal proceedings against, among others, the directors of the company. The claimants asked the court to order the defendants to compensate for losses to the company as a result of alleged fraudulent activity. Wigram VC held that since the company's board of directors was still in existence, and since it was still possible to call a general meeting of the company, there was nothing to prevent the company from obtaining redress in its corporate character and thus the action by the claimants could not be sustained.

The Court further held that the corporation should sue in its own name and in its corporate character, or in the name of someone whom the law has appointed to be its representative. The Court observed that the conduct with which the directors are charged is an injury not to the plaintiff (two minority shareholders) exclusively, it is an injury to the whole corporation. In such cases the rule is that the corporation should come to the Court and sue in its own name and its corporate character. It is not a matter for any individual shareholder or minority shareholders to assume to himself or themselves the right of suing in the name of corporation. In the eye of law, the corporation and aggregate of members of a corporation are not same.

The rule in *Foss* v. *Harbottle* is that a Court will not interfere with the ordinary management of a company acting within its powers and has no jurisdiction to do so at the instance of the shareholders. A shareholder is entitled to institute a suit to enforce his individual rights against the company such as his right to vote, or his right to stand as a director of a company at an election. If the shareholder however intends to obtain redress in respect of a wrong done to the company or to recover monies as damages alleged to be due to the company, the action should ordinarily be brought by the company itself. In order therefore to enable a shareholder to institute a suit in the name of the company; in such a case, there must be the sanction of the majority for corporate action. In ordinary cases, therefore, this principle implies the supremacy of the will of the majority. It is open to a majority always to set right a thing which was done by the majority either illegally or irregularly if the thing complained of was one which the majority of the company were entitled to do legally and was within the powers of the company by calling a fresh meeting. That is the reason why in such cases the Court refuses to interfere at the instance of a a shareholder even in a representative action brought by him. If the majority, however, acts in an oppressive manner, it is not as if the minority are without a remedy.

The underlying principles of *Foss* v. *Harbottle* case may be summerised as follows:

1. The Court would not interfere in the corporate administration if the allegation made by the shareholder or shareholders could be ratified by the company in AGM.
2. The company alone can sue in its own name.
3. The minority shareholders should not assume that they are custodian of company.

[38] *Rajahmundry Electric Supply Corporation Ltd.* v. *A. Nageshwara Rao,* AIR 1956 SC 213.

The rule has several advantages:

1. It prevents members from bringing numerous separate individual actions, i.e., multiplicity of suits.
2. The court is likely to accept the majority decisions and reject individual actions. This would prevent wasteful actions.
3. It would prevent vexatious actions from dissatisfied individual members trying to harass the company.

However, the best known and perhaps the clearest statement of the rule in *Foss* v. *Harbottle* was actually set out by Jenkins LJ in the case of *Edwards* v. *Halliwell*.[39]

> "The rule in Foss v. Harbottle, as I understand it, comes to no more than this. First, the proper plaintiff in an action in respect of a wrong alleged to be done to a company or association of persons is *prima facie* the company or the association of persons itself. Secondly, where the alleged wrong is a transaction which might be made binding on the company or association and on all its members by a simple majority of the members, no individual member of the company is allowed to maintain an action in respect of that matter for the simple reason that, if a mere majority of the members of the company or association is in favour of what has been done, then *cadit quaestio*."[40]

The rule established that where the company suffers harm, the company itself is the true and proper claimant. Therefore, the shareholders cannot generally sue for wrongs done to the company. The *Foss* v. *Harbottle* Rules are well recognized by the Supreme Court of India in *Rajahmundry Electric Supply Co.* v. *Nageshwara Rao* (AIR 1956 SC213).

### Exceptions

It is essential to recognize the rule of majority supremacy in the corporate sectors for smooth functioning of corporate administration and it is also required that minority shareholders' interest must be protected. Therefore, the Companies Act and common law prescribes some exception to the rule of *Foss* v. *Harbottle*. The *Foss* v. *Harbottle* rule may be extended only in situations where the "managerial sins" may be ratified. In other cases, every shareholder may sue in representative character of the corporate interest, i.e., may bring a "derivative action" (as it is called in America.). The exceptions can be categorized under two limbs, i.e., A. Companies Act, and, B. Common law.

#### (A) Companies Act

Following are some of the instances of minority protection under the Companies Act, 2013:—

### The variation of class rights (Sec. 48)

Where the share capital of a company is divided into different classes of shares, the rights attached to the share of any class can be varied as per the MOA or Article of the company. However, it can be done with the consent 3/4th majority of the class or with a special resolution passed at a separate meeting of the holders of the issued shares. Where

39 [1950] 2 All ER 1064.

40 Id at p. 1066 per Jenkins LJ.

the holders of not less than ten per cent of the issued shares of a class did not consent to such variation or vote in favour of the special resolution for the variation, they may apply to the Tribunal to have the variation cancelled.

### Investigation into the affairs of the company (Sec. 213)

Sec. 213 provides that not less than 100 members or members holding not less than one-tenth of the total voting power (in the case of a company having a share capital) may apply to the tribunal seeking for an investigation into the affairs of the company. Similarly in case of a company without share capital, such application can be made by not less than one-fifth of the members of the company. However, for seeking an order for conducting investigation into the affairs of the company the application must be supported with proper evidence.

### Compromise or arrangement (Sec. 230)

This section provides for schemes of compromise or make arrangements with creditors and members. Under Sec. 230 (7) (c) it provides that if the compromise or arrangement results in the variation of the shareholders' rights, it shall be given effect to under the provisions of Section 48. This is already discussed as a provision of minority protection. In addition to this Sec. 230 (7) (e) provides that an order made by the Tribunal shall provide for an exit offer to dissenting shareholders thereby effectively implementing the terms of the compromise or the arrangement.

### Right of dissenting shareholders under an arrangement of take-over (Sec. 235)

When an offer to take-over of all the shares is made by a company (Transferee company) to another company (Transferor company) and the same is accepted by not less than 90% of the holders of the shares of the transferor company, the transferee company may acquire remaining share on the same terms. However, notice has to be given to the dissenting shareholders who have the right to apply to the tribunal praying that their shares should not be allowed to be acquired under the terms of the scheme. The tribunal may make an order as it thinks fit, after hearing both the parties.

### Oppression and mismanagement (Sec. 241)

Sec. 241 is an exception to the majority rule. Any member of a company who complains that the affairs of the company have been or are being conducted in a manner prejudicial to public interest or in a manner prejudicial or oppressive to him or prejudicial to the interests of the company may apply to the Tribunal for an order.

### Class Action (Sec. 245)

In case the members or depositors are of the opinion that the management or conduct of the affairs of the company is being carried out in a manner detrimental to the company's interests or the interests of its members, they have the option to file an application before the Tribunal. This application, filed on behalf of the members or depositors, seeks one or more orders under Sec. 245 of the relevant legislation.

**(B) Common Law**

1. *Ultra Vires acts*

*Ultra vires* means those things which are outside the scope of objective clause of MOA. A shareholder is entitled to bring an action against the company and its officers in respect of matters which are *ultra vires* the company. This exception is based on the rational that acts which are beyond the memorandum are completely illegal and cannot be ratified by the majority. Once the action is *ultra vires* it cannot be validated or ratified by even a unanimous vote. The best example may be *Bharat Insurance Co. Ltd.* v. *Kanhaiya Lal.*[41]

In this case the plaintiff was the shareholder of the respondent company. One of the object clauses was, '*to advance money at interest on the security of land, houses, machinery and other properties situated in India...*' The plaintiff complained that several investments have been made by the company without adequate security and contrary to the provisions of the memorandum and therefore prayed for a perpetual injunction to restrain it from making such investments.

The court observed that the broad rule in such cases is no doubt that in all matters of internal management of a company, the company itself is the best judge of its affairs and the Court should not interfere. But the application of the assets of the company is not a matter of mere internal management. It is alleged that the directors are acting *ultra vires* in their application of the funds of the company. Under these circumstances a single member can maintain a suit for declaration as to the true construction of the article in question.

In *Lowe* v. *Fahey*[42] the funds of the company were diverted to extraneous purposes. The Court held that it had jurisdiction to pass an order for repayment to the company not only against the guilty members and directors but also against third persons who had knowingly received such money or improperly assisted the wrongful diversion.

In such a case the plaintiff shareholder can bring either a personal action, basing himself upon the company's breach of its memorandum, or a derivative action, basing himself upon the wrong done to the company by those who have caused it to act ultra vires. If the action is designed to prevent a threatened *ultra vires* act, the plaintiff may bring either a personal or representative action against the company, and the directors may be joined as co-defendants so that an injunction may be made against them too but if the plaintiff member seeks an order that the company shall recover compensation for an *ultra vires* act which has already been committed, or shall recover property disposed of by an *ultra vires* transaction, the action must be a derivative one.

A shareholder would be barred from bringing an action under this exception if:

(i) the plaintiffs own conduct is not proper, or
(ii) there is an unacceptable delay in filing the action, or
(iii) if the plaintiff is not a proper person to bring an action.

It is the duty of the Court to look at the plaintiff's conduct in order to satisfy itself that the plaintiff is a proper person to bring the action. The plaintiff's own conduct in a

41 AIR 1935 Lah 792.

42 [1988] Ch 114.

particular situation must be proper. If it is found that the plaintiffs conduct was so tainted as to bar an equitable relief, he will not be allowed to bring the action.

Where there is unreasonable, unacceptable, and unexplained delay in filing the action, the plaintiff may be barred from bringing the action.

Where the plaintiff is not the proper person to bring the action he would be barred from taking the benefit of the exception. In a matrimonial proceeding in *Narcombe* v. *Narcombe*[43] where an action was brought by the wife, a minority shareholder, against the wrong doing of her husband as a director, the Court held that she was not a proper plaintiff for a derivative action because she came to know improper profits made by the husband and such profits were taken into consideration in preparing the award.

2. *Fraud on minority*

The rule of *Foss* v. *Harbottle* would not be available if it is proved that the conduct of a majority of shareholders constitutes a "fraud on the minority". The concept of "fraud on the minority" can best be understood with reference to *Menier* v. *Hooper's Telegraph Works*[44] case.

Two companies M and H were in rivalry. The majority of the members of company M were also members of company H. Company M had commenced an action against company H. At a meeting of company M, the majority passed a resolution to compromise the action in a manner which was favourable to company H and unfavourable to M. Thus, they attempted to deprive the company of the benefits which could have been recovered from company H. Consequently, in an action by the minority, the resolution was held invalid. The Court observed that resolution passed by the majority is nothing but a fraud on minority. The majority would be benefited at the cost of minority.

In *Brown* v. *British Abrasive Wheels Co.*[45] a company was in dire need of further capital. The majority shareholders, who control 98% of the shareholding were willing to provide further capital into the company if they could buy up the remaining 2% shares of the minority shareholders. Having failed to buy the 2% shares through agreement, the majority sought to alter the AOA which enables the majority shareholders to acquire the 2% shares of minority shareholders on certain terms and conditions. The minority shareholders refused to surrender their 2% shares and brought an action to test the validity of resolution passed by the majority. The minority shareholders obtained an injunction to restraint the company adopting the alteration.

Justice Astbury in *Brown* case stated that the question is whether the enforcement of the proposed alteration on the minority is within the ordinary principles of justice and whether it is for the benefit of the company as a whole. The Court finds it difficult to follow how it can be just and equitable that a majority, on failing to purchase the shares of a minority by agreement, can take power to do so compulsorily. The defendants (majority shareholders) contend that it is for the benefit of the company as a whole because in default of further capital, the company might go into liquidation. The Court rejected the contention of majority and held that it is nothing but a fraud on minority.

43 [1985] 1 All ER 65 CA.

44 [1874] 9 Ch App 350.

45 [1919] 1 Ch 290.

3. *Resolutions/decisions requiring special majority*

Certain acts can be done only through passing a special resolution at AGM. If the majority without passing special resolution act on these matters because they are unable to get due support from the minority, any member may approach to the Court and the majority would not be allowed to take the advantage of *Foss* v. *Harbottle* case.

4. *Wrongdoers in control*

Company may sue in its own name. In other words, the company itself is to bring an action where it has an interest. Company being an artificial person someone has to represent on behalf of the company. But there may be a situation where the company is itself is controlled by the wrongdoer and no one has been authorized to protect the interest of the company and it may be difficult to conduct AGM where authorization may be issued. In that case for best interest of the company any member of the company would be entitled to approach the court for protecting the interest of the company and thereby rule of *Foss* v. *Harbottle* would not be applied.

5. *Individual membership rights*

Every shareholder has certain personal rights. These rights are conferred upon shareholders either by law or AOA. Such rights are commonly known as "individual membership rights". So far as individual membership right is concerned every shareholder has got the right to assert it in his own name, but if the infringement of a corporate membership right is alleged his remedy is a representative action on behalf of himself and other shareholders or in some instances an action in the name of the company. Individual membership right should not be confused with the rights available for qualified minorities. The question for decision therefore is whether the particular right asserted in a particular case is an individual membership right or a corporate membership right. If it is a corporate membership right it is subject to the will of the majority provided that will is expressed in accordance with the law and the AOC. With respect to this right the principle of supremacy of the majority will apply and the rule in *Foss* v. *Harbottle* will get itself attracted.

*Pender* v. *Lushington*[46] is a leading case in which the law confirms that a company member's right to vote may not be interfered with, because it is a right of property. Furthermore, any interference leads to the personal right of a member to sue in his own name to enforce his right. As Lord Jessel MR put it, a member has a right to say,

> *"Whether I vote in the majority or minority, you shall record my vote, as that is a right of property belonging to my interest in this company, and if you refuse to record my vote I will institute legal proceedings against you to compel you."*

Accordingly, the Court held that Pender could have an injunction for his vote to be recorded. Pender's vote was a property right which could not be interfered with, nor were the motives in this case such as to make the vote invalid. Furthermore, as a matter of litigation, Pender could sue in the name of the company, as well as in his own name. Interference with a personal right created both a derivative claim and a personal action.

The Kerala High Court in *C.L. Joseph* v. *Jos*[47] held that the right of a shareholder to stand for election as a director of the Company is an individual membership right and gives

[46] (1877) 6 Ch D 70.

[47] AIR 1965 Ker 68.

rise to a justiciable issue. In this case the wrong done to the plaintiff is not a wrong which the majority can ratify as it would be against the provisions of the Articles of Association, and it is settled by authorities that a shareholder can insist on the strict observance of the legal rules, statutory provisions and provisions in the memorandum and articles which cannot be waived by a bare majority of shareholders. In these circumstances, the Court was of the view that the contentions that the plaintiff had no right to move the Civil Court must be overruled.

# Chapter XIV Prevention of Oppression and Mismanagement

The majority rule usually prevails in the corporate sectors and it may cause dissatisfaction among the minority shareholders and some time it may be prejudicial to the interest of minority shareholders. Therefore, the Companies Act intends to protect minority shareholders in the case of oppression and mismanagement of the companies' affairs. Sections 241 to 246 of the Companies Act, 2013 empower (i) the Tribunal, and (ii) the Central Government to deal with such situations.

## WHAT IS OPPRESSION?

The term 'oppression' has not been defined under the Act. It may be an act or omission on the part of management which implies majority. Oppression is not confined to minority only. There may be situations where the majority may be oppressed. Therefore, both majority as well as minority can seek relief under the Companies Act. The Supreme Court in *Shanti Prasad Jain* v. *Kalinga Tubes Ltd.*[48] observed that the question in each case is whether the conduct of the affairs of a company by the majority shareholders was oppressive to the minority shareholders and that depends upon the facts of the case. It is not enough to reach into the conclusion that there is just and equitable cause for winding-up the company. It must further be shown that the conduct of the majority shareholders was oppressive to the minority as members and this requires that events have to be considered not in isolation but as a part of a consecutive story. There must be continuous acts on the part of the majority shareholders, continuing up to the date of petition, showing that the affairs of the company were being conducted in a manner oppressive to some part of the members. The conduct must be burdensome, harsh, and wrongful and mere lack of confidence between the majority shareholders and the minority shareholders would not be enough unless the lack of confidence springs from oppression of a minority by a majority in the management of the company's affairs, and such oppression must involve at least an element of lack of probity or fair dealing to a member in the matter of his proprietary rights as a shareholder. It is in the light of these principles that the Court has to consider the facts in the case with reference to oppression and mismanagement.

In 1965 the Supreme Court in *Shanti Prasad Jain* case referred few English cases and following observations are made which are to be kept in mind before invoking provisions relating to oppression and *mismanagement* and they are as follows:

[48] AIR 1965 SC 1535. This case was decided under Section 397 of the Companies Act, 1956.

(1) The oppression of which a petitioner complains must relate to the manner in which the affairs of the company concerned are being conducted; and the conduct complained of must be such as to oppress a minority of the members (including the petitioners) qua shareholders

(2) It follows that the oppression complained of must be shown to be brought about by a majority of members exercising as shareholders a predominant voting power in the conduct of the company's affairs.

(3) Although the facts relied on by the petitioner may appear to furnish grounds for the making of a winding-up order under the 'just and equitable' rules, those facts must be relevant to disclose also that the making of a winding-up order would unfairly prejudice the minority members qua shareholders.

(4) Although the word 'oppressive is not defined, it is possible, by way of illustration, to figure a situation in which majority shareholders, by an abuse of their predominant voting power, are' treating the company and its affairs as if they were their own property' to the prejudice of the minority shareholders-and in which just and equitable grounds would exist for the making of a winding-up order but in which the 'alternative remedy' provided by the Companies Act by way of an appropriate order might well be open to the minority shareholders with a view to bringing to an end the oppressive conduct of the majority.

(5) The power-conferred on the Court to grant a remedy in an appropriate case appears to envisage a reasonably wide discretion vested in the Court in relation to the order sought by a complainer as the appropriate equitable alternative to a winding-up order.

In 1981 the Supreme Court in *Needle Industries (India) Ltd.* v. *Needle Industries Newey (India) Holdings Ltd.*[49] held that in an application under Sec. 397 ( now Sec. 241 of the Companies Act, 2013) before grating relief the Tribunal has to satisfy itself that to wind-up the company will unfairly prejudice the members complaining of oppression, but that otherwise the facts will justify the making of a winding-up order on the ground that it is just and equitable that the company should be wound up. An isolated act, which is contrary to law may not necessarily and by itself support the inference that the law violated with a mala fide intention or that such violation was burdensome, harsh, and wrongful. But a series of illegal acts following upon one another can, in the context, lead justifiably to the conclusion that they are a part of the same transaction, of which the object is to cause or commit the oppression of persons against whom those acts are directed. On a true construction of Sec. 397(now Sec. 241 of the Companies Act, 2013), the unwise, inefficient, or careless conduct of a Director in the performance of his duties cannot give rise to a claim for relief under that section. The person complaining of oppression must show that he has been constrained to submit to a conduct which lacks in probity, conduct which is unfair to him and which causes prejudice to him in the exercise of his legal and proprietary rights as shareholder.

For better understanding the topic relating to oppression and mismanagement, it is highly essential to read actual verbatims of Sec. 241 of the Companies Act, 2013.

[49] AIR 1981 SC 1298.

**Section 241: Application to Tribunal for relief in cases of oppression, etc.—**

(1) Any member of a company who complains that—

(a) the affairs of the company have been or are being conducted in a manner prejudicial to public interest or in a manner prejudicial or oppressive to him or any other member or members or in a manner prejudicial to the interests of the company; or

(b) the material change, not being a change brought about by, or in the interests of, any creditors, including debenture-holders or any class of shareholders of the company, has taken place in the management or control of the company, whether by an alteration in the Board of Directors, or manager, or in the ownership of the company's shares, or if it has no share capital, in its membership, or in any other manner whatsoever, and that by reason of such change, it is likely that the affairs of the company will be conducted in a manner prejudicial to its interests or its members or any class of members,

may apply to the Tribunal, provided such member has a right to apply under Section 244 for an order under this Chapter.

(2) The Central Government, if it is of the opinion that the affairs of the company are being conducted in a manner prejudicial to public interest, it may itself apply to the Tribunal for an order under this Chapter.

Provided that the applications under this sub-section, in respect of such company or class of companies, as may be prescribed, shall be made before the Principal Bench of the Tribunal which shall be dealt with by such Bench.

(3) Where in the opinion of the Central Government there exist circumstances suggesting that—

(a) any person concerned in the conduct and management of the affairs of a company is or has been in connection therewith guilty of fraud, misfeasance, persistent negligence, or default in carrying out his obligations and functions under the law or of breach of trust;

(b) the business of a company is not or has not been conducted and managed by such person in accordance with sound business principles or prudent commercial practices;

(c) a company is or has been conducted and managed by such person in a manner which is likely to cause, or has caused, serious injury or damage to the interest of the trade, industry or business to which such company pertains; or

(d) the business of a company is or has been conducted and managed by such person with intent to defraud its creditors, members or any other person or otherwise for a fraudulent or unlawful purpose or in a manner prejudicial to public interest, the Central Government may initiate a case against such person and refer the same to the Tribunal with a request that the Tribunal may inquire into the case and record a decision as to whether or not such person is a fit and proper person to hold the office of director or any other office connected with the conduct and management of any company.

(4) The person against whom a case is referred to the Tribunal under sub-section (3), shall be joined as a respondent to the application.

(5) Every application under sub-section (3)—

(a) shall contain a concise statement of such circumstances and materials as the Central Government may consider necessary for the purposes of the inquiry; and

(b) shall be signed and verified in the manner laid down in the Code of Civil Procedure, 1908, for the signature and verification of a plaint in a suit by the Central Government.

The phrase used in Sec. 241 *"are being conducted"* implies that there must be continuous acts constituting oppression till the date of petition. However mere illegal, invalid or irregular acts done by the majority would not constitute oppression. After considering the different case studies it is found that the following acts or omissions have been considered as oppression by the Courts/Tribunal and they are as follows:

(i) An attempt to force new and more risky objects upon an unwilling minority may in some circumstances amount to oppression.

(ii) Loans given to other companies at a lower rate in which directors are interested.

(iii) Causing benefit to other companies where one of the groups has interest.

(iv) Non-declaration of dividend, when there is adequate profit in the background of understanding between the parties that they will have some regular income.

(v) Further issue of shares in such a way that existing percentage holding gets changed to the disadvantage of one group.

(vi) High remuneration paid to director.

(vii) An attempt to deprive a member of his ordinary membership rights.

(viii) Person not appointed as director when it was understood that he would be entitled to participate in the management.

(ix) Cornering shares by one group to disturb the percentage holding the other group or transferring or refusing to transfer of shares.

(x) Amending the articles or refusing to amend the articles contrary to understanding.

(xi) Usurpation of office of Director.

(xii) Short notice of meeting intended to overshadow minority shareholders.

## WHAT IS MISMANAGEMENT?

The term *'mismanagement'* is used only in the title of the Chapter XVI of the Companies Act,2013 whereas the word *'mismanagement'* could not be found in the body of the provision. Sec. 241 of the Act provides that any members of a company who have rights to apply in virtue of Sec. 244 may complain—

(i) that the affairs of the company are being conducted in a manner prejudicial to the interests of the company, or

(ii) that a material change has taken place in the management or control of the company and that by reason of such change, it is likely that the affairs of the company will be conducted in a manner prejudicial to the interest of the company.

On such application being made, if the Tribunal is of opinion that the affairs of the company are being conducted in a manner prejudicial to the interests of the company, or any material change has taken place in the management leading to prejudicial to the interest of the company, the Tribunal may, with a view to bringing to an end or preventing the matters complained of or apprehended, make such order as it thinks fit.[50]

## POWERS OF TRIBUNAL ON APPLICATION UNDER SECTION 241

**Section 242: Powers of Tribunal:**

(1) If, on any application made under Section 241, the Tribunal is of the opinion—

(a) that the company's affairs have been or are being conducted in a manner prejudicial or oppressive to any member or members or prejudicial to public interest or in a manner prejudicial to the interests of the company; and

(b) that to wind up the company would unfairly prejudice such member or members, but that otherwise the facts would justify the making of a winding-up order on the ground that it was just and equitable that the company should be wound up, the Tribunal may, with a view to bringing to an end the matters complained of, make such order as it thinks fit.

(2) Without prejudice to the generality of the powers under sub-section (1), an order under that sub-section may provide for—

(a) the regulation of conduct of affairs of the company in future;

(b) the purchase of shares or interests of any members of the company by other members thereof or by the company;

(c) in the case of a purchase of its shares by the company as aforesaid, the consequent reduction of its share capital;

(d) restrictions on the transfer or allotment of the shares of the company;

(e) the termination, setting aside or modification, of any agreement, howsoever arrived at, between the company and the managing director, any other director or manager, upon such terms and conditions as may, in the opinion of the Tribunal, be just and equitable in the circumstances of the case;

(f) the termination, setting aside or modification of any agreement between the company and any person other than those referred to in clause (e): Provided that no such agreement shall be terminated, set aside, or modified except after due notice and after obtaining the consent of the party concerned;

(g) the setting aside of any transfer, delivery of goods, payment, execution, or other act relating to property made or done by or against the company

[50] *Shanti Prasad Jain* v. *Kalinga Tubes Ltd.*, AIR 1965 SC 1535.

within three months before the date of the application under this section, which would, if made or done by or against an individual, be deemed in his insolvency to be a fraudulent preference;

(h) removal of the managing director, manager, or any of the directors of the company;

(i) recovery of undue gains made by any managing director, manager, or director during the period of his appointment as such and the manner of utilisation of the recovery including transfer to Investor Education and Protection Fund or repayment to identifiable victims;

(j) the manner in which the managing director or manager of the company may be appointed subsequent to an order removing the existing managing director or manager of the company made under clause (h);

(k) appointment of such number of persons as directors, who may be required by the Tribunal to report to the Tribunal on such matters as the Tribunal may direct;

(l) imposition of costs as may be deemed fit by the Tribunal;

(m) any other matter for which, in the opinion of the Tribunal, it is just and equitable that provision should be made.

(3) A certified copy of the order of the Tribunal under sub-section (1) shall be filed by the company with the Registrar within thirty days of the order of the Tribunal.

(4) The Tribunal may, on the application of any party to the proceeding, make any interim order which it thinks fit for regulating the conduct of the company's affairs upon such terms and conditions as appear to it to be just and equitable.

(5) Where an order of the Tribunal under sub-section (1) makes any alteration in the memorandum or articles of a company, then, notwithstanding any other provision of this Act, the company shall not have power, except to the extent, if any, permitted in the order, to make, without the leave of the Tribunal, any alteration whatsoever which is inconsistent with the order, either in the memorandum or in the articles.

(6) Subject to the provisions of sub-section (1), the alterations made by the order in the memorandum or articles of a company shall, in all respects, have the same effect as if they had been duly made by the company in accordance with the provisions of this Act and the said provisions shall apply accordingly to the memorandum or articles so altered.

(7) A certified copy of every order altering, or giving leave to alter, a company's memorandum or articles, shall within thirty days after the making thereof, be filed by the company with the Registrar who shall register the same.

(8) If a company contravenes the provisions of sub-section (5), the company shall be punishable with fine which shall not be less than one lakh rupees but which may extend to twenty-five lakh rupees and every officer of the company who is in default shall be punishable with imprisonment for a term which may extend

to six months or with fine which shall not be less than twenty-five thousand rupees but which may extend to one lakh rupees, or with both.

## WHO CAN SEEK THE REMEDY?

Sec. 244 of the Act empowers the following members of a company to apply to the Tribunal for relief under and they are as follows:

(a) in the case of a company having a share capital, not less than one hundred members of the company or not less than one-tenth of the total number of its members, whichever is less or any members or members holding not less than one-tenth of the issued share capital of the company.

(b) in the case of a company not having a share capital, not less than one-fifth of the total number of its members.

However, the tribunal may, on an application made to it, may waive any condition or conditions specified in Sec. 244.

In *TCS* v. *Cyrus Investment*[51] which is popularly known as *Tata* v. *Cyrus Mistry* case. The tussle between Tata Sons and Cyprus Mistry case is a landmark case on oppression and mismanagement issues. Cyrus Mistry was first appointed as the 'Executive Deputy Chairman' in Tata Sons Limited on 16th March 2012, for a period of 5 years with effect from 1st April 2012 to 31st March 2017. Then he was appointed as the Executive Chairman which was approved by the Board of Directors in its meeting held on 18th December 2012, while Mr. Ratan Tata had the position of Chairman Emeritus.

Mr. Cyrus Mistry, Executive Chairman of Tata Sons was removed from the Tata Sons Limited vide resolution passed by the Board of Directors of the Tata Sons Limited dated 24th October 2016. The Cyrus Investments Private Limited and Sterling Investment Corporation Pvt. Ltd., the minority group of shareholders moved to the NCLT under Sec. 241-242 of the Companies Act, 2013 alleging prejudicial and oppressional acts of the majority shareholders (Tata Groups). From the record it was found that the Tata Trusts and Tata Group companies along with Tata Family Members collectively held 81% of total shareholding while the other group holds 18% of the equity share capital of Tata Limited. The Cyrus Investments Private Limited & Another also filed an application for waiver under Sec. 244 of the Companies Act, 2013.

The NCLT dismissed the petition filed by Cyrus Mistry on ground of the maintainability of the petition and held that they could not meet the criteria of 10 per cent ownership in a company for the filing of a case of alleged oppression of minority shareholders under the Companies Act. The NCLT further observed that removal of Cyrus Mistry as the executive chairman cannot be projected as oppression of minority shareholders.

Cyrus Investments Pvt. Ltd. filed an appeal to the NCLAT against order passed by NCLT. NCLAT held that the removal and other actions taken against Cyrus Mistry is declared illegal and is set aside. Thereby, Cyrus Mistry is restored to his original position

[51] 2021SCC On Line SC 272.

as Executive Chairman of Tata Sons Limited and he will continue for rest of the tenure. The outcome of the decision of NCLAT was that the person who has been appointed as Executive Chairman in place of Cyrus Mistry is declared illegal.

Tata Sons approached the Supreme Court and challenged the decision of NCLAT. On March 26, 2021, the Supreme Court decided in favour of Tat Sons reversing the order of NCLAT and observed that removing the Executive Chairman is not a case of oppression and mismanagement.

## CLASS ACTION—SEC. 245

The provision of Class Action Suit was inserted in the Companies Act, 2013 on the recommendation of the JJ Irani Committee as there was no such provision under the Companies Act, 1956. In January 2009, India witnessed one of its biggest corporate scandals—the 'Satyam scandal'. The Satyam case opened the eyes of the law maker and it is felt necessary to have a provision in the law to give a right to the Shareholders and other stakeholders in cases where the Company fails to fulfil its responsibility towards them.

The concept of class action was first introduced in the US in the year 1938. 'Class Action', which is also known as 'Representative Action', is actually a form of lawsuit where a large group of people collectively brings a claim to the court through a representative. A class action suit is filed when a number of people have suffered the same or similar injuries. Often many of the individuals' injuries are relatively minor, such that they might not pursue legal redress on their own. Together, however, the value of the claims of the class add up, and claiming as a class helps consolidate the attorneys, evidence, witnesses, and most other aspects of the litigation.

The provision of Class Action under the Act is provided under two Sections which deals with two different kinds of Class Action Suit. Sec. 37 deals with Securities Class Action whereas Sec. 245 deals with Specialized Class Action by Members and Depositors in the case of oppression and mismanagement.

## AGAINST WHOM CLASS ACTION SUIT CAN BE FILED UNDER COMPANIES ACT, 2013?

The Class Action Suit can be filed and Orders can be sought against the:

1. Company;
2. Directors of the Company;
3. Auditor including Auditor Firm of the Company for any improper or misleading statement made in audit report or any fraudulent, unlawful, or wrongful act or conduct;
4. Expert or advisor or consultant or any other person for incorrect or misleading statement made to the Company or any fraudulent, unlawful, or wrongful act or conduct.

## WHAT ORDERS THAT CAN BE SOUGHT BY THE APPLICANT [SECTION 245(1)]:

1. To restrain the company from committing an act which is *ultra vires* the articles or memorandum of the Company;
2. To restrain the Company from committing breach of any provision of the Company's MOA or AOA;
3. To declare a resolution altering the MOA or AOA of the Company as void if the resolution was passed by suppression of material facts or obtained by misstatement to the members or depositors;
4. To restrain the Company and its directors from acting on such resolution;
5. To restrain the Company from doing an act which is contrary to the provision of the Act or any other law for the time being in force;
6. To restrain the Company from taking action contrary to any resolution passed by the members;
7. To claim damages or compensation or demand any other suitable action from or against—
   - (a) The Company or its directors for any fraudulent, unlawful, or wrongful act or omission or conduct or any likely act or omission or conduct on its or their part;
   - (b) The auditor including Audit Firm of the Company for any improper or misleading statement of particulars made in his audit report or for any fraudulent, unlawful, or wrongful act or conduct, or;
   - (c) Any expert or advisor or consultant or any other person for any incorrect or misleading statement made to the Company or for any fraudulent, unlawful, or wrongful act or conduct or any likely act or conduct on his part;
8. To seek any other remedy as the Tribunal may deem fit.

## REQUISITE NUMBER OF MEMBERS/DEPOSITORS: [SECTION 245(3)]

The requisite Number of Members who may file an Application before the Tribunal shall be as under:

1. ***In case of Company having a Share Capital:*** Not less than 100 Members or Not less than 5% of the total number of its members, whichever is less or any member or members holding not less than 5% of the issued share capital in case of the unlisted Company and not less than 2% of the issued share capital in case of listed Company, subject to the condition that such member/s have paid all calls and other dues on the shares.
2. ***In case of Company not having a Share Capital:*** Not less than 1/5th of the total number of its Members.

## CONDITIONS FOR CONSIDERING ADMISSIBILITY OF APPLICATION FILED

Sec. 245(4) imposed a mandatory obligation on the Tribunal to look into following factors before accepting the Application:

(a) whether the member or depositor is acting in good faith in making the Application for seeking an order [Section 245(4)(a)];

(b) any evidence before it as to involvement of any person other than directors or officers of the Company) [Section 245(4) (b)];

(c) whether the cause of action is one which the member/depositor could pursue in his own right than through an order under this section. [Section 245(4)(c)];

(d) any evidence before it as to the views of the members/depositors of the Company who have no personal interest, direct or indirect in the matter being proceeded under this section [Section 245(4)(d)];

(e) where the cause of action is an act or omission is yet to occur, whether the act or omission could be and in circumstances would be likely to be—

  (i) authorized by the Company before it occurs; or

  (ii) ratified by the Company after it occurs [Sec. 245(4)(e)].

(f) where the cause of action is an act of omission that has already occurred, whether the act or omission could be and in the circumstances would be likely to be ratified by the Company [Sec. 245(4)(f)].

## BINDING EFFECT OF THE ORDERS OF THE TRIBUNAL [SEC. 245(6)]

Any Orders passed by the Tribunal Shall be binding on—

(a) The Company, and

(b) All its members/depositors, and

(c) Auditor including Audit Firm Expert,

(d) Consultant or Advisor or any other person associated with the Company. [Section 245(6)].

## NON-COMPLIANCE OF ORDER [SECTION 245(7)]

In case of non-compliance of the Order passed by the Tribunal: The Company shall be punishable with a minimum fine of ₹ 5 lakh which may extend to ₹ 25 lakhs and every Officer in default shall be punishable with the imprisonment for a term which may extend to 3 years and with a minimum fine of ₹ 25,000 which may extend to ₹ 1 lakh.

# Chapter XV Winding-up of a Company

Winding-up of a company is a process by which the life of a company is brought to an end and its property administered for the benefit of its members and creditors. An administrator, called the liquidator, is appointed and he takes control of the company, collects its assets, pays debts, and finally distributes any surplus among the members in accordance with their rights. At the end of winding-up, the company will have no assets or liabilities. When the affairs of a company are completely wound up, the dissolution of the company takes place. On dissolution, the company's name is struck off from the register of the companies and its legal personality as a corporation comes to an end. The commencement of winding-up does not mean that the company is dissolved. Its corporate character and status continue as such. Winding-up precedes dissolution.

## DEFINITION OF WINDING-UP

As per Section 2 (94A) of the Companies Act 2013, Winding-up means winding-up under this Act or liquidation under the Insolvency and Bankruptcy Code, 2016, as applicable.

## DIFFERENCE BETWEEN WINDING-UP AND DISSOLUTION OF A COMPANY

| S. No. | Winding-up | Dissolution |
|---|---|---|
| 1. | Winding-up is one of the methods by which the dissolution of a company is brought about. | Dissolution is the end result of winding-up. |
| 2. | The legal entity of the company continues at the commencement of the winding-up. | Dissolution brings about an end to the legal entity of the company. |
| 3. | A company may be allowed to continue its business as far it is necessary for the beneficial winding-up of the company | The company ceases to exist on its dissolution. |

## WHO CAN APPLY FOR WINDING-UP?

Following person or authorities are authorized under Sec. 272 of 2013 Act to make an application to the Tribunal for the winding-up of the company:

**(a) Petition by the Company:** The company itself makes an application for winding-up. However, it is necessary that the company has passed a special resolution to that effect.

**(b) Petition by Contributory or contributories:** A contributory or contributories shall be entitled to present a petition before the Tribunal for the winding-up of the company, notwithstanding that, he may be the holder of fully paid-up shares or that the company may have no assets at all, or may have no surplus assets left for distribution among the holders after the satisfaction of its liabilities. It is no more required of a contributory making petition to have tangible interest in the assets of the company.

**(c) Petition by the Registrar:** Registrar may with the previous sanction of the Central Government make petition to the Tribunal for the winding-up the company only in the following cases:

(i) If the company has made a default in filing with the Registrar its financial statements or annual returns for immediately preceding five consecutive financial years;

(ii) If the company has acted against the interests of the sovereignty and integrity of India the security of the State friendly relations with foreign States, public order, decency, or morality;

(iii) If on an application made by the Registrar or any other person authorized by the Central Government by notification under this Act, the Tribunal is of the opinion that the affairs of the company have been conducted in a fraudulent manner or the company was formed for a fraudulent and unlawful purpose or the persons concerned in the formation or management of its affairs have been guilty of fraud, misfeasance or misconduct in connection therewith and that it is proper that the.

**(d) Petition by the Central Government or a State Government:** Either the Central Government or the State Government may file the petition for winding-up on the ground that company has acted against the interests of the sovereignty and integrity of India, the security of the State, friendly relations with foreign States, public order, decency, or morality.

An interesting question of law relating to the right of workmen employed in a company to appear and oppose a petition for winding-up of the company came before the Supreme Court for consideration in *National Textile Workers' Union* v. *P.R. Ramakrishnan.*[52] The controversy between the parties arises out of a petition for winding-up a private limited company called Ramakrishna Industries (P) Limited (herein-after referred to as a company). The Company has three units, one a textile mill in the name of Jotie Mills which employs about 500 workmen, another, a workshop for manufacture of textile and other machinery which employs about 400 workmen and the third a printing press which brings out a Tamil daily, called "Nav India' and employs about 100 workmen. It is a closed company in which there are two groups of shareholders, one group consisting of respondents Nos. 1 to 5 and the other consisting of respondents Nos. 7 to 14. Respondents Nos. 1 to 5 hold 608 shares and respondents Nos. 7 to 14, 687 shares while the remaining 300 shares belong to a Trust in which both the groups are equally represented on the Board of Trustees. It appears that a serious dispute arose between respondents Nos. 1 to 5 on the one hand and respondents Nos. 7 to 14, on the other in regard to the management of the affairs of the Company and since the dispute could not be settled amicably, respondents Nos. 1 to 5 filed a petition for winding-up the Company on two grounds that the Company is unable to pay its debts and the other was that it is just and equitable that the Company should be wound up.

The National Textile Workers Union, with a view to protecting the interests of its members made an application for impleading itself as a respondent.

The question that arises before the Supreme Court for determination is that:

1. When a petition for winding-up a company is filed in Court, are the workmen of the company entitled to ask the Court to implead them as parties in the winding-up petition? or,

[52] AIR 1983 SC 75.

2. To allow the workmen to appear and contest the winding-up petition? or,
3. Workmen have no *locus standi* at all so far as winding-up petition is concerned and they must helplessly watch the proceedings as outsiders though the result of the winding-up petition may be to bring about termination of their services, and thus, affect them vitally by depriving them of their means of livelihood?

The Court observed that the workers of a Company are entitled to appear at the hearing of the winding-up petition whether to support or to oppose it so long as no winding-up order is made by the Court. The workers have a *locus standi* to appear and be heard in the winding-up petition both before the winding-up petition is admitted and an order for advertisement is made as also after the admission and advertisement of the winding-up petition until an order is made for winding-up the company. If a winding-up order is made and the workers are aggrieved by it, they would also be entitled to prefer an appeal and contend in the appeal that no winding-up order should have been made by the Company Judge. But when a winding-up order is made and it has become final, the workers ordinarily would not have any right to participate in any proceeding in the course of winding-up the company though there may be rare cases where in a proceeding in the course of winding-up, the interest of the workers may be involved and in such a case it may be possible to contend that the workers must be heard before an order is made by the Court. Even when an application for appointment of a provisional liquidator is made by the petitioner in a winding-up petition, the workers will have a right to be heard if they so wish because the appointment of a provisional liquidator may adversely affect the interest of the workers. But neither the petitioner nor the Court would be under any obligation to give notice of such application to the workers. It would be for the workers to apply for being heard and if they do so, they would be entitled to appear and be heard on the application for appointment of provisional liquidator.

The Court further observed as follows:[53]

> "It is not only the shareholders who have supplied capital and who are interested in the enterprise which is being run by a company but the workers who supply labour are also equally, if not, more interested because what is produced by the enterprise is the result of labour as well as capital. While the shareholders invest only a part of their moneys, the workers invest their sweat and toil, in fact their life itself. The workers therefore have a special place in a socialist pattern of society. They are not mere vendors of toil; they are not a marketable commodity to be purchased by the owners of capital. They are producers of wealth as much as capital - nay, very much more. In view of the Preamble, the Directive Principles of State Policy and particularly introduction of Article 43-A it is not idle to contend that the workers should have no voice in the determination of the question whether the enterprise should continue to run or be shut down under an order of the Court."[53]

The Court accordingly held that it is no doubts true that the Companies Act confers the right to present a winding-up petition only on certain specifically enumerated persons and the workers are not included in that enumeration and therefore obviously, the workers have no right to prefer a petition for winding-up of a company. But from this exclusion of the workers from the right to present a winding-up petition, it does not follow as a necessary

[53] Id at p. 83 per Bhagwati, J.

consequence that the workers have no right to appear and be heard in a winding-up petition filed by one or more of the persons specified in the Companies Act.

The *audi alteram partem* rule which mandates that no one shall be condemned unheard is one of the basic principles of natural justice and if this rule has been held to be applicable in a quasi-judicial or even in an administrative proceeding involving adverse civil consequences, it would a *fortiori* apply in a judicial proceeding such as a petition for winding-up of a company. It is difficult to imagine how any system of law which is designed to promote justice through fair play in action can permit the Court to make a winding-up order which has the effect of bringing about termination of the services of the workers without giving them an opportunity of being heard against the making of such order. It would be violative of the basic principles of fair procedure and unless there is express provision in the Companies Act which forbids the workers from appearing at the hearing of the winding-up petition and participating in it, the workers must be held entitled to appear and be heard in the winding-up petition.

The Companies Act deal with different provisions of the winding-up proceedings but there is no provision in the Companies Act which in so many terms exclude the workers from appearing at the hearing of the winding-up petition. Merely because the right to apply for winding-up a company is not expressly given to the workers it does not mean that they cannot appear to support or oppose a winding-up petition which is properly filed before the Court.

## WINDING-UP BY THE TRIBUNAL

Section 271 of the 2013 Act prescribes following circumstances for the winding-up of the company by the Tribunal and they are as follows:

(a) if the company has, by special resolution, resolved that the company be wound up by the Tribunal;

(b) if the company has acted against the interests of the sovereignty and integrity of India, the security of the State, friendly relations with foreign States, public order, decency, or morality;

(c) if on an application made by the Registrar or any other person authorised by the Central Government by notification under this Act, the Tribunal is of the opinion that the affairs of the company have been conducted in a fraudulent manner or the company was formed for fraudulent and unlawful purpose or the persons concerned in the formation or management of its affairs have been guilty of fraud, misfeasance or misconduct in connection therewith and that it is proper that the company be wound up;

(d) if the company has made a default in filing with the Registrar its financial statements or annual returns for immediately preceding five consecutive financial years; or

(e) if the Tribunal is of the opinion that it is just and equitable that the company should be wound up.

The provisions of the Companies Act vis-a-vis the jurisdiction of the Tribunal must be considered having regard to the complex situation(s) which may arise in the corporate sectors. No hard and fast rule can be laid down. The function of a Tribunal in the case of winding-up is first to see as to how the interest of the Company vis-a-vis its shareholders can be safeguarded. The Tribunal must also make an endeavour to find out as to whether an order of winding-up will serve the interest of the company or subvert the same. Further, if an application is filed under Sec. 272 of 2013 Act, an order of winding-up may be passed, but the Tribunal in a winding-up application may refuse to do so, if any other remedy is available.

***By special resolution:***

A special resolution is a formal decision passed by the shareholders or members of a company, which requires a higher majority of votes in favor compared to an ordinary resolution. It is typically used for making important decisions that significantly affect the company's structure, governance, or operations. According to Section 114 of the Companies Act, 2013, a special resolution requires the approval of not less than three-fourth (75%) of the shareholders present and voting at a general meeting. The company may be wound up if the company itself has passed a special resolution in the general meeting to this effect. However, the Tribunal is not bound to pass an order of winding-up even though the company has resolved so. It is purely a discretionary power of the Tribunal. The Tribunal would evaluate the interest of public as well as other stake holders. If any alternative or way out is possible, the Tribunal may prefer such alternative or way out rather than passing an order of winding-up. The order of winding-up would be the last resort for the Tribunal to pass if any other alternative is not available for the Tribunal.

***Just and equitable ground:***

The principle of 'just and equitable' clause needs a precise definition or meanings. It must rest with the judicial discretion of the court depending upon the facts and circumstances of each case. These are necessarily equitable considerations and may, in a given case, be imposed on law. Whether it would be so done in a particular case cannot be put in the straitjacket of an inflexible formula. In an application of this type allegations in the petition are of primary importance. A *prima facie* case has to be made out before the tribunal can take any action in the matter. Even admission of a petition which will lead to advertisement of the winding-up proceedings is likely to cause immense injury to the company if ultimately the application has to be dismissed. The interest of the applicant alone is not of predominant consideration. The interests of the shareholders of the company as a whole apart from those of other interests have to be kept in mind at the time of consideration as to whether the application should be admitted on the allegations mentioned in the petition.

It is now well established that, the fifth clause, namely, 'just and equitable' is not to be read as being *"ejusdem generic"* with the preceding four clauses. While the four earlier clauses prescribed definite conditions to be fulfilled for the one or the other to be attracted in a given case, the just and equitable clause leaves the entire matter to the wide and wise judicial discretion of the court or tribunal. The only limitations are the force and content of the words themselves, 'just and equitable'.

Section 271 (e) under which this application has been made has to be read with Sec. 273 (2) of the Act. Under the latter provisions where the petition is presented on the ground that it is 'just and equitable' that the company should be wound up, the tribunal may refuse to make an order of winding-up if it is of opinion that some other remedy is available to the petitioners and that they are acting unreasonably in seeking to have the company wound up instead of pursuing that other remedy.[54] Further the Apex Court in another case observed that the words 'just and equitable' are not to be construed *'ejusdem generis'* with the matters mentioned in Sec. 271 of the Act. Therefore, whether mismanagement of the directors would be a ground for a winding-up becomes a question to be decided on the facts of each case. Where nothing more is established than that the directors have misappropriated the fund of the company, an order for winding-up would not be just or equitable, because if it is a sound concern such an order must operate harshly on the rights of the shareholders. But if, in addition to such misconduct, circumstances exist which render it desirable in the interests of the shareholders that the company should be wound up, there is nothing in the Act which bars the jurisdiction of the tribunal to make such an order.[55]

The Court has applied so far, the just and equitable grounds for winding-up the company and they are as follows:

(i) Loss of substratum.
(ii) When there is deadlock in the management of the company.
(iii) When there is no hope to make any profit.
(iv) Oppression and Mismanagement of the company's affairs.
(v) Against the public policy.
(vi) Company is existed only for illegal purposes.

## WHAT IS LOSS OF SUBSTRATUM?

A company's substratum means the very purpose for which the company is formed and registered. If the company, for any reasons whatsoever, is unable to achieve the objects for which it is formed, means the company lost its substratum. If it is proved in the tribunal, the tribunal may pass an order for its winding-up.

The Court[56] has laid down the following tests to determine as to whether the company has lost its substratum:

(a) where the subject-matter of the company has gone; or
(b) the object for which it was incorporated has substantially failed; or
(c) it is impossible to carry on the business of the company except at a loss which means that there is no reasonable hope that the object of trading at a profit can be attained; or
(d) the existing or probable assets are insufficient to meet the existing liabilities.

[54] *Hind Overseas Private Ltd. v. Raghunath Prasad Jhunjhunwalla*, AIR 1976 SC 565.
[55] *Rajahmundry Electric Supply Corporation Ltd.* v. *A. Nageshwara Rao*, AIR 1956 SC 213.
[56] *Virendra Singh Bahadur* v. *Nandlal Bhandari & Sons Ltd.* [1982] 52 Comp. Cas. 36 ( MP).

In *Re Dunlop India Ltd.*,[57] the Dunlop India Ltd., was a tyre manufacturing company; however, its two manufacturing facilities became defunct for a long period of time. Properties of ₹ 2,300 crores were removed from company without paying debts to the creditors or wages and salaries to its workmen and other employees. In such circumstances, instant petition was filed seeking winding-up of Dunlop company. It was noted that no workmen or employee of company had appeared to resist order of winding-up. Further, company had been unable to show any prospects of it carrying on any business in near future. Furthermore, it was also proved that the management of company in fraudulently selling off assets estimated at ₹ 2,300 crores, which may be construed as just and equitable for company to be wound up. Accordingly, the Court allowed petition for winding-up of the company.

## POWERS OF THE TRIBUNAL (SECTION 273 OF 2013 ACT)

Section 273 of 2013 Act provides the powers of the Tribunal on receipt of a petition for winding-up under Section 272. The Tribunal may, pass any of the following orders, namely:

1. Dismiss it, with or without costs;
2. Make any interim order as it thinks fit;
3. Appoint a provisional liquidator of the company till the making of a winding-up order;
4. Make an order for the winding-up of the company with or without costs; or
5. Any other order as it thinks fit.

The tribunal needs to pass an order within ninety days from the date of presentation of the petition. The Tribunal shall not refuse to make a winding-up order on the ground only that the assets of the company have been mortgaged for an amount equal to or in excess of those assets, or that the company has no assets. Where a petition is presented on the ground that it is just and equitable that the company should be wound up, the Tribunal may refuse to make an order of winding-up, if it is of the opinion that some other remedy is available to the petitioners and that they are acting unreasonably in seeking to have the company wound up instead of pursuing the other remedy.

## APPEAL FROM ORDERS OF TRIBUNAL (SECTION 421)

If any person is aggrieved by an order of the Tribunal, he may prefer an appeal to the Appellate Tribunal. However, there shall not be any appeal to the Appellate Tribunal from an order made by the Tribunal if such order is passed with the consent of parties. Every appeal shall be filed within a period of forty-five days from the date on which a copy of the order of the Tribunal is made available to the person aggrieved. However, the Appellate Tribunal may entertain an appeal after the expiry of forty-five days if the Appellant Tribunal is satisfied that the appellant was prevented by sufficient cause from filing the appeal within forty-five days.

57 [2013] 31 taxmann.com 135 (Calcutta).

The Appellate Tribunal shall, after giving the parties to the appeal a reasonable opportunity of being heard, pass such orders thereon as it thinks fit, confirming, modifying, or setting aside the order of the Tribunal. The Appellate Tribunal shall send a copy of every order made by it to the Tribunal and the parties to appeal.

## APPEAL TO SUPREME COURT (SECTION 423)

Any person aggrieved by any order of the Appellate Tribunal may file an appeal to the Supreme Court within sixty days from the date of receipt of the order of the Appellate Tribunal to him on any question of law arising out of such order. Provided that the Supreme Court may, if it is satisfied that the appellant was prevented by sufficient cause from filing the appeal within the said period, allow it to be filed within a further period not exceeding sixty days.

## CONSEQUENCE OF WINDING-UP ORDER

1. **Effect of winding-up order:** The order for the winding-up of a company shall operate in favour of all the creditors and all contributories of the company as if it had been made out on the joint petition of creditors and contributories (Sec. 278).
2. **Stay of Suits, etc., on winding-up order:** When a winding-up order has been passed or a provisional liquidator has been appointed, no suit or other legal proceeding shall be commenced. However, if any legal proceedings are pending at the date of the winding-up order, it shall be proceeded with the leave of the Tribunal (Sec. 279).
3. **Submission of report by Company Liquidator:** (Sec. 281) Where the Tribunal has made a winding-up order or appointed a Company Liquidator, such liquidator shall submit to the Tribunal, a report containing the following particulars within sixty days from the order, namely:—
   (a) the nature and details of the assets of the company including their location and value, stating separately the cash balance in hand and in the bank, if any, and the negotiable securities, if any, held by the company;
   (b) amount of capital issued, subscribed and paid-up.
   (c) the existing and contingent liabilities of the company including names, addresses and occupations of its creditors;
   (d) the debts due to the company and the names, addresses and occupations of the persons from whom they are due and the amount likely to be realised on account thereof;
   (e) guarantees, if any, extended by the company;
   (f) list of contributories and dues, if any, payable by them and details of any unpaid call;
   (g) details of trademarks and intellectual properties, if any, owned by the company;

(h) details of subsisting contracts, joint ventures and collaborations, if any;
(i) details of holding and subsidiary companies, if any;
(j) details of legal cases filed by or against the company; and
(k) any other information which the Tribunal may direct or the Company Liquidator may consider necessary to include.

4. **Custody of Company's properties:** Where a winding-up order has been made or where a provisional liquidator has been appointed, the Company Liquidator or the provisional liquidator, as the case may be, shall take all necessary steps to protect and preserve the properties of the company. Once the winding-up order is passed by the tribunal, all properties of the company shall be under the custody and control of the liquidator (Sec. 283).
5. **Transfer, etc., after commencement of winding-up to be void:** In the case of a winding-up by the Tribunal, any disposition of the property including actionable claims, of the company and any transfer of shares in the company or alteration in the status of its members, made after the commencement of the winding-up shall, unless the Tribunal otherwise orders, be void (Sec. 334).
6. **Certain attachments, executions, etc., in winding-up by Tribunal to be void:** Where any company is being wound up by the Tribunal, any attachment, distress or execution put in force, sale of any of the properties without leave of the Tribunal after such commencement, shall be void (Sec. 335).
7. **Prosecution of delinquent officers and members of company:** If it appears to the Tribunal in the course of a winding-up by the Tribunal, that any person, who is or has been an officer, or any member, of the company has been guilty of any offence in relation to the company, the Tribunal may, either on the application of any person interested in the winding-up or *suo motu*, direct the liquidator to prosecute the offender or to refer the matter to the Registrar (Sec. 342).
8. **Liability for fraudulent conduct of business:** If in the course of the winding-up of a company, it is found that any business of the company has been carried on for any fraudulent purpose with intent to defraud creditors of the company or any other persons or for any fraudulent purpose, the Tribunal, on the application of the Official Liquidator, or the Company Liquidator or any creditor or contributory of the company, may declare that any person, who is or has been a director, manager, or officer of the company or any persons who were knowingly parties to the carrying on of the business in the fraudulent manner shall be personally responsible, without any limitation of liability, for all or any of the debts or other liabilities of the company (Sec. 339).

## PREFERENTIAL PAYMENTS

In the case of winding-up of a company, certain payments are ranked in priority than others. Secs. 326 and 327 deal with the issue of payments. Section 326 is entitled as "Overriding preferential payments" whereas Section 327 is entitled as "Preferential Payments".

The following debts shall be paid in priority to all other debts:—(Secs. 326 & 327)

(a) workmen's dues; and secured creditor's dues

For the better understanding workmen's dues include—all wages or salary; all accrued holiday remuneration; PF, Gratuity, retrenchment compensations, lay-off compensation, injury compensation, etc.

(b) all revenues, taxes, cesses and rates due from the company to the Central Government or a State Government or to a local authority at the relevant date and having become due.

(c) the expenses of any investigation held in pursuance of Sections 213 and 216, in so far as they are payable by the company.

(d) preferential debts.

(e) floating charge.

(f) unsecured creditors.

# 5

# The Arbitration and Conciliation Act, 1996

An Act to consolidate and amend the law relating to domestic arbitration, international commercial arbitration, and enforcement of foreign arbitral awards as also to define the law relating to conciliation and for matters connected therewith or incidental thereto.

## PREAMBLE

WHEREAS the United Nations Commission on International Trade Law (UNCITRAL) has adopted the UNCITRAL Model Law on International Commercial Arbitration in 1985;

AND WHEREAS the General Assembly of the United Nations has recommended that all countries give due consideration to the said Model Law, in view of the desirability of uniformity of the law of arbitral procedures and the specific needs of international commercial arbitration practice;

AND WHEREAS the UNCITRAL has adopted the UNCITRAL Conciliation Rules in 1980;

AND WHEREAS the General Assembly of the United Nations has recommended the use of the said Rules in cases where a dispute arises in the context of international commercial relations and the parties seek an amicable settlement of that dispute by recourse to conciliation;

AND WHEREAS the said Model Law and Rules make significant contribution to the establishment of a unified legal framework for the fair and efficient settlement of disputes arising in international commercial relations;

AND WHEREAS it is expedient to make law respecting arbitration and conciliation, taking into account the aforesaid Model Law and Rules;

BE it enacted by Parliament in the Forty-seventh Year of the Republic of India as follows:

## INTRODUCTION

It is important to note that before the enactment of the 1996 Act, India operated under the Arbitration Act of 1940, which primarily addressed domestic arbitration matters, lacking provisions for handling foreign awards. Regarding foreign awards, the Arbitration (Protocol and Convention) Act, 1937, and the Foreign Awards (Recognition and Enforcement) Act, 1961, were in place. The necessity for an alternative dispute resolution system, particularly in commercial disputes, became apparent due to the burgeoning global trade and the sluggish pace of case disposal in courts across various nations. Recognizing the global trend towards expeditious resolution of commercial disputes, the United Nations Commission on International Trade Law adopted the UNCITRAL Model Law of International Commercial Arbitration in 1985. Subsequently, numerous countries, including India, incorporated aspects of this model into their respective legal frameworks. Thus, the Arbitration and Conciliation Act of 1996 was introduced in India, supplanting the Indian Arbitration Act of 1940, which originated during British colonial rule, aligning with the principles outlined in the UNCITRAL Model Law.

The Arbitration Act of 1996 extends its scope beyond domestic arbitration to encompass international commercial arbitration. Compared to previous legislation, the Indian law governing the enforcement of foreign arbitration awards grants greater autonomy to the arbitral process and restricts judicial intervention to a narrower extent. This shift was prompted by the need to instill confidence within the international business community and accommodate India's expanding trade and commercial relations following the government's liberalization policies. The enactment of the Arbitration and Conciliation Act of 1996 aligned with the UNCITRAL Model was a deliberate effort to harmonize Indian arbitration law with international standards. Therefore, when interpreting any provision of the 1996 Act, courts must consider the objectives and purposes underlying its enactment. A direct comparison between the provisions of the Arbitration Act of 1940 and those of the Arbitration and Conciliation Act of 1996 clearly illustrates that the latter seeks to minimize court intervention in the arbitral process. It is evident that the legislative intent behind the 1996 Act was not to subject every order issued by an authority under the Act to judicial scrutiny.

Under the new law the grounds on which an award of an arbitrator could be challenged before the Court have been severely cut down and such challenge is now permitted on the basis of invalidity of the agreement, want of jurisdiction on the part of the arbitrator or want of proper notice to a party of the appointment of the arbitrator or of arbitral proceedings. The powers of the arbitrator have been amplified by insertion of specific provisions of several matters. Obstructive tactics adopted by the parties in arbitration proceedings are sought to be thwarted by an express provision inasmuch as if a party knowingly keeps silent and then suddenly raises a procedural objection will not be allowed to do so. The role of institutions in promoting and organizing arbitration has been recognized. The power to nominate arbitrators has been given to the Chief Justice or to an institution or person designated by him. The time limit for making awards has been deleted.

The existing provisions in 1940 Act relating to arbitration through intervention of Court, when there is no suit pending or by order of the Court when there is a suit pending, have been removed. The importance of transnational commercial arbitration has been recognized and it has been specifically provided that even where the arbitration is held in India, the parties to the contract would be free to designate the law applicable to the substance of the dispute. Under the new law unless the agreement provides otherwise, the arbitrators are required to give reasons for the award. The award itself has now been vested with status of a decree, inasmuch as the award itself is made executable as a decree and it will no longer be necessary to apply to the Court for a decree in terms of the award. All these aim at achieving the sole object to resolve the dispute as expeditiously as possible with the minimum intervention of a Court of Law so that the trade and commerce is not affected on account of litigations before a Court. When United Nations established the Commission on International Trade Law it is on account of the fact that the General Assembly recognized that disparities in national laws governing international trade created obstacles to the flow of trade. The General Assembly regarded the Commission on International Trade Law as a medium which could play a more active role in reducing or removing obstacles. Such Commission, therefore, was given a mandate for progressive harmonization and unification of the law of International Trade. With that objective when UNCITRAL Model has been prepared and the Parliament in our country enacted the Arbitration and Conciliation Act of 1996 adopting UNCITRAL Model, it would be appropriate to bear the said objective in mind while interpreting any provision of the Act.[1]

This Act is amended in 2015, 2019 and 2021. The important changes have been made in 2015 Amendment Act, 2015 are as follows:

1. The definition of "Court" in Section 2 has been amended to refer only to a High Court in the case of International Commercial Arbitration.
2. The provision for setting aside an award on grounds of public policy has been modified to include those awards that are (i) in contravention with the fundamental policy of Indian law, or (ii) in conflict with the notions of morality or justice, in addition to the grounds already specified in the Act.
3. The Act of 2015 prescribed time limits for the conclusion of arbitral process.
4. The parties to arbitration can also choose to conclude the proceeding in a fast track manner.
5. Any challenge to an arbitral award must be disposed of within a period of 1 (one) year.

## OBJECT OF THE ACT

The Arbitration and Conciliation Act aims to facilitate the prompt resolution of commercial disputes through private arbitration, ensuring the smooth operation of businesses and industries. Globally, there is a consensus that commercial disputes should ideally be resolved through arbitration rather than traditional judicial processes, leading to the need for Alternate Dispute Resolution (ADR). ADR encompasses four methods: negotiation, mediation, conciliation, and arbitration. Negotiation, being the most economical and straightforward, is typically attempted first. If unsuccessful, mediation with a neutral

[1] *Konkan Railway Corpn. Ltd. v. M/s. Mehul Construction Co.*, AIR 2000 SC 2821.

mediator is pursued. Should mediation fail, conciliation and arbitration are viable options. The Arbitration and Conciliation Act provides for conciliation and arbitration as ADR mechanisms. An arbitrator serves as a private adjudicator, appointed with the mutual consent of both parties. The primary objective of arbitration is to settle disputes swiftly, conveniently, cost-effectively, and privately, preempting potential future litigation between the involved parties.

## SCHEME OF THE ACT

The Act is divided in to four parts and contains seven schedules and they are as follows:

(a) Part I—Domestic arbitration
(b) Part II—Enforcement of foreign awards
(c) Part III—Conciliation procedures
(d) Part IV—Supplementary provisions
(e) First Schedule—Convention on recognition and enforcement of foreign arbitral award as per New York convention
(f) Second Schedule—Protocol on Arbitration clauses
(g) Third Schedule—Convention on the execution of foreign arbitral awards as per Geneva Convention.
(h) Fourth Schedule—Model Fee
(i) Fifth Schedule—Justifiable doubts as to the independence or impartiality of arbitrators
(j) Sixth Schedule—Work Experience of Arbitrator
(k) Seventh Schedule—Arbitrator Relationship with Parties and Others

## LAW BASED ON UNCITRAL MODEL LAW

The present Act is based on model law drafted by United Nations Commission on International Trade Laws (UNCITRAL), both on domestic arbitration as well as international commercial arbitration, to provide uniformity and certainty to both categories of cases.

## MATTERS NOT REFERABLE TO ARBITRATION

Certain matters which are not within the scope of arbitrator are—Suits for divorce or restitution of conjugal rights; Taxation, Non-payment of admitted liability, and Criminal matters.

## PRELIMINARY

### Section 1: Short title, extent, and commencement

(1) This Act may be called the Arbitration and Conciliation Act, 1996.

(2) It extends to the whole of India.

(3) It shall come into force on such date as the Central Government may, by notification in the Official Gazette, appoint.

The main question for consideration before the Supreme Court in *Delhi Transport Corpn. Ltd.* v. *Rose Advertising*[2] is as to whether Arbitration Act, 1940 (the old Act) would apply in the facts and circumstances of the case or the case will have to be dealt with under the Arbitration and Conciliation Act, 1996.

The facts of the case are that the parties had entered into an agreement on 15-1-1993 regarding display of advertisements on the body of DTC (Delhi Transport Corporation) buses. The agreement was made for a period of 3 years commencing from 15-1-1993 up to 14-1-1996 which contained an Arbitration Clause. The High Court held that the parties went for arbitration with clear understanding and belief that the proceedings were being conducted under the 1996 Act. It was noted that the appointment of arbitrator was made after the new Act had come into force and the parties participated in the arbitration proceeding with the understanding and belief that the proceedings are governed under the 1996 Act. In the award itself the arbitrator noted that both the parties submitted claims before arbitrator under the Arbitration and Conciliation Act, 1996. The Delhi Transport Corporation has come up in appeal before the Supreme Court against the said judgment of the High Court.

In the present case, Clause 25 of the agreement is the arbitration clause. Sub-clause (d) of Clause 25 has a bearing on the controversy in hand and, therefore, same is reproduced as under:

> "Subject to as aforesaid, the provision of the Arbitration Act, 1940 or any statutory modification or re-enactment thereof and the rules made there under and for the time being in force shall apply to the arbitration proceedings under this clause."

The Supreme Court observed after referring above clause that the parties agreed to be governed by the law as in force at the relevant time. The conduct of the arbitration proceedings and the participation of the parties therein show that the parties acted under the 1996 Act. Even the arbitrator proceeded on that understanding and gave his award in pursuance of the 1996 Act. Therefore, the Supreme Court held that the view taken by the High Court on this issue was justified.

# PART I Arbitration

## Chapter I General Provisions

### Section 2: Definitions

(1) In this Part, unless the context otherwise requires,—

(a) **"arbitration"** means any arbitration whether or not administered by permanent arbitral institution;

(b) **"arbitration agreement"** means an agreement referred to in Section 7;

---

[2] AIR 2003 SC 2523.

A bare perusal of the definition of arbitration agreement would clearly show that an arbitration agreement is not required to be in any particular form. What is required to be ascertained is whether the parties have agreed that if any dispute arises between them in respect of the subject matter of the contract; such dispute shall be referred to arbitration. In that case such agreement would certainly spell out an arbitration agreement.[3] However, from the definition of the arbitration agreement, it is also clear that the agreement must be in writing and to interpret the agreement as an 'arbitration agreement' one has to ascertain the intention of the parties and also treatment of the decision as final. If the parties had desired and intended that a dispute must be referred to arbitration for decision and they would undertake to abide by that decision, there cannot be any difficulty to hold that the intention of the parties to have an arbitration agreement; that is to say, an arbitration agreement immediately comes into existence.

The Supreme Court has formulated the following essential elements of an arbitration agreement in *Bihar State Mineral Dev. Corpn.* v. *Encon Builders (I) Pvt. Ltd.*[4] and they are as follows:

(1) There must be a present or a future difference in connection with some contemplated affair.

(2) There must be the intention of the parties to settle such difference by a private Tribunal.

(3) The parties must agree in writing to be bound by the decision of such Tribunal.

(4) The parties must be *ad idem*.

Work Order between the parties can be interpreted to be an arbitration agreement even though the term "arbitration" is not expressly mentioned in the agreement. After reading the agreement one can read the mind of the parties to the agreement where one can safely reach to the conclusion that in the case of dispute or differences the matter would be decided by the arbitrator.

For the purpose of constituting the valid arbitration agreement, it is not necessary that the conditions as regards adduction of evidence by the parties or giving an opportunity of hearing to them must specifically be mentioned therein. Such conditions are implicit in the decision-making process in the arbitration proceedings. Compliance of the principles of natural justice in an arbitration process is a *sine qua non*. Once the principles of natural justice are not complied with, the Award made by the Arbitrator would be rendered invalid. The arbitration clause does not necessitate spelling out of a duty on the part of the arbitrator to hear both parties before deciding the question before him.[5]

(c) **"arbitral award"** includes an interim award;

(d) **"arbitral Tribunal"** means a sole arbitrator or a panel of arbitrators;

(e) **"court"** means:

---

[3] *Punjab State* v. *Dina Nath*, AIR 2007 SC 2157.

[4] AIR 2003 SC 3688.

[5] *Mallikarjun* v. *Gulbarga University*, AIR 2004 SC 716.

(i) in the case of an arbitration other than international commercial arbitration, the principal Civil Court of original jurisdiction in a district, and includes the High Court in exercise of its ordinary original civil jurisdiction, having jurisdiction to decide the questions forming the subject-matter of the arbitration if the same had been the subject-matter of a suit, but does not include any Civil Court of a grade inferior to such principal Civil Court, or any Court of Small Causes;

(ii) in the case of international commercial arbitration, the High Court in exercise of its ordinary original civil jurisdiction, having jurisdiction to decide the questions forming the subject-matter of the arbitration if the same had been the subject-matter of a suit, and in other cases, a High Court having jurisdiction to hear appeals from decrees of courts subordinate to the High Court.

(f) "international commercial arbitration" means an arbitration relating to disputes arising out of legal relationships, whether contractual or not, considered as commercial under the law in force in India and where at least one of the parties is—

(i) an individual who is a national of, or habitually resident in, any country other than India; or

(ii) a body corporate which is incorporated in any country other than India; or

(iii) an association or a body of individuals whose central management and control is exercised in any country other than India; or

(iv) the Government of a foreign country.

(g) "legal representative" means a person who in law represents the estate of a deceased person, and includes any person who intermeddles with the estate of the deceased, and, where a party acts in a representative character, the person on whom the estate devolves on the death of the party so acting;

(h) "party" means a party to an arbitration agreement.

(2) This Part shall apply where the place of arbitration is in India.

Provided that subject to an agreement to the contrary, the provisions of Sections 9, 27 and clause (a) of sub-section (1) and sub-section (3) of Section 37 shall also apply to international commercial arbitration, even if the place of arbitration is outside India, and an arbitral award made or to be made in such place is enforceable and recognised under the provisions of Part II of this Act.

(3) This Part shall not affect any other law for the time being in force by virtue of which certain disputes may not be submitted to arbitration.

(4) This Part except sub-section (1) of Section 40, Sections 41 and 43 shall apply to every arbitration under any other enactment for the time being in force, as if the arbitration were pursuant to an arbitration agreement and as if that other enactment were an arbitration agreement, except insofar as the provision of this Part are inconsistent with that other enactment or with any rules made thereunder;

(5) Subject to the provisions of sub-section (4) and save in so far as is otherwise provided by any law for the time being in force or in any agreement in force between India and any other country or countries, this Part shall apply to all arbitrations and to all proceedings relating thereto.

## APPLICABILITY OF PART I

The provisions of Part I would apply to all arbitrations and to all proceedings relating thereto. Where such arbitration is held in India the provisions of Part I would compulsory apply, and parties are free to deviate only to the extent permitted by the derogable provisions of Part I. In cases of international commercial arbitrations held out of India provisions of Part I would apply unless the parties by agreement, express or implied, exclude all or any of its provisions. In that case the laws or rules chosen by the parties would prevail. Any provision in Part I that is contrary to or excluded by that law or rules will not apply.

(6) Where this part, except Section 28, leaves the parties free to determine a certain issue, that freedom shall include the right of the parties to authorize any person including an institution, to determine that issue.

(7) An arbitral award made under this Part shall be considered as a domestic award.

(8) Where this Part—

(a) refers to the fact that the parties have agreed or that they may agree, or

(b) in any other way refers to an agreement of the parties,

that agreement shall include any arbitration rules referred to in that agreement.

(9) Where this Part, other than clause (a) of Section 25 or clause (a) of sub-section (2) of Section 32, refers to a claim, it shall also apply to a counterclaim, and when it refers to a defence, it shall also apply to a defence to that counterclaim.

### Section 3: Receipt of written communications

(1) Unless otherwise agreed by the parties,—

(a) any written communication is deemed to have been received if it is delivered to the addressee personally or at his place of business, habitual residence or mailing address, and

(b) if none of the places referred to in clause (a) can be found after making a reasonable inquiry, a written communication is deemed to have been received if it is sent to the addressee's last known place of business, habitual residence or mailing address by registered letter or by any other means which provides a record of the attempt to deliver it.

(2) The communication is deemed to have been received on the day it is so delivered.

(3) This section does not apply to written communications in respect of proceedings of any judicial authority.

### Section 4: Waiver of right to object

A party who knows that—

(a) any provision of this Part from which the parties may derogate, or

(b) any requirement under the arbitration agreement,

has not been complied with and yet proceeds with the arbitration without stating his objection to such non-compliance without undue delay or, if a time limit is provided for stating that objection, within that period of time, shall be deemed to have waived his right to so object.

Referring to Sec. 4 of the Act, if a party knows that a requirement under the arbitration agreement has not been complied with and still proceeds with the arbitration without filing an objection thereto, waives their right to object. In *Bharat Sanchar Nigam Ltd.* v. *Motorola India Pvt. Ltd.*[6] Where the High Court had appointed an arbitrator in response to the petition filed by the appellant. At this point, the matter was closed unless further objections were to be raised. If further objections were to be made after this order, they should have been made prior to the first arbitration hearing. But the appellant had not raised any such objections. The appellant therefore had clearly failed to meet the stated requirement to object to arbitration without delay. As such their right to object is deemed to be waived.

### Section 5: Extent of judicial intervention

Notwithstanding anything contained in any other law for the time being in force, in matters governed by this Part, no judicial authority shall intervene except where so provided in this Part.

### Section 6: Administrative assistance

In order to facilitate the conduct of the arbitral proceedings, the parties, or the arbitral Tribunal with the consent of the parties, may arrange for administrative assistance by a suitable institution or person.

## Chapter II Arbitration Agreement

### Section 7: Arbitration agreement

(1) In this Part, "arbitration agreement" means an agreement by the parties to submit to arbitration all or certain disputes which have arisen, or which may arise between them in respect of a defined legal relationship, whether contractual or not.

(2) An arbitration agreement may be in the form of an arbitration clause in a contract or in the form of a separate agreement.

---

[6] AIR 2009 SC 357.

(3) An arbitration agreement shall be in writing.

(4) An arbitration agreement is in writing if it is contained in—

(a) a document signed by the parties;

(b) an exchange of letters, telex, telegrams or other means of telecommunication which provide a record of the agreement; or

(c) an exchange of statements of claim and defence in which the existence of the agreement is alleged by one party and not denied by the other.

(5) The reference in a contract to a document containing an arbitration clause constitutes an arbitration agreement if the contract is in writing and the reference is such as to make that arbitration clause part of the contract.

### *The Essentials of an Arbitration Agreement*

In *K. K. Modi* v. *K. N. Modi*[7] the Supreme Court enumerated the following attributes of a valid arbitration agreement:

(i) The arbitration agreement must contemplate that the decision of the Tribunal will be binding on the parties to the agreement,

(ii) that the jurisdiction of the Tribunal to decide the rights of parties must derive either from the consent of the parties or from an order of the Court or from a statute, the terms of which make it clear that the process is to be an arbitration,

(iii) the agreement must contemplate that substantive rights of parties will be determined by the agreed tribunal,

(iv) that the tribunal will determine the rights of the parties in an impartial and judicial manner, with the tribunal owing an equal obligation of fairness towards both sides,

(v) that the agreement of the parties to refer their disputes to the decision of the Tribunal must be intended to be enforceable in law, and lastly,

(vi) the agreement must contemplate that the tribunal will make a decision upon a dispute which is already formulated at the time when a reference is made to the Tribunal.

Following *K.K. Modi* case, the Supreme Court further listed the following as the essential elements of an arbitration agreement in *Bihar State Mineral Development Corporation* v. *Encon Builders (IP) Ltd.*,[8]

(i) There must be a present or a future difference in connection with some contemplated affair;

(ii) There must be the intention of the parties to settle such difference by a private tribunal;

---

[7] AIR 1998 SC 1297.

[8] AIR 2003 SC 3688.

(iii) The parties must agree in writing to be bound by the decision of such tribunal; and

(iv) The parties must be *ad idem*.

In 2007 in *Jagdish Chander* v. *Ram Chandra*[9], the Supreme Court set out the following principles in regard to what constitutes an arbitration agreement:

(i) The intention of the parties to enter into an arbitration agreement shall have to be gathered from the terms of the agreement. If the terms of the agreement clearly indicate an intention on the part of the parties to the agreement to refer their disputes to a private tribunal for adjudication and a willingness to be bound by the decision of such tribunal on such disputes, it is arbitration agreement. While there is no specific form of an arbitration agreement, the words used should disclose a determination and obligation to go to arbitration and not merely contemplate the possibility of going for arbitration. Where there is merely a possibility of the parties agreeing to arbitration in future, as contrasted from an obligation to refer disputes to arbitration, there is no valid and binding arbitration agreement.

(ii) Even if the words 'arbitration' and 'arbitral tribunal (or arbitrator)' are not used with reference to the process of settlement or with reference to the private tribunal which has to adjudicate upon the disputes, in a clause relating to settlement of disputes, it does not detract from the clause being an arbitration agreement if it has the attributes or elements of an arbitration agreement. They are: (a) The agreement should be in writing. (b) The parties should have agreed to refer any disputes (present or future) between them to the decision of a private tribunal. (c) The private tribunal should be empowered to adjudicate upon the disputes in an impartial manner, giving due opportunity to the parties to put forth their case before it. (d) The parties should have agreed that the decision of the Private Tribunal in respect of the disputes will be binding on them.

(iii) Where the clause provides that in the event of disputes arising between the parties, the disputes shall be referred to Arbitration, it is an arbitration agreement. Where there is a specific and direct expression of intent to have the disputes settled by arbitration, it is not necessary to set out the attributes of an arbitration agreement to make it an arbitration agreement. But where the clause relating to settlement of disputes contains words which specifically excludes any of the attributes of an arbitration agreement or contains anything that detracts from an arbitration agreement, it will not be an arbitration agreement. For example, where an agreement requires or permits an authority to decide a claim or dispute without hearing or requires the authority to act in the interests of only one of the parties or provides that the decision of the Authority will not be final and binding on the parties, or that if either party is not satisfied with the decision of the Authority, he may file a civil suit seeking relief, it cannot be termed as an arbitration agreement.

[9] 2007 (5) SCC 719.

(iv) But mere use of the word 'arbitration' or 'arbitrator' in a clause will not make it an arbitration agreement if it requires or contemplates further or fresh consent of the parties for reference to arbitration. For example, use of words such as "parties can, if they so desire, refer their disputes to arbitration" or "in the event of any dispute, the parties may also agree to refer the same to arbitration" or "if any disputes arise between the parties, they should consider settlement by arbitration" in a clause relating to settlement of disputes, indicate that the clause is not intended to be an arbitration agreement. Similarly, a clause which states that "if the parties so decide, the disputes shall be referred to arbitration" or "any disputes between parties, if they so agree, shall be referred to arbitration" is not an arbitration agreement. Such clauses merely indicate a desire or hope to have the disputes settled by arbitration, or a tentative arrangement to explore arbitration as a mode of settlement if and when a dispute arises. Such clauses require the parties to arrive at a further agreement to go to arbitration, as and when the disputes arise. Any agreement or clause in an agreement requiring or contemplating a further consent or consensus before a reference to arbitration is not an arbitration agreement, but an agreement to enter into an arbitration agreement in future.

### Section 8: Power to refer parties to arbitration where there is an arbitration agreement

(1) A judicial authority, before which an action is brought in a matter which is the subject of an arbitration agreement shall, if a party to the arbitration agreement or any person claiming through or under him, so applies not later than the date of submitting his first statement on the substance of the dispute, then, notwithstanding any judgment, decree or order of the Supreme Court or any Court, refer the parties to arbitration unless it finds that *prima facie* no valid arbitration agreement exists.

(2) The application referred to in sub-section (1) shall not be entertained unless it is accompanied by the original arbitration agreement or a duly certified copy thereof.

Provided that where the original arbitration agreement or a certified copy thereof is not available with the party applying for reference to arbitration under sub-section (1), and the said agreement or certified copy is retained by the other party to that agreement, then, the party so applying shall file such application along with a copy of the arbitration agreement and a petition praying the Court to call upon the other party to produce the original arbitration agreement or its duly certified copy before that Court.

(3) Notwithstanding that an application has been made under sub-section (1) and that the issue is pending before the judicial authority, and arbitration may be commenced or continued and an arbitral award made.

An analysis of Sec. 8 provides that for its applicability, the following conditions must be satisfied:

- that there exists an arbitration agreement;
- that action has been brought to the Court by one party to the arbitration agreement against the other party;

- that the subject-matter of the suit is same as the subject-matter of the arbitration agreement;
- that the other party before he submits his first statement of the substance of the dispute, moves the Court for referring the parties to arbitration; and
- that along with the application the other party tenders the original arbitration agreement or duly certified copy thereof.

The scope of the Court to examine the *prima facie* validity of an arbitration agreement as specified in Sec. 8(1) of the Act which includes only:

- Whether the arbitration agreement was in writing?, or
- Whether the arbitration agreement was contained in an exchange of letters, telecommunication etc? or
- Whether the core contractual ingredients qua the arbitration agreement were fulfilled?, or
- On rare occasions, whether the subject matter of the dispute is arbitrable?

**Section 9: Interim measures, etc. by Court**

(1) A party may, before, or during arbitral proceedings or at any time after the making of the arbitral award but before it is enforced in accordance with Section 36, apply to a Court—

(i) for the appointment of a guardian for a minor or person of unsound mind for the purposes of arbitral proceedings; or

(ii) for an interim measure of protection in respect of any of the following matters, namely:—

(a) the preservation, interim custody or sale of any goods which are the subject-matter of the arbitration agreement;

(b) securing the amount in dispute in the arbitration;

(c) the detention, preservation or inspection of any property or thing which is the subject-matter of the dispute in arbitration, or as to which any question may arise therein and authorising for any of the aforesaid purposes any person to enter upon any land or building in the possession of any party, or authorising any samples to be taken or any observation to be made, or experiment to be tried, which may be necessary or expedient for the purpose of obtaining full information or evidence;

(d) interim injunction or the appointment of a receiver;

(e) such other interim measure of protection as may appear to the Court to be just and convenient,

and the Court shall have the same power for making orders as it has for the purpose of, and in relation to, any proceedings before it.

(2) Where, before the commencement of the arbitral proceedings, a Court passes an order for any interim measure of protection under sub-section (1), the arbitral proceedings shall be commenced within a period of ninety days from the date of such order or within such further time as the Court may determine.

(3) Once the arbitral tribunal has been constituted, the Court shall not entertain an application under sub-section (1), unless the Court finds that circumstances exist which may not render the remedy provided under Section 17 efficacious.

## Chapter III Composition of Arbitral Tribunal

### Section 10: Number of arbitrators

(1) The parties are free to determine the number of arbitrators, provided that such number shall not be an even number.

(2) Failing the determination referred to in sub-section (1), the arbitral Tribunal shall consist of a sole arbitrator.

Sec. 10 deviates from the UNCITRAL law only in the sense that Sec. 10(1) of the Act provides that despite the freedom given to the parties to determine the number of arbitrators such numbers shall not be even number. But in default of determination of the number, Sec. 10(2) provides the tribunal is to consist of a sole arbitrator. Therefore, scheme of Sec. 10(2) of the Act is virtually similar to that of the UNCITRAL model law.

Sec. 10 deals with the number of arbitrators. Sec. 10 (1) says that the parties are free to determine the number of arbitrators, provided that such number shall not be an even number. Sect. 10(2) then says that failing the determination referred to in Sec. 10 (1), the arbitral tribunal shall consist of a sole arbitrator.

It must be remembered that arbitration is a creature of an agreement. There can be no arbitration unless there is an arbitration agreement in writing between the parties. Any agreement which permits the parties to appoint an even number of arbitrators would not be contrary to provision of Sec. 10. Such an agreement would not be invalid and void as the Arbitral Tribunal would be validly constituted. Composition of the Arbitral Tribunal itself being valid the proceedings and the Award, even if one be passed, would be invalid and unenforceable.

### Section 11: Appointment of arbitrators

(1) A person of any nationality may be an arbitrator, unless otherwise agreed by the parties.

(2) Subject to sub-section (6), the parties are free to agree on a procedure for appointing the arbitrator or arbitrators.

(3) Failing any agreement referred to in sub-section (2), in an arbitration with three arbitrators, each party shall appoint one arbitrator, and the two appointed arbitrators shall appoint the third arbitrator who shall act as the presiding arbitrator.

(4) If the appointment procedure in sub-section (3) applies and—

(a) a party fails to appoint an arbitrator within thirty days from the receipt of a request to do so from the other party; or

(b) the two appointed arbitrators fail to agree on the third arbitrator within thirty days from the date of their appointment, the appointment shall be made upon request of a party, by the the Supreme Court or, as the case may be, the High Court or any person or institution designated by such Court.

(5) Failing any agreement referred to in sub-section (2), in an arbitration with a sole arbitrator, if the parties fail to agree on the arbitrator within thirty days from receipt of a request by one party from the other party to so agree the appointment shall be made, upon request of a party, by the the Supreme Court or, as the case may be, the High Court or any person or institution designated by such Court.

(6) Where, under an appointment procedure agreed upon by the parties,—

(a) a party fails to act as required under that procedure; or

(b) the parties, or the two appointed arbitrators, fail to reach an agreement expected of them under that procedure; or

(c) a person, including an institution, fails to perform any function entrusted to him or it under that procedure,

a party may request the the Supreme Court or, as the case may be, the High Court or any person or institution designated by such Court to take the necessary measure, unless the agreement on the appointment procedure provides other means for securing the appointment.

(6A) The Supreme Court or, as the case may be, the High Court, while considering any application under sub-section (4) or sub-section (5) or sub-section (6), shall, notwithstanding any judgment, decree or order of any Court, confine to the examination of the existence of an arbitration agreement.

(6B) The designation of any person or institution by the Supreme Court or, as the case may be, the High Court, for the purposes of this Section shall not be regarded as a delegation of judicial power by the Supreme Court or the High Court.

(7) A decision on a matter entrusted by sub-section (4) or sub-section (5) or sub-section (6) to the Supreme Court or, as the case may be, the High Court or the person or institution designated by such Court is final and no appeal including Letters Patent Appeal shall lie against such decision.

(8) The Supreme Court or, as the case may be, the High Court or the person or institution designated by such Court, before appointing an arbitrator, shall seek a disclosure in writing from the prospective arbitrator in terms of sub-section (1) of Section 12, and have due regard to—

(a) any qualifications required for the arbitrator by the agreement of the parties; and

(b) the contents of the disclosure and other considerations as are likely to secure the appointment of an independent and impartial arbitrator.

(9) In the case of appointment of sole or third arbitrator in an international commercial arbitration, the Supreme Court or the person or institution designated by that Court may appoint an arbitrator of a nationality other than the nationalities of the parties where the parties belong to different nationalities.

(10) The Supreme Court or, as the case may be, the High Court, may make such scheme as the said Court may deem appropriate for dealing with matters entrusted by sub-section (4) or sub-section (5) or sub-section (6), to it.

(11) Where more than one request has been made under sub-section(4) or sub-section (5) or sub-section (6) to different High Courts or their designates, the High Court or its designate to whom the request has been first made under the relevant sub-section shall alone be competent to decide on the request.

(12) (a) Where the matters referred to in sub-sections (4), (5), (6),(7), (8) and sub-section (10) arise in an international commercial arbitration, the reference to the "Supreme Court or, as the case may be, the High Court" in those sub-sections shall be construed as a reference to the "Supreme Court"; and

(b) where the matters referred to in sub-sections (4), (5), (6), (7), (8) and sub-section (10) arise in any other arbitration, the reference to "the Supreme Court or, as the case may be, the High Court" in those sub-sections shall be construed as a reference to the "High Court" within whose local limits the principal Civil Court referred to in clause (e) of Sub-section (1) of Section 2 is situate, and where the High Court itself is the Court referred to in that clause, to that High Court.

(13) An application made under this section for appointment of an arbitrator or arbitrators shall be disposed of by the Supreme Court or the High Court or the person or institution designated by such Court, as the case may be, as expeditiously as possible and an endeavour shall be made to dispose of the matter within a period of sixty days from the date of service of notice on the opposite party.

(14) For the purpose of determination of the fees of the arbitral tribunal and the manner of its payment to the arbitral tribunal, the High Court may frame such rules as may be necessary, after taking into consideration the rates specified in the Fourth Schedule.

***Explanation***: For the removal of doubts, it is hereby clarified that this sub-section shall not apply to international commercial arbitration and in arbitrations (other than international commercial arbitration) in case where parties have agreed for determination of fees as per the rules of an arbitral institution.

The marginal heading of Sec. 11 is '*Appointment of arbitrators*'. Sub-Section (1) indicates that a person of any nationality may be an arbitrator, unless otherwise agreed to by the parties. Under sub-section (2), subject to sub-section (6), the parties are free to agree on a procedure for appointing the arbitrator or arbitrators. Under sub-section (3), failing any agreement in terms of sub-section (2), in arbitration with three arbitrators, each party could appoint one arbitrator, and the two arbitrators so appointed, could appoint the third arbitrator, who would act as the presiding arbitrator. Under sub-section (4), the Chief Justice or any person or institution designated by him could make the appointment, in a case where sub-section (3) has application and where either the party or parties had failed to nominate their arbitrator or arbitrators or the two nominated arbitrators had failed to agree on the presiding arbitrator. In the case of a sole arbitrator, sub-section (5) provides for the Chief Justice or any person or institution designated by him, appointing an arbitrator on a request being made by one of the parties, on fulfillment of the conditions laid down therein. Sub-section (6) provides that a party may request the Supreme Court or High Court or any institution designated by the Court to appoint an arbitrator where a party fails to act as required under that procedure; or the parties, or the two appointed arbitrators, fail to reach an agreement expected of them under that procedure; or a person, including an institution, fails to perform any function entrusted to him.

The Supreme Court in *IBI Consultancy* v. *DSC Ltd.*[10] observed that it is a cardinal principle of the Arbitration and Conciliation Act that the parties are free to decide the number of arbitrators, provided, it is an odd number, as well as the procedure for appointing them. However, if the parties are not able to agree on the said procedure, or constitute the Arbitral Tribunal to their mutual satisfaction, either of the party has an option to route to an appropriate remedy under Sec. 11 of the Act, which provides detailed machinery for appointment of Arbitrator through judicial intervention.

In *Swastik Gas* v. *Indian Oil Corporation*[11] the question arose before the Supreme Court in relation to jurisdiction of the High Court for an appointment of arbitrator under Sec. 11(12(b) of the Act.

The question is whether parties by virtue of clause 18 of the agreement have agreed to exclude the jurisdiction of the courts at Jaipur or, in other words, whether in view of clause 18 of the agreement, the jurisdiction of Chief Justice of the Rajasthan High Court has been excluded.

For answer to the above question, we have to see the effect of the jurisdiction clause in the agreement which provides that the agreement shall be subject to jurisdiction of the courts at Kolkata. It is a fact that whilst providing for jurisdiction clause in the agreement the words like 'alone', 'only', 'exclusive' or 'exclusive jurisdiction' have not been used. The Supreme Court held that these words are not decisive and does not make any material difference. The intention of the parties—by having clause 18 in the agreement—is clear and unambiguous that the courts at Kolkata shall have jurisdiction which means that the courts at Kolkata alone shall have jurisdiction. It is so because for construction of jurisdiction clause, like clause 18 in the agreement, the maxim *expressio unius est exclusio alterius* comes into play as there is nothing to indicate to the contrary. This legal maxim means that expression of one is the exclusion of another. By making a provision that the agreement is subject to the jurisdiction of the courts at Kolkata, the parties have impliedly excluded the jurisdiction of other courts.

### Section 11A: Power of Central Government to amend Fourth Schedule

(1) If the Central Government is satisfied that it is necessary or expedient so to do, it may, by notification in the Official Gazette, amend the Fourth Schedule and thereupon the Fourth Schedule shall be deemed to have been amended accordingly.

(2) A copy of every notification proposed to be issued under sub-section (1), shall be laid in draft before each House of Parliament, while it is in session, for a

[10] AIR 2018 SC 2907.

[11] 2013(9)SCC32.

total period of thirty days which may be comprised in one session or in two or more successive sessions, and if, before the expiry of the session immediately following the session or the successive sessions aforesaid, both Houses agree in disapproving the issue of the notification or both Houses agree in making any modification in the notification, the notification shall not be issued or, as the case may be, shall be issued only in such modified form as may be agreed upon by the both Houses of the Parliament.

### Section 12: Grounds for challenge

(1) When a person is approached in connection with his possible appointment as an arbitrator, he shall disclose in writing any circumstances,—

(a) such as the existence either direct or indirect, of any past or present relationship with or interest in any of the parties or in relation to the subject-matter in dispute, whether financial, business, professional or other kind, which is likely to give rise to justifiable doubts as to his independence or impartiality; and

(b) which are likely to affect his ability to devote sufficient time to the arbitration and in particular his ability to complete the entire arbitration within a period of twelve months.

***Explanation* 1:** The grounds stated in the Fifth Schedule shall guide in determining whether circumstances exist which give rise to justifiable doubts as to the independence or impartiality of an arbitrator.

***Explanation* 2:** The disclosure shall be made by such person in the form specified in the Sixth Schedule.

(2) An arbitrator, from the time of his appointment and throughout the arbitral proceedings, shall, without delay, disclose to the parties in writing any circumstances referred to in sub-section (1) unless they have already been informed of them by him.

(3) An arbitrator may be challenged only if—

(a) circumstances exist that give rise to justifiable doubts as to his independence or impartiality, or

(b) he does not possess the qualifications agreed to by the parties.

(4) A party may challenge an arbitrator appointed by him, or in whose appointment he has participated, only for reasons of which he becomes aware after the appointment has been made.

(5) Notwithstanding any prior agreement to the contrary, any person whose relationship, with the parties or counsel or the subject-matter of the dispute, falls under any of the categories specified in the Seventh Schedule shall be ineligible to be appointed as an arbitrator:

Provided that parties may, subsequent to disputes having arisen between them, waive the applicability of this sub-section by an express agreement in writing.

Sec. 12 imposes upon a person approached to be an arbitrator the obligation to disclose to the parties in writing any circumstance that may give rise to justifiable doubts as to his independence and impartiality. An arbitrator can be challenged if there are circumstances that give rise to justifiable doubts about his independence and impartiality or if he does not possess the qualifications agreed to by the parties, but such challenge can be made only for reasons which the party challenging becomes aware of after the appointment has been made.

### Section 13: Challenge procedure

(1) Subject to sub-section (4), the parties are free to agree on a procedure for challenging an arbitrator.

(2) Failing any agreement referred to in sub-section (1), a party who intends to challenge an arbitrator shall, within fifteen days after becoming aware of the constitution of the arbitral Tribunal or after becoming aware of any circumstances referred to in sub-section (3) of Section 12, send a written statement of the reasons for the challenge to the arbitral Tribunal.

(3) Unless the arbitrator challenged under sub-section (2), withdraws from his office or the other party agrees to the challenge, the arbitral Tribunal shall decide on the challenge.

(4) If a challenge under any procedure agreed upon by the parties or under the procedure under sub-section (2) is not successful, the arbitral Tribunal shall continue the arbitral proceedings and make an arbitral award.

(5) Where an arbitral award is made under sub-section (4), the party challenging the arbitrator may make an application for setting aside such an arbitral award in accordance with Section 34.

(6) Where an arbitral award is set aside on an application made under sub-section (5), the Court may decide as to whether the arbitrator who is challenged is entitled to any fees.

Sec. 13(1) provides that party would be free to agree on a procedure for challenging an arbitrator. Sec. 13(2) provides that failing any such agreement, a party intending to challenge an arbitrator, either on grounds of independence or impartiality or on the grounds of lack of requisite qualifications, shall within 15 days of becoming aware of the constitution of the Tribunal send a written statement for the challenge to the Tribunal itself. Sec. 13(3) provides that unless the arbitrator withdraws or the other party agrees to the challenge, the Tribunal shall decide on the challenge itself. Sub-section (4) of Sec. 13 mandates an arbitrator to continue the arbitral proceedings and to make an award.

### Section 14: Failure or impossibility to act

(1) The mandate of an arbitrator shall terminate and he shall be substituted by another arbitrator, if—

(a) he becomes de jure or de facto unable to perform his functions or for other reasons fails to act without undue delay; and

(b) he withdraws from his office or the parties agree to the termination of his mandate.

(2) If a controversy remains concerning any of the grounds referred to in clause.(a) of sub-section (1), a party may, unless otherwise agreed by the parties, apply to the Court to decide on the termination of the mandate.

(3) If, under this section or sub-section (3) of Section 13, an arbitrator withdraws from his office or a party agrees to the termination of the mandate of an arbitrator, it shall not imply acceptance of the validity of any ground referred to in this section or sub-section (3) of Section 12.

## Section 15: Termination of mandate and substitution of arbitrator

(1) In addition to the circumstances referred to in Section 13 or Section 14, the mandate of an arbitrator shall terminate—

(a) where he withdraws from office for any reason; or

(b) by or pursuant to agreement of the parties.

(2) Where the mandate of an arbitrator terminates, a substitute arbitrator shall be appointed according to the rules that were applicable to the appointment of the arbitrator being replaced.

(3) Unless otherwise agreed by the parties, where an arbitrator is replaced under sub-section (2), any hearings previously held may be repeated at the discretion of the arbitral Tribunal.

(4) Unless otherwise agreed by the parties, an order or ruling of the arbitral Tribunal made prior to the replacement of an arbitrator under this section shall not be invalid solely because there has been a change in the composition of the arbitral Tribunal.

In *Yashwith Constructions (P) Ltd.* v. *Simplex Concrete Piles India Ltd.*,[12] where the Managing Director of the respondent company appointed an arbitrator in terms of the arbitration clause. The arbitrator resigned. Thereupon the Managing Director of the respondent company, in view of the mandate in the arbitration agreement promptly appointed another arbitrator. At that stage, the petitioner approached the Chief Justice of the High Court under Sec. 11(5) read with Sec. 15(2) of the Arbitration and Conciliation Act, 1996, praying that the Chief Justice may appoint a substitute arbitrator to resolve the disputes between the parties. The Chief Justice found that the appointment of the second arbitrator by the Managing Director, after the resignation of the first arbitrator, was valid in law since it was permissible under the contract and the right to make such an appointment was saved by Sec. 15(2) of the Act. The argument that Sec. 15(2) of the Act referred to statutory rules providing for appointment of Arbitrators and not to a contractual provision for such appointment was rejected by the learned Chief Justice. It was held by him that no occasion arose for him to appoint an arbitrator under Sec. 11(6) of the Act in the case. Thus, the application was dismissed leaving the parties to pursue their claims before the arbitrator appointed by the Managing Director in terms of arbitration agreement between the parties.

The petitioner challenged the decision of the learned Chief Justice by way of a Writ Petition in the High Court. The Division Bench noticed the decision of the Supreme Court in *SBP and Co.* v. *Patel Engineering Ltd. and another* (AIR 2006 SC 450) holding that the order

[12] AIR 2006 SC 2798.

passed by the Chief Justice is a judicial order and no Writ Petition would lie in the High Court challenging such an order and only an appeal could be filed in the Supreme Court invoking Article 136 of the Constitution of India. But the Division Bench thought that since that decision saved appointments made on or before the date that decision was rendered by the Apex Court, the Writ Petition filed by the petitioner would also be saved and the Writ Petition could be decided on merits. The Division Bench held that in terms of Sec. 15(2) of the Act, the Managing Director could, on the basis of the arbitration agreement, appoint another arbitrator when the originally appointed arbitrator resigned, thus attracting Sec. 15(1)(a) of the Act. It further held that Sec. 15(2) covered not only cases of appointments under statutory rules or rules framed under the Act, but it would also take in the terms of the agreement between the parties for appointment of an arbitrator and in that view, the Managing Director, in the case on hand and on the terms of the arbitration agreement, would have the right to appoint a substitute arbitrator. Thus, it was held that the learned Chief Justice was right in rejecting the application made by the petitioner. Thus, the Writ Petition was dismissed. This decision of the Division Bench was challenged before the Supreme Court and the Supreme Court held as follows:

> "When the arbitrator originally appointed in terms of the arbitration agreement withdrew for health reasons, the Managing Director, as authorized originally by the arbitration agreement, promptly appointed a substitute arbitrator. It is true that in the arbitration agreement there is no specific provision authorizing the Managing Director to appoint a substitute arbitrator if the original appointment terminates or if the originally appointed arbitrator withdraws from the arbitration. But, this so called omission in the arbitration agreement is made up by the specific provision contained in Section 15(2) of the Act. The withdrawal of an arbitrator from the office for any reason is within the purview of Section 15(1)(a) of the Act. Obviously, therefore Section 15(2) would be attracted and a substitute arbitrator has to be appointed according to the rules that are applicable for the appointment of the arbitrator to be replaced.

Sec. 15(2), which regulates appointment of a substitute arbitrator, requires that such an appointment shall be made according to the Rules which were applicable to the appointment of an original arbitrator. The term 'Rules' used in this sub-section is not confined to statutory rules or the rules framed by the competent authority in exercise of the power of delegated legislation but also include the terms of agreement entered into between the parties.

## Chapter IV Jurisdiction of Arbitral Tribunals

### Section 16: Competence of arbitral Tribunal to rule on its jurisdiction

(1) The arbitral Tribunal may rule on its own jurisdiction, including ruling on any objections with respect to the existence or validity of the arbitration agreement, and for that purpose,—

(a) an arbitration clause which forms part of a contract shall be treated as an agreement independent of the other terms of the contract; and

(b) a decision by the arbitral Tribunal that the contract is null and void shall not entail *ipso jure* the invalidity of the arbitration clause.

---

[13] Id at pp. 2799-2800 per P. K. Balasubramanyan, J.

(2) A plea that the arbitral Tribunal does not have jurisdiction shall be raised not later than the submission of the statement of defence; however, a party shall not be precluded from raising such a plea merely because that he has appointed, or participated in the appointment of, an arbitrator.

(3) A plea that the arbitral Tribunal is exceeding the scope of its authority shall be raised as soon as the matter alleged to be beyond the scope of its authority is raised during the arbitral proceedings.

(4) The arbitral Tribunal may, in either of the cases referred to in sub-section (2) or sub-section (3), admit a later plea if it considers the delay justified.

(5) The arbitral Tribunal shall decide on a plea referred to in sub-section (2) or sub-section (3) and, where the arbitral Tribunal takes a decision rejecting the plea, continue with the arbitral proceedings and make an arbitral award.

(6) A party aggrieved by such an arbitral award may make an application for setting aside such an arbitral award in accordance with Section 34.

Sec. 16 of the Act only makes explicit what is even otherwise implicit, namely, that the arbitral tribunal constituted under the Act has the jurisdiction to rule on its own jurisdiction, including ruling on objections with respect to the existence or validity of the arbitration agreement. Sub-section (2) of Sec. 16 enjoins that a party wanting to raise a plea that the arbitral tribunal does not have jurisdiction, has to raise that objection not later than the submission of the statement of defence, and that the party shall not be precluded from raising the plea of jurisdiction merely because he has appointed or participated in the appointment of an arbitrator. Sub-section (3) lays down that a plea that the arbitral tribunal is exceeding the scope of its authority shall be raised as soon as the matter alleged to be beyond the scope of its authority is raised during the arbitral proceedings. When the Tribunal decides these two questions, namely, the question of jurisdiction and the question of exceeding the scope of authority or either of them, the same is open to immediate challenge in an appeal, when the objection is upheld and only in an appeal against the final award, when the objection is overruled. Sub-section (5) enjoins that if the arbitral tribunal overrules the objections under sub-section (2) or sub-section (3), it should continue with the arbitral proceedings and make an arbitral award. Sub-section (6) provides that a party aggrieved by such an arbitral award overruling the plea on lack of jurisdiction and the exceeding of the scope of authority, may make an application on these grounds for setting aside the award in accordance with Sec. 34 of the Act.

## Section 17: Interim measures ordered by arbitral Tribunal

(1) A party may, during the arbitral proceedings or at any time after the making of the arbitral award but before it is enforced in accordance with Section 36, apply to the arbitral tribunal—

(i) for the appointment of a guardian for a minor or person of unsound mind for the purposes of arbitral proceedings; or

(ii) for an interim measure of protection in respect of any of the following matters, namely:—

(a) the preservation, interim custody or sale of any goods which are the subject-matter of the arbitration agreement;
(b) securing the amount in dispute in the arbitration;
(c) the detention, preservation or inspection of any property or thing which is the subject-matter of the dispute in arbitration, or as to which any question may arise therein and authorising for any of the aforesaid purposes any person to enter upon any land or building in the possession of any party, or authorising any samples to be taken, or any observation to be made, or experiment to be tried, which may be necessary or expedient for the purpose of obtaining full information or evidence;
(d) interim injunction or the appointment of a receiver;
(e) such other interim measure of protection as may appear to the arbitral tribunal to be just and convenient,

and the arbitral tribunal shall have the same power for making orders as the Court has for the purpose of, and in relation to, any proceedings before it.

(2) Subject to any orders passed in an appeal under Section 37, any order issued by the arbitral tribunal under this Section shall be deemed to be an order of the Court for all purposes and shall be enforceable under the Code of Civil Procedure, 1908 (5 of 1908), in the same manner as if it were an order of the Court.

## Chapter V Conduct of Arbitral Proceedings

### Section 18: Equal treatment of parties

The parties shall be treated with equality and each party shall be given a full opportunity to present his case.

### Section 19: Determination of rules of procedure

(1) The arbitral Tribunal shall not be bound by the Code of Civil Procedure, 1908 (5 of 1908) or the Indian Evidence Act, 1872 (1 of 1872).
(2) Subject to this Part, the parties are free to agree on the procedure to be followed by the arbitral Tribunal in conducting its proceedings.
(3) Failing any agreement referred to in sub-section (2), the arbitral Tribunal may, subject to this Part, conduct the proceedings in the manner it considers appropriate.
(4) The power of the arbitral Tribunal under sub-section (3) includes the power to determine the admissibility, relevance, materiality and weight of any evidence.

### Section 20: Place of arbitration

(1) The parties are free to agree on the place of arbitration.
(2) Failing any agreement referred to in sub-section (1), the place of arbitration shall be determined by the arbitral Tribunal having regard to the circumstances of the case, including the convenience of the parties.

(3) Notwithstanding sub-section (1) or sub-section (2), the arbitral Tribunal may, unless otherwise agreed by the parties, meet at any place it considers appropriate for consultation among its members, for hearing witnesses, experts or the parties, or for inspection of documents, goods or other property.

In *Sanshin Chemicals Industry* v. *Oriental Carbons and Chemicals Ltd.*[14] the question came before the Supreme Court for consideration is whether a decision regarding the venue of the arbitration proceedings could be assailed in appeal under Sec. 34 of the Arbitration and Conciliation Act, 1996. The court held that a conjoint reading of Sec. 2(6) and Sec. 20 therefore leads to the conclusion that in the event where parties do not agree with regard to the place of arbitration, though they are free to determine the same then they have the right to authorize any person including an institution for deciding the venue of the arbitration and such decision will not partake the character of adjudication of a dispute arising out of the agreement, so as to clothe it the character of an award. The decision on the question of venue under Sec. 20 would not come within making of an arbitral award or an interim award so as to be appealable under Sec. 34 of the Act.

## Section 21: Commencement of arbitral proceedings

Unless otherwise agreed by the parties, the arbitral proceedings in respect of a particular dispute commence on the date on which a request for that dispute to be referred to arbitration is received by the respondent.

The purpose of Sec. 21 of the Act is to determine the date of commencement of the arbitration proceedings, relevant mainly for deciding whether the claims of the claimant are barred by limitation or not. To say on basis of Sec. 21 that arbitral proceedings can commence only in regard to a dispute in respect of which notice has been served by a claimant upon the other party, requesting such dispute to be referred to arbitration; and therefore, a counterclaim can be entertained by the arbitrator only if it has been referred to him.[15]

## Section 22: Language

(1) The parties are free to agree upon the language or languages to be used in the arbitral proceedings.

(2) Failing any agreement referred to in sub-section (1), the arbitral Tribunal shall determine the language or languages to be used in the arbitral proceedings.

(3) The agreement or determination, unless otherwise specified, shall apply to any written statement by a party, any hearing and any arbitral award, decision, or other communication by the arbitral Tribunal.

(4) The arbitral Tribunal may order that any documentary evidence shall be accompanied by a translation into the language or languages agreed upon by the parties or determined by the arbitral Tribunal.

---

14 AIR 2001 SC 1219.

15 *State of Goa* v. *Praveen Enterprises*, AIR 2011 SC 3814.

## Section 23: Statements of claim and defence

(1) Within the period of time agreed upon by the parties or determined by the arbitral Tribunal, the claimant shall state the facts supporting his claim, the points at issue and the relief or remedy sought, and the respondent shall state his defence in respect of these particulars, unless the parties have otherwise agreed as to the required elements of those statements.

(2) The parties may submit with their statements all documents they consider to be relevant or may add a reference to the documents or other evidence they will submit.

(2A) The respondent, in support of his case, may also submit a counterclaim or plead a set-off, which shall be adjudicated upon by the arbitral tribunal, if such counterclaim or set-off falls within the scope of the arbitration agreement.

(3) Unless otherwise agreed by the parties, either party may amend or supplement his claim or defence during the course of the arbitral proceedings, unless the arbitral Tribunal considers it inappropriate to allow the amendment or supplement having regard to the delay in making it.

(4) The statement of claim and defence under this section shall be completed within a period of six months from the date of arbitrator or all the arbitrators, as the case may be, received notice, in writing of their appointment.

Sec. 23 of the Act makes it clear that when the arbitrator is appointed, the claimant is required to file the statement and the respondent has to file his defence statement before the Arbitrator. The claimant is not bound to restrict his statement of claim to the claims already raised by him by notice, *"unless the parties have otherwise agreed as to the required elements"* of such claim statement. It is also made clear that *"unless otherwise agreed by the parties"* the claimant can also subsequently amend or supplement the claims in the claim statement. That is, unless the arbitration agreement requires the Arbitrator to decide only the specifically referred disputes, the claimant can while filing the statement of claim or thereafter, amend or add to the claims already made. Similarly, Sec. 23 read with Sec. 2(9) makes it clear that a respondent is entitled to raise a counterclaim *"unless the parties have otherwise agreed"* and also add to or amend the counterclaim, *"unless otherwise agreed"*. In short, unless the arbitration agreement requires the Arbitrator to decide only the specifically referred disputes, the respondent can file counterclaims and amend or add to the same, except where the arbitration agreement restricts the arbitration to only those disputes which are specifically referred to arbitration, both the claimant and respondent are entitled to make any claims or counterclaims and further entitled to add to or amend such claims and counterclaims provided they are arbitrable and within limitation.[16]

## Section 24: Hearings and written proceedings

(1) Unless otherwise agreed by the parties, the arbitral Tribunal shall decide whether to hold oral hearings for the presentation of evidence or for oral argument, or

[16] *State of Goa* v. *Praveen Enterprises*, AIR 2011 SC 3814.

whether the proceedings shall be conducted on the basis of documents and other materials:

Provided that the arbitral Tribunal shall hold oral hearings, at an appropriate stage of the proceedings, on a request by a party, unless the parties have agreed that no oral hearing shall be held.

Provided further that the arbitral tribunal shall, as far as possible, hold oral hearings for the presentation of evidence or for oral argument on day-to-day basis, and not grant any adjournments unless sufficient cause is made out, and may impose costs including exemplary costs on the party seeking adjournment without any sufficient cause.

(2) The parties shall be given sufficient advance notice of any hearing and of any meeting of the arbitral Tribunal for the purposes of inspection of documents, goods or other property.

(3) All statements, documents or other information supplied to, or applications made to, the arbitral Tribunal by one party shall be communicated to the other party and any expert report or evidentiary document on which the arbitral Tribunal may rely in making its decision shall be communicated to the parties.

**Section 25: Default of a party**

Unless otherwise agreed by the parties, where, without showing sufficient cause,—

(a) the claimant fails to communicate his statement of claim in accordance with sub-section (1) of Section 23, the arbitral Tribunal shall terminate the proceedings;

(b) the respondent fails to communicate his statement of defence in accordance with sub-section (1) of Section 23, the arbitral tribunal shall continue the proceedings without treating that failure in itself as an admission of the allegations by the claimant and shall have the discretion to treat the right of the respondent to file such statement of defence as having been forfeited;

(c) a party fails to appear at an oral hearing or to produce documentary evidence, the arbitral Tribunal may continue the proceedings and make the arbitral award on the evidence before it.

**Section 26: Expert appointed by arbitral Tribunal**

(1) Unless otherwise agreed by the parties, the arbitral Tribunal may—

(a) appoint one or more experts to report to it on specific issues to be determined by the arbitral Tribunal; and

(b) require a party to give the expert any relevant information or to produce, or to provide access to, any relevant documents, goods or other property for his inspection.

(2) Unless otherwise agreed by the parties, if a party so requests or if the arbitral Tribunal considers it necessary, the expert shall, after delivery of his written or oral report, participate in an oral hearing where the parties have the opportunity

to put questions to him and to present expert witnesses in order to testify on the points at issue.

(3) Unless otherwise agreed by the parties, the expert shall, on the request of a party, make available to that party for examination all documents, goods, or other property in the possession of the expert with which he was provided in order to prepare his report.

**Section 27: Court assistance in taking evidence**

(1) The arbitral Tribunal, or a party with the approval of the arbitral Tribunal, may apply to the Court for assistance in taking evidence.

(2) The application shall specify—

(a) the names and addresses of the parties and the arbitrators;

(b) the general nature of the claim and the relief sought;

(c) the evidence to be obtained, in particular,—

(i) the name and address of any person to be heard as witness or expert witness and a statement of the subject-matter of the testimony required;

(ii) the description of any document to be produced or property to be inspected.

(3) The Court may, within its competence and according to its rules on taking evidence, execute the request by ordering that the evidence be provided directly to the arbitral Tribunal.

(4) The Court may, while making an order under sub-section (3), issue the same processes to witnesses as it may issue in suits tried before it.

(5) Persons failing to attend in accordance with such process, or making any other default, or refusing to give their evidence, or guilty of any contempt to the arbitral Tribunal during the conduct of arbitral proceedings, shall be subject to the like disadvantages, penalties, and punishments by order of the Court on the representation of the arbitral Tribunal as they would incur for the like offences in suits tried before the Court.

(6) In this section the expression "Processes" includes summonses and commissions for the examination of witnesses and summonses to produce documents.

# Chapter VI Making of Arbitral Award and Termination of Proceedings

**Section 28: Rules applicable to substance of dispute**

(1) Where the place of arbitration is situated in India,—

(a) in an arbitration other than an international commercial arbitration, the arbitral Tribunal shall decide the dispute submitted to arbitration in accordance with the substantive law for the time being in force in India;

(b) in international commercial arbitration,—

(i) the arbitral Tribunal shall decide the dispute in accordance with the rules of law designated by the parties as applicable to the substance of the dispute;

(ii) any designation by the parties of the law or legal system of a given country shall be construed, unless otherwise expressed, as directly referring to the substantive law of that country and not to its conflict of laws/rules;

(iii) failing any designation of the law under clause (a) by the parties, the arbitral Tribunal shall apply the rules of law it considers to be appropriate given all the circumstances surrounding the dispute.

(2) The arbitral Tribunal shall decide *ex aequo et bono* or as amiable compositeur only if the parties have expressly authorised it to do so.

(3) While deciding and making an award, the arbitral tribunal shall, in all cases, take into account the terms of the contract and trade usages applicable to the transaction.

## Section 29: Decision-making by panel of arbitrators

(1) Unless otherwise agreed by the parties, in arbitral proceedings with more than one arbitrator, any decision of the arbitral Tribunal shall be made by a majority of all its members.

(2) Notwithstanding sub-section (1), if authorised by the parties or all the members of the arbitral Tribunal, questions of procedure may be decided by the presiding arbitrator.

## Section 29A: Time limit for arbitral award

(1) The award in matters other than international commercial arbitration shall be made by the arbitral tribunal within a period of twelve months from the date of completion of pleadings under sub-section (4) of Section 23.

Provided that the award in the matter of international commercial arbitration may be made as expeditiously as possible and endeavor may be made to dispose of the matter within a period of twelve months from the date of completion of pleadings under sub-section (4) of Section 23.

(2) If the award is made within a period of six months from the date the arbitral tribunal enters upon the reference, the arbitral tribunal shall be entitled to receive such amount of additional fees as the parties may agree.

(3) The parties may, by consent, extend the period specified in sub-section (1) for making award for a further period not exceeding six months.

(4) If the award is not made within the period specified in sub-section (1) or the extended period specified under sub-section (3), the mandate of the arbitrator(s) shall terminate unless the Court has, either prior to or after the expiry of the period so specified, extended the period:

Provided that while extending the period under this sub-section, if the Court finds that the proceedings have been delayed for the reasons attributable to the arbitral tribunal, then, it may order reduction of fees of arbitrator(s) by not exceeding five per cent for each month of such delay.

Provided further that where an application under sub-section (5) is pending, the mandate of the arbitrator shall continue till the disposal of the said application:

Provided also that the arbitrator shall be given an opportunity of being heard before the fees is reduced.

(5) The extension of period referred to in sub-section (4) may be on the application of any of the parties and may be granted only for sufficient cause and on such terms and conditions as may be imposed by the Court.

(6) While extending the period referred to in sub-section (4), it shall be open to the Court to substitute one or all of the arbitrators and if one or all of the arbitrators are substituted, the arbitral proceedings shall continue from the stage already reached and on the basis of the evidence and material already on record, and the arbitrator(s) appointed under this section shall be deemed to have received the said evidence and material.

(7) In the event of arbitrator(s) being appointed under this section, the arbitral tribunal thus reconstituted shall be deemed to be in continuation of the previously appointed arbitral tribunal.

(8) It shall be open to the Court to impose actual or exemplary costs upon any of the parties under this section.

(9) An application filed under sub-section (5) shall be disposed of by the Court as expeditiously as possible and endeavour shall be made to dispose of the matter within a period of sixty days from the date of service of notice on the opposite party.

**Section 29B: Fast track procedure**

(1) Notwithstanding anything contained in this Act, the parties to an arbitration agreement, may, at any stage either before or at the time of appointment of the arbitral tribunal, agree in writing to have their dispute resolved by fast-track procedure specified in sub-section (3).

(2) The parties to the arbitration agreement, while agreeing for resolution of dispute by fast-track procedure, may agree that the arbitral tribunal shall consist of a sole arbitrator who shall be chosen by the parties.

(3) The arbitral tribunal shall follow the following procedure while conducting arbitration proceedings under sub-section (1),—

(a) the arbitral tribunal shall decide the dispute on the basis of written pleadings, documents and submissions filed by the parties without any oral hearing;

(b) the arbitral tribunal shall have power to call for any further information or clarification from the parties in addition to the pleadings and documents filed by them;

(c) an oral hearing may be held only, if, all the parties make a request or if the arbitral tribunal considers it necessary to have oral hearing for clarifying certain issues;

(d) the arbitral tribunal may dispense with any technical formalities, if an oral hearing is held, and adopt such procedure as deemed appropriate for expeditious disposal of the case.

(4) The award under this section shall be made within a period of six months from the date the arbitral tribunal enters upon the reference.

(5) If the award is not made within the period specified in sub-section.

(4) the provisions of sub-sections (3) to (9) of Section 29A shall apply to the proceedings.

(6) The fees payable to the arbitrator and the manner of payment of the fees shall be such as may be agreed between the arbitrator and the parties.

### Section 30: Settlement

(1) It is not incompatible with an arbitration agreement for an arbitral Tribunal to encourage settlement of the dispute and, with the agreement of the parties; the arbitral Tribunal may use mediation, conciliation, or other procedures at any time during the arbitral proceedings to encourage settlement.

(2) If, during arbitral proceedings, the parties settle the dispute, the arbitral Tribunal shall terminate the proceedings and, if requested by the parties and not objected to by the arbitral Tribunal, record the settlement in the form of an arbitral award on agreed terms.

(3) An arbitral award on agreed terms shall be made in accordance with Section 31 and shall state that it is an arbitral award.

(4) An arbitral award on agreed terms shall have the same status and effect as any other arbitral award on the substance of the dispute.

### Section 31: Form and contents of arbitral award

(1) An arbitral award shall be made in writing and shall be signed by the members of the arbitral Tribunal.

(2) For the purposes of sub-section (1), in arbitral proceedings with more than one arbitrator, the signatures of the majority of all the members of the arbitral Tribunal shall be sufficient so long as the reason for any omitted signature is stated.

(3) The arbitral award shall state the reasons upon which it is based, unless—

(a) the parties have agreed that no reasons are to be given, or

(b) the award is an arbitral award on agreed terms under Section 30.

(4) The arbitral award shall state its date and the place of arbitration as determined in accordance with Section 20 and the award shall be deemed to have been made at that place.

(5) After the arbitral award is made, a signed copy shall be delivered to each party.

(6) The arbitral Tribunal may, at any time during the arbitral proceedings, make an interim arbitral award on any matter with respect to which it may make a final arbitral award.

(7) (a) Unless otherwise agreed by the parties, where and insofar as an arbitral award is for the payment of money, the arbitral Tribunal may include in the sum for which the award is made interest, at such rate as it deems reasonable, on the whole or any part of the money, for the whole or any part of the period between the date on which the cause of action arose and the date on which the award is made.

(b) A sum directed to be paid by an arbitral award shall, unless the award otherwise directs, carry interest at the rate of two per cent higher than the current rate of interest prevalent on the date of award, from the date of award to the date of payment.

***Explanation***: The expression "current rate of interest" shall have the same meaning as assigned to it under clause (b) of Section 2 of the Interest Act, 1978 (14 of 1978).

(8) The costs of an arbitration shall be fixed by the arbitral tribunal in accordance with Section 31A.

***Explanation***: For the purpose of clause (a), "costs" means reasonable costs relating to—

(i) the fees and expenses of the arbitrators and witnesses,

(ii) legal fees and expenses,

(iii) any administration fees of the institution supervising the arbitration, and

(iv) any other expenses incurred in connection with the arbitral proceedings and the arbitral award.

## Section 31A: Regime for costs

(1) In relation to any arbitration proceeding or a proceeding under any of the provisions of this Act pertaining to the arbitration, the Court or arbitral tribunal, notwithstanding anything contained in the Code of Civil Procedure, 1908 (5 of 1908), shall have the discretion to determine—

(a) whether costs are payable by one party to another;

(b) the amount of such costs; and

(c) when such costs are to be paid.

***Explanation***: For the purpose of this sub-section, "costs" means reasonable costs relating to—

(i) the fees and expenses of the arbitrators, Courts and witnesses;

(ii) legal fees and expenses;

(iii) any administration fees of the institution supervising the arbitration; and

(iv) any other expenses incurred in connection with the arbitral or Court proceedings and the arbitral award.

(2) If the Court or arbitral tribunal decides to make an order as to payment of costs,—

(a) the general rule is that the unsuccessful party shall be ordered to pay the costs of the successful party; or

(b) the Court or arbitral tribunal may make a different order for reasons to be recorded in writing.

(3) In determining the costs, the Court or arbitral tribunal shall have regard to all the circumstances, including—

(a) the conduct of all the parties;

(b) whether a party has succeeded partly in the case;

(c) whether the party had made a frivolous counterclaim leading to delay in the disposal of the arbitral proceedings; and

(d) whether any reasonable offer to settle the dispute is made by a party and refused by the other party.

(4) The Court or arbitral tribunal may make any order under this Section including the order that a party shall pay—

(a) a proportion of another party's costs;

(b) a stated amount in respect of another party's costs;

(c) costs from or until a certain date only;

(d) costs incurred before proceedings have begun;

(e) costs relating to particular steps taken in the proceedings;

(f) costs relating only to a distinct part of the proceedings; and

(g) interest on costs from or until a certain date.

(5) An agreement which has the effect that a party is to pay the whole or part of the costs of the arbitration in any event shall be only valid if such agreement is made after the dispute in question has arisen.

**Section 32: Termination of proceedings**

(1) The arbitral proceedings shall be terminated by the final arbitral award or by an order of the arbitral Tribunal under sub-section (2).

(2) The arbitral Tribunal shall issue an order for the termination of the arbitral proceedings where—

(a) the claimant withdraws his claim, unless the respondent objects to the order and the arbitral Tribunal recognises a legitimate interest on his part in obtaining a final settlement of the dispute,

(b) the parties agree on the termination of the proceedings, or

(c) the arbitral Tribunal finds that the continuation of the proceedings has for any other reason become unnecessary or impossible.

(3) Subject to Section 33 and sub-section (4) of Section 34, the mandate of the arbitral Tribunal shall terminate with the termination of the arbitral proceedings.

### Section 33: Correction and interpretation of award; additional award

(1) Within thirty days from the receipt of the arbitral award, unless another period of time has been agreed upon by the parties—

(a) a party, with notice to the other party, may request the arbitral Tribunal to correct any computation errors, any clerical or typographical errors or any other errors of a similar nature occurring in the award;

(b) if so agreed by the parties, a party, with notice to the other party, may request the arbitral Tribunal to give an interpretation of a specific point or part of the award.

(2) If the arbitral Tribunal considers the request made under sub-section (1) to be justified, it shall make the correction or give the interpretation within thirty days from the receipt of the request and the interpretation shall form part of the arbitral award.

(3) The arbitral Tribunal may correct any error of the type referred to in clause (a) of sub-section (1), on its own initiative, within thirty days from the date of the arbitral award.

(4) Unless otherwise agreed by the parties, a party with notice to the other party, may request, within thirty days from the receipt of the arbitral award, the arbitral Tribunal to make an additional arbitral award as to claims presented in the arbitral proceedings but omitted from the arbitral award.

(5) If the arbitral Tribunal considers the request made under sub-section (4) to be justified, it shall make the additional arbitral award within sixty days from the receipt of such request.

(6) The arbitral Tribunal may extend, if necessary, the period of time within which it shall make a correction, give an interpretation or make an additional arbitral award under sub-section (2) or sub-section (5).

(7) Section 31 shall apply to a correction or interpretation of the arbitral award or to an additional arbitral award made under this section.

## Chapter VII Recourse Against Arbitral Award

### Section 34: Application for setting aside arbitral award

(1) Recourse to a Court against an arbitral award may be made only by an application for setting aside such award in accordance with sub-section (2) and sub-section (3).

(2) An arbitral award may be set aside by the Court only if—

(a) the party making the application furnishes proof that—

(i) a party was under some incapacity; or

(ii) the arbitration agreement is not valid under the law to which the parties have subjected it or, failing any indication thereon, under the law for the time being in force; or

(iii) the party making the application was not given proper notice of the appointment of an arbitrator or of the arbitral proceedings or was otherwise unable to present his case; or

(iv) the arbitral award deals with a dispute not contemplated by or not falling within the terms of the submission to arbitration, or it contains decisions on matters beyond the scope of the submission to arbitration:

Provided that, if the decisions on matters submitted to arbitration can be separated from those not so submitted, only that part of the arbitral award which contains decisions on matters not submitted to arbitration may be set aside; or

(v) the composition of the arbitral Tribunal or the arbitral procedure was not in accordance with the agreement of the parties, unless such agreement was in conflict with a provision of this Part from which the parties cannot derogate, or, failing such agreement, was not in accordance with this Part; or

(b) the Court finds that—

(i) the subject-matter of the dispute is not capable of settlement by arbitration under the law for the time being in force, or

(ii) the arbitral award is in conflict with the public policy of India.

*Explanation* **1:** For the avoidance of any doubt, it is clarified that an award is in conflict with the public policy of India, only if,—

(i) the making of the award was induced or affected by fraud or corruption or was in violation of Section 75 or Section 81; or

(ii) it is in contravention with the fundamental policy of Indian law; or

(iii) it is in conflict with the most basic notions of morality or justice.

*Explanation* **2:** For the avoidance of doubt, the test as to whether there is a contravention with the fundamental policy of Indian law shall not entail a review on the merits of the dispute.

(2A) An arbitral award arising out of arbitrations other than international commercial arbitrations, may also be set aside by the Court, if the Court finds that the award is vitiated by patent illegality appearing on the face of the award:

Provided that an award shall not be set aside merely on the ground of an erroneous application of the law or by re-appreciation of evidence.

(3) An application for setting aside may not be made after three months have elapsed from the date on which the party making that application had received the arbitral award, or, if a request had been made under Section 33, from the date on which that request had been disposed of by the arbitral tribunal:

Provided that if the Court is satisfied that the applicant was prevented by sufficient cause from making the application within the said period of three months it may entertain the application within a further period of thirty days, but not thereafter.

Provided further that where the Court is satisfied that a *prima facie* case is made out that,—

(a) the arbitration agreement or contract which is the basis of the award; or
(b) the making of the award,

was induced or effected by fraud or corruption, it shall stay the award unconditionally pending disposal of the challenge under Section 34 to the award.

***Explanation***: For the removal of doubts, it is hereby clarified that the above proviso shall apply to all court cases arising out of or in relation to arbitral proceedings, irrespective of whether the arbitral or court proceedings were commenced prior to or after the commencement of the Arbitration and Conciliation (Amendment) Act, 2015.

(4) On receipt of an application under sub-section (1), the Court may, where it is appropriate and it is so requested by a party, adjourn the proceedings for a period of time determined by it in order to give the arbitral tribunal an opportunity to resume the arbitral proceedings or to take such other action as in the opinion of arbitral tribunal will eliminate the grounds for setting aside the arbitral award.

(5) An application under this section shall be filed by a party only after issuing a prior notice to the other party and such application shall be accompanied by an affidavit by the applicant endorsing compliance with the said requirement.

(6) An application under this section shall be disposed of expeditiously, and in any event, within a period of one year from the date on which the notice referred to in sub-section (5) is served upon the other party.

## Chapter VIII Finality and Enforcement of Arbitral Awards

### Section 35: Finality of arbitral awards

Subject to this Part an arbitral award shall be final and binding on the parties and persons claiming under them respectively.

### Section 36: Enforcement

(1) Where the time for making an application to set aside the arbitral award under Section 34 has expired, then, subject to the provisions of sub-section (2), such award shall be enforced in accordance with the provisions of the Code of Civil Procedure, 1908 (5 of 1908), in the same manner as if it were a decree of the Court.

(2) Where an application to set aside the arbitral award has been filed in the Court under Section 34, the filing of such an application shall not by itself render that award unenforceable, unless the Court grants an order of stay of the operation

of the said arbitral award in accordance with the provisions of sub-section (3), on a separate application made for that purpose.

(3) Upon filing of an application under sub-section (2) for stay of the operation of the arbitral award, the Court may, subject to such conditions as it may deem fit, grant stay of the operation of such award for reasons to be recorded in writing:

Provided that the Court shall, while considering the application for grant of stay in the case of an arbitral award for payment of money, have due regard to the provisions for grant of stay of a money decree under the provisions of the Code of Civil Procedure, 1908 (5 of 1908).

Provided further that where the Court is satisfied that a *Prima facie* case is made out that,—

(a) the arbitration agreement or contract which is the basis of the award; or

(b) the making of the award, was induced or effected by fraud or corruption, it shall stay the award unconditionally pending disposal of the challenge under Section 34 to the award.

***Explanation***: For the removal of doubts, it is hereby clarified that the above proviso shall apply to all court cases arising out of or in relation to arbitral proceedings, irrespective of whether the arbitral or court proceedings were commenced prior to or after the commencement of the Arbitration and Conciliation (Amendment) Act, 2015 (3 of 2016).

## Chapter IX Appeals

### Section 37: Appealable orders

(1) Notwithstanding anything contained in any other law for the time being in force, an appeal shall lie from the following orders (and from no others) to the Court authorised by law to hear appeals from original decrees of the Court passing the order, namely:—

(a) refusing to refer the parties to arbitration under Section 8;

(b) granting or refusing to grant any measure under Section 9;

(c) setting aside or refusing to set aside an arbitral award under Section 34.

(2) Appeal shall also lie to a court from an order of the arbitral Tribunal—

(a) accepting the plea referred to in sub-section (2) or sub-section (3) of Section 16; or

(b) granting or refusing to grant an interim measure under Section 17.

(3) No second appeal shall lie from an order passed in appeal under this section, but nothing in this section shall affect or take away any right to appeal to the Supreme Court.

# Chapter X Miscellaneous

## Section 38: Deposits

(1) The arbitral Tribunal may fix the amount of the deposit or supplementary deposit, as the case may be, as an advance for the costs referred to in sub-section (8) of Section 31, which it expects will be incurred in respect of the claim submitted to it:

Provided that where, apart from the claim, a counterclaim has been submitted to the arbitral Tribunal, it may fix separate amount of deposit for the claim and counterclaim.

(2) The deposit referred to in sub-section (1) shall be payable in equal shares by the parties:

Provided that where one party fails to pay his share of the deposit, the other party may pay that share:

Provided further that where the other party also does not pay the aforesaid share in respect of the claim or the counterclaim, the arbitral Tribunal may suspend or terminate the arbitral proceedings in respect of such claim or counterclaim, as the case may be.

(3) Upon termination of the arbitral proceedings, the arbitral Tribunal shall render an accounting to the parties of the deposits received and shall return any unexpended balance to the party or parties, as the case may be.

## Section 39: Lien on arbitral award and deposits as to costs

(1) Subject to the provisions of sub-section (2) and to any provision to the contrary in the arbitration agreement, the arbitral Tribunal shall have a lien on the arbitral award for any unpaid costs of the arbitration.

(2) If in any case an arbitral Tribunal refuses to deliver its award except on payment of the costs demanded by it, the Court may, on an application in this behalf, order that the arbitral Tribunal shall deliver the arbitral award to the applicant on payment into Court by the applicant of the costs demanded, and shall, after such inquiry, if any, as it thinks fit, further order that out of the money so paid into Court there shall be paid to the arbitral Tribunal by way of costs such sum as the Court may consider reasonable and that the balance of the money, if any, shall be refunded to the applicant.

(3) An application under sub-section (2) may be made by any party unless the fees demanded have been fixed by written agreement between him and the arbitral Tribunal, and the arbitral Tribunal shall be entitled to appear and be heard on any such application.

(4) The Court may make such orders as it thinks fit respecting the costs of the arbitration where any question arises respecting such costs and the arbitral award contains no sufficient provision concerning them.

## Section 40: Arbitration agreement not to be discharged by death of party thereto

(1) An arbitration agreement shall not be discharged by the death of any party thereto either as respects the deceased or as respects any other party but shall in such event be enforceable by or against the legal representative of the deceased.

(2) The mandate of an arbitrator shall not be terminated by the death of any party by whom he was appointed.

(3) Nothing in this section shall affect the operation of any law by virtue of which any right of action is extinguished by the death of a person.

It is clear from Sec. 40 of the Arbitration Act that an arbitration agreement is not discharged by the death of any party thereto and on such death it is enforceable by or against the legal representatives of the deceased, nor is the authority of the arbitrator revoked by the death of the party appointing him, subject to the operation of any law by virtue of which the death of a person extinguishes the right of action of that person.

It is necessary to have a look to Sec. 2 (1) (g) which defines "legal representative".

> "Legal Representative" means a person who in law represents the estate of a deceased person and includes any person who intermeddles with the estate of the deceased person, and, where a party acts in a representative character, the person on whom the estate develops on the death of the party so acting."

The definition of 'legal representative' became necessary because such representatives are bound by and also entitled to enforce an arbitration agreement. Sec. 40 of Arbitration Act clearly says that an arbitration agreement is not discharged by the death of a party. The agreement remains enforceable by or against the legal representatives of the deceased.

## Section 41: Provisions in case of insolvency

(1) Where it is provided by a term in a contract to which an insolvent is a party that any dispute arising thereout or in connection therewith shall be submitted to arbitration, the said term shall, if the receiver adopts the contract, be enforceable by or against him so far as it relates to any such dispute.

(2) Where a person who has been adjudged an insolvent had, before the commencement of the insolvency proceedings, become a party to an arbitration agreement, and any matter to which the agreement applies is required to be determined in connection with, or for the purposes of, the insolvency proceedings, then, if the case is one to which sub-section (1) does not apply, any other party or the receiver may apply to the judicial authority having jurisdiction in the insolvency proceedings for an order directing that the matter in question shall be submitted to arbitration in accordance with the arbitration agreement, and the judicial authority may, if it is of opinion that, having regard to all the circumstances of the case, the matter ought to be determined by arbitration, make an order accordingly.

(3) In this section the expression "receiver" includes an Official Assignee.

## Section 42: Jurisdiction

Notwithstanding anything contained elsewhere in this Part or in any other law for the time being in force, where with respect to an arbitration agreement any application under this Part has been made in a Court, that Court alone shall have jurisdiction over the arbitral proceedings and all subsequent applications arising out of that agreement and the arbitral proceedings shall be made in that Court and in no other Court.

## Section 42A: Confidentiality of information

Notwithstanding anything contained by any other law for the time being in force, the arbitrator, the arbitral institution and the parties to the arbitration agreement shall maintain confidentially of all arbitral proceedings except award where its disclosure is necessary for the purpose of implementation and enforcement of award.

## Section 42B: Protection of action taken in good faith

No suit or other legal proceedings shall lie against the arbitrator for anything which is in good faith done or intended to be done under this Act or the rules or regulations made thereunder.

## Section 43: Limitations

(1) The Limitation Act, 1963 (36 of 1963), shall apply to arbitrations as it applies to proceedings in court.

(2) For the purposes of this section and the Limitation Act, 1963 (36 of 1963), an arbitration shall be deemed to have commenced on the date referred in Section 21.

(3) Where an arbitration agreement to submit future disputes to arbitration provides that any claim to which the agreement applies shall be barred unless some step to commence arbitral proceedings is taken within a time fixed by the agreement and a dispute arises to which the agreement applies, the Court, if it is of opinion that in the circumstances of the case under hardship would otherwise be caused, and notwithstanding that the time so fixed has expired, may on such terms, if any, as the justice of the case may require, extend the time for such period as it thinks proper.

(4) Where the Court orders that an arbitral award be set aside, the period between the commencement of the arbitration and the date of the order of the Court shall be excluded in computing the time prescribed by the Limitation Act, 1963 (36 of 1963), for the commencement of the proceedings (including arbitration) with respect to the dispute so submitted.

Sec. 43(1) of the 1996 Act provides that the Limitation Act shall apply to arbitrations as it applies to proceedings in Court. The purpose of Sec. 43 of 1996 Act is not to make Limitation Act inapplicable to proceedings before Court, but on the other hand, make Limitation Act applicable to arbitrations. Sec. 43 of the 1996 Act, apart from making the provisions of Limitation Act, 1963 applicable to arbitrations, reiterates that Limitation Act applies to proceedings in Court. Therefore, the provisions of Limitation Act, 1963 apply to all proceedings under the 1996 Act, both in Court and in arbitration, except to the extent expressly excluded by the provisions of the 1996 Act.[17]

# PART IA Arbitration Council of India

## Section 43A: Definitions in this Part, unless the context otherwise requires

(a) "Chairperson" means the Chairperson of the Arbitration Council of India appointed under clause (a) of sub-section (1) of Section 43C;

(b) "Council" means the Arbitration Council of India established under Section 43B;

(c) "Member" means a Member of the Council and includes the Chairperson.

## Section 43B: Establishment and incorporation of Arbitration Council of India

(1) The Central Government shall, by notification in the Official Gazette, establish, for the purposes of this Act, a Council to be known as the Arbitration Council of India to perform the duties and discharge the functions under this Act.

(2) The Council shall be a body corporate by the name aforesaid, having perpetual succession and a common seal, with power, subject to the provisions of this Act, to acquire, hold and dispose of property, both movable and immovable, and to enter into contract, and shall, by the said name, sue or be sued.

(3) The head office of the Council shall be at Delhi.

(4) The Council may, with the prior approval of the Central Government, establish offices at other places in India.

## Section 43C: Composition of Council

(1) The Council shall consist of the following Members, namely:—

(a) a person, who has been, a Judge of the Supreme Court or, Chief Justice of a High Court or, a Judge of a High Court or an eminent person, having special knowledge and experience in the conduct or administration of arbitration, to be appointed by the Central Government in consultation with the Chief Justice of India–Chairperson;

(b) an eminent arbitration practitioner having substantial knowledge and experience in institutional arbitration, both domestic and international, to be nominated by the Central Government–Member;

(c) an eminent academician having experience in research and teaching in the field of arbitration and alternative dispute resolution laws, to be appointed by the Central Government in consultation with the Chairperson–Member;

[17] *Consolidated Engineering Enterprises, M/s.* v. *Principal Secretary, (Irrigation Department)*, AIR 2009 SC (Supp) 396.

(d) Secretary to the Government of India in the Department of Legal Affairs, Ministry of Law and Justice or his representative not below the rank of Joint Secretary–Member, *ex officio;*

(e) Secretary to the Government of India in the Department of Expenditure, Ministry of Finance, or his representative not below the rank of Joint Secretary–Member, *ex officio;*

(f) one representative of a recognised body of commerce and industry, chosen on rotational basis by the Central Government–Part-time Member; and

(g) Chief Executive Officer-Member-Secretary, *ex officio.*

(2) The Chairperson and Members of the Council, other than *ex officio* Members, shall hold office as such, for a term of three years from the date on which they enter upon their office: Provided that no Chairperson or Member, other than *ex officio* Member, shall hold office as such after he has attained the age of seventy years in the case of Chairperson and sixty-seven years in the case of Member.

(3) The salaries, allowances and other terms and conditions of the Chairperson and Members referred to in clauses (b) and (c) of sub-section (1) shall be such as may be prescribed by the Central Government.

(4) The Part-time Member shall be entitled to such travelling and other allowances as may be prescribed by the Central Government.

**Section 43D: Duties and functions of Council**

(1) It shall be the duty of the Council to take all such measures as may be necessary to promote and encourage arbitration, mediation, conciliation, or other alternative dispute resolution mechanism and for that purpose to frame policy and guidelines for the establishment, operation and maintenance of uniform professional standards in respect of all matters relating to arbitration.

(2) For the purposes of performing the duties and discharging the functions under this Act, the Council may—

(a) frame policies governing the grading of arbitral institutions;

(b) recognise professional institutes providing accreditation of arbitrators;

(c) review the grading of arbitral institutions and arbitrators;

(d) hold training, workshops, and courses in the area of arbitration in collaboration of law firms, law universities and arbitral institutes;

(e) frame, review, and update norms to ensure satisfactory level of arbitration and conciliation;

(f) act as a forum for exchange of views and techniques to be adopted for creating a platform to make India a robust centre for domestic and international arbitration and conciliation;

(g) make recommendations to the Central Government on various measures to be adopted to make provision for easy resolution of commercial disputes;

(h) promote institutional arbitration by strengthening arbitral institutions;

(i) conduct examination and training on various subjects relating to arbitration and conciliation and award certificates thereof;

(j) establish and maintain depository of arbitral awards made in India;

(k) make recommendations regarding personnel, training and infrastructure of arbitral institutions; and

(l) such other functions as may be decided by the Central Government.

### Section 43E: Vacancies, etc., not to invalidate proceedings of Council

No act or proceeding of the Council shall be invalid merely by reason of—

(a) any vacancy or any defect in the constitution of the Council;

(b) any defect in the appointment of a person acting as a Member of the Council; or

(c) any irregularity in the procedure of the Council not affecting the merits of the case.

### Section 43F: Resignation of Members

The Chairperson or the Full-time or Part-time Member may, by notice in writing, under his hand addressed to the Central Government, resign his office:

Provided that the Chairperson or the Full-time Member shall, unless he is permitted by the Central Government to relinquish his office sooner, continue to hold office until the expiry of three months from the date of receipt of such notice or until a person duly appointed as his successor enters upon his office or until the expiry of his term of office, whichever is earlier.

### Section 43G: Removal of Member

(1) The Central Government may, remove a Member from his office if he—

(a) is an undischarged insolvent; or

(b) has engaged at any time (except Part-time Member), during his term of office, in any paid employment; or

(c) has been convicted of an offence which, in the opinion of the Central Government, involves moral turpitude; or

(d) has acquired such financial or other interest as is likely to affect prejudicially his functions as a Member; or

(e) has so abused his position as to render his continuance in office prejudicial to the public interest; or

(f) has become physically or mentally incapable of acting as a Member.

(2) Notwithstanding anything contained in sub-section (1), no Member shall be removed from his office on the grounds specified in clauses (d) and (e) of that sub-section unless the Supreme Court, on a reference being made to it in this behalf by the Central Government, has, on an inquiry, held by it in accordance

with such procedure as may be prescribed in this behalf by the Supreme Court, reported that the Member, ought on such ground or grounds to be removed.

### Section 43H: Appointment of experts and constitution of Committees thereof

The Council may appoint such experts and constitute such Committees of experts as it may consider necessary to discharge its functions on such terms and conditions as may be specified by the regulations.

### Section 43I: General norms for grading of arbitral institutions

The Council shall make grading of arbitral institutions on the basis of criteria relating to infrastructure, quality and caliber of arbitrators, performance, and compliance of time limits for disposal of domestic or international commercial arbitrations, in such manner as may be specified by the regulations.

### Section 43J: Norms for accreditation of arbitrators

The qualifications, experience, and norms for accreditation of arbitrators shall be such as may be specified by the regulations.

### Section 43K: Depository of awards

The Council shall maintain an electronic depository of arbitral awards made in India and such other records related thereto in such manner as may be specified by the regulations.

### Section 43L: Power to make regulations by Council

The Council may, in consultation with the Central Government, make regulations, consistent with the provisions of this Act and the rules made thereunder, for the discharge of its functions and perform its duties under this Act.

### Section 43M: Chief Executive Officer

(1) There shall be a Chief Executive Officer of the Council, who shall be responsible for day-to-day administration of the Council.

(2) The qualifications, appointment and other terms and conditions of the service of the Chief Executive Officer shall be such as may be prescribed by the Central Government.

(3) The Chief Executive Officer shall discharge such functions and perform such duties as may be specified by the regulations.

(4) There shall be a Secretariat to the Council consisting of such number of officers and employees as may be prescribed by the Central Government.

(5) The qualifications, appointment and other terms and conditions of the service of the employees and other officers of the Council shall be such as may be prescribed by the Central Government.

# Part II Enforcement of Certain Foreign Awards

## Chapter I New York Convention Awards

### Section 44: Definition

In this Chapter, unless the context otherwise requires, "foreign award" means an arbitral award on differences between persons arising out of legal relationships, whether contractual or not, considered as commercial under the law in force in India, made on or after the 11th day of October, 1960—

(a) in pursuance of an agreement in writing for arbitration to which the Convention set forth in the First Schedule applies, and

(b) in one of such territories as the Central Government, being satisfied that reciprocal provisions have been made may, by notification in the Official Gazette, declare to be territories to which the said Convention applies.

### Section 45: Power of judicial authority to refer parties to arbitration

Notwithstanding anything contained in Part I or in the Code of Civil Procedure, 1908 (5 of 1908), a judicial authority, when seized of an action in a matter in respect of which the parties have made an agreement referred to in Section 44, shall, at the request of one of the parties or any person claiming through or under him, refer the parties to arbitration, unless it *prima facie* finds that the said agreement is null and void, inoperative or incapable of being performed.

Sec. 45 uses the expression 'shall' in respect of referring the parties to arbitration, unless judicial authority finds that the said agreement is null and void, inoperative or incapable of being performed. The term 'shall' in its ordinary significance is mandatory and the court shall ordinarily give that interpretation unless such an interpretation leads to some absurd or inconvenient consequence or be at variance with the intent of the legislature, to be collected from other parts of the statute. The words 'shall' and 'unless' appearing in Sec. 45 mandates that before referring the parties to arbitration, the judicial authority should be satisfied that the arbitration agreement is not null and void, inoperative or incapable of being performed.[18]

### Section 46: When foreign award binding

Any foreign award which would be enforceable under this Chapter shall be treated as binding for all purposes on the persons as between whom it was made and may accordingly be relied on by any of those persons by way of defence, set off or otherwise in any legal proceedings in India and any references in this Chapter to enforcing a foreign award shall be construed as including references to relying on an award.

[18] *Shin-Etsu Chemical Co. Ltd.* v. *M/s. Aksh Optifibre Ltd.*, AIR 2005 SC 3766.

## Section 47: Evidence

(1) The party applying for the enforcement of a foreign award shall, at the time of the application, produce before the Court—

(a) the original award or a copy thereof, duly authenticated in the manner required by the law of the country in which it was made;

(b) the original agreement for arbitration or a duly certified copy thereof; and

(c) such evidence as may be necessary to prove that the award is a foreign award.

(2) If the award or agreement to be produced under sub-section (1) is in a foreign language, the party seeking to enforce the award shall produce a translation into English certified as correct by a diplomatic or consular agent of the country to which that party belongs or certified as correct in such other manner as may be sufficient according to the law in force in India.

*Explanation*: In this section and in the sections following in this Chapter, "Court" means the High Court having original jurisdiction to decide the questions forming the subject-matter of the arbitral award if the same had been the subject-matter of a suit on its original civil jurisdiction and in other cases, in the High Court having jurisdiction to hear appeals from decrees of courts subordinate to such High Court.

## Section 48: Condition for enforcement of foreign awards

(1) Enforcement of a foreign award may be refused, at the request of the party against whom it is invoked, only if that party furnishes to the Court proof that—

(a) the parties to the agreement referred to in Section 44 were, under the law applicable to them, under some incapacity, or the said agreement is not valid under the law to which the parties have subjected it or, failing any indication thereon, under the law of the country where the award was made; or

(b) the party against whom the award is invoked was not given proper notice of the appointment of the arbitrator or of the arbitral proceedings or was otherwise unable to present his case; or

(c) the award deals with a difference not contemplated by or not falling within the terms of the submission to arbitration, or it contain decisions on matters beyond the scope of the submission to arbitration :

Provided that, if the decisions on matters submitted to arbitration can be separated from those not so submitted, that part of the award which contains decisions on matters submitted to arbitration may be enforced; or

(d) the composition of the arbitral authority or the arbitral procedure was not in accordance with the agreement of the parties, or, failing such agreement, was not in accordance with the law of the country where the arbitration took place; or

(e) the award has not yet become binding on the parties or has been set aside or suspended by a competent authority of the country in which, or under the law of which, that award was made.

(2) Enforcement of an arbitral award may also be refused if the Court finds that—

(a) the subject-matter of the difference is not capable of settlement by arbitration under the law of India; or

(b) the enforcement of the award would be contrary to the public policy of India.

*Explanation* **1:** For the avoidance of any doubt, it is clarified that an award is in conflict with the public policy of India, only if,—

(i) the making of the award was induced or affected by fraud or corruption or was in violation of Section 75 or Section 81; or

(ii) it is in contravention with the fundamental policy of Indian law; or

(iii) it is in conflict with the most basic notions of morality or justice.

*Explanation* **2:** For the avoidance of doubt, the test as to whether there is a contravention with the fundamental policy of Indian law shall not entail a review on the merits of the dispute.

(3) If an application for the setting aside or suspension of the award has been made to a competent authority referred to in clause (e) of sub-section (1) the Court may, if it considers it proper, adjourn the decision on the enforcement of the award and may also, on the application of the party claiming enforcement of the award, order the other party to give suitable security.

### Section 49: Enforcement of foreign awards

Where the Court is satisfied that the foreign award is enforceable under this Chapter, the award shall be deemed to be a decree of that Court.

### Section 50: Appealable orders

(1) An appeal shall lie from the order refusing to—

(a) refer the parties to arbitration under Section 45;

(b) enforce a foreign award under Section 48,

to the Court authorised by law to hear appeals from such order.

(2) No second appeal shall lie from an order passed in appeal under this section, but nothing in this section shall affect or take away any right to appeal to the Supreme Court.

### Section 51: Saving

Nothing in this Chapter shall prejudice any rights which any person would have had of enforcing in India of any award or of availing himself in India of any award if this Chapter had not been enacted.

### Section 52: Chapter II not to apply

Chapter II of this Part shall not apply in relation to foreign awards to which this Chapter applies.

# Chapter II Geneva Convention Awards

## Section 53: Interpretation

In this Chapter "foreign award" means an arbitral award on differences relating to matters considered as commercial under the law in force in India made after the 28th day of July, 1924,—

(a) in pursuance of an agreement for arbitration to which the Protocol set forth in the Second Schedule applies, and

(b) between persons of whom one is subject to the jurisdiction of someone of such Powers as the Central Government, being satisfied that reciprocal provisions have been made, may, by notification in the Official Gazette, declare to be parties to the Convention set forth in the Third Schedule, and of whom the other is subject to the jurisdiction of some other of the Powers aforesaid, and

(c) in one of such territories as the Central Government, being satisfied that reciprocal provisions have been made, may, by like notification, declare to be territories to which the said Convention applies,

and for the purposes of this Chapter an award shall not be deemed to be final if any proceedings for the purpose of contesting the validity of the award are pending in the country in which it was made.

## Section 54: Power of judicial authority to refer parties to arbitration

Notwithstanding anything contained in Part I or in the Code of Civil Procedure, 1908 (5 of 1908), a judicial authority, on being seized of a dispute regarding a contract made between persons to whom Section 53 applies and including and arbitration agreement, whether referring to present or future differences, which is valid under that section and capable of being carried into effect, shall refer the parties on the application of either of them or any person claiming through or under him to the decision of the arbitrators and such reference shall not prejudice the competence of the judicial authority in case the agreement or the arbitration cannot proceed or becomes inoperative.

## Section 55: Foreign awards when binding

Any foreign award which would be enforceable under this Chapter shall be treated as binding for all purposes on the persons as between whom it was made and may accordingly be relied on by any of those persons by way of defence, set off or otherwise in any legal proceedings in India and any references in this Chapter to enforcing a foreign award shall be construed as including references to relying on an award.

## Section 56: Evidence

(1) The party applying for the enforcement of a foreign award shall, at the time of the application produce before the Court—

(a) the original award or a copy thereof, duly authenticated in the manner required by the law of the country in which it was made;

(b) evidence proving that the award has become final; and

(c) such evidence as may be necessary to prove that the conditions mentioned in clauses (a) and (c) of sub-section (1) of Section 57 are satisfied.

(2) Where any document requiring to be produced under sub-section (1) is in a foreign language, the party seeking to enforce the award shall produce a translation into English certified as correct by a diplomatic or consular agent of the country to which that party belongs or certified as correct in such other manner as may be sufficient according, to the law in force in India.

*Explanation*: In this section and in the sections following in this Chapter, "Court" means the High Court having original jurisdiction to decide the questions forming the subject-matter of the arbitral award if the same had been the subject-matter of a suit on its original civil jurisdiction and in other cases, in the High Court having jurisdiction to hear appeals from decrees of courts subordinate to such High Court.

## Section 57: Conditions for enforcement of foreign awards

(1) In order that a foreign award may be enforceable under this Chapter, it shall be necessary that—

(a) the award has been made in pursuance of a submission to arbitration which is valid under the law applicable thereto;

(b) the subject-matter of the award is capable of settlement by arbitration under the law of India;

(c) the award has been made by the arbitral Tribunal provided for in the submission to arbitration or constituted in the manner agreed upon by the parties and in conformity with the law governing the arbitration procedure;

(d) the award has become final in the country in which it has been made, in the sense that it will not be considered as such if it is open to opposition or appeal or if it is proved that any proceedings for the purpose of contesting the validity of the award are pending; and

(e) the enforcement of the award is not contrary to the public policy or the law of India.

*Explanation* **1:** For the avoidance of any doubt, it is clarified that an award is in conflict with the public policy of India, only if,—

(i) the making of the award was induced or affected by fraud or corruption or was in violation of Section 75 or Section 81; or

(ii) it is in contravention with the fundamental policy of Indian law; or

(iii) it is in conflict with the most basic notions of morality or justice.

*Explanation* **2:** For the avoidance of doubt, the test as to whether there is a contravention with the fundamental policy of Indian law shall not entail a review on the merits of the dispute.

(2) Even if the conditions laid down in sub-section (1) are fulfilled, enforcement of the award shall be refused if the Court is satisfied that—

(a) the award has been annulled in the country in which it was made;

(b) the party against whom it is sought to use the award was not given notice of the arbitration proceedings in sufficient time to enable him to present his case; or that, being under a legal incapacity, he was not properly represented; and

(c) the award does not deal with the differences contemplated by or falling within the terms of the submission to arbitration or that it contains decisions on matters beyond the scope of the submission to arbitration:

Provided that if the award has not covered all the differences submitted to the arbitral Tribunal, the Court, may, if it thinks fit, postpone such enforcement or grant it subject to such guarantee as the Court may decide.

(3) If the party against whom the award has been made proves that under the law governing the arbitration procedure there is a ground, other than the grounds referred to in clauses (a) and (c) of sub-section (1) and clauses (b) and (c) of sub-section (2) entitling him to contest the validity of the award, the Court may, if it thinks fit, either refuse enforcement of the award or adjourn the consideration thereof, giving such party a reasonable time within which to have the award annulled by the competent Tribunal.

### Section 58: Enforcement of foreign awards

Where the Court is satisfied that the foreign award is enforceable under this Chapter, the award shall be deemed to be a decree of the Court.

### Section 59: Appealable orders

(1) An appeal shall lie from the order refusing—

(a) to refer the parties to arbitration under Section 54; and

(b) to enforce a foreign award under Section 57,

to the court authorised by law to hear appeals from such order.

(2) No second appeal shall lie from an order passed in appeal under this section, but nothing in this section shall affect or take away any right to appeal to the Supreme Court.

### Section 60: Saving

Nothing in this Chapter shall prejudice any rights which any person would have had of enforcing in India of any award or of availing himself in India of any award if this Chapter had not been enacted.

## PART III Conciliation

### Section 61: Application and scope

(1) Save as otherwise provided by any law for the time being in force and unless the parties have otherwise agreed, this Part shall apply to conciliation of disputes

arising out of legal relationship, whether contractual or not and to all proceedings relating thereto.

(2) This part shall not apply where by virtue of any law for the time being in force certain disputes may not be submitted to conciliation.

The Arbitration and Conciliation Act, 1996, as the name itself suggests, deals with two types of proceedings; arbitration proceedings and conciliation proceedings. While provisions relating to arbitration proceedings are contained in Part I, in which are included Chapters I to X, the conciliation proceedings are dealt with in Part III which includes Sections 61 to 81. On perusal of the provisions of the Act the position is manifest that a clear distinction is maintained in the statute between arbitration proceedings and conciliation proceedings.

Sec. 61 which deals with, Application and Scope of the provisions, in Part III provides, inter alia, that save as otherwise provided by any law for the time being in force and unless the parties have otherwise agreed, this Part shall apply to conciliation of disputes arising out of legal relationship, whether contractual or not and to all proceedings relating thereto.

## DIFFERENCE BETWEEN ARBITRATION AND CONCILIATION

1. The person appointed for the process of arbitration is called arbitrator. Appointment of Arbitrator is done under provision of Sec. 11 of Arbitration and Conciliation act 1996. While the person appointed for the process of Conciliation is called conciliator. Appointment of conciliator is done under the provisions of Sec. 64 of Arbitration and Conciliation act 1996.
2. An arbitrator has the power to enforce his decision. While the person appointed to settle the dispute do not have power to enforce the decision taken by him.
3. To settle the dispute through the process of arbitration, prior agreement is required. While, to settle the dispute through the process of Conciliation no prior agreement is required.
4. Arbitration is available for existing and future dispute as well but conciliation is available for existing disputes only, it does not focus on the future dispute.
5. Arbitration is a legal proceeding while conciliation is not a legal proceeding.

Both arbitrator and conciliator guiding by the principle of fairness and justice. They conduct the proceedings in such a manner which consider appropriate. They help to settle the dispute between the parties.

### Section 62: Commencement of conciliation proceedings

(1) The party initiating conciliation shall send to the other party a written invitation to conciliate under this Part, briefly identifying the subject of the dispute.

(2) Conciliation proceedings shall commence when the other party accepts in writing the invitation to conciliate.

(3) If the other party rejects the invitation, there will be no conciliation proceedings.

(4) If the party initiating conciliation does not receive a reply within thirty days from the date on which he sends the invitation, or within such other period of time as specified in the invitation, he may elect to treat this as a rejection of the invitation to conciliate and if he so elects, he shall inform in writing the other party accordingly.

**Section 63: Number of conciliators**

(1) There shall be one conciliator unless the parties agree that there shall be two or three conciliators.

(2) Where there is more than one conciliator, they ought, as a general rule, to act jointly.

**Section 64: Appointment of conciliators**

(1) Subject to sub-section (2),—

(a) in conciliation proceedings with one conciliator, the parties may agree on the name of a sole conciliator;

(b) in conciliation proceedings with two conciliators, each party may appoint one conciliator;

(c) in conciliation proceedings with three conciliators, each party may appoint one conciliator and the parties may agree on the name of the third conciliator who shall act as the presiding conciliator.

(2) Parties may enlist the assistance of a suitable institution or person in connection with the appointment of conciliators, and in particular,—

(a) a party may request such an institution or person to recommend the names of suitable individuals to act as conciliator; or

(b) the parties may agree that the appointment of one or more conciliators be made directly by such an institution or person:

Provided that in recommending or appointing individuals to act as conciliator, the institution or person shall have regard to such consideration as are likely to secure the appointment of an independent and impartial conciliator and, with respect to a sole or third conciliator, shall take into account the advisability of appointing a conciliator of a nationality other than the nationalities of the parties.

**Section 65: Submission of statements to conciliator**

(1) The conciliator, upon his appointment, may request each party to submit to him a brief written statement describing the general nature of the dispute and the points at issue. Each party shall send a copy of such statement to the other party.

(2) The conciliator may request each party to submit to him a further written statement of his position and the facts and grounds in support thereof, supplemented by any documents and other evidence that such party deems appropriate. The party

shall send a copy of such statement, documents and other evidence to the other party.

(3) At any stage of the conciliation proceedings, the conciliator may request a party to submit to him such additional information as he deems appropriate.

*Explanation*: In this section and all the following sections of this Part, the term "conciliator" applies to a sole conciliator, two or three conciliators, as the case may be.

### Section 66: Conciliator not bound by certain enactments

The conciliator is not bound by the Code of Civil Procedure, 1908 (5 of 1908) or the Indian Evidence Act, 1872 (1 of 1872).

### Section 67: Role of conciliator

(1) The conciliator shall assist the parties in an independent and impartial manner in their attempt to reach an amicable settlement of their dispute.

(2) The conciliator shall be guided by principles of objectivity, fairness and justice, giving consideration to, among other things, the rights and obligations of the parties, the usages of the trade concerned and the circumstances surrounding the dispute, including any previous business practices between the parties.

(3) The conciliator may conduct the conciliation proceedings in such a manner as he considers appropriate, taking into account the circumstances of the case, the wishes the parties may express, including any request by a party that the conciliator hear oral statements, and the need for a speedy settlement of the dispute.

(4) The conciliator may, at any stage of the conciliation proceedings, make proposals for a settlement of the dispute. Such proposals need not be in writing and need not be accompanied by a statement of the reasons therefor.

### Section 68: Administrative assistance

In order to facilitate the conduct of the conciliation proceedings, the parties, or the conciliator with the consent of the parties, may arrange for administrative assistance by a suitable institution or person.

### Section 69: Communication between conciliator and parties

(1) The conciliator may invite the parties to meet him or may communicate with them orally or in writing. He may meet or communicate with the parties together or with each of them separately.

(2) Unless the parties have agreed upon the place where meetings with the conciliator are to be held, such place shall be determined by the conciliator, after consultation with the parties, having regard to the circumstances of the conciliation proceedings.

### Section 70: Disclosure of information

When the conciliator receives factual information concerning the dispute from a party, he shall disclose the substance of that information to the other party in order that the other party may have the opportunity to present any explanation which he considers appropriate:

Provided that when a party gives any information to the conciliator subject to a specific condition that it be kept confidential, the conciliator shall not disclose that information to the other party.

### Section 71: Co-operation of parties with conciliator

The parties shall in good faith co-operate with the conciliator and, in particular, shall endeavour to comply with requests by the conciliator to submit written materials, provide evidence and attend meetings.

### Section 72: Suggestions by parties for settlement of dispute

Each party may, on his own initiative or at the invitation of the conciliator, submit to the conciliator suggestions for the settlement of the dispute.

### Section 73: Settlement agreement

(1) When it appears to the conciliator that there exist elements of a settlement which may be acceptable to the parties, he shall formulate the terms of a possible settlement and submit them to the parties for their observations. After receiving the observations of the parties, the conciliator may reformulate the terms of a possible settlement in the light of such observations.

(2) If the parties reach agreement on a settlement of the dispute, they way draw up and sign a written settlement agreement. If requested by the parties, the conciliator may draw up, or assist the parties in drawing up, the settlement agreement.

(3) When the parties sign the settlement agreement, it shall be final and binding on the parties and persons claiming under them respectively.

(4) The conciliator shall authenticate the settlement agreement and furnish a copy thereof to each of the parties.

The question that arises in *Mysore Cements Ltd.* v. *Svedala Barmac Ltd.*[19] before the Supreme Court for consideration in this appeal is whether a Letter of Comfort furnished on the same day of a Settlement arrived at during conciliation signed by both the parties and authenticated by the Conciliators is enforceable in the same manner as an arbitration award under Sec. 74 of the Arbitration and Conciliation Act, 1996?

From the statutory provisions contained in 1996 Act the position is manifest that a conciliator is a person who is to assist the parties to settle the disputes between them amicably. For this purpose, the conciliator is vested with wide powers to decide the

[19] AIR 2003 SC 3493.

procedure to be followed by him untrammeled by the procedural law like the Code of Civil Procedure or the Indian Evidence Act, 1872. When the parties are able to resolve the dispute between them by mutual agreement and it appears to the conciliator that their exists an element of settlement which may be acceptable to the parties he is to proceed in accordance with the procedure laid down in Sec. 73, formulate the terms of a settlement and make it over to the parties for their observations; and the ultimate step to be taken by a conciliator is to draw up a settlement in the light of the observations made by the parties to the terms formulated by him. The settlement takes shape only when the parties draw up the settlement agreement or request the conciliator to prepare the same and affix their signatures to it. Under Sec. 73 (3) the settlement agreement signed by the parties is final and binding on the parties and persons claiming under them. It follows therefore that a successful conciliation proceeding comes to an end only when the settlement agreement signed by the parties comes into existence. It is such an agreement which has the status and effect of legal sanctity of an arbitral award under Sec. 74.

If the Settlement Agreement comes into existence under Sec. 73 satisfying the requirements stated therein, it gets the status and effect of an arbitral award on agreed terms on the substance of the dispute rendered by an arbitral tribunal under Sec. 30 of the Act. The submission that when there was substantial compliance with the requirements of Sec. 73, as in the present case, when the parties have arrived at a Settlement Agreement like the parties before any Civil Court filing a compromise petition, there should be no impediment to take up execution based on such a compromise or agreement cannot be accepted. Even a compromise petition signed by both the parties and filed in the Court *per se* cannot be enforced resorting to execution proceedings unless such a compromise petition is accepted by the Court and the Court puts seal of approval for drawing a decree on the basis of compromise petition. The Court further observed that the Letter of Comfort cannot be accorded the status of Settlement Agreement to bring it within the meaning of Sec. 74 of the Act to treat it as an arbitral award under Sec. 30 of the Act so as to enforce it under Sec. 36 of the Act. In the present case, the Conciliation proceedings were not terminated but they were only adjourned. Under Sec. 76 of the Act, the proceedings shall be terminated as per clauses (a) to (d) of the said Section. If there was Settlement Agreement under Sec. 73, Conciliation Proceedings would have been terminated under Sec. 76 (a) of the Act. This is yet another pointer against the appellant's case. It is also not possible to agree with the submission that this Memorandum of Conciliation and the Letter of Comfort could be treated as interim award in the absence of any Settlement Agreement. It is not every agreement or arrangement between parties to the disputes, arrived at in whatever manner or form, during the pendency of conciliation proceedings that automatically acquires the status of a settlement agreement within the meaning of Sec. 73 of the Act so as to have the same status and effect as if it is an arbitral award, for being enforced as if it were a decree of the Court. It is only that agreement which has been arrived at in conformity with the manner stipulated and form envisaged and got duly authenticated in accordance with Sec. 73 of the Act, alone can be assigned the status of a settlement agreement, within the meaning of and for effective purposes of the Act, and not otherwise. We find in spite of our careful scrutiny, serious deliberations, and analysis of the materials on record, particularly the Memorandum of Conciliation Proceedings and the Letter of Comfort, that either taken individually or even together—they or anyone of them can legitimately claim to be entitled to or assigned the status of a settlement agreement within the meaning of Sec. 73, for purposes of the Act.

**Section 74: Status and effect of settlement agreement**

The settlement agreement shall have the same status and effect as if it is an arbitral award on agreed terms on the substance of the dispute rendered by an arbitral Tribunal under Section 30.

**Section 75: Confidentiality**

Notwithstanding anything contained in any other law for the time being in force, the conciliator and the parties shall keep confidential all matters relating to the conciliation proceedings. Confidentiality shall extend also to the settlement agreement, except where its disclosure is necessary for purposes of implementation and enforcement.

**Section 76: Termination of conciliation proceedings**

The conciliation proceedings shall be terminated—

(a) by the signing of the settlement agreement by the parties, on the date of the agreement; or

(b) by a written declaration of the conciliator, after consultation with the parties, to the effect that further efforts at conciliation are no longer justified, on the date of the declaration; or

(c) by a written declaration of the parties addressed to the conciliator to the effect that the conciliation proceedings are terminated, on the date of the declaration; or

(d) by a written declaration of a party to the other party and the conciliator, if appointed, to the effect that the conciliation proceedings are terminated, on the date of the declaration.

**Section 77: Resort to arbitral or judicial proceedings**

The parties shall not initiate, during the conciliation proceedings, any arbitral or judicial proceedings in respect of a dispute that is the subject-matter of the conciliation proceedings except that a party may initiate arbitral or judicial proceedings where, in his opinion, such proceedings are necessary for preserving his rights.

**Section 78: Costs**

(1) Upon termination of the conciliation proceedings, the conciliator shall fix the costs of the conciliation and give written notice thereof to the parties.

(2) For the purpose of sub-section (1), "costs" means reasonable costs relating to—

(a) the fee and expenses of the conciliator and witnesses requested by the conciliator with the consent of the parties;

(b) any expert advice requested by the conciliator with the consent of the parties;

(c) any assistance provided pursuant to clause (b) of sub-section (2) of Section 64 and Section 68; and

(d) any other expenses incurred in connection with the conciliation proceedings and the settlement agreement.

(3) The costs shall be borne equally by the parties unless the settlement agreement provides for a different apportionment. All other expenses incurred by a party shall be borne by that party.

## Section 79: Deposits

(1) The conciliator may direct each party to deposit an equal amount as an advance for the costs referred to in sub-section (2) of Section 78 which he expects will be incurred.

(2) During the course of the conciliation proceedings, the conciliator may direct supplementary deposits in an equal amount from each party.

(3) If the required deposits under sub-sections (1) and (2) are not paid in full by both parties within thirty days, the conciliator may suspend the proceedings or may make a written declaration of termination of the proceedings to the parties, effective on the date of that declaration.

(4) Upon termination of the conciliation proceedings, the conciliator shall render an accounting to parties of the deposits received and shall return any unexpended balance to the parties.

## Section 80: Role of conciliator in other proceedings

Unless otherwise agreed by the parties,—

(a) the conciliator shall not act as an arbitrator or as a representative or counsel of a party in any arbitral or judicial proceeding in respect of a dispute that is the subject of the conciliation proceedings; and

(b) the conciliator shall not be presented by the parties as a witness in any arbitral or judicial proceedings.

## Section 81: Admissibility of evidence in other proceedings

The parties shall not rely on or introduce as evidence—in arbitral or judicial proceedings, whether or not such proceedings relate to the dispute that is the subject of the conciliation proceedings,—

(a) views expressed or suggestions made by the other party in respect of a possible settlement of the dispute;

(b) admissions made by the other party in the course of the conciliation proceedings;

(c) proposals made by the conciliator; and

(d) the fact that the other party had indicated his willingness to accept a proposal for settlement made by the conciliator.

# PART IV Supplementary Provisions

## Section 82: Power of High Court to make rules

The High Court may make rules consistent with this Act as to all proceedings before the Court under this Act.

## Section 83: Removal of difficulties

(1) If any difficulty arises in giving effect to the provisions of this Act, the Central Government may, by order published in the Official Gazette, make such provisions, not inconsistent with the provisions of this Act as appear to it to be necessary or expedient for removing the difficulty:

Provided that no such order shall be made after the expiry of a period of two years from the date of commencement of this Act.

(2) Every order made under this section shall, as soon as may be after it is made, be laid before each House of Parliament.

## Section 84: Power to make rules

(1) The Central Government may, by notification in the Official Gazette, make rules for carrying out the provisions of this Act.

(2) Every rule made by the Central Government under this Act shall be laid, as soon as may be, after it is made before each House of Parliament while it is in session, for a total period of thirty days which may be comprised in one session or in two or more successive sessions, and if, before the expiry of the session immediately following the sessions or the successive sessions aforesaid, both Houses agree in making any modification in the rule or both Houses agree that the rule should not be made, the rule shall thereafter have effect only in such modified form or be of no effect, as the case may be; so, however, that any such modification or annulment shall be without prejudice to the validity of anything previously done under that rule.

## Section 85: Repeal and savings

(1) The Arbitration (Protocol and Convention) Act, 1937 (6 of 1937), the Arbitration Act, 1940 (10 of 1940) and the Foreign Awards (Recognition and Enforcement) Act, 1961 (45 of 1961) are hereby repealed.

(2) Notwithstanding such repeal,—

(a) the provisions of the said enactments shall apply in relation to arbitral proceedings which commenced before this Act came into force unless otherwise agreed by the parties but this Act shall apply in relation to arbitral proceedings which commenced on or after this Act comes into force; and

(b) all rules made and notifications published, under the said enactments shall, to the extent to which they are not repugnant to this Act, be deemed respectively to have been made or issued under this Act.

**Section 86: Repeal and saving**

(1) The Arbitration and Conciliation (Third) Ordinance, 1996 (27 of 1996) is hereby repealed.

(2) Notwithstanding such repeal, any order, rule, notification or scheme made or anything done or any action taken in pursuance of any provision of the said Ordinance shall be deemed to have been made, done or taken under the corresponding provisions of this Act.

**Section 87: Effect of arbitral and related court proceedings commenced prior to 23rd October, 2015**

Unless the parties otherwise agree, the amendments made to this Act by the Arbitration and Conciliation (Amendment) Act, 2015 shall—

(a) not apply to—

(i) arbitral proceedings commenced before the commencement of the Arbitration and Conciliation (Amendment) Act, 2015 (23rd October, 2015);

(ii) court proceedings arising out of or in relation to such arbitral proceedings irrespective of whether such court proceedings are commenced prior to or after the commencement of the Arbitration and Conciliation (Amendment) Act, 2015.

(b) apply only to arbitral proceedings commenced on or after the commencement of the Arbitration and Conciliation (Amendment) Act, 2015 and to court proceedings arising out of or in relation to such arbitral proceedings.

# THE FIRST SCHEDULE

[See Section 44]

# Convention on the Recognition and Enforcement of Foreign Arbitral Awards

## Article I

1. This Convention shall apply to the recognition and enforcement of arbitral awards made in the territory of a State other than the State where the recognition and enforcement of such awards are sought, and arising out of differences between persons, whether physical or legal. It shall also apply to arbitral awards not considered as domestic awards in the State where their recognition and enforcement are sought.

2. The term "arbitral awards" shall include not only awards made by arbitrators appointed for each case but also those made by permanent arbitral bodies to which the parties have submitted.
3. When signing, ratifying, or acceding to this Convention, or notifying extension under article X hereof, any State may on the basis of reciprocity declare that it will apply the Convention to the recognition and enforcement of awards made only in the territory of another Contracting State. It may also declare that it will apply the Convention only to differences arising out of legal relationships, whether contractual or not, which are considered as commercial under the national law of the State making such declaration.

## Article II

1. Each Contracting State shall recognise an agreement in writing under which the parties undertake to submit to arbitration all or any differences which have arisen or which may arise between them in respect of defined legal relationship, whether contractual or not, concerning a subject-matter capable of settlement by arbitration.
2. The term "agreement in writing" shall include an arbitral clause in a contract or an arbitration agreement, signed by the parties or contained in an exchange of letters or telegrams.
3. The court of a Contracting State, when seized of an action in a matter in respect of which the parties have made an-agreement within the meaning of this article, shall, at the request of one of the parties, refer the parties to arbitration, unless it finds that the said agreement is null and void, inoperative or incapable of being performed.

## Article III

Each Contracting State shall recognize arbitral awards as binding and enforce them in accordance with the rules of procedure of the territory where the award is relied upon, under the conditions laid down in the following articles. There shall not be imposed substantially more onerous conditions or higher fees or charges on the recognition or enforcement of arbitral awards to which this Convention applies than are imposed on the recognition or enforcement of domestic arbitral awards.

## Article IV

1. To obtain the recognition and enforcement mentioned in the preceding article, the party applying for recognition and enforcement shall, at the time or the application, supply:—
   (a) the duly authenticated original award or a duly certified copy thereof;
   (b) the original agreement referred to in article II or a duly certified copy thereof.

2. If the said award or agreement is not made in an official language of the country in which the award is relied upon, the party applying for recognition and enforcement of the award shall produce a translation of these documents into such language. The translation shall be certified by an official or sworn translator or by a diplomatic or consular agent.

## Article V

1. Recognition and enforcement of the award may be refused, at the request of the party against whom it is invoked, only if that party furnishes to the competent authority where the recognition and enforcement is sought, proof that—
   (a) the parties to the agreement referred to in article II were, under the law applicable to them, under some incapacity, or the said agreement is not valid under the law to which the parties have subjected it or, failing any indication thereon, under the law of the country where the award was made; or
   (b) the party against whom the award is invoked was not given proper notice of the appointment of the arbitrator or of the arbitration proceedings or was otherwise unable to present his case; or
   (c) the award deals with a difference not contemplated by or not falling within the terms of the submission to arbitration, or it contains decisions on matters beyond the scope of the submission to arbitration, provided that, if the decisions on matters submitted to arbitration can be separated from those not so submitted, that part of the award which contains decisions on matters submitted to arbitration may be recognised and enforced; or
   (d) the composition of the arbitral authority or the arbitral procedure was not in accordance with the agreement of the parties, or, failing such agreement, was not in accordance with the law of the country where the arbitration took place; or
   (e) the award has not yet become binding on the parties, or has been set aside or suspended by a competent authority of the country in which, or under the law of which, that award was made.

2. Recognition and enforcement of an arbitral award may also be refused if the competent authority in the country where recognition and enforcement is sought finds that—
   (a) the subject-matter of the difference is not capable of settlement by arbitration under the law of that country; or
   (b) the recognition or enforcement of the award would be contrary to the public policy of that country.

## Article VI

If an application for the setting aside or suspension of the award has been made to a competent authority referred to in article V(l)(e), the authority before which the award is sought to be relied upon may, if it considers it proper, adjourn the decision on the enforcement of the award and may also, on the application of the party claiming enforcement of the award, order the other party to give suitable security.

## Article VII

1. The provisions of the present Convention shall not affect the validity of multilateral or bilateral agreements concerning the recognition and enforcement of arbitral awards entered into by the Contracting States nor deprive any interested party of any right he may have to avail himself of an arbitral award in the manner and to the extent allowed by the law or the treaties of the country where such award is sought to be relied upon.
2. The Geneva Protocol on Arbitration Clauses of 1923 and the Geneva Convention on the Execution of Foreign Arbitral Awards of 1927 shall cease to have effect between Contracting States on their becoming bound and to the extent that they become bound by this Convention.

## Article VIII

1. This Convention shall be open until 31st December, 1958 for signature on behalf of any Member of the United Nations and also on behalf of any other State which is or hereafter becomes member of any specialised agency of the United Nations, or which is or hereafter becomes a party to the Statute of the International Court of Justice, or any other State to which an invitation has been addressed by the General Assembly of the United Nations.
2. This Convention shall be ratified and the instrument of ratification shall be deposited with the Secretary-General of the United Nations.

## Article IX

1. This Convention shall be open for accession to all States referred to in article VIII.
2. Accession shall be effected by the deposit of an instrument of accession with the Secretary-General of the United Nations.

## Article X

1. Any State may, at the time of signature, ratification, or accession, declare that this Convention shall extend to all or any of the territories for the international

relations of which it is responsible. Such a declaration shall take effect when the Convention enters into force for the State concerned.

2. At any time thereafter any such extension shall be made by notification addressed to the Secretary-General of the United Nations and shall take effect as from the ninetieth day after the day of receipt by the Secretary-General of the United Nations of this notification, or as from the date of entry into force of the Convention for the State concerned, whichever is the later.

3. With respect to those territories to which this Convention is not extended at the time of signature, ratification or accession, each State concerned shall consider the possibility of taking the necessary steps in order to extend the application of this Convention to such territories, subject, where necessary for constitutional reasons, to the consent of the Governments of such territories.

## Article XI

In the case of a federal or non-unitary State, the following provisions shall apply—

(a) with respect to those articles of this Convention that come within the legislative jurisdiction of the federal authority, the obligations of the federal Government shall to this extent be the same as those of Contracting States which are not federal States;

(b) with respect to those articles of this Convention that come within the legislative jurisdiction of constituent States or provinces which are not, under the constitutional system of the federation, bound to take legislative action, the federal Government shall bring such articles with a favourable recommendation to the notice of the appropriate authorities of constituent States or provinces at the earliest possible moment;

(c) a federal State Party to this Convention shall, at the request of any other Contracting State transmitted through the Secretary-General of the United Nations, supply a statement of the law and practice of the federation and its constituent units in regard to any particular provision of this Convention, showing the extent to which effect has been given to that provision by legislative or other action.

## Article XII

1. This Convention shall come into force on the ninetieth day following the date of deposit of the third instrument of ratification or accession.

2. For each State ratifying or acceding to this Convention after the deposit of the third instrument of ratification or accession, this Convention shall enter into force on the ninetieth day after deposit by such State of its instrument of ratification or accession.

## Article XIII

1. Any Contracting State may denounce this Convention by a written notification to the Secretary-General of the United Nations. Denunciation shall take effect one year after the date of receipt of the notification by the Secretary-General.
2. Any State which has made a declaration or notification under Article X may, at any time thereafter, by notification to the Secretary-General of the United Nations, declare that this Convention shall cease to extend to the territory concerned one year after the date of the receipt of the notification by the Secretary-General.
3. This Convention shall continue to be applicable to arbitral awards in respect of which recognition or enforcement proceedings have been instituted before the denunciation takes effect.

## Article XIV

A Contracting State shall not be entitled to avail itself of the present Convention against other Contracting States except to the extent that it is itself bound to apply the Convention.

## Article XV

The Secretary-General of the United Nations shall notify the States contemplated in article VIII of the following:—

(a) signatures and ratifications in accordance with article VIII;
(b) accessions in accordance with article IX;
(c) declarations and notifications under articles I, X and XI;
(d) the date upon which this Convention enters into force in accordance with article XII;
(e) denunciations and notifications in accordance with article XIII.

## Article XVI

1. This Convention, of which the Chinese, English, French, Russian and Spanish texts shall be equally authentic shall be deposited in the archives of the United Nations.
2. The Secretary-General of the United Nations shall transmit a certified copy of this Convention to the States contemplated in article XIII.

# THE SECOND SCHEDULE

[See Section 53]

# Protocol on Arbitration Clauses

The undersigned, being duly authorised, declare that they accept, on behalf of the countries which they represent, the following provisions:—

1. Each of the Contracting States recognises the validity of an agreement whether relating to existing or future differences between parties subject respectively to the jurisdiction of different Contracting States by which the parties to a contract agree to submit to arbitration all or any differences that may arise in connection with such contract relating to commercial matters or to any other matter capable of settlement by arbitration, whether or not the arbitration is to take place in a country to whose jurisdiction none of the parties is subject.

   Each Contracting State reserves the right to limit the obligation mentioned above to contracts which are considered as commercial under its national law. Any Contracting State which avails itself of this right will notify the Secretary-General of the League of Nations in order that the other Contracting States may be so informed.

2. The arbitral procedure, including the constitution of the arbitral Tribunal, shall be governed by the will of the parties and by the law of the country in whose territory the arbitration takes place.

   The Contracting States agree to facilitate all steps in the procedure which require to be taken in their own territories, in accordance with the provisions of their law governing arbitral procedure applicable to existing differences.

3. Each Contracting State undertakes to ensure the execution by its authorities and in accordance with the provisions of its national laws of arbitral awards made in its own territory under the preceding articles.

4. The Tribunals of the Contracting Parties, on being seized of a dispute regarding a contract made between persons to whom article 1 applies and including an Arbitration Agreement whether referring to present or future differences which is valid in virtue of the said article and capable of being carried into effect, shall refer the parties on the application of either of them to the decision of the Arbitrators.

   Such reference shall not prejudice the competence of the judicial Tribunals in case the agreement or the arbitration cannot proceed or becomes inoperative.

5. The present Protocol, which shall remain open for signature by all States, shall be ratified. The ratification shall be deposited as soon as possible with the Secretary-General of the League of Nations, who shall notify such deposit to all the Signatory States.

6. The present Protocol will come into force as soon as two ratifications have been deposited. Thereafter it will take effect, in the case of each Contracting State, one month after the notification by the Secretary-General of the deposit of its ratification.

7. The present Protocol may be denounced by any Contracting State on giving one year's notice. Denunciation shall be effected by a notification addressed to the Secretary-General of the League, who will immediately transmit copies of such notification to all the other Signatory States and inform them of the date on which it was received. The denunciation shall take effect one year after the date on which it was notified to the Secretary-General and shall operate only in respect of the notifying State.

8. The Contracting States may declare that their acceptance of the present Protocol does not include any or all of the undermentioned territories: that is to say, their colonies, overseas possessions or territories, protectorates, or the territories over which they exercise a mandate.

The said States may subsequently adhere separately on behalf of any territory thus excluded. The Secretary-General of the League of Nations shall be informed as soon as possible of such adhesions. He shall notify such adhesions to all Signatory States. They will take effect one month after the notification by the Secretary-General to all Signatory States.

The Contracting States may also denounce the Protocol separately on behalf of any of the territories referred to above. Article 7 applies to such denunciation.

# THE THIRD SCHEDULE

[See Section 53]

## Convention on the Execution of Foreign Arbitral Awards

### Article I

(1) In the territories of any High Contracting Party to which the present Convention applies, an arbitral award made in pursuance of an agreement, whether relating to existing or future differences (hereinafter called "a submission to arbitration") covered by the Protocol on Arbitration Clauses opened at Geneva on September 24, 1923, shall be recognised as binding and shall be enforced in accordance with the rules of the procedure of the territory where the award is relied upon, provided that the said award has been made in a territory of one of the High Contracting Parties to which the present Convention applies and between persons who are subject to the jurisdiction of one of the High Contracting Parties.

(2) To obtain such recognition or enforcement, it shall, further, be necessary:—

(a) that the award has been made in pursuance of a submission to arbitration which is valid under the law applicable thereto;

(b) that the subject-matter of the award is capable of settlement by arbitration under the law of the country in which the award is sought to be relied upon;

(c) that the award has been made by the Arbitral Tribunal provided for in the submission to arbitration or constituted in the manner agreed upon by the parties and in conformity with the law governing the arbitration procedure;

(d) that the award has become final in the country in which it has been made, in the sense that it will not be considered as such if it is open to opposition, appeal or *pourvoien cassation* (in the countries where such forms of procedure exist) or if it is proved that any proceedings for the purpose of contesting the validity of the award are pending;

(e) that the recognition or enforcement of the award is not contrary to the public policy or to the principles of the law of the country in which it is sought to be relied upon.

## Article II

Even if the conditions laid down in Article 1 hereof are fulfilled, recognition and enforcement of the award shall be refused if the Court is satisfied:—

(a) that the award has been annulled in the country in which it was made;

(b) that the party against whom it is sought to use the award was not given notice of the arbitration proceedings in sufficient time to enable him to present his case; or that, being under a legal incapacity, he was not properly represented;

(c) that the award does not deal with the differences contemplated by or falling within the terms of the submission to arbitration or that it contains decisions on matters beyond the scope of the submission to arbitration.

If the award has not covered all the questions submitted to the arbitral Tribunal, the competent authority of the country where recognition or enforcement of the award is sought can, if it thinks fit, postpone such recognition or enforcement or grant it subject to such guarantee as that authority may decide.

## Article III

If the party against whom the award has been made proves that, under the law governing the arbitration procedure, there is a ground, other than the grounds referred to in Article 1 (a) and (c), and Article 2(b) and (c), entitling him to contest the validity of the award in a Court of Law, the Court may, if it thinks fit, either refuse recognition or enforcement of the award or adjourn the consideration thereof, giving such party a reasonable time within which to have the award annulled by the competent Tribunal.

## Article IV

The party relying upon an award or claiming its enforcement must supply, in particular:—

(1) the original award or a copy thereof duly authenticated, according to the requirements of the law of the country in which it was made;

(2) documentary or other evidence to prove that the award has become final, in the sense defined in Article 1(d), in the country in which it was made;

(3) when necessary, documentary, or other evidence to prove that the conditions laid down in Article 1, paragraph (1) and paragraph (2)(a) and (c), have been fulfilled.

A translation of the award and of the other documents mentioned in this Article into the official language of the country where the award is sought to be relied upon may be demanded. Such translations must be certified correct by a diplomatic or consular agent of the country to which the party who seeks to rely upon the award belongs or by a sworn translator of the country where the award is sought to be relied upon.

## Article V

The provisions of the above Articles shall not deprive any interested party of the right of availing himself of an arbitral award in the manner and to the extent allowed by the law or the treaties of the country where such award is sought to be relied upon.

## Article VI

The present Convention applies only to arbitral awards made after the coming into force of the Protocol on Arbitration Clauses opened at Geneva on September 24, 1923.

## Article VII

The present Convention, which will remain open to the signature of all the signatories of the Protocol of 1923 on Arbitration Clauses, shall be ratified.

It may be ratified only on behalf of those Members of the League of Nations and Non-Member States on whose behalf the Protocol of 1923 shall have been ratified.

Ratification shall be deposited as soon as possible with the Secretary-General of the League of Nations, who will notify such deposit to all the signatories.

## Article VIII

The present Convention shall come into force three months after it shall have been ratified on behalf of two High Contracting Parties. Thereafter, it shall take effect, in the case of each High Contracting Party, three months after the deposit of the ratification on its behalf with the Secretary-General of the League of Nations.

## Article IX

The present Convention may be denounced on behalf of any Member of the League or Non-Member State. Denunciation shall be notified in writing to the Secretary-General of the League of Nations, who will immediately send a copy thereof, certified to be in conformity with the notifications, to all the other Contracting Parties, at the same time informing them of the date on which he received it.

The denunciation shall come into force only in respect of the High Contracting Party which shall have notified it and one year after such notification shall have reached the Secretary-General of the League of Nations.

The denunciation of the Protocol on Arbitration Clauses shall entail, ipso facto, the denunciation of the present Convention.

### Article X

The present Convention does not apply to the Colonies, Protectorates or territories under suzerainty or mandate of any High Contracting Party unless they are specially mentioned.

The application of this Convention to one or more of such Colonies, Protectorates or territories to which the Protocol on Arbitration Clauses opened at Geneva on September 24, 1923, applies, can be effected at any time by the means of a declaration addressed to the Secretary-General of the League of Nations by one of the High Contracting Parties.

Such declaration shall take effect three months after the deposit thereof.

The High Contracting Parties can at any time denounce the Convention for all or any of the Colonies, Protectorates or territories referred to above. Article 9 hereof applied to such denunciation.

### Article XI

A certified copy of the present Convention shall be transmitted by the Secretary-General of the League of Nations of every Member of the League of Nations and to every Non-Member State which signs the same.

## THE FOURTH SCHEDULE

[See Section 11(14)]

| Sum in dispute | Model fee |
|---|---|
| Up to ₹ 5,00,000 | ₹ 45,000 |
| Above ₹ 5,00,000 and up to ₹ 20,00,000 | ₹ 45,000 plus 3.5 per cent of the claim amount over and above ₹ 5,00,000 |
| Above ₹ 20,00,000 and up to ₹ 1,00,00,000 | ₹ 97,500 plus 3 per cent of the claim amount over and above ₹ 20,00,000 |
| Above ₹ 1,00,00,000 and up to ₹ 10,00,00,000 | ₹ 3,37,500 plus 1 per cent of the claim amount over and above ₹ 1,00,00,000 |
| Above ₹ 10,00,00,000 and up to ₹ 20,00,00,000 | ₹ 12,37,500 plus 0.75 per cent of the claim amount over and above ₹ 1,00,00,000 |
| Above ₹ 20,00,00,000 | ₹ 19,87,500 plus 0.5 per cent of the claim amount over and above ₹ 20,00,00,000 with a ceiling of ₹ 30,00,000 |
| **Note:** In the event, the arbitral tribunal is a sole arbitrator, he shall be entitled to an additional amount of twenty-five per cent on the fee payable as per the table set out above. | |

# THE FIFTH SCHEDULE

[See Section 12 (1) (b)]

The following grounds give rise to justifiable doubts as to the independence or impartiality of arbitrators:

## Arbitrator's relationship with the parties or counsel

1. The arbitrator is an employee, consultant, advisor or has any other past or present business relationship with a party.
2. The arbitrator currently represents or advises one of the parties or an affiliate of one of, the parties.
3. The arbitrator currently represents the lawyer or law firm acting as counsel for one of the parties.
4. The arbitrator is a lawyer in the same law firm which is representing one of the parties.
5. The arbitrator is a manager, director or part of the management, or has a similar controlling influence, in an affiliate of one of the parties if the affiliate is directly involved in the matters in dispute in the arbitration.
6. The arbitrator's law firm had a previous but terminated involvement in the case without the arbitrator being involved himself or herself.
7. The arbitrator's law firm currently has a significant commercial relationship with one of the parties or an affiliate of one of the parties.
8. The arbitrator regularly advises the appointing party or an affiliate of the appointing party even though neither the arbitrator nor his or her firm derives a significant financial income therefrom.
9. The arbitrator has a close family relationship with one of the parties and in the case of companies with the persons in the management and controlling the company.
10. A close family member of the arbitrator has a significant financial interest in one of the parties or an affiliate of one of the parties.
11. The arbitrator is a legal representative of an entity that is a party in the arbitration.
12. The arbitrator is a manager, director, or part of the management, or has a similar controlling influence in one of the parties.
13. The arbitrator has a significant financial interest in one of the parties or the outcome of the case.
14. The arbitrator regularly advises the appointing party or an affiliate of the appointing party, and the arbitrator or his or her firm derives a significant financial income therefrom.

## Relationship of the arbitrator to the dispute

15. The arbitrator has given legal advice or provided an expert opinion on the dispute to a party or an affiliate of one of the parties.
16. The arbitrator has previous involvement in the case.

## Arbitrator's direct or indirect interest in the dispute

17. The arbitrator holds shares, either directly or indirectly, in one of the parties or an affiliate of one of the parties that is privately held.
18. A close family member of the arbitrator has a significant financial interest in the outcome of the dispute.
19. The arbitrator or a close family member of the arbitrator has a close relationship with a third party who may be liable to recourse on the part of the unsuccessful party in the dispute.

## Previous services for one of the parties or other involvement in the case

20. The arbitrator has within the past three years served as counsel for one of the parties or an affiliate of one of the parties or has previously advised or been consulted by the party or an affiliate of the party making the appointment in an unrelated matter, but the arbitrator and the party or the affiliate of the party have no ongoing relationship.
21. The arbitrator has within the past three years served as counsel against one of the parties or an affiliate of one of the parties in an unrelated matter.
22. The arbitrator has within the past three years been appointed as arbitrator on two or more occasions by one of the parties or an affiliate of one of the parties.
23. The arbitrator's law firm has within the past three years acted for one of the parties or an affiliate of one of the parties in an unrelated matter without the involvement of the arbitrator.
24. The arbitrator currently serves, or has served within the past three years, as arbitrator in another arbitration on a related issue involving one of the parties or an affiliate of one of the parties.

## Relationship between an arbitrator and another arbitrator or counsel

25. The arbitrator and another arbitrator are lawyers in the same law firm.
26. The arbitrator was within the past three years a partner of, or otherwise affiliated with, another arbitrator or any of the counsel in the same arbitration.
27. A lawyer in the arbitrator's law firm is an arbitrator in another dispute involving the same party or parties or an affiliate of one of the parties.
28. A close family member of the arbitrator is a partner or employee of the law firm representing one of the parties, but is not assisting with the dispute.

29. The arbitrator has within the past three years received more than three appointments by the same counsel or the same law firm.

**Relationship between arbitrator and party and others involved in the arbitration**

30. The arbitrator's law firm is currently acting adverse to one of the parties or an affiliate of one of the parties.
31. The arbitrator had been associated within the past three years with a party or an affiliate of one of the parties in a professional capacity, such as a former employee or partner.

**Other circumstances**

32. The arbitrator holds shares, either directly or indirectly, which by reason of number or denomination constitute a material holding in one of the parties or an affiliate of one of the parties that is publicly listed.
33. The arbitrator holds a position in an arbitration institution with appointing authority over the dispute.
34. The arbitrator is a manager, director or part of the management, or has a similar controlling influence, in an affiliate of one of the parties, where the affiliate is not directly involved in the matters in dispute in the arbitration.

*Explanation* **1:** The term "close family member" refers to a spouse, sibling, child, parent or life partner.

*Explanation* **2:** The term "affiliate" encompasses all companies in one group of companies including the parent company.

*Explanation* **3:** For the removal of doubts, it is clarified that it may be the practice in certain specific kinds of arbitration, such as maritime or commodities arbitration, to draw arbitrators from a small, specialised pool. If in such fields it is the custom and practice for parties frequently to appoint the same arbitrator in different cases, this is a relevant fact to be taken into account while applying the rules set out above.

## THE SIXTH SCHEDULE

[See Section 12 (1) (b)]

NAME:

CONTACT DETAILS:

PRIOR EXPERIENCE (INCLUDING EXPERIENCE WITH ARBITRATIONS):

NUMBER OF ONGOING ARBITRATIONS:

CIRCUMSTANCES DISCLOSING ANY PAST OR PRESENTRELATIONSHIP WITH OR INTEREST IN ANY OF THE PARTIES OR IN RELATION TO THE SUBJECT-MATTER

IN DISPUTE, WHETHER FINANCIAL, BUSINESS, PROFESSIONAL OR OTHER KIND, WHICH IS LIKELY TO GIVE RISE TO JUSTIFIABLE DOUBTS AS TO YOUR INDEPENDENCE OR IMPARTIALITY (LIST OUT):

CIRCUMSTANCES WHICH ARE LIKELY TO AFFECT YOUR ABILITY TO DEVOTE SUFFICIENT TIME TO THE ARBITRATION AND IN PARTICULAR YOUR ABILITY TO FINISH THE ENTIRE ARBITRATION WITHIN TWELVE MONTHS (LIST OUT):

# THE SEVENTH SCHEDULE

[See Section 12 (5)]

### Arbitrator's relationship with the parties or counsel

1. The arbitrator is an employee, consultant, advisor or has any other past or present business relationship with a party.
2. The arbitrator currently represents or advises one of the parties or an affiliate of one of the parties.
3. The arbitrator currently represents the lawyer or law firm acting as counsel for one of the parties.
4. The arbitrator is a lawyer in the same law firm which is representing one of the parties.
5. The arbitrator is a manager, director, or part of the management, or has a similar controlling influence, in an affiliate of one of the parties if the affiliate is directly involved in the matters in dispute in the arbitration.
6. The arbitrator's law firm had a previous but terminated involvement in the case without the arbitrator being involved himself or herself.
7. The arbitrator's law firm currently has a significant commercial relationship with one of the parties or an affiliate of one of the parties.
8. The arbitrator regularly advises the appointing party or an affiliate of the appointing party even though neither the arbitrator nor his or her firm derives a significant financial income therefrom.
9. The arbitrator has a close family relationship with one of the parties and in the case of companies with the persons in the management and controlling the company.
10. A close family member of the arbitrator has a significant financial interest in one of the parties or an affiliate of one of the parties.
11. The arbitrator is a legal representative of an entity that is a party in the arbitration.
12. The arbitrator is a manager, director, or part of the management, or has a similar controlling influence in one of the parties.
13. The arbitrator has a significant financial interest in one of the parties or the outcome of the case.
14. The arbitrator regularly advises the appointing party or an affiliate of the appointing party, and the arbitrator or his or her firm derives a significant financial income therefrom.

## Relationship of the arbitrator to the dispute

15. The arbitrator has given legal advice or provided an expert opinion on the dispute to a party or an affiliate of one of the parties.
16. The arbitrator has previous involvement in the case.

## Arbitrator's direct or indirect interest in the dispute

17. The arbitrator holds shares, either directly or indirectly, in one of the parties or an affiliate of one of the parties that is privately held.
18. A close family member of the arbitrator has a significant financial interest in the outcome of the dispute.
19. The arbitrator or a close family member of the arbitrator has a close relationship with a third party who may be liable to recourse on the part of the unsuccessful party in the dispute.

*Explanation* **1:** The term "close family member" refers to a spouse, sibling, child, parent or life partner.

*Explanation* **2:** The term "affiliate" encompasses all companies in one group of companies including the parent company.

*Explanation* **3:** For the removal of doubts, it is clarified that it may be the practice in certain specific kinds of arbitration, such as maritime or commodities arbitration, to draw arbitrators from a small, specialised pool. If in such fields it is the custom and practice for parties frequently to appoint the same arbitrator in different cases, this is a relevant fact to be taken into account while applying the rules set out above.

# 6

# The Negotiable Instruments Act, 1881

## INTRODUCTION

In the business world, goods and/or services are bought and sold for cash as well as on credit. All these transactions require flow of cash either immediately or after due date. Therefore, a huge sum of money is required to be carried along which may be inconvenient to the business people and risky for either of the parties who makes or receives the payments in cash. Therefore, it is a common practice for businessmen to make use of certain documents as a means of making payment and thereby to avoid unnecessary risk. Some of these documents are called negotiable instruments which are well defined in the Negotiable Instruments Act (hereafter referred to as NI Act).

The NI Act was passed in 1881. Some provisions of the Act have become redundant, may be due to the passage of time or change of technology. However, the basic principles of the Act are still valid and the Act is able to satisfy the requirements of the time. The Act extends to the whole of India. The object of the Act is to regulate the commercial transactions and therefore it is drafted to suit the requirements of business conditions which are prevailing at present.

The negotiable instrument is mainly an instrument of credit readily convertible into money and easily transferable.

## OBJECT OF THE ACT

The object of the Act is as follows:

An Act to define and amend the law relating to Promissory Notes, Bills of Exchange and Cheques.

Whereas it is expedient to define and amend the law relating to promissory notes, bills of exchange and cheques;

It is hereby enacted as follows:

The Act was enacted with a specified object of making a special provision by incorporating a strict liability so far as a negotiable instrument is concerned. The law relating to negotiable instrument is the law of commercial world legislated to facilitate the activities in trade and commerce, making provision of giving sanctity to the instruments of credit which could be deemed to be convertible into money and easily passable from one person to another. In the absence of such instruments, including a cheque, trade and commerce activities, in the present-day world, are likely to be adversely affected as it is impracticable for the trading community to carry the currency in force. The negotiable instruments are in fact the instruments of credit being convertible on account of legality of being negotiated and are easily passable from one hand to another. To achieve the objectives of the Act, the Legislature has, in its wisdom, thought it proper to make provisions in the Act which confer such privileges the mercantile instruments contemplated under it and provide special penalties and procedure in case the obligations under the instruments are not discharged. The laws relating to the Act are, therefore, required to be interpreted in the light of the objects intended to be achieved by it despite there being deviations from the general law and the procedure provided for the redressal of the grievances of the litigants. Efforts to defeat the objectives of law by resorting to innovative measures and methods are to be discouraged, otherwise it may affect the commercial and mercantile activities in a smooth and healthy manner, ultimately affecting the economy of the country.[1]

## SALIENT FEATURES OF NEGOTIABLE INSTRUMENTS

After considering the whole Act and various types of negotiable instruments created under the Act, the important features emerge as follows:

1. A negotiable instrument is freely transferable.
   The formalities which are required for transfer of any property like registration, payment of stamp duty, etc. are not required while transferring a negotiable instrument. The ownership is changed by mere delivery (when payable to the bearer) or by valid endorsement and delivery (when payable to order). Further, while transferring the instruments, it is also not required to give any notice to the previous holder.
2. Negotiability confers absolute and valid title on the transferee.
   It means that a person who receives a negotiable instrument has a clear and undisputable title to the instrument only if he has got the instrument in good faith, for a consideration and no knowledge of the defect of the title.
3. A negotiable instrument must be in writing.
4. In every negotiable instrument, there must be an unconditional order or promise for payment.
5. The instrument must involve payment of a certain sum of money only.
6. The time of payment must be certain.
   It means that the instrument must be payable at a particular time which must be certain to arrive. If the time mentioned in the document is ambiguous and does not specify any certain time, it would not be considered a negotiable instrument.

[1] *Dalmia Cement (Bharat) Ltd., M/s. v. M/s. Galaxy Traders and Agencies Ltd.*, AIR 2001 SC 676.

For example, if it is mentioned *'when convenient'*, it is not a negotiable instrument. However, if the time of payment is linked to the death of a particular person, it is nevertheless a negotiable instrument as death is certain and going to happen one day.

7. The payee must be a certain person.

   The term 'person' includes individuals, body corporates, trade unions, even secretary, director or chairman of an institution. The payee can also be more than one person.
8. A negotiable instrument must bear the signature of its maker.
9. Delivery of the instrument is essential.
10. Stamping of Bills of Exchange and Promissory Notes is mandatory. This is required as per the Indian Stamp Act, 1899. The value of stamp depends upon the value of the pronote or bill and the time of their payment.

## INFORMATION TECHNOLOGY ACT, 2000 vis-a-vis NI ACT, 1881

Referring to Sec. (1)(4)(a) of the Information Technology Act and read with the First Schedule of the Act, it may be very well construed that the Information Technology Act will not apply to Bill of Exchange and Promissory Notes. Thus, a Bill of Exchange or Promissory Note cannot be made by electronic mode. However, cheque is covered under the Information Technology Act and hence can be made and/or sent by electronic mode. Therefore, Sec. 6 of the NI Act was amended in 2002 that came into force from 6 February, 2003.

### NI Act and Principle of *nemo dat quod non habet*

*Nemo dat quod non habet* means no one can transfer better title than he himself has. The same principle is applied in case of transfer of movable and immovable property as well. Section 27 of the Sale of Goods Act would be the right example so far as transfer of goods is concerned; of course, there are certain exceptions to it. *Nemo dat quod non habet* signifies that a person cannot transfer better title to property that he himself has even though he has purchased the product in good faith without knowing the defects of the title of the said product. *Nemo dat quod non habet* principle is not applicable to negotiable instruments if a person acquires it in good faith and without the knowledge of defect in title of the transferor, the transferee can get better title to the negotiable instrument, even if the title of the transferor was defective. This is really to ensure free negotiability of instrument so that persons can deal in the instrument without any fear.

## Chapter I Preliminary

### Section 1: Short title

This Act may be called the Negotiable Instruments Act, 1881.

**Local extent. Saving of usages relating to hundis, etc.**—It extends to the whole of India but nothing herein contained affects the Indian Paper Currency Act, 1871 (3 of 1871), Section 21, or affects any local usage relating to any instrument in an oriental language:

Provided that such usages may be excluded by any words in the body of the instrument which indicate an intention that the legal relations of the parties thereto shall he governed by this Act;

Commencement—and it shall come into force on the first day of March, 1882.

It extends to the whole of India but nothing herein contained affects the Indian Paper Currency Act, 1871 (3 of 1871), Section 21, or affects any local usage relating to any instrument in an oriental language:

### Commencement

Provided that such usages may be excluded by any words in the body of the instrument, which indicate an intention that the legal relations of the parties thereto shall be governed by this Act; and it shall come into force on the first day of March, 1882.

### Section 2: Repeal of enactment

### Section 3: Interpretation clause

In this Act—

**"Banker".**

"Banker" includes any person acting as a banker and any post office saving bank.

## Chapter II Of Notes, Bills and Cheques

### Section 4: "Promissory note"

A "promissory note" is an instrument in writing (not being a bank-note or a currency-note) containing an unconditional undertaking, signed by the maker, to pay a certain sum of money only to, or to the order of, a certain person, or to the bearer of the instrument.

### Illustrations

A signs instruments in the following terms:—

(a) "I promise to pay B or order ₹500."

(b) "I acknowledge myself to be indebted to B in ₹1,000, to be paid on demand, for value received."

(c) "Mr. B, I.O.U. ₹1,000."

(d) "I promise to pay B ₹500 and all other sums which shall be due to him."

(e) "I promise to pay B ₹500 first deducting there out any money which he may owe me."

(f) "I promise to pay B ₹500 seven days after my marriage with C."

(g) "I promise to pay B ₹500 on D's death, provided D leaves me enough to pay that sum."

(h) "I promise to pay B ₹500 and to deliver to him my black horse on 1st January next."

The instruments respectively marked (a) and (b) are promissory notes. The instruments respectively marked (c), (d), (e), (f), (g) and (h) are not promissory notes.

Section 4 of the Act recognises three kinds of promissory notes:

(1) Payable to a specified person
(2) Payable to the order of a specified person
(3) Payable to a bearer

A promissory note cannot be made payable to the bearer on demand. It has been prohibited under the RBI Act.

### *Parties to a promissory note*

There are primarily two parties involved in a promissory note. They are:

(1) Maker or drawer—the person who makes the note and promises to pay the amount stated therein.
(2) Payee—the person to whom the amount is payable.
(3) Endorser—the person who endorses the note in favour of another person.
(4) Endorsee—the person in whose favour the note is negotiated by endorsement.

### *Essentials of a promissory note*

Following are the essentials of a promissory note:

(1) It must be in writing.
(2) The promissory note must contain an express promise or undertaking to pay. An implied undertaking cannot make a document a promissory note.
(3) The promise to pay must be unconditional or subject to only such conditions which, according to the ordinary experience of mankind, is bound to happen.
(4) There must be a promise to pay money only.
(5) A definite sum of money. Certainty (a) as to the amount, and (b) as to the persons by whose order and to whom payment is to be made.
(6) The instrument must be signed by the maker.
(7) The person to whom the promise is made must be a definite person. The payee must be a certain person. Where the name of the payee is not mentioned as a party, the instrument becomes invalid. It is to be kept in mind that a promissory note cannot be made payable by the maker himself. Thus, a note which runs *"I promise to pay myself"* is not a promissory note and hence invalid. However, it would become valid when it is endorsed by the maker. A promissory note must point out with certainty the person who is entitled to receive the money. Where it is made payable to the bearer, the bearer is the definite person to whom payment is to be made. The words 'certain person' means a person who

is capable of being ascertained at the time of making the instrument. Therefore, if any person has not been named in the instrument but sufficient description of such person has been included therein by which such person may be ascertained, the requirement is fulfilled.[2]

(8) It may be payable in instalment (refer Sec. 5, para 3 of the NI Act).

(9) Place and date of making it need not be mentioned. A promissory note on which date is not mentioned is deemed to have been drawn on the date of its delivery.

(10) It cannot be made payable to the bearer on demand or payable to the bearer after a certain time (Sec. 31 of the Reserve Bank of India Act).

(11) It cannot be payable to the bearer on demand (Sec. 31 of the Reserve Bank of India Act).

Section 31 of the Reserve Bank of India Act, 1934:
Issue of demand bills and notes

(1) No person in India other than the Bank or, as expressly authorised by this Act, the Central Government shall draw, accept, make or issue any bill of exchange, hundi, promissory note or engagement for the payment of money payable to bearer on demand, or borrow, owe or take up any sum or sums of money on the bills, hundis or notes payable to bearer on demand of any such person:
Provided that cheques or drafts, including hundis, payable to bearer on demand or otherwise may be drawn on a person's account with a banker, shroff or agent.

(2) Notwithstanding anything contained in the Negotiable Instruments Act, 1881 (26 of 1881), no person in India other than the Bank or, as expressly authorised by this Act, the Central Government shall make or issue any promissory note expressed to be payable to the bearer of the instrument.

(12) It must be duly stamped as per the State laws in which it is executed, under the Indian Stamp Act. A promissory note which is not stamped is a nullity. Stamping may be before or after the execution.

The document must be read as a whole and no single sentence from it can be torn out and considered separately for the purpose of deciding the question as to whether the document is an agreement or a promissory note. No amount of judicial authority can decide this question since the matter must rest on the circumstances of each case. Two tests may be applied in deciding the question, the first being the intention of the parties at the time the document was made. The second test would be whether the document as drawn out can be said to be negotiable, that is to say, could a third person file a suit on the strength of this document. Where the intention underlying the document was that after certain credit and debit entries had been made and taken into consideration, a certain amount would be due which the applicant undertook to pay, the document is not a promissory note but an agreement.[3]

[2] *Ponnuswami* v. *Velliamuthu*, AIR 1957 Mad 355.

[3] *Bherulal* v. *Ram Rikh*, AIR 1951 AJMER 71.

## Section 5: "Bill of exchange"

A "bill of exchange" is an instrument in writing containing an unconditional order, signed by the maker, directing a certain person to pay a certain sum of money only to, or to the order of, a certain person or to the bearer of the instrument.

A promise or order to pay is not "conditional", within the meaning of this section and Section 4, by reason of the time for payment of the amount or any instalment thereof being expressed to be on the lapse of a certain period after the occurrence of a specified event which, according to the ordinary expectation of mankind, is certain to happen, although the time of its happening may be uncertain.

The sum payable may be "certain", within the meaning of this section and Section 4, although it includes future interest or is payable at an indicated rate of exchange, or is according to the course of exchange, and although the instrument provides that, on default of payment of an instalment, the balance unpaid shall become due.

The person to whom it is clear that the direction is given or that payment is to be made may be a "certain person", within the meaning of this section and Section 4, although he is mis-named or designated by description only.

### *Characteristic of a bill of exchange*

1. It must be in writing: The Bill of Exchange must be in writing.
2. Order to pay: There must be an order to pay. It is of the essence of the bill that its drawer orders the drawee to pay money to the payee. The term 'order' does not mean command. Any request or direction or other words, which show an intention of the drawer to cause a payment being made by the drawee is sufficient. Politeness may be admissible but excessive politeness may prompt one to disregard it as an order.
3. Unconditional order: This order must be unconditional, as the bill is payable at all events. It is absolutely necessary for the drawer's order to the drawee to be unconditional. The order must not make the payment of the bill dependent on a contingent event. A conditional bill of exchange is invalid.
4. Signature of the drawer: The drawee must sign the instrument. The instrument without the proper signature will be inchoate (unclear or unformed or undeveloped) and hence ineffective. It is permissible to add the signature at any time after the issue of the bill.
5. Drawee: A bill, in order to be perfect, must indicate a drawee who should be called upon to accept or pay it.
6. Parties: The drawer, the drawee (acceptor) and the payee—the parties to a bill—are to be specified in the instrument with reasonable certainty.
7. Certainty of amount: The sum must be certain.
8. Payment in kind not valid: The medium of payment must be money and money only. The distinctive order to pay anything in kind will vitiate the bill.
9. Stamping: A Bill of Exchange, to be valid, must be duly stamped as per the Indian Stamp Act.

10. Cannot be made payable to bearer on demand: A Bill of Exchange as originally drawn cannot be made payable to the bearer on demand.

***Parties to the bill of exchange***

1. Drawer: The maker of a bill of exchange or cheque is called drawer.
2. Drawee: The person who is directed to pay by the drawer.
3. Acceptor: One who accepts the bill. Generally, the drawee is the acceptor but a stranger may accept it on behalf of the drawee.
4. Payee: Person to whom the sum stated in the bills is payable.
5. Holder: Section 8 of the Negotiable Instruments Act states that "the 'holder' of a promissory note, bill of exchange or cheque means *"any person entitled in his own name to the possession thereof and to receive or recover the amount due thereon from the parties thereto."*
6. Holder in due course: A person who for consideration becomes the possessor of a promissory note, bill of exchange or cheque (if payable to bearer).
7. Endorser: Holder who endorses the bill in favour of any other person.
8. Endorsee: Person in whose favour the bill is endorsed by the endorser.
9. Drawee in case of need: When in the bill or in any endorsement thereon the name of any person is given in addition to the drawee to be resorted to in case of need, such person is called the 'drawee in case of need'.
10. Acceptor for honour: When a bill of exchange has been noted and protested for non-acceptance or for better security, any other person accepts it supra protest for honour of the drawer or of any of the endorsers, such person is called the 'acceptor for honour'.

The distinctive features of Promissory Note and Bill of Exchange are given below:

| Promissory Note | Bill of Exchange |
|---|---|
| 1. It contains a promise to pay. | 1. It contains an order to pay. |
| 2. In the case of a promissory note, there are only two parties, viz., the maker (debtor) and the payee (creditor). | 2. There are three parties, viz, drawer, drawee and payee; however, the drawer and the payee may be the same person. |
| 3. The liability of the maker of a note is primary and absolute (Sec. 32). | 3. The liability of the drawer of a bill is secondary and conditional. |
| 4. It is presented for payment without any previous acceptance by the maker. | 4. If a bill is payable some time after sight, it is required to be accepted either by the drawee himself or by someone else on his behalf, before it can be presented for payment. |
| 5. The maker of a promissory note stands in immediate relationship with the payee and is primarily liable to the payee or the holder. | 5. The maker or drawer of an accepted bill stands in immediate relationship with the acceptor and the payee. |
| 6. It cannot be made payable to the maker himself. The maker and the payee cannot be the same person. | 6. The drawer and the payee or the drawee and the payee may be the same person. |

(Contd.)

| Promissory Note | Bill of Exchange |
|---|---|
| 7. A promissory note can never be conditional. | 7. A bill of exchange too cannot be drawn conditionally, but it can be accepted conditionally with the consent of the holder. |
| 8. In case of dishonour, no notice of dishonour is required to be given. | 8. A notice of dishonour must be given in case of dishonour of a bill of exchange. |

**Section 6: "Cheque"**

A "cheque" is a bill of exchange drawn on a specified banker and not expressed to be payable otherwise than on demand and it includes the electronic image of a truncated cheque and a cheque in the electronic form.

*Explanation I*: For the purposes of this section, the expressions—

(a) "a cheque in the electronic form" means a cheque drawn in electronic form by using any computer resource and signed in a secure system with digital signature (with or without biometrics signature) and asymmetric crypto system or with electronic signature, as the case may be;

(b) "a truncated cheque" means a cheque which is truncated during the course of a clearing cycle, either by the clearing house or by the bank whether paying or receiving payment, immediately on generation of an electronic image for transmission, substituting the further physical movement of the cheque in writing.

*Explanation II*: For the purposes of this section, the expression "clearing house" means the clearing house managed by the Reserve Bank of India or a clearing house recognised as such by the Reserve Bank of India.

*Explanation III*: For the purposes of this section, the expressions "asymmetric crypto system", "computer resource", "digital signature", "electronic form" and "electronic signature" shall have the same meanings respectively assigned to them in the Information Technology Act, 2000 (21 of 2000).

From a bare perusal of Secs. 5 and 6 of the Act, it would appear that the Bill of Exchange is a negotiable instrument in writing containing an instruction to a third party to pay a stated sum of money at a designated future date or on demand. On the other hand, a 'cheque' is a Bill of Exchange drawn on a bank by the holder of an account payable on demand. Under Sec. 6 of the Act, a 'cheque' is also a bill of exchange but it is drawn on a banker and payable on demand. A bill of exchange even though drawn on a banker, if it is not payable on demand, it is not a cheque. A post-dated cheque is not payable till the date which is shown thereon arrives and will become cheque on the said date and prior to that date the same remains Bill of Exchange.[4]

***Characteristics of a Cheque***

(1) A cheque is an unconditional order on a specified banker where the drawer has his account.

[4] *Ashok Yeshwant Badeve* v. *Surendra Madhavrao Nighojakar*, AIR 2001 SC 1315.

(2) A cheque can be drawn for a certain sum of money.
(3) Cheque is payable by the banker only on demand.
(4) A cheque does not require acceptance by the banker as in the case of Bill of Exchange.
(5) A cheque may be drawn up in three forms, i.e. (i) Bearer cheque; (ii) Order cheque (Sec. 18); and (iii) Crossed cheque.
(6) All cheques are Bills of Exchange but all Bills of Exchange are not cheques.

The differences between cheque and bill of exchange are given below:

| Cheque | Bill of Exchange |
|---|---|
| 1. **Drawee:** Cheque can be drawn only on a banker. | 1. The drawee may be any person. |
| 2. **Time of payment:** A cheque is payable on demand. | 2. A bill may be drawn payable on demand or on expiry of certain period after date or sight. |
| 3. **Grace period:** Cheque is payable on demand and no grace period is allowed. | 3. While calculating maturity three day's grace is allowed. |
| 4. **Notice of dishonour**: Notice of dishonour is not necessary. | 4. A notice of dishonour is required. |
| 5. **Payee:** A cheque can be drawn to bearer and made payable on demand. | 5. A bill cannot be made bearer if it is payable on demand. A bill drawn 'payable to bearer on demand' is void. |
| 6. **Acceptance:** A cheque is not required to be presented for acceptance. It needs to be presented only for payment. | 6. Bills, sometimes, require presentment for acceptance and it is advisable to present them for acceptance even when it is not essential to do so. |
| 7. **Stamping:** No stamp duty is payable on cheques. | 7. Affixation of proper stamps is necessary in case of Bills of Exchange. |
| 8. **Crossing:** A cheque may be crossed. | 8. A Bill of Exchange cannot be crossed. |
| 9. **Noting and protesting:** There is no system for noting and protesting in case of dishonour. | 9. In case of dishonour of a bill, proper noting and protesting is necessary. |
| 10. **Discharge of drawer:** The drawer does not get discharged from his liability because of delay in presenting the cheque to the bank for payment. | 10. The drawer of the bill stands discharged from his liability if it is not duly presented for payment. |
| 11. **Liability of drawee for dishonour:** In case of dishonour of cheque, the drawee is liable to the drawer and not to the payee. | 11. In case of dishonour of the bill by non-payment on an accepted Bill of Exchange, the drawee becomes liable to the payee. |
| 12. **Validity period:** A cheque is usually valid for a period of six months. | 12. A bill may be drawn for any period. |

## Section 7: "Drawer", "Drawee"

The maker of a bill of exchange or cheque is called the "drawer"; the person thereby directed to pay is called the "drawee".

**"Drawee in case of need"**

When in the bill or in any indorsement thereon the name of any person is given in addition to the drawee to be resorted to in case of need, such person is called a "drawee in case of need".

**"Acceptor"**

After the drawee of a bill has signed his assent upon the bill, or, if there are more parts thereof than one, upon one of such parts, and delivered the same, or given notice of such signing to the holder or to some person on his behalf, he is called the "acceptor".

**"Acceptor for honour"**

When a bill of exchange has been noted or protested for non-acceptance or for better security, and any person accepts it *supra protest* for honour of the drawer or of anyone of the endorsers, such person is called an "acceptor for honour".

**"Payee"**

The person named in the instrument, to whom or to whose order the money is by the instrument directed to be paid, is called the "payee".

## Section 8: "Holder"

The "holder" of a promissory note, bill of exchange or cheque means any person entitled in his own name to the possession thereof and to receive or recover the amount due thereon from the parties thereto.

Where the note, bill or cheque is lost or destroyed, its holder is the person so entitled at the time of such loss or destruction.

To be a holder under Sec. 8 of the Act, he must be entitled to:

(a) the possession of the instrument in his own name; and

(b) receive or recover the amount due thereon from the parties liable thereto.

Possession of the instrument does not mean that he should have the actual possession of the instrument, it is sufficient if he has a 'de facto' control over the instrument in question. Any person in wrongful possession of the instrument cannot be the holder under Sec. 8 of the Act. Therefore, the finder of a lost instrument payable to bearer, or a person in wrongful possession of such instrument, is not a holder.

## Section 9: "Holder in due course"

"Holder in due course" means any person who for consideration became the possessor of a promissory note, bill of exchange or cheque if payable to bearer, or the payee or endorsee thereof, if payable to order, before the amount mentioned in it became payable, and without having sufficient cause to believe that any defect existed in the title of the person from whom he derived his title.

The definition makes it clear that to be a *'holder in due course'*, a person must be a holder for consideration and the instrument must have been transferred to him before it becomes overdue and he must be a transferee in good faith and another important condition is that the transferee, namely the person who for consideration becomes the possessor of the cheque should not have any reason to believe that there was any defect in the title of the transferor.

A holder, to be a holder in due course, must not only have acquired the bill, note or cheque for valid consideration but should have acquired the cheque without having sufficient cause to believe that any defect existed in the title of the person from whom he derived his title. This condition requires that he should act in good faith and with reasonable caution. However, mere failure to prove bona fide or absence of negligence on his part would not negative his claim. But in a given case, it is left to the Court to decide whether the negligence on the part of the holder is so gross and extraordinary as to presume that he had sufficient cause to believe that such title was defective. However, when the presumption in his favour as provided under Sec. 118(g) gets rebutted under the circumstances mentioned therein, then the burden of proving that he is a *'holder in due course'* lies upon him. The Court, while examining these requirements including valid consideration, must also go into the question whether there was a contract express or implied for crediting the proceeds to the account of the bearer before receiving the same. The enquiry regarding the satisfaction of this requirement invariably depends upon the facts and circumstances in each case. The words *"without having sufficient cause to believe"* incorporated in Sec. 9 of the Act have to be understood in this background.[5]

### *Prerequisites for being holder in due course*

A person who claims to be 'holder in due course' is required to prove that:

(i) That he is a holder;

(ii) That he is a holder for consideration;

(iii) Acquisition before maturity;

(iv) That he has no knowledge of defective title;

(v) That instrument was complete at the time of possession.

Differences between holder and holder in due course

1. *Meaning*: Holder means any person who is entitled to the negotiable instrument in his possession and in his own name and to recover or receive the amount due thereon from the parties thereto. A holder in due course, on the other hand, means a holder who takes the instrument in good faith for a consideration before it is overdue and without any knowledge of defect in the title of the person who transferred it to him.
2. *Consideration*: A holder may become the possessor or payee of an instrument even without consideration, whereas a holder in due course is one who acquires possession for consideration.

[5] *U. Ponnappa Moothan, M/s. Sons, Palghat* v. *Catholic Syrian Bank Ltd.*, AIR 1991 SC 441.

3. *Title*: Holder of negotiable instrument does not acquire a better title than that of the person from whom he acquired the instrument. Thus, a holder does not acquire a good title if the title of any of the prior parties is defective. But a holder in due course gets a good and valid title even though there was a defect in the title of any prior parties to the instrument.
4. *Liability*: A holder in due course can sue all prior parties to a negotiable instrument until the instrument is duly satisfied, whereas a holder of the instrument can enforce it against the person who has signed it and also against the transferor from whom he obtained it.
5. *Maturity*: A person will be a holder in due course only if he acquires the instrument before the amount mentioned in it becomes payable. But a holder may acquire the instrument even after it has become due for payment.

### *Privileges of a holder in due course*

The NI Act provides certain privileges to the holder in due course which are not available to the holder and they are as follows:

1. ***Estoppel against inchoate stamped instrument (Sec. 20)***: A person who has signed and delivered to another a paper stamped in India but otherwise it is an inchoate instrument (an incomplete financial instrument that can be completed by the addition of a payee's name or an amount) thereby he would be estopped from denying his liability to a holder in due course on the ground that the instrument has not been filled in accordance with the authority given by him.
2. ***Acceptor of a bill drawn in fictitious name (Sec. 42)***: If a bill of exchange is drawn on behalf of a fictitious person and is payable to his order, the acceptor is not relieved of his liability to the holder in due course because of the fictitious name. It is essential though that the holder in due course proves that the document bears the endorsement with signature in the same hand as that of the drawer and purporting to be made by the drawer.
3. ***Instrument obtained by unlawful means or for unlawful consideration (Sec. 58)***: A person liable on a negotiable instrument cannot defend himself against a holder in due course on the ground that the instrument was lost or obtained from him by means of an offence or for an unlawful consideration.
4. ***Liability of prior parties to holder in due course (Sec. 36)***: Every prior party to a negotiable instrument is liable thereon to a holder in due course until the instrument is duly satisfied.
5. ***Estoppel against denying validity of instrument (Sec. 120)***: No maker of a promissory note, and no drawer of a bill of exchange or cheque, and no acceptor of a bill of exchange for the honour of the drawer shall, in a suit thereon by holder in due course, be permitted to deny the validity of the instrument as originally made or drawn.
6. ***Estoppel against denying capacity of payee to indorse (Sec. 121)***: No maker of a promissory note and no acceptor of a bill of exchange payable to order shall, in a suit thereon by a holder in due course, be permitted to deny the payee's capacity at the date of note or bill, to endorse the same.

7. ***Estoppel against denying signature or capacity of prior party (Sec. 122):*** No endorser of a negotiable instrument shall, in a suit thereon by a subsequent holder, be permitted to deny the signature or capacity of any prior party to the instrument.

## Section 10: "Payment in due course"

"Payment in due course" means payment in accordance with the apparent tenor of the instrument in good faith and without negligence to any person in possession thereof under circumstances which do not afford a reasonable ground for believing that he is not entitled to receive payment of the amount therein mentioned.

## Section 11: "Inland instrument"

A promissory note, bill of exchange or cheque drawn or made in India and made payable in, or drawn upon any person resident in India shall be deemed to be an inland instrument.

## Section 12: "Foreign instrument"

Any such instrument not so drawn, made or made payable shall be deemed to be a foreign instrument.

## Section 13: "Negotiable instrument"

(1) A "negotiable instrument" means a promissory note, bill of exchange or cheque payable either to order or to bearer.

*Explanation (i)*: A promissory note, bill of exchange or cheque is payable to order which is expressed to be so payable or which is expressed to be payable to a particular person, and does not contain words prohibiting transfer or indicating an intention that it shall not be transferable.

*Explanation (ii)*: A promissory note, bill of exchange or cheque is payable to bearer which is expressed to be so payable or on which the only or last indorsement is an indorsement in blank.

*Explanation (iii)*: Where a promissory note, bill of exchange or cheque, either originally or by indorsement, is expressed to be payable to the order of a specified person, and not to him or his order, it is nevertheless payable to him or his order at his option.

(2) A negotiable instrument may be made payable to two or more payees jointly, or it may be made payable in the alternative to one of two, or one or some of several payees.

## Section 14: Negotiation

When a promissory note, bill of exchange or cheque is transferred to any person, so as to constitute that person the holder thereof, the instrument is said to be negotiated.

### Section 15: Indorsement

When the maker or holder of a negotiable instrument signs the same, otherwise than as such maker, for the purpose of negotiation, on the back or face thereof or on a slip of paper annexed thereto, or so signs for the same purpose a stamped paper intended to be completed as a negotiable instrument, he is said to indorse the same, and is called the "indorser".

### Section 16: Indorsement "in blank" and "in full"

(1) If the indorser signs his name only, the indorsement is said to be "in blank", and if he adds a direction to pay the amount mentioned in the instrument to, or to the order of, a specified person, the indorsement is said to be "in full"; and the person so specified is called the "indorsee" of the instrument.

*"Indorsee"*

(2) The provisions of this Act relating to a payee shall apply with the necessary modifications to an indorsee.

### Section 17: Ambiguous instruments

Where an instrument may be construed either as a promissory note or bill of exchange, the holder may at his election treat it as either and the instrument shall be thence forward treated accordingly.

### Section 18: Where amount is stated differently in figures and words

If the amount undertaken or ordered to be paid is stated differently in figures and in words, the amount stated in words shall be the amount undertaken or ordered to be paid.

### Section 19: Instruments payable on demand

A promissory note or bill of exchange, in which no time for payment is specified, and a cheque, are payable on demand.

### Section 20: Inchoate stamped instruments

Where one person signs and delivers to another a paper stamped in accordance with the law relating to negotiable instruments then in force in India, and either wholly blank or having written thereon an incomplete negotiable instrument, he thereby gives *prima facie* authority to the holder thereof to make or complete, as the case may be, upon it a negotiable instrument, for any amount specified therein and not exceeding the amount covered by the stamp. The person so signing shall be liable upon such instrument, in the capacity in which he signed the same, to any holder in due course for such amount:

Provided that no person other than a holder in due course shall recover from the person delivering the instrument anything in excess of the amount intended by him to be paid thereunder.

### Section 21: "At sight", "On presentment", "After sight"

In a promissory note or bill of exchange the expressions "at sight" and "on presentment" mean on demand. The expression "after sight" means, in a promissory note, after presentment for sight, and, in a bill of exchange, after acceptance, or noting for non-acceptance, or protest for non-acceptance.

### Section 22: "Maturity"

The maturity of a promissory note or bill of exchange is the date at which it falls due.

**Days of grace**

Every promissory note or bill of exchange which is not expressed to be payable on demand, at sight or on presentment is at maturity on the third day after the day on which it is expressed to be payable.

### Section 23: Calculating maturity of bill or note payable so many months after date or sight

In calculating the date at which a promissory note or bill of exchange, made payable a stated number of months after date or after sight, or after a certain event, is at maturity, the period stated shall be held to terminate on the day of the month which corresponds with the day on which the instrument is dated, or presented for acceptance or sight, or noted for non-acceptance, or protested for non-acceptance, or the event happens, or, where the instrument is a bill of exchange made payable a stated number of months after sight and has been accepted for honour, with the day on which it was so accepted. If the month in which the period would terminate has no corresponding day, the period shall be held to terminate on the last day of such month.

### Illustrations

(a) A negotiable instrument, dated 29th January, 1878, is made payable at one month after date. The instrument is at maturity on the 3rd day after the 28th February, 1878.

(b) A negotiable instrument, dated 30th August, 1878, is made payable three months after date. The instrument is at maturity on the 3rd December, 1878.

(c) A promissory note or bill of exchange, dated 31st August, 1878, is made payable three months after date. The instrument is at maturity on the 3rd December, 1878.

### Section 24: Calculating maturity of bill or note payable so many days after date or sight

In calculating the date at which a promissory note or bill of exchange made payable a certain number of days after date or after sight or after a certain event is at maturity, the day of the date, or of presentment for acceptance or sight, or of protest for non-acceptance, or on which the event happens, shall be excluded.

### Section 25: When day of maturity is a holiday

When the day on which a promissory note or bill of exchange is at maturity is a public holiday, the instrument shall be deemed to be due on the next preceding business day.

*Explanation*: The expression "public holiday" includes Sundays and any other day declared by the Central Government, by notification in the Official Gazette, to be a public holiday.

## Chapter III Parties to Notes, Bills and Cheques

### Section 26: Capacity to make, etc., the promissory notes, etc.

Every person capable of contracting, according to the law to which he is subject, may bind himself and be bound by the making, drawing, acceptance, indorsement, delivery and negotiation of a promissory note, bill of exchange or cheque.

**Minor**

A minor may draw, indorse, deliver and negotiate such instruments so as to bind all parties except himself.

Nothing herein contained shall be deemed to empower a corporation to make, indorse or accept such instruments except in cases in which, under the law for the time being in force, they are so empowered.

### Section 27: Agency

Every person capable of binding himself or of being bound, as mentioned in Section 26, may so bind himself or be bound by a duly authorised agent acting in his name. A general authority to transact business and to receive and discharge debts does not confer upon an agent the power of accepting or indorsing bills of exchange so as to bind his principal.

An authority to draw bills of exchange does not of itself import an authority to indorse.

### Section 28: Liability of agent signing

An agent who signs his name to a promissory note, bill of exchange or cheque without indicating thereon that he signs as agent, or that he does not intend thereby to incur personal responsibility, is liable personally on the instrument, except to those who induced him to sign upon the belief that the principal only would be held liable.

### Section 29: Liability of legal representative signing

A legal representative of a deceased person who signs his name to a promissory note, bill of exchange or cheque is liable personally thereon unless he expressly limits his liability to the extent of the assets received by him as such.

### Section 30: Liability of drawer

The drawer of a bill of exchange or cheque is bound, in case of dishonour by the drawee or acceptor thereof, to compensate the holder, provided due notice of dishonour has been given to, or received by, the drawer as hereinafter provided.

### Section 31: Liability of drawee of cheque

The drawee of a cheque having sufficient funds of the drawer in his hands properly applicable to the payment of such cheque must pay the cheque when duly required so to do, and, in default of such payment, must compensate the drawer for any loss or damage caused by such default.

### Section 32: Liability of maker of note and acceptor of bill

In the absence of a contract to the contrary, the maker of a promissory note and the acceptor before maturity of a bill of exchange are bound to pay the amount thereof at maturity according to the apparent tenor of the note or acceptance respectively, and the acceptor of a bill of exchange at or after maturity is bound to pay the amount thereof to the holder on demand.

In default of such payment as aforesaid, such maker or acceptor is bound to compensate any party to the note or bill for any loss or damage sustained by him and caused by such default.

The drawee of a negotiable instrument is not liable on it to the payee, unless he has accepted it. Under Sec. 32, the liability of the drawee arises only when he accepts the bill. There is no provision in the Act that the drawee is as such liable on the instrument, the only exception being under Sec. 31 in the case of a drawee of a cheque having sufficient funds of the customer in his hands; and even then, the liability is only towards the drawer and not the payee.[6] This is elementary law, and was laid down by West, J. in *Khandas Narandas* v. *Dahiabhai*,[7] that where there is no acceptance, no cause of action can have arisen to the payee against the drawee.

### Section 33: Only drawee can be acceptor except in need or for honour

No person except the drawee of a bill of exchange, or all or some of several drawees, or a person named therein as a drawee in case of need, or an acceptor for honour, can bind himself by an acceptance.

### Section 34: Acceptance by several drawees not partners

Where there are several drawees of a bill of exchange who are not partners, each of them can accept it for himself, but none of them can accept it for another without his authority.

### Section 35: Liability of indorser

In the absence of a contract to the contrary, whoever indorses and delivers a negotiable instrument before maturity, without, in such indorsement, expressly excluding or making conditional his own liability, is bound thereby to every subsequent holder, in case of dishonour by the drawee, acceptor or maker, to compensate such holder for any loss or damage caused to him by such dishonour, provided due notice of dishonour has been given to, or received by, such indorser as hereinafter provided.

Every indorser after dishonour is liable as upon an instrument payable on demand.

---

[6] *Jagjivan Mavji Vithalani* v. *Messrs. Ranchhoddas Meghji*, AIR 1954 SC 554.

[7] 3 Bom 182.

### Section 36: Liability of prior parties to holder in due course

Every prior party to a negotiable instrument is liable thereon to a holder in due course until the instrument is duly satisfied.

### Section 37: Maker, drawer and acceptor principals

The maker of a promissory note or cheque, the drawer of a bill of exchange until acceptance, and the acceptor are, in the absence of a contract to the contrary, respectively liable thereon as principal debtors, and the other parties thereto are liable thereon as sureties for the maker, drawer or acceptor, as the case may be.

### Section 38: Prior party a principal in respect of each subsequent party

As between the parties so liable as sureties, each prior party is, in the absence of a contract to the contrary, also liable thereon as a principal debtor in respect of each subsequent party.

### Illustration

A draws a bill payable to his own order on B, who accepts. A afterwards indorses the bill to C, C to D and D to E. As between E and B, B is the principal debtor, and A, C and D are his sureties. As between E and A, A is the principal debtor, and C and D are his sureties. As between E and C, C is the principal debtor and D is his surety.

### Section 39: Suretyship

When the holder of an accepted bill of exchange enters into any contract with the acceptor which, under Section 134 or 135 of the Indian Contract Act, 1872 (9 of 1872), would discharge the other parties, the holder may expressly reserve his right to charge the other parties, and in such case they are not discharged.

### Section 40: Discharge of indorser's liability

Where the holder of a negotiable instrument, without the consent of the indorser, destroys or impairs the indorser's remedy against a prior party, the indorser is discharged from liability to the holder to the same extent as if the instrument had been paid at maturity.

### Illustration

A is the holder of a bill of exchange made payable to the order of B, which contains the following indorsements in blank—

First indorsement, "B".

Second indorsement, "Peter Williams".

Third indorsement, "Wright & Co".

Fourth indorsement, "John Rozario".

This bill A puts in suit against John Rozario and strikes out, without John Rozario's consent, the indorsement by Peter Williams and Wright & Co. A is not entitled to recover anything from John Rozario.

### Section 41: Acceptor bound although indorsement forged

An acceptor of a bill of exchange already indorsed is not relieved from liability by reason that such indorsement is forged, if he knew or had reason to believe the indorsement to be forged when he accepted the bill.

### Section 42: Acceptance of bill drawn in fictitious name

An acceptor of a bill of exchange drawn in a fictitious name and payable to the drawer's order is not, by reason that such name is fictitious, relieved from liability to any holder in due course claiming under an indorsement by the same hand as the drawer's signature, and purporting to be made by the drawer.

### Section 43: Negotiable instrument made, etc., without consideration

A negotiable instrument made, drawn, accepted, indorsed, or transferred without consideration, or for a consideration which fails, creates no obligation of payment between the parties to the transaction. But if any such party has transferred the instrument with or without indorsement to a holder for consideration, such holder, and every subsequent holder deriving title from him, may recover the amount due on such instrument from the transferor for consideration or any prior party thereto.

*Exception I*: No party for whose accommodation a negotiable instrument has been made, drawn, accepted or indorsed can, if he has paid the amount thereof, recover thereon such amount from any person who became a party to such instrument for his accommodation.

*Exception II*: No party to the instrument who has induced any other party to make, draw, accept, indorse or transfer the same to him for a consideration which he has failed to pay or perform in full shall recover thereon an amount exceeding the value of the consideration (if any) which he has actually paid or performed.

### Section 44: Partial absence or failure of money-consideration

When the consideration for which a person signed a promissory note, bill of exchange or cheque consisted of money, and was originally absent in part or has subsequently failed in part, the sum which a holder standing in immediate relation with such signer is entitled to receive from him is proportionally reduced.

*Explanation*: The drawer of a bill of exchange stands in immediate relation with the acceptor. The maker of a promissory note, bill of exchange or cheque stands in immediate relation with the payee, and the indorser with his indorsee. Other signers may by agreement stand in immediate relation with a holder.

### Illustration

A draws a bill on B for ₹500 payable to the order of A. B accepts the bill, but subsequently dishonours it by non-payment. A sues B on the bill. B proves that it was accepted for value as to ₹400, and as an accommodation to the plaintiff as to the residue. A can only recover ₹400.

### Section 45: Partial failure of consideration not consisting of money

Where a part of the consideration for which a person signed a promissory note, bill of exchange or cheque, though not consisting of money, is uncertainable in money without collateral enquiry, and there has been a failure of that part, the sum which a holder standing in immediate relation with such signer is entitled to receive from him is proportionally reduced.

### Section 45A: Holder's right to duplicate of lost bill

Where a bill of exchange has been lost before it is overdue, the person who was the holder of it may apply to the drawer to give him another bill of the same tenor, giving security to the drawer, if required, to indemnify him against all persons whatever in case the bill alleged to have been lost shall be found again.

If the drawer on request as aforesaid refuses to give such duplicate bill, he may be compelled to do so.

## Chapter IV Of Negotiation

### Section 46: Delivery

The making, acceptance or indorsement of a promissory note, bill of exchange or cheque is completed by delivery, actual or constructive.

As between parties standing in immediate relation, delivery to be effectual must be made by the party making, accepting or indorsing the instrument, or by a person authorised by him in that behalf.

As between such parties and any holder of the instrument other than a holder in due course, it may be shown that the instrument was delivered conditionally or for a special purpose only, and not for the purpose of transferring absolutely the property therein.

A promissory note, bill of exchange or cheque payable to bearer is negotiable by the delivery thereof.

A promissory note, bill of exchange or cheque payable to order is negotiable by the holder by indorsement and delivery thereof.

### Section 47: Negotiation by delivery

Subject to the provisions of Section 58, a promissory note, bill of exchange or cheque payable to bearer is negotiable by delivery thereof.

*Exception*: A promissory note, bill of exchange or cheque delivered on condition that it is not to take effect except in a certain event is not negotiable (except in the hands of a holder for value without notice of the condition) unless such event happens.

### Illustrations

(a) A, the holder of a negotiable instrument payable to bearer, delivers it to B's agent to keep for B. The instrument has been negotiated.

(b) A, the holder of a negotiable instrument payable to bearer, which is in the hands of A's banker, who is at the time the banker of B, directs the banker to transfer the instrument to B's credit in the banker's account with B. The banker does so, and accordingly now possesses the instrument as B's agent. The instrument has been negotiated, and B has become the holder of it.

### Section 48: Negotiation by indorsement

Subject to the provisions of Section 58, a promissory note, bill of exchange or cheque payable to order, is negotiable by the holder by indorsement and delivery thereof.

### Section 49: Conversion of indorsement in blank into indorsement in full

The holder of a negotiable instrument indorsed in blank may, without signing his own name, by writing above the indorser's signature a direction to pay to any other person as indorsee, convert the indorsement in blank into an indorsement in full; and the holder does not thereby incur the responsibility of an indorser.

### Section 50: Effect of indorsement

The indorsement of a negotiable instrument followed by delivery transfers to the indorsee the property therein with the right of further negotiation; but the indorsement may, by express words, restrict or exclude such right, or may merely constitute the indorsee an agent to indorse the instrument, or to receive its contents for the indorser, or for some other specified person.

### Illustrations

B signs the following indorsements on different negotiable instruments payable to bearer:

(a) "Pay the contents to C only".
(b) "Pay C for my use."
(c) "Pay C or order for the account of B."
(d) "The within must be credited to C."

These indorsements exclude the right of further negotiation by C

(e) "Pay C."
(f) "Pay C value in account with the Oriental Bank."
(g) "Pay the contents to C, being part of the consideration in a certain deed of assignment executed by C to the indorser and others."

These indorsements do not exclude the right of further negotiation by C.

### Section 51: Who may negotiate

Every sole maker, drawer, payee or indorsee, or all of several joint makers, drawers, payees or indorsees, of a negotiable instrument may, if the negotiability of such instrument has not been restricted or excluded as mentioned in Section 50, indorse and negotiate the same.

***Explanation***: Nothing in this section enables a maker or drawer to indorse or negotiate an instrument, unless he is in lawful possession or is holder thereof; or enables a payee or indorsee to indorse or negotiate an instrument, unless he is holder thereof.

### Illustration

A bill is drawn payable to A or order. A indorses it to B, the indorsement not containing the words "or order" or any equivalent words, B may negotiate the instrument.

### Section 52: Indorser who excludes his own liability or makes it conditional

The indorser of a negotiable instrument may, by express words in the indorsement, exclude his own liability thereon, or make such liability or the right of the indorsee to receive the amount due thereon depend upon the happening of a specified event, although such event may never happen. Where an indorser so excludes his liability and afterwards becomes the holder of the instrument, all intermediate indorsers are liable to him.

### Illustrations

(a) The indorser of a negotiable instrument signs his name, adding the words—"Without recourse". Upon this indorsement he incurs no liability.

(b) A is the payee and holder of a negotiable instrument. Excluding personal liability by an indorsement "without recourse", he transfers the instrument to B, and B indorses it to C, who indorses it to A. A is not only reinstated in his former rights, but has the rights of an indorsee against B and C.

### Section 53: Holder deriving title from holder in due course

A holder of a negotiable instrument who derives title from a holder in due course has the rights thereon of that holder in due course.

### Section 54: Instrument indorsed in blank

Subject to the provisions hereinafter contained as to crossed cheques, a negotiable instrument indorsed in blank is payable to the bearer thereof even although originally payable to order.

### Section 55: Conversion of indorsement in blank into indorsement in full

If a negotiable instrument, after having been indorsed in blank, is indorsed in full, the amount of it cannot be claimed from the indorser in full, except by the person to whom it has been indorsed in full, or by one who derives title through such person.

### Section 56: Indorsement for part of sum due

No writing on a negotiable instrument is valid for the purpose of negotiation if such writing purports to transfer, only a part of the amount appearing to be due on the instrument; but where such amount has been partly paid, a note to that effect may be indorsed on the instrument, which may then be negotiated for the balance.

### Section 57: Legal representative cannot by delivery only negotiate instrument indorsed by deceased

The legal representative of a deceased person cannot negotiate by delivery only a promissory note, bill of exchange or cheque payable to order and indorsed by the deceased but not delivered.

### Section 58: Instrument obtained by unlawful means or for unlawful consideration

When a negotiable instrument has been lost, or has been obtained from any maker, acceptor or holder thereof by means of an offence or fraud, or for an unlawful consideration, no possessor or indorsee who claims through the person who found or so obtained the instrument is entitled to receive the amount due thereon from such maker, acceptor or holder, or from any party prior to such holder, unless such possessor or indorsee is, or some person through whom he claims was, a holder thereof in due course.

### Section 59: Instrument acquired after dishonour or when overdue

The holder of a negotiable instrument, who has acquired it after dishonour, whether by non-acceptance or non-payment, with notice thereof, or after maturity, has only, as against the other parties, the rights thereon of his transferor.

*Accommodation note or bill.*

Provided that any person who, in good faith and for consideration, becomes the holder, after maturity, of a promissory note or bill of exchange made, drawn or accepted without consideration, for the purpose of enabling some party thereto to raise money thereon, may recover the amount of the note or bill from any prior party.

### Illustration

The acceptor of a bill of exchange, when he accepted it, deposited with the drawer certain goods as a collateral security for the payment of the bill, with power to the drawer to sell the goods and apply the proceeds in discharge of the bill if it were not paid at maturity. The bill not having been paid at maturity, the drawer sold the goods and retained the proceeds, but indorsed the bill to A. A's title is subject to the same objection as the drawer's title.

### Section 60: Instrument negotiable till payment or satisfaction

A negotiable instrument may be negotiated (except by the maker, drawee or acceptor after maturity) until payment or satisfaction thereof by the maker, drawee or acceptor at or after maturity, but not after such payment or satisfaction.

## Chapter V Of Presentment

### Section 61: Presentment for acceptance

A bill of exchange payable after sight must, if no time or place is specified therein for presentment, be presented to the drawee thereof for acceptance, if he can, after reasonable search, be found, by a person entitled to demand acceptance, within a reasonable time after it is drawn, and in business hours on a business day. In default of such presentment, no party thereto is liable thereon to the person making such default. If the drawee cannot, after reasonable search, be found, the bill is dishonoured.

If the bill is directed to the drawee at a particular place, it must be presented at that place; and if at the due date for presentment he cannot, after reasonable search, be found there, the bill is dishonoured.

Where authorised by agreement or usage, a presentment through the post office by means of a registered letter is sufficient.

### Section 62: Presentment of promissory note for sight

A promissory note, payable at a certain period after sight, must be presented to the maker thereof for sight (if he can after reasonable search be found) by a person entitled to demand payment, within a reasonable time after it is made and in business hours on a business day. In default of such presentment, no party thereto is liable thereon to the person making such default.

### Section 63: Drawee's time for deliberation

The holder must, if so required by the drawee of a bill of exchange presented to him for acceptance, allow the drawee forty-eight hours (exclusive of public holidays) to consider whether he will accept it.

### Section 64: Presentment for payment

(1) Promissory notes, bills of exchange and cheques must be presented for payment to the maker, acceptor or drawee thereof respectively, by or on behalf of the holder as hereinafter provided. In default of such presentment, the other parties thereto are not liable thereon to such holder.

Where authorised by agreement or usage, a presentment through the post office by means of a registered letter is sufficient.

*Exception*: Where a promissory note is payable on demand and is not payable at a specified place, no presentment is necessary in order to charge the maker thereof.

(2) Notwithstanding anything contained in Section 6, where an electronic image of a truncated cheque is presented for payment, the drawee bank is entitled to demand any further information regarding the truncated cheque from the bank holding the truncated cheque in case of any reasonable suspicion about the genuineness of the apparent tenor of instrument, and if the suspicion is that of any fraud, forgery, tampering or destruction of the instrument, it is entitled to further demand the presentment of the truncated cheque itself for verification:

Provided that the truncated cheque so demanded by the drawee bank shall be retained by it, if the payment is made accordingly.

In a bill payable after sight, there are two distinct stages, firstly when it is presented for acceptance, and later when it is presented for payment. Section 61 deals with *'presentment for acceptance'* where as Sec. 64 deals with *'presentment for payment'*. Presentment for acceptance must always and in every case precede presentment for payment. But when the bill is payable on demand, both the stages synchronise, and there is only one presentment, which is both for acceptance and for payment. When the bill is paid, it involves an acceptance; but when it is not paid, it is really dishonoured for non-acceptance. But whether the bill is payable after sight or at sight or on demand, acceptance by the drawee is necessary before he can be fixed with liability on it. It is acceptance that establishes privity on the instrument between the payee and the drawee.[8]

**Section 65: Hours for presentment**

Presentment for payment must be made during the usual hours of business, and, if at a banker's within banking hours.

**Section 66: Presentment for payment of instrument payable after date or sight**

A promissory note or bill of exchange, made payable at a specified period after date or sight thereof, must be presented for payment at maturity.

**Section 67: Presentment for payment of promissory note payable by installments**

A promissory note payable by installments must be presented for payment on the third day after the date fixed for payment of each installment; and non-payment on such presentment has the same effect as non-payment of a note at maturity.

**Section 68: Presentment for payment of instrument payable at specified place and not elsewhere**

A promissory note, bill of exchange or cheque made, drawn or accepted payable at a specified place and not elsewhere must, in order to charge any party thereto, be presented for payment at that place.

**Section 69: Instrument payable at specified place**

A promissory note or bill of exchange made, drawn or accepted payable at a specified place must, in order to charge the maker or drawer thereof, be presented for payment at that place.

**Section 70: Presentment where no exclusive place specified**

A promissory note or bill of exchange, not made payable as mentioned in Sections 68 and 69, must be presented for payment at the place of business (if any), or at the usual residence, of the maker, drawee or acceptor thereof, as the case may be.

**Section 71: Presentment when maker, etc., has no known place of business or residence**

If the maker, drawee or acceptor of a negotiable instrument has no known place of business or fixed residence, and no place is specified in the instrument for presentment for acceptance or payment, such presentment may be made to him in person wherever he can be found.

**Section 72: Presentment of cheque to charge drawer**

Subject to the provisions of Section 84 a cheque must, in order to charge the drawer, be presented at the bank upon which it is drawn before the relation between the drawer and his banker has been altered to the prejudice of the drawer.

[8] *Jagjivan Mavji Vithalani* v. *Messrs. Ranchhoddas Meghji*, AIR 1954 SC 554.

**Section 73: Presentment of cheque to charge any other person**

A cheque must, in order to charge any person except the drawer, be presented within a reasonable time after delivery thereof by such person.

**Section 74: Presentment of instrument payable on demand**

Subject to the provisions of Section 31, a negotiable instrument payable on demand must be presented for payment within a reasonable time after it is received by the holder.

**Section 75: Presentment by or to agent, representative of deceased, or assignee of insolvent**

Presentment for acceptance or payment may be made to the duly authorised agent of the drawee, maker or acceptor, as the case may be, or, where the drawee, maker or acceptor has died, to his legal representative, or, where he has been declared an insolvent, to his assignee.

**Section 75A: Excuse for delay in presentment for acceptance or payment**

Delay in presentment for acceptance or payment is excused if the delay is caused by circumstances beyond the control of the holder, and not imputable to his default, misconduct or negligence. When the cause of delay ceases to operate, presentment must be made within a reasonable time.

**Section 76: When presentment unnecessary**

No presentment for payment is necessary, and the instrument is dishonoured at the due date for presentment, in any of the following cases:

(a) if the maker, drawee or acceptor intentionally prevents the presentment of the instrument, or

if the instrument being payable at his place of business, he closes such place on a business day during the usual business hours, or

if the instrument being payable at some other specified place, neither he nor any person authorized to pay it attends at such place during the usual business hours, or

if the instrument not being payable at any specified place, he cannot after due search be found;

(b) as against any party sought to be charged therewith, if he has engaged to pay notwithstanding non-presentment;

(c) as against any party if, after maturity, with knowledge that the instrument has not been presented—

he makes a part payment on account of the amount due on the instrument, or promises to pay the amount due therein whole or in part,

or otherwise waives his right to take advantage of any default in presentment for payment;

(d) as against the drawer, if the drawer could not suffer damage from the want of such presentment.

### Section 77: Liability of banker for negligently dealing with bill presented for payment

When a bill of exchange, accepted payable at a specified bank, has been duly presented there for payment and dishonoured, if the banker so negligently or improperly keeps, deals with or delivers back such bill as to cause loss to the holder, he must compensate the holder for such loss.

## Chapter VI Of Payment and Interest

### Section 78: To whom payment should be made

Subject to the provisions of Section 82, Clause (c), payment of the amount due on a promissory note, bill of exchange or cheque must, in order to discharge the maker or acceptor, be made to the holder of the instrument.

### Section 79: Interest when rate specified

When interest at a specified rate is expressly made payable on a promissory note or bill of exchange, interest shall be calculated at the rate specified, on the amount of the principal money due thereon, from the date of the instrument, until tender or realisation of such amount, or until such date after the institution of a suit to recover such amount as the Court directs.

### Section 80: Interest when no rate specified

When no rate of interest is specified in the instrument, interest on the amount due thereon shall, notwithstanding any agreement relating to interest between any parties to the instrument, be calculated at the rate of eighteen per centum per annum from the date at which the same ought to have been paid by the party charged, until tender or realisation of the amount due thereon, or until such date after the institution of a suit to recover such amount as the Court directs.

***Explanation***: When the party charged is the indorser of an instrument dishonoured by non-payment, he is liable to pay interest only from the time that he receives notice of the dishonour.

### Section 81: Delivery of instrument on payment or indemnity in case of loss

(1) Any person liable to pay, and called upon by the holder thereof to pay, the amount due on a promissory note, bill of exchange or cheque is before payment entitled to have it shown, and is on payment entitled to have it delivered up, to him, or if the instrument is lost or cannot be produced, to be indemnified against any further claim thereon against him.

(2) Where the cheque is an electronic image of a truncated cheque, even after the payment the banker who received the payment shall be entitled to retain the truncated cheque.

(3) A certificate issued on the foot of the printout of the electronic image of a truncated cheque by the banker who paid the instrument, shall be *prima facie* proof of such payment.

## Chapter VII Of Discharge from Liability on Notes, Bills and Cheques

### Section 82: Discharge from liability

The maker, acceptor or indorser respectively of a negotiable instrument is discharged from liability thereon—

*by cancellation.*

(a) to a holder thereof who cancels such acceptor's or indorser's name with intent to discharge him, and to all parties claiming under such holder;

*by release.*

(b) to a holder thereof who otherwise discharges such maker, acceptor or indorser, and to all parties deriving title under such holder after notice of such discharge;

*by payment.*

(c) to all parties thereto, if the instrument is payable to bearer, or has been indorsed in blank, and such maker, acceptor or indorser makes payment in due course of the amount due thereon.

### Section 83: Discharge by allowing drawee more than forty-eight hours to accept

If the holder of a bill of exchange allows the drawee more than forty-eight hours, exclusive of public holidays, to consider whether he will accept the same, all previous parties not consenting to such allowance are thereby discharged from liability to such holder.

### Section 84: When cheque not duly presented and drawer damaged thereby

(1) Where a cheque is not presented for payment within a reasonable time of its issue, and the drawer or person on whose account it is drawn had the right, at the time when presentment ought to have been made, as between himself and the banker, to have the cheque paid and suffers actual damage through the delay, he is discharged to the extent of such damage, that is to say, to the extent to which such drawer or person is a creditor of the banker to a larger amount than he would have been if such cheque had been paid.

(2) In determining what is a reasonable time, regard shall be had to the nature of the instrument, the usage of trade and of bankers, and the facts of the particular case.

(3) The holder of the cheque as to which such drawer or person is so discharged shall be a creditor, in lieu of such drawer or person, of such banker to the extent of such discharge and entitled to recover the amount from him.

## Illustrations

(a) A draws a cheque for ₹1,000, and, when the cheque ought to be presented, has funds at the bank to meet it. The bank fails before the cheque is presented. The drawer is discharged, but the holder can prove against the bank for the amount of the cheque.

(b) A draws a cheque at Umballa on a bank in Calcutta. The bank fails before the cheque could be presented in ordinary course. A is not discharged, for he has not suffered actual damage through any delay in presenting the cheque.

### Section 85: Cheque payable to order

(1) Where a cheque payable to order purports to be indorsed by or on behalf of the payee, the drawee is discharged by payment in due course.

(2) Where a cheque is originally expressed to be payable to bearer, the drawee is discharged by payment in due course to the bearer thereof, notwithstanding any indorsement whether in full or in blank appearing thereon, and notwithstanding that any such indorsement purports to restrict or exclude further negotiation.

In a case, a bank (plaintiff) agreed to give cash credit facilities to the defendant against cloth bales upon certain terms. The defendant needed an amount for purchasing cloth allotted to it. The bank agreed to advance the amount on condition that it would not be paid to the defendant but would be paid to the wholesaler directly by the bank and the cloth bales would be retained as further security. The defendant drew a cheque which was encashed but the money was entrusted by the bank to its servant who accompanied the defendant to the place where the money was to be paid. The servant, however, absconded with the amount with the result that the money was not paid to the wholesaler. The bank sued the defendant for recovery of money paid on the cheque relying on Secs. 85 and 118 of the Negotiable Instruments Act. The defendant denied the liability contending that the money was never paid to it, it having remained throughout with the bank's servant. It was stated by the bank that even assuming that its servant misappropriated the money, it was not responsible for the loss as the servant's act was criminal, and was entitled to recover the money from the defendant.

Held (i) it is sufficient to say that before the provisions of Sec. 85 can assist the Bank, it had to be established that payment had in fact been made to the Firm or to a person on behalf of the Firm. Payment to a person who had nothing to do with the Firm or a payment to an agent of the bank would not be a payment to the Firm. Therefore, Sec. 118 (presumptions as to negotiable instruments) also did not apply.

(ii) The principle of vicarious liability was not attracted. Vicarious liability could, in appropriate cases, rest on the master with respect to his servant's acts but it could not rest on a stranger with respect to the criminal acts of a servant of another. That principle could have no application for founding a liability against a stranger from whom the servant could in no sense be regarded as deriving any authority.[9]

---

[9] *Bank of Bihar* v. *Mahabir Lal*, AIR 1964 SC 377.

## Section 85A: Drafts drawn by one branch of a bank on another payable to order

Where any draft, that is an order to pay money, drawn by one office of a bank upon another office of the same bank for a sum of money payable to order on demand, purports to be indorsed by or on behalf of the payee, the bank is discharged by payment in due course.

## Section 86: Parties not consenting discharged by qualified or limited acceptance

If the holder of a bill of exchange acquiesces in a qualified acceptance, or one limited to part of the sum mentioned in the bill, or which substitutes a different place or time for payment, or which, where the drawees are not partners, is not signed by all the drawees, all previous parties whose consent is not obtained to such acceptance are discharged as against the holder and those claiming under him, unless on notice given by the holder they assent to such acceptance.

*Explanation*: An acceptance is qualified—

(a) where it is conditional, declaring the payment to be dependent on the happening of an event therein stated;

(b) where it undertakes the payment of part only of the sum order to be paid;

(c) where, no place of payment being specified on the order, it undertakes the payment at a specified place, and not otherwise or elsewhere; or where, a place of payment being specified in the order, it undertakes the payment at some other place and not otherwise or elsewhere;

(d) where it undertakes the payment at a time other than that at which under the order it would be legally due.

## Section 87: Effect of material alteration

Any material alteration of a negotiable instrument renders the same void as against anyone who is a party thereto at the time of making such alteration and does not consent thereto, unless it was made in order to carry out the common intention of the original parties;

*Alteration by indorsee.*

and any such alteration, if made by an indorsee, discharges his indorser from all liability to him in respect of the consideration thereof.

The provisions of this section are subject to those of Sections 20, 49, 86 and 125.

A material alteration is one which varies the rights, liabilities, or legal position of the parties ascertained by the deed in its original State or otherwise varies the legal effect of the instrument as originally expressed, or reduces to certainty some provision which was originally unascertained and as such void, or may otherwise prejudice the party bound by the deed as originally executed. The effect of making such an alteration without the consent of the party bound is exactly the same as that of cancelling the deed.[10] The general rule in English law followed in India is that a party having custody or control of a document produced in evidence must explain the alteration. When the instrument on its production appears to have been altered, it is a general rule that the party offering it in evidence must

[10] *Nathu Lal* v. *Mt. Gomti Kuar*, AIR 1940 PC 160.

explain its appearance, because every alteration in the case of a negotiable instrument renders it suspicious. It is only reasonable that the party claiming under it should remove the suspicion. It must be remembered that it is not any and every alteration that avoids the instrument. To have that effect the alteration must be in a material particular. A material alteration can be brought about by change of date or time of drawing or of the place of payment or by change in the sum payable, etc., etc. It is thus evident that the date of a promissory note is a material portion of it, and any alteration of such date will naturally avoid the promissory note, unless, of course, as stated in the section, such an alteration is made with the consent of the other party, or is made to effectuate the common intention of the original parties. It is wrong to assume that the date of the promissory note is merely a description. It indicates the time when the promissory note was executed. In most cases the date is very material in calculating the date of the performance of the contract and more often fixing the period of limitation within which the plaintiff will have to institute the suit on the foot of such promissory note. It is immaterial whether the alteration is made in the date or month or year. Any such alteration being material must necessarily result in the avoidance of the promissory note.[11]

The first paragraph of Sec. 87 makes it clear that the party who consents to the alteration as well as the party who made the alteration are disentitle to complain against such alteration, e.g. if the drawer of the cheque himself altered the cheque for validating or re-validating the same instrument he cannot take advantage of it later by saying that the cheque became void as there is material alteration thereto. Further, even if the payee or the holder of the cheque made the alteration with the consent of the drawer thereof, such alteration also cannot be used as a ground to resist the right of the payee or the holder thereof. It is always a question of fact whether the alteration was made by the drawer himself or whether it was made with the consent of the drawer. It requires evidence to prove the aforesaid question whenever it is disputed. A cheque which has become invalid because of the expiry of the stipulated period could be made valid by alteration of dates. There is no provision in the Negotiable Instruments Act or in any other law which stipulates that a drawer of a negotiable instrument cannot re-validate it. It is always open to a drawer to voluntarily re-validate a negotiable instrument, including a cheque.[12]

### Section 88: Acceptor or indorser bound notwithstanding previous alteration

An acceptor or indorser of a negotiable instrument is bound by his acceptance or indorsement notwithstanding any previous alteration of the instrument.

### Section 89: Payment of instrument on which alteration is not apparent

(1) Where a promissory note, bill of exchange or cheque has been materially altered but does not appear to have been so altered,

or where a cheque is presented for payment which does not at the time of presentation appear to be crossed or to have had a crossing which has been obliterated,

[11] *A. Subba Reddy* v. *Neelapa Reddi*, AIR 1966 AP 267.

[12] *Veera Exports* v. *T. Kalavathy*, AIR 2002 SC 38.

payment thereof by a person or banker liable to pay, and paying the same according to the apparent tenor thereof at the time of payment and otherwise in due course, shall discharge such person or banker from all liability thereon; and such payment shall not be questioned by reason of the instrument having been altered, or the cheque crossed.

(2) Where the cheque is an electronic image of a truncated cheque, any difference in apparent tenor of such electronic image and the truncated cheque shall be a material alteration and it shall be the duty of the bank or the clearing house, as the case may be, to ensure the exactness of the apparent tenor of electronic image of the truncated cheque while truncating and transmitting the image.

(3) Any bank or a clearing house which receives a transmitted electronic image of a truncated cheque, shall verify from the party who transmitted the image to it, that the image so transmitted to it and received by it, is exactly the same.

### Section 90: Extinguishment of rights of action on bill in acceptor's hands

If a bill of exchange which has been negotiated is, at or after maturity, held by the acceptor in his own right, all rights of action thereon are extinguished.

## Chapter VIII Of Notice of Dishonour

### Section 91: Dishonour by non-acceptance

A bill of exchange is said to be dishonoured by non-acceptance when the drawee, or one of several drawees not being partners, makes default in acceptance upon being duly required to accept the bill, or where presentment is excused and the bill is not accepted.

Where the drawee is incompetent to contract, or the acceptance is qualified, the bill may be treated as dishonoured.

### Section 92: Dishonour by non-payment

A promissory note, bill of exchange or cheque is said to be dishonoured by non-payment when the maker of the note, acceptor of the bill or drawee of the cheque makes default in payment upon being duly required to pay the same.

### Section 93: By and to whom notice should be given

When a promissory note, bill of exchange or cheque is dishonoured by non-acceptance or non-payment, the holder thereof, or some party thereto who remains liable thereon, must give notice that the instrument has been so dishonoured to all other parties whom the holder seeks to make severally liable thereon, and to someone of several parties whom he seeks to make jointly liable thereon.

Nothing in this section renders it necessary to give notice to the maker of the dishonoured promissory note, or the drawee or acceptor of the dishonoured bill of exchange or cheque.

### Section 94: Mode in which notice may be given

Notice of dishonour may be given to a duly authorised agent of the person to whom it is required to be given, or, where he has died, to his legal representative, or, where he has been declared an insolvent, to his assignee; may be oral or written; may, if written, be sent by post; and, may be in any form; but it must inform the party to whom it is given, either in express terms or by reasonable intendment that the instrument has been dishonoured, and in what way, and that he will be held liable thereon; and it must be given within a reasonable time after dishonour, at the place of business or (in case such party has no place of business) at the residence of the party for whom it is intended.

If the notice is duly directed and sent by post and miscarries, such miscarriage does not render the notice invalid.

### Section 95: Party receiving must transmit notice of dishonour

Any party receiving notice of dishonour must, in order to render any prior party liable to himself, give notice of dishonour to such party within a reasonable time, unless such party otherwise receives due notice as provided by Section 93.

### Section 96: Agent for presentment

When the instrument is deposited with an agent for presentment, the agent is entitled to the same time to give notice to his principal as if he were the holder giving notice of dishonour, and the principal is entitled to a further like period to give notice of dishonour.

### Section 97: When party to whom notice given is dead

When the party to whom notice of dishonour is dispatched is dead, but the party dispatching the notice is ignorant of his death, the notice is sufficient.

### Section 98: When notice of dishonour is unnecessary

No notice of dishonour is necessary—

(a) when it is dispensed with by the party entitled thereto;

(b) in order to charge the drawer, when he has countermanded payment;

(c) when the party charged could not suffer damage for want of notice;

(d) when the party entitled to notice cannot after due search be found; or the party bound to give notice is, for any other reason, unable without any fault of his own to give it;

(e) to charge the drawers, when the acceptor is also a drawer;

(f) in the case of a promissory note which is not negotiable;

(g) when the party entitled to notice, knowing the facts, promises unconditionally to pay the amount due on the instrument.

# Chapter IX Of Noting and Protest

## Section 99: Noting

When a promissory note or bill of exchange has been dishonoured by non-acceptance or non-payment, the holder may cause such dishonour to be noted by a notary public upon the instrument, or upon a paper attached thereto, or partly upon each.

Such note must be made within a reasonable time after dishonour, and must specify the date of dishonour, the reason, if any, assigned for such dishonour, or, if the instrument has not been expressly dishonoured, the reason why the holder treats it as dishonoured, and the notary's charges.

## Section 100: Protest

When a promissory note or bill of exchange has been dishonoured by non-acceptance or non-payment, the holder may, within a reasonable time, cause such dishonour to be noted and certified by a notary public. Such certificate is called a protest.

*Protest for better security.*

When the acceptor of a bill of exchange has become insolvent, or his credit has been publicly impeached, before the maturity of the bill, the holder may, within a reasonable time, cause a notary public to demand better security of the acceptor, and on its being refused may, with a reasonable time, cause such facts to be noted and certified as aforesaid. Such certificate is called a protest for better security.

## Section 101: Contents of protest

Protest under Section 100 must contain—

(a) either the instrument itself, or a literal transcript of the instrument and of everything written or printed thereupon;

(b) the name of the person for whom and against whom the instrument has been protested;

(c) a statement that payment or acceptance, or better security, as the case may be, has been demanded of such person by the notary public; the terms of his answer, if any, or a statement that he gave no answer, or that could not be found;

(d) when the note or bill has been dishonoured, the place and time of dishonour, and, when better security has been refused, the place and time of refusal;

(e) the subscription of the notary public making the protest;

(f) in the event of an acceptance for honour or of a payment for honour, the name of the person by whom, of the person for whom, and the manner in which, such acceptance or payment was offered and effected.

A notary public may make the demand mentioned in clause (c) of this section either in person or by his clerk or, where authorised by agreement or usage, by registered letter.

## Section 102: Notice of protest

When a promissory note or bill of exchange is required by law to be protested, notice of such protest must be given instead of notice of dishonour, in the same manner and subject to the same conditions; but the notice may be given by the notary public who makes the protest.

### Section 103: Protest for non-payment after dishonour by non-acceptance

All bills of exchange drawn payable at some other place than the place mentioned as the residence of the drawee, and which are dishonoured by non-acceptance, may, without further presentment to the drawee, be protested for non-payment, in the place specified for payment, unless paid before or at maturity.

### Section 104: Protest of foreign bills

Foreign bills of exchange must be protested for dishonour when such protest is required by the law of the place where they are drawn.

### Section 104A: When noting equivalent to protest

For the purposes of this Act, where a bill or note is required to be protested within a specified time or before some further proceeding is taken, it is sufficient that the bill has been noted for protest before the expiration of the specified time or the taking of the proceeding; and the formal protest may be extended at any time thereafter as of the date of the noting.

## Chapter X Of Reasonable Time

### Section 105: Reasonable time

In determining what is a reasonable time for presentment for acceptance or payment, for giving notice of dishonour and for noting, regard shall be had to the nature of the instrument and the usual course of dealing with respect to similar instruments; and, in calculating such time, public holidays shall be excluded.

### Section 106: Reasonable time of giving notice of dishonour

If the holder and the party to whom notice of dishonour is given carry on business or live (as the case may be) in different places, such notice is given within a reasonable time if it is dispatched by the next post or on the day next after the day of dishonour.

If the said parties carry on business or live in the same place, such notice is given within a reasonable time if it is dispatched in time to reach its destination on the day next after the day of dishonour.

### Section 107: Reasonable time for transmitting such notice

A party receiving notice of dishonour, who seeks to enforce his right against a prior party, transmits the notice within a reasonable time if he transmits it within the same time after its receipt as he would have had to give notice if he had been the holder.

# Chapter XI Of Acceptance and Payment for Honour and Reference in Case of Need

## Section 108: Acceptance for honour

When a bill of exchange has been noted or protested for non-acceptance or for better security, any person not being a party already liable thereon may, with the consent of the holder, by writing on the bill, accept the same for the honour of any party thereto.

## Section 109: How acceptance for honour must be made

A person desiring to accept for honour must, by writing on the bill under his hand, declare that he accepts under protest the protested bill for the honour of the drawer or of a particular indorser whom he names, or generally for honour.

## Section 110: Acceptance not specifying for whose honour it is made

Where the acceptance does not express for whose honour it is made, it shall be deemed to be made for the honour of the drawer.

## Section 111: Liability of acceptor for honour

An acceptor for honour binds himself to all parties subsequent to the party for whose honour he accepts to pay the amount of the bill if the drawee do not; and such party and all prior parties are liable in their respective capacities to compensate the acceptor for honour for all loss or damage sustained by him in consequence of such acceptance.

But an acceptor for honour is not liable to the holder of the bill unless it is presented, or (in case the address given by such acceptor on the bill is a place other than the place where the bill is made payable) forwarded for presentment, not later than the day next after the day of its maturity.

## Section 112: When acceptor for honour may be charged

An acceptor for honour cannot be charged unless the bill has at its maturity been presented to the drawee for payment, and has been dishonoured by him, and noted or protested for such dishonour.

## Section 113: Payment for honour

When a bill of exchange has been noted or protested for non-payment any person may pay the same for the honour of any party liable to pay the same : Provided that the person so paying or his agent in that behalf has previously declared before a notary public the party for whose honour he pays, and that such declaration has been recorded by such notary public.

## Section 114: Right of payer for honour

Any person so paying is entitled to all the rights, in respect of the bill, of the holder at the time of such payment, and may recover from the party for whose honour he pays all sums so paid, with interest thereon and with all expenses properly incurred in making such payment.

### Section 115: Drawee in case of need

Where a drawee in case of need is named in a bill of exchange, or in any indorsement thereon, the bill is not dishonoured until it has been dishonoured by such drawee.

### Section 116: Acceptance and payment without protest

A drawee in case of need may accept and pay the bill of exchange without previous protest.

## Chapter XII Of Compensation

### Section 117: Rules as to compensation

The compensation payable in case of dishonour of a promissory note, bill of exchange or cheque, by any party liable to the holder or any indorsee, shall be determined by the following rules:—

(a) The holder is entitled to the amount due upon the instrument, together with the expenses properly incurred in presenting, noting and protesting it;
(b) When the person charged resides at a place different from that at which the instrument was payable, the holder is entitled to receive such sum at the current rate of exchange between the two places;
(c) An indorser who, being liable, has paid the amount due on the same is entitled to the amount so paid with interest at eighteen per centum per annum from the date of payment until tender or realisation thereof, together with all expenses caused by the dishonour and payment;
(d) When the person charged and such indorser reside at different places, the indorser is entitled to receive such sum at the current rate of exchange between the two places;
(e) The party entitled to compensation may draw a bill upon the party liable to compensate him, payable at sight or on demand, for the amount due to him, together with all expenses properly incurred by him. Such bill must be accompanied by the instrument dishonoured and the protest thereof (if any). If such bill is dishonoured, the party dishonouring the same is liable to make compensation thereof in the same manner as in the case of the original bill.

## Chapter XIII Special Rules of Evidence

### Section 118: Presumptions as to negotiable instruments

Until the contrary is proved, the following presumptions shall be made:—

*of consideration.*

(a) that every negotiable instrument was made or drawn for consideration, and that every such instrument, when it has been accepted, indorsed, negotiated or transferred, was accepted, indorsed, negotiated or transferred for consideration;

*as to date.*

(b) that every negotiable instrument bearing a date was made or drawn on such date;

*as to time of acceptance.*

(c) that every accepted bill of exchange was accepted within a reasonable time after its date and before its maturity;

*as to time of transfer.*

(d) that every transfer of a negotiable instrument was made before its maturity;

*as to order of indorsements.*

(e) that the indorsements appearing upon a negotiable instrument were made in the order in which they appear thereon;

*as to stamps.*

(f) that a lost promissory note, bill of exchange or cheque was duly stamped;

*that holder is a holder in due course.*

(g) that the holder of a negotiable instrument is a holder in due course: provided that, where the instrument has been obtained from its lawful owner, or from any person in lawful custody thereof, by means of an offence or fraud, or has been obtained from the maker or acceptor thereof by means of an offence or fraud, or for unlawful consideration, the burden of proving that the holder is a holder in due course lies upon him.

### *Presumption as to negotiable instrument*

In case of dispute, the Court has the power to presume in respect of rights of parties involved in a bill of exchange and they are as follows:

1. **Consideration:** That every negotiable instrument is made or drawn for a consideration. Thus, this need not necessarily be mentioned.
2. **Date:** That the negotiable instrument was drawn on the date shown on the face of it.
3. **Acceptance before maturity:** That the bill of exchange was accepted before its maturity, i.e., before it became overdue.
4. **Transfer before maturity:** That the negotiable instrument was transferred before its maturity.
5. **Order of endorsements:** That the endorsements appearing upon a negotiable instrument were made in the order in which they appear.

6. **Stamping of the instrument:** That an instrument which has been lost was properly stamped.
7. **Holder is holder in due course:** That the holder of a negotiable instrument is the 'holder in due course', except where the instrument has been obtained from its lawful owner or its lawful custodian by means of offence or fraud.
8. **Proof of dishonour:** If a suit is filed upon an instrument which has been dishonoured, the Court shall, on proof of the protest, presume the fact of dishonour unless it is disproved (Sec. 119).

In order to determine the question whether offence punishable under Sec. 138 of the Act is made out against the appellant, it will be necessary to examine the scope and ambit of presumptions to be raised as envisaged by the provisions of Secs. 118 and 139 of the Act. In a suit to enforce a simple contract, the plaintiff has to aver in his pleading that it was made for good consideration and must substantiate it by evidence. But to this rule, the negotiable instruments are an exception. In a significant departure from the general rule applicable to contracts, Sec. 118 of the Act provides certain presumptions to be raised. This section lays down some special rules of evidence relating to presumptions. The reason for these presumptions is that, negotiable instrument passes from hand to hand on endorsement and it would make trading very difficult and negotiability of the instrument impossible, unless certain presumptions are made. The presumption, therefore, is a matter of principle to facilitate negotiability as well as trade. Section 118 of the Act provides presumptions to be raised until the contrary is proved (i) as to consideration, (ii) as to date of instrument, (iii) as to time of acceptance, (iv) as to time of transfer, (v) as to order of indorsements, (vi) as to appropriate stamp and (vii) as to holder being a holder in due course.[13]

In a case where the signature in the cheque is admitted to be that of the accused, the presumption envisaged in Sec. 118 of the Act can legally be inferred that the cheque was made or drawn for consideration on the date which the cheque bears. Sec. 139 of the Act enjoins on the Court to presume that the holder of the cheque received it for the discharge of any debt or liability. The burden was on the accused to rebut the aforesaid presumption.[14]

Section 118 of the NI Act needs to be discussed in the light of Section 114 of the Indian Evidence Act, 1872 where Sec. 114 deals with presumption of existence of certain facts. Sec. 114 of the Evidence Act reads:

**Section 114 of the Evidence Act:- Court may presume existence of certain facts**
The Court may presume the existence of any fact which it thinks likely to have happened, regard being had to the common course of natural events, human conduct and public and private business, in their relation to the facts of the particular case.

**Illustrations**

The Court may presume—

(a) That a man who is in possession of stolen goods after the theft is either the thief or has received the goods knowing them to be stolen, unless he can account for his possession;

[13] *Kumar Exports, M/s.* v. *M/s. Sharma Carpets*, AIR 2009 SC 1518.

[14] *K. Bhaskaran* v. *Sankaran Vaidhyan Balan*, AIR 1999 SC 3762.

(b) That an accomplice is unworthy of credit, unless he is corroborated in material particular;

(c) That a bill of exchange, accepted or endorsed, was accepted or endorsed for good consideration;

(d) That a thing or State of things which has been shown to be in existence within a period shorter than that within which such things or State of things usually cease to exist, is still in existence;

(e) That judicial and official acts have been regularly performed;

(f) That the common course of business had been followed in particular cases;

(g) That evidence which could be and is not produced would, if produced be unfavourable to the person who withholds it;

(h) That if a man refuses to answer a question which he is not compelled to answer by law, the answer, if given, would be unfavourable to him;

(i) That when a document creating an obligation is in the hands of the obligor, the obligation has been discharged.

But the Court shall also have regard to such facts as the following, in considering whether such maxims do or do not apply to the particular case before it—

As to illustration (a)—A shop-keeper has in his till a marked rupee soon after it was stolen, and cannot account for its possession specifically, but is continually receiving rupees in the course of his business;

As to illustration (b)—A, a person of the highest character, is tried for causing a man's death by an act of negligence in arranging certain machinery. B, a person of equally good character, who also took part in the arrangement, describes precisely what was done, and admits and explains the common carelessness of A and himself;

As to illustration (b)—A crime is committed by several persons. A, B and C, three of the criminals, are captured on the spot and kept apart from each other. Each gives an account of the crime implicating D, and the accounts corroborate each other in such a manner as to render previous concert highly improbable;

As to illustration (c)—A, the drawer of a bill of exchange, was a man of business. B, the acceptor, was young and ignorant person, completely under A's influence;

As to illustration (d)—It is proved that a river ran in a certain course five years ago, but it is known that there have been floods since that time which might change its course;

As to illustration (e)—A judicial act, the regularity of which is in question, was performed under exceptional circumstances;

As to illustration (f)—The question is, whether a letter was received. It is shown to have been posted, but the usual course of the post was interrupted by disturbances;

As to illustration (g)—A man refuses to produce a document which would bear on a contract of small importance on which he is sued, but which might also injure the feelings and reputation of his family;

As to illustration (h)—A man refuses to answer a question which he is not compelled by law to answer, but the answer to it might cause loss to him in matters unconnected with the matter in relation to which it is asked;

As to illustration (i)—A bond is in possession of the obligor, but the circumstances of the case are such that he may have stolen it.

Section 114 of the Indian Evidence Act authorises the Court to presume the existence of any fact which it thinks likely to have happened, regard being had to the common course of natural events, human conduct and public and private business in their relation to the facts of the particular case. Under the third illustration of Sec. 114 the Court may presume that a bill of exchange accepted or endorsed was accepted for good consideration. But the section provides that the Court shall also have regard to other material facts in considering whether the maxim does or does not apply in the particular case before it, it is therefore open to the Court to consider in its proper setting, the fact that the drawer of a bill of exchange was a man of business, and the acceptor was a young and ignorant person completely under the former's influence. This is one illustrative fact which the Court may consider in raising the presumption. There may be other circumstances which may also justify the Court in declining to raise the presumption. Mr. Pathak, the learned counsel for the respondents urged that the Indian Evidence Act was enacted in 1872 and the Negotiable Instruments Act having been enacted in 1881, and as the two provisions conflict or overlap, Sec. 118 of the Negotiable Instruments Act must supersede Sec. 114 of the Evidence Act. But the Court is unable to accept that contention. The Court held that undoubtedly Sec. 114 of the Evidence Act is a general provision which enables the Court to presume, though not obliged to do so, that a bill of exchange or a promissory note was founded on a good consideration. Section 118 of the Negotiable Instruments Act, however, enacts a special rule of evidence which operates between parties to the instrument of persons claiming under them in a suit or proceeding relating to the bill of exchange and does not affect the rule contained in Sec. l14 of the Evidence Act, in cases not falling within Sec. 118 of the Negotiable Instruments Act.[15]

### Section 119: Presumption on proof of protest

In a suit upon an instrument which has been dishonoured, the Court shall, on proof of the protest, presume the fact of dishonour, unless and until such fact is disproved.

### Section 120: Estoppel against denying original validity of instrument

No maker of a promissory note, and no drawer of a bill of exchange or cheque, and no acceptor of a bill of exchange for the honour of the drawer shall, in a suit thereon by a holder in due course, be permitted to deny the validity of the instrument as originally made or drawn.

### Section 121: Estoppel against denying capacity of payee to indorse

No maker of a promissory note and no acceptor of a bill of exchange payable to order shall, in a suit thereon by a holder in due course, be permitted to deny the payee's capacity, at the rate of the note or bill, to indorse the same.

### Section 122: Estoppel against denying signature or capacity of prior party

No indorser of a negotiable instrument shall, in a suit thereon by a subsequent holder, be permitted to deny the signature or capacity to contract of any prior party to the instrument.

---

[15] *Official Receiver, Kanpur* v. *Abdul Shakoor*, AIR 1965 SC 920.

Estoppel in its broadest sense is a legal term referring to a series of legal and equitable doctrines that preclude a person from denying or asserting anything to the contrary of that which has been established as the truth by his own act which may be expressed or implied. Estoppel is essentially a rule of evidence whereby a person is barred from denying the truth of a fact that has already been settled. The object of estoppel is to prevent fraud and secure justice between the parties by promotion of honesty and good faith. The business community believes other contracting parties and thereby making the contract or accepting the legal documents only on good faith. That may be the reasons the NI Act deals with the rule of estoppel which runs from Sec. 120 to Sec. 122. Section 115 of the Indian Evidence Act, 1872 defines estoppel as follows:

> When one person has by his declaration, act or omission, intentionally caused or permitted another person to believe a thing to be true and to act upon such belief, neither he nor his representative shall be allowed, in any suit or proceeding between himself and such person or his representative, to deny the truth of that thing.
>
> **Illustration**
>
> A intentionally and falsely leads B to believe that certain land belongs to A, and thereby induces B to buy and pay for it.
>
> The land afterwards becomes the property of A, and A seeks to set aside the sale on the ground that, at the time of the sale, he had no title. He must not be allowed to prove his want of title.

### *Rules of estoppel applicable to negotiable instruments*

Certain rules of estoppel are applicable to negotiable instruments. These are as follows:

(1) Estoppel against denying original validity of instrument: The persons who are directly responsible for bringing into existence promissory note, bill of exchange or cheque, like the maker of the note and the drawer of the bill of exchange or cheque, would not be allowed to deny the validity of such instruments once they are made (Sec. 120).

(2) Estoppel against denying capacity of the payee to endorse: The maker of a promissory note or an acceptor of a bill shall not, in a suit by holder in due course, be allowed to deny the capacity of the payee to endorse the bill (Sec. 121).

(3) Estoppel against denying signature or capacity of prior party: An endorser of a negotiable instrument shall not be allowed to deny the signature or capacity to contract of any prior party to the instrument (Sec. 122).

# Chapter XIV Of Crossed Cheques

### Section 123: Cheque crossed generally

Where a cheque bears across its face an addition of the words "and company" or any abbreviation thereof, between two parallel transverse lines, or of two parallel transverse lines simply, either with or without the words "not negotiable", that addition shall be deemed a crossing, and the cheque shall be deemed to be crossed generally.

### Section 124: Cheque crossed specially

Where a cheque bears across its face an addition of the name of a banker, either with or without the words "not negotiable", that addition shall be deemed a crossing, and the cheque shall be deemed to be crossed specially, and to be crossed to that banker.

### Section 125: Crossing after issue

Where a cheque is uncrossed, the holder may cross it generally or specially.

Where a cheque is crossed generally, the holder may cross it specially.

Where a cheque is crossed generally or specially, the holder may add the words "not negotiable".

Where a cheque is crossed specially, the banker to whom it is crossed may again cross it specially to another banker, his agent, for collection.

### Section 126: Payment of cheque crossed generally

Where a cheque is crossed generally, the banker on whom it is drawn shall not pay it otherwise than to a banker.

**Payment of cheque crossed specially**

Where a cheque is crossed specially, the banker on whom it is drawn shall not pay it otherwise than to the banker to whom it is crossed, or his agent for collection.

### Section 127: Payment of cheque crossed specially more than once

Where a cheque is crossed specially to more than one banker, except when crossed to an agent for the purpose of collection, the banker on whom it is drawn shall refuse payment thereof.

### Section 128: Payment in due course of crossed cheque

Where the banker on whom a crossed cheque is drawn has paid the same in due course, the banker paying the cheque, and (in case such cheque has come to the hands of the payee) the drawer thereof, shall respectively be entitled to the same rights, and be placed in the same position in all respects, as they would respectively be entitled to and placed in if the amount of the cheque had been paid to and received by the true owner thereof.

### Section 129: Payment of crossed cheque out of due course

Any banker paying a cheque crossed generally otherwise than to a banker, or a cheque crossed specially otherwise than to the banker to whom the same is crossed, or his agent for collection, being a banker, shall be liable to the true owner of the cheque for any loss he may sustain owing to the cheque having been so paid.

### Section 130: Cheque bearing "not negotiable"

A person taking a cheque crossed generally or specially, bearing in either case the words "not negotiable", shall not have, and shall not be capable of giving, a better title to the cheque than that which the person from whom he took it had.

### Section 131: Non-liability of banker receiving payment of cheque

A banker who has in good faith and without negligence received payment for a customer of a cheque crossed generally or specially to himself, shall not, in case the title to the cheque proves defective, incur any liability to the true owner of the cheque by reason only of having received such payment.

*Explanation I*: A banker receives payment of a crossed cheque for a customer within the meaning of this section notwithstanding that he credits his customer's account with the amount of the cheque before receiving payment thereof.

*Explanation II*: It shall be the duty of the banker who receives payment based on an electronic image of a truncated cheque held with him, to verify the *prima facie* genuineness of the cheque to be truncated and any fraud, forgery or tampering apparent on the face of the instrument that can be verified with due diligence and ordinary care.

### Section 131A: Application of Chapter to drafts

The provisions of this Chapter shall apply to any draft, as defined in Section 85A, as if the draft were a cheque.

## Chapter XV Of Bills in Sets

### Section 132: Set of bills

Bills of exchange may be drawn in parts, each part being numbered and containing a provision that it shall continue payable only so long as the others remain unpaid. All the parts together make a set; but the whole set constitutes only one bill, and is extinguished when one of the parts, if a separate bill, would be extinguished.

*Exception*: When a person accepts or indorses different parts of the bill in favour of different persons, he and the subsequent indorsers of each part are liable on such part as if it were a separate bill.

### Section 133: Holder of first acquired part entitled to all

As between holders in due course of different parts of the same set, he who first acquired title to his part is entitled to the other parts and the money represented by the bill.

## Chapter XVI Of International Law

### Section 134: Law governing liability of maker, acceptor or indorser of foreign instrument

In the absence of a contract to the contrary, the liability of the maker or drawer of a foreign promissory note, bill of exchange or cheque is regulated in all essential matters by the law of the place where he made the instrument and the respective liabilities of the acceptor and indorser by the law of the place where the instrument is made payable.

#### Illustration

A bill of exchange was drawn by A in California, where the rate of interest is 25%, and accepted by B, payable in Washington, where the rate of interest is 6%. The bill is indorsed in India, and is dishonoured. An action on the bill is brought against B in India. He is liable to pay interest at the rate of 6% only; but if A is charged as drawer, A is liable to pay interest at the rate of 25%.

### Section 135: Law of place of payment governs dishonour

Where a promissory note, bill of exchange or cheque is made payable in a different place from that in which it is made or indorsed, the law of the place where it is made payable determines what constitutes dishonour and what notice of dishonour is sufficient.

#### Illustration

A bill of exchange drawn and indorsed in India, but accepted payable in France, is dishonoured. The indorsee causes it to be protested for such dishonour, and gives notice thereof in accordance with the law of France, though not in accordance with the rules herein contained in respect of bills which are not foreign. The notice is sufficient.

### Section 136: Instrument made, etc., out of India, but in accordance with the law of India

If a negotiable instrument is made, drawn, accepted or indorsed outside India, but in accordance with the law of India, the circumstance that any agreement evidenced by such instrument is invalid according to the law of the country wherein it was entered into does not invalidate any subsequent acceptance or indorsement made thereon within India.

### Section 137: Presumption as to foreign law

The law of any foreign country regarding promissory notes, bills of exchange and cheques shall be presumed to be the same as that of India, unless and until the contrary is proved.

## Chapter XVII Of Penalties in Case of Dishonour of Certain Cheques for Insufficiency of Funds in the Accounts

### Section 138: Dishonour of cheque for insufficiency, etc., of funds in the account

Where any cheque drawn by a person on an account maintained by him with a banker for payment of any amount of money to another person from out of that account for the discharge, in whole or in part, of any debt or other liability, is returned by the bank unpaid, either because of the amount of money standing to the credit of that account is insufficient to honour the cheque or that it exceeds the amount arranged to be paid from that account by an agreement made with that bank, such person shall be deemed to have committed an offence and shall, without prejudice to any other provisions of this Act, be punished with imprisonment for a term which may extend to two years, or with fine which may extend to twice the amount of the cheque, or with both:

Provided that nothing contained in this section shall apply unless—

(a) the cheque has been presented to the bank within a period of six months from the date on which it is drawn or within the period of its validity, whichever is earlier;

(b) the payee or the holder in due course of the cheque, as the case may be, makes a demand for the payment of the said amount of money by giving a notice, in writing, to the drawer of the cheque, within thirty days of the receipt of information by him from the bank regarding the return of the cheque as unpaid; and

(c) the drawer of such cheque fails to make the payment of the said amount of money to the payee or, as the case may be, to the holder in due course of the cheque, within fifteen days of the receipt of the said notice.

***Explanation***: For the purposes of this section, "debt or other liability" means a legally enforceable debt or other liability.

Chapter XVII of the Act which runs from Sec. 138 to Sec. 142 was inserted by the Banking, Public Financial Institutions and Negotiable Instruments Laws (Amendment) Act, 1988 (66 of 1988). The object of bringing Sec. 138 into the statute is to inculcate faith in the efficacy of banking operations and credibility in transacting business on negotiable instruments. It is to enhance the acceptability of cheques in settlement of liabilities by making the drawer liable for penalties in case of bouncing of cheques due to insufficient arrangements made by the drawer, with adequate safeguards to prevent harassment of honest drawers. If the cheque is dishonoured for insufficiency of funds in the drawer's account or if it exceeds the amount arranged to be paid from that account, the drawer is to be punished with imprisonment for a term which may extend to two years, or with fine which may extend to twice the amount of the cheque, or with both. It may be noted that when the offence was inserted in the statute in 1988, it carried the provision for imprisonment up to one year, which was revised to two years following the amendment to the Act in 2002. It is quite evident that the legislative intent was to provide a strong criminal remedy in order to deter the worryingly high incidence of dishonour of cheques. While the possibility of imprisonment up to two years provides a remedy of a punitive nature, the provision for imposing a *'fine which may extend to twice the amount of the cheque'* serves a compensatory purpose. What must be remembered is that the dishonour of a cheque can be best described as a regulatory offence that has been created to serve the public interest in ensuring the reliability of these instruments. The impact of this offence is usually confined to the private parties involved in commercial transactions.[16]

[16] *Damodar S. Prabhu* v. *Sayed Babalal H.*, AIR 2010 SC 1907

Section 138 of the Act makes a civil transaction to be an offence by fiction of law. Where any cheque drawn by a person on an account maintained by him with a banker for payment of any amount of money to another person is returned by the bank unpaid either because of the amount or money standing to the credit of that person being insufficient to honour the cheque or that it exceeds the amount arranged to be paid from that account, such person, subject to the other conditions, shall be deemed to have committed an offence under the section and be punished for a term which may extend to one year or with fine which may extend to twice the amount of cheque or with both. To make the dishonour of the cheque an offence, the aggrieved party is required to present the cheque to the bank within a period of six months from the date on which it is drawn or within the period of its validity, whichever is earlier, and the payee or the holder in due course of the cheque makes a demand for payment of the cheque amount by giving a notice in writing to the drawer of the cheque within 15 days of the receipt of information by him from the bank regarding the return of the cheque as unpaid and the drawer of the such cheque fails to make the payment of the amount within 15 days of the receipt of the said notice. Section 139 refers to presumption that unless the contrary is proved, the holder received the cheque of the nature referred to under Sec. 138 for the discharge in whole or in part or of any debt or other liability. Section 140 restricts the defence in any prosecution under Sec. 138 of the Act and Sec. 141 refers to such offence committed by the companies. Section 142 provides that notwithstanding anything contained in the Code of Criminal Procedure, no Court shall take cognizance of an offence under the Section except upon a complaint in writing made by the payee or as the case may be, the holder of the cheque and that such complaint is made within one month of the date on which the cause of action arose under clause (c) of proviso to Sec. 138 of the Act.[17]

The Supreme Court in *K. Bhaskaran* v. *Sankaran Vaidhyan Balan*[18] categorically discussed two important issues.

(i) Criteria to invoke Sec. 138 of the Act; and

(ii) Jurisdiction of criminal Court to entertain the case made under Sec. 138 of the Act.

The Court held that the offence under Section 138 of the Act can be completed only with the concatenation of a number of acts. Following are the acts which are components of the said offence: (i) Drawing of the cheque, (ii) Presentation of the cheque to the bank, (iii) Returning the cheque unpaid by the drawee bank, (iv) Giving notice in writing to the drawer of the cheque demanding payment of the cheque amount, (v) failure of the drawer to make payment within 15 days of the receipt of the notice.

So far as the jurisdiction of the trail Court is concerned, the Court further observed that It is not necessary that all the above five acts should have been perpetrated at the same locality. It is possible that each of those five acts could be done at five different localities. But concatenation of all the above five is a *sine qua non* for the completion of the offence under Sec. 138 of the Act. In this context, a reference to Sec. 178(d) of the Code of Criminal Procedure is useful and it reads as follows:

---

[17] *Dalmia Cement (Bharat) Ltd., M/s.* v. *M/s. Galaxy Traders and Agencies Ltd.*, AIR 2001 SC 676.

[18] AIR 1999 SC 3762.

> "Where the offence consists of several acts done in different local areas, it may be inquired into or tried by a Court having jurisdiction over any of such local areas."

Thus, it is clear that if the five different acts are done in five different localities, anyone of the Courts exercising jurisdiction in one of the five local areas can become the place of trial for the offence under Sec. 138 of the Act. In other words, the complainant can choose anyone of those Courts having jurisdiction over anyone of the local areas within the territorial limits of which anyone of those five acts was done.

The conditions relating to the notice, which is to be given to the drawer, have been formulated and incorporated in Clauses. (b) and (c) of the proviso to Sec. 138 of the Act. On the part of the payee, he has to make a demand by *"giving a notice"* in writing. If that was the only requirement to complete the offence on the failure of the drawer to pay the cheque amount within 15 days from the date of such "giving", the travails of the prosecution would have been very much lessened. But the Legislature says that failure on the part of the drawer to pay the amount should be within 15 days *"of the receipt"* of the said notice. It is, therefore, clear that *"giving notice"* in the context is not the same as receipt of notice. Giving is a process of which receipt is the accomplishment. It is for the payee to perform the former process by sending the notice to the drawer in the correct address. No doubt, Sec. 138 of the NI Act does not require that the notice should be given only by "post". Nonetheless, the principle incorporated in Sec. 27 of the General Clauses Act can profitably be imported in a case where the sender has dispatched the notice by post with the correct address written on it. Then it can be deemed to have been served on the sendee unless he proves that it was not really served and that he was not responsible for such non-service. Any other interpretation can lead to a very tenuous position as the drawer of the cheque who is liable to pay the amount would resort to the strategy of subterfuge by successfully avoiding the notice.[19]

It is one thing to say that sending of a notice is one of the ingredients for maintaining the complaint, but it is another thing to say that dishonour of a cheque by itself constitutes an offence. For the purpose of proving its case that the accused had committed an offence under Sec. 138 of the Negotiable Instruments Act, the ingredients thereof are required to be proved. What would constitute an offence is stated in the main provision. The proviso appended thereto, however, imposes certain further conditions which are required to be fulfilled before cognizance of the offence can be taken. If the ingredients for constitution of the offence laid down in the provisos (a), (b) and (c) appended to Sec. 138 of the Negotiable Instruments Act intended to be applied in favour of the accused, there cannot be any doubt that receipt of a notice would ultimately give rise to the cause of action for filing a complaint. As it is only on receipt of the notice, the accused at his own peril may refuse to pay the amount. Clauses (b) and (c) of the proviso to Sec. 138 therefore must be read together. Issuance of notice would not by itself give rise to a cause of action but communication of the notice would.[20]

---

[19] *K. Bhaskaran* v. *Sankaran Vaidhyan Balan*, AIR 1999 SC 3762.

[20] *Harman Electronics (P) Ltd., M/s.* v. *M/s. National Panasonic India Ltd.*, AIR 2009 SC 1168.

In 2010, the question that came before the Supreme Court for consideration in *P.J. Agro Tech. Ltd.* v. *Water Base Ltd.*[21] was whether a complaint under Sec. 138 of the Act would be maintainable against a person who was not the drawer of the cheque from an account maintained by him, which ultimately came to be dishonoured on presentation. The Court observed that after reading Sec. 138 of the Act, it is very clear that in order to attract the provisions thereof, a cheque which is dishonoured will have to be drawn by a person on an account maintained by him with the banker for payment of any amount of money to another person from out of that account for the discharge, in whole or in part of any debt or other liability. It is only such a cheque which is dishonoured which would attract the provisions of Sec. 138 of the above Act against the drawer of the cheque. In the instant case, the cheque which had been dishonoured may have been issued by Respondent No. 11 for discharging the dues of Appellant No. 1 Company and its Directors to Respondent No. 1 Company and the Respondent. The company may have a good case against Appellant No. 1 Company for recovery of its dues before other fora, but it would not be sufficient to attract the provisions of Sec. 138 of the Act. The Appellant Company and its Directors cannot be made liable under Sec. 138 of the Act for a default committed by Respondent No. 11. An action in respect of a criminal or a quasi-criminal provision has to be strictly construed in keeping with the provisions alleged to have been violated. The proceedings in such matters are in personam and cannot be used to foist an offence on some other person, who under the statute was not liable for the commission of such offence.

In *Indo Automobiles, M/s.* v. *M/s. Jai Durga Enterprises,*[22] it was admitted that a notice under Sec. 138 of the Act was sent to the respondents through registered post and under a certificate of posting on the correct address of the respondents. The High Court had quashed proceeding on the ground that although notice through registered post and also under certificate of posting was sent by the appellant/complainant to the respondents but because of the endorsement of the postal peon, the service could not be said to have been effected. The Supreme Court held that the High Court was not justified in holding that service of notice could not be found to be valid. The Court relied on *K. Bhaskaran* v. *Sankaran Vaidhyan Balan and anr.*[23] where it has been held that Sec. 138 of the Act invites a liberal interpretation favouring the person who has the statutory obligation to give notice under the Act because he must be presumed to be the loser in the transaction and provision itself has been made in his interest and if a strict interpretation is asked for, that would give a handle to the trickster cheque drawer. It is also well settled that once notice has been sent by registered post with acknowledgment due in a correct address, it must be presumed that the service has been made effective. Therefore, the Supreme Court held that the order of the High Court is set aside and appeal is allowed.

In *Goaplast Pvt. Ltd.* v. *Shri Chico Ursula D'Souza,*[24] the issue is regarding payment of a post-dated cheque being countermanded before the date mentioned on the face of the cheque. For the purpose of considering the issue, it is relevant to see Sec. 139 of the Act which creates a presumption in favour of the holder of a cheque. The said section

---

[21] AIR 2010 SC 2596.

[22] AIR 2009 SC 386.

[23] [1999 (7) SCC 510].

[24] AIR 2003 SC 2035.

provides that *"it shall be presumed that, unless the contrary is proved, that the holder of a cheque received that cheque of the nature referred to in Section 138 for the discharge, in whole or in part, or any debt or other liability"*. Thus, it has to be presumed that a cheque is issued in discharge of any debt or other liability. The presumption can be rebutted by adducing evidence and the burden of proof is on the person who wants to rebut the presumption. This presumption, coupled with the object of Chapter XVII of the Act which is to promote the efficacy of banking operation and to ensure credibility in business transactions through banks, persuades us to take a view that by countermanding payment of post-dated cheque, a party should not be allowed to get away from the penal provision of Sec. 138 of the Act. A contrary view would render Sec. 138 a dead letter and will provide a handle to persons trying to avoid payment under legal obligations undertaken by them through their own acts which, in other words, can be said to be taking advantage of one's own wrong. If we hold otherwise, by giving instructions to banks to stop payment of a cheque after issuing the same against a debt or liability, a drawer will easily avoid penal consequences under Sec. 138. Once a cheque is issued by a drawer, a presumption under Sec. 139 must follow and merely because the drawer issued notice to the drawee or to the bank for stoppage of payment, it will not preclude an action under Sec. 138 of the Act by the drawee or the holder of the cheque in due course. A post-dated cheque will lose its credibility and acceptability if its payment can be stopped routinely. A cheque is a well-recognised mode of payment and post-dated cheques are often used in various transactions in daily life. Thus, the purpose of a post-dated cheque is to provide some accommodation to the drawer of the cheque. Therefore, it is all the more necessary that the drawer of the cheque should not be allowed to abuse the accommodation given to him by a creditor by way of acceptance of post-dated cheque. If stoppage of payment of a post-dated cheque is permitted to take the case out of the purview of Sec. 138 of the Act, it will amount to allowing the party to take advantage of his own wrong.

In the case of *Modi Cements Ltd.* v. *Kuchil Kumar Nandi,*[25] it has been held that even though the cheque is dishonoured by reason of 'stop payment' instruction, an offence under Sec. 138 could still be made out. It is held that presumption under Sec. 139 is attracted in such a case also. The authority shows that even when the cheque is dishonoured by reason of stop payment instructions by virtue of Sec. 139, the Court has to presume that the cheque was received by the holder for the discharge, in whole or in part, of any debt or liability. Of course this is a rebuttable presumption. The accused can thus show that the "stop payment" instructions were not issued because of insufficiency or paucity of funds. If the accused shows that in his account there was sufficient funds to clear the amount of the cheque at the time of presentation of the cheque for encashment at the drawer bank and that the stop payment notice had been issued because of other valid causes including that there was no existing debt or liability at the time of presentation of cheque for encashment, then offence under Sec. 138 would not be made out. The important thing is that the burden of so proving would be on the accused. Thus, a Court cannot quash a complaint on this ground.

Reading Sec. 138 as a whole, the words *"said amount of money"* in Clauses (b) and (c) of proviso to Sec. 138 refers to the words *"payment of any amount of money"* occurring in

---

[25] (1998) 3 SCC 249.

main Sec. 138, i.e. the cheque amount. So in notice, under Clause (b) to the proviso, demand has to be made for the cheque amount. It is a well settled principle of law that the notice has to be read as a whole. In the notice, demand has to be made for the *"said amount"*, i.e. cheque amount. If no such demand is made, the notice, no doubt, would fall short of its legal requirement. Where in addition to *"said amount"* there is also a claim by way of interest, cost, etc. whether the notice is bad would depend on the language of the notice. If in a notice while giving break-up of the claim, the cheque amount, interest, damages, etc. are separately specified, other such claims for interest, cost, etc. would be superfluous and these additional claims would be severable and will not invalidate the notice. If, however, in the notice an omnibus demand is made without specifying what was due under the dishonoured cheque, the notice might well fail to meet the legal requirement and may be regarded as bad. In Sec. 138, Legislature clearly stated that for the dishonoured cheque, the drawer shall be liable for conviction if the demand is not made within 15 days of the receipt of notice but this is without prejudice to any other provision of the Act. If the cheque amount is paid within the above period or before the complaint is filed, the legal liability under Sec. 138 will cease and for recovery of other demands as compensation, costs interest, etc. a civil proceeding will lie. Therefore, if in a notice any other sum is indicated in addition to the *"said amount"*, the notice cannot be faulted.[26]

### Whether a 'pay order' is a cheque

A 'pay order' is a 'cheque' within the meaning of Sec. 138 of the NI Act. A cheque is a bill of exchange drawn on a specified banker and not expressed to be payable otherwise than on demand. The quintessence of a bill of exchange is that the maker or the drawer of a bill of exchange must direct a *'certain perso'* to pay a particular sum of money. It cannot be said that in every Bill of exchange there must necessarily be three parties, the maker, the payee and the person to whom direction is given to pay and as a draft or a pay order contains only two persons, i.e. the drawer and the payee, a draft may at best be a promissory note. The indispensable postulate for a promissory note is that there should be an unconditional undertaking to pay a certain sum by the drawer. Such an undertaking cannot be read out from a pay order. A pay order is closer to a bill of exchange because of the unconditional order of its maker to the person concerned *'to pay a certain sum'*. The postulate in Sec. 5 of the Act that the bill of exchange shall contain an unconditional order directing 'a certain person to pay' need not necessarily refer to a third person. Such 'a certain person' could as well be the bank which has drawn the bill of exchange. Even Sec. 85A of the Act renders a draft a negotiable instrument. Moreover, Sec. 131A makes all the provisions for crossing of cheques applicable to the drafts also. Section 131A is intended to widen the scope of crossed drafts as to contain all incidences of a crossed cheque and is not intended to limit the operation of a draft as a cheque only for crossing purposes. Even if it is possible to construe the draft either as a promissory note or as a bill of exchange, law has given the option to the holder to treat it as he chooses. Once the holder, which in this case is the complainant-bank, has elected to treat the instrument as a cheque it cannot but be treated

---

[26] *Suman Sethi* v. *Ajay K. Churiwal*, AIR 2000 SC 828.

as a cheque, thereafter. This is an irretrievable corollary of exercising such an election by the holder himself.[27]

## Section 139: Presumption in favour of holder

It shall be presumed, unless the contrary is proved, that the holder of a cheque received the cheque of the nature referred to in Section 138 for the discharge, in whole or in part, of any debt or other liability.

The provision under Sec. 139 has been inserted to regulate the growing business, trade, commerce and industrial activities of the country and the strict liability to promote greater vigilance in financial matters and to safeguard the faith of the creditor in the drawer of the cheque which is essential to the economic life of a developing country like India. This, however, shall not mean that the Courts shall turn a blind eye to the ground realities. Statute mandates raising of presumption but it stops at that. It does not say how presumption drawn should be held to have rebutted. Other important principles of legal jurisprudence, namely, presumption of innocence as human rights and the doctrine of reverse burden introduced by Sec. 139 should be delicately balanced. Such balancing acts, indisputably, would largely depend upon the factual matrix of each case, the materials brought on record and having regard to legal principles governing the same. The Courts must be on guard to see that merely on the application of presumption as contemplated under Sec. 139, the same may not lead to injustice or mistaken conviction.[28]

The presumption mandated by Sec. 139 of the Act does indeed include the existence of legally enforceable debt or liability. This is of course in the nature of a rebuttable presumption and it is open to the accused to raise a defence wherein the existence of a legally enforceable debt or liability can be contested. However, there can be no doubt that there is an initial presumption which favours the complainant. Section 139 of the Act is an example of a reverse onus clause that has been included in furtherance of the legislative objective of improving the credibility of negotiable instruments. While Sec. 138 of the Act specifies a strong criminal remedy in relation to the dishonour of cheques, the rebuttable presumption under Sec. 139 is a device to prevent undue delay in the course of litigation. However, it must be remembered that the offence made punishable by Sec. 138 can be better described as a regulatory offence since the bouncing of a cheque is largely in nature of a civil wrong whose impact is usually confined to the private parties involved in commercial transactions. In such a scenario, the test of proportionality should guide the construction and interpretation of reverse onus clauses and the accused/defendant cannot be expected to discharge an unduly high standard of proof. In the absence of compelling justifications, reverse onus clauses usually impose an evidentiary burden and not a persuasive burden. Keeping this in view, it is a settled position that when an accused has to rebut the presumption under Sec. 139, the standard of proof for doing so is that of *'preponderance of probabilities'*. Therefore, if the accused is able to raise a probable defence which creates doubts about the existence of a legally enforceable debt or liability, the prosecution can fail. The accused can rely on the materials submitted by the complainant in order to raise such

---

[27] *Punjab and Sind Bank* v. *Vinkar Sahakari Bank Ltd.*, AIR 2001 SC 3641.

[28] *Krishna Janardhan Bhat* v. *Dattatraya G. Hegde*, AIR 2008 SC 1325.

a defence and it is conceivable that in some cases, the accused may not need to adduce evidence of his/her own.[29]

The use of the phrase *"until the contrary is proved"* in Sec. 118 of the Act and use of the words *"unless the contrary is proved"* in Sec. 139 of the Act read with definitions of *"may presume"* and *"shall presume"* as given in Sec. 4 of the Evidence Act, makes it at once clear that presumptions to be raised under both the provisions are rebuttable.

Section 4 of the Indian Evidence Act reads:

"(a) 'may presume'—Whenever it is provided by this Act that the Court may presume a fact, it may either regard such fact as proved, unless and until it is disproved or may call for proof of it.

(b) 'shall presume'—Whenever it is directed by this Act that the Court shall presume a fact, it' shall regard such fact as proved, unless and until it is disproved."

When a presumption is rebuttable, it only points out that the party on whom lies the duty of going forward with evidence, on the fact presumed and when that party has produced evidence fairly and reasonably tending to show that the real fact is not as presumed, the purpose of the presumption is over. The accused in a trial under Sec. 138 of the Act has two options. He can either show that consideration and debt did not exist or that under the particular circumstances of the case, the non-existence of consideration and debt is so probable that a prudent man ought to suppose that no consideration and debt existed. To rebut the statutory presumptions, an accused is not expected to prove his defence beyond reasonable doubt as is expected of the complainant in a criminal trial. The accused may adduce direct evidence to prove that the note in question was not supported by consideration and that there was no debt or liability to be discharged by him. However, the Court need not insist in every case that the accused should disprove the non-existence of consideration and debt by leading direct evidence because the existence of negative evidence is neither possible nor contemplated. At the same time, it is clear that bare denial of the passing of the consideration and existence of debt, apparently, would not serve the purpose of the accused. Something which is probable has to be brought on record for getting the burden of proof shifted to the complainant. To disprove the presumptions, the accused should bring on record such facts and circumstances, upon consideration of which The Court may either believe that the consideration and debt did not exist or their non-existence was so probable that a prudent man would, under the circumstances of the case, act upon the plea that they did not exist. Apart from adducing direct evidence to prove that the note in question was not supported by consideration or that he had not incurred any debt or liability, the accused may also rely upon circumstantial evidence and if the circumstances so relied upon are compelling, the burden may likewise shift again on to the complainant. The accused may also rely upon presumptions of fact, for instance, those mentioned in Sec. 114 of the Evidence Act to rebut the presumptions arising under Secs. 118 and 139 of the Act. The accused has also an option to prove the non-existence of consideration and debt or liability either by letting in evidence or in some clear and exceptional cases, from the case set out by the complainant, that is, the averments in the complaint, the case set out in the statutory notice and evidence adduced by the complainant during the trial. Once such rebuttal evidence is adduced and accepted by the Court, having

---

[29] *Rangappa* v. *Mohan*, AIR 2010 SC 1898.

regard to all the circumstances of the case and the preponderance of probabilities, the evidential burden shifts back to the complainant and, thereafter, the presumptions under Secs. 118 and 139 of the Act will not again come to the complainant's rescue.[30]

Section 139 provides that *"it shall be presumed, unless the contrary is proved, that the holder of a cheque received the cheque, of the nature referred to in Section 138 for the discharge, in whole or in part, of any debt or other liability."* The effect of these presumptions is to place the evidential burden on the accused of proving that the cheque was not received by the complainant towards the discharge of any liability. Because both Secs. 138 and 139 require that the Court *"shall presume"* the liability of the drawer of the cheques for the amounts for which the cheques are drawn, as noted in it is obligatory on the Court to raise this presumption in every case where the factual basis for raising of the presumption had been established. It introduced an exception to the general rule as to the burden of proof in criminal cases and shifts the onus on to the accused. Such a presumption is a presumption of law, as distinguished from a presumption of fact which describes provisions by which the Court *"may presume"* a certain State of affairs. Presumptions are rules of evidence and do not conflict with the presumption of innocence, because by the latter all that is meant is that the prosecution is obliged to prove the case against the accused beyond reasonable doubt. The obligation on the prosecution may be discharged with the help of presumptions of law or fact unless the accused adduces evidence showing the reasonable possibility of the nonexistence of the presumed fact.[31]

## Section 140: Defence which may not be allowed in any prosecution under Section 138

It shall not be a defence in a prosecution for an offence under Section 138 that the drawer had no reason to believe when he issued the cheque that the cheque may be dishonoured on presentment for the reasons stated in that section.

## Section 141: Offences by companies

(1) If the person committing an offence under Section 138 is a company, every person who, at the time the offence was committed, was in charge of, and was responsible to, the company for the conduct of the business of the company, as well as the company, shall be deemed to be guilty of the offence and shall be liable to be proceeded against and punished accordingly:

Provided that nothing contained in this sub-section shall render any person liable to punishment if he proves that the offence was committed without his knowledge, or that he had exercised all due diligence to prevent the commission of such offence:

Provided further that where a person is nominated as a Director of a company by virtue of his holding any office or employment in the Central Government or State Government or a financial corporation owned or controlled by the Central Government or the State Government, as the case may be, he shall not be liable for prosecution under this Chapter.

[30] *Kumar Exports, M/s. v. M/s. Sharma Carpets*, AIR 2009 SC 1518.

[31] *Hiten P. Dalal* v. *Bratindranath Banerjee*, AIR 2001 SC 3897.

(2) Notwithstanding anything contained in sub-section (1), where any offence under this Act has been committed by a company and it is proved that the offence has been committed with the consent or connivance of, or is attributable to, any neglect on the part of, any director, manager, secretary or other officer of the company, such director, manager, secretary or other officer shall also be deemed to be guilty of that offence and shall be liable to be proceeded against and punished accordingly.

***Explanation***: For the purposes of this section,—

(a) "company" means any body corporate and includes a firm or other association of individuals; and

(b) "director", in relation to a firm, means a partner in the firm.

The legal position concerning the vicarious liability of a director in a company which is being prosecuted for the offence under Sec. 138 of the NI Act has come up for consideration before the Supreme Court on more than one occasion. In the case of *S.M.S. Pharmaceuticals Ltd.* v. *Neeta Bhalla and another*[32], the following questions were referred to a 3-Judge Bench for determination:

(a) Whether for purposes of Sec. 141 of the Negotiable Instruments Act, 1881, it is sufficient if the substance of the allegation read as a whole fulfils the requirements of the said section and it is not necessary to specifically State in the complaint that the person accused was in charge of, or responsible for, the conduct of the business of the company.

(b) Whether a director of a company would be deemed to be in charge of, and responsible to, the company for conduct of the business of the company and, therefore, deemed to be guilty of the offence unless he proves to the contrary.

(c) Even if it is held that specific averments are necessary, whether in the absence of such averments the signatory of the cheque or the managing directors or joint managing director who admittedly would be in charge of the company and responsible to the company for conduct of its business could be proceeded against.

The Supreme Court answered the aforesaid questions as follows:

(a) It is necessary to specifically aver in a complaint under Sec. 141 that at the time the offence was committed, the person accused was in charge of, and responsible for, the conduct of business of the company. This averment is an essential requirement of Sec. 141 and has to be made in a complaint. Without this averment being made in a complaint, the requirements of Sec. 141 cannot be said to be satisfied.

(b) The answer to the question posed in sub-para (b) has to be in the negative. Merely being a director of a company is not sufficient to make the person liable under Sec. 141 of the Act. A director in a company cannot be deemed to be in charge of and responsible to the company for the conduct of its business. The requirement of Sec. 141 is that the person sought to be made liable should be in

[32] AIR 2005 SC 3512.

charge of and responsible for the conduct of the business of the company at the relevant time. This has to be averred as a fact as there is no deemed liability of a director in such cases.

(c) The answer to Question (c) has to be in the affirmative. The question notes that the managing director or joint managing director would be admittedly in charge of the company and responsible to the company for the conduct of its business. When that is so, holders of such positions in a company become liable under Sec. 141 of the Act. By virtue of the office they hold as managing director or joint managing director, these persons are in charge of and responsible for the conduct of business of the company. Therefore, they get covered under Sec. 141. So far as the signatory of a cheque which is dishonoured is concerned, he is clearly responsible for the incriminating act and will be covered under sub-section (2) of Sec. 141.

In *N. Rangachari* v. *Bharat Sanchar Nigam Ltd.*,[33] a 2-Judge Bench of the Supreme Court discussed and considered *S.M.S. Pharmaceuticals Ltd.* case and observed as follows:

> ".......The scope of Section 141 has been authoritatively discussed in the decision in S.M.S. Pharmaceuticals Ltd. [2005 (8) SCC 89] binding on us and there is no scope for redefining it in this case. Suffice it to say, that a prosecution could be launched not only against the company on behalf of which the cheque issued has been dishonoured, but it could also be initiated against every person who at the time the offence was committed, was in charge of and was responsible for the conduct of the business of the company. In fact, Section 141 deems such persons to be guilty of such offence, liable to be proceeded against and punished for the offence, leaving it to the person concerned, to prove that the offence was committed by the company without his knowledge or that he has exercised due diligence to prevent the commission of the offence. Sub-section (2) of Section 141 also roped in Directors, Managers, Secretaries or other officers of the company, if it was proved that the offence was committed with their consent or connivance. But as has already been noticed, the decision in S.M.S. Pharmaceuticals Ltd. [2005 (8) SCC 89]: (AIR 2005 SC 3512) binding on us, has postulated that a Director in a company cannot be deemed to be in charge of and responsible to the company for the conduct of his business in the context of Section 141 of the Act. Bound as we are by that decision no further discussion on this aspect appears to be warranted."[34]

In the case of *K.K. Ahuja* v. *V.K. Vora and another*,[35] a 2-Judge Bench of the Supreme Court had an occasion to consider the earlier decisions of this Court including the decision in the case of *S.M.S. Pharmaceuticals Ltd.* case and accordingly it was held that mere fact that at some point of time an officer of a company had played some role in the financial affairs of the company, that will not be sufficient to attract the constructive liability under Sec. 141 of the NI Act. The Court summarised the legal position as follows:

(i) If the accused is the Managing Director or a Joint Managing Director, it is not necessary to make an averment in the complaint that he is in charge of, and is responsible to the company, for the conduct of the business of the company. It is sufficient if an averment is made that the accused was the Managing Director

[33] AIR 2007 SC 1682.

[34] Cited in *Harshendra Kumar D.* v. *Rebatilata Koley*, AIR 2011 SC 1090 at pp. 1094–95.

[35] (2009) 10 SCC 48.

or Joint Managing Director at the relevant time. This is because the prefix "Managing" to the word "Director" makes it clear that they were in charge of and are responsible to the company, for the conduct of the business of the company.

(ii) In the case of a Director or an officer of the company who signed the cheque on behalf of the company, there is no need to make a specific averment that he was in charge of and was responsible to the company, for the conduct of the business of the company or make any specific allegation about consent, connivance or negligence. The very fact that the dishonoured cheque was signed by him on behalf of the company, would give rise to responsibility under sub-section (2) of Sec. 141.

(iii) In the case of a Director, secretary or manager as defined in Sec. 2(24) of the Companies Act or a person referred to in clauses (e) and (f) of Sec. 5 of the Companies Act, an averment in the complaint that he was in charge of, and was responsible to the company, for the conduct of the business of the company is necessary to bring the case under Sec. 141(1) of the Act. No further averment would be necessary in the complaint, though some particulars will be desirable. They can also be made liable under Sec. 141(2) by making necessary averments relating to consent and connivance or negligence, in the complaint, to bring the matter under that sub-section.

(iv) Other officers of a company cannot be made liable under sub-section (1) of Sec. 141. Other officers of a company can be made liable only under sub-section (2) of Sec. 141, by averring in the complaint their position and duties in the company and their role in regard to the issue and dishonour of the cheque, disclosing consent, connivance or negligence.

In the *K.K. Ahuja* case, the Court observed that if a mere reproduction of the wording of Sec. 141(1) in the complaint was sufficient to make a person liable to face prosecution, virtually every officer/employee of a company without exception could be impleaded as accused by merely making an averment that at the time when the offence was committed, they were in charge of and were responsible to the company for the conduct and business of the company.

In a recent decision in the case of *National Small Industries Corporation Limited* v. *Harmeet Singh Paintal and another*[36], after survey of earlier decisions wherein legal position concerning Sec. 138 and Sec. 141 of the NI Act was considered, the Supreme Court culled out the following principles:

(i) The primary responsibility is on the complainant to make specific averments as are required under the law in the complaint so as to make the accused vicariously liable. For fastening the criminal liability, there is no presumption that every Director knows about the transaction.

(ii) Section 141 does not make all the Directors liable for the offence. The criminal liability can be fastened only on those who, at the time of the commission of the

[36] 2010 AIR SCW 1508.

offence, were in charge of and were responsible for the conduct of the business of the company.

(iii) Vicarious liability can be inferred against a company registered or incorporated under the Companies Act, 1956 only if the requisite statements, which are required to be averred in the complaint/petition, are made so as to make the accused therein vicariously liable for offence committed by the company along with averments in the petition containing that the accused were in charge of and responsible for the business of the company and by virtue of their position they are liable to be proceeded with.

(iv) Vicarious liability on the part of a person must be pleaded and proved and not inferred.

(v) If the accused is a Managing Director or a Joint Managing Director, then it is not necessary to make specific averment in the complaint and by virtue of their position they are liable to be proceeded with.

(vi) If the accused is a Director or an officer of a company who signed the cheques on behalf of the company then also it is not necessary to make specific averment in the complaint.

(vii) The person sought to be made liable should be in charge of and responsible for the conduct of the business of the company at the relevant time. This has to be averred as a fact as there is no deemed liability of a Director in such cases.

Section 141 provides for a constructive liability. A legal fiction has been created thereby. The statute being a penal one, should receive strict construction. It requires strict compliance of the provision, specific averments in the complaint petition so as to satisfy the requirements of Section 141 are imperative. Mere fact that at one point of time some role has been played by the accused may not by itself be sufficient to attract the constructive liability under Sec. 141.[37]

## Section 142: Cognizance of offences

(1) Notwithstanding anything contained in the Code of Criminal Procedure, 1973 (2 of 1974),—

(a) no Court shall take cognizance of any offence punishable under Section 138 except upon a complaint, in writing, made by the payee or, as the case may be, the holder in due course of the cheque;

(b) such complaint is made within one month of the date on which the cause of action arises under clause (c) of the proviso to Section 138:

Provided that the cognizance of a complaint may be taken by the Court after the prescribed period, if the complainant satisfies the Court that he had sufficient cause for not making a complaint within such period;

(c) no Court inferior to that of a Metropolitan Magistrate or a Judicial Magistrate of the first class shall try any offence punishable under Section 138.

[37] *DCM Financial Services Ltd.* v. *J. N. Sareen*, AIR 2008 SC 2255.

(2) The offence under Section 138 shall be inquired into and tried only by a court within whose local jurisdiction,—

(a) if the cheque is delivered for collection through an account, the branch of the bank where the payee or holder in due course, as the case may be, maintains the account, is situated; or

(b) if the cheque is presented for payment by the payee or holder in due course, otherwise through an account, the branch of the drawee bank where the drawer maintains the account, is situated.

*Explanation:* For the purposes of clause (a), where a cheque is delivered for collection at any branch of the bank of the payee or holder in due course, then, the cheque shall be deemed to have been delivered to the branch of the bank in which the payee or holder in due course, as the case may be, maintains the account.

The payee of the cheque is M/s. Shankar Finance and Investments. The complaint is filed by "M/s. Shankar Finance and Investments, a proprietary concern of Sri Atmakuri Sankara Rao, represented by its Power of Attorney Holder Sri Thamada Satyanarayana". It is therefore evident that the complaint is in the name of and on behalf of the payee. Section 142(a) of the Act requires that no Court shall take cognizance of any offence punishable under Sec. 138 except upon a complaint made in writing by the payee. Thus, the two requirements are that (a) the complaint should be made in writing (in contradistinction from an oral complaint); and (b) the complainant should be the payee (or the holder in due course, where the payee has endorsed the cheque in favour of someone else). The payee, as noticed above, is M/s. Shankar Finance and Investments. Once the complaint is in the name of the 'payee' and is in writing, the requirements of Sec. 142 are fulfilled. Who should represent the payee where the payee is a company, or how the payee should be represented where payee is a sole proprietary concern is not a matter that is governed by Sec. 142. The next question is where a proprietary concern carries on business through an Attorney holder, whether the Attorney holder can lodge the complaint. The Attorney holder is the agent of the grantor. When the grantor authorises the Attorney holder to initiate legal proceedings and the Attorney holder accordingly initiates legal proceedings, he does so as the agent of the grantor and the initiation is by the grantor represented by his Attorney holder, and not by the Attorney holder in his personal capacity.[38]

## Section 142A: Validation for transfer of pending cases

(1) Notwithstanding anything contained in the Code of Criminal Procedure, 1973 (2 of 1974) or any judgment, decree, order or direction of any court, all cases transferred to the court having jurisdiction under sub-section (2) of Section 142, as amended by the Negotiable Instruments (Amendment) Ordinance, 2015 (Ord. 6 of 2015), shall be deemed to have been transferred under this Act, as if that sub-section had been in force at all material times.

(2) Notwithstanding anything contained in sub-section (2) of Section 142 or sub-section (1), where the payee or the holder in due course, as the case may be, has

---

[38] *Shankar Finance and Investments, M/s.* v. *State of A.P.*, AIR 2009 SC 422.

filed a complaint against the drawer of a cheque in the court having jurisdiction under sub-section (2) of Section 142 or the case has been transferred to that court under sub-section (1) and such complaint is pending in that court, all subsequent complaints arising out of Section 138 against the same drawer shall be filed before the same court irrespective of whether those cheques were delivered for collection or presented for payment within the territorial jurisdiction of that court.

(3) If, on the date of the commencement of the Negotiable Instruments (Amendment) Act, 2015 (26 of 2015), more than one prosecution filed by the same payee or holder in due course, as the case may be, against the same drawer of cheques is pending before different courts, upon the said fact having been brought to the notice of the court, such court shall transfer the case to the court having jurisdiction under sub-section (2) of Section 142, as amended by the Negotiable Instruments (Amendment) Ordinance, 2015 (Ord. 6 of 2015), before which the first case was filed and is pending, as if that sub-section had been in force at all material times.

**Section 143: Power of Court to try cases summarily**

(1) Notwithstanding anything contained in the Code of Criminal Procedure, 1973 (2 of 1974), all offences under this Chapter shall be tried by a Judicial Magistrate of the first class or by a Metropolitan Magistrate and the provisions of Sections 262 to 265 (both inclusive) of the said Code shall, as far as may be, apply to such trials:

Provided that in the case of any conviction in a summary trial under this section, it shall be lawful for the Magistrate to pass a sentence of imprisonment for a term not exceeding one year and an amount of fine exceeding five thousand rupees:

Provided further that when at the commencement of, or in the course of, a summary trial under this section, it appears to the Magistrate that the nature of the case is such that a sentence of imprisonment for a term exceeding one year may have to be passed or that it is, for any other reason, undesirable to try the case summarily, the Magistrate shall after hearing the parties, record an order to that effect and thereafter recall any witness who may have been examined and proceed to hear or rehear the case in the manner provided by the said Code.

(2) The trial of a case under this section shall, so far as practicable, consistently with the interests of justice, be continued from day to day until its conclusion, unless the Court finds the adjournment of the trial beyond the following day to be necessary for reasons to be recorded in writing.

(3) Every trial under this section shall be conducted as expeditiously as possible and an endeavour shall be made to conclude the trial within six months from the date of filing of the complaint.

**Section 143A: Power to direct interim compensation**

(1) Notwithstanding anything contained in the Code of Criminal Procedure, 1973, the Court trying an offence under Section 138 may order the drawer of the cheque to pay interim compensation to the complainant—

(a) in a summary trial or a summons case, where he pleads not guilty to the accusation made in the complaint; and

(b) in any other case, upon framing of charge.

(2) The interim compensation under sub-section (1) shall not exceed twenty per cent of the amount of the cheque.

(3) The interim compensation shall be paid within sixty days from the date of the order under sub-section (1), or within such further period not exceeding thirty days as may be directed by the Court on sufficient cause being shown by the drawer of the cheque.

(4) If the drawer of the cheque is acquitted, the Court shall direct the complainant to repay to the drawer the amount of interim compensation, with interest at the bank rate as published by the Reserve Bank of India, prevalent at the beginning of the relevant financial year, within sixty days from the date of the order, or within such further period not exceeding thirty days as may be directed by the Court on sufficient cause being shown by the complainant.

(5) The interim compensation payable under this section may be recovered as if it were a fine under Section 421 of the Code of Criminal Procedure, 1973 (2 of 1974).

(6) The amount of fine imposed under Section 138 or the amount of compensation awarded under Section 357 of the Code of Criminal Procedure, 1973 (2 of 1974), shall be reduced by the amount paid or recovered as interim compensation under this section.

In the statement of objects and reasons, it was stated that unscrupulous drawers of the cheques prolong the proceedings of a complaint under Section 138 by filing appeals and obtaining a stay. Therefore, injustice is caused to the payee of a dishonoured cheque, who has to spend considerable time and resources in Court proceedings to realise the value of the cheque. It was further observed that such delays compromise the sanctity of the cheque transactions. Therefore, it was proposed to amend the N.I. Act to address the issue of undue delay in the final resolution of the cheque dishonour cases. It was also stated that the proposed amendments would strengthen the credibility of cheques and help trade and commerce. The Supreme Court in 2024 in *Rakesh Ranjan Shrivastava* v. *The State of Jharkhand & Anr* [2024] 3 S.C.R. 438, provides a guideline for the court that the court should adhere the following guidelines before awarding interim compensation under Section 143A.

(1) The exercise of power under sub-section (1) of Section 143A is discretionary. The provision is directory and not mandatory. The word "may" used in the provision cannot be construed as "shall."

(2) While deciding the prayer made under Section 143A, the Court must record brief reasons indicating consideration of all relevant factors.

(3) The broad parameters for exercising the discretion under Section 143A are as follows:

(a) The Court will have to *prima facie* evaluate the merits of the case made out by the complainant and the merits of the defence pleaded by the accused in the reply to the application. The financial distress of the accused can also be a consideration.

(b) A direction to pay interim compensation can be issued, only if the complainant makes out a *prima facie* case.

(c) If the defence of the accused is found to be *prima facie* plausible, the Court may exercise discretion in refusing to grant interim compensation.

(d) If the Court concludes that a case is made out to grant interim compensation, it will also have to apply its mind to the quantum of interim compensation to be granted. While doing so, the Court will have to consider several factors such as the nature of the transaction, the relationship, if any, between the accused and the complainant, etc.

(e) There could be several other relevant factors in the peculiar facts of a given case, which cannot be exhaustively stated. The parameters stated above are not exhaustive.

**Section 144: Mode of service of summons**

(1) Notwithstanding anything contained in the Code of Criminal Procedure, 1973 (2 of 1974), and for the purposes of this Chapter, a Magistrate issuing a summons to an accused or a witness may direct a copy of summons to be served at the place where such accused or witness ordinarily resides or carries on business or personally works for gain, by speed post or by such courier services as are approved by a Court of Session.

(2) Where an acknowledgement purporting to be signed by the accused or the witness or an indorsement purported to be made by any person authorised by the postal department or the courier services that the accused or the witness refused to take delivery of summons has been received, the Court issuing the summons may declare that the summons has been duly served.

**Section 145: Evidence on affidavit**

(1) Notwithstanding anything contained in the Code of Criminal Procedure, 1973 (2 of 1974), the evidence of the complainant may be given by him on affidavit and may, subject to all just exceptions be read in evidence in any enquiry, trial or other proceeding under the said Code.

(2) The Court may, if it thinks fit, and shall, on the application of the prosecution or the accused, summon and examine any person giving evidence on affidavit as to the facts contained therein.

Under Sec. 145, the Court subject to just exception may allow the complainant to give evidence by way of affidavit. Such evidence by way of affidavit had been made admissible in evidence in any enquiry, trial or other proceedings under the Code. Whereas sub-section (1) of Sec. 145 uses the term *'may'*, sub-section (2) thereof uses the term *'shall.'* The first part of the aforementioned provision must be read with sub-section (1) of Sec. 145. It therefore merely points out to the discretionary power of the Court conferred upon it by reason thereof. The Court, however, has no other option but to summon and examine any person who has given evidence on affidavit as to the facts contained therein if an application is filed either by the prosecution or the accused. Section 145 must be read reasonably. If affidavit in terms of the provisions of Sec. 145 of the Act is to be considered to be an evidence, it is difficult to comprehend as to why the Court will ask the deponent of the said affidavit to examine himself with regard to the contents thereof once over again. He may be cross-examined and upon completion of his evidence, he may be re-examined. Thus, the words *"examine any person giving evidence on affidavit as to the facts contained therein"* in the event the deponent is summoned by the Court in terms of sub-section (2) of Sec. 146 of the Act would mean for the purpose of cross-examination. The provision seeks to attend a salutary purpose. The object of enactment of the said provision is for the purpose of expedition of the trial. The deponent cannot be summoned again under Sec. 145(2) for his examination-in-chief.[39]

## Section 146: Bank's slip *prima facie* evidence of certain facts

The Court shall, in respect of every proceeding under this Chapter, on production of bank's slip or memo having thereon the official mark denoting that the cheque has been dishonoured, presume the fact of dishonour of such cheque, unless and until such fact is disproved.

## Section 147: Offences to be compoundable

Notwithstanding anything contained in the Code of Criminal Procedure, 1973 (2 of 1974), every offence punishable under this Act shall be compoundable.

The tendency of litigants to adopt compounding as a last resort to compound offence of dishonour of cheque is putting unnecessary strain on judicial system and contributing to increase in number of pending cases. Moreover, the free and easy compounding of offences at any stage, however belated, gives an incentive to the drawer of the cheque to delay settling the cases for years. An application for compounding made after several years not only results in the system being burdened but the complainant is also deprived of effective justice. Section 147, which permits compounding, does not carry any guidance on how to proceed with the compounding offences under the Act. The Scheme contemplated under Sec. 320 of the Cr.P.C. cannot be followed in the strict sense. In view of legislative vacuum, the Supreme Court directed Courts to follow a graded system of levying costs on parties so as to encourage them to go in for early compounding. The Supreme Court framed the following guidelines:[40]

(a) Directions can be given that the writ of Summons be suitably modified making it clear to the accused that he could make an application for compounding of the offences at the first or second hearing of the case and that if such an application is made, compounding may be allowed by the Court without imposing any costs on the accused.

[39] *Radhey Shyam Garg* v. *Naresh Kumar Gupta*, AIR 2010 SC 3210.

[40] *Damodar S. Prabhu* v. *Sayed Babalal H.*, AIR 2010 SC 1907.

(b) If the accused does not make an application for compounding as aforesaid, then if an application for compounding is made before the Magistrate at a subsequent stage, compounding can be allowed subject to the condition that the accused will be required to pay 10% of the cheque amount to be deposited as a condition for compounding with the Legal Services Authority, of such authority as the Court deems fit.

(c) Similarly, if the application for compounding is made before the Sessions Court or a High Court in revision or appeal, such compounding may be allowed on the condition that the accused pays 15% of the cheque amount by way of costs.

(d) Finally, if the application for compounding is made before the Supreme Court, the figure would increase to 20% of the cheque amount.

## Section 148: Power of Appellate Court to order payment pending appeal against conviction

(1) Notwithstanding anything contained in the Code of Criminal Procedure, 1973 (2 of 1974), in an appeal by the drawer against conviction under Section 138, the Appellate Court may order the appellant to deposit such sum which shall be a minimum of twenty per cent of the fine or compensation awarded by the trial Court:

Provided that the amount payable under this sub-section shall be in addition to any interim compensation paid by the appellant under Section 143A.

(2) The amount referred to in sub-section (1) shall be deposited within sixty days from the date of the order, or within such further period not exceeding thirty days as may be directed by the Court on sufficient cause being shown by the appellant.

(3) The Appellate Court may direct the release of the amount deposited by the appellant to the complainant at any time during the pendency of the appeal:

Provided that if the appellant is acquitted, the Court shall direct the complainant to repay to the appellant the amount so released, with interest at the bank rate as published by the Reserve Bank of India, prevalent at the beginning of the relevant financial year, within sixty days from the date of the order, or within such further period not exceeding thirty days as may be directed by the Court on sufficient cause being shown by the complainant.

# Index


Agency, 162
- agent and principal, 162
- agent's authority, 164
- effect of agency on contracts with third person, 175
- ratification, 167
- sub-agent, 165
- termination of agency, 168

Agreement, 3
- by way of wager void, 78
- effect of wagering contract, 79
- in restraint of marriage void, 67
- in restraint of trade void, 67
- in restraint of legal proceedings void, 74
- void for uncertainty, 77

Arbitration, 453
- appointment of arbitrator, 462
- arbitral award, 475
- arbitral proceeding, 471
- arbitral tribunal, 469, 470, 471, 474
- arbitration agreement, 457
- arbitration council, 487
- international commercial arbitration, 475
- jurisdiction of arbitral tribunal, 469

Article of Association, 356
- alteration, 358
- constructive notice, 359
- contents, 357
- exception to doctrine of indoor management, 361
- indoor management, 359

Bailment, 149
- actual delivery, 151
- bailor and bailee, 150
- constructive delivery, 151
- delivery of possession, 150
- duties and liabilities of bailor and bailee, 153 – 156
- general lien, 157
- lien, 157

Breach of contract, 121
- compensation for loss or damage, 121
- compensation where penalty stipulated for, 128
- liquidated damages and penalty, 131

Cheque, 529
- bearing not negotiable, 565
- crossed generally, 564
- crossed specially, 564
- electronic form, 529
- payable to order, 550
- truncated, 529

Communication and acceptance, 24
- offer to the world at large, 24
- performing condition and receiving consideration, 33
- promises, express or implied, 34
- revocation of proposal, 31

Company, 328
- definition, 328
- kinds, 336
- lifting the corporate veil, 333

Compensation, 270
both to consumer and beneficiaries, 260
for harassment, mental agony or oppression, 270
for negligence, 258
Conciliation, 497
appointment of conciliator, 498
cost, 503
proceedings, 498
role of conciliator, 499
settlement agreement, 500
termination of conciliation proceedings, 502
Conditions and Warranties, 192
condition, 192
distinction, 193
implied terms and conditions, 195
stipulation, 192
warranty, 193
Consent, 38
*consensus ad idem, 38*
Consideration, 60
agreement without consideration, 65
executory consideration, 67
executed consideration, 67
exceptions to consideration, 67
Consumer, 243
commercial purpose, 247
consumer dispute, 248
contract of service and contract for service, 254
defect, 248
deficiency, 249
goods, 250
manufacturer, 251
Consumer protection councils, 283
central council, 283
object of district council, 284
object of state council, 283
Contingent contract, 80
contacts contingent on an event happening, 80
contracts contingent on an event not happening, 81
contingent on impossible event void, 82
Contract of sale, 186
auction sale, 232
CIF contract, 215
delivery and payment, 188
FOB contracts, 215
formalities of, 188
hire purchase, 182
offer and acceptance, 188
repudiation of contract, 230
sale and agreement to sell, 182
sale vis-à-vis agreement to sell, 185
seller and buyer, 187
Contracts which need not be performed, 102
alteration of contract, 102
novation of contract, 103
rescission of contract, 103

Damages, 229
for non-acceptance, 229
for non-delivery, 229
interest by way of damages and special damages, 230
Debenture, 385
holders, 389
types, 386, 388
Delivery of goods, 212
buyer to apply for, 212
effect of part, 212
instalment, 214
of wrong quantity, 213
rules as to, 213
to carrier or wharfinger, 214
Directors, 393
appointment, 396
duties, 398
liabilities, 402
meetings, 407
position, 393
power, 400
removal, 398
remuneration, 408
Dishonour of cheque, 566
by non-acceptance, 553
by non-payment, 553
notice of dishonour, 554
of cheque for insufficiency of funds, 566

Enforcement of foreign award, 505
conditions for enforcement of foreign awards, 495
Geneva convention awards, 494
New York convention awards, 491

Free consent, 38
bars to rescission, 53
coercion, 39

contracts *uberrimae fidei*, 52
duress, 41
effect of mistake as to law, 57
fraud, 47
grounds of coercion, 41
guidelines as to constitute misrepresentation, 50
misrepresentation, 50
mistake as to different subject matter in mind, 59
mistake as to identity, 57
mistake as to subject matter, 58
mistake as to title, 59
mistake, 56
remedies for coercion, 41
remedies for misrepresentation, 52
remedies of undue influence, 47
undue influence, 42

Goods, 180
effect of perishing of goods, 189
existing or future goods, 188
perishing of goods, 189

Impossibility for performance, 94
destruction of the subject matter, 94
effects of frustration, 98
non-occurrence of a specified event, 95
personal incapacity, 95
supervening illegality, 97
Indemnity and guarantee, 134
continuing guarantee, 139
contacts of guarantee, 137
contracts of indemnity, 134
discharge of surety, 141
Insurance and principle of indemnity, 135
revocation of continuing guarantee, 139
rights of the indemnity-holder, 136
rights of surety, 145
surety's liability, 138
Inchoate Stamped Instruments, 535
ambiguous instruments, 535
foreign instrument, 534
in blank and in full, 535
indorsement, 535
inland instrument, 534
instruments payable on demand, 535
negotiable instrument, 534
negotiation, 534

Meetings, 410
annual general, 410
chairman, 412
duties, 412
extraordinary, 410
ordinary resolution, 416
quorum, 418
requisites of a valid, 410
resolutions, 416
types, 416
voting, 413
Memorandum of association, 347
contents, 347
consequences of ultra vires transactions, 352
doctrine of the ultra vires, 350

Negotiable instruments features, 522
delivery of the instrument, 523
freely transferable, 522
payment of a certain sum of money, 522
presumptions as to negotiable instruments, 558
signature of its maker, 523
unconditional order or promise for payment, 522
writing, 522
Negotiation, 541
delivery, 541
effect of indorsement, 542
indorsement for part of sum due, 543
indorsement in blank, 543
indorsement in full, 543
negotiation by delivery, 541
negotiation by indorsement, 542

Offer, 3
offer and invitation to treat, 4
rules with regard to offer, 3
tender, 6
Oppression and mismanagement, 428
powers of tribunal, 432
remedy, 434

Parties to a promissory note, 525
endorser and endorsee, 525
maker or drawer, 525
payee, 525
Parties to the Bill of Exchange, 528
acceptor, 531

acceptor for honour, 531
drawee, 531
drawee in case of need, 531
drawer, 531
endorsee, 528
endorser, 528
holder in due course, 531
holder, 531
payee, 528
Performance of contracts, 82
obligation of parties to contract, 82
performance of reciprocal promises, 87
time and place for performance, 85
time whether essence of contract, 90
Pledge, 160
by mercantile agent, 161
pawnor and pawnee, 160
pawnor's right to redeem, 161
Presentment, 544
for acceptance, 544
for payment, 545
hours for presentment, 546
of promissory note for sight, 545
Promissory note, 524
payable to a bearer, 525
payable to a specified person, 525
payable to the order of a specified person, 525
Prospectus, 362
contents, 366
deemed prospectus, 366
definition, 362
kinds, 363
public issue, 364
red-herring prospectus, 365
shelf prospectus, 364
statement in lieu of prospectus, 404

Quasi contract, 110
claim for necessaries, 110
non-gratuitous act, 112
principle, 109
*quantum meruit*, 118
responsibility of finder of goods, 115

Registration and incorporation, 343
certificate as conclusive evidence, 344
commencement of business, 345
pre-incorporation contract, 345

Sale, 182
by description as well as sample, 196
by description, 195
by one of joint owners, 209
by person in possession under voidable contract, 209
by person not the owner, 207
by sample, 200
duties of seller and buyer, 211
*nemo dat quod non habet*, 207
seller or buyer in possession after sale, 210
Services, 255
banking services, 265
goods carrier services, 273
medical services, 255
postal service, 278
services marketing, 255
Share and share capital, 369
allotment of shares, 381
buyback of shares, 416
definition and meaning, 369
equity share, 371
preference share, 372
share certificate and share warrant, 380
shareholders and members, 382
shares at a premium, 374
shares at discount, 374
sweat equity share, 378

Unpaid seller, 223
seller's lien, 224
termination of lien, 225
unpaid sellers rights, 224

Voidable contracts and void agreements, 35
a minor, 36
a person disqualified by law, 36
a person of unsound mind, 36
effect of minors contract, 37
who are competent to contract, 36

Warranties, 192
distinction between warranty and condition, 193
Winding-up of a company, 437
voluntary winding-up, 400
who can apply for, 438